LANCHESTER LIBRARY, Coventry University
Gosford Street, Coventry CV1 5DD Telephone 024 7688 7555

This book is due to be returned not later than the date and
time stamped above. Fines are charged on overdue books

FINANCIAL

STATEMENT

ANALYSIS

FINANCIAL STATEMENT ANALYSIS

George Foster

Stanford University

Prentice-Hall, Inc., Englewood Cliffs, New Jersey 07632

Library of Congress Cataloging in Publication Data

Foster, George,
  Financial statement analysis.

  Includes bibliographies.
  1. Financial statements   I. Title.
HF5681.B2F64   657'.3   77-28890
ISBN   0-13-316273-7

Printed in the United States of America

10   9   8   7   6

PRENTICE-HALL INTERNATIONAL, INC., *London*
PRENTICE-HALL OF AUSTRALIA PTY. LIMITED, *Sydney*
PRENTICE-HALL OF CANADA, LTD., *Toronto*
PRENTICE-HALL OF INDIA PRIVATE LIMITED, *New Delhi*
PRENTICE-HALL OF JAPAN, INC., *Tokyo*
PRENTICE-HALL OF SOUTHEAST ASIA PTE. LTD., *Singapore*
WHITEHALL BOOKS LIMITED, *Wellington, New Zealand*

CONTENTS

Contents

PREFACE

This book provides an intensive study of financial statement analysis. This area has undergone marked change as researchers have utilized developments in accounting and the related disciplines of economics, finance, and statistics. We now understand these developments well enough to present them in the traditional textbook package of text followed by problem or case material.

Some details on the development of the book may place the approach taken in perspective. Starting mainly in the early to mid 1960's there developed in the accounting and finance literature a heavily empirical-based line of research. Topics such as the ability of financial ratios to predict bankruptcy or bond ratings and the work on the random-walk behavior of security prices are illustrative of this research. Subsequently, this line of research has expanded in the topics examined and the methodologies applied. There have also been important attempts to provide theoretical foundations for the methodologies used and the issues addressed. Instructors who first used this material in financial statement analysis courses generally handed out packages containing 20 to 30 of the original articles. Many students found confronting the original literature a difficult task. Individual articles differed in notation, were frequently addressed to those on the research frontier, and often required a knowledge of statistics or econometrics beyond most students' grasp. Baruch Lev's *Financial Statement Analysis* (Prentice-Hall, 1974) monograph provided the first attempt to synthesize much of this literature into a comprehensible package. My early experience in teaching in this area convinced me that a combination of text, problems/cases and selected original articles was a good medium to convey the material to students. This book is an outgrowth of my efforts to provide University of Chicago M.B.A. students with the text and problem/cases for that combination. The reaction of those M.B.A. students has been very encouraging. This book especially benefited from the four M.B.A. classes who in 1976/77 used and gave feedback on drafts of each chapter.

The text is aimed at second year M.B.A. or Masters students in business and final year students in Undergraduate accounting or business programs. It should also be of interest to practicing investment and credit analysts. I have covered the material in both one quarter and one semester courses. In a one semester course, I supplement the text and problem/cases with a broader selection of original articles than is possible in a one quarter course.

FEATURES OF THE APPROACH

Several features of my approach to financial statement analysis warrant stressing. I have sought to describe and explain:

(i) the properties of accounting numbers derived from financial statements,

(ii) the key aspects of decisions which use financial statement information, and

(iii) the features of the environment in which these decisions are made.

As part of this attempt to describe and explain (i) (ii) and (iii), empirical evidence is emphasized more than is customary in financial statement analysis texts. Many issues in financial statement analysis can only be resolved finally at an empirical level. It is important that students be exposed to this situation and be able to evaluate critically the existing modes of empirical testing. At the time of writing the text, the existing empirical evidence on the properties of accounting numbers was widely scattered and of highly variable quality. For this reason, I have presented in Chapters 3 through 6 considerable new evidence and have updated prior studies in this area.

Another feature of the approach adopted is the relatively greater emphasis given to describing and explaining key aspects of decisions which use financial statement information and the features of the environment in which these decisions are made. My philosophy is that much richer inferences about the usefulness of financial statement information can be gained by simultaneously considering such aspects and features than can be gained from the more traditional textbook approach of concentrating on the procedures by which financial statement information is derived. Thus, topics such as portfolio theory, asset pricing models and the efficient markets paradigm are given considerable attention. I have sought to present both the evidence relating to efficient capital markets, and to discuss its implication for investment decision-making. Unfortunately, there is much misunderstanding about the latter and it is necessary to also discuss the nonimplications of efficient capital markets.

Where extensive reference has been made to the original research literature, I have deliberately refrained from detailed criticism of individual papers. Rather, criticisms are made in sections titled "Some General Comments". These criticisms are presented for several reasons. Those who use the results from specific research areas should know the limitations of the published research results. Too often one reads that "X found" or "Y demonstrated" without any apparent attempt to evaluate the methodology used or the approach taken by X or Y. The criticisms are also presented so that those who do research will be able to improve upon and extend the existing literature. At various times I have also noted the unsettled nature of the research in specific areas. For example, theory and evidence relating to asset pricing models is noted to be such an area.

STRUCTURE OF THE BOOK

The book is structured into five modules.

I. An introductory chapter (1) on information and decisions that stresses the derived nature of the demand for financial statement information.

II. Five chapters (2 to 6) on properties of accounting numbers e.g., their time series behavior and the importance of economy and industry influences on the numbers of individual firms.

III. Six chapters (7 to 12) on the relationship between the pricing of capital assets and financial statement information. The final chapter in this module discusses the implications of the material examined for investment decisions.

IV. Three chapters (13 to 15) that examine the ability of financial statement information to predict events of interest e.g. bond ratings, corporate bankruptcy and default on commercial and consumer loans.

V. A final chapter (16) that takes a more global perspective inherent in policy decisions about regulating the flow of information that firms provide to investors and creditors.

I strongly recommend doing modules I and II in sequence. Then the reader is reasonably flexible as regards rearranging or omitting any of the remaining modules e.g., various possible sequences could be I, II, III; I, II, IV; I, II, III, V, and I, II, III, IV, V.

Unavoidably, some chapters are more difficult than others. I have assumed the reader has a background in introductory statistics, including some probability theory. Where statistical tools have been used, they are described and illustrated. I have found that students with minimal statistical background (e.g., no prior exposure to ordinary least squares regression) find parts of Chapters 4 and 5 heavy reading. Chapter 8 may prove rather terse to those with no prior exposure to modern finance theory. For chapters that I have observed students finding the most difficult, there are questions that very closely relate to the examples given in the text, (e.g. Question 4.1, Question 5.1 and Question 8.1). My experience is that through working on these questions most students can comprehend any relatively abstract concepts that are in the text. A solutions manual is available for instructors. In addition to containing detailed solutions to each question, this manual contains teaching suggestions and recommendations for additional reading material.

ACKNOWLEDGMENTS

Many people helped in the development of this book. A special note of appreciation is due to William Beaver, Nicholas Dopuch and Baruch Lev for their detailed comments on the manuscript. Ray Ball, Philip Brown, Sydney Davidson, David Green, Charles Horngren, John Ingersoll, John Shank, Myron Scholes, Shyam Sunder and Roman Weil all gave helpful suggestions. Considerable assistance was also received from University of Chicago students—especially Haji Izan, John King, Yves Marois, Jeff Skelton, Tom Stober and Jeff Watts. Jane Hilmers, Vicky Longawa and Evelyn Shropshire provided professional secretarial support. Financial assistance from Coopers and Lybrand helped provide both time and resources to ensure the manuscript was completed in reasonable time. Frank Enenbach and Ron Ledwith of Prentice-Hall provided much encouragement and Kim Field supervised the production with care and patience.

INTRODUCTION

CHAPTER 1

INFORMATION AND DECISIONS

Why might a decision maker decide to invest scarce resources in acquiring or analyzing accounting information? At a very general level, the answer is that he thinks he will make a better decision with the accounting information than without it. This "general" answer, however, raises further questions such as "What do we mean by a better decision?" and "How may accounting information facilitate the making of a better decision?" In this chapter we shall describe a general approach to decision making under uncertainty in which answers to these questions may be found. We stress at the outset that the approach to be described is offered as a "general philosophy." In many cases a more simplified approach to that offered here will be adopted. These simplifications, however, are not inconsistent with the approach to be presented when it is recognized that acquiring information about the alternatives available, the consequences of these alternatives, etc., is a costly activity.

The general approach to decision making under uncertainty will be illustrated by a bank loan decision. The loan decision is necessarily a simplified one, although it does illustrate some important points about choice under uncertainty:

> ILLUSTRATIVE CASE: A steel manufacturing corporation (*ABC Corp.*) has approached a bank for a loan of $1 million at a 10% interest rate for a one-year period. The corporation has provided the bank with financial statements covering the last five years and budgeted financial statements for the next year.
>
> Based on its prior experience with similar firms and a preliminary analysis of *ABC's* financial statements, the bank makes the following assessments: The probability that *ABC* will default on the loan is .2; in the case of default, it is estimated that $200,000 will be spent on legal fees, etc., in selling assets pledged as collateral for the $1 million loan and any accrued interest on that loan.
>
> The bank's best alternative use of the $1 million is an investment in a risk-free one-year government bond at a 7% interest rate.

Initially it will be assumed that the only uncertainty facing the bank is whether *ABC* will default on the loan. In Section 1.1, we shall outline the steps in deciding whether, on the basis of existing information, to grant the loan to *ABC*. In Sections 1.2A and 1.2B we shall outline the steps in deciding whether to acquire more accounting information prior to making the decision to grant or refuse the loan to *ABC*. In Section 1.2C we shall relax the assumption that the only uncertainty relates to the default/non-default of *ABC*. Once this assumption is relaxed, the role of accounting information in decision making is considerably expanded.

4

The basic approach to decision making under uncertainty that will be exposited has been termed *decision analysis*—see Raiffa and Schlaifer [1961]. An extension of this approach to incorporate prior information choice is found in Demski and Feltham [1976].

1.1   DECISION ANALYSIS APPROACH TO CHOICE UNDER UNCERTAINTY

A decision analysis approach to the bank loan problem involves five steps:

Step One: *Determine the Objective of the Decision Maker.*   It will be assumed that the decision maker's objective is to maximize expected utility.[1] To make this objective operational, it is necessary to specify his utility function—such a function encodes a decision maker's preferences for alternative outcomes. It is assumed in this chapter that the decision maker has a linear utility function. For this utility function, maximize expected utility is equivalent to maximize expected monetary payoff.

Step Two: *Determine the Set of Collectively Exhaustive and Mutually Exclusive Actions Available to the Decision Maker.*   In the bank loan problem it is assumed that there are two available actions:

a_1 = lend the $1 million to ABC,

and

a_2 = invest the $1 million in risk-free government bonds,

where a_i is the notation for available action i.

Step Three: *Determine the Set of Collectively Exhaustive and Mutually Exclusive States of Nature (or Outcomes).*   Two possible outcomes are assumed possible in the bank loan problem:

$s_1 = ABC$ repays loan and interest,

and

$s_2 = ABC$ defaults on repayment, and the bank outlays $200,000
     to recover the principal and interest,

where s_i is the notation for state i.

Step Four: *Determine the Probabilities of Each Available State.*   The problem specified the following probabilities:

$$\phi(s_1) = .8$$
$$\phi(s_2) = .2,$$

where $\phi(s_i)$ is the notation for the probability of state i occurring. These assessments were "based on the bank's prior experience with similar firms and a preliminary analysis of $ABC's$ financial statements."

Step Five: *Determine the End-of-Period Wealth for Each State of Nature (Outcome), Conditional upon a Particular Action Being Taken.*[2] A convenient way to summarize this information is via the following *payoff matrix*:

s_i $\diagdown$ a_j	s_1 ABC Not Default	s_2 ABC Defaults
a_1 Lend to ABC	$1,100,000	$ 900,000
a_2 Invest in Risk-free Bonds	$1,070,000	$1,070,000

That is, if the bank lends to ABC (a_1) and ABC defaults (s_2), it will receive $900,000 (the $1,100,000 principal and accrued interest less the $200,000 required to recover the $1,100,000).

The above stages are sufficient to structure the problem facing the bank. Prior to determining what decision should be made, some more notation will be introduced. Let $E(U|a_j)$ be the expected utility of action j. Then

$$E(U|a_j) = \sum_{i=1}^{S} U(s_i, a_j) \cdot \phi(s_i),$$

where $U(s_i, a_j)$ is the utility of the payoff to the bank if s_i occurs and a_j is taken. We are now in a position to choose the preferred action.

$$E(U|a_j) = U(s_1, a_j) \times \phi(s_1) + U(s_2, a_j) \times \phi(s_2)$$
$$E(U|a_1) = \$1,100,000 \times .8 + \$900,000 \times .2 = \$1,060,000$$
$$E(U|a_2) = \$1,070,000 \times .8 + \$1,070,000 \times .2 = \$1,070,000.$$

Given the bank's objective of maximizing expected utility (which in the example is equivalent to maximizing expected monetary payoff), the preferred action is to invest the $1 million in risk-free government securities.

It is important to note that we assume the criterion of a good decision is one that maximizes *expected* utility. This does not guarantee that the actual outcome of the decision will be that preferred by the bank. North [1968] is particularly eloquent on this point:

Choosing an alternative that is consistent with [our] preferences and present knowledge does not guarantee that we will choose the alternative that by

hindsight turns out to be most profitable. We must distinguish between a good
decision and a good *outcome*.... Decision theory is not a substitute for the
fortune teller. It is rather a procedure that takes account of all available
information to give us the best possible logical decision. It will minimize the
consequence of getting an unfavorable outcome, but we cannot expect our
theory to shield us from all "bad luck." The best protection we have against a
bad outcome is a good decision. (pp. 200–201)

The temptation to use *hindsight* to evaluate past decisions is often overwhelming. Such use of hindsight ignores the fact that a decision made at t
can be made only on the basis of information available at time t.

1.2 DECISION ANALYSIS APPROACH TO PRIOR INFORMATION CHOICE

The only uncertainty assumed in the above problem is whether ABC
will or will not default on the loan. The assessments of $\phi(s_1)=.8$ and
$\phi(s_2)=.2$ were based on the bank's "prior experience with similar firms and
a preliminary analysis of ABC's financial statements." Prior to making
loan decisions, a bank often has the option of extending its information
set. This extension may take various forms, e.g., requesting more information from ABC or doing a more detailed analysis of the information
contained in ABC's financial statements.

Such options to extend the existing information set are rarely cost-
free. The question naturally arises whether it is cost-effective to make this
extension. In this section, a structured approach to making this information choice decision is presented. In Section 1.2A, the case of perfect state
revelation by an information system is analyzed. This case is important in
that it allows one to set a maximum amount one would be willing to pay
for additional accounting information in a specific decision setting. In
Section 1.2B we shall discuss the more general case of an information
system yielding imperfect revelation about which future state will occur.

A Expected Value of Perfect Information

A calculation, termed the expected value of perfect information
(hereafter EVPI), is designed to indicate an upper bound on the amount
one would be willing to pay for additional information in a specific
decision context. There are three steps in determining EVPI:

Step One: *Determine the Optimal Action Conditional upon Knowing What
State Will Occur.* If the bank is told that ABC will not default on the
loan (s_1), the optimal action is to grant the loan (a_1)—end-of-period
wealth is $1,100,000. The optimal action if the bank is told that ABC will

default on the loan (s_2) is to invest in the risk-free government bills (a_2)—end-of-period wealth is $1,070,000.

Step Two: *Determine the Probabilities of Each State Being Revealed After You Have Purchased Advance State Revelation.* Given the problem facing the bank, the best estimate of either state being revealed is the current assessed probability of each occurring, i.e., $\phi(s_1)=.8$ and $\phi(s_2)=.2$.

Given the data from Steps One and Two it is possible to calculate the bank's expected utility when the actual state to occur is revealed prior to making the loan decision to *ABC*.

$$E(U \mid \text{advance state revelation}) = \sum_{i=1}^{S} \left\{ \max_{a \in A} U(s_i, a) \right\} \cdot \phi(s_i)$$
$$= \$1,100,000 \times .8 + \$1,070,000 \times .2$$
$$= \$1,094,000.$$

Step Three: *Determine the Expected Utility of the Optimal Action, Based on the Existing Set of Information Available to the Decision Maker.* From Section 1.1, the expected utility of the optimal act $[E(U|a^*)]$ is $1,070,000.
The notation for calculating EVPI is

$$\text{EVPI} = \sum_{i=1}^{S} \left\{ \max_{a \in A} U(s_i, a) \right\} \phi(s_i) - E(U|a^*)$$
$$= \$1,100,000 \times .8 + \$1,070,000 \times .2 - \$1,070,000$$
$$= \$24,000.$$

Thus, the maximum that the bank would be willing to pay to acquire or analyze additional information in the bank loan decision is $24,000. This $24,000 is the difference between the expected utility given advance state revelation and the expected utility of the optimal action given the existing set of information.

B   Information Choice in a Structured Environment

The most that available information systems can provide the bank is a revision in its probability assessments to less than or equal to $\phi(s_1)=1$ or $\phi(s_1)=0$. Suppose a proposal is made that the bank further analyze the financial statements of *ABC*. The question naturally arises whether it is cost-effective to conduct such an analysis. In making such a decision there is a two-step procedure:

(1) Is the cost of the new information system (i.e., from the additional analysis) less than EVPI? *If* yes, then

(2) Is the expected utility with the new information system greater than the expected utility from using currently available information?

If the answer to (1) is no, then (2) becomes irrelevant. This is the importance of calculating EVPI. In many cases, knowledge of EVPI allows one to reject information options *without* analysis of their properties. As such an analysis is a costly activity, the avoidance of it is important.

In many cases the answer to (1) is yes. In addressing (2), there are five steps in a formal analysis of the information system choice problem. To illustrate these steps, the following problem faced by the bank will be examined. It is a continuation of the problem examined in Section 1.1.

> ILLUSTRATIVE CASE: The bank determines that the most critical factor affecting whether *ABC* will default is next period's operating expenses to sales ratio. For simplicity, we shall assume that the bank is interested only in predicting if this ratio is ≤ 1 *or* > 1. Based on prior experience with similar loan applicants, the bank assesses that the probability of next period's expense to sales ratio being ≤ 1, given that *ABC* does not default, is .9. The probability of this ratio being > 1, given that *ABC* does default, is assessed to be .7.
>
> Prior to making the loan decision, the bank has the option to develop a model to predict next period's expenses to sales ratio. This development requires collecting details of this ratio over the past 20 years, analysis of the time-series behavior of this ratio, and computer estimation of a specific time-series model. The total cost is estimated to be $1,000.

Is it cost-effective for the bank to make this $1,000 investment in information production prior to making the loan decision? There are five steps in examining this question:

Step One: *Determine the Set of Mutually Exclusive and Collectively Exhaustive Signals the Information System May Produce.* In the above problem, it will be assumed that the time-series model will give one of two signals:

$$y_1 = \text{Expense to sales ratio} \leq 1,$$

and

$$y_2 = \text{Expense to sales ratio} > 1,$$

where y_i is a signal from an information system denoted by η.

Step Two: *Determine the Probability of Receiving Each Signal of the Information System.* Using the information available in the problem, the following probabilities were calculated[3]:

$$\phi(y_1) = .78$$
$$\phi(y_2) = .22.$$

Step Three: *Determine the Revised Probabilities of Each State Occurring, Conditional upon Receiving a Particular Signal from the Information System.* Using the information from Step Two and other information available in the problem, the revised probabilities were[4]

$$\phi(s_1|y_1,\eta) = .92$$
$$\phi(s_2|y_1,\eta) = .08$$
$$\phi(s_1|y_2,\eta) = .36$$
$$\phi(s_2|y_2,\eta) = .64.$$

Step Four: *Determine the Optimal Action Conditional upon Each Signal from the Information System.* Each signal will, in general, cause the bank's revised probability assessments of default to be different from the initial probability assessments. The action that was optimal based on the initial probability assessments may no longer be optimal for the revised assessments. Thus, it is necessary to redo the five-step analysis in Section 1.1 for each signal of the information system. The revised payoff matrix after incorporation of the $1,000 cost of developing a model to predict the expense to sales ratio is

s_i a_j	s_1 ABC Not Default	s_2 ABC Defaults
a_1 Lend to ABC	$1,099,000	$ 899,000
a_2 Invest in Risk-free bonds	$1,069,000	$1,069,000

The general notation for the revised probability case is

$$E(U|a,y,\eta) = \sum_{i=1}^{S} U(s_i,a)\cdot\phi(s_i|y,\eta).$$

If y_1 is received by the bank (i.e., the expense to sales ratio is predicted to be $\leqslant 1$),

$$E(U|a_1,y_1,\eta) = \$1,099,000 \times .92 + \$899,000 \times .08$$
$$= \$1,083,000$$
$$E(U|a_2,y_1,\eta) = \$1,069,000 \times .92 + \$1,069,000 \times .08$$
$$= \$1,069,000.$$

That is, a_1 (grant the loan to *ABC*) is the optimal action if signal y_1 is received.

If y_2 is received by the bank (i.e., the expense to sales ratio is predicted to be >1),

$$E(U|a_1,y_2,\eta) = \$1,099,000 \times .36 + \$899,000 \times .64$$
$$= \$971,000$$
$$E(U|a_2,y_2,\eta) = \$1,069,000 \times .36 + \$1,069,000 \times .64$$
$$= \$1,069,000.$$

That is, a_2 (invest in risk-free government securities) is the optimal action if signal y_2 is received.

Step Five: *Determine the Expected Utility with the Information System.* The notation for determining this is

$$E(U|\eta) = \sum_{k=1}^{Y} (U|a_{y_k}^*,\eta) \cdot \phi(y_k|\eta),$$

where $a_{y_k}^*$ is the optimal action conditional upon receiving y_k.

$$E(U|\eta) = \$1,083,000 \times .78 + \$1,069,000 \times .22$$
$$= \$1,079,920.$$

Should the bank invest in this modeling of the expense to sales ratio in order to predict next period's ratio? The expected utility from using only the existing set of information (let $\mathscr{E}$ be this existing set of information) is

$$E(U|\mathscr{E}) = \$1,070,000.$$

The expected utility if the modeling of the expense to sales ratio is undertaken prior to the loan decision is

$$E(U|\eta) = \$1,079,920.$$

Thus, it is cost-effective (by \$9,920) to invest resources in the modeling of the expense to sales ratio.

It was noted at the outset that a decision maker chooses to invest scarce resources in acquiring and analyzing accounting information because he thinks he will make a better decision with the accounting information than without it. The above bank loan example has enabled us to make this comment more specific. A better decision is one that leads to an increase in expected utility. The expected utility prior to analyzing the expense to sales ratio is \$1,070,000; the expected utility after deciding to invest \$1,000 in the analysis of the expense to sales ratio is \$1,079,920. It is also instructive to see *why* this increase in expected utility occurs. By further analyzing accounting information, the bank is able to revise its probability assessments about *ABC* defaulting on the loan. Moreover, this revision is sufficient to change the actions the bank may take. Prior to

modeling the financial ratio series, the bank would reject the loan application. Subsequent to modeling the financial series, the bank will grant the
loan if the forecasted expense to sales ratio is ≤ 1 and reject the loan if the
forecasted ratio is > 1.

The term *information needs* of a decision maker has not been used in
the prior discussion. In a decision analysis framework, the demand for
information is *derived* from the increase in utility a decision maker expects
to obtain from its acquisition in a specific decision context(s). Information
is not "needed" in isolation of any decision context(s).[5] The issue of
whether the bank found it cost-effective to invest the \$1,000 in information
production was addressed by how it would affect its actions in the loan
decision and through these actions its expected utility. One factor that
affected this expected utility was the cost of the information system. Had
the cost of the information production alternative exceeded \$10,920, the
bank would not have found it cost-effective to make the information
investment. (Why?)

C   Information Choice in a Less Structured Environment[6]

The example in Section 1.2B is obviously very simplified. Making the
bank loan decision more realistic could take various approaches. One
approach is to admit to more actions and more outcomes of these actions
but still retain the assumption that the only uncertainty pertains to state
occurrence. For example, instead of considering only two available actions
(lend/not lend) we could allow for lending at various interest rates and
various time periods and for various amounts. The role of accounting
information in this expanded problem would remain the same as that
exposited in Section 1.2B, i.e., to aid in the revision of probability assessments about which possible outcome will occur.

Alternatively, the example could be made more realistic by admitting
to uncertainty as regards actions possible to the banker and the possible
consequences of these actions. For instance, there may be uncertainty
about the future realizable values of the assets ABC is willing to pledge as
collateral for the loan. In this case, the bank may decide it is cost-effective
to acquire more information about the past market values of these assets
and the various factors that affect these values. Similarly, the bank may be
uncertain as to the restrictions to include in debt covenants related to the
loan. In this case, the bank may deem it cost-effective to undertake
research into which financial ratios of steel manufacturing companies are
the best predictors of loan default. The results of this research could affect
the ratios which the bank includes in a restrictive covenant agreement that
it requires ABC to sign when borrowing from the bank.

When the costs of acquiring information about the alternatives available to a decision maker, the consequences of these alternatives, and the probability of these consequences are recognized, it is apparent that simplified approaches to decision making under uncertainty may be cost-effective. In subsequent chapters we shall illustrate several such simplifications. For instance, in Chapter 8 the use of the *market model* to reduce the number of parameters to be estimated in portfolio analysis is discussed.

1.3 SUMMARY

The decision analysis framework outlined in this chapter is a highly structured approach to decision making under uncertainty. It is not contended that all decisions to utilize financial statement information do (or should) methodically proceed through the five steps outlined in Section 1.2B. Rather, the framework is presented more as a general philosophy to be followed in decisions on the acquisition or analysis of financial statement information. In subsequent chapters, we shall examine in some detail the decisions that external parties such as investors and creditors make. Emphasis will be placed on the potential use of financial statement information in these decisions.

NOTES

[1]Some "heady" issues in choice under uncertainty are subsumed when we refer to the "decision maker's utility function." One could assume it is the utility function of the specific loan evaluation officer. Alternatively it could refer to the utility function of the shareholders of the bank. In the latter case, if one makes certain assumptions about capital markets (e.g., they are complete and perfect), the objective of maximize the market value of the bank's shares is appropriate. If these assumptions are not made, then deriving the "decision maker's utility function" involves difficult problems of aggregating the diverse utility functions of individual shareholders. See Sen [1970] for a basic reference on these issues and Demski and Feltham [1976, Chapters 2 and 8] for discussion of these issues in an accounting context.

[2]The "end-of-period wealth" presented in Step Five is for the bank loan problem. Given the assumption of a linear utility function, it is valid to ignore the total end-of-period wealth of the bank. For most other utility

functions, however, this restriction to the effects of only the bank loan decision could lead to the choice of alternatives inconsistent with a maximize expected utility choice criterion.

[3]These probabilities were calculated via the following formula:

$$\phi(y_k) = \sum_{i=1}^{S} \phi(y_k|s_i) \cdot \phi(s_i).$$

Details of $\phi(y_k|s_i)$ were given in the problem—$\phi(y_1|s_1) = .9$ and $\phi(y_2|s_2) = .7$. Details of $\phi(s_i)$ were given in Section 1.1—$\phi(s_1) = .8$ and $\phi(s_2) = .2$. Then

$$\phi(y_1) = \phi(y_1|s_1) \cdot \phi(s_1) + \phi(y_1|s_2) \cdot \phi(s_2)$$
$$= .9 \times .8 + .3 \times .2 = .78.$$

Similarly,

$$\phi(y_2) = \phi(y_2|s_1) \cdot \phi(s_1) + \phi(y_2|s_2) \cdot \phi(s_2)$$
$$= .1 \times .8 + .7 \times .2 = .22.$$

[4]These probabilities were calculated using Bayes's theorem:

$$\phi(s_i|y_k) = \frac{\phi(y_k|s_i) \cdot \phi(s_i)}{\phi(y_k)}.$$

Details of the calculations are as follows: If $y_1 \leqslant 1$,

	$\phi(s_i)$	$\phi(y_1|s_i)$	$\phi(y_1,s_i)$	$\phi(s_i|y_1,\eta)$
s_1	.8	.9	.72	.92
s_2	.2	.3	.06	.08
			.78	

If $y_2 > 1$,

	$\phi(s_i)$	$\phi(y_2|s_i)$	$\phi(y_2,s_i)$	$\phi(s_i|y_2,\eta)$
s_1	.8	.1	.08	.36
s_2	.2	.7	.14	.64
			.22	

[5]The phrase "information need" is often used in the accounting literature in reference to a specific decision model. For example, if a bank uses a decision model of refuse credit if an applicant's expense to sales ratio exceeds 1, it "needs" to know the expense to sales ratio of each applicant. Note, however, that the basic issue of what decision model a bank uses is itself an object of choice. There are many other models a bank

could use in credit decisions, and their information inputs vary considerably. Thus, from a decision analysis perspective, the bank does not need to know the applicant's expense to sales ratio. It is quite possible that it is cost-effective to use a decision model other than refuse credit if the expense to sales ratio exceeds 1.

[6]See Demski and Feltham [1976, Chapter 3] for further discussion of issues raised in this section.

QUESTIONS

QUESTION 1.1:   Philosophy of Information Choice Decisions

Demski and Feltham [1976] describe the basic philosophy to accounting information acquisition/analysis decisions that was exposited in Chapter 1 as follows:

> Desirability [of accounting information] is determined in a conventional economic manner. That is, we explicitly consider available opportunities and prevailing tastes and beliefs. By implication...*the focus is on analysis and not on prescription.* In consumer demand theory, for example, we analyze the question of how much butter an individual should consume, but we do not categorically state a preferred amount of butter. Rather, this is a function of the individual's opportunities, tastes and beliefs. Treating accounting measures as an economic commodity quite naturally produces the same outcome. We analyze the question of which [accounting] measurements should be produced in a particular setting, but we do not categorically state preferred types of measurements. Rather, these are a function of the individual's *opportunities, tastes and beliefs.* (p. 8, emphasis added)

REQUIRED

(1) What corresponds to the bank's "opportunities," "tastes," and "beliefs" in the lending decision illustration in Chapter 1?
(2) Explain the statement "the focus is on analysis and not on prescription" by reference to the lending decision illustration in Chapter 1.

QUESTION 1.2:   Good Decisions and Bad Outcomes

A 1931 court judgment in a case finding negligence on the part of an investment trustee included the following statement:

> It was common knowledge, not only amongst bankers and trust companies, but the general public as well, that the stock market condition at the time [August 1929]...was an unhealthy one, that values were very much inflated, and that a crash was almost sure to occur. (quoted in Langbein and Posner [1976, p. 61])

(1) In the decision analysis framework outlined in Chapter 1, what is the criterion for judging if a decision was a "good" one?

(2) Comment on the above 1931 statement in the light of your answer to (1).

QUESTION 1.3: Information Needs of Investors

In an article titled "Information Needs of Individual Investors," Baker and Haslem [1973] reported the results of a questionnaire study. The population examined was common stock investors in metropolitan Washington, D.C. Questionnaires were sent to a sample of 1,623 individual investors on the customer lists of five stock brokerage firms—851 completed questionnaires were received. Investors were asked to indicate the "relative importance" of 33 individual factors in their investment decisions. A five-point scale (5 = maximum importance,..., 1 = no importance) was used. The mean ratings for several factors were

1. Future economic outlook of the company (4.34),
2. Quality of management (4.13),
3. Future economic outlook of the industry in which the firm is a part (4.05),
4. Expected future growth in sales (3.93),

.

.

.

31. Expected future level of long-term interest rate on corporate bonds (2.48),
32. Size of the company (2.31), and
33. Ease with which the company can sell its assets in case of failure (2.23).

(1) What role does the information need notion play in the decision analysis framework exposited in Chapter 1? Explain your answer.

(2) Evaluate the questionnaire approach to determining the importance of individual factors in common stock investment decisions.

QUESTION 1.4: Information Choice Decisions Under Uncertainty:
Down-Under Bank

1. The *Down-Under Bank* has been approached by a customer named Gough for a personal loan of $2,000 for one year. Interest on personal loans is currently at 12%. Gough proposes to repay both the principal and

interest at the end of the one-year loan period. Based on Gough's educa-
tion level, job, salary, and other personal characteristics, *Down-Under*
assesses the probability of default on the loan at .15. If Gough defaults,
both the interest and principal are fully written off by the bank. The
bank's alternative use of the $2,000 is investment in a risk-free asset at 5%.
It chooses between actions using a "maximize expected monetary payoff"
criterion.

REQUIRED

(1) Should *Down-Under* grant the loan to Gough? (Assume s_1 = no default, s_2 = default.)
(2) What is the expected value of perfect information (EVPI) about
whether Gough will default on the loan? Of what use is the EVPI
calculation to *Down-Under*?

2. Prior to making the personal loan decision, *Down-Under* can
acquire information on the credit-worthiness of Gough from a credit rating
agency. The agency charges $30 for each report. The credit report will
contain one of two signals. The first signal (y_1) is that Gough is a good
credit risk, while the second signal (y_2) is that he is a bad credit risk.
Down-Under assesses that $\phi(y_1|s_1)=.98$ and $\phi(y_1|s_2)=.3$. Using these prob-
ability assessments and other information given in the problem, *Down-
Under* determines that $\phi(s_1|y_1)=.949$ and $\phi(s_1|y_2)=.139$. The probability
of the credit agency reporting that Gough is a good credit risk is determined to be .878.

REQUIRED

(1) The manager of *Down-Under* comments that the information provided by the credit rating agency is potentially useful but too expensive to obtain. Do you agree?
(2) The credit agency decides to reduce its charge for each report to $15.
Should the manager of *Down-Under* revise his decision not to
purchase the credit rating on Gough?

QUESTION 1.5:   Information Choice Decisions Under Uncertainty:
                On the Move Corp.

1. *On the Move Corp.* is a company active in the "takeover game." At
present, it is considering acquiring a publicly listed company—*XYZ Corp.*
On the Move can acquire *XYZ* for $2 million. The key issue in the takeover
decision is the value of the assets of *XYZ*. *XYZ*'s latest balance sheet
shows cash of $1 million and municipal bonds of $3 million. *XYZ* has no
liabilities. The municipal bonds mature in one year. The interest rate on
the bond is 20%. *On the Move* can invest cash at 10% with its bank.

On the Move is concerned with the possibility of the municipality defaulting on the bonds. Indeed, it assesses the probability of such a default at .8. A default would mean *On the Move* would receive nothing for the $3 million bond or the accrued interest of $600,000. *On the Move* chooses projects on an expected monetary payoff basis.

REQUIRED

(1) Should *On the Move* take over *XYZ*, or should it invest the $2 million with its bank? (Hint: Let state 1 be no default, state 2 be default; express all amounts in end of period 1 values.)

(2) What is the expected value of perfect information about whether the municipality will default on the bond?

2. *On the Move* decides to consider purchasing more information about the municipal bond. It approaches a merchant bank which offers *On the Move* two alternatives:

Alternative A. For $100,000 it will use its automated bond rating program. This program will yield one of two signals:

$$y_1: \quad \text{rating} \geqslant B$$
$$y_2: \quad \text{rating} < B.$$

On the Move assesses that $\phi(y_1|s_1)=.6$ and $\phi(y_1|s_2)=.3$. Using these assessments and other information in the problem, *On the Move* determines that

$$\phi(s_1|y_1)= .33; \qquad \phi(s_2|y_1)= .67; \qquad \phi(y_1)=.36$$
$$\phi(s_1|y_2)=.125; \qquad \phi(s_2|y_2)=.875; \qquad \phi(y_2)=.64.$$

Alternative B. For $200,000 it will engage its super new MBA graduate—Hobie Leland, Jr.—to rate the bonds. Hobie will also report two signals:

$$y_1: \quad \text{rating} \geqslant B$$
$$y_2: \quad \text{rating} < B.$$

On the Move assesses that $\phi(y_1|s_1)=.9$ and $\phi(y_1|s_2)=.25$. Using these assessments and other information in the problem, *On the Move* determines that

$$\phi(s_1|y_1)=.47; \qquad \phi(s_2|y_1)=.53; \qquad \phi(y_1)=.38$$
$$\phi(s_1|y_2)=.03; \qquad \phi(s_2|y_2)=.97; \qquad \phi(y_2)=.62.$$

REQUIRED

(1) On what basis would *On the Move* assess the $\phi(y_k|s_i)$ probabilities given above?

(2) Should *On the Move* adopt alternative A, or alternative B, or neither? Why? (Express all amounts in end of period 1 values. Assume the $100,000 under Alternative A and the $200,000 under Alternative B are not paid until the end of the period 1.)

(3) Information can be potentially useful in a decision but too costly to acquire. Is there any evidence that this situation exists for alternative A or alternative B?

REFERENCES

BAKER, H. K., and HASLEM, J. A. "Information Needs of Individual Investors." *Journal of Accountancy* (Nov. 1973): 64–69.

DEMSKI, J. S., and FELTHAM, G. A. *A Conceptual Approach to Cost Determination.* Iowa State University Press, Ames, 1976.

LANGBEIN, J. H., and POSNER, R. A. "Market Funds and Trust-Investment Law." *American Bar Foundation Research Journal* No. 1 (1976): 1–34.

NORTH, D. W. "A Tutorial Introduction to Decision Theory." *IEEE Transactions on Systems Science and Cybernetics* (Sept. 1968): 200–210.

RAIFFA, H., and SCHLAIFER, R. *Applied Statistical Decision Theory.* M.I.T. Press, Cambridge, Mass., 1961.

SEN, A. *Collective Choice and Social Welfare.* Holden-Day, Inc., San Francisco, 1970.

PROPERTIES OF ACCOUNTING NUMBERS

CHAPTER 2

FINANCIAL STATEMENT ANALYSIS: AN OVERVIEW

Financial statement analysis has traditionally concerned itself with the study of relationships within a set of financial statements *at a point in time* and with the trends in these relationships *over time*. In this chapter we shall outline various techniques that have been developed for these tasks. Further analysis of their rationale and assumptions is made in Chapters 3–6. Cross-sectional techniques and time-series techniques of financial statement analysis will be examined.

The financial statements of *Jos. Schlitz Brewing Company* (hereafter *Schlitz*) will be used to illustrate these techniques. Tables 2.1–2.3 contain summary (1) balance sheets, (2) income statements, and (3) changes in financial position statements of *Schlitz* for the 1971–1975 period. The information presented for each year in these tables is as reported in the annual report of the respective year. *Schlitz* is the second largest brewer in the United States, accounting for 15.5% of total domestic consumption in 1975. It is one of the three major publicly listed brewing companies in the United States which market their brands nationally. The other two major national brewers are *Anheuser-Busch, Incorporated* (1975 market share,

TABLE 2.1   Jos. Schlitz Brewing Company
Comparative Balance Sheets: 1971–1975 ($000's)

	1971	1972	1973	1974	1975
Assets					
1. Cash	6,015	12,606	9,687	9,215	12,571
2. Marketable securities	26,119	64,577	48,472	11,418	7,519
3. Accounts receivable	28,609	30,426	26,456	35,647	31,053
4. Inventories	31,756	38,794	53,657	53,524	56,521
5. Other current assets	7,515	4,481	6,923	17,799	9,470
6. Investments and other assets	33,290	32,355	34,181	37,562	29,818
7. Plant and equipment	236,361	240,015	276,976	400,363	523,283
8. Total assets	369,665	423,254	456,352	565,528	670,235
Liabilities and Equity					
9. Accounts payable	18,644	31,857	37,480	36,709	44,343
10. Other current liabilities	31,689	50,389	41,360	33,598	39,816
11. Long-term debt	70,879	64,800	62,026	143,828	212,717
12. Deferred tax	18,108	23,708	30,008	36,133	46,840
13. Shareholders' equity	230,345	252,500	285,478	315,260	326,519
	369,665	423,254	456,352	565,528	670,235

TABLE 2.2 Jos. Schlitz Brewing Company
Comparative Income Statements: 1971–1975 ($000's)

		1971	1972	1973	1974	1975
14.	Sales	669,178	779,359	892,745	1,015,978	1,130,439
15.	Other income	2,592	4,599	6,218	8,013	1,484
16.	Cost of goods sold	360,819	422,490	498,901	619,949	728,861
17.	Excise taxes	147,084	168,082	189,703	201,454	207,452
18.	Marketing, administrative, and general expenses	86,570	95,462	94,373	100,932	110,641
19.	Interest expense	5,910	5,747	6,071	7,857	14,526
20.	Other expenses	1,340	2,420	466	0	9,528
21.	Earnings before tax	70,047	89,757	109,451	93,799	60,915
22.	Tax	34,798	43,918	54,241	44,817	30,019
23.	Earnings after tax	35,249	45,839	55,210	48,982	30,896
24.	Extraordinary items[a]	0	(8,300)	(1,535)	0	0
25.	Earnings after extra. items	35,249	37,539	53,675	48,982	30,896
26.	Earnings (before tax) per share	1.22[b]	1.58	1.90	1.69	1.06
27.	Market price per share (Dec. 31)	$36.375	$58.375	$56	$16	$19.125

[a] The 1972 and 1973 extraordinary losses related to the closing of breweries in Brooklyn and Kansas City, respectively. The 1973 *Annual Report* noted that both breweries "lacked production efficiency and expansion potential" (p. 3).

[b] Adjusted for 3 for 1 stock split in 1972.

23.4%—hereafter *Busch*) and *Pabst Brewing Company* (1975 market share, 10.4%—hereafter *Pabst*).[1] In addition to competing with national brewing companies, *Schlitz* competes with regional brewing companies in geographical segments of the U.S. market (e.g., *Adolph Coors Company* in the west and *F & M Schaefer* in the east).

2.1 CROSS-SECTIONAL TECHNIQUES

Two frequently discussed cross-sectional techniques of financial statement analysis are (1) common-size statements and (2) financial ratio analysis. In both techniques, the results for a specific firm are compared to some bench mark—e.g., the results of another firm, the average results for the industry, or some "ideal" bench mark. "Ideal" bench marks are

TABLE 2.3 Jos. Schlitz Brewing Company Comparative Statements of Changes in Financial Position: 1971–1975 ($000's)

	1971	1972	1973	1974	1975
Working Capital Provided by					
28. Net earnings	35,249	45,839	55,210	48,892	30,896
29. Depreciation	13,496	16,654	18,636	21,692	25,301
30. Deferred tax	6,445	8,100	6,300	6,125	10,707
31. Extraordinary items	0	(5,600)[a]	(1,535)	0	0
32. Issue of long-term debt	54,010	7,500	4,462	83,195	75,000
33. Other sources	8,298	5,219	10,345	5,933	17,319
	117,498	77,712	93,418	165,927	159,223
Working Capital Used for					
34. Additions to plant and equipment	48,223	28,923	64,105	150,500	165,417
35. Cash dividends declared	14,940	16,056	17,677	19,466	19,760
36. Retirement of long-term debt	46,517	13,579	7,236	1,393	6,111
37. Other uses	66	(935)	6,683	3,627	(7,744)
	109,746	57,623	95,701	174,986	183,544
Net Change in Working Capital	7,752	20,089	(2,283)	(9,059)	(24,321)
Other Information					
38. Barrels of beer sold	16,708	18,906	21,343	22,661	23,279
39. Plant capacity in barrels	18,000	20,500	21,700	24,000	25,300

[a] Extraordinary items, net of portion not affecting working capital.

discussed in Chapter 3. In this chapter, the results of *Schlitz* will be compared with (1) the other two major national brewers and (2) arithmetically weighted brewing industry averages.[2] Chapter 3 also contains a discussion of arithmetically weighted averages and other procedures for computing industry financial statements.

A Common-Size Statements

One impetus to the development of the common-size statement technique came from the problems in comparing the financial statements of firms which differ in size. Suppose Company A has long-term debt of $10 million and Company B has long-term debt of $8 million. Due to possible size differences between Companies A and B, it would be misleading to always infer that Company A was more highly levered than Company B. One way of controlling for these size differences is to express the components of the balance sheet as a percentage of total assets and the components of the income statement as a percentage of total revenue. The derived statements are termed common-size statements. For instance, in 1975 *Schlitz* had accounts receivable of $31,053,000, inventories of $56,521,000, and total assets of $670,235,000. The common-size balance sheet of *Schlitz* would show:

accounts receivable of 4.6% ($31,053,000/$670,235,000) and inventories of 8.4% ($56,521,000/$670,235,000).

Table 2.4 illustrates the 1975 common-size balance sheets and income

TABLE 2.4   Common-Size Statements: 1975

A. *Common-Size Balance Sheet*

Assets	Schlitz	Busch	Pabst	Industry Average
Cash and marketable securities	3.0	18.7	17.0	10.71
Accounts receivable	4.6	4.8	4.3	9.44
Inventories	8.4	11.4	15.2	14.92
Other current assets	1.4	0	1.3	2.30
Plant and equipment	78.1	60.3	62.2	51.38
Investments and other assets	4.5	4.8	0	11.25
	100	100	100	100

Liabilities + Equity				
Accounts payable	6.6	6.6	6.6	9.00
Other current liabilities	6.0	6.8	11.0	11.13
Long-term debt	31.7	28.5	0	17.30
Deferred tax	7.0	8.7	7.7	5.44
Stockholders's equity	48.7	49.4	74.7	57.13
	100	100	100	100

B. *Common-Size Income Statement*

Revenues	100	100	100	100
	100	100	100	100

Expenses				
Cost of goods sold	64.4	65.6	65.7	62.01
Excise taxes	18.3	19.1	21.0	20.37
Marketing, general, and administrative expenses	9.8	6.2	7.6	11.66
Interest expense	1.3	1.1	0	.78
Other expense	.8	0	.1	1.01
Tax	2.7	3.9	2.5	2.79
Income after tax	2.7	4.1	3.1	1.38
	100	100	100	100

statements of *Schlitz, Busch, Pabst,* and the brewing industry. [Common-size statements are a convenient way to compare the composition of financial statements across companies.] For instance, it is readily apparent that *Schlitz* in 1975 had a much lower percentage of total assets in cash and marketable securities (3.0%) than either of its two main competitors (*Busch,* 18.7%; *Pabst,* 17.0%) or the industry average of 10.71%. Similarly, it is apparent that *Schlitz* spent more on advertising, general, and administrative expenses (9.8% of revenue) than either *Busch* (6.2%) or *Pabst* (7.6%). These comparisons may lead to further analysis to account for or explain the difference between the percentages across companies or between a company and an industry average.

B Financial Ratio Analysis

The most extensively discussed cross-sectional tool is financial ratio analysis. Many alternative categories of financial ratios and numerous individual ratios have been proposed in the literature.[3] The following four categories and ratios within each category are meant to be illustrative rather than exhaustive:

(1) Liquidity ratios.

(2) Leverage/capital structure ratios.

(3) Profitability ratios.

(4) Turnover ratios.

Common stock security ratios are discussed in Subsection (5).

(1) Liquidity Ratios

Liquidity refers to the ability of a firm to meet its short-term financial obligations when and as they fall due. Several ratios provide evidence on liquidity.

Current Ratio

$$\frac{\text{Current assets}}{\text{Current liabilities}}$$

This ratio has a long history in liquidity analysis. Foulke [1968, p. 181] cites usage of the terms *current assets* and *current liabilities* by a corporation (*Pennsylvania Railroad Co.*) as early as 1891.[4] The main categories of assets in the numerator are cash, short-term marketable securities, accounts receivable, inventories, and prepaid expenses. The main categories in the denominator include accounts payable, dividends, taxes due within one year, and short-term bank loans.

Quick Ratio

$$\frac{\text{Cash} + \text{Short-term marketable securities} + \text{Accounts receivable}}{\text{Current liabilities}}$$

Concerns with the liquidity of inventories and prepaid expenses led to proposals for the quick ratio. The assets in the numerator are referred to as *quick assets*. Both the current and quick ratios have been criticized on the basis that they do not incorporate information about the timing and magnitude of future cash inflows and outflows—see Walter [1957] and Lemke [1970]. These criticisms, in turn, led to proposals for cash-based and *funds-flow*-based liquidity ratios. One such ratio is the *defensive interval* measure.   *magnitude*

Defensive Interval Measure

$$\frac{\text{Total defensive assets}}{\text{Projected daily operating expenditures}}$$

Davidson et al. [1964] describe the components of the measure as follows:

> Defensive assets include cash, short-term marketable securities and accounts receivable. Inventories are not included in the total, nor are current liabilities deducted from the total. The denominator includes all projected operating costs requiring the use of defensive assets. Ideally, this would be based on the cash budget for the next year or shorter period. Since this information is unlikely to be available to external analysts, the total of operating expenses on the income statement for the prior period will usually serve as a basis for calculating the projected expenditures. Two adjustments must be made to the total expense figure on that statement:
>
> (1) Depreciation, deferred taxes and other expenses that do not utilize defensive assets must be subtracted.
>
> (2) Adjustments should be made for known changes in planned operations. (p. 23)

The ratio is an estimate of the number of days the *defensive assets* could service the projected daily operating expenditures of the firm.

Brewing Industry Liquidity Ratios. Three short-term 1975 liquidity ratios for *Schlitz, Busch, Pabst,* and the industry average are presented in Table 2.5.[5] Note that all three ratios point in the same direction—i.e., *Schlitz* is in a less liquid position than either of its two main national competitors or the industry average. Of the nine brewers included in the industry average, only one has a 1975 current ratio lower than that of *Schlitz*—*Lone Star Brewing Company's* 1975 current ratio was 1.32. *Schlitz* had a lower defensive interval measure (18.04 days) than any of the other brewers examined.

TABLE 2.5   Liquidity Ratios: 1975

	Schlitz	Busch	Pabst	Industry Average
1. Current ratio	1.39	2.60	2.14	1.82
2. Quick ratio	.61	1.75	1.21	.99
3. Defensive interval (days)	18.04	56.65	39.99	36.83

In evaluating liquidity it is also useful to examine information such as revolving credit agreements with banks. For instance, *Schlitz* issued the following news release in February 1976:

> The Chairman...announced today that the company had entered into a six-year standby revolving credit agreement with nine domestic banks. Initially, this agreement provides $70 million in credit with declining amounts available during the last two years.... This new credit facility is in addition to a $75 million revolving credit agreement arranged with six banks in late 1974. Both agreements are designed to provide working capital needs in addition to the current capital expenditure program.

The existence of such agreements by *Schlitz* and other brewers can obviously be very important when assessing the liquidity position of *Schlitz* vis-à-vis other firms in the industry.[6]

The use of different asset and liability valuation rules across firms means that a less than literal interpretation of the exact numerical magnitudes of each firm's current ratio, quick ratio, etc., may be appropriate. Consider inventory valuation rules. The 1975 Annual Reports of the brewing companies examined indicate some diversity in this respect. For instance, while all firms used "lower of cost or market," they differed with regard to methods used to determine cost, e.g.,

Schlitz: LIFO for 81% of inventory; average cost for 19%.

Busch: LIFO for 64% of inventory; average cost for 36%.

Pabst: "primarily on the moving average basis."

Coors: LIFO for 49%; FIFO for 51%.

Olympia: LIFO for 70%; average cost for 30%.

Heileman: LIFO for 45%; FIFO for 55%.

The effect on reported inventories of using alternative valuation rules is sometimes provided in footnotes. For instance, *Busch* noted that had the average cost method been used for the inventories calculated using LIFO, the 1975 inventory would have been approximately $33,111,000 higher —this would have increased the reported current ratio of 2.60 to 2.81. Similarly, *Heileman* noted that had the FIFO method been used for the entire inventory, the 1975 inventory figure would have been $776,000 higher—this would have increased the reported current ratio of 1.95 to 1.99. In cases where information is not available in published footnotes, an analyst may resort to an approximating technique to make the adjustment. In Chapter 6 we shall outline one such technique for FIFO to LIFO adjustments.

(2) Leverage/Capital Structure Ratios

These ratios provide evidence on (1) the extent to which nonequity capital is used in a firm and (2) the long-run ability of a firm to meet payments to nonequity suppliers of capital.

Long-Term Debt to Equity Ratio

$$\frac{\text{Long-term debt}}{\text{Shareholders' equity}}$$

The components to include in the numerator and the denominator depend on how one defines liabilities and shareholders' equity. Unfortunately, there is general agreement neither in the accounting literature nor in published financial reports on the precise distinction between liabilities and equity. Issues such as the treatment of deferred tax, preferred stock, etc., must be decided when computing the above ratio.

Total Debt to Equity Ratio

$$\frac{\text{Current liabilities} + \text{Long-term debt}}{\text{Shareholders' equity}}$$

From an equity shareholder's viewpoint, a debt to equity ratio may indicate the extent to which external parties are financing the assets of the firm. This viewpoint suggests the inclusion of current as well as long-term debt in the numerator of balance sheet leverage ratios.

Valuation questions arise in computing debt to equity ratios; e.g., should long-term debt be at book value or at market prices? Another important valuation issue relates to the inclusion or exclusion of lease financing from the long-term component of the ratio. In industries which make heavy use of lease financing—e.g., the airline industry—the treatment of leases can be a very important issue. As with the short-term liquidity ratios derived from the balance sheet, the above leverage ratios have been criticized for not focusing on the cash (or funds) flow necessary to service long-term debt payments. These criticisms have, in part, motivated proposals for interest coverage ratios.

Times Interest Earned Ratio

$$\frac{\text{Operating income}[7]}{\text{Annual interest payments}}$$

Many variations of this ratio have been proposed—e.g., (1) an adjustment to the numerator for the tax benefit received for interest payments and (2) an adjustment to the denominator for interest payments other than interest on long-term debt (e.g., annual lease payments).[8]

    Brewing Industry Leverage Ratios.   Details of three 1975 long-term leverage ratios are provided in Table 2.6.[9] One interesting feature of Table 2.6 is the differences in capital structure of the three major national brewers. Both *Schlitz* and *Busch* have raised considerable funds by issuing long-term debentures. In contrast, *Pabst* has no long-term debentures in its capital structure. *Pabst's* capital structure is not unique in the brewing industry. *Coors, Olympia* (up to 1974), and *Genesee* all make minimal use of long-term debt financing. The industry average long-term debt/shareholders' equity ratio of .52 in 1975 is heavily weighted by *Schaefer's* 1975 ratio of 3.05. In computing these ratios deferred tax was treated as part of shareholders' equity. The leverage ratios were also computed with deferred tax *consistently* treated as part of long-term debt. Inferences drawn about *Schlitz's* relative leverage position were not affected by this alternative treatment of deferred tax. The relative rankings of individual firms also did not appear to be significantly affected by whether deferred tax was treated as part of debt or equity (the Spearman rank correlation between the long-term debt to shareholders' equity ratios with the two different treatments of deferred tax for the nine companies in the brewing industry was .95).

TABLE 2.6   Leverage/Capital Structure Ratios: 1975

	Schlitz	Busch	Pabst	Industry Average
1. Long term debt/shareholders' equity	.57	.49	0	.52
2. Total debt/shareholders' equity	.80	.72	.21	.90
3. Times interest earned	5.75	7.75	91.25	N/C[a]

[a] N/C means not calculated.

    The times interest earned ratio also indicates that *Schlitz* was more highly levered in 1975 than *Busch* and *Pabst*; e.g., interest charges were only covered 5.75 times by *Schlitz's* operating income, whereas *Busch's* interest charges were covered 7.75 times by 1975 operating income. The industry average ratio was not calculated due to computational reasons. For firms with zero fixed interest charges (e.g., *Genesee*) the ratio is undefined. For firms with minimal fixed charges, the ratio is very large (e.g., *Pabst*)—such a figure could dominate an equally weighted industry average. Note also that the ratio is undefined for firms which make a net loss (e.g., *Schaefer's*). In a case like this, it may be instructive to compare *Schlitz's* coverage ratios with those of other individual firms, making adjustments for factors such as those noted above on a firm-by-firm basis.

Information provided in published footnotes may be useful in extending coverage ratios to include annual fixed payments for long-term obligations such as lease and pension fund payments. For instance, in a footnote in its 1975 Annual Report, *Pabst* reveals details about (1) future rental commitments of the company under all noncancellable leases —"mainly for machinery and equipment" and (2) total annual lease rental expenses. In 1975, the total lease rental expense was $7,162,000. The 1975 operating income to interest coverage ratio, excluding this rental expense, is 91.25. Adjusting the numerator and denominator for this expense, the interest coverage ratio becomes 5.60. Neither *Schlitz* nor *Busch* reports the use of any lease financing in their 1975 Annual Reports or Form 10-K Statements.

(3) Profitability Ratios

Profitability refers to the ability of a firm to generate revenues in excess of expenses. In examining this ability, it is useful to control for differences across firms in their resource base. The following three ratios illustrate alternative ways of expressing *relative profitability*.

Return on Total Assets

$$\frac{\text{Net income after tax} + \text{Interest expense} - \text{Tax benefit of interest expense}}{\text{Total assets}}$$

This ratio measures how efficiently total assets are being utilized by a firm. The use of total assets is an attempt to eliminate the effect of the different methods firms use in the financing of assets. An adjustment is usually made to the numerator to take into account the tax savings from the interest charges included in net income.

Return on Equity

$$\frac{\text{Net income available to common}}{\text{Common shareholders' equity}}$$

This ratio measures the efficiency with which common shareholders' equity is being employed within the firm. The numerator of this ratio is usually net income available to common, i.e., after preferred dividend payments. As with the debt to equity ratio, the return on equity ratio implicitly requires one to define debt and equity—e.g., when deciding to include or exclude deferred tax from the denominator.

The average of the opening and closing balances of total assets or shareholders' equity is usually recommended as the denominator—the motivation is that this average is seen as a better approximation of the assets generating the period income than is either the opening or closing total assets or shareholders' equity.

Expenses to Revenue

$$\frac{\text{Expenses (before tax)}}{\text{Revenues}}$$

This ratio indicates how much of each revenue dollar is taken up by before-tax expenses. A ratio over 1 indicates the firm is not generating sufficient revenues to meet before-tax expenses. There are many variants of the above ratio—e.g., operating income ratio [(sales − cost of goods sold − selling and administrative expenses)/sales].

Brewing Industry Profitability Ratios. Three profitability ratios for 1975 are presented in Table 2.7.[10] Note that the return on total assets ratio, return on shareholders' equity, and the expenses/revenue ratio all indicate a similar picture. Of the three major national brewers, *Busch* was the most profitable in 1975, while *Schlitz* and *Pabst* performed approximately the same. The 1975 industry average return on shareholders' equity ratio is − .012. This average is heavily influenced by *F & M Schaefer Corporation* having a large negative return of − .689 in 1975. In such a case, one may compute the industry average excluding such an *outlier*.[11] Alternatively, one may examine other aspects of the distribution of return on equity ratio. For instance, the following presentation may give a better perspective on industry profitability:

Ranking of Companies on 1975 Return on Shareholders' Equity

1.	*Coors*	.146
2.	*Genesee*	.142
3.	*Busch*	.128
4.	*Heileman*	.121
5.	*Schlitz*	.085
6.	*Pabst*	.082
7.	*Lone Star*	.071
8.	*Olympia*	.050
9.	*Falstaff*	−.161
10.	*Schaefer*	−.689

This presentation also indicates that *Schlitz's* 1975 profitability is below that of several large brewing companies.

In attempting to explain differences in profitability across firms one may examine a variety of factors, e.g., (1) the age of the brewing plant, (2) the distance between the location of a brewery and the markets served by

TABLE 2.7 Profitability Ratios: 1975

	Schlitz	Busch	Pabst	Industry Average
1. Return on total assets	.062	.090	.068	.061
2. Return on shareholders' equity	.085	.128	.082	−.012
3. Expenses/revenues	.946	.919	.944	.958

the brewery, and (3) the relative wage rates paid at the brewing operations. One may also want to examine if there are differences in accounting methods across firms; e.g., are all the brewers with higher reported earnings using straight-line depreciation, while all the brewers with lower reported earnings are using accelerated depreciation methods? Such does not seem to be the case for the ten brewing companies examined. The "Statement of Accounting Policies" in the 1975 Annual Reports of all ten brewing companies reported the use of the straight-line depreciation method. *Busch*, in its 1975 Annual Report, noted that it had switched (effective January 1, 1975) to the straight-line method from the sum-of-the years' digits method—the reason given for the change was "the desire to conform to prevailing industry practice" (p. 30).

(4) Turnover Ratios

Various aspects of the efficiency with which assets are utilized can be gleaned from turnover ratios as well as from the previously examined profitability ratios.

Total Asset Turnover

$$\frac{Sales}{Average\ total\ assets}$$

This ratio indicates how many times annual sales cover total assets. In examining this ratio it is important to examine also the related earnings/sales ratio.[2] Firms may trade off an increase in the asset turnover ratio for a decrease in the earnings/sales ratio.

Accounts Receivable Turnover

$$\frac{Sales}{Average\ (net)\ accounts\ receivable}$$

As accounts receivable pertain only to credit sales, it is often recommended that the numerator include only credit sales. In many cases, total sales are used due to precise information of cash and credit sales not being provided in published annual reports. By dividing 365 by the accounts receivable turnover ratio, one obtains an estimate of the average collection period of credit sales.

Inventory Turnover

$$\frac{\text{Sales}}{\text{Average inventory}}$$

As the denominator is usually valued at some variant of cost (LIFO, FIFO, current costs, etc.), the above numerator is often replaced by cost of goods sold:

$$\frac{\text{Cost of goods sold}}{\text{Average inventory}}.$$

Average inventory is most often calculated as an equally weighted average of opening and closing yearly inventory figures.

Brewing Ratios. Table 2.8 includes 1975 turnover ratios for *Schlitz*, *Busch*, *Pabst*, and the brewing industry.[13] Note that *Schlitz* has higher inventory turnover ratios—sales/average inventories = 20.55; COGS/ average inventories = 13.25—than either *Busch* or *Pabst* or the industry average. The reasons an analyst may consider in explaining this difference include (1) more efficient inventory policies, (2) a shorter production cycle for beer requiring a lower work-in-process inventory, and (3) differential accounting valuation rules for *Schlitz's* inventory vis-à-vis other firms in the brewing industry.

TABLE 2.8 Turnover Ratios: 1975

		Schlitz	Busch	Pabst	Industry Average
1.	Sales/total assets	1.83	1.91	2.16	2.35
2.	Sales/accounts receivable	33.90	37.32	45.62	28.57
3.	Sales/inventories	20.55	16.29	13.72	16.67
4.	COGS/inventories	13.25	10.75	9.05	10.53

(5) Common Stock Security Ratios

Many items from the balance sheet, income statement, and statement of changes in financial position are often expressed on a per share basis. A frequently used ratio is *earnings per share* (*EPS*):

$$\frac{\text{Net income available for common}}{\text{Number of shares outstanding}}.$$

The denominator of the EPS ratio is usually a weighted average of the amount of common stock outstanding during the year. When the capital structure includes items such as stock options and convertible securities, the calculation of the denominator is a complex task. *APB No. 15* ("*Earnings Per Share*"), issued in 1969, examines the computation of EPS in considerable detail.

Differences in EPS across firms, at a point of time, are difficult to interpret. Two firms with same assets, same earnings, etc., could have different EPS figures because of an arbitrary choice made many years ago about the number of shares to issue. Similarly, the interpretation of differences in EPS over time is less than clear-cut. For instance, a change in dividend policy by a corporation can cause changes in the EPS of subsequent years that are not related to any change in efficiency with which each dollar of shareholders' capital is being used.

Examples of other frequently computed per-share-based ratios include

$$\text{Book value per share} = \frac{\text{Shareholders' equity}}{\text{Number of shares outstanding}}$$

and

$$\text{Dividends per share} = \frac{\text{Dividends paid on common}}{\text{Number of shares outstanding}}.$$

Published investment service information (e.g., *Value Line, Moody's,* and *Standard & Poor's*) often present the above and other financial items on a per share basis.

2.2 TIME-SERIES TECHNIQUES

One objective of financial statement analysis is the prediction of future earnings, sales, etc., or the prediction of future ratios. Several financial statement analysis tools have been proposed to provide insight into this prediction issue. These tools are discussed below. A more detailed discussion of time-series techniques for predicting accounting numbers is presented in Chapter 4.

A Trend Statements

Constructing trend statements involves choosing one financial statement as a base year and then expressing subsequent statement items as percentages of their value in the base year. Consider the cost of goods sold item in successive income statements of *Schlitz*:

1971	1972	1973	1974	1975
$360,819	$422,490	$498,901	$619,949	$728,861

If 1971 is chosen as the base year, then the 1972 COGS item in a trend statement is 117.1% ($422,490/$360,819). The COGS items in a trend statement for the 1971–1975 period would be

1971	1972	1973	1974	1975
100%	117.1%	138.3%	171.8%	202.0%

Trend statements for selected items of the income statement for the 1971–1975 period are presented in Table 2.9.

TABLE 2.9   Trend Statement of Selected Income Items: 1971–1975

	1971	1972	1973	1974	1975
Schlitz					
Sales and other income	100	116.7	133.8	152.4	168.5
Cost of goods sold	100	117.1	138.3	171.8	202.0
Excise taxes	100	114.3	129.0	137.0	141.0
Marketing, general, and administrative					
expenses	100	110.3	109.0	116.6	127.8
Busch					
Sales and other income	100	108.5	123.0	153.0	173.6
Cost of goods sold	100	110.0	132.9	180.3	203.9
Excise taxes	100	109.1	122.9	139.8	144.5
Marketing, general, and administrative					
expenses	100	99.9	104.5	98.7	116.6
Pabst					
Sales and other income	100	107.7	113.8	134.4	159.7
Cost of goods sold	100	107.9	120.4	157.6	194.1
Excise taxes	100	107.5	111.9	121.8	133.9
Marketing, general, and administrative					
expenses	100	105.7	113.4	126.7	138.1
Industry Average					
Sales and other income	100	111.3	122.2	138.3	159.0
Cost of goods sold	100	114.2	132.5	163.8	196.7
Excise tax	100	111.2	118.9	123.9	131.3
Marketing, general, and administrative					
expenses	100	113.0	114.6	114.1	127.8

One feature apparent from Table 2.9 is that *Schlitz's* cost of goods sold increased at a much faster rate than sales over the 1971–1975 period; e.g., the trend percentage for sales and other income was 168.5% in 1975 (1971 = 100%), whereas the cost of goods sold percentage in 1975 was 202% (1971 = 100%). Comments made in the annual reports of several brewers over this period provide some explanations for the patterns in Table 2.9.

For instance, *Busch* made the following comment on price increases for beer over this period:

> During the years 1965–1970, price increases for beer averaged approximately 2% per year. From 1971 through 1973, increases in beer selling prices were constrained by competitive pressures and price control regulations under the Economic Stabilization Program. Price increases for beer in 1974 were unprece-dented and approximated the inflationary rate for all consumer goods. These price increases were implemented in an attempt to recover the significantly higher costs which the company incurred in 1972, 1973, and 1974. Price increases implemented during 1974 were not sufficient to totally achieve this objective. (*Busch, 1974 Annual Report*, p. 32)

One way to gain insight into the reasons for sales dollar increases is to compute trend percentages for (a) sales dollars and (b) sales units (barrels of beer; see item No. 38 in Table 2.3). These are presented below for *Schlitz*:

	1971	1972	1973	1974	1975
Sales (dollars)	100	116.5	133.8	152.4	168.5
Sales (units)	100	113.2	127.7	135.62	139.3

From 1971 to 1973 *Schlitz's* sales dollar gains were mainly from increases in barrels of beer sold. In 1974 and 1975, price increases accounted for a larger percentage of sales dollar increases.

Schlitz made the following comments on increases in the cost of goods sold item:

> Unprecedented cost increases were the major cause of the company's reduced [1974] earnings. Selling prices were raised, but not enough to offset the widespread cost inflation. The following schedule details the material cost increases which faced the entire industry in 1974:

	Percent Increase
Brewing Materials	
Malt	40
Corn	125
Packaging Materials	
Cans and lids	30
Bottles	20
Other packaging materials	30

> It is expected that cost pressures will continue in 1975, but at a reduced rate. (*Schlitz, 1974 Annual Report*, p. 4)

> In 1975, operating cost increases exceeded beer price increases. Agricultural products on an annual average basis were about 25 percent higher in 1975 than in 1974, and packaging costs were about 15 percent higher. On the same basis, Jos. Schlitz Brewing Company beer prices were only ten percent higher.

> The outlook for 1976 is more encouraging.... Barley, corn and rice prices currently are below the levels of a year ago. (*Schlitz, 1975 Annual Report*, p. 4)

By examining the trend statements of *Schlitz*, vis-à-vis the industry average, one can gain insight into possible reasons (e.g., industry factors or firm-specific factors) for the observed trends. For example, *Schlitz's* cost of goods sold item was 202% in 1975 as compared to the 1975 industry average of 197.7% (1971 = 100%). Industry factors appear to be an important cause of the increase in *Schlitz's* cost of goods sold over the 1971–1975 period. In Chapter 5 additional techniques (index models) for examining these issues are described in detail.

In computing trend percentages, it is advisable to examine if there have been any accounting changes over the period being examined. For instance, in 1974 *Heileman* switched from FIFO to LIFO for certain components of their inventories:

> Effective January 1, 1974 the Company adopted the LIFO method of determining inventory costs for approximately 33 percent of its inventory; it had previously used the FIFO method for the entire inventory.... The LIFO method is considered preferable because it reduces the impact that inflation has on earnings; under the LIFO method, current costs are charged to cost of sales for the year. Under the FIFO method of accounting, inventories would have been $700,000 higher than those reported at December 13, 1974.... This change had the effect of reducing net income for 1974 by $342,000 below that which would have been reported using FIFO. (*Heileman, 1974 Annual Report*, pp. 3, 12)

The 1975 Annual Report also gave information to estimate the FIFO inventory figure. With this disclosure in the 1974 and 1975 Annual Reports, one could compute trend income statements for *Heileman* with a consistent inventory valuation method (FIFO) used over the 1971–1975 period. In cases where the effect of the accounting change is not disclosed in annual reports, an analyst has several options. One option is to use an approximating technique to convert the financial items to those that would have been reported using consistent accounting policies over the period. Another option is to reduce the time frame covered by the trend statements to that in which a company followed consistent accounting policies. Yet another option is to ignore the accounting change on the assumption that its effect on the analysis at hand is immaterial. The last option, if taken, should be the product of deliberate choice rather than being made by the nonconsideration of other available options.

B Common-Size Statements

The common-size statement technique (see Section 2.1A) can also be used in time-series analysis. By comparing successive common-size statements of the one firm over time, changes in composition of assets, financial structure, etc., can be highlighted. Table 2.10 contains common-size balance sheets of *Schlitz* for the 1971–1975 period. Note the increase in the plant and equipment percentage over the 1972–1975 period (from 56.7% in 1972 to 78.1% in 1975). Note also the increase in the long-term debt percentage over the same 1972–1975 period (from 15.3% in 1972 to 31.7% in 1975). These two changes are not unrelated. Since 1973 *Schlitz* has undertaken a substantial program to expand existing and build new brewing and can manufacturing plants. The "additions to plant and equipment" item in the statement of changes in financial position over the 1971–1975 period (see Table 2.3, item No. 34) indicates this rapid increase in capital outlays. Part of this expansion program has been financed through a $75 million issue in 1974 of sinking fund debentures and a $75 million issue in 1975 of ten-year notes payable to banks.

TABLE 2.10 Common-Size Balance Sheets of Schlitz: 1971–1975

	1971	*1972*	*1973*	*1974*	*1975*
Assets					
Cash + marketable securities	8.7	18.2	12.7	3.6	3.0
Accounts receivable	7.7	7.2	5.8	6.3	4.6
Inventories	8.6	9.2	11.8	9.5	8.4
Other current assets	2.0	1.1	1.5	3.1	1.4
Plant and equipment	63.9	56.7	60.7	70.8	78.1
Investment and other assets	9.1	7.6	7.5	6.7	4.5
	100	100	100	100	100
Liabilities + Equity					
Accounts payable	5.0	7.5	8.2	6.5	6.6
Other current liabilities	8.6	11.9	9.1	5.9	6.0
Long-term debt	19.2	15.3	13.6	25.4	31.7
Deferred tax	4.9	5.6	6.5	6.4	7.0
Stockholders' equity	62.3	59.7	62.6	55.8	48.7
	100	100	100	100	100

C Financial Ratio Analysis

Analysis of time-series trends in financial ratios is another technique used in financial statement analysis. In some cases this analysis is quite heuristic; e.g., an analyst may attempt to extrapolate a general trend based on (say) the current ratio over the past five years. In other cases, a more systematic analysis is made of the past sequence of (say) a firm's return on assets ratio prior to making predictions of next year's return on assets ratio. In Chapter 4 we shall examine time-series tools that are used in the systematic analysis of accounting numbers.

TABLE 2.11   Comparative Financial Ratios: 1971–1975

	1971	1972	1973	1974	1975
Current Ratio					
Schlitz	1.99	1.83	1.84	1.81	1.39
Busch	2.17	2.04	1.77	2.23	2.60
Pabst	1.93	2.28	2.35	2.03	2.14
Industry average	2.22	2.20	2.09	1.86	1.82
Long-Term Debt / Equity					
Schlitz	.29	.23	.20	.41	.57
Busch	.25	.19	.16	.31	.49
Pabst	0	0	0	0	0
Industry average	.35	.43	.39	.35	.52
Return on Total Assets					
Schlitz	.108	.123	.132	.104	.062
Busch	.119	.118	.093	.083	.090
Pabst	.105	.106	.083	.062	.068
Industry average	.087	.071	.062	.065	.061
Inventory Turnover Ratio *(COGS / inventories)*					
Schlitz	11.10	11.98	10.79	11.57	13.25
Busch	10.45	12.17	13.81	13.17	10.75
Pabst	10.06	11.07	10.81	9.15	9.05
Industry average	11.20	12.05	11.43	10.53	10.53

Table 2.11 details the 1971–1975 values of one ratio in each of the four categories discussed in Section 2.1B. Note that many of the inferences drawn from trend statements and successive common-size balance sheets are supported by the trends observed in Table 2.11. For instance, *Schlitz's* debt/equity ratio has increased from .20 in 1973 to .57 in 1975—as noted previously, this increase was due to increased use of debentures and long-term bank notes.

2.3   SUMMARY

Our purpose in this chapter was to introduce various tools of financial statement analysis. In Chapters 3–6 a more detailed examination of these tools and other properties of accounting data is made. The material in Chapters 3–6 provides an important underpinning to the discussion in subsequent chapters. These subsequent chapters examine investor and creditor decisions, the use of accounting information in these decisions, and aspects of the environment in which such decisions are made.

NOTES

[1] *Miller Brewing Company* is also a major national brewer. Published financial statements of *Miller's*, however, are not available as it is a subsidiary of *Philip Morris Incorporated*.

[2] The industry averages are based on the following companies (1975 sales in $000's are in brackets): (1) *Anheuser-Busch* [$2,036,687], (2) *Pabst Brewing Company* [$665,291], (3) *Adolph Coors Company* [$663,422], (4) *F & M Schaefer* [$287,215], (5) *Olympia Brewing Company* [$259,624], (6) *Falstaff Brewing Company* [$211,490], (7) *G. Heileman Brewing* [$209, 824], (8) *Genesee Brewing* [$100,714], and (9) *Lone Star Brewing* [$60,391].

[3] For details of the history of financial ratio analysis, see Horrigan [1967]. Section 6.2C (Chapter 6) contains a discussion of an alternative approach to developing categories of financial ratios.

[4] Foulke [1968, Chapter VI] also reported the following comment by a banker in 1919:

> Common practice has developed only one general theory...the "two for one rule" and consists of the principle that, in order to establish a good credit proportion, the subjects statement must show at least two dollars of current assets for every dollar of current liability.

[5] The three liquidity ratios were calculated as follows (numbers refer to items in Tables 2.1–2.3):

(1) Current ratio = (No. 1 + No. 2 + No. 3 + No. 4 + No. 5)/(No. 9 + No. 10).
(2) Quick ratio = (No. 1 + No. 2 + No. 3)/(No. 9 + No. 10).
(3) Defensive interval = [(No. 1 + No. 2 + No. 3) × 365]/[(No. 16 + No. 17 + No. 18 + No. 19 + No. 20) − (No. 29 + No. 30)].

[6] Several other firms in the brewing industry also have revolving credit agreements with banks. For example, *Busch* disclosed the following in a footnote in their 1975 Annual Report:

> In June, 1974, the company entered into a $125,000,000 revolving credit agreement with sixteen banks for the period June 28, 1974 to December 31, 1976. Interest on any borrowings the company might choose to make would be at the prime rate during that period. The company has agreed to pay a fee of $\frac{1}{2}$ of 1% per annum on the unused portion of the commitment. (p. 29)

[7] As with many other accounting terms, there is less than general agreement on a definition of operating income. We use the term to refer to sales less operating expenses (cost of goods sold, marketing and general administrative costs, and, in the case of brewers, excise taxes).

[8]When a firm has several bonds outstanding, each with differing priority in their claims to earnings, coverage ratios applicable to each bond are sometimes computed—see the discussion of "cumulative-deduction-coverage ratios" in Williams and Findlay [1974, Chapter 7].

[9]The three leverage ratios were calculated as follows (numbers refer to items in Tables 2.1–2.3):

(1) Long-term debt/shareholders' equity = (No. 11)/(No. 12 + No. 13).

(2) Total debt/shareholders' equity = (No. 9 + No. 10 + No. 11)/(No. 12 + No. 13).

(3) Times interest earned = [(No. 14) − (No. 16 + No. 17 + No. 18)]/(No. 19).

[10] The three profitability ratios were calculated as follows (numbers refer to items in Tables 2.1–2.3):

(1) Return on total assets = (No. 23 + No. 19 − .5 × No. 19)/(No. 8).

(2) Return on shareholders' equity = (No. 23)/(No. 12 + No. 13).

(3) Expenses/revenues = (No. 16 + No. 17 + No. 18 + No. 19 + No. 20)/(No. 14 + No. 15).

An average of the opening and closing book values for the denominator was used in calculating the first two ratios. A 50% effective tax rate was assumed in computing the return on total assets ratio.

[11]Chapter 4 contains details of the circumstances surrounding *Schaefer's* large loss in 1975.

[12]These two ratios and the return on assets ratio comprise the so-called DuPont system of ratio analysis:

$$\frac{\text{Sales}}{\text{Average total assets}} \times \frac{\text{Earnings}}{\text{Sales}} = \frac{\text{Earnings}}{\text{Average total assets}}.$$

[13]The four turnover ratios were calculated as follows (numbers refer to items in Tables 2.1–2.3):

(1) Sales/total assets = (No. 14)/(No. 8).

(2) Sales/accounts receivable = (No. 14)/(No. 3).

(3) Sales/inventories = (No. 14)/(No. 4).

(4) COGS/inventories = (No. 16)/(No. 4).

An average of the opening and closing book values of the denominator was used for all four ratios.

QUESTIONS

QUESTION 2.1:   Computation of the Inventory Turnover Ratio

The use of an average of the opening and closing balances of inventory is often proposed for the denominator of the inventory turnover ratio. Sprouse and Swieringa [1972] note some problems in this proposal for companies using a *natural business year* for financial reporting:

> A natural business year usually ends on a date of low business activity.... The probability that the amounts of inventories...reported on the balance sheet will be representative of those on hand throughout the year decreases with the use of the natural business year. (p. 20)

REQUIRED

(1) What *evidence* could an external analyst use in deciding whether the average of the opening and closing balances of inventories is "representative of those on hand throughout the year?"

(2) What analogous problems occur in computing earnings per share? What approach to computing the denominator of the earnings per share ratio is generally adopted in published annual reports? Could this approach be adopted for computing the inventory turnover ratio?

QUESTION 2.2:   Cash Flow Coverage Ratios

Robert Morris Associates [1975], in their *Annual Statement Studies: 1975 Edition*, propose the following ratio to measure "the ability to retire term debt each year from cash generated by operations":

$$\frac{\text{Cash flow}}{\text{Current maturities of long-term debt}}.$$

They described the rationale behind the ratio as follows:

> Cash flow or "throw-off" is the primary source of regular repayment of long-term debt, and this ratio measures the coverage of such debt service. Often much if not all of the depreciation will be needed for fixed asset replacements and expenditures but similarly some part of net profits may be committed to dividends. Although thus misleading to think that all cash flow is available for debt service, the ratio is a valid measure of the optimum coverage and a very useful calculation in all considerations of term lending. (p. 10)

REQUIRED

(1) Evaluate this rationale for the use of the above ratio in a term lending decision.

(2) As a measure of *cash flow*, *Robert Morris Associates* use "net profits plus depreciation and amortization." What noncash items may be included and what cash items may be excluded from this measure of cash flow?

QUESTION 2.3: Computerized Financial Statement Analysis

Several firms market computerized data bases that contain financial information on many companies. For example, the *Compustat* data base marketed by *Standard & Poor's Corp.* contains information on over 120 items for over 2,500 industrial companies. This data base uses a consistent format when presenting these items for each company.

REQUIRED

(1) What specific problems might arise in presenting the accounting items of all companies in a consistent format? Illustrate these problems by reference to the annual reports of several companies.

(2) Another problem in using computerized data bases arises from errors in the recorded data. What sources could give rise to recording errors? What specific procedures might one use to check for possible errors when computing common-size statements, trend statements, or financial ratios?

QUESTION 2.4: Olympia Brewing Company

Olympia Brewing Company is engaged in the business of brewing, packaging, and marketing beer. Its two major brands are Olympia Beer and Hamm's Beer, produced at Tumwater, Washington and St. Paul, Minnesota. Olympia purchased the St. Paul brewery, a malting plant, a can manufacturing building, certain Hamm's brands, and other assets from *Theodore Hamm Company* effective March 1, 1975. The total purchase price was $13,857,571 cash and assumption of $8,594,126 in liabilities. The cost of the assets acquired were allocated as follows, based on "appraised values and negotiated costs":

Inventories	$ 5,180,381
Plant and equipment	$15,298,249
Investments and other assets	$ 1,973,067

The acquisition was accounted for as a "purchase." Tables 2.12–2.14 contain summary financial statement information for *Olympia* over the 1971–1975 period. The information presented for each year is as reported in the annual report of the respective year.

REQUIRED

(1) Evaluate the 1975 financial statements of Olympia, vis-à-vis *Schlitz*, *Busch*, and *Pabst*, as regards liquidity, capital structure, profitability, and turnover. Use both common-size statements and ratio analysis to support your evaluation.

TABLE 2.12 Olympia Brewing Company
Comparative Balance Sheets: 1971–1975 ($000's)

	1971	1972	1973	1974	1975
Assets					
1. Cash	3,547	3,253	2,266	733	1,056
2. Marketable securities	5,000	2,973	0	0	0
3. Accounts receivable	4,495	5,353	5,614	8,939	11,406
4. Inventories	3,568	3,807	5,884	7,159	14,684
5. Other current assets	27	2,830	6,130	7,915	2,540
6. Investments and other assets	10,329	12,032	11,881	8,102	5,608
7. Plant and equipment	21,347	19,444	19,999	22,558	34,047
8. Total assets	48,313	49,692	51,774	55,406	69,341
Liabilities and Equity					
9. Accounts payable	3,946	4,246	4,827	5,986	6,810
10. Other current liabilities	2,009	2,982	3,609	7,231	11,643
11. Long-term debt	0	0	0	0	7,586
12. Deferred tax	0	0	0	0	0
13. Shareholders' equity	42,358	42,464	43,338	42,189	43,302
	48,313	49,692	51,774	55,406	69,341

TABLE 2.13 Olympia Brewing Company
Comparative Income Statements: 1971–1975 ($000's)

	1971	1972	1973	1974	1975
14. Sales	118,549	127,373	140,182	180,611	259,624
15. Other income	573	1,042	1,299	1,405	1,231
16. Cost of goods sold	69,709	76,384	87,703	121,711	177,318
17. Excise taxes	28,188	30,249	32,901	40,672	53,504
18. Marketing, administrative, and general expenses	14,652	15,720	14,263	16,043	25,672
19. Interest expense	0	0	0	0	596
20. Other expenses	0	0	0	990	0
21. Earnings before tax	6,573	6,061	6,513	2,600	3,765
22. Tax	3,140	2,660	2,971	950	1,620
23. Earnings after tax	3,433	3,401	3,542	1,650	2,145
24. Extraordinary items[a]	0	0	0	0	640
25. Earnings after extra. items	3,433	3,401	3,542	1,650	2,785
26. Earnings per share	1.62	1.61	1.69	.79	1.33
27. Market price per share (Dec. 31)	$24.50	$19	$13	$10	$23.50

[a] The 1975 extraordinary gain related to the "net recovery of loss on a short-term investment reported in a prior year."

TABLE 2.14 Olympia Brewing Company
Comparative Statements of Changes in Financial Position: 1971–1975 ($000's)

	1971	1972	1973	1974	1975
Working Capital Provided by					
28. Net earnings	3,433	3,401	3,542	1,650	2,145
29. Depreciation	2,973	2,783	2,777	2,938	4,696
30. Deferred tax	14	379	47	379	217
31. Extraordinary items	0	0	0	0	640
32. Issue of long-term debt	0	0	0	0	3,000
33. Other sources	0	461	353	2,448	8,369
	6,420	7,024	6,719	7,415	19,067
Working Capital Used for					
34. Addition to plant and equipment	1,365	1,941	3,333	5,498	16,146
35. Cash dividends	3,599	2,963	2,514	2,090	1,672
36. Retirement of long-term debt	0	0	0	0	0
37. Other uses	1,058	1,814	403	0	1,544
	6,022	6,718	6,250	7,588	19,362
Net Change in Working Capital	398	306	469	(173)	(295)
Other Information					
38. Barrels of beer sold	3,094	3,330	3,637	4,301	5,574
39. Plant capacity in barrels	N/A[a]	N/A	N/A	N/A	N/A

[a] N/A means not available.

(2) Evaluate major financial trends in *Olympia* over the 1971–1975 period. Is there any evidence that industry factors could partly explain these trends? Use trend statements, common-size statements, and ratio analysis to support your evaluation. [Some 1970 balance sheet items (in $000's) useful for computing 1971 ratios are accounts receivable = $5,607, inventories = $4,089, total assets = $48,951, and shareholders' equity = $42,524.]

(3) What problems for financial statement analysis might arise from the acquisition of the St. Paul, Minnesota brewery of *Theodore Hamm Company*. in February 1975? What techniques might be used to minimize these problems?

REFERENCES

DAVIDSON, S., SORTER, G. H., and KALLE, H. "Measuring the Defensive Position of a Firm." *Financial Analysts Journal* (Jan.–Feb. 1964): 23–29.

FOULKE, R. A. *Practical Financial Statement Analysis*, 6th ed. McGraw-Hill, New York, 1968.

HORRIGAN, J. O. "An Evaluation of Financial Ratio Analysis." Ph.D. Dissertation, University of Chicago, Chicago, 1967.

LEMKE, K. W. "The Evaluation of Liquidity: An Analytical Study." *Journal of Accounting Research* (Spring 1970): 47–77.

ROBERT MORRIS ASSOCIATES. *Annual Statement Studies: 1975 Edition.* Robert Morris Associates, Philadelphia, 1975.

SPROUSE, R. T., and SWIERINGA, R. J. *Essentials of Financial Statement Analysis.* Addison-Wesley, Reading, Mass., 1972.

WALTER, J. E. "Determination of Technical Solvency." *Journal of Business* (Jan. 1957): 30–43.

WILLIAMS, E. E., and FINDLAY, M. C. *Investment Analysis.* Prentice-Hall, Englewood Cliffs, N.J., 1974.

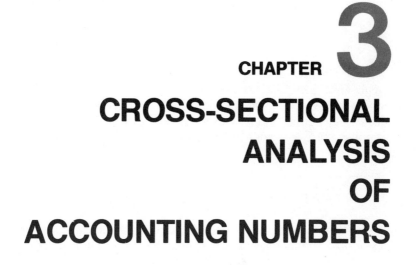

CHAPTER 3

CROSS-SECTIONAL ANALYSIS OF ACCOUNTING NUMBERS

In Chapter 2, two cross-sectional techniques—common-size statements and financial ratio analysis—were outlined. In both techniques the results for a specific firm are compared to standards such as "ideal" bench marks, other firms, industry averages, etc. In this chapter we shall further examine issues and evidence pertaining to the use of these techniques.

3.1 "IDEAL" BENCH MARKS

The notion of "ideal" bench marks for financial ratios has a long history. A 1919 statement by a Detroit banker of the two for one current ratio bench mark is quoted in Foulke [1968]. A typical set of more recent bench marks for industrial firms is found in Dun & Bradstreet's [1975] *Key Business Ratios*:

Fixed assets to tangible net worth. Ordinarily, this relationship should not exceed 100% for a manufacturer and 75% for a wholesaler or retailer.

Current debt to tangible net worth. Ordinarily, a business begins to pile up trouble when this relationship exceeds 80%.

Inventory to net working capital. Ordinarily, the relationship should not exceed 80%.

Funded debts to net working capital. Ordinarily, the relationship should not exceed 100%.

"Ideal" bench marks are also proposed for nonindustrial sectors of the economy. For instance, Williams and Findlay [1974] propose the following bench marks for the ratios of municipalities:

Municipal debt as a percentage of assessed valuation of taxable real estate. Ratios from 8 to 10% are considered acceptable by most analysts.

Per capita debt (the total debt of the municipal authority per resident). Depending on the population of the issuing authority, per capita debt of from $100 to $400 is acceptable.

Debt service as a percentage of the municipal budget. When more than one quarter of a municipal budget goes for debt service, the ability of the authority to meet its obligations is considered in jeopardy. (pp. 167–168)

The above "bench marks" are proposed as *guidelines*—there is generally no implication that these figures are optimal for all firms in all contexts. Rather, the guidelines (or, more precisely, deviations from the guidelines) are viewed as indicators of areas that need further investigation. Unfortunately, *there is a dearth of evidence to support even an "indicator's" interpretation of the above bench marks.* Saying that a deviation from a 2 to 1 current ratio is a possible indicator of liquidity problems may say very little when it is recognized that a firm with a 2 to 1 current ratio may also have liquidity problems. One needs to decide in a specific context what maintaining liquidity entails and then derive a current ratio consistent with this liquidity maintenance.

One problem in using the same bench mark for (say) the current ratio of a cross section of firms is that economic factors that may differentially affect firms are not incorporated into the bench mark. For instance, different expected future price changes for the inventories of firms may lead to differences in their speculative inventory holdings and in their observed current ratios. Economic factors can also explain differences across firms in changes in their financial ratios. Consider the inventory turnover ratio. If one uses an economic order quantity decision model for inventory, the optimal order quantity is a nonlinear function of the period demand. If demand doubles, a less than twofold increase in the economic order quantity is optimal.[1] As the order quantity is one factor affecting the denominator in the inventory turnover ratio, differences across firms in sales growth could help explain differences in the change in their inventory turnover ratios.

At present, there is little developed theory of the economic determinants of the financial ratios of firms.[2] Research on this issue offers promise of providing a richer framework for evaluating the financial ratios of a firm than does the existing "ideal" bench mark framework.

3.2 INDUSTRY NORMS

Comparison of a firm's common-size statements or financial ratios with those of an industry norm occupies an important part in financial statement analysis. Many published sources provide examples of industry norms.[3] For example, Robert Morris Associates' *Annual Statement Studies* contain industry common-size statements and financial ratios for many manufacturing, wholesaling, and retailing industries. Dun & Bradstreet's *Key Business Ratios* also contains extensive data on industry financial ratios. Deriving industry norms for financial ratios and common-size statements involves several key issues that are discussed below—e.g., definition of an industry and estimation of the industry norm.

A Definition of an Industry

Defining what is meant by an industry can raise some "heady" economic issues. One common definition is based on the cross-elasticity of demand notion. Bain [1952] made the following comments on this notion:

> Ideally, an industry is a group of products of firms which are perfect substitutes for each other to a common group of buyers and which are very poor substitutes for all other products in the economy. Products within a group are perfect substitutes for each other if they are regarded as absolutely identical and interchangeable by buyers, if they are sold to a common group of buyers, and if, therefore, a price for any one product in the group which is lower than those of the others will tend to attract all buyers of the commodity the industry produces.
>
> [Several] types of complications are found [in actual economies], and the definition of an industry must be elaborated to take account of each of them. A first complication is that the products of various firms producing a given sort of commodity are in most cases not identical or perfect substitutes. ...In most cases,...products are differentiated one from another by design, quality, packaging, advertising, or direct sales promotion. ...[Another] major complication in defining an industry stems from the fact that not all the firms producing a given range of potentially close-substitute products will necessarily sell to a common market or group of buyers. The world market for most goods is broken up into continental submarkets by the force of transport costs. ...(pp. 24–26)

Bain subsequently defined an industry as a "group of close-substitute products, each of which is sold entirely to a common group of buyers" (p. 26). The economics literature contains much debate on both conceptual and implementation problems with this and other definitions of an industry—Schnabel [1976] is a useful reference source on these debates.

In the financial statement analysis literature, the typical assumption is that an industry is a set of products which are "reasonably homogeneous with respect to *end product*." The frequent use of the Standard Industrial Classification (SIC) of industries is consistent with this *end-product* definition of an industry. The SIC code distinguishes among two-, three-, and four-digit industries. A two-digit classification is the broadest definition of an industry; a four digit classification is the narrowest definition. Consider the two-, three-, and four-digit SIC industry groups in which *Jos. Schlitz Brewing Company* is included. The two-digit code short title (#20) is "food and kindred products." The three-digit code short title (#208) is "beverages." The four-digit code title (#2082) is "malt beverages." That is, using a "narrower" SIC code results in firms with more homogeneous *end products* being classified as being in the same industry.

Another approach to defining an industry uses several criteria—e.g., end-product similarity, size similarity, and geographical location similarity. For instance, Kruger [1975] presents financial averages for three classes of general freight carriers (A, B, and C) in the U.S. "motor carrier industry." These classes are based on a gross revenue size criterion. These classes are also cross-categorized along geographical bases—e.g., New England, Rocky Mountains, and Pacific. The presentation of these subcategories is based on the assumption that a comparison of a carrier with similar-sized companies operating in the same geographical area is likely to yield more meaningful inferences about relative profitability, liquidity, etc. For example, carriers operating in New England may be expected to have higher operating expenses than Pacific carriers in winter months.[4]

In general, the decision problem at hand should guide the choice of an industry definition (and indeed the choice of whether one is "appropriate" to the problem). The framework outlined in Chapter 1 provides the basic philosophy in approaching the industry definition decision; i.e., it should be based on cost-benefit criteria. Unfortunately, the published literature provides little guidance on what factors will determine when one industry definition is more likely to be preferred to other definitions.

B Corporation Diversification and Industry Norms

The existence of corporate diversification creates problems in computing industry norms for firms in similar end-product industries. For instance, not all firms in the SIC four-digit "malt beverages" industry are 100% brewing companies. Consider *Anheuser Busch, Inc.* In 1975, the net sales dollars of the Beer Division (*Budweiser, Busch,* and *Michelob* beers) were approximately 90% of consolidated net sales. The other 10% was derived from such diverse activities as (1) production of yeast—*Anheuser Busch* supplies 40% of total yeast industry sales, (2) family entertainment parks—Busch Gardens, (3) real estate development, and (4) a National League baseball team—the St. Louis Cardinals. Consider also *Lone Star Brewing Company*. Of the 1975 net sales dollars, 21.2% was from the Truck Rental Division. Note that many of the nonbrewing interests of *Busch* and of *Lone Star* are far removed from even those encompassed by the two-digit SIC industry in which both firms are included. The consequence of such corporate diversification is that the resultant industry ratios do not represent purely brewing industry norms.

Another problem caused by corporate diversification is that industry norms based on, say, SIC codes will generally not include all firms in that industry. For instance, a firm may be a subsidiary of another company whose major activity is not in the industry being examined. Consider *The Miller Brewing Company*—a fully owned subsidiary of *Philip Morris Incorporated. Philip Morris's* major activity is cigarette manufacturing and is included in the "tobacco and cigarette manufacturing" four-digit SIC industry (#2111). In 1975, *Miller Brewing Company* constituted 18.1% of

Philip Morris's consolidated operating revenues and 5.8% of consolidated operating income. Insufficient information is available in *Philip Morris's* annual reports to compute and thus include most financial ratios of *Miller's* in an industry average.[5] Excluding *Miller's* from an industry average means excluding the fourth largest brewing company (on the basis of sales) in 1975. Companies may also be omitted from industry averages due to financial data not being publicly available. For instance, *The Stroh Brewing Company*—the tenth largest brewing company in 1975— is a private company and does not publish annual reports.

These omissions can affect the industry averages if there are systematic differences between the companies included and excluded from the average. For instance, omitting *Miller's* means excluding the company with the largest percentage gains in unit volume and sales of all U.S. brewers in both 1974 and 1975.

C Estimation of the Industry Norm

Some technical issues in computing industry norms are also worth considering. For instance, should it be the mean or the median ratio in the industry? Computation of the mean is discussed below. The median is found by ranking ratios from lowest (highest) to highest (lowest) and choosing the middle ratio. For instance, the ranking of the nine brewing companies used as the brewing industry in Chapter 2 on the 1975 total debt to equity ratio is

	Rank	Company	Total Debt to Equity
	1	Pabst	.159
	2	Coors	.258
	3	Genesee	.334
	4	Lone Star	.583
Median⇒	5	Olympia	.611
	6	Falstaff	.692
	7	Busch	.720
	8	Heileman	.753
	9	Schaefer	3.905

The median ratio is used as the measure of central tendency in both Robert Morris Associates' *Annual Statement Studies* and Dun & Bradstreet's *Key Business Ratios*.

Equal- vs. Value-Weighted Mean

If the industry mean is chosen as the norm, should it be an equally weighted mean of all firms' ratios or a value-weighted mean? The following example illustrates the computation of equal- and value-weighted industry earnings/common equity ratios. Suppose an industry with three firms:

	A	B	C
Earnings available for common	$240	$860	$1,400
Common equity—book value	$1,200	$8,600	$20,000
Earnings/common equity ratio	20%	10%	7%
Common stock outstanding— market value	$2,000	$10,000	$20,000

The equal-weighted industry average is

$$\frac{1}{3} \times (20\% + 10\% + 7\%) = 12.33\%.$$

Computation of a value-weighted index requires choice of a weighting scheme. Two alternatives are illustrated.

(1) Weighted by the book value of common equity (denominator of ratio):

$$(\$240 + \$860 + \$1,400)/(\$1,200 + \$8,600 + \$20,000) = 8.39\%.$$

(2) Weighted by the market value of common stock outstanding:

$$\left(20\% \times \frac{\$2,000}{\$32,000}\right) + \left(10\% \times \frac{\$10,000}{\$32.000}\right) + \left(7\% \times \frac{\$20,000}{\$32,000}\right) = 8.75\%.$$

TABLE 3.1 Equal- vs. Value-Weighted Total Debt to Equity Ratios of Brewing Industry: 1975

Company	Total Debt ($000's)	Equity ($000's)	Total Debt to Equity
Busch	503,433	698,683	.720
Pabst	55,442	348,994	.159
Coors	118,235	458,080	.258
Schaefer	131,568	33,693	3.905
Olympia	26,039	43,302	.601
Falstaff	27,842	40,208	.692
Heileman	37,178	49,384	.753
Genesee	9,969	29,832	.334
Lone Star	12,287	21,061	.583
	$\Sigma = 921,993$	$\Sigma = 1,723,237$	

$$\text{Equal-weighted average} = \frac{.720 + .159 + \ldots + .583}{9} = .889$$

$$\frac{\text{Value-weighted average}}{\text{(weighted by equity)}} = \frac{921,993}{1,723,237} = .535$$

The equal-weighted average 1975 total debt to equity ratio for the nine brewing companies detailed above is .889; the value-weighted average ratio is .535—see Table 3.1. Thus, use of the equal-weighted average as the industry norm would result in *Schlitz's* 1975 ratio of .795 being below the industry average. In contrast, use of the value-weighted average would indicate *Schlitz* had a 1975 ratio above the industry average.[6]

Other Technical Issues

Other technical issues in computing industry mean accounting ratios also arise. Consider computing the return on equity ratio when a firm has negative reported common equity. In this case, an expedient such as deleting the firm when computing the industry average is often adopted. This procedure, for instance, is adopted by Robert Morris Associates when computing the "profit before taxes to tangible net worth" ratio—see Robert Morris Associates [1976]. It is also possible that a computed ratio may be very large due to the denominator of the ratio approaching zero. Such a ratio could dominate an equally weighted industry mean. An expedient such as truncating the ratio at a certain value is often adopted in this case. For example, all times-interest-earned ratios ≥ 500 will be set at 500.[7] In this and similar cases, it must be admitted that the solutions chosen are ad hoc. Moreover, there seem to be no universally accepted means of handling such technical problems.

3.3 INDUSTRY DIFFERENCES IN FINANCIAL RATIOS

An important assumption of industry ratio analysis is that significant differences in the distributions of industry ratios exist. If, for example, the distribution of the current ratio of each industry were the same, there would be little point in separately examining deviations of a firm's current ratio from its industry average. Comparison of a firm's ratio with the economy average would be sufficient in this situation.

A Evidence of Industry Differences

Some evidence on the extent of numerical differences among the ratios of various industries is provided in Table 3.2. Equally weighted 1975 industry averages of 12 financial ratios for 14 four-digit SIC industries are presented. These industries were those for which there were more than 25 firms available on the 1976 *Compustat* Annual Industrial Tape with data

TABLE 3.2 Financial Ratio Averages for Selected Industries

Financial Ratios: 1975 Industry Averages

SIC Code	Short Industry Title	CR	QR	DI	DE	LTDE	TIE	ES	ROA	ROE	TAT	IT	ART
1311	Oil—crude producers	1.55	1.21	236	.76	.46	7.94	.19	.09	.17	.48	17.6	4.9
2200	Textile products	2.98	1.56	87	.91	.45	3.20	.02	.03	-.03	1.40	5.8	6.6
2300	Textile apparel mfg.	3.49	1.73	82	.98	.41	6.05	.02	.06	.09	1.69	5.1	7.5
3311	Steel—minor	3.25	1.57	64	.90	.45	6.29	.04	.07	.10	1.41	5.4	8.9
3679	Electronic components	3.17	1.45	90	1.07	.50	5.22	.01	.04	.05	1.37	4.0	6.2
3714	Auto parts and accessories	2.78	1.23	71	.87	.45	4.99	.03	.07	.14	1.55	4.9	7.6
3999	MFG inds	2.77	1.38	82	1.38	.69	8.66	.04	.07	.16	1.52	4.9	7.0
4210	Trucking	1.49	1.01	53	1.28	.73	3.55	.02	.05	.12	1.70	64.7	12.2
4511	Air transport	1.33	1.03	80	2.12	1.33	2.97	.02	.04	.06	1.15	38.2	10.3
4911	Electric utilities—flow thru	1.15	N/A	N/A	1.31	1.05	2.71	.13	.06	.12	.39	N/A	N/A
4912	Electric utilities—normalized	.79	N/A	N/A	1.21	.93	2.68	.11	.06	.11	.36	N/A	N/A
4924	Natural gas companies	1.02	N/A	N/A	1.35	.96	2.80	.07	.06	.13	.68	N/A	N/A
5311	Retail department stores	2.11	.88	51	1.17	.54	5.15	.02	.05	.09	2.17	6.9	29.9
5411	Retail—food chains	1.73	.56	15	1.15	.42	6.22	.01	.05	.10	5.28	16.9	100.7

NOTE: N/A means data not available.

available to compute at least 8 of the 12 financial ratios. The 12 financial ratios are

Liquidity
1. Current ratio (CR)
2. Quick ratio (QR)
3. Defensive interval (DI)

Leverage
4. Debt (total) to shareholders' equity (DE)
5. Long-term debt to shareholders' equity (LTDE)
6. Times interest earned (TIE)

Profitability
7. Earnings to sales (ES)
8. Return on assets (ROA)
9. Return on equity (ROE)

Turnover
10. Total asset turnover (TAT)
11. Inventory turnover (IT)
12. Accounts receivable turnover (ART)

One limitation of the results in Table 3.2 is that no statistical significance tests are applied to the data. Results in the literature—e.g., Bowen and Huber [1972]—strongly suggest that the differences across industries observed in Table 3.2 are statistically significant.

Bowen and Huber examined the average total debt to total assets ratio of ten firms in each of nine four-digit SIC industries. The ten firms were randomly chosen from a set of firms which met two criteria: (1) They had complete financial data for the above leverage measure over the 1951–1969 period, and (2) they were members of a four-digit SIC industry with at least ten firms. The statistical test used was a one-way parametric analysis of variance (ANOV).[8] The null hypothesis tested was that the mean industry leverage ratio of each of the nine industries was the same. The alternative hypothesis was that at least one industry mean ratio was significantly different from the other eight industry mean ratios. Average industry leverage ratios for three selected years (1951, 1960, and 1969) are given in Table 3.3. Note that there are differences across some industries each year (e.g., steel = .35 and air transportation = .60 in 1969) and differences over years for some industries (e.g., textile products = .29 in 1951 and = .47 in 1969). In each year examined, the null hypothesis was rejected at the .01 significance level. This evidence is consistent with one premise of industry financial statement analysis having descriptive validity, i.e., that significant industry differences in ratios exist.

TABLE 3.3   Total Debt to Total Assets Ratio of Nine Industries

		1951	*1960*	*1969*
1.	Textile products (2200)	.29	.38	.47
2.	Chemicals (2800)	.38	.38	.42
3.	Oil—integ. domestic (2912)	.32	.31	.37
4.	Steel (3310)	.37	.32	.35
5.	Auto parts (3714)	.38	.26	.34
6.	Aerospace (3721)	.52	.48	.54
7.	Air transportation (4511)	.44	.63	.60
8.	Retail dept. stores (5311)	.37	.41	.48
9.	Retail food chains (5411)	.45	.42	.46

SOURCE: Bowen and Huber [1972, Table B].

B   Explaining Industry Differences

Assuming that significant interindustry differences in financial ratios exist, the substantive question of *why* such differences exist arises. At present, there is limited theoretical or empirical analysis that bears on this question. One area in which some analysis has been conducted is interindustry differences in accounting rates of return. In perfect markets under certainty, the rates of return of all industries would be the same—see Stigler [1963]. Many authors have attempted to explain interindustry differences in accounting rates of return by relaxing either (1) the certainty assumption or (2) the perfect market assumption.

Consider relaxing the certainty assumption. Stigler [1963] hypothesized that differences in industry accounting rates of return could be explained by differences in business risk—risk-averse entrepreneurs would require higher rates of return in industries in which there is higher business risk and vice versa. In an empirical study, Cootner and Holland [1970] reported a significant positive relationship between mean industry rates of return and standard deviations of firm rates of return about industry means (the standard deviation was used as a measure of business risk). Consider now relaxing the perfect market assumption. Several authors have examined if differences in accounting rates of return can be explained by differences in industry concentration ratios or barriers to entry. For example, Bain [1951] reported finding a correlation coefficient of .28 between rates of return on net worth of 42 industries and concentration ratios of these industries. Weiss [1971] surveyed over 30 more recent studies and noted that most also reported a significant positive relationship between profitability and industry concentration. It should be noted that criticism has been made of both the theoretical underpinnings and the empirical techniques used in the above empirical studies.[9] At this stage, it would be premature to accept such explanations of interindustry differences in profitability ratios as part of "established knowledge."

Differences in observed industry (and firm) financial ratios are jointly determined by (1) differences in the underlying economic conditions and (2) differences in the accounting techniques used in computing the items in the ratio. Attempts have been made to control for accounting technique differences in research in this area. For instance, Stigler [1963] made adjustments for the effect of some accounting techniques (e.g., depreciation) in a study of concentration ratios and industry rates of return. Similarly, Ayanian [1975] made adjustments for research and development accounting techniques when examining whether cross-sectional differences in rates of return could be explained by differences in advertising policy. Hopefully, as techniques for adjusting for differences in the accounting techniques of firms become more refined (see Chapter 6), more reliable inferences about what nonaccounting technique factors explain industry differences in financial ratios will be drawn.[10]

3.4 INDUSTRY NORMS AS TARGET FINANCIAL RATIOS

A premise in many expositions of financial ratio analysis is that the industry norm represents a target ratio for firms in that industry. The analyst usually places the onus of justifying a certain ratio level on firms whose ratio differs from the industry norm. For instance, Weston and Brigham [1972] state

> If a firm's ratios are very far removed from the average of its industry, then the analyst must be concerned about why this variance occurs; that is, a deviation from the industry average should signal the analyst to check further.... (p. 20)

If substantive reasons for the deviation do not exist, the implication is that the firm with a ratio deviating from the industry mean should take steps so that its ratio approximates the industry mean.

What evidence is there that industry mean ratios are perceived as target ratios by firms in that industry? Lev [1969] addressed this issue for 245 firms over the 1947–1966 period. These firms (1) had a full 20 years of annual financial data available over the 1947–1966 period and (2) belonged to a four-digit SIC industry with at least 10 firms. The following model was used in the analysis:

$$z_t - z_{t-1} = \beta(z_t^* - z_{t-1}), \qquad 0 < \beta \leqslant 1, \qquad (3.1)$$

where z_t is a firm's financial ratio in time t and z_t^* is a firm's target financial ratio for time t. Lev specified z_t^* to be the industry mean (presumably equally weighted) ratio in time $t-1$. Thus, (3.1) "postulates that when the firm observes a deviation between its ratio and the industry mean, it will adjust its ratio in the next period so that the observed deviation will be partially eliminated.... The speed of adjustment is determined by the size of β; the closer β is to 1, the faster the period adjustment" (p. 292). Ordinary least squares (OLS) was used in estimating the following equation for each firm:

$$Y_i = \hat{\alpha} + \hat{\beta} X_i + \hat{e}_i, \qquad (3.2)$$

where

$$Y_i = z_t - z_{t-1}$$
$$X_i = z_t^* - z_{t-1}.$$

Appendix 3.A contains a description and illustration of the OLS estimation technique.

The mean $\hat{\beta}$, $t(\hat{\beta})$, and R^2 of (3.2) for the 245 firms in Lev [1969], and the .1, .5, and .9 fractiles of the distribution, are presented in Table 3.4.[11] The .1, .5, and .9 fractiles are the values of the pertinent statistic [$\hat{\beta}$, $t(\hat{\beta})$, or R^2] at which 10%, 50%, and 90% of its distribution for the 245 firms lies below. Thus, for instance, the .9 fractile of .43 for the R^2 of the quick ratio means that the R^2 of (3.2) for 90% of the 245 firms was below .43. The results in Table 3.4 support the hypothesis that financial ratios are adjusted toward the industry mean over time. For instance, the mean $\hat{\beta}$ for the inventory turnover ratio is .38, while the mean $\hat{\beta}$ for the quick ratio is .51.[12] Differences across ratios in their speed of adjustment (i.e., $\hat{\beta}$) were hypothesized to be a function of "two conflicting types of costs: (1) the cost of adjustment and (2) the cost of being out of equilibrium" (p. 296).

3.5 SUMMARY

In this chapter we have discussed issues and evidence pertaining to cross-sectional financial statement analysis. In general, comparisons of a firm's ratios or common-size statements with those of "ideal" bench marks or industry norms are exposited as a preliminary step in financial analysis. There is a trend, however, toward more explicit integration of the material in this chapter with specific decision models of creditors and investors. For instance, proposals have been made for building industry-specific quantitative models, using financial ratios, for the prediction of corporate solvency —e.g., Harmelink [1973]. This requires one to define what is meant by an *industry*—an issue discussed in Section 3.2A. This proposal also assumes that differences in ratios exist across industries—an issue discussed in Section 3.3A. Moreover, in several studies, the relationship between a

TABLE 3.4 Industry Averages as Target Financial Ratios

	Means and Fractiles	$\hat{\beta}$	$t(\hat{\beta})$	R^2
Quick ratio	Mean	.51	2.1	.22
	.1	.12	.82	.04
	.5	.50	2.09	.20
	.9	.95	3.60	.43
Current ratio	Mean	.48	1.93	.19
	.1	.10	.53	.02
	.5	.46	1.97	.20
	.9	.84	3.12	.36
Equity/total debt	Mean	.30	1.64	.16
	.1	.05	.40	.01
	.5	.25	1.52	.12
	.9	.65	2.94	.34
Net operating income/ total assets	Mean	.43	1.75	.17
	.1	.10	.46	.02
	.5	.40	1.71	.15
	.9	.91	3.15	.37
Sales/inventory	Mean	.38	1.78	.19
	.1	.07	.46	.02
	.5	.37	1.78	.16
	.9	.82	3.28	.39

SOURCE: Lev [1969, Table 1].

company's ratio and an industry norm is an important variable in models to discriminate between bankrupt and nonbankrupt firms, e.g., Edmister [1971] and Altman [1973]. This step requires estimation of an industry norm—an issue discussed in Section 3.2C. That is, many of the recent attempts to apply more quantitative tools to financial statement analysis need to address issues long encountered in the application of more traditional techniques of analysis. This point will become more apparent in subsequent chapters.

APPENDIX 3.A ORDINARY LEAST-SQUARES REGRESSION

OLS is a frequently used technique for estimating the coefficients of a linear model, e.g.,

$$Y_i = \hat{\alpha} + \hat{\beta}_1 X_i + \hat{e}_i, \qquad i = 1 \text{ to } N, \tag{3.3}$$

where Y_i is the dependent variable in period t, X_i is the independent variable, and e_i is a random error (residual) term. OLS yields estimates of α and β_1 such that the sum of the squared residuals $(\sum_{i=1}^{N} \hat{e}_i^2)$ is a minimum. For the two-variable model in (3.3),

$$\hat{\beta} = \frac{N \sum X_i Y_i - \sum X_i \sum Y_i}{N \sum X_i^2 - \left(\sum X_i \right)^2}$$

and

$$\hat{\alpha} = \frac{\sum Y_i - \beta \sum X_i}{N}.$$

Given additional assumptions (e.g., residuals normally distributed), the OLS estimates of α and β are maximum likelihood estimates of the population values.

The following data for the current ratios of *Schlitz* and the brewing industry over the 1961–1971 period will be used to illustrate ordinary least squares. The illustration is based on the Lev [1969] model described in Section 3.4. Let $Y_i = z_t - z_{t-1}$ and $X_i = z_t^* - z_{t-1}$; z_t^* is the target financial ratio for time t which is assumed to be the industry average for time $t - 1$:

	Current Ratio of Schlitz	Current Ratio of Brewing Industry	Y_i	X_i
1961	3.22	2.78		
1962	3.11	2.67	-.11	-.44
1963	2.82	2.62	-.29	-.44
1964	2.05	1.57	-.77	-.20
1965	1.62	2.37	-.43	-.48
1966	2.46	2.45	.84	.75
1967	2.44	2.46	-.02	-.01
1968	1.98	2.10	-.46	.02
1969	1.73	2.08	-.25	.12
1970	1.78	1.99	.05	.35
1971	1.99	2.21	.21	.21

For the data in the example,

$$\sum Y_i = -1.23 \qquad \sum Y_i^2 = 1.9007$$
$$\sum X_i = -.12 \qquad \sum X_i^2 = 1.4016$$
$$\sum X_i Y_i = 1.189$$
$$N = 10.$$

Using this information, the estimates of α and β are

$$\hat{\alpha} = -.113$$
$$\hat{\beta} = .839.$$

This model predicts that if *Schlitz* observes that the industry current ratio at $t-1$ is 2.5 and its current ratio at $t-1$ is 1.8, then it adjusts its current ratio by the following amount next period:

$$\hat{Y}_t = -.113 + .839 \times (2.5 - 1.8) = .474.$$

That is, the current ratio in t becomes 2.274, the $t-1$ value of 1.8 plus the .474 adjustment.

A measure of the goodness of fit of the model in (3.3) is the R^2 statistic. This measure is estimated by

$$R^2 = 1 - \frac{\sum \hat{e}_i^2}{\sum (Y_i - \bar{Y})^2},$$

where $\bar{Y}=$ the mean of the Y_i series. The $\hat{e}_i$ series (the residuals) is estimated as

$$\hat{e}_i = Y_i - (\hat{\alpha} + \hat{\beta} X_i)$$
$$= Y_i - (-.113 + .839 X_i).$$

For the data in the example,

$$\sum \hat{e}_i^2 = .765 \qquad \sum (Y_i - \bar{Y})^2 = 1.749.$$

Thus,

$$R^2 = .563.$$

In empirical work an adjustment is often made to the R^2 statistic to take into account the degrees of freedom used to estimate the OLS model. The resultant statistic—termed the adjusted R^2—is usually calculated by (see Montgomery and Morrison [1973])

$$\text{ADJ. } R^2 = 1 - (1 - R^2)\left(\frac{N-1}{N-K}\right),$$

where $N=$number of observations in the sample, and

$\qquad K=$number of degrees of freedom used (number of independent variables plus 1).

For the data in the example,

$$\text{ADJ. } R^2 = .508.$$

This indicates that the linear model in (3.3) explains approximately 51% of the variation in the one-period change in *Schlitz's* current ratio over the 1961–1971 period.

It is often of interest to assess the statistical significance of the estimated β coefficients. This is done by reference to a t test, which is computed as follows (assuming the null hypothesis of $\beta = 0$):

$$t_\beta = \frac{\hat{\beta}}{\hat{S}_\beta}$$

where $\hat{S}_\beta = $ estimated standard error of β,

$$\hat{S}_\beta = \frac{\sqrt{\Sigma (Y_i - \bar{Y})^2 / (N - K)}}{\sqrt{\Sigma (X_i - \bar{X})^2}},$$

where

$$\bar{Y} = \text{mean of the } Y_i \text{ series, and}$$
$$\bar{X} = \text{mean of the } X_i \text{ series.}$$

For the data in the example,

$$\Sigma (Y_i - \bar{Y})^2 = 1.749 \qquad \Sigma (X_i - \bar{X})^2 = 1.400.$$

Thus, $t_\beta = 3.210$.

A useful rule of thumb is that with samples of 20 to 50 observations, a t statistic ≥ 2 indicates that the estimated coefficient is statistically different from zero at at least the .05 level.

An assumption usually made when using OLS regression is that the residuals are serially uncorrelated. Given this assumption (and others, such as normally distributed residuals), the estimated α and β can be shown to have some important properties; e.g., they are minimum variance, unbiased, and maximum likelihood estimators of the population α and β values. If, however, the residuals are not serially uncorrelated, then the OLS estimates of α and β will be inefficient; i.e., there is another set of estimates of α and β that have a lower variance. One test for (first-order) serial correlation in the residuals is the Durbin-Watson statistic:

$$\text{D.W.} = \frac{\displaystyle\sum_{t=2}^{T} (\hat{e}_t - \hat{e}_{t-1})^2}{\displaystyle\sum_{t=1}^{T} \hat{e}_t^2}$$

$$= 1.64.$$

This statistic ranges between 0 and 4; a value of 2 indicates no serial correlation in the $\hat{e}_t$ series. A bench mark for suspecting positive serial correlation in the residuals in samples of 30 observations is a D.W. < 1.35. A corresponding bench mark for suspecting negative correlation is a D.W. > 2.65.

For further discussion of ordinary least squares, see Johnston [1972] and Theil [1978].

NOTES

[1]A simple economic order quantity model is

$$q^* = \sqrt{\frac{2 \cdot C_p \cdot D}{C_s}}$$

where q^* = economic order quantity,
C_p = cost of placing an order,
D = demand for the period, and
C_s = cost of storing one unit of inventory for the period.

Consider a case where $C_p = \$5$ and $C_s = \$1$. Then for $D = 100$, $q = 31.62$; $D = 200$, $q = 44.72$; $D = 400$, $q = 63.24$; and $D = 800$, $q = 89.44$. That is, for an eightfold increase in demand from 100 to 800, q^* increases from 31.62 to 89.44 (only a 283% increase).

[2]In developing analytical models of factors affecting firms' financial ratios, there are two related issues:

(1) Modeling how ratios change with changes in the components of the ratio, and

(2) Modeling what factors affect components of the ratio.

Beranek [1966, Chapter 3] provides some analytical results for the behavior of the current ratio when changes in current assets or current liabilities occur. Heston [1962] and Gupta and Huefner [1972] provide some preliminary empirical explorations of the latter issue.

[3]An early example of industry breakdowns of financial ratios is Wall [1919]. Wall presented data for 7 different ratios of 981 firms. He stratified these firms by industry and geographical location.

[4]Yet another approach is to define an industry in terms of firms with similar composition of assets, liabilities, revenues, and expenses in their financial statements. Lev [1974, Chapter 4] illustrates the use of "decomposition measures" to examine such similarities in the financial statements of aerospace firms.

[5]One problem in using line-of-business information from multiactivity firms, to increase the representativeness of industry norms, arises from the lack of a consistent breakdown of lines of business by firms. FASB Statement No. 14 (*Financial Reporting for Segments of a Business Enterprise*) argues that "no single set of characteristics is universally applicable

in determining the industry segments of all enterprises nor is any single characteristic determinative in all cases. Consequently, determination of an enterprise's industry segments must depend to a considerable extent on the judgment of the management of the enterprise" (p. 8). The FASB considered requiring all firms to report lines-of-business along SIC four-digit industry codes but rejected this idea in favor of the above approach.

[6]See Sunder [1977] for some evidence on the numerical effect of equal- vs. value-weighting schemes on profitability ratios for the petroleum industry.

[7]This example illustrates the often "thorny" problem of deciding what is an *outlier* in an empirical study. Values of the ratio in prior years and values of the ratio for other firms in the same industry often provide useful evidence when deciding if an observation is an *outlier*.

[8]See Hays and Winkler [1971, Chapter 11] for a description of the analysis of variance test.

[9]See, for instance, comments made in Brozen [1971] and Demsetz [1973].

[10]Institutional factors may well be an important factor when explaining financial ratio differences between regulated and nonregulated industries. For instance, Peltzman [1970] reported finding that commercial banks substitute FDIC (Federal Deposit Insurance Corp.) insurance of their liabilities for capital in their financial structure. Firms in the unregulated sector rarely have access to such insurance for their liabilities (albeit the U.S. government did "insure" *Lockheed Aircraft Corporation*).

[11]Lev [1969] did not present evidence on the serial correlation of the residuals in the regression of each firm. If there was substantial positive serial correlation in these residuals, the estimated α and β coefficients are not minimum variance estimators of the population coefficients. Indeed, for the distributed lags model used by Lev, positive correlation of the residuals is to be expected—see Griliches [1967].

[12]Lev and Pekelman [1975] present a more rigorously developed model than (3.1) of the adjustment by firms toward a target financial leverage ratio. This model was based on the assumption that the costs of deviating from the target ratio could be approximated by a quadratic function.

QUESTIONS

QUESTION 3.1: Computation of Industry Norms

The following data are the 1975 sales and the 1975 average accounts receivable balance of the nine companies used as the brewing industry in Chapter 2:

	Sales	Accounts Receivable
Busch	2,036,687	54,574
Pabst	665,291	14,582
Coors	633,422	26,280
Schaefer	287,215	21,743
Olympia	259,624	10,173
Falstaff	211,490	11,365
Heileman	209,824	5,654
Genesee	100,714	6,967
Lone Star	60,391	1,752

REQUIRED

(1) *Schlitz's* 1975 accounts receivable ratio was 33.89. How does this compare to

   (a) The median industry ratio,

   (b) An equally weighted industry ratio,

   (c) A value-weighted industry ratio, where the weights are based on the denominator of the accounts receivable ratio, and

   (d) A value-weighted industry ratio, where the weights are based on company sales relative to industry sales?

   Explain any differences among (a), (b), (c), and (d).

(2) One industry association argues that "medians are used [as industry norms] because they are considered more reliable and more representative than averages." Comment on this argument.

QUESTION 3.2: Industry Norms and Outliers

The treatment of *outliers* is, in practice, an important yet little discussed problem. For example, Rosenberg and Marathe [1975] note the following:

> No matter how robust a formula is, a few extraordinarily low or high values for firms in peculiar circumstances may be generated. Sometimes the formula is so constructed that *these values represent equally extreme states of the underlying characteristic.* In this case, the descriptor should be left as it is. But in other cases, *the extreme values exaggerate the differences between the firm and the population of firms with ordinary values.* In this case, it is appropriate to "pull in" the extreme value toward a more ordinary one.... This can be done by defining a lower and upper bound for the descriptor and redefining all values that fall outside the bounds to equal the bounds: Any value that falls below the lower bound is transformed to equal the lower bound; any value that is above the upper bound is transformed to equal the upper bound. This process may be called...truncation. (p. 155, emphasis added)

(1) How would one determine whether extreme values of a financial ratio represent "extreme states of the underlying characteristic" or "exaggerate the differences between the firm and the population of firms with ordinary values?"

(2) What approaches other than *truncation* may be used to handle *outliers* when computing industry ratios?

(3) What specific factors would you consider in evaluating the alternative approaches to handling *outliers*?

QUESTION 3.3:   Industry Financial Ratios and Industry Characteristics

Gupta and Huefner [1972] examined "financial ratios at a macro level for broad industry classes, seeking a correspondence between the accounting numbers and basic attributes" (p. 77). They examined the 1967 inventory turnover ratios of 20 manufacturing industries, defined according to the Standard Industrial Classification (two-digit level). They classified the industries into the following four groups, based on similarities in their inventory turnover ratios:

Group	Industry	Inventory Turnover	Group Mean
I	Petroleum	12.35	11.55
	Printing	11.62	
	Food	10.67	
II(A)	Paper	7.93	6.77
	Motor vehicles	7.68	
	Stone clay & glass	7.06	
	Chemicals	6.72	
	Lumber & wood	6.49	
	Furniture & fixtures	6.35	
	Apparel	6.32	
	Leather	6.30	
	Fabricated metal	6.09	
II(B)	Primary metal	5.61	4.98
	Textile	5.58	
	Rubber & plastic	5.57	
	Electrical equipment	4.95	
	Scientific instruments	4.83	
	Machinery	4.39	
	Transportation equipment	3.94	
III	Tobacco	2.18	

The industries in each group were then examined to see if they exhibited common characteristics. They concluded the following:

Examination of industry characteristics yielded the following:

(1) Product life. Industries producing a product with a very short life may be expected to have low inventories and a high turnover. Short life may be due to rapid obsolescence (as in the case of newspapers) or perishability (as in the case of some food products).

(2) Holding costs. High costs of holding inventories are a second factor that would be expected to result in low inventories and a high turnover. The short product life situation is one factor that would contribute toward high holding costs. In some industries, physical holding costs are very high. This is especially true in the Petroleum industry, where specialized storage facilities are required.

(3) Production period. Industries with a long production period may be expected to have high inventories and a low turnover. This has been particularly true in the Tobacco industry where a long aging process has been common. (pp. 87–88)

Dun & Bradstreet [1975] present 1974 industry turnover ratios for 71 different manufacturing industries. The 10 industries in the Dun & Bradstreet survey with the highest inventory turnover ratios were

Line of Business	Industry Median Ratio
Meat packing plants	31.7
Bakery products	24.5
Dairy products	22.0
Soft drinks, bottled and canned	16.6
Petroleum refining	13.8
Malt liquors	13.1
Blouses and waists: Women's and misses'	10.9
Dresses: Women's and misses'	10.0
Grain mill products	10.0
Nonferrous foundries	10.0

The 10 industries with the lowest inventory turnover ratios were

Line of Business	Industry Median Ratio
Equipment and plumbing fixtures	4.1
General industrial machinery and equipment	4.1
Household appliances	4.0
Instruments: Measuring and controlling	3.9
Work clothing: Men's and boys'	3.8
Farm machinery and equipment	3.8
Construction: Mining and handling equipment	3.8
Engineering, laboratory, and scientific instruments	3.7
Books: Publishing and printing	3.6
Computing and accounting machines	3.3

REQUIRED

(1) What evidence is there that the above characteristics outlined by Gupta and Huefner [1972] help discriminate between industries with high turnover ratios and those with low turnover ratios in the Dun & Bradstreet survey?

(2) Can you determine any other characteristics that discriminate between the above two groups of industries?

(3) Evaluate the Gupta-Huefner [1972] approach of examining if there is a "correspondence between accounting numbers and basic industry attributes" (p. 77).

(4) Describe an alternative approach of examining if there is a "correspondence between accounting numbers and basic industry attributes" (p. 77).

QUESTION 3.4:   McDonald's Corporation

Financial statement analysis often involves a comparison of the financial ratios of a cross section of "similar" firms. In many instances similarity is defined in terms of end products, e.g., *Schlitz* vis-à-vis *Busch* and *Pabst*. Consider the following analysis in which similarity is defined in terms of stocks with "comparable" price to earnings (P/E) ratios.

McDonald's Corporation operates a chain of fast-food restaurants. In 1975, over 3,700 restaurants were in operation in the United States, Canada, and other countries such as Australia, Germany, and Japan. Over the 1966–1975 period, *McDonald's* was consistently in the upper spectrum of U.S. stocks with high P/E ratios. A set of ten firms whose P/E ratio was consistently ranked high over the 1966–1975 period was chosen as a comparison set for *McDonald's*. These ten firms and their P/E ratios over the 1970–1975 period were

		1970	1971	1972	1973	1974	1975
1.	Economics Laboratory	38	42	53	42	22	20
2.	Texas Instruments	30	41	42	29	17	35
3.	Perkin-Elmer Corp.	26	43	49	36	17	19
4.	Coca-Cola	34	43	47	35	16	21
5.	Becton, Dickinson & Co.	35	34	35	26	16	20
6.	Eli Lilly & Co.	35	40	43	33	26	20
7.	Merck & Co.	32	36	45	34	24	23
8.	Burroughs Corp.	29	38	46	35	21	20
9.	Avery International	43	50	48	25	13	53
10.	Xerox Corp.	36	46	47	32	12	12
	Average	34	41	45	33	18	24

PROPERTIES OF ACCOUNTING NUMBERS 74

The P/E ratios of *McDonald's* over this period were

1970	1971	1972	1973	1974	1975
31	55	81	44	17	27

The above P/E ratios were calculated using the December 31 closing stock price of the financial year to which each earnings number pertained.

For each of eight financial ratios, (equally weighted) averages of the above ten stocks were computed. Equally weighted averages of these eight

TABLE 3.5 Financial Ratios of (1) McDonald's, (2) Portfolio of High P/E Stocks and (3) the Economy

	1970	1971	1972	1973	1974	1975
1. Current ratio						
McDonald's	1.50	1.62	1.14	1.26	1.10	1.13
P/E portfolio	2.82	2.87	2.97	2.46	2.24	2.52
Economy	2.50	2.51	2.54	2.26	2.14	2.46
2. Defensive interval (days)						
McDonald's	84	80	78	68	61	58
P/E portfolio	117	137	134	137	120	133
Economy	102	103	104	100	92	95
3. Total debt to equity						
McDonald's	.92	.97	.81	1.07	1.20	1.18
P/E portfolio	.65	.66	.59	.60	.66	.62
Economy	1.25	1.18	1.30	1.28	1.31	1.26
4. Times interest earned						
McDonald's	4.10	4.48	7.49	6.35	4.07	3.79
P/E portfolio	23.37	17.85	17.42	18.59	13.72	10.44
Economy	5.49	6.12	7.14	6.30	5.68	5.24
5. Earnings to sales						
McDonald's	.093	.094	.095	.089	.094	.094
P/E portfolio	.086	.083	.088	.093	.089	.082
Economy	.057	.062	.069	.070	.054	.051
6. Return on equity						
McDonald's	.290	.267	.255	.254	.251	.253
P/E portfolio	.184	.168	.182	.194	.187	.160
Economy	.120	.118	.136	.184	.140	.135
7. Inventory turnover						
McDonald's	123.0	114.7	119.2	116.4	96.6	103.5
P/E portfolio	6.8	6.3	6.6	6.8	5.9	5.5
Economy	11.6	11.1	12.3	12.6	12.1	11.3
8. Receivables turnover						
McDonald's	27.4	25.8	30.0	39.1	36.6	37.8
P/E portfolio	7.4	6.7	6.7	6.6	6.2	6.1
Economy	8.9	8.8	9.2	9.5	9.6	9.4

ratios for all companies on the *Compustat* file were also computed—these represent economy averages. The eight financial ratios were

(1) Current ratio
(2) Defensive interval
(3) Total debt to equity
(4) Times interest earned
(5) Earnings to sales
(6) Return on equity*
(7) Inventory turnover*
(8) Receivables turnover*

* denotes the average of the opening and closing balances used in the denominator.

Table 3.5 details the 1970–1975 values of these ratios for (1) *McDonald's*, (2) the above portfolio of high P/E stocks, and (3) the economy. The rank of *McDonald's* ratio for each year, vis-à-vis the ratios of the above ten high P/E stocks, was also computed. Table 3.6 details these rankings for each ratio and each year over the 1970–1975 period.

TABLE 3.6 Ranking of Financial Ratios of McDonald's Vis-à-vis Ten Companies with High P/E Ratios

	1970	1971	1972	1973	1974	1975
1. Current ratio	11	11	11	11	11	11
2. Defensive interval	9	10	11	11	11	11
3. Total debt to equity	2	2	3	1	1	1
4. Times interest earned	10	9	8	9	11	10
5. Earnings to sales	4	5	5	6	4	4
6. Return on equity	1	1	3	3	2	2
7. Inventory turnover	1	1	1	1	1	1
8. Receivables turnover	1	1	1	1	1	1

REQUIRED

(1) What inferences can you draw about the financial ratios of *McDonald's* vis-à-vis those of the ten stocks with high P/E ratios? In making this cross-sectional analysis, which presentation of the data (Table 3.5 vs. Table 3.6; equally weighted averages vs. ranks) do you find most useful? Why?

(2) What features of *McDonald's* ratios appear to be related to the nature of its business? What features of *McDonald's* ratios appears to be related to its having a high P/E ratio?

(3) What financial variables, in addition to the eight ratios examined, might explain the high P/E ratio of *McDonald's*?

(4) Using an end-product definition of an industry, what firms would you compare *McDonald's* financial ratios with? What problems may arise in making this comparison?

REFERENCES

ALTMAN, E. I. "Predicting Railroad Bankruptcies in America." *Bell Journal of Economics & Management Science* (Spring 1973): 184–211.

AYANIAN, R. "Advertising and Rate of Return." *Journal of Law and Economics* (Oct. 1975): 479–506.

BAIN, J. S. "Relation of Profit Rate to Industry Concentration: American Manufacturing, 1936–40." *Quarterly Journal of Economics* (1951): 293–324.

———. *Price Theory*. Wiley, New York, 1952.

BERANEK, W. *Working Capital Management*. Wadsworth, Belmont, Calif., 1966.

BOWEN, R. M., and HUBER, C. C. "An Investigation of Industry Effects on Financial Structure." Unpublished Paper, Stanford University, Stanford, Calif., 1972.

BROZEN, Y. "Bain's Concentration and Rates of Return Revisited." *Journal of Law and Economics* (Oct. 1971): 351–369.

COOTNER, P., and HOLLAND, D. "Rate of Return and Business Risk." *Bell Journal of Economics & Management Science* (Autumn 1970): 211–226.

DEMSETZ, H. *The Market Concentration Doctrine*. Hoover Institution on War, Revolution & Peace, Stanford University, Stanford, Calif., 1973.

DUN & BRADSTREET. *Key Business Ratios*. Dun & Bradstreet, New York, 1975.

EDMISTER, R. O. "Financial Ratios and Credit Scoring for Small Business Loans." *Journal of Commercial Bank Lending* (Sept. 1971): 10–23.

FOULKE, R. A. *Practical Financial Statement Analysis*. McGraw-Hill, New York, 1968.

GRILICHES, Z. "Distributed Lags: A Survey." *Econometrica* (Jan. 1967): 16–49.

GUPTA, M. C., and HUEFNER, R. J. "A Cluster Analysis Study of Financial Ratios and Industry Characteristics." *Journal of Accounting Research* (Spring 1972): 77–95.

HARMELINK, P. J. "An Empirical Examination of the Predictive Ability of Alternative Sets of Insurance Company Accounting Data." *Journal of Accounting Research* (Spring 1973): 146–158.

Hays, W. L., and Winkler, R. L. *Statistics: Probability, Inference, and Decision.* Holt, Rinehart and Winston, Inc., New York, 1971.

Heston, A. W. "An Empirical Study of Cash, Securities and Other Current Accounts of Large Corporations." *Yale Economic Essays* (Spring 1962): 116–168.

✓ Johnston, J. *Econometric Methods* 2nd ed. McGraw-Hill, New York, 1972.

Kruger, D. W. *1975 Financial Analysis of the Motor Carrier Industry.* First National Bank of Boston, Boston, 1975.

Lev, B. "Industry Averages as Targets for Financial Ratios." *Journal of Accounting Research* (Autumn 1969): 290–299.

———. *Financial Statement Analysis: A New Approach.* Prentice-Hall, Englewood Cliffs, N.J., 1974.

Lev, B., and Pekelman, D. "A Multiperiod Adjustment Model for the Firm's Capital Structure." *Journal of Finance* (Mar. 1975): 75–91.

Montgomery, D. B., and Morrison, D. G. "A Note on Adjusting R^2." *Journal of Finance* (Sept. 1973): 1009–1013.

Peltzman, S. "Capital Investment in Commercial Banking and Its Relationship to Portfolio Regulation." *Journal of Political Economy* (Jan.–Feb. 1970): 1–26.

Robert Morris Associates. *Annual Statement Studies: 1975 Edition.* Robert Morris Associates, Philadelphia, 1976.

Rosenberg, B., and Marathe, V. "The Prediction of Investment Risk: Systematic and Residual Risk." *Proceedings of the Seminar on the Analysis of Security Prices.* Center for Research in Security Prices, University of Chicago (Nov. 1975): 85–226.

Schnabel, M. "Defining a Product." *Journal of Business* (*Oct.* 1976): 517–529.

Stigler, G. J. *Capital and Rates of Return in Manufacturing Industries.* Princeton University Press, Princeton, N.J., 1963.

Sunder, S. *Oil Industry Profits.* American Enterprise Institute for Public Policy Research, 1977.

Theil, H. *Introduction to Econometrics.* Prentice-Hall, Englewood Cliffs, N.J., 1978.

Wall, A. "Study of Credit Barometrics." *Federal Reserve Bulletin* (Mar. 1919): 229–243.

Weiss, L. "Quantitative Studies of Industrial Organization." In M. D. Intriligator (ed.), *Frontiers of Quantitative Economics.* North-Holland, Amsterdam, 1971: 362–411.

Weston, J. F., and Brigham, E. F. *Managerial Finance,* 4th ed. Holt, Rinehart and Winston, Inc., New York, 1972.

Williams, E. E., and Findlay, M. C. *Investment Analysis.* Prentice-Hall, Englewood Cliffs, N.J., 1974.

CHAPTER

TIME-SERIES ANALYSIS OF ACCOUNTING NUMBERS

What factors are important when deciding how to forecast the earnings or sales of a firm? What problems arise when using accounting numbers in forecasting? What evidence is there of systematic patterns in the time-series behavior of accounting numbers? These and similar issues are discussed in this chapter. Major emphasis is placed on time-series approaches to forecasting. Other approaches are noted and contrasted with time-series approaches to forecasting.

4.1 IMPORTANCE OF TIME-SERIES ANALYSIS

The prediction of earnings plays a major role in investment analysis and financial statement analysis. For instance, Graham et al. [From *Security Analysis* by Graham et al. Copyright © 1962 by McGraw-Hill, Inc. Used with permission of McGraw-Hill Book Company.] note that expected earnings is the major factor determining the *intrinsic value* of a security:

> The most important single factor determining a stock's value is now held to be the *indicated average future earning power*, i.e., the estimated average earnings for a future span of years. Intrinsic value would then be found by first forecasting this earning power and then multiplying that prediction by an appropriate "capitalization factor." (p. 28)

In an interview survey, Opinion Research Corporation [1973] asked 534 analysts which factors they considered important in appraising companies. The factor cited most often was an "estimate of future earnings" followed by "competence of management" and "competitive position in an industry."

Bernstein [1974] also stresses the key importance of earnings predictions in financial statement analysis:

> For decision-making purposes by external analysts, the importance of determining the level of enterprise earnings or "earnings power" lies primarily in its use of *forecasting future earnings*. Security, credit, and most other types of financial analysis are oriented towards the future so that past and present results derive most of their value from their use as a basis for earnings projection. (p. 494)

Given the often-stated importance of earnings prediction in the investment and financial analysis literature, it is surprising how little analysis of (and evidence pertaining to) prediction issues is contained in this literature. For instance, proposals are made for the use of "average earnings over...five to ten years" in predicting future earnings without evidence to support the descriptive validity of such a model. Evidence presented in Sections 4.5 and 4.6 suggests that models quite different from those involving moving averages of past earnings have greater descriptive validity. Similarly, the use of trend statements (see Chapter 2) is often proposed for predicting earnings, sales, expenses, etc. Again, this proposal is made without support from any empirical analysis. *The basic philosophy in this chapter is that (1) the prediction of a variable such as earnings is enhanced by a model of how the variable behaves over time, and (2) the results of time-series analysis provide important information in the development of such a model.*

A second reason for studying the time-series properties of accounting variables relates to the capital markets/accounting information area (see Chapters 7–12). In this area, inferences are made about the degree of association between, say, accounting earnings and security returns. A key factor in examining this association is the development of a model of unexpected earnings changes for each firm. Again, this model development is facilitated by evidence of a time-series kind.

Yet another reason for examining models to predict accounting numbers relates to task allocation in auditing. There is a trend toward the more frequent use of quantitative tools when deciding what accounts to audit in detail and what procedures to use in these audits—see Stringer [1975] and Kinney [1978]. One approach is to predict various financial variables and then pay particular audit attention to those variables with the largest forecast error. This approach is obviously affected by the accuracy of the forecast model. In subsequent sections, evidence that is important in developing models to forecast a variety of accounting numbers is presented.[1]

4.2 ALTERNATIVE FORECASTING APPROACHES

In this chapter we shall concentrate on time-series techniques for forecasting accounting numbers. To place our concentration in perspective, it is useful to note briefly several alternative approaches to forecasting that can be adopted.

(1) Ad Hoc Approach. This approach is characterized by an arbitrary choice of a forecast model and of the parameters of the chosen model. By arbitrary is meant that there is no formal statistical or economic modeling of the financial series being forecast. One model often used in this approach is the equally weighted moving-average model, e.g.,

$$E(Z_t|Z_{t-1}\ldots Z_{t-n}) = \frac{1}{4}\sum_{i=1}^{4} Z_{t-i}$$
$$= .25 \times Z_{t-1} + .25 \times Z_{t-2} + .25 \times Z_{t-3} + .25 \times Z_{t-4}, \qquad (4.1)$$

where Z_t = value of the financial series in period t. Another variant of this model is a weighted moving-average model, e.g.,

$$E(Z_t|Z_{t-1}...Z_{t-n}) = .7 \times Z_{t-1} + .2 \times Z_{t-2} + .1 \times Z_{t-3}. \quad (4.2)$$

Accounting and investment textbooks often exposit such models in chapters on "forecasting techniques," "earnings predictions," etc.[2] These expositions rarely attempt to justify the particular models examined or the particular parameters of the chosen models.

(2) *Statistical Modeling Approach.* The distinctive feature of this approach is that a detailed *statistical* analysis of the financial series is an integral part of the forecast model choice. Box-Jenkins time-series modeling (see Appendix 4.A) is one example of this approach.[3] In some instances, the models chosen in this approach are models that may be chosen in the ad hoc approach—however, this choice is not an arbitrary one. Rather, it is the result of a detailed statistical analysis of the financial series.

(3) *Causal Modeling Approach.* This approach attempts to provide a *theoretical* underpinning for the specific model used in forecasting. The FRB-MIT-PENN(FMP) structural econometric forecasting model of the U.S. economy is an example of this approach. This model has theoretical underpinnings in Keynesian macroeconomic theory. Forecasts are obtained from the model by simultaneous solution of an equation system, after historical values of endogenous and exogenous variables and projected future values of exogenous variables have been provided. Most work on building such structural econometric models has been done at the economy or industry level—see Klein and Burmeister [1976]. In comparison, work on causal modeling of the financial series of individual firms is relatively less developed.

The above approaches to forecasting are obviously not mutually exclusive. For instance, in an econometric model, predictions of exogenous variables may be based on a time-series modeling approach. The exposition in this chapter will concentrate on the time-series modeling approach to forecasting accounting series. The causal modeling approach will be discussed briefly in Section 4.7.

4.3 TIME-SERIES ANALYSIS TOOLS

The set of models that we shall examine in studying the time-series behavior of a firm's accounting variables belong to the general class of discrete linear stochastic processes. Box and Jenkins [1976] and Nelson [1973] describe this class of models in some detail. This section draws on these sources. *Our purpose in this section is to provide an intuitive apprecia-*

tion of some important aspects of these models. When we say an earnings series can be described as a stochastic process, we mean that the sequence of earnings observations evolves through time according to some probability law. Such an evolution is in marked contrast to a sequence evolving through time in a deterministic pattern. A stochastic process is a discrete linear process if each observation z_t may be expressed in the form

$$z_t = \mu + u_t + \psi_1 u_{t-1} + \psi_2 u_{t-2} + \ldots + \psi_k u_{t-k}, \tag{4.3}$$

where μ and the ψ_i are fixed parameters of the process. The u_t term is referred to as a disturbance term. One important feature of (4.3) is that the time series $(u_t, u_{t-1}, \ldots, u_{t-k})$ is a sequence of independently and identically distributed (i,i,d) random disturbances with mean zero and variance σ_u^2. The process in (4.3) is discrete because each z_t observation is taken at a discrete (and equally spaced) interval. The process in (4.3) is linear because the z_t are a linear combination of the current and past disturbances. Several examples of specific discrete linear stochastic processes will illustrate the above comments.

A   A Random-Walk Model

One commonly discussed model is the random-walk model:

$$z_t = z_{t-1} + u_t. \tag{4.4}$$

This model implies that the best (in the minimum mean-square forecast error sense) forecast of z_t is z_{t-1}:

$$E(z_t) = z_{t-1}. \tag{4.5}$$

There is no other forecast, conditioned on only the past sequence of z_t, that can produce forecast errors whose squared values will on the average be smaller. Suppose the earnings series of *Jos. Schlitz Brewing Company* could be adequately described as a random walk. Then the best estimate of the 1976 earnings would be the 1975 earnings of $30,896,000.

How would one detect if a firm's earnings series could be adequately described as a random walk? This involves a comparison of known theoretical properties of this model's autocorrelation function and the sample autocorrelation function for the firm's earnings series.

AUTOCORRELATION FUNCTION: This function displays the autocorrelation structure of a series up to a specified lag. The jth-order autocorrelation coefficient measures the extent to which the z_t and z_{t+j} observations move together. If a higher (lower) than average observation tends to be followed by another higher (lower) than average observation j periods later, the z_t and z_{t+j} observations are said to be positively autocorrelated. If a higher than average observation (z_t) tends to be followed by a lower than average observation j

periods later, the z_t and z_{t+j} observations are negatively autocorrelated. The jth-order autocorrelation coefficient is estimated as

$$r_j = \frac{(1/T)\sum_{t=1}^{T-j}\left[(z_t-\bar{z})(z_{t+j}-\bar{z})\right]}{\gamma_0}, \qquad (4.6)$$

where $\bar{z}$ is the mean of the stationary series, γ_0 is the variance of the stationary series and T is the number of observations.[4] The range of r_j for $j=1$ to $T-j$ is from -1 to $+1$.

A theoretical property of the random-walk model is that the autocorrelations of the $\{\{z_t-z_{t-j}, z_{t-1}-z_{t-j-1}, z_{t-2}-z_{t-j-2}, \ldots \text{ for } j=1 \text{ to } N\}$ sequence are zero. This property implies that

$$r_j = 0 \qquad \text{for } j=1 \text{ to } N,$$

where N is the number of autocorrelations computed. Thus, testing whether a firm's earnings series behaves as a random walk involves estimating the r_j's for the $\{z_t-z_{t-j}, z_{t-1}-z_{t-j-1}, \ldots\}$ series and comparing them with the theoretical predictions of the random-walk model. The following data (in $000's) are the net income series of *Abbott Laboratories* over the 1955–1975 period. This company is included in the SIC 2835 four-digit industry group (drugs—ethical):

1955	$ 9,683	1966	$26,741
1956	$10,859	1967	$28,081
1957	$12,681	1968	$31,595
1958	$12,873	1969	$35,249
1959	$12,989	1970	$40,021
1960	$12,385	1971	$23,378
1961	$12,005	1972	$39,436
1962	$14,831	1973	$45,997
1963	$17,663	1974	$55,009
1964	$22,574	1975	$70,670
1965	$24,663		

The autocorrelations for the $\{z_t-z_{t-j}, z_{t-1}-z_{t-j-1}, \ldots\}$ series for $j=1$ to 6 are

r_1	r_2	r_3	r_4	r_5	r_6
$-.133$	.113	.072	$-.229$	.039	.026

Even if a random-walk model is a "true" description of the underlying time-series model for *Abbott*, one does not expect that the estimated autocorrelations in any finite sample will all be exactly zero. Significance tests are often very useful in deciding if the estimated autocorrelations are statistically different from zero. The standard error (SE) of each r_j indicates the standard deviation of a distribution with $r_j = 0$ for the sample size (T) used to estimate r_j. For r_j,

$$SE(r_j) = \sqrt{\frac{1}{T}}$$

given that the underlying series has $r_j = 0$ for all lags. A general rule of thumb is that r_j is significantly different from zero if the sample estimate is more than two standard errors from zero. If the sample r_j is no more than two standard errors from zero, one can accept the null hypothesis that the population $r_j = 0$ at the 95% confidence level. For estimating r_1 of *Abbott*, $T = 20$ and $SE(r_1) = .224$. Thus, even though the sample estimate of r_1 is not zero (it is $-.133$), one cannot reject the hypothesis that the underlying r_1 of *Abbott* is zero at a 95% confidence level. A similar conclusion applies to r_2 through r_6 of *Abbott*. Thus, based on the above estimated autocorrelations, *Abbott's* net income series appears to be well described by the random-walk model.

The random-walk model turns out to be an important model for forecasting accounting data. For instance, it is difficult to find models that yield more efficient forecasts of the earnings of individual firms than does the random-walk model (see Section 4.5).

B An Autoregressive Model

Suppose that one computed the autocorrelations for the first differences of the sales series of a firm and found significant positive autocorrelations at lag $1(r_1 = .80)$, lag $2(r_2 = .60)$, lag $3(r_3 = .40)$, and lag $4(r_4 = .15)$. This would imply that there is a systematic pattern in the past sequence of changes that can be exploited in forecasting future values of the series. One model suggested by such a pattern in the sample autocorrelation estimates is

$$z_t - z_{t-1} = .8(z_{t-1} - z_{t-2}) + u_t \qquad (4.7)$$

This model—termed an autoregressive model of order 1—has the property that the theoretical autocorrelation at lag k is $(\phi_1)^k$, where an estimate of ϕ_1 is the first-order autocorrelation coefficient. Suppose such a model describes the time-series behavior of *Schlitz's* sales series. Then for computing the one-step-ahead forecasts of sales (in $000's), (4.7) is rearranged to

$$E(z_t) = z_{t-1} + .8(z_{t-1} - z_{t-2}). \qquad (4.8)$$

Using the data for *Schlitz* in Table 2.2,

$$E(z_{1973}) = z_{1972} + .8 \times (z_{1972} - z_{1971})$$
$$= 779{,}359 + .8 \times (779{,}359 - 669{,}178) = \$867{,}504$$
$$E(z_{1974}) = z_{1973} + .8 \times (z_{1973} - z_{1972})$$
$$= 892{,}745 + .8 \times (892{,}745 - 779{,}359) = \$983{,}454.$$

The implications of this model are quite different from the random-walk model. The random-walk model would imply that successive changes in sales are serially uncorrelated. The model in (4.7) implies that successive changes in sales are positively correlated. That is, if a firm has experienced a sales increase in the past period, there is a high probability that it will experience a sales increase next period. These differences in the implied theoretical autocorrelation functions of different models play an important role in choosing an appropriate time-series model for a firm's sales, earnings, etc.

C A Seasonal Model

The quarterly sales and net income series of *Marshall Field and Company* (a Chicago-based retail department chain) provide a convenient way to introduce the third example of a time-series model. Table 4.1 lists both series for the 1960–1975 period. The fiscal year-end is January 31; the first quarter covers the February–April months...the fourth quarter covers the November–January months. In modeling a time series, one examines if there are any systematic patterns in the series that can be exploited in forecasting. Several such systematic patterns appear in both the quarterly sales and net income series of *Marshall Field and Company*. One pattern in both series is of a seasonal kind. In particular, note that the fourth quarter in every year has the highest sales and net income. For a retail department store this is hardly surprising—the fourth quarter includes the heavy Christmas buying period. Note also that the third quarter results generally exceed those of either the first or second quarters—the third quarter includes the "back-to-school" and "winter-wardrobe" buying periods. A second pattern in both series is the increase (upward drift) in both sales and net income over the 1960–1975 period. Several factors could account for this increase. First, *Marshall Field* has reinvested much of its earnings in expanding into many suburban areas of Chicago (and also Cleveland and Seattle). Second, inflation has caused nominal sales to increase over this period.

In forecasting (say) the sales of *Marshall Field*, one would attempt to exploit these seasonality and drift features. One possible model could be

$$z_t = z_{t-4} + \delta + u_t, \tag{4.9}$$

TABLE 4.1   Quarterly Net Sales and Net Income of Marshall Field and
Company: 1960–1975

	First Quarter	Second Quarter	Third Quarter	Fourth Quarter
	Net Sales			
1960	50,147	49,325	57,948	76,781
1961	48,617	50,898	58,517	77,691
1962	50,862	53,028	58,849	79,660
1963	51,640	54,119	65,681	85,175
1964	56,405	60,031	71,486	92,183
1965	60,800	64,900	76,997	103,337
1966	67,279	69,869	81,029	107,192
1967	69,110	76,084	87,160	113,829
1968	73,567	79,360	97,324	136,036
1969	78,071	84,382	100,422	139,632
1970	79,823	84,750	96,724	140,586
1971	97,015	103,137	114,402	152,135
1972	101,984	108,562	121,749	160,499
1973	108,152	114,499	127,292	171,965
1974	115,673	125,995	136,255	169,677
1975	111,905	127,872	145,367	188,635
	Net Income			
1960	973	997	2,132	4,759
1961	993	1,167	2,319	4,628
1962	1,187	1,150	2,168	4,656
1963	924	1,027	2,489	4,928
1964	1,391	1,733	3,632	5,685
1965	1,752	2,216	4,190	6,672
1966	2,343	2,446	3,949	7,014
1967	2,012	2,877	4,359	7,429
1968	1,892	2,560	4,473	8,323
1969	2,351	2,942	4,428	7,836
1970	1,500	2,432	4,074	8,073
1971	1,989	2,935	4,371	9,757
1972	2,106	3,083	5,050	11,218
1973	2,564	3,164	4,530	10,644
1974	2,647	3,659	4,942	9,063
1975	637	3,347	5,226	10,116

where δ is the average change in sales between the corresponding quarters
of (say) the last two years. Thus, for predicting fourth-quarter 1976 sales,
(4.9) becomes

$$E(z_t) = z_{t-4} + \delta \tag{4.10}$$
$$E(z_{1976,4}) = Z_{1975,4} + .5 \times (z_{1975,4} - z_{1973,4})$$
$$= \$188,635 + .5 \times \$16,670 = \$196,970.$$

This model is one possible model that captures the above-noted systematic features in the past series. Appendix 4.A contains a more detailed analysis of model identification for the net income to sales ratio series of *Marshall Field and Company*. The important feature of this analysis is the attempt to model systematic patterns in a firm's past time series and then exploit these patterns when forecasting.

D Forecast Error Measures

In this section, a variety of summary forecast error measures are discussed and illustrated. Two commonly used forecast error measures provide evidence on the dispersion of the forecast error—the mean absolute error (MABE) and the mean-square error (MSE). These two measures are computed (in percentage form) as follows:

$$\text{MABE } (\%) = \frac{1}{N} \sum_{t=1}^{N} \left| \frac{E(X_{it}) - X_{it}}{X_{it}} \right|$$

$$\text{MSE } (\%) = \frac{1}{N} \sum_{t=1}^{N} \left[\frac{E(X_{it}) - X_{it}}{X_{it}} \right]^2,$$

where X_{it} = realization of the forecast variable of the ith firm in period t,
N = number of forecasts examined.
The MABE measure gives equal weighting to all forecast errors. The MSE measure gives greatest weight to large forecast errors.

Another error measure—the average error (AVE)—provides evidence on the bias of a forecast. A forecast is said to be unbiased if the expected value of the forecast error is zero. The AVE is computed (in percentage form) as follows:

$$\text{AVE } (\%) = \frac{1}{N} \sum_{t=1}^{N} \frac{E(X_{it}) - X_{it}}{X_{it}}.$$

Forecast errors of differing sign are allowed to cancel each other out. The concern of the AVE is not with each individual forecast error but rather with the average error over all forecasts. A significant negative AVE would imply that the forecast method, *on average*, is underestimating the realizations of the series being forecast.

The quarterly net income series of *Pabst Brewing Company* for 1974–1975 will be used to illustrate these error measures. The relevant data (in $000's) are

	First Quarter	Second Quarter	Third Quarter	Fourth Quarter
1974	$2,609	$3,918	$6,400	$5,403
1975	$3,957	$5,569	$6,174	$4,995

Assume a model that predicts that the quarterly earnings of *Pabst* in quarter t is the earnings of the corresponding quarter in the prior year, i.e.,

$$E(Q_t) = Q_{t-4}, \tag{4.11}$$

where Q_t = quarterly earnings in period t. For the first quarter of 1975, this model predicts earnings will be the 1974 first-quarter earnings of $2,609. The above error metrics for this model are

$$\text{MABE } (\%) = \left| \frac{2,609 - 3,957}{3,957} \right| = .341$$

$$\text{MSE } (\%) = \left[\frac{2,609 - 3,957}{3,957} \right]^2 = .1163$$

$$\text{AVE } (\%) = \frac{2,609 - 3,957}{3,957} = -.341.$$

For all four quarters of 1975,

	MABE (%)	MSE (%)	AVE (%)
First quarter	.341	.1163	−.341
Second quarter	.296	.0876	−.296
Third quarter	.037	.0014	.037
Fourth quarter	.082	.0067	.082
Average	.189	.053	−.129

As a standard of comparison, the forecast error measures were computed from a model predicting next quarter's earnings to be the same as last quarter's earnings, i.e.,

$$E(Q_t) = Q_{t-1} \tag{4.12}$$

The averages for this model over all four quarters of 1975 were

MABE (%)	MSE (%)	AVE (%)
.247	.071	.053

Thus for 1975, (4.11) yields less dispersed forecasts than (4.12). However, the forecasts of (4.11) have a larger bias than those of (4.12).

The above summary measures are often used in forecast evaluation. It is important to realize that in specific decision contexts they may not be appropriate measures of the loss from using a specific model. For instance, a credit evaluation officer may place a higher penalty on overestimating the earnings of a loan applicant than on underestimating earnings. Such an asymmetrical payoff as regards forecast errors would need to be explicitly considered in choosing among alternative earnings forecast models. In general, the model which yields forecasts having the highest *expected payoff* to the decision maker should be chosen. The framework outlined in Chapter 1 illustrates the basic approach to making this forecast model choice in a specific context. Demski and Feltham [1972] provide an insightful discussion of various factors that influence the expected payoffs of alternative forecasting models in several specific contexts.[5]

4.4 ISSUES IN MODELING THE TIME-SERIES BEHAVIOR OF ACCOUNTING NUMBERS

Several important issues must be considered when identifying and estimating time-series models from accounting data.

A   Absence of a Theory of Time-Series Behavior of Accounting Data

A major problem in choosing between a set of time-series models is the lack of an underlying theory of how the time series of accounting variables might be expected to behave. There is at present little theory to use in forming a prior probability about a time-series model.[6] Several important issues need to be explored. Consider viewing the reported earnings series as being a transformation (via accounting techniques) on some basic series (which is a function of the financing, investment, and production decisions of firms):

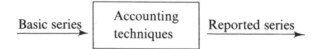

Under this viewpoint, the reported accounting numbers are a joint product of (1) the basic series and (2) the accounting techniques used by the firm.[7]

At present, we lack a theory which would specify the characteristics of the basic series. Variables such as the concentration of firms in the industry, barriers to entry, and the shape of cost functions are likely candidates. Moreover, we also have little analysis of how specific accounting techniques transform the basic series, e.g., the effect of LIFO vs. FIFO on the reported series. Assertions are often made about the effect on reported earnings of using accounting alternatives without any attempt to examine if they apply under only certain conditions. For instance, it is often asserted that the use of LIFO over FIFO will result in lower reported earnings if input prices are rising. Note, however, that if a firm is reducing its inventory, the use of LIFO over FIFO may well produce higher reported earnings even if input prices are rising, i.e., when the firm "dips" into older LIFO layers.[8]

A consequence of this limited knowledge about the type of time-series models to be expected for accounting data is that heavy weight is often placed on patterns in the sample of observations examined. As illustrated below, care must be taken in using the small samples commonly encountered with accounting data.

B   Sampling Variation and Model Identification

Sampling variation in small samples is quite high. A consequence is that one must be careful *not* to assume that differences across firms in their sample autocorrelation functions imply differences in the underlying time-series models of firms. Consider the following model:

$$z_t = \phi_1(z_{t-1}) + u_t, \tag{4.13}$$

with a "true" value of $\phi_1 = .5$. In any one sample of observations generated by this model, it is quite possible to observe sample estimates of ϕ_1 different from .5. To examine this, we simulated 100 z_t values for (4.13) and from the last 30 simulated values estimated the sample autocorrelations up to lag 8. This was repeated ten times. Table 4.2 has the results of this experiment. The theoretical model that generated the data implies $\phi_1 = .5$, $\phi_2 = .25$, $\phi_3 = .125$, etc. Note, however, that the *sample* estimates of ϕ_1 ranged from .139 to .582. Similarly, the sample estimates of ϕ_2 ranged from $-.024$ to .313. That is, the sample estimate of ϕ_i's from a finite sample can be very different from that implied by the underlying time-series model.[9] Note that in any situation one does not obtain 10 independent realizations of 30 observations of a specific firm. One obtains *one* set of observations and must infer the model from the sample and other available information. The patterns of r_1 to r_8 for the 10 realizations in Table 4.2 suggest that with small samples it is quite difficult to identify anything but a crude approximation of the underlying time-series model.

Several steps might be taken when faced with sampling variation in time-series analysis. The *first* step would be not to read too much into all patterns in the sample autocorrelation function. One presumes that the basic model to be identified is a reasonably parsimonious one. For

TABLE 4.2 Theoretical Autocorrelations for Process $z_t = .5z_{t-1} + u_t$ and Sample Autocorrelations for Ten Independent Realizations of $T = 30$

Lag	Theoretical Autocorrelations	Sample Autocorrelations for r_j for 10 Independent Realizations									
		1	2	3	4	5	6	7	8	9	10
1	.50	.537	.139	.498	.491	.388	.582	.503	.459	.145	.429
2	.25	.140	-.024	.172	.165	.178	.055	.295	.173	.313	.175
3	.125	-.042	.286	.047	.063	.142	-.276	.173	.336	-.057	-.144
4	.0625	-.129	.010	-.083	-.051	.137	-.222	.096	.571	-.101	-.131
5	.0312	-.026	-.214	-.216	-.016	.216	-.005	.272	.506	.034	-.227
6	.0156	-.071	-.033	-.213	.038	-.085	-.008	.089	.119	-.174	-.183
7	.0078	-.210	.074	-.108	.071	.018	-.142	.036	.037	-.085	-.156
8	.0039	-.213	-.191	-.128	.096	-.076	-.264	-.120	.201	-.218	.063

instance, the prior probability may be that the random-walk model describes a firm's earnings series. One would then examine the sample autocorrelation function to see if there is strong evidence that this is not an adequate time-series model. A *second* step might be to use both the sample autocorrelation function and simulation analysis in identifying a time-series model—for examples, see the Beaver [1970], Ball and Watts [1972], and Foster [1977] papers. A *third* step would be to examine the predictive ability of the fitted models on a set of data not used to identify and estimate them—for example, see the Watts [1970] and Foster [1977] papers. These steps will be further discussed in Section 4.5.

C Structural Change and Time-Series Analysis

The problems that structural change poses for model fitting also need to be considered. Here there are two offsetting considerations. For estimation efficiency, one wants to have a large sample size. In a time-series context, this means going back a long period of time. However, the farther one goes back in time, the more one expects to encounter a structurally different firm. In one study—Watts [1970]—annual earnings of U.S. railroads over the 1927–1964 period were used for model identification and estimation. Over this 38-year period, there are some indications that the railroad industry may have undergone structural change. For instance, it was over this period that competition from the road transportation industry became more marked—at the start of this period, road transportation was in its infancy. Changes such as this may affect the underlying time series of earnings. Watts did examine this issue for his sample and found some evidence that the variance of the accounting series examined had changed over this 1927–1964 period.[10]

Structural change can occur for a variety of reasons—e.g., (1) changes in the lines of business or (2) take-overs and mergers. These two may, of course, occur simultaneously. Data of *The Greyhound Corporation* over the 1966–1975 period illustrate the effect that mergers/change of activity may have on the time sequence of an accounting series; see Table 4.3. From 1965 to 1969 the total revenues series has a reasonably constant rate of increase—it varies from a 5.18% to a 6.98% increase. Then in 1970 the level of the total revenues series increased 426.22%. Prior to 1969 *Greyhound* derived most of its revenues from passenger bus operations. In 1970 it acquired 100% ownership of *Armour & Company*—a company specializing in food processing. In predicting 1970 total revenues, one would probably want to adjust the results of a time-series prediction model that incorporated only pre-1970 total revenues. Columns (4) and (5

TABLE 4.3   The Greyhound Corporation: 1966–1975

	Total Revenues (1)	Net Income (2)	Total Assets (3)	Net Income / Total Revenues (4)	Net Income[a] / Total Assets (5)
1966	552,112	46,723	446,172	.085	—
1967	590,505	45,449	470,287	.077	.099
1968	621,084	43,233	525,081	.070	.087
1969	663,118	43,928	707,797	.069	.071
1970	2,826,363	55,460	1,189,570	.020	.058
1971	2,626,644	70,542	1,143,182	.027	.060
1972	2,952,217	70,104	1,237,039	.024	.059
1973	3,421,447	76,408	1,309,159	.022	.060
1974	3,469,281	57,955	1,357,328	.017	.043
1975	3,748,224	81,220	1,427,964	.022	.058

[a] Averages of opening and closing balances of total assets used as the denominator.

SOURCE: *Moody's Transportation Manuals* (1967–1976).

contains two ratio series of *Greyhound*. The net income/total revenues ratio series appears to be more affected by the merger than does the net income/total assets series. (Why?)

The possibility of structural change means one may choose a time period for model identification that is shorter than the available data set. Unfortunately, in this chapter we can do little more than raise the problem of structural change. Techniques for handling these problems are quite involved. Moreover, they have not been extensively developed for a wide class of contexts in which structural change occurs. Note that when structural change occurs, each new observation in the series serves a dual function—it provides new information about the time sequence of the series, and it provides new information about the underlying time-series model.

Restated Accounting Data

To reduce the problems associated with structural change, annual reports often disclose *restated figures*. The issue of whether to use (say) the earnings as reported or the *restated* earnings is a difficult one. Even if one decides to use restated earnings, additional complications arise. Consider an investor predicting the 1974 net income series of *ITT* (International Telephone & Telegraph Corporation) based on the 1967–1973 series. Over the 1967–1973 period, *ITT* was actively involved in acquiring and divesting firms. The 1973 Annual Report disclosed the following restated figures (in

$000's) for the prior five years:

1973	$521,291
1972	$477,296
1971	$428,061
1970	$382,212
1969	$321,650

The 1972 Annual Report disclosed a different restated series for the overlapping time period:

1972	$476,626
1971	$427,372
1970	$381,920
1969	$321,465
1968	$285,496

The 1971 Annual Report disclosed yet another restated series for the overlapping time period:

1971	$406,834
1970	$362,541
1969	$304,701
1968	$270,987
1967	$231,180

Thus, if the investor wanted to use data over the 1967–1973 period to identify a time-series model, it is far from obvious what series to use. If he decided to use the 1973 Annual Report restated series, the question of the number to use for 1968 arises—the 1972 Annual Report figure of $285,496 or the 1971 Annual Report figure of $270,987. Due to mergers and divestitures, neither 1968 figure relates to the activities included in the 1973 Annual Report restated series. There are no easy answers to these questions. As a first step, it is useful to examine if the investment decision is sensitive to the choice between the *as-reported* series and the *restated* series.

D Accounting Classification and Measurement Changes

Use of accounting time-series data requires care in analysis. Over time, firms may voluntarily or involuntarily change (1) the classification of certain balance sheet/income statement items or (2) the measurement rules underlying these statements. Consider the accounts of *F & M Schaefer Corporation* (the largest regional Eastern U.S. brewing company) over the 1968–1975 period—see Table 4.4.

Prior to 1969, *Schaefer* manufactured beer at its Albany and Brooklyn breweries. Then in 1969 management decided to build a new plant at Lehigh Valley, Penn. The new plant began operations in 1972. In 1972, the

TABLE 4.4 F & M Schaefer Corporation: 1968–1975 ($000's)

	Sales	Operating Profit	Net Income (NI) [bef. ext (BE)]	Net Income [after ext (AE)]	Stockholders' Equity (SE)	Total Assets (TA)
1968	201,347	13,549	3,763	3,763	36,860	158,979
1969	223,186	16,621	5,633	5,633	43,943	153,049
1970	242,726	17,104	5,794	5,794	50,658	163,164
1971	280,822	14,562	4,348	4,348	55,006	191,918
1972	280,569	4,659	(1,005)	(6,393)^a	48,629	198,569
1973	286,727	9,305	973	973	49,637	198,422
1974	308,868	10,012	675	675	50,338	196,487
1975	287,215	1,433	(32,511)^b	(33,091)^c	17,269	165,261

Financial Ratios

	Operating Profit / Sales	NI (BE) / Sales	NI (AE) / Sales	NI (BE)* / SE	NI (BE)* / TA
1968	.067	.019	.019		
1969	.074	.025	.025	.139	.036
1970	.070	.024	.024	.122	.037
1971	.052	.015	.015	.082	.024
1972	.017	−.004	−.023	−.019	−.005
1973	.032	.003	.003	.020	.005
1974	.032	.002	.002	.014	.003
1975	−.005	−.113	−.115	−.962	−.180

* denotes an average of the opening and closing balances used as the denominator.

^{a} An extraordinary charge of $5,387,000 related to the closing of the Albany brewery.

^{b} Includes a $26,136,000 charge related to the closing of the Brooklyn brewery—shown as a separate line in the income statement but *not* shown as an extraordinary charge.

^{c} Extraordinary charge of $580,000 in 1975 was "an adjustment for estimated closing costs and a reduction of the estimated net realizable value of the remaining assets" at the Albany brewery.

SOURCE: Annual reports of *F & M Schaefer Corporation*.

Albany plant was closed due to its "manufacturing costs [being] out-of-line with competition." The 1972 income statement included an extraordinary charge of $5,387,080 related to "closing of its Albany brewery and brewing operations." In 1975 the company closed its Brooklyn brewing plant—"it had become economically obsolete and inefficient compared with larger, automated, high-speed plants that have been erected by brewers over the last few years" (p. 4). The 1975 income statement included a separate line item of $26,136,000 related to closing of the Brooklyn plant. The item was *not* treated as an extraordinary item due to a change in guidelines for items qualifying as extraordinary (*APB Opinion No. 30*). Thus, a time-series trend of the net income before extraordinaries series includes the $26,136,000 item in 1975 but excludes the $5,387,080 item in 1972. In a Box-Jenkins time-series model of this series (or the net income to stockholder's equity ratio series), the 1975 observation could dramatically affect the coefficients that will minimize the sum of the squared residuals. In this context, an analyst may decide to use a different definition of extraordinary items than that used in the published financial statements. Alternatively, he may use a profitability ratio less affected by the 1972 and 1975 brewing plant closings, e.g., the operating profit to sales ratio.

A related problem arises when firms change their accounting techniques; e.g., many U.S. steel companies switched from accelerated to straight-line depreciation in the 1960s. Similarly, in 1974 many companies switched from the FIFO to LIFO inventory valuation method. These changes may induce changes in the time-series model of the reported series. Dopuch and Watts [1972] provide an interesting discussion of this issue as regards depreciation switches in the steel industry. At a minimum, the possibility of changes in the time series being due to accounting changes rather than changes in the underlying basic time series should be recognized and investigated.

4.5 TIME-SERIES PROPERTIES OF EARNINGS

The time-series behavior of earnings has been examined in some detail. In this literature, different earnings variables have been examined, different samples have been used, and different methodologies have been applied. We shall distinguish studies making inferences based on mean or median results for samples of firms from studies making inferences based on detailed analysis of the time series of individual firms. We shall also distinguish studies examining annual earnings from studies examining interim earnings.

A Annual Earnings—Inferences Based on Mean or Median Results

The typical approach in mean/median studies is to compute statistics (e.g., autocorrelations) for each firm and then present the mean or median results for all firms in the sample. There are several reasons such mean/median results are important. The *first* reason relates to sampling error. The number of annual earnings observations that are available on machine-readable sources is quite limited. For instance, the *Compustat* file for annual data covers only the post-1946 period. Such small data bases mean that the sampling error, when attempts are made to identify and estimate the time-series models of individual firms, is quite large. By aggregating the results over many firms, it is hoped that there is a reduction in this sampling error. A *second* reason for examining mean/ median results is the use that such information can play in forming prior probabilities of the time-series models for individual firms. That is, one can combine prior information from mean/median studies with the information contained in the sample autocorrelations of an individual firm to form a revised probability of the appropriate time-series model. In the case of recently formed firms, such prior information could be critical as there may be only three or four years of firm-specific annual data available as sample evidence.

Empirical Evidence

Work in this area has a long history; e.g., see the early studies by Little [1962] and Little and Rayner [1966] on U.K. companies and by Brealey [1969] on U.S. companies. The most detailed study is by Ball and Watts [1972], which we shall examine in some detail. The sample of firms examined was taken from the *Compustat* file. Firms were required to have data for the full 1947–1966 period. Ball and Watts describe their study as follows:

> This study is a descriptive exercise since we do not have theories of the firm or of the measurement of income. Further, due to our limited number of observations for each firm, the results we obtain may be sensitive to violations of the assumptions of each test. Analytical results for most tests are for "large" samples. We attempt to avoid both issues by subjecting the income data to a number of different tests. (p. 668)

The first test used was a *runs test*. This test examined if the signs of successive changes in earnings were independent.

RUNS TEST: A runs test examines if there is a systematic pattern in a sequence of observations. Consider the net income series ($000's) of *Faberge, Inc.* and *Monroe Auto Equipment Company* over the 1966–1975 period:

Year	Faberge		Monroe	
	$000's	Sign of Change	$000's	Sign of Change
1966	8,370		8,223	
1967	9,405	+	9,869	+
1968	8,550	−	11,930	+
1969	9,670	+	13,902	+
1970	2,557	−	17,788	+
1971	7,112	+	20,464	+
1972	8,088	+	22,525	+
1973	8,740	+	18,622	−
1974	5,622	−	6,681	−
1975	3,167	−	5,411	−

What evidence is there of a systematic pattern in the sign of the net income changes for *Faberge* or *Monroe*? *Monroe* appears to exhibit a more systematic pattern relative to *Faberge*. Defining a run as a succession of identical observations, *Faberge* has six runs of + or −, while *Monroe* has only two runs. A runs test is a statistical test that can buttress our intuitive analysis of the above sequences of +'s and −'s. The null hypothesis of this test is that the sequence of observations is random. The mean number of runs expected under this null hypothesis is

$$\mu_r = \frac{2N_1 N_2}{N_1 + N_2} + 1,$$

where N_1 = number of + signs,
$\quad\quad N_2$ = number of − signs.

The standard deviation of the number of runs under the null hypothesis is

$$\sigma_r = \sqrt{\frac{2N_1 N_2 (2N_1 N_2 - N_1 - N_2)}{(N_1 + N_2)^2 (N_1 + N_2 - 1)}}.$$

The significance test can be made by computing the following statistic:

$$z = \frac{\mu_r - r}{\sigma_r},$$

where r = the number of runs in the sample. The z statistic is approximately normally distributed.[11] Thus, if z is >2, one can reject the null hypothesis of randomness at the 95% confidence level. See Dyckman and Thomas [1977, Chapter 18] for further discussion of the runs test.

For *Faberge*, $N_1 = 5$, $N_2 = 4$, and $r = 6$. Thus,

$$\mu_r = 5.444$$
$$\sigma_r = 1.383$$
$$z = -.402.$$

For *Monroe*, $N_1 = 6$, $N_2 = 3$, and $r = 2$. Thus,

$$\mu_r = 5$$
$$\sigma_r = 1.247$$
$$z = 2.406.$$

These z scores accord with our conclusions based on visual inspection of each series. For *Monroe*, one can reject the null hypothesis of randomness at the 95% confidence level, while for *Faberge* one cannot reject the randomness hypothesis at this significance level.

TABLE 4.5   Runs in Signs of Income Changes

	Net Income		EPS	
	Number	Percent	Number	Percent
Firms with more runs than expected under independence	348	48.7	326	48.0
Firms with fewer runs than expected under independence	366	51.3	353	52.0
	714	100.0	679	100.0
Total runs in sample	6,522	100.0	6,338	99.8
Total expected runs, assuming independence	6,524	100.0	6,350	100.0

SOURCE: Ball and Watts [1972, Table 2].

Results of the Ball and Watts runs test for the 1947–1966 period are presented in Table 4.5. Note that for all firms there were 6,522 runs for the net income series—the total expected runs assuming independence was 6,524. This result is consistent with successive changes in earnings of firms, *on average*, being independent.

The second major test was examination of the autocorrelation function of the firms in the sample. Recall from Section 4.3 that the random-walk model implies that the autocorrelations for all lags of earnings changes are zero. Ball and Watts computed autocorrelations (up to lag 5) for each firm and then examined aspects of the cross-sectional distribution of these statistics for the firms in their sample. Summary results are presented in Table 4.6. The .1, .5, and .9 deciles in Table 4.6 refer to that "point" on the distribution of r_j at which 10%, 50%, and 90% of the distribution of all firms lies below. Thus, the .9 decile of .388 for the r_1 of

TABLE 4.6   Distribution of Autocorrelation Coefficients: Net Income Changes and EPS Changes

Lag r_j	Net Income				EPS			
	Mean	.1 Decile	.5 Decile	.9 Decile	Mean	.1 Decile	.5 Decile	.9 Decile
1	−.030	−.386	−.075	.388	−.200	−.453	−.198	.057
2	−.040	−.368	−.067	.315	−.076	−.375	−.081	.208
3	.006	−.306	.001	.321	−.061	−.331	−.073	.259
4	−.007	−.320	−.013	.313	.023	−.300	−.052	.319
5	.055	−.277	.047	.403	.010	−.346	−.024	.318

SOURCE: Ball and Watts [1972, Tables 3 and 4].

the net income series means that 90% of the firms in the sample had an r_1 less than .388. The mean and median (.5 decile) autocorrelations for net income are all close to the zero values implied by a random-walk model—e.g., the mean $r_1 = -.030$, $r_2 = -.040$, and $r_3 = .006$. There is some small evidence in the mean/median results of the EPS series of negative autocorrelation at lower lags—e.g., the mean $r_1 = -.200$, $r_2 = -.076$, and $r_3 = -.061$. Ball and Watts comment as follows: "The most extreme mean or median coefficient is $-.200$. This is not only an extreme observation; it also implies a mere 4 percent explanatory power for an autoregressive prediction model" (p. 671). Note that the .1 and .9 decile values of r_1 to r_5 for each series all seem quite different from zero. This does not necessarily mean that the time series implied by the mean/median results does not adequately describe these .1 and .9 fractile firms. With 19 observations (successive earnings changes) for each firm, some dispersion across firms' *sample* autocorrelations is to be expected even if a random-walk model describes the underlying time series of net income or EPS.

The final test used by Ball and Watts [1972] involved the following class of forecast models:

$$\hat{y}_t = \alpha y_{t-1} + (1 - \alpha)\hat{y}_{t-1}, \qquad 0 \leqslant \alpha \leqslant 1, \tag{4.14}$$

where $\hat{y}_t$ is forecasted earnings in period t and y_t is actual earnings in period t. For successive values of α from 0 to 1 (increments of .05), predictions of $\hat{y}_t$ over the 1948–1966 period were computed. The mean absolute error (MABE)

$$|y_t - \hat{y}_t|$$

of each forecast for each year and for each firm were then computed for the successive increments of α. The optimum α values (defined on ranks of MABE) for all forecasts and all firms were

Net income	$\alpha = .95$
EPS	$\alpha = .95$
Net income/total assets	$\alpha = .85$

For a random-walk model, the theoretical value of α is 1. Thus, the results of this test are also consistent with the net income and EPS series described by a model closely resembling a random walk. As with other results in the Ball and Watts paper, this inference is based on mean/median results for the sample of firms.

The results of the three tests used by Ball and Watts [1972] were thus all consistent with the net income and EPS series of firms being well described by a random-walk model. Similar results have been reported for the earnings and EPS series by many authors, e.g., Little and Rayner [1966] on U.K. companies and Brealey [1969] on U.S. companies.

Unresolved Issues

The Ball and Watts [1972] study raised some important unresolved issues. One issue concerns the time-series behavior of the deflated earnings series. Ball and Watts provided some evidence on the net income to total assets ratio series for the partial-adjustment model—the optimal α of .85 was less consistent with a random-walk model than was the optimal α of .95 for the net income series. Other authors have also provided evidence inconsistent with the random-walk model for the return on equity or return on total assets ratio series.[12] At present, suffice it to note that further evidence on this issue is necessary. Note also that there is no reason the undeflated and the deflated series should follow the same time-series process. For instance, one would expect an upward drift in the undeflated series for firms reinvesting earnings within the firm. Similarly, inflation may induce upward drift in the undeflated series. By using (say) total assets as the deflator, the effect that reinvestment and inflation have on the undeflated series may not occur for the deflated series.

A second unresolved issue is estimation of the upward drift factor that may be important in models of the undeflated earnings series. Recall that the random-walk model is:

$$z_t = z_{t-1} + u_t \tag{4.15}$$

where the u_t sequence is independently and identically distributed (iid) with $E(u_t|u_{t-1}\ldots)=0$. The drift factor can be incorporated into (4.15) as:

$$z_t = z_{t-1} + \delta + v_t \tag{4.16}$$

where δ is the drift term and $E(v_t|v_{t-1}\ldots)=0$. Ball *et al.*, (1976) presented evidence that the longer the period used to compute δ, the lower the mean absolute forecast error. These forecast errors, however, were computed over the 1958–1967 period...a period of relatively low inflation. One would need to be careful in extrapolating this result to periods of higher inflation. (The model in (4.15) is sometimes referred to as a martingale— for the martingale model, however, there is no restriction that the u_t series be iid. The model in (4.16) is sometimes referred to a sub-martingale; again, for this model there is no restriction that the v_t series be iid.)

A third unresolved issue is whether there are industry similarities in the time-series behavior of firms' earnings. *If* factors such as concentration and barriers to entry influence the time-series behavior of earnings, then some differences across industries in the time-series behavior are to be expected.[13] This is but one of several areas where a closer interplay between the accounting and the industrial organization literature may yield important insights into the time-series behavior of accounting variables.

B Annual Earnings—Inferences Based on Analysis of Firm-Specific Models

Much of financial statement analysis is concerned with evaluating individual firms. A natural issue in this analysis is the construction of firm-specific models for a firm's earnings series. Is there evidence that the random-walk results Ball and Watts [1972] report for a large sample of firms apply also to individual firms? Watts [1970] provides preliminary evidence on this question. Watts used the Box-Jenkins methodology to identify and estimate the time-series behavior of the "earnings available to common" series of 32 firms over the 1927–1964 period. The 32 firms were in 3 industries—railroads, petroleum, and metals. Several examples of identifying and estimating Box-Jenkins models for annual and quarterly accounting data are contained in Appendix 4.A. Briefly, there is a four-step approach to modeling the time series of each firm. The first step is analyzing and plotting the data. The second step is model identification. This involves, among other things, a comparison of the sample autocorrelations with theoretical patterns of particular autoregressive-moving average models. The third step is model estimation. The parameters of the model are usually estimated via a nonlinear estimation procedure. The final step is diagnostic checking. For instance, the residuals from the identified model are examined to see if they are serially uncorrelated.

Watts found diversity across firms in the time-series models identified on the 1927–1964 data. There was also evidence of some industry similarities in the identified models. Watts summarized the results of the identification and estimation stage as follows:

> There does appear to be an industry effect for the generating process, at least for railroads and petroleums. Of the 10 railroads only one does not have a first order autoregressive generating process. Of the 11 petroleum firms only three do not have generating processes that are first order moving averages in the first differences.... The metals do not seem to tend to have similar generating processes.... However, one point must be remembered. In fitting these models to the particular time period, a large number of degrees of freedom have been consumed. Therefore, it is necessary to compare the forecasts of the models outside the interval over which they were fitted. (pp. 113, 118)

The one-year-ahead forecasts of the Box-Jenkins model for each firm over the 1965–1968 period were compared to those of (1) a random-walk model and (2) a random-walk and drift (i.e., martingale) model. Table 4.7 contains summary results of these comparisons. Although the Box-Jenkins models had more first places than either of the other two models, there was little evidence from the sum of ranks comparisons of important differences among the models. Results from sum of squared forecasts error tests also were consistent with the sum of ranks comparisons in Table 4.7. Watts

TABLE 4.7   Box-Jenkins Models Fitted over 1927–1964 Vis-à-vis Naive
Models for Predicting 1965–1968

	Box-Jenkins Models		Random Walk		Random Walk + Drift	
	Sum of Ranks[a]	1st[b]	Sum of Ranks	1st	Sum of Ranks	1st
Railroads	18	6	18	2	24	2
Petroleum	20	4	26	0	14	6
Metals	21	6	20	3	25	2
Total	59	16	64	5	63	10

[a] Each prediction model was placed 1, 2, or 3 for each firm depending on which had the minimum sum of squared errors over the years 1965–1968. Then the ranks were summed across firms.

[b] The number of 1st's is the number of firms for which the particular prediction model ranked 1st under the minimum sum of squares as described above.

SOURCE: Watts [1970, Table A.4].

concluded that although the firm-specific models did "perform better on the basis of the criteria [used],... the difference between them and the naive (i.e., random walk and martingale) models is small" (p. 121). One important implication of the Watts forecasting results is that part of the diversity in the identified Box-Jenkins models of different firms is explained by sample variation in the model-fit period. It is important not to place undue weight on all patterns in a firm's sample autocorrelation function.

Note that the Watts [1970] sample is far from a random one. It would be premature to conclude that differences in time-series models across all firms are "small." There is not sufficient evidence to justify the strong conclusion that there are no systematic patterns in the annual earnings series of individual firms that can be exploited for forecasting.[14]

C   Interim Earnings—Inferences Based on Mean or Median Results

Quarterly accounting data provide a much larger data base for identifying time-series models than do annual accounting data. It is partly this enlarged data base that has led to intensive analysis of the time-series properties of quarterly data. An enlarged data base, other things being equal, means more observations are available to use in identifying and estimating the parameters of specific models. Other things, however, are not equal. At a minimum, issues of seasonality occur in using quarterly data.

Evidence on the time-series behavior of quarterly earnings is taken from Foster [1977]. The sample comprised 69 NYSE firms with quarterly earnings and quarterly sales data available over the 1946–1974 period. For each firm, the autocorrelations for several combinations of first differencing (d) and seasonal differencing (D) were computed:

1. $d=1, D=0$
2. $d=0, D=1$.

Seasonal differencing involves four periods (quarters) per seasonal cycle. The estimated standard error for r_j up to a lag of 8 is approximately .09 for each combination of differencing. If a random-walk model adequately describes quarterly earnings, the sample autocorrelations for the $d=1$, $D=0$ (i.e., first differences in quarterly earnings) combination would all be insignificantly different from zero. The average autocorrelations for the 69 firms for the $d=1$, $D=0$ combination were

$\bar{r}_1$	$\bar{r}_2$	$\bar{r}_3$	$\bar{r}_4$	$\bar{r}_5$	$\bar{r}_6$	$\bar{r}_7$	$\bar{r}_8$
−.296	−.125	−.153	.408	−.162	−.076	−.139	.344

These results provide strong evidence of seasonality in quarterly earnings changes—$\bar{r}_4=.408$ and $\bar{r}_8=.344$. A random-walk model does not adequately describe the time-series behavior of quarterly earnings. The average autocorrelations for the $d=0$, $D=1$ combination were

$\bar{r}_1$	$\bar{r}_2$	$\bar{r}_3$	$\bar{r}_4$	$\bar{r}_5$	$\bar{r}_6$	$\bar{r}_7$	$\bar{r}_8$
.445	.244	.128	−.121	.001	.019	−.017	−.034

Taking seasonal differences in quarterly earnings appears to be an effective way of capturing the seasonality in the series—$\bar{r}_4$ and $\bar{r}_8$ for the $d=0$, $D=1$ combination are both within two standard errors of zero. Note, however, that $\bar{r}_1=.445$ and $\bar{r}_2=.244$ for this combination. This implies that quarterly earnings in time t are not only related to quarterly earnings in time $t-4$ but also to the quarterly earnings reported between time $t-1$ and $t-5$.

In summary, the mean sample results in Foster [1977] suggest that quarterly earnings has (1) an adjacent quarter-to-quarter component and (2) a seasonal component.[15] A major concern to analysts, credit officers, etc., is whether models incorporating these two components can be efficiently estimated at the *individual firm level*. This issue is examined in the next section.

D   Interim Earnings—Inferences Based on
Analysis of Firm-Specific Models

Detailed analysis of this issue is provided in the Foster [1977] paper discussed above. Box-Jenkins models (termed model 6) were identified for each of the 69 firms in the sample using the 1946–1961 quarterly data. Then, the forecasts of these models over the 1962–1974 period were contrasted with the forecasts of the following five models:

$$\text{Model 1:} \quad E(Q_t) = Q_{t-4}$$
$$\text{Model 2:} \quad E(Q_t) = Q_{t-4} + \delta_1$$
$$\text{Model 3:} \quad E(Q_t) = Q_{t-1}$$
$$\text{Model 4:} \quad E(Q_t) = Q_{t-1} + \delta_2$$
$$\text{Model 5:} \quad E(Q_t) = Q_{t-4} + \phi_1(Q_{t-1} - Q_{t-5}) + \delta_3.$$

Models 1 and 2 are a random walk and submartingale in the seasonal series. Models 3 and 4 are a random walk and submartingale in the regular series. The δ_1 and δ_2 drift terms were calculated on corresponding seasonal quarters (δ_1) and on all corresponding quarters (δ_2), respectively. For model 5 a preliminary estimate of ϕ_1 is the first-order serial correlation coefficient of the differenced series; δ_3 is estimated as $u(1-\phi_1)$, where u is the mean of the seasonally differenced quarterly series. Model 6 (the Box-Jenkins model) is based on analysis of each firm's autocorrelation function—examples of the type of analysis used to derive each firm's model are given in Appendix 4.A.

Model 5 was chosen for several reasons: (1) It was reasonably consistent with the 1946–1961 mean autocorrelations across the sample; (2) Box-Jenkins firm-specific models generally involve estimation of more parameters than model 5, and thus model 5 may be an attractive alternative due to more efficient estimation of its parameters; and (3) the identification of Box-Jenkins firm-specific models in finite samples runs the danger of *search bias*—much of the observed variation across firms' autocorrelation functions could be due to sampling variation. Note that with model 5 both ϕ_1 and δ_3 were estimated separately for each firm over the 1946–1961 period; that is, diversity across firms as regards ϕ_1 and δ_3 is admitted in model 5.

Table 4.8 contains the MABE (%) and MSE (%) for each of the six models over all four quarters combined and separately for each of the four fiscal year quarters. Note that model 5 performs best on both error measures; e.g., the average MABE = .258 and MSE = .152 compared to MABE = .283 and MSE = .167 for the seasonal random walk + drift model (model 2). This result indicates that it is possible to efficiently estimate, at the individual firm level, the systematic patterns in the quarterly earnings

TABLE 4.8 Summary Statistics for One-Step-Ahead Forecasting for Quarterly Earnings
Series: 1962–1974

Models	All Four Quarters		First Quarter		Second Quarter		Third Quarter		Fourth Quarter	
	MABE (%)	MSE (%)	MABE (%)	MSE (%)	MABE (%)	MSE (%)	MABE (%)	MSE (%)	MABE (%)	MSE (%)
Model 1	.287	.166	.304	.185	.256	.129	.296	.180	.292	.169
Model 2	.283	.167	.300	.185	.251	.130	.290	.180	.290	.173
Model 3	.346	.226	.396	.285	.335	.206	.308	.197	.343	.215
Model 4	.346	.227	.398	.287	.332	.204	.311	.200	.343	.217
Model 5	.258	.152	.287	.181	.218	.109	.264	.163	.262	.153
Model 6	.288	.171	.323	.215	.244	.121	.293	.177	.292	.169

SOURCE: Foster [1977, Table 3].

time series that were apparent in the mean/median results discussed in
Section 4.5C. Moreover, this result also suggests that recognizing differences across firms leads to more efficient forecasts of quarterly earnings.
The main issue, unresolved by the Foster [1977] paper, is how detailed the
recognition of these interfirm differences should be.

Care should be taken in generalizing the results noted in Table 4.8.
Recall that all models were fitted on the 1946–1961 period and then used
to predict over the 1962–1974 period. It is possible that model 5 is more
robust to structural change over the post-model-fit period than is model 6.
Indeed, subperiod results presented in Foster [1977] suggest that the
forecasting performance of model 6 is slightly better than that of model 5
in the 1962 period (e.g., MSE of model 5 = .169, MSE of model 6 = .156)
but declines vis-à-vis model 5 the farther one moves away from the
model-fit period. An interesting extension of Foster [1977] would be to
compare model 5 vis-à-vis model 6 when the parameters of both are
reestimated each quarter. One could also examine the effect of reidentify-
ing as well as reestimating a Box-Jenkins model each quarter.

4.6 TIME-SERIES PROPERTIES OF FINANCIAL RATIOS

At present there is very little published evidence on the time-series
behavior of financial ratios. The following analysis was conducted to gain
some preliminary descriptive evidence on this issue. A second motivation
for the analysis was to update the previous studies on the time-series
behavior of accounting earnings.

Autocorrelations for 12 financial ratios were computed for all firms with available data on the *Compustat* tape for the 1957–1975 period. These 12 ratios were

Liquidity

1. Current ratio (CR)
2. Quick ratio (QR)
3. Defensive interval (DI)

Leverage

4. Debt to equity (DE)
5. Long-term debt to equity (LTDE)
6. Times interest earned (TIE)

Profitability

7. Earnings to sales (ES)
8. Return on assets (ROA)
9. Return on equity (ROE)

Turnover

10. Total assets turnover (TAT)
11. Inventory turnover (IT)
12. Accounts receivable turnover (ART)

Autocorrelations were also computed for two additional profitability series:

13. Net income (NI)
14. Earnings per share (EPS)

Autocorrelations were computed for both the levels of each series $\{z_t, z_{t-1}, \ldots\}$ and the first differences of each series $\{z_t - z_{t-1}, z_{t-1} - z_{t-2}, \ldots\}$.

Average autocorrelations for all firms in the sample are presented in Table 4.9. The number of firms used to compute the average autocorrelations for each ratio is also included in Table 4.9. The autocorrelations for the first differenced series suggest that a random-walk model could, *on average*, have considerable descriptive validity. There are 18 observations used to compute the r_j's for the first differenced series—this implies $SE(r_1) = .236$. Thus, the average r_1 for the first differenced series of each of the 14 variables in Table 4.9 is within one standard error of r_1 being zero. Note that for the first differenced net income series $\bar{r}_1 = .013$, $\bar{r}_2 = -.075$, and $\bar{r}_3 = -.043$. These results are consistent with those that Ball and Watts [1972] reported for a smaller (overlapping) sample over the 1947–1966 period.[16]

TABLE 4.9   Average Autocorrelations of Accounting Variables

		Levels				First Differences				No. of
		$\bar{r}_1$	$\bar{r}_2$	$\bar{r}_3$	$\bar{r}_4$	$\bar{r}_1$	$\bar{r}_2$	$\bar{r}_3$	$\bar{r}_4$	Firms
1.	CR	.495	.282	.168	.084	−.214	−.102	−.048	.005	647
2.	QR	.500	.267	.160	.086	−.193	−.130	−.043	.002	640
3.	DI	.474	.246	.127	.043	−.182	−.101	−.054	−.018	600
4.	DE	.658	.436	.272	.141	−.062	−.067	−.044	−.038	646
5.	LTDE	.528	.308	.190	.106	−.196	−.102	−.039	.011	646
6.	TIE	.608	.363	.202	.081	−.006	−.114	−.062	−.078	542
7.	ES	.537	.261	.114	.004	−.053	−.104	−.062	−.052	776
8.	ROA	.517	.239	.084	−.033	−.070	−.122	−.065	−.072	660
9.	ROE	.496	.195	.051	−.048	−.058	−.139	−.066	−.060	733
10.	TAT	.599	.327	.163	.023	−.006	−.097	−.052	−.089	742
11.	IT	.607	.312	.173	.065	.008	−.181	−.051	−.044	619
12.	ART	.645	.420	.254	.109	.006	−.116	−.020	−.075	617
13.	NI	.631	.402	.262	.169	.013	−.075	−.043	−.026	786
14.	EPS	.452	.156	.002	−.083	−.144	−.104	−.069	−.062	623

4.7   FORECASTING ACCOUNTING NUMBERS: EXTENSIONS

The exposition in earlier sections of this chapter concentrated on time-series analysis of a single financial series. A variety of extensions of this analysis has been made. Two such extensions are considered below.

A   Forecasting Aggregate Series from Disaggregate Series

An important forecasting issue is the level of aggregation to adopt in time-series modeling. Consider forecasting the sales of a multidivisional firm. One alternative is to build separate time-series models of each division, make forecasts from these models, and then aggregate the forecasts to obtain a forecast of the firm's sales. Another alternative is to aggregate the divisional sales, build a time-series model for the aggregate series, and then forecast with this model. Which approach should be adopted?

Initial attempts to address this issue in accounting have been of an empirical kind. For example, Kinney [1971] examined whether the "disaggregation of consolidated earnings of 24 companies will permit better prediction of next year's earnings" (p. 127). These companies voluntarily disclosed *subentity earnings data* in 1967. Predictions of the 1968 and 1969 earnings of models using subentity data and models using consolidated data were compared. Kinney reported that "the additional information contained in the segment sales and earnings data...did allow a statistically significant reduction in uncertainty in predicting the earnings of the test companies" (p. 133). Collins [1976], using a similar methodology on a larger sample of firms, reported similar results for the 1969–1971 period.

These empirical studies suffer from the fact that they do not provide any generalizable results on the aggregation question. Analytical models are also needed to show the conditions under which disaggregation may improve or impair forecasting ability. With such models, one could then examine the properties of the data available and ex ante predict the consequences of aggregation on predictive ability. Work in the economometrics literature on similar aggregation issues needs to be incorporated into the analysis when deciding such issues in accounting contexts.[17]

B Forecasting with Econometric Models

In Section 4.2 we noted that one approach to forecasting accounting variables is causal modeling as exemplified by an econometric model. Very little work at the individual firm level has been done in this area. The Elliot and Uphoff [1972] paper is representative of the existing state of the art. This paper illustrated the use of econometric models in forecasting the "monthly management income statement of a large consumer nondurables producer" (p. 260). They describe the specific econometric model as follows:

> The model of the [income] statement is structured with an equation to explain each line [e.g., net sales, cost of goods sold, marketing expense, etc.]. In this approach, the value of each line item is explained partially by the value of other line items and partially by forces external to the model. The resulting model includes seven *relational equations* and four *definitional equations*. Endogenous variables in the model include each line item in the income statement. The exogenous variables include an industrial production index, a materials price index, a package cost index, total industry unit sales, a population series and dummy variables representing the effects of strikes and labor cost increments. In addition, lagged endogenous variables are present at various points in the model. (p. 261)

As an example of one of the *relational equations*, consider the cost of goods sold variable. This variable was estimated as a function of net sales dollars plus the following three exogenous variables: materials price index, package price index, and a labor cost dummy variable. The net sales dollars estimate was derived from an equation which included such independent variables as market share, population, and advertising. A typical *definitional equation* is the familiar accounting identity

$$\text{Net sales} - \text{Cost of goods sold} = \text{Gross margin.}$$

The econometric model was estimated over the January 1969 to March 1971 period. Forecasts from this model were compared to forecasts from time-series models for such variables as net sales, cost of goods sold, and operating margin, On balance, the forecasts from the econometric model had a lower average percentage error. Elliot and Uphoff [1972] concluded that "every indication of our study is that the use of econometric models may be expected to improve the accuracy of short-term forecasts" (p. 273).[18]

One motivation in using an econometric model for forecasting a firm's earnings, sales, etc., is to exploit more information than is in the past sequence of the variable being forecast. In Chapter 5, additional forecasting models (i.e., index models) that have a similar motivation are examined.

4.8 SUMMARY

The basic philosophy in this chapter is that (1) the prediction of an accounting variable is enhanced by a model of how the variable behaves over time, and (2) the results of analysis of the past series provide important information in the development of a time-series model. In analyzing the past data, one attempts to exploit any systematic patterns in the observed series. In Sections 4.5 and 4.6 we provided evidence on systematic patterns in the time-series behavior of annual and quarterly accounting data.

In Section 4.7 we outlined some alternative approaches to forecasting financial series. It is important to note that the alternative forecasting approaches outlined in this chapter are not mutually exclusive. Indeed, it is possible that an approach combining the forecasts of say a time-series model and the forecasts of an econometric model will yield more accurate predictions than will exclusive reliance on either time-series models or econometric models.[19] Work on combining diverse information sets when forecasting represents one of the more important areas on which analysis is warranted.

APPENDIX 4.A   BOX-JENKINS TIME-SERIES MODELING
OF ACCOUNTING DATA

The Box-Jenkins methodology is being applied to accounting data with increasing frequency. This appendix provides several examples to illustrate the steps in using this methodology. In Section 4.A.1 of this appendix we shall examine the *annual* net income to sales (I to S) ratio series of *Inland St el Company*. Brief analysis is also made of the sales and net income series of *Inland Steel*. In Section 4.A.2 we shall examine the *quarterly* net income to sales (*I* to *S*) ratio series of *Marshall Field and Company*. A step-by-step approach to the Box-Jenkins methodology is outlined primarily to structure the exposition. In many applications, the process is more heuristic than is presented below.

4.A.1 Inland Steel Company

Net Income to Sales Ratio Series

Table 4.10 details this series for the 1928–1975 period. The 1928–1973 period was used for model identification and estimation.

TABLE 4.10 Financial Series of Inland Steel Company

Year	Net Income ($000's)	Sales ($000's)	Net Income/ Sales
1928	9,334	64,310	.145
1929	11,712	68,585	.171
1930	6,498	51,756	.126
1931	1,263	31,606	.040
1932	− 3,320	15,173	− .219
1933	166	27,554	.006
1934	3,729	40,404	.092
1935	9,417	62,544	.151
1936	12,800	98,903	.129
1937	12,665	110,744	.114
1938	4,916	74,058	.066
1939	10,931	115,346	.095
1940	14,450	142,173	.102
1941	14,824	202,755	.073
1942	10,721	189,612	.057
1943	10,801	203,680	.053
1944	10,249	221,161	.046
1945	9,861	217,386	.045
1946	15,556	217,739	.071
1947	29,888	315,031	.094
1948	38,606	392,708	.098
1949	25,013	345,861	.072
1950	38,015	403,378	.094
1951	34,398	518,684	.066
1952	23,775	458,043	.052
1953	33,867	575,590	.059
1954	41,287	533,113	.077
1955	52,466	659,706	.080
1956	52,998	727,151	.073
1957	58,876	763,950	.077

TABLE 4.10 Continued

Year	Net Income ($000's)	Sales ($000's)	Net Income/ Sales
1958	47,869	655,966	.073
1959	45,065	705,087	.064
1960	47,050	747,096	.063
1961	54,674	724,596	.075
1962	52,487	760,142	.069
1963	56,139	808,090	.069
1964	71,074	873,715	.081
1965	68,377	967,562	.071
1966	64,498	1,054,490	.061
1967	52,786	991,926	.053
1968	75,820	1,073,720	.071
1969	58,662	1,216,430	.048
1970	52,300	1,195,090	.044
1971	47,779	1,253,610	.038
1972	65,913	1,469,800	.045
1973	83,129	1,828,950	.045
1974	148,009	2,450,289	.060
1975	83,350	2,107,418	.040

Step One: *Plot the data.* This step serves several important functions. First, one can check for possible errors/outliers in the data, e.g., due to a transposed decimal point. Second, one can check for evidence of structural change in the series being examined, e.g., due to a merger or a change in lines of business. Third, one can check for evidence of possible nonstationarity in the series. Nonstationarity occurs when a series exhibits no affinity for a mean value. The sales series of most firms and many macroeconomic series exhibit nonstationarity due to having an upward drift over time. When estimating a Box-Jenkins model, it is first necessary to derive a stationary series. If nonstationarity is evidenced in the raw series, a technique such as taking the first differences of the raw series or the natural logarithms of the raw series is employed to obtain a stationary series. Note that one rarely expects that stationarity will be a perfect description of the series to be used in Box-Jenkins analysis. Rather, one seeks to obtain a series for which stationarity appears to be a useful working assumption. Moreover, note that for some accounting series (e.g., many profitability series) a technique such as taking logarithms of the raw series is not always feasible due to the possibility of negative values in the raw series.

Figure 4.1 contains a plot of the I/S ratio for the 1928–1973 period. This series appears to be a reasonably stationary one. Note, however, that the variance of the series in recent years is lower than in the early period

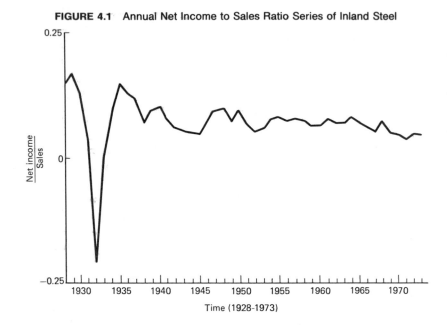

FIGURE 4.1 Annual Net Income to Sales Ratio Series of Inland Steel

covered by the data. The first ten years (1928–1937) include a major depression period. The high variance in this period suggested estimating the model on (say) the 1938–1973 period rather than the full 1928–1973 period. The effect of using the full 1928–1973 period will be examined subsequently.

Step Two: *Preliminary model identification.* This step involves identifying possible Box-Jenkins models consistent with the data being analyzed. This entails, among other things, a comparison of the sample autocorrelations with theoretical autocorrelation patterns of particular autoregressive-moving average models. The *sample* autocorrelations for the 1938–1973 period are

	Lag								Standard Error
	1	*2*	*3*	*4*	*5*	*6*	*7*	*8*	
r_j	.59	.19	−.05	−.19	−.34	−.11	.22	.24	.17

Two possible models were entertained for this series:

(1) An autoregressive model of order 1—AR(1):

$$z_t = \phi_1 z_{t-1} + \delta + u_t.$$

(2) A moving-average model of order 1—MA(1):

$$z_t = u_t - \theta_1 u_{t-1} + \delta.$$

In both the above models a constant (δ) was identified as being of potential importance.

The theoretical autocorrelation functions implied by these two models, assuming the sample r_1 estimate is the population value, are

				Lag				
	1	*2*	*3*	*4*	*5*	*6*	*7*	*8*
AR(1) r_j	.59	.35	.21	.12	.07	.04	.02	.01
MA(1) r_j	.59	.00	.00	.00	.00	.00	.00	.00

As noted in Section 4.4B, one does not expect an exact correspondence between the sample autocorrelation function and any theoretical autocorrelation function. Moreover, with 36 observations the sampling variation in the estimated autocorrelation function is quite high. Indeed, the problem of identifying theoretical models in samples of the size encountered in many economic contexts makes this step in the Box-Jenkins approach a relatively heuristic one.

Step Three: *Model estimation.* For the preliminary models identified in Step Two, estimates of their parameters are next obtained. This estimation was done via a nonlinear estimation procedure available at the University of Chicago. The estimates for the AR(1) model were

$$z_t = .549 z_{t-1} + .033 + u_t.$$
$$\quad\quad t=4.312 \quad\quad t=3.293$$

The estimates for the MA(1) model were

$$z_t = \underset{t=18.82}{.067} + .570 u_{t-1} + u_t.$$
$$\quad\quad\quad t=3.925$$

Step Four: *Diagnostic checking.* Several checks need to be made on the adequacy of the model estimated in Step Three. One check is the significance of the coefficients of the estimated model. For the AR(1) model, the coefficients on both the autoregressive term and the constant term are significant at conventional levels. Similarly, both coefficients in the MA(1) model are significant at conventional levels.

Another check on the estimated models is whether their residuals are *random noise*. The aim of the model identification is to obtain a model with the u_t series being serially uncorrelated. If this series is not serially uncorrelated, there is additional information in the past sequence of the series that can be exploited in forecasting. The autocorrelations of the residuals for the two models examined are

					Lags				Standard
	1	*2*	*3*	*4*	*5*	*6*	*7*	*8*	Error
AR(1)	.12	−.21	−.12	−.04	.09	−.13	−.04	−.01	.17
MA(1)	.19	.23	−.11	−.01	−.33	−.08	.23	.16	.17

Note that the AR(1) model appears to be a better specified model as regards nonserial correlation of the residuals. A statistic that examines autocorrelation in the residuals is the Box-Pierce Q statistic. This statistic indicated a high probability of the residuals from the AR(1) model being serially uncorrelated; there was a lower probability that the residuals from the MA(1) model were serially uncorrelated. Given this evidence, AR(1) was chosen as the appropriate model.

In this diagnostic checking step, it may be found that none of the models tentatively identified in Step Two satisfy the above diagnostic tests. In this case, one tentatively identifies other possible time-series models and then repeats the model estimation and diagnostic checking steps in the Box-Jenkins methodology.

Step Five: *Forecasting.* The 1974 and 1975 observations were withheld from the model estimation sample to illustrate the use of Box-Jenkins models for forecasting. The AR(1) model for one-step-ahead forecasts becomes

$$E(Z_t|Z_{t-1}...) = .549\, z_{t-1} + .033.$$

Thus, the forecast of the 1974 I/S ratio, given the 1973 I/S ratio of .045, is

$$E(I/S_{1974}) = .549 \times .045 + .033 = .058.$$

Similarly, the forecast of the 1975 I/S ratio, given the 1974 I/S ratio of .060, is

$$E(I/S_{1975}) = .549 \times .060 + .033 = .066.$$

General Note

The above process was repeated using the full 1928–1973 data deck of the I/S series. The sample autocorrelations were

					Lag				Standard
	1	2	3	4	5	6	7	8	Error
r_j	.40	−.13	−.46	−.36	−.10	.08	.04	−.03	.15

Note how different these sample autocorrelations are from those for the 1938–1973 period; i.e., including the first ten observations has a marked effect on the sample autocorrelations. The most reasonable model for the 1928–1973 data appeared to be the following AR(2) model:

$$z_t = .553z_{t-1} - .367z_{t-2} + .056 + u_t.$$

This model yielded residuals that were reasonably nonautocorrelated. However, in several respects (e.g., standard deviation of regression residuals) the AR(1) model estimated on the 1938–1973 period appeared to be a better fit. This AR(2) model also had a poorer one-step-ahead prediction performance over the 1974–1975 period than the AR(1) model.

The deletion of the 1928–1937 observations was, of course, an arbitrary choice. Statistical tests, however, are available to test for the stability of the variance of the residuals over the sample estimation period. One such test was applied to the *Inland Steel* data and supported the above decision to delete the 1928–1937 observations.

Annual Sales Series and Annual Net Income Series

The above steps were repeated for the annual sales and the annual net income series of *Inland Steel*. The two series appeared to be non-stationary—both exhibited a marked upward drift over time. One feature of a nonstationary series is that the autocorrelation function at successive lags does not die out quickly. This is apparent for both the sales and net income series over the 1928–1973 period. The autocorrelations for the raw series are

		Lags: Raw Series								*Standard Error*
		1	*2*	*3*	*4*	*5*	*6*	*7*	*8*	
Sales	r_j	.87	.79	.73	.68	.60	.55	.50	.43	.15
Net income	r_j	.87	.79	.76	.73	.67	.60	.59	.53	.15

These patterns indicate that a procedure such as first-differencing the raw series is necessary to achieve a stationary series. The first differenced sales and the first differenced net income series both appeared reasonably stationary. The autocorrelation patterns for these series are

		Lags: First Differenced Series								*Standard Error*
		1	*2*	*3*	*4*	*5*	*6*	*7*	*8*	
Sales	r_j	.14	−.03	.06	.22	−.04	−.02	.06	.06	.15
Net income	r_j	−.11	−.13	−.20	.08	−.14	−.17	.18	.05	.15

Using a rule of thumb that an autocorrelation coefficient less than two standard errors away from zero is insignificant, a random-walk model would be the preliminary model identified for both the net income and sales series. Subsequent analysis with other possible models confirmed this preliminary identification of a random-walk model.

The above analysis was repeated using the 1938–1973 data of *Inland Steel*. For both the sales and earnings series, a random-walk model also appeared to be a descriptively valid model.

4.A.2 Marshall Field and Company

The data in the *Inland Steel* examples comprised annual observations. The data to be examined for *Marshall Field* comprise quarterly observations. When examining quarterly (or monthly) data, the issue of seasonality is often encountered.

Net Income to Sales Ratio Series

Step One: *Plot the Data.*   Table 4.11 contains the 1960–1975 quarterly I/S ratios of *Marshall Field*. The 1960–1973 period was used for model estimation, with the 1974–1975 period used to illustrate forecasting with seasonal Box-Jenkins models. Figure 4.2 contains a plot of the 1960–1973 I/S ratios. The strong seasonal pattern in the data is readily apparent. This pattern is also evident in the autocorrelations of the raw series:

Lags: Raw Series

	1	2	3	4	5	6	7	8	Standard Error
r_j	−.04	−.53	−.11	.88	−.05	−.50	−.12	.76	.13
	9	10	11	12	13	14	15	16	
r_j	−.07	−.48	−.12	.66	−.08	−.45	−.13	.56	.13

Note that there is evidence of nonstationarity at seasonal lags; i.e., $r_4 = .88$, $r_8 = .76$, $r_{12} = .66$, and $r_{16} = .56$.

A common technique used to take seasonality into account is to seasonally difference the series, i.e., derive a new series $z_{t-1} - z_{t-5}$, $z_{t-2} - z_{t-6}$, etc. The autocorrelations for this new series are

Lags: Seasonally Differenced Series

	1	2	3	4	5	6	7	8	Standard Error
r_j	.52	.26	.05	−.07	.03	.10	.05	−.09	.14
	9	10	11	12	13	14	15	16	
r_j	−.14	−.27	−.20	−.05	.13	.10	.03	−.11	.14

On balance, stationarity appears a good working assumption for this series.

TABLE 4.11 Quarterly Net Income to Sales Ratio of
Marshall Field and Company: 1960–1975

	First Quarter	Second Quarter	Third Quarter	Fourth Quarter
1960	.019	.020	.037	.062
1961	.020	.023	.040	.060
1962	.023	.022	.037	.059
1963	.018	.019	.038	.058
1964	.025	.029	.051	.062
1965	.029	.034	.054	.065
1966	.035	.035	.049	.065
1967	.029	.038	.050	.065
1968	.026	.032	.046	.061
1969	.030	.035	.044	.056
1970	.019	.029	.042	.057
1971	.021	.028	.038	.064
1972	.021	.028	.041	.070
1973	.024	.028	.036	.062
1974	.023	.029	.036	.053
1975	.006	.026	.036	.054

FIGURE 4.2 Quarterly Net Income to Sales Ratio Series of Marshall Field

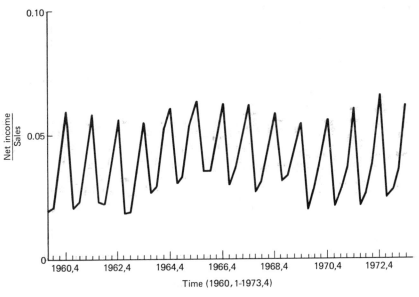

Step Two: *Preliminary Model Identification.* The pattern of autocorrelations above suggests an autoregressive model of order 1 in the seasonally differenced series:

$$X_t = \phi_1 X_{t-1} + \delta + u_t,$$

where $X_t = Z_t - Z_{t-4}$.

The theoretical autocorrelation function of this model, assuming the r_1 of .52 is the population value, is

				Lags				
	1	*2*	*3*	*4*	*5*	*6*	*7*	*8*
r_j	.52	.27	.14	.07	.04	.02	.01	.01
	9	*10*	*11*	*12*	*13*	*14*	*15*	*16*
r_j	.00	.00	.00	.00	.00	.00	.00	.00

The correspondence between the theoretical autocorrelation function and the sample function is quite high given the sample size of 52 observations.

Step Three: *Model Estimation.* Using a nonlinear estimation technique, the following model resulted:

$$X_t = .555 X_{t-1} + u_t$$
$$t = 4.572$$

The above model was estimated with the constant (δ) term suppressed to zero. When the model was estimated with the constant included, the sample estimate of δ was insignificantly different from zero.

Step Four: *Diagnostic Checking.* The above model appeared to be a reasonable one. The coefficient on the X_{t-1} term is significant. Moreover, the Box-Pierce statistic indicated a high probability that the estimated residuals are serially uncorrelated. The autocorrelation function for the residuals is

				Lags				
	1	*2*	*3*	*4*	*5*	*6*	*7*	*8*
r_j	−.00	.07	−.05	−.18	.01	.10	.08	−.07
	9	*10*	*11*	*12*	*13*	*14*	*15*	*16*
r_j	−.02	−.20	−.12	−.03	.14	.10	.04	.03

With this evidence, it appears that the AR(1) model in the seasonally differenced series is a descriptively valid one.

Step Five: *Forecasting.* The estimated model is

$$X_t = .555X_{t-1} + u_t,$$

where

$$X_t = z_t - z_{t-4}$$

An alternative form of the estimated model is

$$z_t - z_{t-4} = .555(z_{t-1} - z_{t-5}) + u_t.$$

For forecasting z_t, this model becomes

$$E(Z_t|Z_{t-1}\ldots) = z_{t-4} + .555(z_{t-1} - z_{t-5}).$$

Thus, the one-step-ahead (quarter) forecast for the 1974 first-quarter I/S ratio is

$$E(z_{1974,1}) = z_{1973,1} + .555(z_{1973,4} - z_{1972,4})$$
$$= .024 + .555 * (.062 - .070) = .019.$$

The one-step-ahead forecasts, actuals, and forecast errors for 1974 and 1975 are

	Forecast	*Actual*	*Forecast Error*
1974, 1	.019	.023	− .004
1974, 2	.027	.029	− .002
1974, 3	.037	.036	.001
1974, 4	.062	.053	+ .009
1975, 1	.018	.006	+ .012
1975, 2	.019	.026	− .007
1975, 3	.035	.036	− .001
1975, 4	.053	.054	− .001

Note how the Box-Jenkins model has incorporated seasonal patterns into its one-step-ahead forecasts.

General Comment

This appendix is intended to provide some intuitive appreciation of the Box-Jenkins methodology. Those who wish to explore the subject further should consult Box-Jenkins [1976] and Nelson [1973].

NOTES

[1]Other reasons for studying the time-series behavior of earnings are discussed in Beaver [1970] and Ball and Watts [1972].

[2]See, for example, Bernstein [1974, Chapter 22].

[3]Another example of the statistical modeling approach is spectral analysis—see Jenkins and Watts [1968].

[4]When computing autocorrelation coefficients, it is important that the series be stationary. Box and Jenkins [1976] state that "a stochastic process is said to be...stationary if its properties are unaffected by a change of time origin: ...for a discrete process to be...stationary, the joint distribution of any set of observations must be unaffected by shifting all the times of observation forward or backward by any integer amount k" (p. 26). Most accounting series such as earnings and sales are nonstationary in their levels. In many cases, however, a simple procedure like first-differencing the series will result in the series being reasonably described as stationary. Nelson [1973, Chapters 2–4] provides a good discussion of stationarity and its importance in time-series analysis.

[5]For further discussion of forecast model evaluation, see Platt [1974] and Brandon and Jarrett [1976].

[6]By a theory we mean something akin to that developed by Samuelson [1965] to predict the time-series behavior of the prices of futures contracts in commodity markets.

[7]This viewpoint is, of course, not a new one. For instance, Brown and Niederhoffer [1968, p. 490] noted that both factors are important when deciding on an appropriate prediction model for quarterly earnings. For an extended discussion of this viewpoint, see Gonedes and Dopuch [1976].

[8]Beaver [1970] is an important preliminary exercise on the effect of accounting alternatives on the time-series properties of the reported series. He examined the effect of depreciation rules on the time-series properties of accounting rates of return. See also Brigham [1968], Fogelberg [1971], and Dopuch and Watts [1972].

[9]See Nelson [1973] for further examination of sampling variation for (4.13) using sample sizes of 100 observations. It is often asserted that 50 observations are required before one can use Box-Jenkins time-series techniques, described in Appendix 4.A. This assertion is based on a misinterpretation of a comment by Box-Jenkins [1976, p. 18]. These authors argue that where there are less than 50 observations, one must place greater weight on "experience and past information" in identifying a preliminary time-series model. In time-series analysis, there are no universal "golden rules" such as use 50 or 100 observations. What is needed is an appreciation of the statistical properties of the tools one uses when deciding issues such as the size of the sample used for model identification and estimation.

[10]The Watts [1970] paper is further described in Section 4.5.

[11]The z statistic is approximately normally distributed when $N_1 + N_2 >$ 20 and N_1 and N_2 are close to equal. The example in the text is used to illustrate the runs test, even though strictly speaking the normal approximation is less appropriate for the case where $N_1 + N_2 = 9$—see Dyckman and Thomas [1977, Chapter 18].

[12]See, for example, Beaver [1970] and Lookabill [1976]. Beaver [1970] hypothesized that *accounting measurement rules* in addition to *economic factors* (e.g., competition) may explain the observed mean reversion of rates of return in his sample. He supported this hypothesis with simulation results examining the effect of depreciation rules on the reported rate of return series.

[13]See Weiss [1971] for evidence of industry differences in concentration and barriers to entry. Lev [1977] provides some evidence on the association between various economic factors and dependence in the time-series behavior of earnings. He concluded that "product type factor (nondurables and services vs. durables) had the most significant and persistent association with positive dependence in the changes of both the earnings and earnings/equity series" (p. 27).

[14]Watts and Leftwich [1977] updated the Watts [1970] study and reported that there was little evidence that the firm-specific models performed significantly better than the random-walk model. In contrast, Brooks and Buckmaster [1976] argued that "a substantial and identifiable portion of income time-series do not appear to follow a submartingale process" (p. 1,370). See also Albrecht et al. [1977]. Suffice it to note that the issue of whether there are systematic patterns in the annual earnings series of individual firms *that can be exploited for forecasting* is very much an unresolved question.

[15]Griffin [1977] reports similar results for a sample of 94 firms over the 1958–1971 period.

[16]The interpretation of the data in Table 4.9 depends on one's priors about stationarity of the levels and first differences of each series. My priors are strong that due to earnings reinvestment, inflation, etc., first differencing is generally necessary to achieve a stationary series for net income and EPS. For the first 12 ratio series in Table 4.9, my priors about the necessity for first differencing are more diffuse. Thus, it is possible that (say) autoregressive models in the levels could, *on average*, describe the time-series behavior of several of the financial ratio series detailed in Table 4.9.

[17]See, for instance, Orcutt et al. [1968] and Zellner [1969].

[18]One problem in interpreting the forecasts made by the econometric model was that perfect foreknowledge of the exogenous variables in the forecast period was assumed. In practice, the predictive ability of an econometric model will be jointly dependent on the structure of the model and the ability to forecast the exogenous variables. Cooper and Nelson

[1975] discuss the different motivations for using the actual and forecasted values of the exogenous variables when examining the forecasts of an econometric model.

[19]See Cooper and Nelson [1975] for an illustration of how combining the forecasts of econometric models and Box-Jenkins time-series models can lead to improved forecasting ability of macroeconomic aggregates.

QUESTIONS

QUESTION 4.1:   Caterpillar Tractor Co.

Caterpillar Tractor is a producer of heavy-type tractors, motor graders, and earth-moving equipment. The following data are reported in the 1975 Annual Report of *Caterpillar Tractor Co.* (dollar amounts are in millions except those stated on a percentage basis):

Year	Sales	Profit	Profit to Sales Ratio
1925	$ 13.8	$ 3.3	23.7
1926	20.7	4.3	20.9
1927	26.9	5.7	21.3
1928	35.1	8.7	24.9
1929	51.8	12.4	24.0
1930	45.4	9.1	20.1
1931	24.1	1.6	6.5
1932	13.3	(1.6)	(12.2)
1933	14.4	.4	2.5
1934	23.8	3.8	16.0
1935	35.4	6.2	17.2
1936	54.1	10.2	18.9
1937	63.2	10.6	16.7
1938	48.2	3.2	6.7
1939	58.4	6.0	10.3
1940	73.1	7.8	10.7
1941	102.0	7.7	7.6
1942	142.2	7.0	4.9
1943	171.4	7.6	4.4
1944	242.2	7.3	3.0
1945	230.6	6.5	2.8
1946	128.4	6.1	4.8
1947	189.1	13.5	7.1

Year	Sales	Profit	Profit to Sales Ratio
1948	218.0	17.5	8.0
1949	254.9	17.2	6.7
1950	337.3	29.2	8.7
1951	394.3	15.8	4.0
1952	480.8	22.7	4.7
1953	437.8	20.6	4.7
1954	406.7	25.9	6.4
1955	533.0	36.0	6.8
1956	685.9	55.5	8.1
1957	649.9	40.0	6.2
1958	585.2	32.2	5.5
1959	742.3	46.5	6.3
1960	716.0	42.6	6.0
1961	734.3	55.8	7.6
1962	827.0	61.9	7.5
1963	966.1	77.3	8.0
1964	1,216.6	129.1	10.6
1965	1,405.3	158.5	11.3
1966	1,524.0	150.1	9.9
1967	1,472.5	106.4	7.2
1968	1,707.1	121.6	7.1
1969	2,001.6	142.5	7.1
1970	2,127.8	143.8	6.8
1971	2,175.2	128.3	5.9
1972	2,602.2	206.4	7.9
1973	3,182.4	246.8	7.8
1974	4,082.1	229.2	5.6
1975	4,963.7	398.7	8.0

REQUIRED

(1) What systematic patterns in the profit series are apparent over the 1925–1975 period. Autocorrelations for the first-differenced profit series are: $r_1 = -.039$; $r_2 = .016$; $r_3 = .282$; $r_4 = -.007$; and $r_5 = -.065$.

(2) Assume you are asked to develop a time-series model to predict the 1976 profit to sales ratio for *Caterpillar*. What factors would you consider in deciding the number of observations used to identify and estimate the time-series model?

(3) In September 1975, several analysts were predicting *Caterpillar's* 1975 profit to be $380–$385 million. Among the factors cited as underlying their predictions were sales of heavy equipment in Alaska and increased "pace of construction contract awards." Why might these predictions be more accurate than a model predicting annual

profit to follow a random walk: i.e., the expected profit for 1975 is the 1974 profit of $229.2 million?

QUESTION 4.2:   Time-Series Properties of Annual Earnings

The evidence examined in Chapter 4 indicated that, *on average*, first differences in the annual earnings of U.S. companies were serially uncorrelated. The following data are for the *net income* earnings series (in $000's) of three companies over the 1967–1975 period:

	McDonald's Corp.	Pizza Hut, Inc.	Sambo's Restaurant
1967	6,250	481	691
1968	8,841	1,238	898
1969	12,641	1,042	1,793
1970	17,691	1,279	2,415
1971	25,798	1,895	3,678
1972	36,225	3,505	5,997
1973	51,992	5,162	8,910
1974	67,396	10,024	12,846
1975	86,881	15,261	17,641

The estimated autocorrelation functions for first differences of these series are

	Autocorrelation Coefficients		
	r_1	r_2	r_3
McDonald's	.621	.337	−.085
Pizza Hut	.580	.117	−.079
Sambo's	.610	.281	−.042

REQUIRED

(1) Reconcile the above autocorrelations with the following mean autocorrelations reported in the Ball and Watts [1972] paper described in Chapter 4:

r_1	r_2	r_3
−.030	−.040	.006

(2) The above companies are often referred to as *growth stocks* by security analysts. One variable that analysts consider before applying this term to a company is its compound annual growth rate in earnings. This growth rate (r) is calculated via the following formula:

$$\frac{x}{y} = (1+r)^n,$$

where $X =$ earnings of nth year,

$\quad\quad y =$ earnings of base year,

$\quad\quad r =$ compound growth rate,

$\quad\quad n =$ number of years excluding base year.

Estimate the compound annual growth rate of each of the above three companies for the 1967–1975 period. Is there an upper limit to the time period over which any of these companies can continue their 1967–1975 compound annual growth rate?

(3) What additional information would you acquire before forecasting the future net income of *McDonald's, Pizza Hut*, and *Sambo's*?

QUESTION 4.3:   Forecasting Models for Quarterly
                Accounting Data: Marshall Field and Company

Appendix 4.A illustrated the Box-Jenkins modeling of the quarterly income to sales ratio series of *Marshall Field and Company*. Using the 1960–1973 data, the following Box-Jenkins model was identified as appropriate for forecasting the series:

$$E(Z_t|Z_{t-1}\ldots) = Z_{t-4} + .555(Z_{t-1} - Z_{t-5}),$$

where $Z_t =$ quarterly income to sales ratio in quarter t.

REQUIRED

(1) Evaluate the one-quarter-ahead forecasting performance of the above Box-Jenkins model over the 1974,1 to 1975,4 period vis-à-vis the performance of the following two *naive* forecasting models:

$$E(Z_t|Z_{t-1}\ldots) = Z_{t-1}$$
$$E(Z_t|Z_{t-1}\ldots) = Z_{t-4}.$$

The MABE (%) and MSE (%) of the forecasts from the alternative models should be used in this evaluation. Comment on the results.

(2) The evaluation in (1) examined the relative forecasting ability of the Box-Jenkins model in a time period different from that used to identify and estimate the specific model. What limitations would exist if we evaluated the relative forecasting ability of the Box-Jenkins model over the same time period used to identify and estimate the specific model?

(3) Suppose you are a credit analyst of a bank. *Marshall Field* applies for a loan, and you decide that forecasts of their future quarterly earnings are important in deciding the terms of the loan. What factors would you consider in choosing one of the above (or other) forecasting models?

(4) Brown and Niederhoffer [1968] used variants of the above naive forecasting models in a study on the predictive ability of interim data. In discussing the limitations of their study they noted:

> It is possible to continue creating imaginary situations in which other [forecast models] could be expected to do best, but there is little advantage to be gained by doing so. It clearly depends on the nature of the [quarterly] earnings process (and the accountant's interpretation of it), a process that is yet to be studied rigorously. (p. 490)

Comment on the above statement. What aspects of the quarterly earnings process are yet to be studied rigorously?

QUESTION 4.4: Time-Series Behavior of Numbers of Alternative Accounting Systems: Indiana Telephone Corporation*

Although the debate on historical cost (HC) accounting vs. general price level accounting (GPLA) has occupied the accounting literature for many decades, very few companies have continuously reported both historical cost and general price-level accounting financial statements over an extended period. *Indiana Telephone Corporation* is one exception to this general pattern. Since 1954, both sets of financial statements have been published in their annual reports. The following extracts are taken from annual reports over the 1954–1975 period:

> While we will continue for the present to keep records as prescribed by the "Uniform System of Accounts" [for utilities], we have decided this does not supply us with accurate information which we ought to have for the purpose of our own thinking and informing others. We are now prepared to procure more accurate and truthful information ourselves and the reports herewith for the first time will share this information with you.
>
> The present value figures have been developed...by applying to the dollars of cost in each of the plant accounts appropriate conversion factors which translate the actual cost as incurred by the Company for labor and material into an estimate of what these costs would be if incurred as of January 1, 1954....
>
> ...[Such costs] have been brought forward to December 31, 1954 using as a single adjusting factor the government index of wholesale prices, "All commodities other than farm and foods," issued by the Department of Labor.

*Helen E. Schultz of the *Indiana Telephone Corporation* kindly assisted in the preparation of this question.

In addition to informing management and others it is hoped that the completion
of this information and making it public will (a) result in accurate information and
show the true situation, (b) sufficiently inform others so that it may be helpful in
correcting the present regulatory inaccuracies and inequities, and (c) be helpful
in procuring ultimately a change in the income tax law so that true replacement
expense (customarily called depreciation) will be allowed as a tax deductible
item. (1954 Annual Report)

In 1965, the GNP implicit price deflator was chosen as the appropriate
index:

In the accompanying financial statements...historical cost [is] restated for
change in purchasing power of dollar. These dollars of cost have been restated
in terms of the price level at December 31, 1964 and 1965, as measured by the
Gross National Product Implicit Price Deflator, to recognize the inflation experienced to the date of these statements. (1965 Annual Report)

In 1969 the inflation adjustments were extended from "plant accounts" to
also include gain or loss on short-term monetary items. However, they
explicitly rejected inflation adjustments for price level gains or loss on
currently held long-term bonds and preferred stock:

It is neither necessary nor meaningful to attempt annually to reflect the effects
of changes in purchasing power on the bonds and preferred stock. It would
convey no facts for no facts exist until the bonds and/or preferred stocks are
actually retired or refinanced at which time the facts will be known and truthful.
At that time it will be known whether the Corporation and its customers have
been able to survive the effects of monetary inflation. (1969 Annual Report)

Details of the net income series for the 1954–1975 period, for both the HC
and GPLA systems, are presented in Table 4.12.

The sample autocorrelations for the net income series (1954–1975)
are

	r_1	r_2	r_3	r_4	r_5
HC					
Levels	.824	.700	.534	.367	.229
First differences	−.176	−.078	.240	.063	−.139
GPLA					
Levels	.763	.667	.552	.354	.217
First differences	−.279	−.355	.261	.036	−.190

TABLE 4.12 Indiana Telephone Corporation

	Net Income	
	HC	GPLA
1954	158	54
1955	146	45
1956	43	− 66
1957	254	140
1958	368	258
1959	450	333
1960	488	366
1961	414	260
1962	565	411
1963	632	478
1964	582	414
1965	638	447
1966	700	506
1967	664	465
1968	1,039	811
1969	1,391	1,054
1970	1,540	1,089
1971	1,702	1,154
1972	2,031	1,570
1973	2,219	1,461
1974	1,932	941
1975	2,448	1,558

REQUIRED

(1) (a) What evidence is there that the time-series behavior of the net income series over the 1954–1975 period for the HC series is different from that for the GPLA series? What factors could explain these results?

(b) What problems arise in using the data in Table 4.12 to make inferences about the effect of HC procedures vis-à-vis GPLA procedures on the time-series behavior of the reported net income series?

(2) (a) It is often argued that one "limitation" of using the net income figure of the most recent year for forecasting is that it is affected by "erratic and extraordinary factors as well as by cyclical factors." Due to these "limitations," proposals are made for using average net income over periods such as the most recent five years. What evidence is there that a five-year average of

prior years' net income provides more "reliable" forecasts of next year's net income than does use of last year's net income figure? Your evaluation should include forecasts of the 1970–1975 net income (HC) figures of *Indiana Telephone* and include the AVE (%), and MABE (%) forecast error metrics. What factors could explain these results?

(b) Repeat (a) for the GPLA net income series.

QUESTION 4.5: Accounting Materiality Decisions
              and Time-Series Analysis

When firms change accounting techniques, questions relating to the materiality of the change arise. If the change is deemed by an auditor to be material, disclosure of both the change and its effect on the financial statements is generally required. Criteria for deciding materiality questions have been proposed by many authors. One set of criteria considers the percentage effect of the change on reported income; e.g., if an accounting change affects reported income by more than 10%, it is deemed to be material. Dopuch and Watts [1972] note the arbitrariness of this approach and propose using the Box-Jenkins time-series methodology to address the materiality issue:

> We propose to evaluate the significance of accounting changes on the basis of an evaluation of the time-series characteristics of income numbers. However, our approach differs from previous attempts in two respects. First, instead of an arbitrary choice of a time-series model to describe the income-generating processes of firms, we use [Box-Jenkins] procedures to identify the model which best fits those processes under a given accounting measurement technique. ...Second, we define a change to another accounting technique as being significant only if we can reject at some probability level the hypothesis that the reported income-generating process has not been altered by the new measurement technique. In effect, we assume that if the use of an alternative measurement technique does not require a respecification of the parameters of the identified time-series model, a shift to this new technique has no potential impact on the decisions of users of accounting reports. (p. 184)

The reception of the Dopuch and Watts proposal has not been overwhelming. For instance, Kaplan [1975] noted the following:

> Two problems arise with this [approach to materiality]. First, Box-Jenkins analysis requires an enormous amount of data to estimate the underlying process which presumably is remaining stationary during this time. Secondly, at the time the accounting change is made there is no evidence of what the future series

will look like to see if a different time series model is operating. It does not seem helpful to recommend that auditors should wait fifteen years to garner enough data to decide whether a change made fifteen years previous was, in fact, material. (pp. 35–36)

REQUIRED

(1) Evaluate the Dopuch and Watts [1972] approach in the light of the above criticisms. Do you agree with these criticisms? What data would be necessary to overcome these criticisms?

(2) Do you perceive any other problems in using the Dopuch and Watts approach to materiality?

(3) Propose and defend an alternative method for assessing the materiality of an accounting change.

REFERENCES

ALBRECHT, W. S., LOOKABILL, L. L., and MCKEOWN, J. C. "The Time Series Properties of Annual Earnings." *Journal of Accounting Research* (Autumn 1977: in press).

BALL, R., and WATTS, R. "Some Times Series Properties of Accounting Income." *Journal of Finance* (June 1972): 663–682.

BALL, R., LEV, B., and WATTS, R. "Income Variation and Balance Sheet Compositions." *Journal of Accounting Research* (Spring 1976): 1–9.

BEAVER, W. H. "The Time Series Behavior of Earnings." *Empirical Research in Accounting: Selected Studies 1970* (1970): 62–99.

BERNSTEIN, L. P. *Financial Statement Analysis.* Irwin, Homewood, Ill., 1974.

BOX, G. E. P., and JENKINS, G. M. *Time-Series Analysis: Forecasting and Control,* rev. ed. Holden-Day, Inc., San Francisco, 1976.

BRANDON, C. H., and JARRETT, J. E. "Evaluating Accounting Forecasts." *Journal of Business, Finance and Accounting* (Autumn 1976): 67–78.

BREALEY, R. A. *An Introduction to Risk and Return from Common Stocks.* M.I.T. Press, Cambridge, Mass., 1969.

BRIGHAM, E. F. "The Effects of Alternative Depreciation Policies on Reported Profits." *The Accounting Review* (Jan. 1968): 46–61.

BROOKS, L. D., and BUCKMASTER, D. A. "Further Evidence of the Time Series Properties of Accounting Income." *Journal of Finance* (Dec. 1976): 1359–1373.

BROWN, P., and NIEDERHOFFER, V. "The Predictive Content of Quarterly Earnings." *Journal of Business* (Oct. 1968): 488–497.

COLLINS, D. W. "Predicting Earnings with Sub-Entity Data: Some Further Evidence." *Journal of Accounting Research* (Spring 1976): 163–177.

COOPER, J. P., and NELSON, C. R. "The Ex Ante Prediction Performance of the St. Louis and FRB-MIT-PENN Econometric Models and Some Results on Composite Predictors." *Journal of Money, Credit and Banking* (Mar. 1975): 1–32.

DEMSKI, J. S., and FELTHAM, G. A. "Forecast Evaluation." *The Accounting Review* (July 1972): 533–548.

DOPUCH, N., and WATTS, R. "Using Time-Series Models To Assess the Significance of Accounting Changes." *Journal of Accounting Research* (Spring 1972): 180–194.

DYCKMAN, T. R., and THOMAS, J. L. *Business Statistics.* Prentice-Hall, Englewood Cliffs, N.J., 1977.

ELLIOT, J. W., and UPHOFF, H. L. "Predicting the Near Term Profit and Loss Statement with an Econometric Model: A Feasibility Study." *Journal of Accounting Research* (Autumn 1972): 259–274.

FOGELBERG, G. "Interim Income Determination: An Examination of the Effects of Alternative Measurement Techniques." *Journal of Accounting Research* (Autumn 1971): 215–235.

FOSTER, G. "Quarterly Accounting Data: Time-Series Properties and Predictive-Ability Results." *The Accounting Review* (Jan. 1977): 1–21.

GONEDES, N. J., and DOPUCH, N. "Economic Analyses and Accounting Techniques: Perspective and Proposals." Report 7644, Center for Mathematical Studies in Business and Economics, University of Chicago, Chicago, 1976.

GRAHAM, B., DODD, D. L., and COTTLE, S. *Security Analysis: Principles and Techniques*, 4th ed. McGraw-Hill, New York, 1962.

GRIFFIN, P. A. "The Time-Series Behavior of Quarterly Earnings: Preliminary Evidence." *Journal of Accounting Research* (Spring 1977): 71–83.

JENKINS, G. M., and WATTS, D. G. *Spectral Analysis and Its Applications.* Holden-Day, Inc., San Francisco, 1968.

KAPLAN, R. S. "The Information Content of Financial Accounting Numbers: A Survey of Empirical Evidence." Paper Presented at Symposium on the Impact of Research in Financial Accounting and Disclosure on Accounting Practice, Duke University, Durham, N.C., Dec. 1975.

KINNEY, W. R. "Predicting Earnings: Entity versus Subentity Data." *Journal of Accounting Research* (Spring 1971): 127–136.

—— "ARIMA and Regression in Analytical Review: An Empirical Test." *The Accounting Review* (Jan. 1978: in press).

KLEIN, L. R., and BURMEISTER, E. *Econometric Model Performance.* University of Pennsylvania Press, Philadelphia, 1976.

LEV, B. "Economic Determinants of Some Time-Series Properties of Earnings." Report 7705, Center for Mathematical Studies in Business and Economics, University of Chicago, Chicago, Jan. 1977.

LITTLE, I. M. D. "Higgledy Piggledy Growth." *Bulletin of the Oxford Institute of Economics and Statistics* (Nov. 1962): 389–412.

LITTLE, I. M. D., and RAYNER, A. C. *Higgledy Piggledy Growth Again.* Blackwell's, Oxford, 1966.

LOOKABILL, L. L. "Some Additional Evidence on the Time Series Properties of Accounting Earnings." *Accounting Review* (Oct. 1976): 724–738.

MOODY'S INVESTORS SERVICE, *Moody's Transportation Manuals*, Moody's Investor Service Inc., New York (1967–76 issues).

NELSON, C. R. *Applied Time Series Analysis for Managerial Forecasting.* Holden-Day, Inc., San Francisco, 1973.

OPINION RESEARCH CORPORATION. *ORC Public Opinion Index Report to Management.* Opinion Research Corporation, Princeton, N.J., 1973.

ORCUTT, G. H., WATTS, H. W., and EDWARDS, J. B. "Data Aggregation and Information Loss." *American Economic Review* (Sept. 1968): 773–787.

PLATT, R. B. "Statistical Measures of Forecast Accuracy." In W. F. Butler, R. A. Kavesh, and R. B. Platt (eds.), *Methods and Techniques of Business Forecasting.* Prentice-Hall, Englewood Cliffs, N.J., 1974: 597–610.

SAMUELSON, P. A. "Proof that Properly Anticipated Prices Fluctuate Randomly." *Industrial Management Review* (Spring 1965): 41–49.

STRINGER, K. W. "A Statistical Technique for Analytical Review." *Studies on Statistical Methodology in Auditing*, Supplement to *Journal of Accounting Research* (1975): 1–9.

WATTS, R. "The Time Series of Accounting Earnings." Appendix A to "The Information Content of Dividends." Unpublished Ph.D. Dissertation, University of Chicago, Chicago, 1970.

WATTS, R. L., and LEFTWICH, R. W. "The Time Series of Annual Accounting Earnings." *Journal of Accounting Research* (Autumn 1977: in press).

WEISS, L. "Quantitative Studies of Industrial Organization." In M. D. Intrilligator (ed.), *Frontiers of Quantitative Economics.* North-Holland, Amsterdam, 1971: 362–411.

ZELLNER, A. "On the Aggregation Problem: A New Approach to a Troublesome Problem." In K. A. Fox et al. (eds.), *Economic Models, Estimation and Risk Programming, Essays in Honor of Gerhard Tinter.* Springer, Berlin, 1969: 365–374.

CHAPTER **5**

ACCOUNTING NUMBERS: ECONOMY AND INDUSTRY INFLUENCES

It is commonly argued that changes in the earnings and other financial series of firms are influenced by economy and industry factors. For instance, the following statements were made in the 1975 Annual Reports of three companies:

(1) *Marshall Field and Company*

Reflecting the change in the national *economy*, operating results for your company improved during 1975 from the recession-weakened first half to a strong recovery in the second half.

(2) *Crown Zellerbach*

Earnings in 1975...amounted to $74.5 million, compared with $125 million in 1974. [There] were powerful forces at work in the domestic *economy*: the general recession, the greatest year-to-year drop in paper demand in recent history, the lowest level of housing starts since 1946 and continuing inflation in our costs.

(3) *The Continental Corporation*

1975 was in many ways the worst year ever experienced by the property and casualty insurance *industry*, with total underwriting losses estimated to exceed $4 billion. Thus, with 84 percent of our total revenues being derived from property and casualty operations, the year was a difficult one for the Continental Corporation.

In this chapter we shall illustrate how, via *index models*, these economy-wide and industry-wide factors can be explicitly taken into account when analyzing the financial statements of individual firms.

A simple example of an *index model* is

$$(CR_{i,t} - CR_{i,t-1}) = \alpha + \beta_1 (CR_{M,t} - CR_{M,t-1}) + e_{it}, \qquad (5.1)$$

where $CR_{i,t}$ = current ratio of the ith firm in period t,

$CR_{M,t}$ = average current ratio for all the other firms comprising the market in period t.

The model in (5.1) posits that the one-period change in the current ratio of the ith firm is a function of both (1) macroeconomic factors affecting the current ratio of all firms (e.g., a credit squeeze) and (2) firm-specific factors that affect only the current ratio of the ith firm. The model in (5.1) is referred to as a single-index model; there is only one index as an independent variable. A natural extension is to use a multi-index model—say, a two-index model with one index representing economy-wide factors and the other index representing industry-wide factors:

$$(CR_{i,t} - CR_{i,t-1}) = \alpha + \beta_1 (CR_{M,t} - CR_{M,t-1}) + \beta_2 (CR_{I,t} - CR_{I,t-1}) + e_{it}, \qquad (5.2)$$

where $CR_{I,t}$ = the average current ratio for all the other firms in the ith firm's industry. In Sections 5.3 and 5.4 we shall outline the use of index models in financial statement analysis and forecasting. Index models have also been used extensively in research into security market risk assessment (see Chapter 9) and the association between accounting data and security returns (see Chapter 11).[1]

Prior to discussing applications of index models, it is necessary to examine issues relating to the construction of indexes from accounting data—see Section 5.1. It is also useful to examine evidence on the importance of economy-wide and industry-wide factors in explaining variations in a firm's financial ratios. The assumption in developing index models is that such factors are important explanatory variables. Evidence pertaining to this assumption is presented in Section 5.2.

5.1 INDEX CONSTRUCTION ISSUES

Many of the issues discussed in Section 3.2 ("Industry Norms") also apply to the construction of indexes for index models. For instance, if one chooses a two-index model (with economy-wide and industry-wide indexes), it is necessary to first define the economy and the industry. Several specific issues related to accounting index construction are discussed below.

A Populations vs. Samples

A major decision in index construction is whether to (1) include all firms in the population or (2) include a sample of available firms. Often this decision is heavily influenced by data availability considerations. For instance, many accounting indexes are based on data in Standard & Poor's *Compustat* file. This file is not a random selection of all U.S. firms. The initial sample was a set of relatively large firms of potential interest to subscribers to *Compustat*.

Even if one uses a readily available data file such as *Compustat*, there is still a decision on whether to (1) use all firms with available data each year or (2) use a subset of such firms. One commonly used technique is to build indexes from a set of firms which had available data for every year of an extended time period (say, 1947–1975). The main problem with such a technique is that a sizable (and *nonrandom*) proportion of firms are excluded from the index. To exclude firms from the market index in any one year (say, 1975) simply because those firms did not have available data on the *Compustat* file in earlier years (say, 1947) is arbitrary at best. Such a technique imposes what is referred to as a *survivorship* bias on the index.

An alternative (preferable) approach is to construct the economy-wide index from all firms who had available data for the variable in question in each specific year. The result is that as the number of firms in the economy expands (contracts), the number of firms used to construct the index likewise expands (contracts); i.e., the index remains representative of the average ratios of all firms with data in each specific year. Appendix 5.A contains market indexes for 12 accounting ratios over the 1947–1975 period. The number of firms used in constructing the indexes in each year is also detailed. These indexes were built from a merged Annual Industrial *Compustat* tape covering the 1946–1975 period. Several of the indexes in Appendix 5.A will be used in Sections 5.2, 5.3, and 5.4.

B Accounting Fiscal Year Differences

Another index construction issue arises because all firms do not have the same accounting fiscal year. Table 5.1 contains a breakdown of the 1975 fiscal years of all companies listed on the *Compustat* file. Note that a December 31 fiscal year is by far the most common choice—55.4% of all firms.

TABLE 5.1 Fiscal Year Breakdown of *Compustat* Companies

	% of Sample
January	5.0
February	2.5
March	4.5
April	3.2
May	2.2
June	8.7
July	2.8
August	2.5
September	6.5
October	4.1
November	2.6
December	55.4
	100%

Should the indexes be built from all firms with the same fiscal year (e.g., December 31), or should the index be built from all firms regardless of their fiscal years? In practice, both alternatives have been adopted—e.g., Brown and Ball [1967] used the former, while Gonedes [1973] used the latter. There are arguments for the use of both alternatives. Use of all firms regardless of fiscal year means that important industries are not excluded from the index. For instance, most retail department stores have a January 31 fiscal year and are thus excluded when the index is built on only December 31 fiscal year firms. Restriction to December 31 firms does, however, have advantages. The market index in (5.1) is presumed to capture economy-wide factors that affect the current ratios of all firms. If one averages the current ratios of December 31 fiscal year companies and March 31 fiscal year companies, the aggregate index may not represent the average economy-wide ratio pertaining to any one phase of an economic cycle.

C   Equal- vs. Value-Weighted Indexes

The issue of appropriate weighting schemes was discussed in Chapter 3. Appendix 5.A contains both an equal- and a value-weighted economy index for 12 financial ratios. The construction of these indexes will be illustrated by reference to the debt to equity ratio:

$$X_{M,t}^E = \frac{1}{N} \sum_{i=1}^{N} \left(\frac{D_{i,t}}{E_{i,t}} \right)$$

$$X_{M,t}^V = \frac{\sum_{i=1}^{N} D_{i,t}}{\sum_{i=1}^{N} E_{i,t}},$$

where $X_{M,t}^E$ = equally weighted economy index in period t,

$X_{M,t}^V$ = value-weighted economy index in period t,

D_{it} = debt of the ith firm in period t,

E_{it} = average shareholder's equity of the ith firm in period t.

One problem in computing an equal-weighted index is that the index can be markedly affected by extreme values of ratios. Extreme values of a ratio can occur, for instance, when computing a times-interest-earned ratio for firms with minimal interest payments (i.e., the denominator of the ratio is close to zero).[2] In most cases, value-weighted indexes appear to be less affected by extreme values of the ratio of any individual firm.

The indexes in Appendix 5.A provide some useful evidence on financial trends in the U.S. corporate sector. For instance, the average debt to equity ratio (either equal- or value-weighted) has doubled over the 1947–1975 period. In contrast, both the average total asset turnover ratio and the average accounts receivables turnover ratio have declined over the same period. It is important to be aware of such trends when building predictive models using accounting data (see, for example, the models in Chapters 13 and 14). If the time trends in financial ratios are marked, it may be necessary to frequently reestimate the parameters of a predictive model using data from the most recent period.

D Some Empirical Evidence on Indexes

The economy-wide indexes in Appendix 5.A are

(1) Equal-weighted averages of December 31 fiscal year firms, and

(2) Value-weighted averages of December 31 fiscal year firms.

Equal- and value-weighted indexes were also computed for all firms, regardless of accounting fiscal year. The Spearman rank correlation coefficient between pairwise combinations of these indexes was computed to gain insight into the extent to which these indexes move together.

SPEARMAN RANK CORRELATION COEFFICIENT: This coefficient estimates the extent to which two variables move together. It is based on the ranks of the two variables (say X and Y) being examined.

The observations of one variable are ranked, and then the correspondence of these ranks with the rankings of the other variable is examined. The formula used to compute this coefficient is

$$r_s = 1 - \frac{6 \sum d_i^2}{N^3 - N},\qquad(5.3)$$

where d_i is the difference in ranking of X_i and Y_i and N is the number of observations. Critical values of r_s for statistical significance depend on N. Selected values are (from Zar [1972])

	Significance Level	
N	.05	.01
6	.886	1.00
8	.738	.881
10	.648	.794
15	.521	.654
20	.447	.570

The range of values of r_s is -1 to $+1$. A value of 1 (-1) indicates perfect positive (negative) correspondence in ranks. See Siegel [1956] and Hollander and Wolfe [1973] for further discussion of this statistic.

The 1970–1975 equal- (I_M^E) and value- (I_M^V) weighted observations for the return on assets economy-wide index will be used to illustrate computation of r_s. The indexes and their respective rankings for the 1970–1975 period are

	Indexes		Rank			
Year	I_M^E	I_M^V	I_M^E	I_M^V	d_i	d_i^2
1970	.052	.044	6	6	0	0
1971	.055	.045	5	5	0	0
1972	.060	.046	3	4	−1	1
1973	.066	.053	2	2	0	0
1974	.067	.056	1	1	0	0
1975	.057	.047	4	3	1	1
						$\sum d_i^2 = 2$

Note that the only disparity in ranking is for 1972 and 1975. Using (5.3),

$$r_s = 1 - \frac{6 \times 2}{6^3 - 6} = .94.$$

This correlation between I^E and I^V for the return on assets ratio is a statistically significant one at the .05 level.

The Spearman rank correlation examines the correspondence between the rankings of two variables. It is insensitive to the magnitudes of the two variables being examined. If one assumes that the two variables are normally distributed, information about the magnitude of the comovements in the two variables can be captured by the product moment correlation coefficient—see Dyckman and Thomas [1977, Chapter 16].

Table 5.2 details the Spearman rank correlation coefficients between pairwise combinations of the economy indexes for December 31 fiscal year firms/all firms and for equal weightings/value weightings. Note that indexes based on 12/31 fiscal year firms and indexes based on all firms are highly correlated. The lowest correlation in the first and second columns of Table 5.2 is .922. Similarly there is, in general, a high correlation between the equal- and value-weighted indexes of most financial ratios.[3]

TABLE 5.2 Correlations Between Alternative Accounting Market Indexes

	Equal 12/31 Firms vs. Equal All Firms	Value 12/31 Firms vs. Value All Firms	Equal 12/31 Firms vs. Value 12/31 Firms	Equal All Firms vs. Value All Firms
1. Current ratio	.991	.997	.972	.979
2. Quick ratio	.973	.993	.936	.951
3. Defensive interval	.960	.960	.796	.814
4. Debt to equity	.992	.996	.933	.962
5. Long-term debt to equity	.978	.996	.802	.744
6. Times interest earned	.988	.999	.973	.979
7. Earnings to sales	.941	.990	.881	.868
8. Return on assets	.976	.996	.940	.918
9. Return on equity	.922	.984	.778	.765
10. Total assets turnover	.974	.981	.913	.878
11. Inventory turnover	.985	.928	.929	.758
12. Receivables turnover	.984	.992	.967	.980

5.2 IMPORTANCE OF ECONOMY AND INDUSTRY FACTORS ON ACCOUNTING NUMBERS

An important assumption in building single- or multi-index models is that economy-wide or industry-wide factors are important factors affecting an individual firm's accounting numbers. In this section we shall examine evidence on this assumption. The impetus to examining this issue initially arose from research into market and industry-wide factors in security returns. King [1966] examined (via factor analysis) this issue for the monthly price changes of 63 NYSE stocks over the 1927–1960 period. His conclusion was that over the 1927–1952 period, general market movements accounted for over 52% of the price changes in individual stocks; the corresponding figure for the 1952–1960 period was 31%. Industry factors explained an additional 13% over the 1927–1952 period and an additional 12% over the 1952–1960 period.

A An Example: National Steel Corporation

The methodology used to examine the importance of economic and industry factors in accounting numbers will be illustrated by reference to the return on total assets ratio series of *National Steel Corporation*. *National Steel* is a major U.S. steel producer and is in the SIC 3310 industry group (steel—major). Table 5.3 presents the return on total assets ratio for *National Steel* [column (1)], the economy average [column (5)], and the steel industry (SIC #3310) average [column (6)] over the 1951–1974 period. The return on total assets series of the other steel firms in Table 5.3 are used in subsequent parts of this chapter.

The following regressions were run:

$$Y_{i,t} = \hat{\alpha} + \hat{\beta}_1 X_{M,t} + \hat{e}_{it} \tag{5.4}$$

$$Y_{i,t} = \hat{\alpha} + \hat{\beta}_1 X_{M,t} + \hat{\beta}_2 X_{I,t} + \hat{e}_{it} \tag{5.5}$$

$$\Delta Y_{i,t} = \hat{\alpha} + \hat{\beta}_1 \Delta X_{M,t} + \hat{e}_{it} \tag{5.6}$$

$$\Delta Y_{i,t} = \hat{\alpha} + \hat{\beta}_1 \Delta X_{M,t} + \hat{\beta}_2 \Delta X_{I,t} + \hat{e}_{it}, \tag{5.7}$$

where $Y_{i,t}$ = financial ratio of *National Steel* at time t,

$X_{M,t}$ = average economy financial ratio at time t,

$X_{I,t}$ = average steel industry financial ratio at time t,

Δ = first differences operator.

Note that (5.4) and (5.5) use the levels of the financial ratio; (5.6) and (5.7) use first differences in financial ratios. The motivation for including (5.6) and (5.7) is that the first differences version of the model is generally a better specified linear model. Evidence to support this statement is presented on the following page.

TABLE 5.3 Return on Total Assets Series

Year	National Steel (1)	Armco Steel (2)	Lykes-Youngstown (3)	Bethlehem Steel (4)	Economy (value-weighted) (5)	Industry (value-weighted) (6)
1951	.091	.086	.077	.077	.085	.074
1952	.072	.071	.052	.061	.075	.055
1953	.092	.074	.065	.082	.077	.074
1954	.055	.087	.043	.080	.078	.064
1955	.085	.123	.081	.099	.093	.098
1956	.082	.107	.075	.081	.086	.087
1957	.069	.083	.070	.090	.075	.088
1958	.055	.073	.036	.063	.062	.062
1959	.074	.083	.048	.053	.069	.057
1960	.053	.073	.038	.054	.053	.057
1961	.041	.061	.034	.054	.050	.046
1962	.044	.049	.040	.040	.051	.040
1963	.073	.064	.053	.046	.053	.050
1964	.090	.080	.068	.063	.054	.061
1965	.086	.084	.062	.062	.056	.063
1966	.068	.073	.050	.068	.056	.060
1967	.062	.054	.045	.049	.051	.045
1968	.062	.060	.039	.055	.052	.053
1969	.059	.059	.019	.053	.048	.046
1970	.042	.037	.023	.032	.044	.032
1971	.035	.034	.021	.046	.045	.032
1972	.044	.045	.025	.043	.046	.037
1973	.056	.057	.031	.060	.053	.055
1974	.087	.092	.090	.086	.056	.091

If economy-wide factors are important in explaining the variability in a firm's ratios, the average adjusted R^2 for (5.4) will be significant. If industry-wide factors are an important additional factor, the average adjusted R^2 from (5.5) will be significantly above that in (5.4). Similar statements apply to Eqs. (5.6) and (5.7); the focus here is on explaining the variability in the first differences of a firm's ratio. Results of regressions (5.4)–(5.7) for *National Steel* for the 1951–1970 period are as follows:

(1) *Levels*:

$$(5.4) \quad Y_{i,t} = \underset{t=1.894}{.026} + \underset{t=3.140}{.660 X_{M,t}}$$

Adjusted $R^2 = .318$;   Durbin-Watson $= 1.320$

$$(5.5) \quad Y_{i,t} = \underset{t=2.044}{.027} + \underset{t=.212}{.084 X_{M,t}} + \underset{t=1.682}{.591 X_{I,t}}$$

Adjusted $R^2 = .380$;   Durbin-Watson $= 1.151$

(2) *First Differences*:

(5.6) $\Delta Y_{i,t} = .001 + 1.629\Delta X_{M,t}$
$\qquad\qquad\quad t=.273 \qquad\quad t=3.532$

Adjusted $R^2 = .389$; Durbin-Watson $= 2.189$

(5.7) $\Delta Y_{i,t} = .001 + .824\Delta X_{M,t} + .628\Delta X_{I,t}$
$\qquad\qquad\quad t=.189 \qquad\quad t=1.484 \qquad\quad t=2.196$

Adjusted $R^2 = .501$; Durbin-Watson $= 1.977$

How does one choose between these models? One factor to be considered is *economic interpretation*. For example, in (5.5) and (5.7) the sign of the coefficient on the industry variable is expected to be positive —in (5.5) $\hat{\beta}_2 = .591$ and in (5.7) $\hat{\beta}_2 = .628$. A second factor is the *statistical specification* of the OLS model. For instance, are the residuals serially correlated? A third factor is the *strength of the relationship*. Other things being equal, the model with the greatest explanatory power is generally to be preferred.

There is evidence that the first differences versions of the index models for *National Steel* are better specified than models using levels of the financial ratios; e.g., the Durbin-Watson for (5.7) is 1.977 vis-à-vis 1.151 for (5.5).[4] Inferences about economy and industry effects on *National Steel's* return on total assets ratio will be made from the models using (the better specified) first differences of the ratio. The adjusted R^2 of .389 for (5.6) indicates that economy factors account for 38.9% of the variation of $Y_t - Y_{t-1}$ of *National Steel* over the 1948–1974 period. Moreover, steel industry factors account for an *additional* 11.2% of this variation [the difference between the .501 adjusted R^2 for (5.7) and the .389 adjusted R^2 of (5.6)].[5] Thus, the influence of economy and industry factors on changes in this ratio of *National Steel* appear to be considerable.

In some cases, the economy and industry indexes used in models (5.5) and (5.7) will be positively correlated—e.g., the correlation between the economy and steel industry index in (5.5) is .863. In this context the portion of the variation in *National's* return on total assets ratio series that is attributable to (1) market and (2) industry factors will depend on whether an economy or an industry index is entered in the first stage of the analysis. The analysis above entered an economy variable in the first stage. Consider entering an industry variable in the first stage for *National Steel*:

Levels:

$$Y_{i,t} = .028 + .655X_{I,t} \qquad (5.8)$$
$$\qquad\quad t=2.593 \quad t=3.796$$

Adjusted $R^2 = .414$; Durbin-Watson $= 1.149$

First Differences:

$$\Delta Y_{i,t} = -.006 + .908\Delta X_{I,t} \qquad (5.9)$$
$$\qquad\quad t=-.184 \quad t=4.089$$

Adjusted $R^2 = .466$; Durbin-Watson $= 2.254$.

The first differenced version of the index model—(5.9)—is the better specified index model as regards serial correlation of the residuals. By comparing (5.9) with (5.7), we would infer that (1) industry factors explain 46.6% and (2) economy factors explain an additional 3.5% of the variation in *National Steel's* return on total assets ratio series. In some cases, an index model including only an industry index may represent an attractive parsimonious alternative to an index model including both economy and industry indexes.

B Published Evidence

The first study to examine the importance of economy and industry factors on financial numbers was Brown and Ball [1967]. Firms with available data for the 1947–1965 period on the *Compustat* tape were examined. An industry was defined at the two-digit SIC level—only industries with 15 or more firms were examined. Four earnings variables were used: (1) net income, (2) operating income, (3) net income and after-tax interest expense, and (4) adjusted EPS. Equations (5.4) and (5.5) were used in the analysis. The major conclusions were

(1) On average, approximately 35–40 percent of the variability of a firm's annual earnings numbers can be associated with the variability of earnings numbers averaged over all firms, and

(2) On average, a further 10–15 percent can be associated with the industry average (p. 65).

The above conclusions applied to all four forms of the earnings variables examined.

Brealey [1968] examined issues similar to those of Brown and Ball [1967], except that (1) industries were defined at the three-digit rather than the two-digit SIC level and (2) first differences rather than levels of EPS were examined. The period of analysis was 1948–1968. Brealey reported that economy factors explained, *on average*, 21% of the variability of earnings changes of firms; industry factors explained, *on average*, an additional 21% of this variability.[6]

C Some Further Evidence

To extend and update the above results, I conducted the following analysis:

(1) Economy-wide and four-digit SIC industry indexes were built for the 1957–1975 period. The index in each year was the value-weighted average of all December 31 fiscal year firms on the *Compustat* tape which had available data in that year for the accounting variable examined.

(2) Equations (5.4)–(5.7) were estimated for firms in all four-digit SIC industries in which there were at least eight firms (December 31 fiscal year) with available data over the entire 1957–1975 period.

The first series examined was net income. The average adjusted R^2 and Durbin-Watson statistic for (5.4)–(5.7) of the firms that met the above criteria are presented in Table 5.4. The .1, .5, and .9 fractiles of the distribution of each statistic are also presented in Table 5.4. The last two columns of Table 5.4 detail the number of firms and the number of four-digit SIC industries underlying these averages and fractiles. The average Durbin-Watson statistic indicates that first difference versions of the index models are, on average, the better specified models for net income.[7] Using (5.6) and (5.7), economy factors explain 27% of the variations in net income changes of firms over the 1957–1975 period; industry factors explain an additional 18% of this variation. Table 5.5 presents an industry breakdown of the results for (5.6) and (5.7)—average adjusted R^2's for all industries with at least ten firms are detailed. The average adjusted R^2 for (5.6) ranges from .05 for drugs—ethical to .45 for textile products. The average adjusted R^2 for (5.7) ranges from .16 for aerospace to .80 for oil—integrated domestic.

In addition to net income, index models for the following 12 financial ratios were also estimated:

Liquidity
   1.   Current ratio (CR)
   2.   Quick ratio (QR)
   3.   Defensive interval (DI)

Leverage
   4.   Total debt to shareholders' equity (DE)
   5.   Long-term debt to shareholders' equity (LTDE)
   6.   Times interest earned (TIE)

Profitability
   7.   Earnings to sales (ES)
   8.   Return on assets (ROA)
   9.   Return on equity (ROE)

Turnover
   10.   Total asset turnover (TAT)
   11.   Inventory turnover (IT)
   12.   Accounts receivable turnover (ART)

TABLE 5.4 Economy and Industry Influences on Net Income: 1957–1975

	(5.4)	(5.5)	(5.6)	(5.7)	Number of Firms	Number of Industries
A. Adjusted R^2						
Mean	.29	.71	.27	.45	457	30
.1 fractile	.05	.21	.00	.05		
.5 fractile	.28	.85	.22	.48		
.9 fractile	.53	.98	.68	.83		
B. Durbin-Watson						
Mean	.86	1.22	1.81	2.09		
.1 fractile	.48	.63	.99	1.32		
.5 fractile	.76	1.16	1.82	2.14		
.9 fractile	1.38	1.97	2.60	2.85		

TABLE 5.5 Economy and Industry Influences on Net Income: 1957–1975 Industry Breakdown

SIC Code	Industry	Average Adjusted. R^2 for (5.6)	Average Adjusted R^2 for (5.7)	Number of Firms
2200	Textile products	.45	.55	13
2300	Textile apparel mfg	.33	.61	12
2600	Paper	.37	.79	13
2801	Chemicals—major	.29	.56	15
2835	Drugs—ethical	.05	.56	10
2912	Oil—integrated domestic	.31	.80	16
3000	Tire and rubber goods	.22	.51	13
3311	Steel—minor	.20	.36	12
3430	Building material	.12	.27	10
3570	Office and business equipment	.16	.36	10
3714	Auto parts and accessories	.13	.34	18
3721	Aerospace	.15	.16	11
4511	Air transport	.27	.32	19
4911	Electric utilities—flow thru	.37	.54	46
4912	Electric utilities—normalized	.34	.50	70
4924	Natural gas companies	.22	.31	36
5311	Retail—department stores	.34	.60	14
5411	Retail—food chains	.23	.35	16

The average adjusted R^2 and the average Durbin-Watson for (5.4) to (5.7) of these 12 ratios is presented in Table 5.6. Several aspects of the results are noteworthy. *First*, the first differences versions of the index models are, on average, better specified as regards serial correlation of the residuals than the levels versions; i.e., the average Durbin-Watson for first differences is closer to 2. This is a consistent result for all 12 ratios. *Second*, the importance of economy and industry factors varies across ratios. It is strongest for the profitability and turnover ratios and weakest for the liquidity and leverage ratios. On balance, these results are consistent with an implicit assumption made when index models are used in financial statement analysis—i.e., that there are important economy-wide and industry-wide factors affecting the accounting numbers of individual firms.

TABLE 5.6 Economy and Industry Influences on Financial Ratios: 1957–1975

Financial Ratio	Average Adjusted R^2				Average Durbin-Watson				Number of Firms	Number of Industries
	(5.4)	(5.5)	(5.6)	(5.7)	(5.4)	(5.5)	(5.6)	(5.7)		
1. CR	.35	.38	.10	.12	1.36	1.51	2.35	2.33	291	26
2. QR	.35	.39	.07	.11	1.32	1.45	2.30	2.33	287	26
3. DI	.08	.21	.08	.11	1.03	1.25	2.28	2.28	274	25
4. DE	.27	.47	.09	.13	.93	1.14	2.03	2.13	292	26
5. LTDE	.24	.41	.09	.10	.90	1.15	2.07	2.12	283	25
6. TIE	.49	.58	.11	.23	1.03	1.06	1.78	1.93	298	17
7. ES	.21	.38	.14	.26	.95	1.06	1.97	2.04	450	30
8. ROA	.12	.37	.19	.28	.84	1.15	1.99	2.08	309	22
9. ROE	.12	.33	.19	.29	.88	1.09	1.97	2.07	382	29
10. TAT	.16	.42	.11	.27	.72	1.01	1.89	1.99	377	28
11. IT	.14	.34	.14	.25	.86	.99	1.90	1.94	272	25
12. ART	.41	.53	.09	.18	1.02	1.22	1.85	1.93	251	23

5.3 INDEX MODELS IN FINANCIAL STATEMENT ANALYSIS

A major part of financial statement analysis is explaining observed changes in financial ratios, common-size statements, etc. In Section 5.2 we noted that economy-wide and industry-wide factors are two important factors explaining such changes. In this section we shall describe how to use index models to take these factors into account in financial statement analysis. Having controlled for such factors, the analyst is in a better position to determine firm-specific factors affecting a firm's ratios.

A An Example: Pabst Brewing Company

There are several steps in controlling for economy and industry factors. Changes in the return on equity ratio series of *Pabst Brewing Company* will be used to illustrate these steps.

Step One: *Construct Indexes for the Independent Variables in the Index Model*. The following index model was examined:

$$\Delta Y_{i,t} = \hat{\alpha} + \hat{\beta}_1 \Delta X_{M,t} + \hat{\beta}_2 \Delta X_{I,t} + \hat{e}_{i,t}, \qquad (5.10)$$

where $Y_{i,t}$ = return on equity ratio of *Pabst* in period t,

$\quad X_{M,t}$ = average (value-weighted) return on equity ratio of other firms in the economy at time t,

$\quad X_{I,t}$ = average (value-weighted) return on equity ratio of all other firms in the brewing industry at time t,

$\quad \Delta$ = first differences operator.

Values of $Y_{i,t}$, $X_{M,t}$, and $X_{I,t}$ for the 1951–1974 period are presented in Table 5.7.

TABLE 5.7 Return on Equity Ratio Series

	Pabst Brewing Company	Economy	Brewing Industry
1951	.128	.143	.128
1952	.110	.126	.125
1953	.087	.130	.122
1954	.028	.129	.101
1955	.033	.152	.093
1956	−.011	.139	.076
1957	−.043	.127	.082
1958	−.021	.101	.085
1959	.018	.114	.093
1960	.030	.106	.091
1961	.070	.102	.090
1962	.083	.108	.093
1963	.098	.113	.098
1964	.114	.120	.114
1965	.129	.128	.125
1966	.144	.130	.137
1967	.153	.120	.129
1968	.153	.125	.143
1969	.121	.120	.145
1970	.140	.105	.156
1971	.138	.112	.161
1972	.140	.119	.150
1973	.109	.140	.137
1974	.081	.145	.116

Step Two: *Estimate the Coefficients of the Index Model.*   Using ordinary least squares, the following results were obtained for the 1951–1970 period:

$$\Delta Y_{i,t} = -.001 + .262\Delta X_{M,t} + 1.571\Delta X_{I,t} + \hat{e}_{i,t} \quad (5.11)$$
$$t=.211 \qquad\qquad t=.560 \qquad\qquad t=2.843$$

Adjusted $R^2 = .286$;   Durbin-Watson $= 1.585$.

Step Three: *Estimate the Firm-Specific Change in Return on Equity Ratio.*   Using (5.11), the firm-specific change ($\hat{e}_{i,t}$) is

$$\hat{e}_{i,t} = \Delta Y_{i,t} - (-.001 + .262\Delta_{M,t} + 1.571\Delta X_{I,t}). \qquad (5.12)$$

To illustrate (5.12), consider the decrease in *Pabst's* return on equity from .109 in 1973 to .081 in 1974 (i.e., $\Delta Y_{i,t} = -.028$). Over this period, the economy average increased from .140 to .145, and the industry average decreased from .137 to .116. Based on (5.11), the change in *Pabst* is predicted to be

$$E(\Delta Y_{it}|\Delta X_{M,t},\Delta X_{I,t}) = -.001 + .262\times(.005) + 1.571\times(-.021) = -.033.$$

Thus, the firm-specific change is

$$\hat{e}_{i,t} = -.028 - (-.033) = .005.$$

After controlling for economy and industry movements, *Pabst's* return on equity increased (albeit insignificantly) in the 1973–1974 period. The actual changes in *Pabst's* return on equity series and the changes after controlling from economy and industry factors over the 1970–1974 period are

	$\Delta Y_{i,t}$	$\hat{e}_{i,t}$
1971–1970	−.002	−.011
1972–1971	.002	.018
1973–1972	−.031	−.015
1974–1973	−.028	.005

The above steps are not independent of each other. For instance, in step 1 a single-index model may initially be assumed—thus only an economy-wide index is constructed. Then, the estimation results in step 2 may suggest a missing variable in the index model. One obvious such variable would be an industry-wide index. Thus, it is necessary to go back to the step 1 stage of constructing an industry index.

5.4 INDEX MODELS IN FORECASTING

The time-series forecast models examined in Chapter 4 utilized only the past sequence of the accounting variable being forecast. Obviously, a forecaster is not restricted to such a small information set. In this section, the use of index models in forecasting is outlined. A feature of such models is the use of macroeconomic and industry information as well as the past sequence of the accounting variable being forecast.

A An Example: Olympia Brewing Company

The use of an index model in forecasting involves a four-step process. These steps will be illustrated via the forecasting of the profit margin ratio (earnings to sales) of *Olympia Brewing Company*.

Step One: *Construct Indexes for the Independent Variables in the Index Model.* The following model is examined:

$$PM_{i,t} = \hat{\alpha} + \hat{\beta}_1 PM_{M,t} + \hat{\beta}_2 PM_{I,t} + \hat{e}_{i,t}, \qquad (5.13)$$

where $PM_{i,t}$ = profit margin of *Olympia* at time t,

$PM_{M,t}$ = average profit margin of other firms in the economy at time t,

$PM_{I,t}$ = average profit margin of other firms in the brewing industry at time t.

Values for $PM_{i,t}$, $PM_{M,t}$, and $PM_{I,t}$ for the 1951–1974 period are presented in Table 5.8. Both $PM_{M,t}$ and $PM_{I,t}$ were constructed from all firms on *Compustat* with available data for the profit margin in the year the index was being computed. These indexes are value-weighted averages for December 31 fiscal year companies.

Step Two: *Estimate the Coefficients of the Index Model.* Ordinary least squares was used in estimating the model over the 1951–1970 period. The estimated model was

$$PM_{i,t} = -.023 + 1.022 PM_{M,t} + .010 PM_{I,t} + e_{i,t}. \qquad (5.14)$$

This model was also estimated in the first differences version; however, diagnostic tests (e.g., for serial correlation of the residuals) indicated that (5.14) was a better specified model.

Step Three: *Forecast the Future Values of the Indexes.* For illustration, we shall assume that a random-walk model (see Chapter 4) adequately

TABLE 5.8   Operating Margin Ratios

	Olympia Brewing Co.	Economy	Brewing Industry
1951	.0639	.072	.065
1952	.0583	.066	.059
1953	.0523	.064	.055
1954	.0667	.071	.051
1955	.0627	.079	.050
1956	.0589	.079	.049
1957	.0578	.075	.046
1958	.0564	.069	.045
1959	.0569	.076	.049
1960	.0536	.073	.048
1961	.0593	.072	.048
1962	.0543	.074	.049
1963	.0542	.076	.049
1964	.0644	.080	.053
1965	.0654	.082	.057
1966	.0628	.080	.060
1967	.0641	.074	.055
1968	.0539	.072	.056
1969	.0444	.067	.055
1970	.0312	.059	.062
1971	.0288	.061	.061
1972	.0265	.063	.056
1973	.0251	.068	.053
1974	.0091	.059	.040

describes the time-series behavior of both indexes. That is,

$$E(PM_{M, 1971}) = PM_{M, 1970} = .059$$
$$E(PM_{I, 1971}) = PM_{I, 1970} = .062.$$

Step Four: *Forecast the Future Value of the Accounting Variable, Conditional upon Forecasts of the Future Values of the Index.*

$$E(PM_{i, t+1}) = \hat{\alpha} + \hat{\beta}_1 \cdot E(PM_{M, t+1}) + \hat{\beta}_2 \cdot E(PM_{I, t+1})$$
$$E(PM_{i, 1971}) = -.023 + 1.022 \times .059 + .010 \times .062 = .038$$

B   Some General Comments

1. A change in the model used for forecasting $PM_{M, t}$ and $PM_{I, t}$ will obviously lead to different forecasts of $PM_{i, t}$. Suppose a two-year moving-average model provides the most efficient estimates of $PM_{M, t}$ and $PM_{I, t}$.

Then

$$E(\text{PM}_{M,1971}) = .5\text{PM}_{M,1970} + .5\text{PM}_{M,1969}$$
$$= .063$$
$$E(\text{PM}_{I,1971}) = .5\text{PM}_{I,1970} + .5\text{PM}_{I,1969}$$
$$= .0585$$

and

$$E(PM_{i,1971}) = -.023 + 1.22 \times .063 + .010 \times .0585$$
$$= .042.$$

The time-series analysis tools described in Chapter 4 could be used in identifying and estimating a prediction model for each index. It is important to note that use of an index model has transformed rather than solved the forecasting problem. Instead of predicting $\text{PM}_{i,t}$ directly, we transform the problem into predicting $\text{PM}_{M,t}$ and $\text{PM}_{I,t}$. One motivation for this approach is that it may be easier to identify and estimate time-series models for the economy and the industry than it is to identify and estimate a model for an individual firm.[8] Another motivation is that forecasts of economy and industry variables may be readily available in government, bank, trade association, etc., publications.

2. The forecasting ability of an index model is jointly dependent on how efficiently the index model is estimated and how accurate are the forecasts of the independent variables. Useful insights into the forecasting ability of index models can often be gained by computing forecast error metrics with the ex post (i.e., realized) values of the independent variables. Suppose the MABE (%) with the ex post values averaged 1%, whereas it averaged 15% with the forecasted values. This comparison would suggest that it may be cost-effective to devote more resources to developing better forecasts of the independent variables.

C Evidence of Forecasting Ability of Index Models

The most detailed examination of the forecasting ability of index models—vis-à-vis other models—is provided by Gonedes [1973]. Only a single-index model was examined. The single index used by Gonedes was the average (both equal- and value-weighted) of 316 firms which had complete data available for several accounting variables over the entire

1947–1968 period. The main conclusions of this analysis were

(1) The first differences version of the index model generally yielded more efficient forecasts of next period's net income/common equity ratio than did the levels version of the index model,

(2) There was little difference in the forecasting abilities of index models when different economy indexes (value- vs. equal-weighted) were used, and

(3) The first differences version of the index model yielded similar forecasting performance (on MSE and MABE criteria) to the random-walk time-series model.

The forecast errors examined by Gonedes were individual firm forecasts. Another important forecast issue is the average error when forecasting the earnings of a portfolio of firms. In such cases, portfolio-type considerations become important.[9] The lower the cross-sectional correlation in the forecast errors of the individual firms in the portfolio (ceteris paribus), the greater the reduction in forecasting error when one moves from average forecast errors for individual firms to the forecast error for predicting the aggregate portfolio earnings. Gonedes did present evidence that the cross-sectional correlation of forecast errors for the martingale model exceeded those for the index model. This result is not surprising given that the random-walk model ignores important influences affecting the net income/common equity ratio of all firms (i.e., economy and industry influences). A forecaster's concern, however, is not with cross-sectional correlation per se but rather with forecasting ability. Unfortunately, Gonedes did not present details of the portfolio earnings forecasting errors of index models vis-à-vis the forecasting errors of alternatives such as a random-walk time-series model.

5.5 SUMMARY

Financial analysts have long recognized that economy-wide and industry-wide factors affect the financial numbers of individual firms. Index models enable quantification of the effects of these factors. Such quantification can be important when assessing financial trends in a firm and when forecasting fnancial variables. In subsequent chapters, we shall discuss the use of index models in risk assessment (Chapter 9) and in examining the association between accounting data and security returns (Chapter 11).

APPENDIX 5.A   ECONOMY-WIDE INDEXES FOR ACCOUNTING RATIOS

Economy-wide indexes for 12 accounting ratios over the 1947–1975 period are presented in this appendix. The 12 financial ratios are

Liquidity
1. Current ratio
2. Quick ratio
3. Defensive interval (in days)

Leverage
4. Debt to equity ratio
5. Long-term debt to equity ratio
6. Times-interest-earned ratio

Profitability
7. Earnings to sales
8. Return on assets
9. Return on equity

Turnover
10. Total assets turnover
11. Inventory turnover
12. Accounts receivable turnover

The indexes were built from all December 31 fiscal year firms which had available data for the ratio in the year examined. The equal-weighted index is an arithmetic average of all ratios. The value-weighted index is computed by summing the numerator for all firms, summing the denominator for all firms, and then dividing the aggregate numerator by the aggregate denominator.

Liquidity Ratios

Year	Current Ratio			Quick Ratio			Defensive Interval		
	Equal	Value	Number of Firms	Equal	Value	Number of Firms	Equal	Value	Number of Firms
1947	3.17	2.60	514	1.78	1.55	508	108.9	105.1	460
1948	3.13	2.53	516	1.73	1.48	511	101.6	96.6	467
1949	3.73	2.76	542	2.15	1.72	537	112.0	103.3	492
1950	2.95	2.37	552	1.77	1.55	547	120.6	113.7	503
1951	2.64	2.16	555	1.51	1.34	549	108.9	104.9	508
1952	2.88	2.32	563	1.67	1.38	557	106.8	102.4	515
1953	2.98	2.23	572	1.70	1.39	566	102.0	96.6	526
1954	3.17	2.36	585	1.85	1.49	580	112.4	103.0	541
1955	2.97	2.29	600	1.77	1.49	594	113.7	107.0	558
1956	2.97	2.33	609	1.69	1.41	602	104.5	93.5	573
1957	3.06	2.34	630	1.68	1.39	621	98.2	87.9	590
1958	3.33	2.53	642	1.89	1.57	632	108.8	100.0	603
1959	3.10	2.43	650	1.77	1.53	640	106.3	100.4	611
1960	3.11	2.39	993	1.76	1.49	986	100.4	95.9	920
1961	2.82	2.25	1,200	1.75	1.49	1,054	104.2	100.6	981
1962	2.81	2.22	1,282	1.76	1.48	1,137	103.6	100.1	1,067
1963	2.84	2.18	1,346	1.84	1.48	1,202	103.8	101.5	1,115
1964	2.73	2.11	1,389	1.76	1.41	1,243	104.3	97.8	1,160
1965	2.55	1.91	1,407	1.64	1.29	1,261	104.8	95.4	1,175
1966	2.51	1.85	1,467	1.62	1.20	1,321	101.7	91.1	1,237
1967	2.62	1.87	1,462	1.66	1.19	1,318	103.8	90.6	1,238
1968	2.53	1.73	1,491	1.65	1.11	1,349	105.5	91.9	1,261
1969	2.32	1.61	1,537	1.47	1.02	1,395	104.5	89.0	1,328
1970	2.50	1.55	1,514	1.60	.95	1,371	101.7	86.2	1,309
1971	2.51	1.61	1,509	1.61	1.02	1,366	103.4	87.7	1,300
1972	2.54	1.61	1,505	1.68	1.05	1,362	104.3	89.4	1,297
1973	2.26	1.57	1,462	1.43	1.03	1,321	99.8	89.4	1,260
1974	2.14	1.50	1,431	1.23	.92	1,293	92.4	80.0	1,245
1975	2.46	1.54	1,393	1.51	.98	1,254	95.3	80.4	1,209

Leverage Ratios

	Debt to Equity			Long-Term Debt to Equity			Times Interest Earned		
Year	Equal	Value	Number of Firms	Equal	Value	Number of Firms	Equal	Value	Number of Firms
1947	.56	.51	515	.38	.28	515	26.3	13.9	259
1948	.56	.53	516	.36	.29	516	25.7	15.1	290
1949	.49	.49	542	.31	.25	542	20.8	12.5	310
1950	.58	.53	551	.41	.32	551	27.2	13.2	306
1951	.68	.59	554	.49	.37	554	21.2	12.4	355
1952	.69	.59	561	.47	.35	561	18.0	10.8	398
1953	.67	.59	570	.44	.34	570	14.9	9.8	406
1954	.61	.54	584	.39	.30	584	15.5	10.9	413
1955	.65	.56	598	.42	.33	598	17.0	12.4	423
1956	.69	.54	608	.43	.30	608	14.6	8.9	546
1957	.67	.55	629	.40	.29	629	13.0	8.1	583
1958	.72	.52	641	.40	.25	641	11.1	6.7	643
1959	.67	.53	650	.40	.27	650	11.9	6.3	682
1960	.72	.54	994	.43	.27	994	9.3	5.8	910
1961	.84	.62	1,200	.43	.26	1,200	9.1	5.5	964
1962	.86	.63	1,280	.44	.26	1,280	9.4	5.3	1,034
1963	.85	.62	1,338	.44	.27	1,338	9.1	5.2	1,128
1964	.88	.63	1,384	.46	.27	1,384	9.4	4.9	1,168
1965	1.09	.68	1,402	.58	.32	1,402	9.3	4.8	1,208
1966	1.06	.73	1,462	.56	.33	1,462	9.5	4.7	1,313
1967	1.08	.74	1,461	.54	.32	1,461	7.6	4.2	1,357
1968	1.15	.80	1,489	.58	.35	1,489	7.2	3.9	1,408
1969	1.19	.85	1,534	.61	.39	1,534	6.5	3.3	1,484
1970	1.25	.92	1,508	.65	.41	1,509	5.5	2.9	1,514
1971	1.18	.93	1,507	.59	.40	1,507	6.1	3.0	1,522
1972	1.30	.93	1,502	.67	.41	1,502	7.1	3.1	1,524
1973	1.28	.95	1,458	.68	.44	1,459	6.3	2.9	1,500
1974	1.31	1.02	1,426	.70	.50	1,426	5.7	2.6	1,483
1975	1.26	.98	1,389	.65	.46	1,390	5.2	2.5	1,444

Profitability Ratios

	Earnings to Sales			Return on Assets			Return on Equity		
Year	Equal	Value	Number of Firms	Equal	Value	Number of Firms	Equal	Value	Number of Firms
1947	.088	.082	524	.117	.094	437	.219	.155	485
1948	.091	.090	528	.119	.105	461	.204	.179	512
1949	.082	.082	552	.098	.088	466	.163	.146	519
1950	.094	.091	562	.119	.106	489	.203	.176	543
1951	.073	.072	569	.090	.085	502	.155	.143	552
1952	.064	.066	575	.075	.075	510	.133	.126	558
1953	.064	.064	582	.077	.077	522	.131	.130	567
1954	.068	.071	594	.077	.078	532	.129	.129	573
1955	.073	.079	609	.091	.093	546	.160	.152	584
1956	.084	.079	716	.090	.086	562	.148	.139	600
1957	.079	.075	733	.076	.075	675	.130	.127	708
1958	.075	.069	784	.067	.062	694	.110	.101	724
1959	.088	.076	834	.077	.069	746	.134	.114	789
1960	.069	.073	1,195	.065	.053	795	.109	.106	797
1961	.069	.072	1,259	.057	.050	1,094	.123	.102	1,154
1962	.073	.074	1,337	.062	.051	1,171	.112	.108	1,230
1963	.075	.076	1,451	.063	.053	1,224	.117	.113	1,333
1964	.078	.080	1,496	.067	.054	1,334	.129	.120	1,452
1965	.083	.082	1,516	.073	.056	1,346	.148	.128	1,459
1966	.086	.080	1,578	.077	.056	1,407	.159	.130	1,508
1967	.079	.074	1,579	.068	.051	1,445	.144	.120	1,512
1968	.083	.072	1,605	.066	.052	1,481	.140	.125	1,532
1969	.068	.067	1,660	.062	.048	1,553	.138	.120	1,596
1970	.057	.059	1,643	.052	.044	1,573	.120	.105	1,595
1971	.062	.061	1,642	.055	.045	1,573	.118	.112	1,595
1972	.069	.063	1,664	.060	.046	1,582	.136	.119	1,603
1973	.070	.068	1,623	.066	.053	1,583	.184	.140	1,590
1974	.054	.059	1,590	.067	.056	1,561	.140	.145	1,555
1975	.051	.052	1,551	.057	.047	1,522	.135	.121	1,519

Turnover Ratios

Year	Total Asset Turnover			Inventory Turnover			Accounts Receivable Turnover		
	Equal	Value	Number of Firms	Equal	Value	Number of Firms	Equal	Value	Number of Firms
1947	1.55	1.10	469	8.47	5.60	452	16.05	9.53	453
1948	1.57	1.13	494	8.60	5.70	478	16.44	9.54	479
1949	1.44	1.02	502	8.80	5.46	486	15.85	8.68	489
1950	1.53	1.12	526	10.19	6.45	509	15.31	8.89	511
1951	1.54	1.15	536	9.71	6.26	518	15.04	8.65	522
1952	1.48	1.09	543	9.39	5.73	523	14.81	8.00	529
1953	1.51	1.14	553	9.84	6.08	533	15.43	8.19	539
1954	1.40	1.04	561	9.55	5.82	542	14.47	7.65	546
1955	1.49	1.13	573	10.68	6.64	556	14.03	8.10	559
1956	1.49	1.09	589	10.34	6.31	571	13.47	7.36	576
1957	1.28	.94	699	9.47	6.12	583	13.78	7.36	590
1958	1.20	.84	714	9.46	5.74	597	12.62	6.77	606
1959	1.23	.87	773	10.11	6.32	610	13.05	6.98	620
1960	1.14	.64	824	9.57	6.17	618	12.60	6.53	630
1961	1.19	.60	1,174	10.18	6.10	944	12.39	6.32	974
1962	1.26	.62	1,247	11.19	6.38	1,008	12.16	6.29	1,043
1963	1.24	.62	1,327	11.55	6.51	1,077	11.71	6.09	1,123
1964	1.22	.60	1,446	12.44	6.67	1,139	11.45	6.02	1,192
1965	1.22	.61	1,455	12.98	6.82	1,139	10.82	6.05	1,195
1966	1.25	.61	1,513	12.06	6.70	1,177	10.69	5.49	1,249
1967	1.18	.60	1,523	11.45	6.47	1,184	10.33	5.56	1,259
1968	1.19	.60	1,549	11.80	6.70	1,208	10.03	5.80	1,284
1969	1.17	.59	1,612	12.03	6.60	1,267	9.85	5.60	1,347
1970	1.10	.57	1,613	11.58	6.26	1,266	8.92	5.34	1,334
1971	1.09	.56	1,607	11.10	6.35	1,248	8.82	5.44	1,332
1972	1.11	.55	1,619	12.34	6.71	1,249	9.22	5.30	1,332
1973	1.16	.58	1,617	12.63	7.20	1,227	9.52	5.55	1,306
1974	1.21	.64	1,586	12.14	7.33	1,210	9.58	6.10	1,274
1975	1.15	.61	1,548	11.26	6.71	1,173	9.39	5.78	1,237

NOTES

[1]See also Barnea et al. [1975] for discussion of the use of index models in managerial performance evaluation.

[2]Note that extreme values of ratios can also occur due to errors in the underlying data. When using machine-readable data bases, care should always be taken to check for possible errors. See Rosenberg and Houglet [1974].

[3]Several private and government bodies publish "economy-wide" indexes for accounting variables; e.g., the *Federal Reserve Board* publishes a sales series and a profit (after-tax) series for industrial firms. The available evidence indicates that these series are very highly correlated with comparable series based on *Compustat* data—see Brown and Ball [1967, Appendix D].

[4]The Durbin-Watson statistic is a measure of the first-order serial correlation of the residuals of a regression model. It is computed as

$$D.W. = \frac{\sum\limits_{t=2}^{T} (\hat{e}_t - \hat{e}_{t-1})^2}{\sum\limits_{t=1}^{T} \hat{e}_t^2}.$$

The statistic ranges between 0 and 4; a value of 2 indicates no first-order serial correlation in the $\hat{e}_t$ series. A bench mark for suspecting positive serial correlation in the residuals in samples of 30 observations is a $D.W. < 1.35$. A corresponding bench mark for suspecting negative correlation is a $D.W. > 2.65$. If the residuals of a regression model are serially correlated, the ordinary least-squares estimates of α and β will be inefficient; i.e., there is another set of estimates of α and β that have lower variance. See Johnston [1972].

[5]For a statistical test of the significance of the increase in the R^2 when an additional independent variable is added, see Goldberger [1964, pp. 176–177].

[6]See also Gonedes [1973] and Magee [1974] for an examination of issues similar to those of Brown and Ball [1967] and Brealey [1968].

[7]This is not a new result in time-series analysis. Granger and Newbold [1974] discuss the levels vs. differences issue with considerable clarity. Ball and Brown [1969] noted this result for accounting index models: "Changes in the income variables appear to be a more appropriate specification than levels for our estimating procedures" (p. 320). Gonedes [1973] also provides evidence on this issue.

[8]There is considerable debate in the econometric literature on the benefits and costs of estimating models at the aggregate economy level vis-à-vis at the less aggregated levels. See, for instance, Orcutt et al. [1968].

[9]See Chapter 8 for a discussion of portfolio theory.

QUESTIONS

QUESTION 5.1: Index Models for Lykes-Youngstown and Bethlehem Steel

1. *Lykes-Youngstown* is included in the SIC industry code 3310 (steel —major). Table 5.3 details the return on total assets ratio of *Lykes-Youngstown*, the economy, and the steel industry group over the 1951–1974 period. The results from examining a variety of index models using the 1951–1970 period data were

Levels:

$$Y_t = -.064 + .904 X_{M,t}$$
$$t = -.533 \qquad t = 4.908$$

Adjusted $R^2 = .549$; Durbin-Watson $= 1.173$

$$Y_t = -.028 + .887 X_{I,t}$$
$$t = -.332 \qquad t = 6.543$$

Adjusted $R^2 = .688$; Durbin-Watson $= 1.076$

$$Y_t = -.005 + .151 X_{M,t} + .771 X_{I,t}$$
$$t = -.531 \qquad t = .487 \qquad t = 2.811$$

Adjusted $R^2 = .674$; Durbin-Watson $= 1.043$

First Differences:

$$\Delta Y_t = .0008 + 1.684 \Delta X_{M,t}$$
$$t = .277 \qquad t = 4.392$$

Adjusted $R^2 = .504$; Durbin-Watson $= 2.39$

$$\Delta Y_t = -.0008 + .946 \Delta X_{I,t}$$
$$t = -.307 \qquad t = 5.423$$

Adjusted $R^2 = .612$; Durbin-Watson $= 2.251$

$$\Delta Y_t = .0004 + .832 \Delta X_{M,t} + .663 \Delta X_{I,t}$$
$$t = .181 \qquad t = 2.000 \qquad t = 3.095$$

Adjusted $R^2 = .670$; Durbin-Watson $= 1.945$.

where Y_t = return on total assets ratio of *Lykes-Youngstown* in period t,

$X_{M,t}$ = average return on total assets ratio for the economy in period t,

$X_{I,t}$ = average return on total assets ratio of firms in steel—major 3310 industry group in period t,

Δ = first differences operator.

(1) Evaluate the results of the above regressions. Which index model appears to be the best specified one? What inferences can you draw about economy-wide and industry-wide influences on the return on total assets ratio of *Lykes-Youngstown*?

(2) An analyst decides to choose the following model when examining firm-specific changes ($\hat{e}_t$) in *Lykes-Youngstown's* return on total assets ratio:

$$\Delta Y_t = .0004 + .832\Delta X_{M,t} + .663\Delta X_{I,t} + \hat{e}_t.$$

Compute the firm-specific change in the return on total assets ratio in each year of the 1971–1974 period. What inferences can you make from the results?

(3) Discuss any factors you would want to consider when using the index model in (2) to estimate the firm-specific changes in *Lykes-Youngstown's* return on total assets ratio over the 1971–1974 period.

2. [Access to a computer is necessary for this subpart of Question 5.1]. *Bethlehem Steel* is also included in the 3310 SIC industry group. Table 5.3 details the return on total assets ratio of *Bethlehem* over the 1951–1974 period.

Estimate single- and multi-index models for *Bethlehem* using 1951–1970 data. Which index model would you choose for estimating the firm-specific changes in *Bethlehem* over the 1971–1974 period?

QUESTION 5.2:   Models of the Financial Variables of Firms

The Brown and Ball [1967] study discussed in Chapter 5 found that a multi-index model with economy and industry variables explained, *on average*, 45–55% of the variance in the earnings of firms. Cyert [1967] commented on this finding as follows: "One of the interesting aspects of the result is the unexplained variance in profits. Obviously a more complete model is necessary to increase the proportion of the variance explained" (p. 79).

(1) What variables, in addition to those representing economy and industry factors, might be included in an index model explaining variations in the earnings of a firm over time?

(2) On what basis would you decide what variables in (1) warrant explicit inclusion in an index model?

QUESTION 5.3: Industry Influences on Earnings

The Brealey [1968] study discussed in Chapter 5 estimated the importance of economy and industry influences as follows:

$$\Delta Y_{i,t} = \alpha + \beta_1 \Delta X_{M,t} + \hat{e}_{i,t} \tag{5.15}$$

$$\Delta Y_{i,t} = \alpha + \beta_1 \Delta X_{M,t} + \beta_2 \Delta X_{I,t} + \hat{e}_{i,t}, \tag{5.16}$$

where $Y_{i,t}$ = earnings of ith firm in period t,

$X_{M,t}$ = *Standard & Poor's* economy earnings index in period t,

$X_{I,t}$ = earnings of all companies in the industry in period t,

Δ = first differences operator.

The strength of the industry influence was measured by the increase in the average R^2 of (5.16) over the average R^2 of (5.15) for the firms in each industry. Some details of the average R^2 of (5.15) and (5.16) for the industries examined are

	Av. R^2 of (5.15)	Av. R^2 of (5.16)
Aircraft	.11	.16
Autos	.48	.59
Breweries	.11	.18
Cement	.06	.48
Chemicals	.41	.49
Cosmetics	.05	.11
Dept. stores	.30	.67
Drugs	.14	.21
Electricals	.24	.32
Food	.10	.20
Machinery	.19	.35
Nonferrous metals	.26	.51
Office machinery	.14	.20
Oil	.13	.62
Paper	.27	.55
Rubber	.26	.74
Steel	.32	.53
Supermarkets	.06	.39
Textiles and clothing	.25	.54
Tobacco	.08	.27

Brealey commented on the results as follows:

The more homogeneous the product lines or the production process of the members of any industry, the more marked should be the additional comovement.... The results largely confirm prior expectations. Companies in industries characterized by very homogeneous product lines, such as cement, paper, oil, supermarkets and tires, appear to have been most subject to an industry effect. In those industries where there is a diverse range of products or where the

products are distinguished by strong brand loyalties, t
shown to have been relatively weak. This is the case with th
drugs and office machinery groups. Some results, how
notably the strong industry influence in the case of the te
store companies and the very weak effect for chemical a
(p. 7)

REQUIRED

(1) Evaluate the above explanation of the differences across industries in the importance of industry influences on earnings.

(2) What consequence would a trend to corporate diversification have for the analysis by Brealey?

(3) There is a trend toward more detailed disclosure of line-of-business results by multiactivity firms. What problems may arise in deriving the line-of-business results disclosed in annual reports? How could this line-of-business information be utilized in index models?

QUESTION 5.4: Index Models and Forecasting: Armco Steel

Hobie Leland, Jr. has been charged with the task of forecasting the return on total assets (ROA) series of *Armco Steel*. Table 5.3 [column (2)] lists this series as well as the economy and steel industry return on total assets series. Hobie examines a variety of index models and chooses the following:

$$Y_t = .006 + .247 X_{M,t} + .869 X_{I,t} + \hat{e}_{i,t}$$
$$t = .699 \qquad t = .992 \qquad t = 3.946$$
$$\text{Adjusted } R^2 = .825; \qquad \text{Durbin-Watson} = 1.751.$$

For prediction purposes, Hobie decides that the economy and industry ROA series are best described by a random-walk model; i.e., the best prediction of $X_{M,t}$ is $X_{M,t-1}$, and the best prediction of $X_{I,t}$ is $X_{I,t-1}$.

REQUIRED

(1) Hobie decides to evaluate the one-year-ahead forecasting ability of the above index model vis-à-vis a model predicting that *Armco's* ROA series behaves as a random-walk. Use the 1971–1974 period to assess predictive ability and compute the MABE (%) and MSE (%) error measures. Does the index model outperform the random-walk model for *Armco* over this period? Comment on the results.

(2) The error measures for the index model in (1) are based on forecasts of the independent variables $(X_{M,t}, X_{.,t})$ rather than their actual values. Recompute the error measures using the actual values of the independent variables for the year being forecast. Why might Hobie find these error measures informative over and above those computed in (1)?

3) Hobie's superior uses the same data for the 1951–1970 period and argues that the following model is preferable to that chosen by Hobie:

$$Y_{i,t} = .010 + 1.058X_{I,t} + \hat{e}_{i,t}$$
$$t = 1.425 \qquad t = 9.518$$

Adjusted $R^2 = .825$; Durbin-Watson $= 2.016$.

What factors would you consider when choosing among Hobie's model, his superior's model, and the random-walk model for forecasting *Armco's* earnings?

REFERENCES

BALL, R., and BROWN, P. "Portfolio Theory and Accounting." *Journal of Accounting Research* (Autumn 1969): 300–323.

BARNEA, A., SADAN, S., and SCHIFF, M. "Conditional Performance Review." *Management Accounting* (Nov. 1975): 19–22.

BREALEY, R. A. "Some Implications of the Comovement of Company Earnings." Presented at Seminar on the Analysis of Security Prices, University of Chicago, Chicago, Nov. 1968.

BROWN, P., and BALL, R. "Some Preliminary Findings on the Association Between the Earnings of a Firm, Its Industry, and the Economy." *Empirical Research in Accounting: Selected Studies, 1967.* Supplement to *Journal of Accounting Research* (1967): 55–77.

CYERT, R. M "Discussion of Some Preliminary Findings on the Association Between the Earnings of a Firm, Its Industry, and the Economy." *Empirical Research in Accounting: Selected Studies, 1967.* Supplement to *Journal of Accounting Research* (1967): 78–80.

DYCKMAN, T. R., and THOMAS, L. J. *Fundamental Statistics for Business and Economics.* Prentice-Hall, Englewood Cliffs, N.J., 1977.

GOLDBERGER, A. S. *Econometric Theory.* Wiley, New York, 1964.

GONEDES, N. J. "Properties of Accounting Numbers: Models and Tests." *Journal of Accounting Research* (Autumn 1973): 212–237.

GRANGER, C. W. J., and NEWBOLD, P. "Spurious Regressions in Econometrics." *Journal of Econometrics* (No. 2, 1974): 111–120.

HOLLANDER, M., and WOLFE, D. A. *Nonparametric Statistical Methods.* Wiley, New York, 1973.

JOHNSTON, J. *Econometric Methods*, 2nd ed. McGraw-Hill, New York, 1972.

KING, B. F. "Market and Industry Factors in Stock Price Behavior." *Journal of Business* (Jan. 1966): 139–190.

MAGEE, R. P. "Industry-Wide Commonalities in Earnings." *Journal of Accounting Research* (Autumn 1974): 270–287.

ORCUTT, G. H., WATTS, H. W., and EDWARDS, J. B. "Data Aggregation and Information Loss." *American Economic Review* (Sept. 1968): 773–787.

ROSENBERG, B., and HOUGLET, M. "Error Rates in CRSP and Compustat Data Bases and Their Implications." *Journal of Finance* (Sept. 1974): 1303–1310.

SIEGEL, S. *Nonparametric Statistics*. McGraw-Hill, New York, 1956.

ZAR, J. H. "Significance Testing of the Spearman Rank Correlation Coefficient." *Journal of American Statistical Association* (Sept. 1972): 578–580.

CHAPTER

6

FINANCIAL RATIOS: ADDITIONAL ISSUES AND EVIDENCE

Analysis of financial ratios is an important part of financial statement analysis. Although in Chapters 3–5 we discussed many issues relating to this analysis, several important issues remain to be examined. These include (1) the nature of the distribution of financial ratios, (2) the correlation between financial ratios, and (3) the effect of alternative accounting rules on financial ratios. An important part of this chapter is illustrating how these issues can be examined in samples of firms other than those discussed in this chapter.

6.1 THE DISTRIBUTION OF FINANCIAL RATIOS

A Importance of Distribution Evidence

Two areas in which distribution evidence is important are (1) financial statement analysis and (2) statistical tool choice. These are discussed below.

Financial Statement Analysis

It was noted in Chapter 2 that the 1975 inventory turnover ratio (COGS/average inventory) of *Jos. Schlitz Brewing Company* was 13.25 compared to an industry average of 10.53. Is this difference a statistically significant one? To answer this question, it is necessary to examine the distribution of the inventory turnover ratio for brewing companies. If this ratio is normally distributed with a mean of 10.53 and a standard deviation of 1, the above difference between *Schlitz* and the industry average is statistically significant at more than the .05 significance level—it is more than two standard deviations away from the mean of the distribution. What if the inventory turnover ratio of brewing companies is not normally distributed? In this case, one can proceed in several directions. One direction is to examine additional aspects of the distribution, e.g., skewness, kurtosis, and fractiles of the distribution. In Section 6.1B we shall discuss such aspects of distributions. Another direction is to use a distribution-free significance test such as Tchebysheff's inequality.

Tchebysheff's inequality states that for any distribution with finite mean and variance

$$\text{Prob}(|x - \mu| \geqslant t \cdot \sigma) \leqslant \frac{1}{t^2}, \tag{6.1}$$

where $t > 0$.[1] This inequality, for instance, implies that no more than $\frac{1}{9}$ of the distribution lies beyond 3σ from the mean. Thus, in the above example where $\mu = 10.53$, $\sigma = 1$, and $x = 13.25$, *Schlitz's* inventory turnover ratio is not statistically different from the industry mean at the .05 (or .10) level. Tchebysheff's inequality applies to any distribution. Note that if one makes the additional assumption that the distribution is normal, we can specify a tighter confidence interval in which we would expect 95% of the distribution to lie.

Choice of Statistical Tools

The distribution of financial ratios is also an important consideration when choosing statistical tools for any empirical exercise. For instance, the use of a t statistic to assess the significance of an estimated coefficient in an OLS regression model assumes that the residuals are normally distributed. If this assumption is strongly violated by the data, the use of a t statistic may yield misleading inferences about the significance/nonsignificance of a variable. Strong violations of this assumption may lead a researcher to choose an alternative estimation technique to that of minimizing the sum of the squared residuals employed in OLS—e.g., a technique that minimizes the sum of the absolute values of the residuals may be appropriate.[2] At a minimum, strong violation would mean a less than literal interpretation of conventional significance levels for the t distribution. In general, a less than literal interpretation of such levels is always appropriate but more so if one knows that an assumption underlying the derivation of the test is not a descriptively valid one for the data being examined.

B Aspects of Distributions

Some important features of distributions will be illustrated by reference to the 1974 total debt to equity ratio of 67 firms in the SIC two-digit "foods and kindred products" industry. Table 6.1 contains the debt to equity ratios of these 67 firms.

Central Tendency

One important feature of a distribution is its central tendency. The *arithmetic mean* and the *median* are the two most common measures of central tendency. The arithmetic mean (γ_1) is computed as follows:

$$\hat{\gamma}_1 = \frac{\sum\limits_{i=1}^{N} X_i}{N}$$
$$= 1.126, \tag{6.2}$$

where X_i is the debt to equity ratio of the ith firm and N is the number of

TABLE 6.1 1974 Total Debt to Equity Ratios for
67 Firms in Food and Kindred Products Industry

No.	Ticker Symbol	Ratio	No.	Ticker Symbol	Ratio	No.	Ticker Symbol	Ratio
1	CFD	.841	2	GF	.831	3	GIS	1.053
4	GEB	.364	5	K	.358	6	PSY	1.610
7	DAT	1.026	8	SB	1.068	9	ESM	.938
10	FI	2.163	11	GH	2.293	12	G	.884
13	HRL	.642	14	KML	1.131	15	RHP	1.017
16	UB	1.151	17	BRY	.689	18	BN	.874
19	CMK	.832	20	FMF	1.116	21	KRA	.921
22	PET	.730	23	CPB	.243	24	CKE	.907
25	DEL	1.370	26	HNZ	.923	27	LJ	1.019
28	SBC	.818	29	RAL	1.092	30	STA	.873
31	ABA	1.557	32	IBC	1.017	33	TBC	.463
34	WD	6.428	35	NAB	1.291	36	ASR	1.110
37	SUC	9.162	38	ABM	.623	39	HLY	.929
40	HSY	.465	41	TR	.331	42	WWY	.313
43	ADM	1.208	44	ABW	.718	45	CSY	1.139
46	ABUD	.490	47	CKB	.503	48	GHB	.626
49	LONE	.621	50	OLYB	.313	51	PABT	.228
52	PBR	.633	53	ADC	1.040	54	BFD	.549
55	HBL	1.195	56	DR	.590	57	PUL	.507
58	VO	.820	59	HIR	.473	60	KNY	.694
61	KO	.333	62	DOC	.114	63	PCI	1.980
64	PEP	1.146	65	RCC	.544	66	CBF	3.365
67	CHF	2.166						

observations used to compute the mean. The median is computed by ranking the observations from highest (9.162) to lowest (.114) and choosing that ratio which is midway on the distribution—the median of the 67 debt to equity ratios is .874.

Dispersion

Another feature of a distribution is its dispersion. The *standard deviation*—a common measure of dispersion—is estimated as follows:

$$\hat{\gamma}_2 = \sqrt{\frac{\sum_{i=1}^{n}(X_i - \bar{X})^2}{N-1}}$$

$$= 1.320. \tag{6.3}$$

If the debt to equity ratio were normally distributed, knowledge of γ_1 and γ_2 would be sufficient to generate the whole distribution; e.g., approximately two thirds of the distribution would lie within one standard deviation of the mean. A related measure of dispersion is the *variance*. This measure is estimated as the square of the standard deviation ($\gamma_2^2 = 1.742$).

Skewness

Detecting whether the distribution of the debt to equity ratio is normal involves several steps. A useful first step is to plot the sample distribution and compare it with that of a theoretical normal distribution with a mean of 1.126 and standard deviation of 1.320. Figure 6.1 presents the actual distributions of the debt to equity ratio. The theoretical normal distribution is also plotted on Figure 6.1. One feature of Figure 6.1 is that the actual distribution does not have the familiar bell-shaped curve of the theoretical normal distribution. The actual distribution is blunt on the left and has a long tail pointing to the right. The actual distribution in Figure 6.1 provides some evidence of positive skewness. A common measure of this skewness is the *skewness coefficient*:

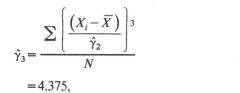

$$\hat{\gamma}_3 = \frac{\sum \left[\frac{\left(X_i - \bar{X} \right)}{\hat{\gamma}_2} \right]^3}{N}$$

$$= 4.375, \tag{6.4}$$

FIGURE 6.1   1974 Debt to Equity Ratios: Food and Kindred Products Industry

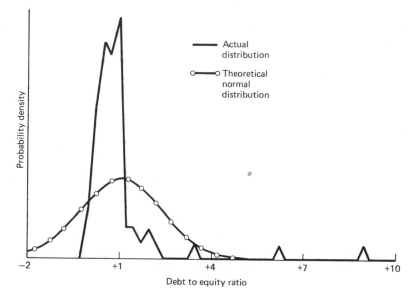

where $\hat{\gamma}_2$ is the estimated standard deviation of the debt to equity ratio. For a normal distribution, $\gamma_3 = 0$. For samples of 20–100 observations, a bench mark for suspecting positive (negative) skewness is $\gamma_3 > +.5 (\gamma_3 < -.5)$.

Kurtosis

A common test for normality is to compare the sample distribution in the tails with the distribution in the tails under a theoretical normal distribution. One statistic used in this comparison is the *kurtosis coefficient*:

$$\hat{\gamma}_4 = \frac{\sum \left(\frac{X_i - \bar{X}}{\hat{\gamma}_2}\right)^4}{N} - 3$$
$$= 21.520. \tag{6.5}$$

The kurtosis coefficient provides evidence on whether the distribution is more or less *fat-tailed* than would be expected from the normal distribution. For a normal distribution, $\gamma_4 = 0$. A convenient rule of thumb for suspecting violations from normality is $\gamma_4 > \pm 1$. A γ_4 of 21.520 is consistent with the debt to equity ratio being not well approximated by a normal distribution.

Studentized Range

Another measure of the dispersion of a distribution is the *studentized range* (S.R.). This statistic is the ratio of the sample range (largest observation minus smallest observation: $9.162 - .114$) to the sample standard deviation (1.320):

$$S.R. = \frac{X_{max} - X_{min}}{\hat{\gamma}_2}$$
$$= 6.854. \tag{6.6}$$

This statistic tends to be "large" for fat-tailed distributions. A rule of thumb for suspecting the underlying distribution to have fat tails when using 50 (100) sample observations is S.R. > 6 (6.5).

Fractiles of the Distribution

Useful insights into the distribution of a variable can often be obtained from the fractiles of the distribution. Computing such fractiles involves ranking the sample observations from highest to lowest and observing the actual (or implied) values at various points on the distribution. The deciles of the distribution (the $.9, .8, \ldots, .2, .1$ fractiles) of the debt to equity ratio are

				Deciles				
.9	.8	.7	.6	.5	.4	.3	.2	.1
1.610	1.151	1.068	.938	.874	.730	.623	.490	.333

A .1 decile of .333 means that 10% of the distribution of the debt to equity ratio lies below .333. Similarly, the .7 decile of 1.068 means that 70% of the distribution lies below 1.068. The .25 (.549) and .75 (1.116) fractiles are referred to as the lower and upper quartiles of the distribution. As noted previously, the .5 fractile is the median.[3]

Transformations as a Technique To Approximate Normality

Due to appealing features of the normal distribution (e.g., two statistics being sufficient to describe the distribution) and its role in many econometric tools, it is often useful to examine if some transformation of financial ratios can yield a distribution better approximating a normal. A common transformation for a positively skewed distribution is the natural logarithmic transformation, i.e.,

$$Z_i = \log(X_i).$$

A comparison of the distributions of X_i (actual debt to equity ratios) and Z_i (logs of debt to equity ratios) yields some interesting results:

	X_i	Z_i
$\hat{\gamma}_1$ (mean)	1.126	−.177
$\hat{\gamma}_2$ (std deviation)	1.320	.706
$\hat{\gamma}_3$ (skewness)	4.375	.474
$\hat{\gamma}_4$ (kurtosis)	21.520	2.003
S.R. (studentized range)	6.854	6.211

The logarithmic transformation has considerably reduced the violations from normality that were apparent in the distribution of the actual debt to equity ratios.

The logarithmic transformation is one of several that may be considered. Other alternatives include the power and square root transformations. Note that some transformations may be defined for only certain ranges of variables; e.g., the logarithm of a negative number is undefined. Thus, a logarithmic transformation may not be used for the distributions of financial ratios in which a negative number is possible, e.g., the return on equity ratio.

Some General Comments

When examining the distribution of a financial ratio, it is important to remember that *one rarely expects that the distribution of any one sample will exactly correspond to that implied by any one theoretical distribution.* Indeed, in small samples (say, 20–30 observations) it is often very hard, due to sampling variation, to identify the underlying distribution. If one were to start with a prior belief that the underlying distribution was normal, one would only look for systematic and substantial deviations from normality in the sample evidence before concluding normality was not a workable description of the underlying distribution.[4]

Care should be taken in interpreting the statistical significance of the skewness and kurtosis coefficients and of the studentized range for financial ratios. Significance tests for these statistics assume that each firm's ratio is an independent observation. The evidence in Chapter 5 suggests that such an assumption is not descriptively valid. Financial ratios appear to be cross-sectionally correlated due (at least) to economy-wide and industry-wide factors. This cross-sectional correlation means that a less than literal interpretation of significance levels for skewness, kurtosis, etc., is particularly appropriate. At a minimum, the degrees of freedom in such tests would appear to be less than if the ratios across firms were independent.

This cross-sectional correlation also has implications for any appeal to the central limit theorem as justification for assuming financial ratios are normally distributed. This theorem states that the sums of N independent and identically distributed random variables will approximate a normal distribution as N becomes large. There are two important provisos in this theorem: First, the random variables are independent. As noted above, this condition does not appear to be a descriptively valid one for many financial ratios. The second condition is that the random variables be identically (although not normally) distributed. Inasmuch as an identical distribution of a ratio across firms is a special case, there appears little economic rationale for expecting this special case to hold. At a minimum, differences across industries as regards concentration, barriers to entry, etc., may well mean that the distribution of a ratio across industries is not identical. In short, an appeal to the central limit theorem for assuming normality of financial ratio distributions is of questionable validity.

C Published Evidence on Distributions

Evidence on the dispersion and symmetry of distributions of financial ratios is presented in the publications of

(1) Dun & Bradstreet's *Key Business Ratios* [1976] and Robert Morris Associates' *Annual Statement Studies* [1976]—both give the .25, .5, and .75 fractiles of distributions of ratios for many industries—and

(2) Federal and state agencies; e.g., the Federal Deposit Insurance Corporations's *Bank Operating Statistics* [1975] gives the .1, .25, .5, .75, and .9 fractiles of the distributions of banking ratios.

Evidence on the symmetry of distributions can be gained by comparing the difference between selected fractiles of the distribution. Consider the net profits to tangible net worth ratio of three industries in Dun & Bradstreet's *Key Business Ratios* [1976]:

	Fractiles		
	.75	*.50*	*.25*
Drugs	18.86%	14.37%	7.46%
Hardware stores	16.38%	8.41%	4.68%
Millwork	12.65%	6.58%	3.27%

Positive (negative) skewness is indicated when the difference between the .75 fractile and the .5 fractile exceeds (is less than) the difference between the .5 fractile and the .25 fractile. Thus, both the hardware stores and millwork industries exhibit positive skewness, whereas the drugs industry exhibits negative skewness.

There is considerable evidence of positive skewness in the ratios of many of the 125 industries detailed in Dun & Bradstreet's *Key Business Ratios* [1976]. Table 6.2 contains the number (and percentage) of the 125 industries in which (upper quartile less median difference) > (median less

ABLE 6.2 Symmetry of Distributions of Financial Ratios for 125 Industries in Dun & Bradstreet [1976]

	Positive Skewness, $(UQ-M)>(M-LQ)$	$(UQ-M)=(M-LQ)$	*Negative Skewness,* $(UQ-M)<(M-LQ)$
Liquidity Current ratio	117 (93.6%)	0	8 (6.4%)
Leverage Total debt to tangible net worth	105 (84%)	0	20 (16%)
Profitability Net profits to tangible net worth	84 (67.2%)	0	41 (32.8%)
Turnover[a] Net sales to inventory	103 (85.8%)	3 (2.5%)	14 (11.7%)

KEY: UQ = upper quartile,
       M = median,
       LQ = lower quartile.

[a] For 5 of the 125 industries, details of this ratio not given.

lower quartile difference). This percentage was computed for one ratio in each of the four main ratio categories discussed in Chapter 2. The percentage of industries exhibiting positive skewness ranges from 67.2% for the profitability ratio to 93.6% for the liquidity ratio. Note that for each of the three ratios exhibiting strongest evidence of positive skewness (liquidity, leverage, and turnover) there is a lower bound of zero on the computed ratio. There is no zero bound on the net profits to tangible net worth ratio. Indeed, in some industries in *Key Business Ratios*, even the .25 fractile is negative for this ratio; e.g., the .25 fractile for the broad woven cotton fabrics industry is −4.18% in 1975.[5]

D Some Additional Evidence

The information in Table 6.2 is based on only the .25, .5, and .75 fractiles of four ratios. To gain additional insight into the distribution of ratios, the deciles of the distribution of 12 ratios were computed. The data base comprised all firms with 1975 data on the Annual Industrial *Compustat* tape. The 12 ratios examined were

Liquidity
  1. Current ratio (CR)
  2. Quick ratio (QR)
  3. Defensive interval (DI)

Leverage
  4. Debt to equity (DE)
  5. Long-term debt to equity (LTDE)
  6. Times interest earned (TIE)

Profitability
  7. Earnings to sales (ES)
  8. Return on assets (ROA)
  9. Return on equity (ROE)

Turnover
  10. Total asset turnover (TAT)
  11. Inventory turnover (IT)
  12. Accounts receivable turnover (ART)

The deciles of the distribution for each ratio are presented in Table 6.3. Note that several ratios exhibit marked positive skewness, e.g., all three liquidity rates, all three leverage ratios, and the inventory turnover and accounts receivable turnover ratios. The skewness (γ_3), kurtosis (γ_4), and studentized range (S.R.) statistics were also computed for each ratio. For

TABLE 6.3 Deciles of Distribution of Financial Ratios—All Industries: 1975

Ratio		.9	.8	.7	.6	Deciles .5	.4	.3	.2	.1	Number of Observations
1.	CR	3.90	3.15	2.69	2.38	2.10	1.84	1.58	1.31	1.03	2,389
2.	QR	2.24	1.70	1.42	1.24	1.09	.97	.86	.71	.50	2,233
3.	DI	147.65	112.81	96.86	84.52	75.04	67.98	59.46	49.60	31.97	2,162
4.	DE	2.23	1.54	1.26	1.06	.91	.75	.62	.48	.30	2,387
5.	LTDE	1.16	.85	.64	.49	.38	.30	.21	.10	.02	2,388
6.	TIE	10.67	6.28	4.69	3.75	3.08	2.62	2.22	1.76	1.15	2,384
7.	ES	.12	.08	.06	.05	.04	.03	.02	.01	−.01	2,546
8.	ROA	.11	.09	.08	.07	.06	.05	.04	.03	.01	2,499
9.	ROE	.24	.18	.16	.14	.12	.10	.08	.04	−.03	2,524
10.	TAT	2.39	1.86	1.61	1.42	1.27	1.10	.87	.54	.27	2,543
11.	IT	21.21	11.36	8.02	6.40	5.56	4.84	4.20	3.60	2.95	2,093
12.	ART	17.61	10.79	8.68	7.66	6.85	6.17	5.53	4.79	3.90	2,196

all 12 ratios, the normal distribution did not appear to be a descriptively valid distribution.[6]

As noted previously, a logarithmic transformation is often used in an attempt to reduce the positive skewness in some ratio distributions. Such a transformation did reduce skewness in the distribution of many ratios detailed in Table 6.3. For instance, the skewness coefficient of the distribution of (1) the actual ratios and (2) the logs of actual ratios for some selected ratios are

	Skewness Coefficient	
	Actual Ratio	Log of Actual Ratio
Current ratio	16.36	−2.56
Quick ratio	20.75	−1.67
Defensive interval	2.60	−.88
Debt to equity	6.47	−.49
Total debt to equity	26.72	−1.00
Total asset turnover	2.69	−1.24
Inventory turnover	5.38	.92
Accounts receivable turnover	5.31	−.29

For the other four ratios (TIE, ES, ROA, and ROE), the logarithmic transformation was inappropriate for the whole distribution, as negative ratios were encountered.

6.2 CORRELATION OF FINANCIAL RATIOS

The number of financial ratios one can compute from financial statements is obviously very high. Even within each of the main categories of ratios described in Chapter 2, there are a minimum of at least three or four different ratios proposed in the literature. How does one determine how many ratios to compute in each category? In general, this will depend on the specific decision context being considered. One important factor in this determination will be the extent to which the ratios in each category overlap in the information they provide about liquidity, leverage, profitability, or turnover. A useful first step in examining this issue is to compute the correlation between various ratios in each category. In Section 6.2A we shall examine the correlation between financial ratios at a point in time; i.e., it is a cross-sectional analysis. In Section 6.2B we shall examine the extent to which financial ratios move together over time; i.e., it is a time-series analysis.

Cross-sectional correlations between financial ratios are important when using such ratios in a statistical model. Consider a multiple regression model. One extreme case is where two ratios are the only independent variables and these two ratios happen to be perfectly collinear. In this case, one would not be able to compute estimates of the coefficients of the model.[7] A less extreme case is where two ratios in a model are less than perfectly correlated. In this case, problems exist in assessing the significance of individual variables in the multiple regression model. One consequence of multicollinearity between independent variables is that it is difficult to disentangle the influence of each variable. Moreover, the coefficients on the individual variables are quite sensitive to the number of observations used to estimate the model. A small change in the number of observations examined can often lead to a marked change in the estimated coefficients of the model (see Johnston [1972]).

A Cross-Sectional Correlation

The evidence in Section 6.1 indicated that a normal distribution is not always a descriptively valid description of the distribution of specific ratios. This evidence has implications when examining the correlation between financial ratios at a point in time. The two main statistics for examining the correlation between two variables are (1) the Pearson moment correlation statistic[8] and (2) the Spearman rank correlation statistic. The Pearson statistic is appropriate if the distribution of the two variables is approximately normal. In contrast, the Spearman statistic does not assume any specific distribution for the two variables. Due to the evidence in Section 6.1, the Spearman statistic is used in this section.

The Spearman rank correlation coefficient was described in Chapter 5. Recall that

$$r_s = 1 - \frac{6\Sigma d_i^2}{N^3 - N}, \qquad (6.7)$$

where d_i = disparity in rankings of the two variables,

N = number of observations.

Consider computing the correlation between the 1975 current and quick ratios of the ten brewing companies referred to in Chapter 2:

	CR	QR	Rank of CR	Rank of QR	d_i	d_i^2
Busch	2.602	1.750	1	1	0	0
Genesee	2.177	1.625	2	2	0	0
Pabst	2.145	1.207	3	3	0	0
Heileman	1.947	.985	4	4	0	0
Olympia	1.609	.675	5	7	-2	4
Coors	1.583	.421	6	10	-4	16
Schaefer	1.553	.800	7	6	1	1
Falstaff	1.441	.870	8	5	3	9
Schlitz	1.392	.608	9	8	1	1
Lone Star	1.320	.592	10	9	-1	1

$$\Sigma d_i^2 = 32$$

$$r_s = 1 - \frac{6 \times 32}{1,000 - 10} = .806.$$

An r_s of .806 for $N = 10$ indicates that there is a significant positive correlation between these two ratios for the brewing companies.

Table 6.4 presents the Spearman rank correlations between the 12 financial ratios outlined in Section 6.1. The correlations are for all firms on the annual industrial *Compustat* tape for 1975. The number of observations ranged from 1,978 for r_s between TIE and IT to 2,538 for r_s between ES and TAT. Some high positive correlations occur where expected; e.g., r_s of CR and QR = .74, DE and LTDE = .80, and ROA and ROE = .80. In part, these high correlations reflect the influence of common items in each ratio. Note, also, that some negative correlations occur where expected; e.g., LTDE and TIE = −.56. When a firm issues new debt, this increases the numerator of the LTDE ratio and increases the denominator of the TIE ratio.

**5.4   Cross-Sectional Correlations of Financial Ratios—All Industries: 1975
(Spearman rank correlation coefficients)**

	CR	QR	DI	DE	LTDE	TIE	ES	ROA	ROE	TAT	IT	ART
CR	1.00											
QR	.74	1.00										
DI	.20	.52	1.00									
DE	−.58	−.52	−.18	1.00								
LTDE	−.39	−.29	−.12	.80	1.00							
TIE	.30	.33	.12	−.59	−.56	1.00						
ES	.02	.32	.40	−.33	−.17	.56	1.00					
ROA	.22	.26	.11	−.40	−.33	.85	.63	1.00				
ROE	.01	.11	.06	−.12	−.13	.64	.60	.80	1.00			
TAT	.25	−.04	−.56	−.09	−.28	.33	−.37	.31	.20	1.00		
IT	−.42	.01	−.15	.05	.09	.16	.10	.18	.26	.23	1.00	
ART	−.10	−.30	−.73	−.05	.00	.15	−.08	.17	.16	.49	.37	1.00

General Comments

A high correlation between financial ratios used in a regression model does not necessarily mean that one wants to delete ratios from the model. The regression model might be specified by some theory (e.g., of corporate failure), and a model excluding certain specified ratios may well not be a test of the descriptive validity of the theoretical model. Note, moreover, that even if one is concerned with building a parsimonious model, deleting financial ratios from the model is not the only alternative open to an analyst. For instance, a statistical tool such as factor analysis can be used prior to estimating the regression model. This tool aims at capturing the information contained in many variables and representing that information by a smaller number of derived variables. In Section 6.2C we shall discuss an application of this tool. Even if there is little theory underlying the choice of ratios in a regression model, it is not always the case that one requires all independent variables to be orthogonal (i.e., uncorrelated with each other). If the concern is with explaining variations in the dependent variable, then including two nonorthogonal ratios may well explain more variation than using either of the ratios as single independent variables.

B   Time-Series Correlation

Financial ratios are also used to assess changes in the liquidity profitability, etc., of firms over time. As with cross-sectional tools, the issue arises of how many ratios to examine in such time-series assessments. One

approach to gaining evidence on this issue is to examine the extent to
which financial ratios move together. Changes in the return on assets
(ROA) and the return on equity (ROE) of *Trans World Airlines* over the
1960–1970 period will be used to illustrate one mode of examination:

	ROA_t	ROE_t	Sign of $ROA_t - ROA_{t-1}$	Sign of $ROE_t - ROE_{t-1}$
1960	.024	.053		
1961	−.014	−.140	−	−
1962	.008	−.069	+	+
1963	.059	.217	+	+
1964	.083	.305	+	+
1965	.091	.268	+	−
1966	.054	.120	−	−
1967	.055	.144	+	+
1968	.030	.069	−	−
1969	.028	.066	−	−
1970	−.032	−.233	−	−

In nine out of the ten yearly changes, both the ROA and the ROE had the
same sign. Only in the 1965–1964 period did they differ—ROA increased,
whereas ROE decreased. In part, this high correlation (90%) in the signs of
the year-to-year changes is due to the common elements found in both
ratios. Another reason for the high correlation is that both ratios are
influenced by common economy-wide and industry-wide factors (see
Chapter 5).

Table 6.5 contains the percentage agreement in the signs of one-year
changes of the 12 ratios detailed in Section 6.1D. The percentages are for

TABLE 6.5 Percentage of Times Ratios Have Same Sign
of Yearly Change—All Industries: 1975

	CR	QR	DI	DE	LTDE	TIE	ES	ROA	ROE	TAT	IT
CR											
QR	85%										
DI	56	67%									
DE	30	34	53%								
LTDE	15	24	52	81%							
TIE	50	52	53	39	48%						
ES	49	52	56	46	51	81%					
ROA	47	49	50	48	54	76	84%				
ROE	45	47	51	53	57	74	82	89%			
TAT	45	46	40	50	56	63	57	72	68%		
IT	46	53	50	50	53	64	61	68	67	75%	
ART	48	47	40	49	52	60	57	64	63	72	65%

all firms listed on the annual industrial *Compustat* tape covering the 1957–1975 period. As with the cross-sectional correlations between ratios, the influence of common components in financial ratios appears to explain many of the high percentage agreements in Table 6.5, e.g., the 85% agreement between CR and QR, the 81% agreement between DE and LTDE, and the 89% agreement between ROA and ROE.[9] One result that is "surprising" in Table 6.5 is the 15% agreement between CR and LTDE; i.e., in 85% of the cases examined, the current ratio and the long-term debt to equity ratio moved in opposite directions. In part, this could be a result of the period examined. Over the 1957–1975 period there has been a systematic decrease in the average current ratios of firms and a systematic increase in the long-term debt to equity ratios of firms—see the economy-wide indexes presented in the appendix to Chapter 5.

C   Categories of Financial Ratios

The categorization of financial ratios outlined in Chapter 2, although frequently exposited in the literature, has little explicit theoretical or empirical underpinnings. There is little in economic theory that suggests that the liquidity, leverage, profitability, and turnover categories constitute either a mutually exclusive or collectively exhaustive set of financial characteristics of a firm. Moreover, until recently there has been little empirical analysis of how different financial ratios reflect different financial characteristics of firms. A study by Pinches et al. [1973] contains some interesting preliminary empirical evidence on this topic.

Pinches et al. criticized the traditional classification schemes of financial ratios as (1) being "ad hoc" and (2) failing to "take account of the empirical relationships existing between and among financial ratios." They then attempted to develop "empirically-based classifications of financial ratios" (p. 389). The sample was 221 *Compustat* industrial firms over the 1951–1969 period. Factor analysis was used to group 40 financial ratios into a smaller number of independent categories. Factor analysis is a statistical technique that attempts to reduce a set of variables into a smaller set of derived factors. These "factor patterns have the property of retaining the maximum amount of information (explaining the maximum variance) contained in the original data matrix" (p. 389).[10] Seven factors or classifications of the financial ratios were identified. Based on the financial ratios that grouped with each factor, Pinches et al. attached the following labels to these seven factors:

(1) Return on investment,

(2) Financial leverage,

(3) Capital intensiveness,

(4) Inventory intensiveness,

(5) Receivables intensiveness,

(6) Short-term liquidity, and

(7) Cash position.

Although several of the factors were similar to traditional ones exposited in the literature, several differences are apparent. Three separate patterns of intensiveness (activity) were identified; under the traditional classification, ratios such as total assets turnover, inventory turnover, and receivables turnover are grouped under one general "activity" category. Note also that cash-based ratios (e.g., cash to total assets, cash to fund expenditures, etc.) were separately grouped from liquidity ratios (e.g., current ratio, quick ratio, etc.). The above seven factors accounted for approximately 90% of the variance in the original data matrix of 40 financial ratios.[11]

One motivation for grouping financial ratios into categories is to facilitate understanding and prediction of financial patterns in a firm. Although the approach of Pinches et al. [1973] offers interesting evidence, it is likely that no one classification will be appropriate for the varied contexts in which financial statements are used. An interesting issue, yet to be explored, is what similarities in contexts exist when one categorization system is deemed preferable to other categorization systems.

6.3 FINANCIAL RATIOS AND ACCOUNTING ALTERNATIVES

In this section, two issues relating to the effect of alternative accounting rules on financial ratios will be discussed:

(1) What is the effect on computed financial ratios of all firms consistently using accounting alternative A vis-à-vis all firms consistently using alternative B?

(2) What is the effect on computed financial ratios if a subset of firms uses accounting alternative A while another subset uses accounting alternative B?

A Uniformity and Financial Ratios

The effect on computed financial ratios of alternative measurement rules for two accounting issues will be discussed: (1) the LIFO vs. FIFO inventory valuation issue and (2) the historical cost vs. general price level adjusted accounting (GPLA) issue. An interesting feature of several studies that have examined these issues is the particular adjustment techniques used to derive accounting numbers not reported in published annual reports.

LIFO vs. FIFO

Derstine and Huefner [1974] examined the effect of the LIFO vs. FIFO inventory valuation methods on several ratios of 24 companies over the 1951–1960 period. One technique used to derive the LIFO and FIFO sets of accounts utilized information made available at the time of an accounting change:

> For companies which changed [inventory] methods, some of the actual data was on a LIFO basis and some on a FIFO basis. For example, if a company switched from FIFO to LIFO in 1956, we would have FIFO data for 1951–55 and LIFO data for 1956–60. For at least the year 1956, both LIFO and FIFO figures would be disclosed. Thus we would need to construct LIFO data for 1951–55 and FIFO data for 1957–60. This second set of financial data was constructed using the Dollar-Value LiFO technique.... This technique adjusts reported FIFO inventory amounts to remove changes in these amounts due solely to price changes. The price change component in inventory is removed by using price indices to express reported inventory amounts in terms of base year prices. Only the actual quantity change (the difference between the current inventory converted to base year prices and the actual base year inventory) is then used as a basis for determining the incremental (or decremental) LIFO layer adjustment to the LIFO inventory.... Industrial price indices were selected, from the *Federal Reserve Bulletin*, to correspond as closely as possible to the industrial classifications of the twenty-four firms in our sample....

> The conversion by the Dollar-Value LIFO method appeared to provide a good estimate of what inventory values would have been under the alternative method. We found forty-seven cases where the inventory value under the alternative method was disclosed in the financial statements. We compared these values to our calculated values, and observed that our calculated values had no apparent bias (twenty-five were higher than the disclosed value, twenty-two lower). In total, our calculated values represented 102 percent of the disclosed values.... (pp. 218–219)

Using the above technique, LIFO and FIFO statements for each of the 24 firms over the 1951–1960 period were computed. For each inventory valuation method the average dividend payout ratio and the average leverage ratio over the 1951–1960 period were computed. The Spearman rank correlation coefficient between the LIFO and FIFO computed average ratio of each of the 24 firms was then computed. The Spearman rank correlation was .971 for the dividend payout ratio and .997 for the leverage ratio (total debt to total assets). An interesting analysis, not presented in Derstine and Huefner [1974], would be to examine the effect of consistent use of LIFO vs. FIFO on ratios in which inventories generally form a larger component of the numerator or denominator—e.g., the current ratio or the inventory turnover ratio.

In an earlier study, Holden [1964] examined the effect of LIFO vs. FIFO on the current ratio, the inventory turnover ratio, and the net profit to sales ratio. Data to convert the accounts to either inventory method were obtained from either the annual report or from private correspondence with companies. The sample comprised 12 companies over the 1950–1958 period. Although Holden [1964] did not compute correlations between the LIFO and FIFO ratios, there is sufficient information in the paper to calculate the Spearman rank correlation coefficient. The correlations for selected years were

	1951	1953	1955	1957
Current ratio	1.00	.822	.969	.958
Inventory turnover ratio	.892	.895	.972	.927
Net profit to sales	.993	.965	.965	.986

These high correlations are consistent with those Derstine and Huefner [1974] reported for the dividend payout and leverage ratios.

Many discussions of the LIFO/FIFO alternatives stress the absolute dollar differences in the resultant inventory or cost of goods sold figures. Often a single instance, with seemingly large numerical differences, is chosen for illustrative purposes. The important features of the Derstine and Huefner [1974] and Holden [1964] papers are (1) larger samples were chosen to analyze the issue, and (2) the instances examined were not ex post chosen because they showed "large differences." The results were quite different from that implied by many LIFO/FIFO discussions. On balance, the results suggest little differences in the ranking of firms if either inventory valuation method is consistently used. It is important, however, not to assume that the above results necessarily apply to all firms in the economy or to inventory price patterns different from that experienced in the periods examined.

Historical Cost vs. General Price Level Adjusted Accounting

Numerous studies have been published in which the historical cost accounts of a company are contrasted with the general price level adjusted (GPLA) accounts of a company. Rosenfield [1969] is illustrative of such studies. In 1963, Accounting Research Study No. 6 (*Reporting the Financial Effects of Price-Level Changes*) was published by the AICPA. To gain more information on "the practical effects" of GPLA restatements, the AICPA conducted a "field test." Eighteen companies adjusted their financial statements for changes in the general price level using the techniques set out in Accounting Research Study No. 6. Rosenfield's conclusions were based on the extent of the numerical differences in net income: "Using net income under general price level accounting as the standard, the field test showed that ignoring inflation in historical-dollar statements results in understating net income for some companies and overstating net income for other companies" (p. 47). One issue ignored by Rosenfield was the correlation between the historical cost rate of return and the GPLA rate of return. On this issue, the similarities between the two measures are more marked than Rosenfield implies. The Spearman rank correlation between the historical cost rate of return and the GPLA rate of return of the 13 companies disclosing these figures was .87 (Pearson correlation coefficient = .98).

The GPLA data examined in Rosenfield were provided by individual companies. An interesting analysis of the effect of GPLA on financial ratios for firms which did not report these numbers is provided by Petersen [1973]. Petersen used some approximating methods to GPLA adjust the statements of 65 companies randomly selected from the May 1970 *Fortune* list of the 500 largest industrial U.S. corporations. Some details of the approximating methods are the following:

> The general solution procedure employed necessarily must be developed on a set of heuristic observations concerning financial information. For example, certain financial statement items like foreign currency and claims to foreign currency, marketable securities (stocks), nonmonetary advances and prepaid assets are most usually acquired during the preceding twelve-month period; therefore, the restatement procedure treats all such items as if they were acquired at the average price level which existed during the preceding twelve-month period. In a like manner the problem of inventories can be handled by making certain observations regarding the nature of the various inventory valuation methods and coupling these observations with some informed guesses regarding probable age. For example, the estimated age of FIFO inventories was developed using inventory turnover as a basic indicator of average age. LIFO and average cost inventory age was estimated by using regression procedures to estimate a functional relationship of the following form:

$$Y = b_0 + b_1(x).$$

> where Y = the dollar magnitude of total basic cost inventories
>
> x = year.

> This functional relation was used in turn to estimate the rate of inventory growth over time and the probable average age of such inventory.

> The average age of Property, Plant and Equipment Accounts was estimated by relating annual depreciation expense to the balance in accumulated depreciation. A separate routine was developed for straight-line, double-declining balance and sum-of-the-years digits methods. Asset cost, accumulated depreciation, and depreciation expense were restated in turn using the information generated by these estimation routines.

> Sales, other expense items, and federal income tax expense items were treated as if they were incurred evenly throughout the accounting period. Cost of sales was determined by assuming that purchases occurred evenly throughout the year and by applying the price-level restated opening and closing inventory restatement determined in the inventory adjustment routine. Finally, owner's equity balances were determined as a function of the numeric relation between all other price-level adjusted balances in the system at a point in time. (pp. 35-36)

Petersen then examined whether these techniques yielded GPLA numbers similar to those reported by companies who had actually issued GPLA statements. Results presented in Petersen [1973] suggest his techniques approximated actual company-reported GPLA numbers quite well. The second stage in Petersen's analysis included a comparison of the rankings of companies based on (1) GPLA numbers and (2) historical cost numbers for the return on equity and net income ratio. The Spearman rank correlation coefficients were .974 for the return on equity ratio and .989 for net income.

The most detailed comparisons between historical cost and GPLA numbers are in the Davidson and Weil [1975] papers. Based on detailed approximating techniques to derive the GPLA numbers, they have presented GPLA figures for a broad cross section of U.S. industry. The correlations between the historical cost and GPLA numbers suggest that general conclusions about the effect of GPLA for all companies are difficult to derive. For instance, for the 30 Dow-Jones Industrials in 1974 the Spearman rank correlation between the historical cost and GPLA rate of return on total stockholders' equity is .771. Table 6.6 presents these rates of return for each company. The comparable correlations in the Rosenfield [1969] and Petersen [1973] studies were .870 and .974, respectively.[12] In part, these differences could be explained by different techniques used to derive the GPLA numbers. Nonetheless, these differences suggest that the effect of GPLA adjustment differs across different samples of firms. An interesting economic issue would be to a priori determine what financial characteristics of firms lead to these differences in the effect of GPLA adjustments.[13]

The above studies are descriptive exercises which provide information on the properties of alternative accounting systems. In interpreting these studies it is important to realize that there is no one-to-one correspondence between correlation coefficients and the information content of alternative accounting systems. The framework outlined in Chapter 1 indicates that the context in which the information system is used is important. In subsequent chapters, the effect of using alternative accounting systems in specific decision contexts is examined in some detail.

TABLE 6.6 Dow Jones Industrials Rate of Return on
Total Stockholders' Equity for 1974

	Historical Cost Basis		GPLA Basis	
	Rate	Rank	Rank	Rate
Union Carbide	19.7%	1	5	11.0%
Anaconda	19.5	2	1	11.6
Exxon	18.2	3	8	10.3
International Paper	18.2	4	12	8.5
Eastman Kodak	17.8	5	10	9.6
International Nickel	17.8	6	2	11.5
General Electric	16.9	7	9	10.0
Texaco	15.2	8	7	10.6
Procter & Gamble	15.0	9/10	6	11.0
Standard Oil of California	15.0	9/10	11	8.5
U.S. Steel	13.6	11	18	5.7
Allied Chemical	13.6	12	15	7.0
American Brands	13.1	13	4	11.0
United Technologies	13.0	14	26	2.3
Bethlehem Steel	12.6	15	19	5.5
Esmark	12.6	16	20	5.2
American Can	12.4	17	16	6.9
Johns Manville	11.6	18	13	7.9
General Foods	10.9	19	21	5.0
Du Pont	10.8	20	23	3.4
Alcoa	10.3	21	17	6.7
Owens-Illinois	9.9	22	14	7.9
AT&T	9.5	23	3	11.1
International Harvester	8.9	24	25	2.8
Goodyear	8.5	25	22	4.7
Sears	8.3	26	27	−.3
General Motors	7.7	27	28	−1.9
Woolworth	6.5	28	24	3.4
Westinghouse Electric	1.4	29	29	−1.6
Chrysler	−1.9	30	30	−3.4
Median	12.6%			7.0%
Interquartile range	16.1%–9.2%			10.5%–3.4%

Source: S. Davidson and R. L. Weil (unpublished).

B Diversity and Financial Ratios

The second issue as regards financial ratios and accounting alternatives arises when a subset of firms uses accounting alternative A (say, straight-line depreciation) and another subset uses alternative B (say, accelerated depreciation). This issue has attracted considerable attention from many authors. A common mode of exposition is to choose a hypothetical company and examine the effect of using different accounting techniques. For instance, Greer [1938] showed that the reported profits of a group of companies over an eight-year period could range from $125 million to $275 million, depending on the specific accounting rules used. Spacek [1959] conducted an exercise that was similar to that of Greer. He showed that by choice of different accounting rules (as to inventory, depreciation, research and development costs, pension plan costs, stock options, and capital gain recognition) the reported earnings per share of a hypothetical company could be as different as $.80 and $1.79. Several comments can be made about these examples. First, the hypothetical cases are explicitly chosen to show large numerical differences in reported income. No details are generally given as to whether the reported differences are representative of those encountered in practice. Second, the use of different accounting alternatives by different companies does not, *in itself*, imply anything about the effect of such diversity on users of financial statement information. Some argue that this diversity is a major limitation of conventional accounting. Several factors need to be considered on this diversity issue.

The context in which the financial data are used is important. Suppose one were only interested in ranking companies in terms of a leverage ratio. If the use of diverse accounting rules did not change the rankings of companies vis-à-vis what they would have been if uniform accounting rules had been used, then the diversity in accounting rules *in this context* would pose no problem. Derstine and Huefner [1974] provided some evidence on this issue in their previously discussed paper. In addition to the consistent use of LIFO vs. consistent use of FIFO, they also examined the consistent use of LIFO (FIFO) vs. a mixed LIFO/FIFO sample. For the leverage ratio, the correlation for the LIFO sample vs. mixed sample was 1.00, while for the FIFO sample vs. mixed sample the correlation was .996. The corresponding correlations for the dividend payout ratio were .981 and .980, respectively.

A second factor to be considered as regards diverse accounting measurements and their effect on users is the availability of methods to adjust reported numbers to reduce such diversity. The adjustment techniques detailed in Derstine and Huefner [1974], Petersen [1973], and Davidson and Weil [1975] are examples of the use of information not found in annual reports to estimate nonreported accounting numbers. Other adjustment techniques are also available. For instance, Comiskey [1969] illustrates how information in the deferred income tax account can be used to estimate the income that an accelerated depreciation company would report if it had used straight-line depreciation. Moreover, in other cases, information disclosed in footnotes may be sufficient to adjust the reported numbers to those reported under an alternative measurement rule. Several examples of using such footnote information were given in Chapter 2. In subsequent chapters use will be made of these adjustment techniques, footnote information, etc., when examining the reaction of investors and creditors to diverse accounting measurements.

The above comments are not intended to imply that diversity in accounting procedures poses no problems in financial analysis. Rather, they are made to illustrate that options to *reduce* these problems do exist. The word reduce rather than eliminate is used deliberately. Consider the option of using adjustment techniques. At present, there is limited evidence on the accuracy of these techniques. For instance, Barefield and Comiskey [1971] used the depreciation adjustment technique outlined by Comiskey [1969]. They assumed a tax rate of 50% for all 26 companies in their analysis and that all the change in the deferred tax liability arose from depreciation items. Both assumptions appear open to question. Yet, the critical issue is how well do the derived estimates approximate those a company would actually report. The information made available at the time firms make accounting changes can be useful in testing these approximations. Firms often disclose the effect of both accelerated and straight-line in the year of a change from accelerated to straight-line. With this disclosure one can test the accuracy of techniques to estimate accelerated (straight-line) income for straight-line (accelerated) reporters. Hopefully, more authors in the future will provide evidence on the accuracy as well as the mechanical aspects of proposed adjustment techniques.

6.4 SUMMARY

In this chapter we have examined various aspects pertaining to financial ratios. Our concern has been to illustrate ways of examining issues such as the distribution of financial ratios and correlations between financial ratios. It is important to obtain some feel for the data being analyzed in any study. Hopefully, one brings to any empirical exercise prior notions of what to expect in the data as regards these issues. These notions could be based on theoretical considerations or on previous empirical experience with financial ratios. The evidence in the sample data can then be combined with these prior notions when deciding such issues as (1) Are a firm's ratios significantly different from the industry norms? (2) How parsimonious a set of ratios should be used when examining the leverage of a firm or an industry? (3) What statistical tool should be used for predicting some event of interest?

NOTES

[1]For proof of this inequality, see Wadsworth and Bryan [1974, Chapter 7].

[2]Sharpe [1971] illustrates the use of this technique in security risk estimation.

[3]It is interesting to note that one financial information service— *Bankcorp.*, a firm that provides information on 50 major banks—reports both the value of a financial ratio for each bank and the decile of the distribution of the ratio for the 50 banks that the ratio falls in.

[4]In examining distributional evidence, it is often useful to see if inferences about nonnormality are heavily affected by one or two extreme observations. One check on this is to delete the highest (9.162) and lowest (.114) observations and then recompute the above statistics for skewness, etc. The statistics for this reduced sample of 65 observations are $\hat{\gamma}_1 = 1.018$, $\hat{\gamma}_2 = .873$, $\hat{\gamma}_3 = 4.006$, $\hat{\gamma}_4 = 20.781$, and S.R. $= 7.105$. That is, one would still reject the normality assumption for the reduced sample. The distribution of the reduced sample is often referred to as a *truncated* distribution.

[5]See also Deakin [1976] for published evidence on the distribution of financial ratios.

[6]These statistics for several ratios were

	γ_3	γ_4	S.R.
Current ratio	16.36	358.55	26.18
Debt to equity	6.47	77.01	22.74
Return on equity	−6.39	135.83	27.97
Inventory turnover	2.69	12.56	9.26

[7]The technical reason for this is that computing the coefficients of a multiple regression model involves inverting a matrix, and an inverse of a matrix does not exist when two columns of a matrix are perfectly collinear.

[8]The Pearson moment correlation statistic is computed as

$$r = \frac{N \Sigma X_i Y_i - (\Sigma X_i)(\Sigma Y_i)}{\sqrt{\left[N \Sigma X_i^2 - (\Sigma X_i)^2 \right]\left[N \Sigma Y_i^2 - (\Sigma Y_i)^2 \right]}},$$

where X_i and Y_i are the two variables being correlated and N is the number of observations. Consider the two variables used to compute the Spearman rank correlation coefficient in Chapter 5, i.e., the equal-weighted (X_i) and value-weighted (Y_i) economy average for the return on total assets ratio:

	X_i	Y_i
1970	.052	.044
1971	.055	.045
1972	.060	.046
1973	.066	.053
1974	.067	.056
1975	.057	.047

$$\Sigma X_i = .357 \qquad \Sigma X_i^2 = .021423 \qquad \Sigma X_i Y_i = .017452.$$
$$\Sigma Y_i = .291 \qquad \Sigma Y_i^2 = .014231$$

These values imply $r = .942$. As with the Spearman rank correlation coefficient, the range of r is from -1 to 1, with 1 (-1) indicating perfect positive (negative) correlation between the two variables.

[9]Davidson et al. [1964] provide evidence similar to that in Table 6.5 for the current ratio and the defensive interval measure over the 1954–1960 period. These two ratios moved in the same direction for 57% of the cases examined.

[10]For further discussion of factor analysis, see Lawley and Maxwell [1971] or Rummell [1970]. Stevens [1973] provides another illustration of the use of factor analysis in a financial context.

[11]In an extension of this study, Pinches et al. [1975] examined the short-term stability of empirically based financial ratio groups over the 1966–1969 time period. They reported finding stability of the factor loadings identified in 1969 in 1966, 1967, and 1968.

[12]Basu and Hanna [1976] and Parker [1977] provide additional evidence on the effect of GPLA procedures on the financial ratios of Canadian and U.S. companies, respectively. Both works provide detailed descriptions of the GPLA approximating techniques used. The Basu and Hanna book is especially interesting due to the attempt to validate the approximating techniques used in the analysis—see Basu and Hanna [1976, Appendix A].

[13]Revsine and Thies [1976] provide an interesting exploratory study on this issue—they examine the effect of productivity changes on the reported numbers of alternative accounting systems.

QUESTIONS

QUESTION 6.1:   Distribution of Bank Financial Ratios

The 1974 issue of *Bank Operating Statistics*, published by the Federal Deposit Insurance Corporation [1975], included the following details on the distribution of financial ratios for "insured commerical banks" (Tables F and G):

Ratio	Fractiles	All Banks (%)
1. Cash and due from banks, U.S. Treasury Securities, & other U.S. govt. issues divided by total assets	10	15.8
	25	19.9
	50	26.0
	75	34.4
	90	44.8
2. Obligations of states, etc., divided by total assets	10	1.4
	25	7.3
	50	12.5
	75	17.3
	90	21.9
3. Total capital accounts divided by total assets	10	6.4
	25	7.2
	50	8.3
	75	9.7
	90	12.0
4. Loans and discounts divided by total deposits	10	46.8
	25	56.2
	50	66.3
	75	74.3
	90	81.6
5. Rate of return on loans	10	7.94
	25	8.42
	50	9.00
	75	9.70
	90	10.46
6. Total operating income divided by total assets	10	6.57
	25	6.94
	50	7.39
	75	7.95
	90	8.59
7. Loan reserves divided by loans	10	.34
	25	.86
	50	1.29
	75	1.56
	90	1.76
8. Provision for loan losses divided by loans	10	.04
	25	.09
	50	.22
	75	.42
	90	.69

REQUIRED

(1) Which ratio has the strongest evidence of positive skewness in its distribution? Which ratio has the strongest evidence of negative skewness in its distribution? Comment on the results.

(2) Suppose that a bank had a "provision for loan losses to loans" ratio of .80 and that the distribution of this ratio for all banks had a mean (X) of .25 and a standard deviation (σ) of .25. Assume the distribution is normally distributed. Is this bank's ratio statistically different (at the .95 level) from the industry mean?

(3) Assume that in answering (2) one decided that the industry distribution was not normally distributed. Using Tchebysheff's inequality, is the bank's loan loss ratio of .8 significantly different (at the .95 level) from the industry mean? Explain any differences in the answers to (2) and (3).

QUESTION 6.2: Distribution of Industry Financial Ratios

Dun & Bradstreet [1976] presents details of the upper quartile (UQ), median (M), and lower quartile (LQ) of the distributions of 14 financial ratios for 125 industries. Table 6.7 presents these data for 12 of these industries for the following three ratios:

Net Profit on Net Sales. Obtained by dividing net earnings of the business, after taxes, by net sales (the dollar volume less returns, allowances, and cash discounts).

Collection Period. Annual net sales are divided by 365 days to obtain average daily credit sales.

Current Debt to Tangible Net Worth. Derived by dividing Current Debt by Tangible Net Worth. (pp. 2–3)

REQUIRED

(1) Which ratio exhibits the most consistent evidence of positive skewness over the 12 industries presented? Present your results in a format similar to Table 6.2. What factors may explain differences across ratios in their skewness?

(2) The data underlying Table 6.7 are ranked from highest to lowest when determining the upper and lower quartiles. In contrast, Dun & Bradstreet arrange the ratios "in order of size—the best ratio at the top, the weakest at the bottom" (p. 2). Thus, for instance, Dun & Bradstreet refer to 58.5 as the lower quartile for the current debt to tangible net worth ratio of the bakery products industry. What problems may arise in deciding what is the "best" ratio and what is the "weakest" ratio as opposed to deciding what is the highest and what is the lowest?

TABLE 6.7 Distribution of Industry Financial Ratios: 1975

Industry	Net Profits on Net Sales (%)			Collection Period (days)			Current Debt to Tangible Net Worth (%)		
	UQ	M	LQ	UQ	M	LQ	UQ	M	LQ
Agricultural chemicals	10.09	6.60	4.35	63	38	16	82.9	53.8	35.3
Bakery products	5.66	2.95	1.78	35	24	17	58.5	34.0	23.3
Broad woven fabrics, cotton	2.63	1.79	-1.48	75	58	40	57.1	34.1	17.9
Dresses: Women's, misses', & juniors'	1.67	.50	-.66	64	51	34	160.5	93.3	36.7
Confectionary & related products	4.39	3.24	-.13	29	16	8	84.1	43.8	16.1
Drugs	10.16	6.15	3.27	77	59	44	59.9	45.0	30.5
Hosiery	3.52	1.41	-1.18	67	49	33	68.3	41.5	16.5
Malt liquors	4.05	3.23	-1.03	19	12	8	49.8	35.2	25.4
Meat packing plants	2.33	1.09	.40	18	15	12	100.0	42.0	21.5
Motor vehicle parts & accessories	4.85	3.51	1.55	60	45	37	71.1	41.2	24.3
Soft drinks, bottled & canned	8.53	6.46	3.62	22	17	14	52.9	31.8	19.0
Work clothing, men's & boys'	5.45	3.37	2.40	58	42	32	97.0	43.7	16.5

PROPERTIES OF ACCOUNTING NUMBERS   198

QUESTION 6.3:   Correlation Between Financial Ratios

There is substantial evidence that financial ratios are correlated, both in cross-sectional and time-series contexts. Horrigan [1965] made the following comment on this collinearity:

> This presence of collinearity is both a blessing and a curse for financial ratio analysis. It means that only a small number of financial ratios are needed to capture most of the information that ratios can provide, but it also means that this small number must be selected very carefully. A selection of collinear ratios which are related to a dependent variable in the same fashion would obscure and possibly worsen the results of multivariate analyses. It is clear that large numbers of financial ratios cannot be computed willy-nilly in an analysis. The collinearity of these ratios requires that a careful and parsimonious selection be carried out. (p. 561)

REQUIRED

(1) What factors could account for the observed correlation between financial ratios?

(2) Evaluate the above argument of Horrigan.

QUESTION 6.4:   R & D Accounting Alternatives and Financial Ratios

FASB Statement No. 2 [1974]—*Accounting for Research & Development Costs*—specifies that expensing is the only acceptable method of reporting research and development (R & D) costs in published financial statements. This specification, however, does not mean that financial analysts are restricted to the expensing alternative. Given the disclosure of annual R & D costs in the income statement, it is possible to approximate what the financial statements would report with R & D capitalized and amortized over (say) five years on a straight-line basis. The relationship between reported figures using the expense alternative and the adjusted figures using the capitalization alternative is approximated by

$$RD_t^C = .2\left(RD_t^R + RD_{t-1}^R + RD_{t-2}^R + RD_{t-3}^R + RD_{t-4}^R\right)$$
$$TA_t^C = TA_t^R + \left(.8 \times RD_t^R + .6 \times RD_{t-1}^R + .4 \times RD_{t-2}^R + .2 \times RD_{t-3}^R\right)$$
$$I_t^C = I_t^R + \left(RD_t^R - RD_t^C\right),$$

where RD_t^R = research and development expense as reported (i.e., under the expense alternative),

RD_t^C = research and development expense under the capitalization alternative,

TA_t^R = total assets as reported,

TA_t^C = total assets under the capitalization alternative,

I_t^R = net income as reported,

I_t^C = net income under the capitalization alternative.

The data in Table 6.8 are RD_t^R, TA_t^R, I_t^R, and sales of seven pharmaceutical firms. The data are in \$000,000's, and RD_t^R has been rounded to the nearest \$5 million (to reduce your computational burden!).

TABLE 6.8 Pharmaceutical Company Data

Companies	Research & Development Expenditures					Net Income,	Sales,	Total Assets,
	1970	1971	1972	1973	1974	1974	1974	1974
1. Abbott Laboratories	25	30	30	35	40	80	765	817
2. Bristol-Myers Co.	35	40	45	50	55	120	1,591	1,041
3. Johnson & Johnson	40	45	55	70	85	162	1,937	1,406
4. Merck & Co.	70	70	80	90	105	210	1,330	1,243
5. Pfizer, Inc.	30	35	45	55	70	135	1,542	1,683
6. Searle (G.D.) & Co.	20	25	35	45	55	72	621	734
7. Smithkline Corp.	30	35	40	40	45	58	518	511

REQUIRED

(1) Estimate the following financial ratios of the seven companies for 1974 with (a) R & D expensed and (b) R & D capitalized and amortized on a straight-line basis over five years:

   (a) Net income to sales,

   (b) Net income to total assets, and

   (c) Sales to total assets.

What is the Spearman rank correlation coefficient for each ratio between the expense and capitalization alternatives?

(2) An executive of a pharmaceutical company described the above capitalization adjustment technique as naive—it assumed the same capitalization and amortization rate for all companies and for all products. On what dimensions could you as an external analyst make the technique more refined? What *evidence* could you use to document that any adjustments you make to the five-year straight-line amortization technique are indeed refinements?

(3) At the time the FASB was considering alternative methods to account for R & D expenditures, it was argued that the alternative adopted would have the following economic consequences:

   (a) Immediate expensing of R & D costs would bias managers against investments in R & D (in comparison with capitalizable investments), and

(b) Immediate expensing of R & D costs, which in many cases would result in lower reported earnings, lower stockholders' equity, and a higher debt to equity ratio, would have an adverse impact on the markets for the securities of research-intensive companies. The resulting higher cost of capital would lead to underinvestment in research-intensive industries.

Comment on these alleged consequences. How would you examine if the adoption of FASB Statement No. 2 did lead to these consequences?

QUESTION 6.5: Leverage Ratios of Airlines and Lease Accounting

FASB Statement No. 13 [1976], *Accounting for Leases*, requires that leases meeting *any* of the following criteria should be capitalized and accounted for as assets and liabilities (*capital* leases) on the balance sheet:

(1) Ownership is transferred to the lessee by the end of the lease.

(2) There is a bargain (less than fair value) purchase option.

(3) The lease term is 75% or more of the leased property's estimated economic life.

(4) The present value of the minimum lease payments is 90% or more of the fair value of the leased property, less any investment credit retained by the lessor.

Leases that do not meet any of the above criteria are classified as *operating* leases for which rentals generally should be charged to operations as they become payable. The statement is effective for leases entered into or revised on or after January 1, 1977. Retroactive application for all leases is encouraged but not required until fiscal years ending after December 24, 1981.

One industry that was opposed to the capitalization of leases alternative chosen by the FASB was the airlines. This industry has traditionally engaged extensively in lease financing when acquiring new aircraft. Prior to FASB Statement No. 13, none of the 11 major airlines showed the future obligations on leases as a liability on the balance sheet. An article in *Barron's* (September 1, 1975) noted that one reason for the airlines opposition to the capitalization alternative related to restrictive covenants in existing loan agreements:

> The airlines are highly concerned about any modification of accounting methods which would outlaw "off balance sheet" financing as currently practiced.... *One of the immediate consequences would be possible technical violation of covenants in earlier loan agreements.* Such agreements must be interpreted under existing accounting rules and not under those in effect when the leases were incurred. The required modification or reopening of previous loan agreements likely would entail higher interest charges and other elements more costly to the borrower.

One financial ratio of importance in loan agreements is the long-t|
to equity ratio. Most airline loan agreements include converti|
ordinated debentures and deferred credits with stockholders' equity wnen
computing this ratio. Information pertinent to calculating the 1975 debt to
equity ratios is provided in the 1975 Annual Reports of these companies.
The following information (in $000,000's) was taken from that source:

		Long-Term Debt	Lease Obligations	Conv. Sub. Debentures	Deferred Credits	Stockholders' Equity
1.	American	279.1	737.2	172.5	166.9	541.8
2.	Braniff	234.9	190.8	—	30.5	167.1
3.	Continental	347.3	62.7	46.5	42.1	147.4
4.	Delta	369.5	216.6	20.9	276.8	483.8
5.	Eastern	497.6	725.3	125.0	18.5	290.3
6.	National	170.2	123.4	—	100.3	194.4
7.	Northwest	246.0	79.7	—	171.6	623.7
8.	Pan American	342.9	437.2	465.0	28.5	256.6
9.	Trans World	724.7	833.9	250.0	60.5	335.2
10.	United	795.6	834.4	182.0	401.3	777.3
11.	Western	78	104.2	29.6	68.9	137.9

Information on the lease obligations was obtained from footnotes to the
financial statements of each company.

REQUIRED

(1) Compute the long-term debt to equity ratios of the above airlines
with

   (a) Lease obligations excluded from the balance sheet, and

   (b) Lease obligations included as long-term debt on the balance
   sheet.

   What is the Spearman rank correlation coefficient between these two
   debt to equity ratios for the 11 airlines? Would the alternative
   accounting treatments of lease obligations affect inferences you
   might make about the relative indebtedness of each airline?

(2) It was stated in the *Barron's* article that one consequence of recognizing future lease obligations as a liability would be "technical violations of covenants in loan agreements." Why would an airline company agree to a set of covenants in loan agreements that can be
violated by accounting changes as well as economic changes in the
airline's financial ability? How could a company make its bond
indenture agreements less vulnerable to violations arising from required accounting changes?

(3) Nelson [1963] earlier examined the effect of lease capitalization on
the debt to equity ratios of 11 companies. (Names of the companies
were not disclosed.) These 11 companies provided sufficient information in footnotes to estimate the capitalized value of the lease rentals.

The Spearman rank correlation of the debt to equity ratios with and without lease capitalization was .345. Nelson concluded the following: "The ranking [of companies] changes after capitalization. This means that, other things remaining equal, the financial analyst could easily have made faulty decisions if he had based his analysis on ratios which were computed from conventional financial statements" (p. 54). Evaluate the conclusion that "the financial analyst could easily have made faulty decisions..."

REFERENCES

BAREFIELD, R. M., and COMISKEY, E. E. "Depreciation Policy and the Behavior of Corporate Profits." *Journal of Accounting Research* (Autumn 1971): 351–358.

BASU, S., and HANNA, J. R. *Inflation Accounting: Alternatives, Implementation Issues and Some Empirical Evidence.* Society of Industrial Accountants of Canada, 1976.

COMISKEY, E. E. "A Note on Depreciation and Statement Comparability." *Financial Analysts Journal* (Jan.–Feb. 1969): 78–80.

DAVIDSON, S., and WEIL, R. L. "Inflation Accounting: What Will General Price Level Adjusted Income Statements Show?" *Financial Analysts Journal* (Jan.–Feb. 1975): 27–31, 70–84.

———. "Inflation Accounting: Public Utilities." *Financial Analysts Journal* (May–June 1975a): 30–34, 62.

———. "Inflation Accounting and 1974 Earnings." *Financial Analysts Journal* (Sept.–Oct. 1975b): 42–54.

DAVIDSON, S., SORTER, G., and KALLE, H. "Measuring the Defensive Position of a Firm." *Financial Analysts Journal* (Jan.–Feb. 1964): 23–29.

DEAKIN, E. B. "Distributions of Financial Accounting Ratios: Some Empirical Evidence." *The Accounting Review* (Jan. 1976): 90–96.

DERSTINE, R. P., and HUEFNER, R. J. "LIFO-FIFO, Accounting Ratios and Market Risk." *Journal of Accounting Research* (Autumn 1974): 216–234.

DUN & BRADSTREET. *Key Business Ratios.* Dun & Bradstreet, New York, 1976.

FASB STATEMENT NO. 2. *Accounting for Research and Development Costs.* FASB, Stamford, Conn., 1974.

FASB STATEMENT NO. 13. *Accounting for Leases.* FASB, Stamford, Conn., 1976.

FEDERAL DEPOSIT INSURANCE CORPORATION. *Bank Operating Statistics: 1974.* Federal Deposit Insurance Corporation, Washington, D.C., 1975.

GREER, H. C. "What Are Accepted Principles of Accounting?" *The Accounting Review* (March 1938): 25–31.

HOLDEN, G. C. "LIFO and Ratio Analysis." *The Accounting Review* (Jan. 1964): 70–85.

HORRIGAN, J. O. "Some Empirical Bases of Financial Ratio Analysis." *The Accounting Review* (July 1965): 558–568.

JOHNSTON, J. *Econometrics*, 2nd ed. McGraw-Hill, New York, 1972.

LAWLEY, D. N., and MAXWELL, A. E. *Factor Analysis as a Statistical* ∨ *Method.* American Elsevier, New York, 1971.

NELSON, A. T. "Capitalizing Leases—The Effect on Financial Ratios." *Journal of Accountancy* (July 1963): 49–58.

PARKER, J. E. "Impacts of Price-Level Accounting." *The Accounting Review* (Jan. 1977): 69–96.

PETERSEN, R. J. "General Price-Level Impact on Financial Information." *The Accounting Review* (Jan. 1973): 34–43.

PINCHES, G. E., EUBANK, A. A., MINGO, K. A., and CARUTHERS, J. K. "The Hierarchical Classification of Financial Ratios." *Journal of Business Research* (Oct. 1975): 295–310.

PINCHES, G. E., MINGO, K. A., and CARUTHERS, J. K. "The Stability of Financial Patterns in Industrial Organizations." *Journal of Finance* (May 1973): 389–396.

REVSINE, L., and THIES, J. B. "Productivity Changes and Alternative Income Series: A Simulation." *The Accounting Review* (Apr. 1976): 255–268.

ROBERT MORRIS ASSOCIATES. *Annual Statement Studies: 1975 Edition.* Robert Morris Associates, Philadelphia, 1976.

ROSENFIELD, P. "Accounting for Inflation—A Field Test." *Journal of Accountancy* (June 1969): 45–50.

RUMMELL, R. J. *Applied Factor Analysis.* Northwestern University Press, Chicago, 1970.

SHARPE, W. F. "Mean-Absolute Deviation Characteristics Lines for Securities and Portfolios." *Management Science* (Oct. 1971): B1–B13.

SPACEK, L. "Business Success Requires an Understanding of Unsolved Problems of Accounting and Financial Reporting." Speech at Harvard University, Cambridge, Mass., Sept. 1959. Reprinted in J. Lorie and R. Brealey (eds.). *Modern Developments in Investment Management.* Praeger, New York, 1972: 630–644.

STEVENS, D. L. "Financial Characteristics of Merged Firms: A Multivariate Analysis." *Journal of Financial and Quantitative Analysis* (Mar. 1973): 149–158.

WADSWORTH, G. P., and BRYAN, J. G. *Applications of Probability and Random Variables*, 2nd ed., McGraw-Hill, New York, 1974.

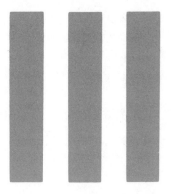

CAPITAL MARKETS AND FINANCIAL INFORMATION

7

CAPITAL MARKETS
AND
INFORMATION

It is commonly argued that the information disclosed in annual reports is important in resource allocation. Norr [1975], for instance, eloquently makes this argument while discussing accounting policy decisions:

> The drama of SEC rules, APB Opinions and FASB Statements unfolds between the lines of annual reports. The struggle over accounting principles marches through financial statements. The flow of savings is influenced; the raising of capital is altered by the outcome. (p. 1)

In this chapter we are concerned with the role of information, especially financial statement information, in capital markets. We shall distinguish between the role of information at (1) the aggregate market level and (2) the individual investor level. The role of information at the aggregate level is manifested in the prices of traded securities. The role of information at the individual level is manifested in the composition of investors' portfolios and in the number of trading decisions made.

In Section 7.1, some analytical results indicating the importance of information in capital markets are noted. In Section 7.2 we shall outline the efficient markets model and the assumptions about information generally made in this model. Various approaches to investment selection are briefly outlined in Section 7.3. Of particular concern is the role of financial statement information in these approaches and the assumptions they make about capital market efficiency. In Appendix 7.A we shall discuss assumptions about capital markets and information made in the accounting literature.

7.1 ASSET PRICES AND INFORMATION

To demonstrate analytically that information has the potential to affect security prices necessarily requires considerable abstraction from the complexities of organized capital markets. Demski [1974] provides one such demonstration for a "simple economy" with one good, two individuals, and two time periods. The *first* stage in the Demski analysis assumed that the single good in the economy was corn, which was traded in a perfectly competitive market. The two time periods were the present period and a future period. The two individuals ($i = 1$ and 2) had different opening endowments of corn. In addition, individual 2 owned a firm which produced corn. The amount of corn produced depended on which of two states ($s=1$ and $s=2$) occurred in the future period. The "securities" traded in this economy were state-contingent claims to corn in the future period; i.e., "corn in the future period when state 1 occurred" was separately traded from "corn in the future period when state 2 occurred." The information system available to $i=1$ and $i=2$ enabled both to observe which future state occurred. Given this scenario, the preferred consumption schedules of $i=1$ and $i=2$ and the market price for each state-contingent claim to corn were determined via optimization techniques for each individual and imposing market clearing conditions for each commodity.

The *second* stage in the Demski analysis adjusted the above scenario in one respect. The information system now only allowed the owner of the firm ($i=2$) to observe which future state occurred. The effect of this restriction was that $i=1$ was not able to separately contract for the state-dependent delivery of future corn; i.e., his preferred consumption schedule was constrained to be the same whether $s=1$ or $s=2$ occurred. Incorporating this constraint in the analysis produced different preferred consumption schedules for $i=1$ and $i=2$ and a different set of market clearing prices for each state-contingent claim to corn.

The above analysis is obviously very simplified. However, it does yield important insights. The *first* insight is the tracing of the effect of information on individual decisions through to the aggregate market prices that equate supply and demand schedules for the securities. *Information was shown to induce changes in both the consumption and production allocations of individuals and firms and through these effects to induce changes in market prices of traded securities.* The *second* insight is that the preferred consumption schedule of $i=2$ was affected by the information made available to $i=1$. Given that $i=2$ observes which state occurs, issues relating to $i=2$ revealing state occurrence to $i=1$ arise. For instance, under what conditions would both $i=1$ and $i=2$ be better off through this revelation by $i=2$, and what procedures could $i=1$ use to verify that $i=2$ reveals the future state that actually occurs? At present, much work in the economics literature is attempting to address these and similar issues.[1]

Information as a Screening Device

In much of the traditional economic price theory literature, the assumption was made that perfect information about traded commodities was costlessly available to all participants in the market. This assumption was made when deriving the equilibrium consumption and production schedules and the market clearing prices in the first stage of the Demski [1974] analysis. In recent economics literature there has been considerable work on alternative assumptions about information availability and the role of information in markets.[2] Some economists have cogently argued that much of traditional economic analysis needs rethinking when analyzing information. For instance, Stiglitz [1975] argues as follows:

> The production and dissemination of information is different in a number of fundamental ways from the production of ordinary commodities. One simply cannot transfer the tools and modes of thinking that have been developed for the latter into the analysis of the production of information.... I would argue that imperfect information necessitates serious modification of the conventional analysis of the production and exchange of commodities. Indeed, even what we mean by a "commodity" is dependent upon our "information structure." There are a number of phenomena with which the conventional theory finds difficulty coping, e.g., the existence of different prices for different commodities, tie-in sales, quantity discounts in excess of the difference in transactions costs—for which the theory which we are about to develop does provide considerable insight. Somewhat loosely, what I am arguing is that it is not as if there is a "commodity" sector for which the conventional theory is applicable and an "information sector" for which a new theory is required; the production of goods and information are so intertwined that an attempt to construct a theory of "information" immediately leads to a reconstruction of at least a part of the conventional theory. (pp. 27–28)

Stiglitz then outlined a theory of *screening* in which the role of information is to aid in discriminating between goods, which in the absence of information "would for economic purposes be treated the same even though it may be known that they differ in perhaps some important ways" (p. 28). Thus, if two securities were both in the brewing industry, the role of firm-specific information could be in discriminating between these two securities along lines such as operating leverage and financial leverage. In this context, the firm-specific accounting information provided could markedly affect the capital market's ability to distinguish between these two securities.

Whether accounting information does enable the capital markets to discriminate between different securities is an empirical question which is examined in detail in subsequent chapters. In interpreting empirical studies on this and other questions it is useful to understand the *efficient markets model*. This model is described in the next section of this chapter.

7.2 EFFICIENT MARKETS MODEL AND INFORMATION

An efficient capital market is one in which market prices "fully reflect" all information available at that time. To examine whether actual capital markets are efficient in this sense, it is necessary to derive some testable implications of this model.

A Efficient Markets Model: Testable Implications

The approach to defining capital market efficiency that we shall adopt draws on Fama [1976]. Let

ϕ_{t-1} = set of information available at time $t-1$,

ϕ_{t-1}^M = set of information the market uses to determine security prices at $t-1$,

$P_{j,t-1}$ = price of security j at time $t-1$, $j=1,2,\ldots,n$, where n is the number of securities,

$f_M\left(P_{1,t+\tau},\ldots,P_{n,t+\tau}|\phi_{t-1}^M\right)$ = joint probability density function for security prices at time $t+\tau (\tau \geq 0)$ assessed by the market at time $t-1$ on the basis of the information set ϕ_{t-1}^M,

$f(P_{1,t+\tau},\ldots,P_{n,t+\tau}|\phi_{t-1})$ = joint probability density function for security prices at time $t+\tau$ $(\tau \geq 0)$ that is "implied by" the information set ϕ_{t-1}.

Note that ϕ_{t-1} includes all information that became public at time $t-1$ and at *all* previous points of time.

Capital market efficiency implies that

$$\phi_{t-1}^M = \phi_{t-1}; \tag{7.1}$$

that is, the information set used by the market to determine security prices at $t-1$ includes all available information. *There is no piece of information relevant to security price determination that is ignored by the market.* This condition implies that

$$f_M\left(P_{1t},\ldots,P_{nt}|\phi_{t-1}^M\right)=f(P_{1t},\ldots,P_{nt}|\phi_{t-1}). \tag{7.2}$$

Sufficient conditions for the above characterization of an efficient market are

(1) There are no transactions costs in trading securities,
(2) All information is costlessly available to all market participants, and
(3) All participants agree on the implications of current information for the current price and distributions of future prices of each security.

The above conditions do not imply a specific equilibrium model of price determination. They simply imply that whatever asset pricing model is used, the resultant set of equilibrium prices "fully incorporates" information available at time $t - 1$.[3]

Two important implications of (7.1) and (7.2) are that (1) capital asset prices adjust instantaneously to new information and (2) capital asset prices adjust to new information in an unbiased manner. Both implications have been the subject of detailed testing. To test whether the efficient capital markets model is a descriptively valid model of actual capital markets, it is necessary to specify in more detail how equilibrium prices at $t - 1$ are determined from ϕ_{t-1}^M. That is, a model of how equilibrium market prices are set is necessary. In Chapter 8 we shall present an analysis of several such equilibrium price setting models.

The efficient markets model is obviously a simplification of *real-world* capital markets. Such simplification is often necessary to yield a model that produces tractable results. An important test of this modeling process is its ability to yield important insights into the phenomena being modeled; e.g., does it enable us to understand the actual operation of real-world capital markets? On this test, the efficient markets model turns out to be one of the most successful of the models developed in the financial economics literature. This observation will become apparent in subsequent chapters of this book.

B Alternative Assumptions About Information

Relaxing the above-noted sufficient conditions for market efficiency can take several directions. For instance, one could recognize costs of acquiring information by market participants. In this context, it is quite possible that such costs could result in less information being impounded into security prices than would be the case with costless information acquisition.[4] Stigler [1967] makes the following comment on this case:

> There is no imperfection in a market possessing incomplete knowledge if it would not be remunerative to acquire (produce) complete knowledge; information costs are the costs of transportation from ignorance to omniscience, and seldom can a trader afford to take the entire trip. (p. 291)

In testing market efficiency, it is necessary to make some assumptions about the information costs incurred by market participants. In many cases, the implicit assumption in empirical studies is that such information costs are zero. Note, however, that if this assumption is invalid, one may make misleading inferences about market efficiency if it is observed that a specific item of information is not instantaneously impounded into security prices. The reason for the noninstantaneous impounding of information may well relate to the nature of information costs rather than to the nature of the market for the firm's securities.[5]

Another traditional assumption in many definitions of market efficiency is that "all information is available to all market participants." This assumption appears to be important when denoting ϕ_{t-1}^M as "the set of information *the market* uses to determine security prices." Who is the market? Whose set of information is impounded into security prices? Answers to these questions are not obvious. One approach is to define *available information* as only that information which has been formally placed in the "public domain," e.g., in the *Wall Street Journal*. This definition, however, would exclude many items of information which may be impounded into security prices and yet have not been formally placed in the "public domain." For instance, it would exclude the potentially rich informal information flows between market participants and corporate officials, e.g., a telephone call from a broker to a corporate vice-president to confirm or disconfirm a possible merger rumor. The available evidence, although not extensive, suggests that such informal flows of information are considerable. As an example, a vice-president of *J. C. Penney Company* —Axelson [1975]—noted that in one year *Penney's* had over 1,000 interviews with security analysts, in addition to their more formal presentations such as the annual and interim reports and speeches before analysts' luncheons, etc.[6]

The ambiguity that is inherent in a phrase such as "that market's set of information" should be well understood when interpreting tests of capital market efficiency. At a minimum, it is important to recognize the many possible channels by which information may become "available" to market participants. For example, it would be premature to conclude that the market was inefficient because it did not react to the announcement in the *Wall Street Journal* (*WSJ*) of an event a researcher had determined was pertinent to security price determination (no easy matter in itself). It may well be that more timely cues had conveyed the information to the "market" prior to the *WSJ* announcement date.

C Defining Inside Information

The ambiguity in defining what is "the market's set of information" is a source of much concern to security analysts. An analyst faces liability under the various antifraud provisions of the federal securities law (in particular, Rule 10b-5) if it can be shown he used to advantage *inside information*.[7] No definitive definition of inside information is given in the federal securities laws. Legal decisions, however, do provide evidence on whether a particular court views a particular set of information as being of a "public" or of an "inside" kind. For instance, in *Cady Roberts and Company*[8] a partner managing discretionary accounts in a brokerage house obtained information about a proposed dividend cut from a director before the dividend cut was formally released by the company. A court held that trading on the basis of this dividend cut constituted the use of inside information. This decision appears to be consistent with the so-called *mosaic theory* that is referred to (but poorly operationalized) by Securities and Exchange Commission officials. Under the mosaic theory it appears that *highly specific information* (e.g., a dividend or earnings announcement) is most likely to fall in the domain of inside information. For instance, an SEC commissioner—Loomis [1972]—made the following comment:

> The Commission's idea of highly specific information is a single concrete event or determination or fact, as opposed to a mosaic of general information, some of which is public and some of which isn't. Skillful assembly of a mosaic may lead an analyst to the conclusion that the company's stock is going up or down a point. We are trying not to inhibit securities research. That's one of the reasons why we refer to a specific event rather than the result of research. (p. 25)

Loomis also noted that the concern was with material information in insider trader cases. Not surprisingly, materiality turns out to be an elusive concept to operationalize. Loomis stated the following:

> The definition of materiality has been very difficult to formulate and is usually pronounced in general terms. Material information is information which an investor would find significant and which—and this is significant—might be expected to have a market impact. (pp. 23-24)

In short, the difficulties alluded to in Section 7.2B of defining what is the "market's set of information" also arise in legal decisions on insider trading.

7.3 INVESTMENT DECISION MAKING AND INFORMATION

A variety of approaches to investment decision making are used in practice. We shall consider three such approaches. Of particular concern is the role of financial statement information in these approaches and the assumptions they make about capital market efficiency.

A Technical Analysis

This approach assumes that there are systematic dependencies in security market prices or returns which can be exploited to yield abnormal returns. Technical analysis is a general term that embraces a variety of specific tools.[9] For instance, *trend analysis* relies on the sequencing of movements (so-called "head and shoulders movements") in returns on individual stocks. *Relative strength analysis* relies on movements in the returns on individual stocks vis-à-vis returns on the market. At a more aggregate level are attempts to use systematic patterns in market indexes to time the market, i.e., to buy long in *bull markets* and sell short in *bear markets*. Technical analysis assumes that the capital market is inefficient—there is information in the past sequence of prices or returns that is ignored by the capital market when assessing the distribution of security prices. Accounting data of specific firms rarely play any role in this approach to investment selection.

The success of technical analysis is very much open to question. For instance, trend analysis assumes there are systematic dependencies in security returns. Yet, the available evidence suggests that, at best, any systematic dependencies in daily security returns are very minor. Daily security returns appear to be well approximated by a random-walk model (see Chapter 4 for a description of this model). Fama [1965] examined the sample autocorrelations of daily returns for each of the 30 Dow-Jones Industrials over the 1957–1962 period. Table 7.1 details these autocorrelations up to a lag of 10. Note that the observed autocorrelations are, in general, close to zero and mostly statistically insignificant from zero. Although the number of stocks having positive autocorrelations between successive daily returns (r_1) is greater than expected under the random-walk model, the largest r_1 is only .118 (*Alcoa*). This r_1 implies that only 1.39% of the variability in $\tilde{R}_{it}$ of *Alcoa* can be explained by the linear relationship between $\tilde{R}_{it}$ and $\tilde{R}_{i,t-1}$. Thus, a random-walk model appears to provide a good approximation of the process generating daily security returns of the Dow-Jones stocks.[10] Many studies similar to Fama [1965] have reported similar results. Indeed, the onus is now on those who advocate technical analysis investment techniques to provide detailed evidence to support their position.[11]

B Fundamental Analysis

This approach to investment decision making assumes that each security has an *intrinsic value* which can be determined on the basis of such fundamentals as earnings, dividends, growth, and capital structure.

TABLE 7.1 Sample Autocorrelations of Daily Return on the Dow-Jones Industrials for Lags $\tau = 1, 2, \ldots, 10$

Stock	Lag(τ)										T^b
	1	2	3	4	5	6	7	8	9	10	
Allied Chemical	.017	-.042	.007	-.001	.027	.004	-.017	-.026	-.017	-.007	1,223
Alcoa	.118[a]	.038	-.014	.022	-.022	.009	.017	.007	-.001	-.033	1,190
American Can	-.087[a]	-.024	.034	-.065[a]	-.017	-.006	.015	.025	-.047	-.040	1,219
AT & T	-.039	-.097[a]	.000	.026	.005	-.005	.002	.027	-.014	.007	1,219
American Tobacco	.111[a]	-.109[a]	-.060[a]	-.065[a]	.007	-.010	.011	.046	.039	.041	1,283
Anaconda	.067[a]	-.061[a]	-.047	-.002	.000	-.038	.009	.016	-.014	-.056	1,193
Bethlehem Steel	.013	-.065[a]	.009	.021	-.053	-.098[a]	-.010	.004	-.002	-.021	1,200
Chrysler	.012	-.066[a]	-.016	-.007	-.015	.009	.037	.056[a]	-.044	.021	1,692
Du Pont	.013	-.033	.060[a]	.027	-.002	-.047	.020	.011	-.034	.001	1,243
Eastman Kodak	.025	.014	-.031	.005	-.022	.012	.007	.006	.008	.002	1,238
General Electric	.011	-.038	-.021	.031	-.001	.000	-.008	.014	-.002	.010	1,693
General Foods	.061[a]	-.003	.045	.002	-.015	-.052	-.006	-.014	-.024	-.017	1,408
General Motors	-.004	-.056[a]	-.037	-.008	-.038	-.006	.019	.006	-.016	.009	1,446
Goodyear	-.123[a]	.017	-.044	.043	-.002	-.003	.035	.014	-.015	.007	1,162
International Harvester	-.017	-.029	-.031	.037	-.052	-.021	-.001	.003	-.046	-.016	1,200

216

										T[b]
International Nickel	.096[a]	−.033	−.019	.020	.027	.059[a]	−.038	−.008	−.016	.034	1,243
International Paper	.046	−.011	−.058[a]	.053[a]	.049	−.003	−.025	−.019	−.003	−.021	1,447
Johns Manville	.006	−.038	−.027	−.023	−.029	−.080[a]	.040	.018	−.037	.029	1,205
Owens Illinois	−.021	−.084[a]	−.047	.068[a]	.086[a]	−.040	.011	−.040	.067[a]	−.043	1,237
Procter and Gamble	.099[a]	−.009	−.008	.009	−.015	.022	.012	−.012	−.022	−.021	1,447
Sears	.097[a]	.026	.028	.025	.005	−.054	−.006	−.010	−.008	−.009	1,236
Standard Oil (Calif.)	.025	−.030	−.051[a]	−.025	−.047	−.034	−.010	.072[a]	−.049[a]	−.035	1,693
Standard Oil (N.J.)	.008	−.116[a]	.016	.014	−.047	−.018	−.022	−.026	−.073[a]	.081[a]	1,156
Swift and Co.	−.004	−.015	−.010	.012	.057[a]	.012	−.043	.014	.012	.001	1,446
Texaco	.094[a]	−.049	−.024	−.018	−.017	−.009	.031	.032	−.013	.008	1,159
Union Carbide	.107[a]	−.012	.040	.046	−.036	−.034	.003	−.008	−.054	−.037	1,118
United Aircraft	.014	−.033	−.022	−.047	−.067[a]	−.053	.046	.037	.015	−.019	1,200
U.S. Steel	.040	−.074[a]	.014	.011	−.012	−.021	.041	.037	−.021	−.044	1,200
Westinghouse	−.027	−.022	−.036	−.003	.000	−.054[a]	−.020	.013	−.014	.008	1,448
Woolworth	.028	−.016	.015	.014	.007	−.039	.013	.003	−.088[a]	−.008	1,445

[a]Sample autocorrelation is at least two standard deviations to the left or to the right of its expected value under the hypothesis that the true autocorrelation is zero.

[b]T is the number of observations.

SOURCE: Fama [1965, Table 10].

An analyst determines the intrinsic value on the basis of these fundamentals and compares this value with the current market price to determine if the security is under- or overvalued.

The most articulate exposition of this approach is in Graham et al. [1962].[12] These authors drew the following distinction between current market price and intrinsic value:

> A general definition of intrinsic value would be "that value which is justified by the facts," e.g., assets, earnings, dividends, definite prospects, including the factor of management. The primary objective in using the adjective "intrinsic" is to emphasize the distinction between *value* and *current market price*, but not to invest this "value" with an aura of permanence. In truth, the computed intrinsic value is likely to change at least from year to year, as the various factors governing that value are modified. But in most cases intrinsic value changes less rapidly and drastically than market price, and the investor usually has an opportunity to profit from any wide discrepancy between the current price and the intrinsic value as determined at the same time.
>
> The most important single factor determining a stock's value is now held to be the *indicated average future earning power*, i.e., the estimated average earnings for a future span of years. Intrinsic value would then be found by first forecasting this earning power and then multiplying that prediction by an appropriate "capitalization factor." (p. 28)

A detailed analysis of accounting statements was proposed as one means of detecting differences between current market price and intrinsic value.

Graham et al. [1962] gave the example of a "clearly undervalued common stock," the detection of which turned on the earnings of an unconsolidated subsidiary. The stock was the *Hoover Company*:

> In addition to its domestic (U.S) business, it controls three foreign subsidiaries of which the most important is the 53 percent owned Hoover, Ltd. of England. The American company has a substantial equity interest in the undistributed earnings of the English affiliate. Since this equity is not reported directly in either the income account or the balance sheet, the parent company's earnings and asset value are both understated.
>
> The Hoover American shares appeared undervalued at the end of 1957 because they were selling at only 4.3 times their *full* 1957 earnings and less than 7 times their 10-year average earnings. (p. 31, emphasis added)

By "full 1957 earnings," Graham et al. meant the 1957 American earnings plus adjustments they made for *Hoover's* equity in the English company's 1957 earnings. The adjustments to the reported U.S. earnings proposed by Graham et al. involved publicly available information—the percent ownership of the English affiliate and the annual report of the English affiliate. The argument that by these accounting adjustments one can detect an undervalued security assumes that $I_t^M \neq I_t$; i.e., there is publicly available information pertinent to security price determination that is overlooked by the capital market.

One implication of an efficient capital market is that capital asset prices adjust instantaneously to new information. Comments in Graham et al. [1962] explicitly assume a very different speed of adjustment. In discussing one limitation of the capitalization of earnings approach to detecting mispriced securities, they note the following:

> Assuming that profits develop as anticipated, there remains...doubt as to whether the multiplier, or capitalization rate, will prove correctly chosen. A valuation may be very skillfully done in the light of all the pertinent data and the soundest judgment of future probabilities; yet *the market price may delay adjusting itself to the indicated value for so long a period* that new conditions may supervene and bring with them a new value. (p. 30)

That is, Graham et al. posit the existence of lags in the adjustment of security prices to publicly available information.

The Graham et al. [1962] exposition is somewhat dated. However, even in more recent expositions of fundamental analysis, statements such as those noted above occur frequently. For example, Bernstein [1975] expressed the following familiar comments on the distinction between *price* and *value*:

> Even if all the information available on a security at a given point in time is impounded in its price, that price may not reflect *value*. It may be under- or over-valued depending on the degree to which an incorrect interpretation or evaluation of the available information has been made by those whose actions determine the market price at a given time. (p. 58)

Bernstein advocated that *value* was to be determined via fundamental analysis. In Chapter 10 we shall outline several specific models that use accounting information to estimate the intrinsic value of a security. Evidence on the ability of these models to earn abnormal returns is also presented in that chapter.

C Portfolio Theory Analysis

Both the technical and fundamental approaches to investment selection concentrate on selecting *individual securities* that are under- or over-valued. In contrast, in portfolio theory the selection of individual securities is approached from a *portfolio perspective*. An investor first decides on the characteristics of his portfolio of securities, e.g., its beta or relative risk level. Then he chooses individual securities to achieve the desired portfolio characteristics. In Chapter 8 we shall describe portfolio theory in considerable detail. The role of accounting information in portfolio theory is examined in Chapter 9. Further discussion of these topics is deferred to these two chapters.

7.4 SUMMARY

The central theme of this chapter was the role of information in capital markets. A distinction was drawn between the role of information at (1) the aggregate market level (i.e., in the setting of equilibrium prices) and (2) the individual level (i.e., in the selection of securities for investment).

The efficient markets model was outlined and its testable implications noted; i.e., (1) capital asset prices adjust instantaneously to new information, and (2) capital asset prices adjust to new information in an unbiased manner. These implications were then contrasted with assumptions made about capital asset prices and information in the investment literature. In Chapters 9–11 we shall provide a detailed analysis of the evidence on the role of financial statement information in capital markets. The implications of this evidence for investment decision making are examined in Chapter 12.

APPENDIX 7.A ASSUMPTIONS ABOUT CAPITAL MARKETS
AND INFORMATION
IN THE ACCOUNTING LITERATURE

The accounting literature contains many statements about what information is (or should be) impounded into security prices. In this section we shall consider some assumptions implicit in these statements. *A common assumption is that there is a mechanistic relation between reported accounting earnings and stock prices.*

An early assertion of such a relation is in MacNeal's [1939, pp. 9–15] *Truth in Accounting.* He presented the hypothetical example of two investment trusts. Both trusts started with $1 million in marketable securities. One trust (American Trust) sold its marketable securities at the end of the year and showed a $200,000 realized profit from securities in addition to $30,000 from dividends. The other trust (National Trust) bought exactly the same marketable securities but did not sell them at the end of the year. It showed only the $30,000 dividends on its income statements—"there was a footnote on the balance sheet stating that the present market value of these securities was $1,230,000" (p. 11):

> Now as soon as the certified financial statements of the American Trust and of the National Trust were mailed to stockholders and printed in the newspapers,

everybody learned that the American Trust had earned 23 percent on its capital stock during the year whereas the National Trust had earned only 3 percent on its capital stock. The price of the American Trust stock therefore rose sharply as many investors rushed to buy it, and the price of the National Trust stock dropped sharply due to selling by disappointed stockholders. (p. 12)

That is, MacNeal posited that because the capital gains were disclosed in a footnote rather than in the income statement, the price of the National Trust stock would decline—this assumes a mechanistic relationship between the reported earnings number and stock prices.

Some recent accounting expositions also reveal a similar mechanistic assumption. Briloff [1972] in Chapter 3 ("Dirty Pooling and Polluted Purchase") of *Unaccountable Accounting* gives a similar scenario for an "Ajax Aero Computer Co." The company had a price to earnings (P/E) ratio of 30. The reported earnings per share for Ajax in $t-1$ was $4; with a P/E multiple of 30 it sold for $120. During the period $t-1$ to t, Ajax acquired another company and accounted for it on a pooling of interest basis. The reported earnings per share in t was $5 (this includes the whole year's earnings of the company acquired)—"the tape watchers remember Ajax's P/E ratio of 30—Ajax shares get marked up to $150" (p. 62).

The above examples of a mechanistic relation being posited may be viewed as extreme or isolated. If one examines statements made elsewhere in the accounting literature, or by industry officials about the possible effects of accounting alternatives, they turn out to be not so extreme nor isolated. Consider the accounting methods used for life insurance companies. In 1972, the AICPA *Committee on Accounting for Life Insurance Companies* issued an audit guide recommending the use of an adjusted underwriting measure over the previously used statutory underwriting measure. The two main differences between the measures relate to (1) the capitalizing versus expensing of the costs of writing new policies and (2) the use of actual versus prescribed minimum interest rate assumptions in computing policy reserves. A member of the AICPA committee made the following comment on the audit guide:

Was it worth the cost and effort...? To answer this...we must look to the interests and needs of shareholders and the investing public. *To the extent that conservative regulatory accounting practices frequently resulted in understated earnings of insurance companies, thus directly affecting the prices of stocks, they clearly did not serve investors' interests and needs.* (Waterfield [1974, p. 4], emphasis added)

Even while life insurance companies published statutory numbers in their annual financial statements, information about the adjusted numbers was available from other sources, e.g., A. M. Best Co. and Standard & Poor's. Many companies even reported the adjusted numbers in the president's letter or elsewhere in the annual report. To imply that the use of a statutory number in the income statement "directly affected the prices of stocks" is to imply that these other sources of adjusted underwriting earnings are ignored.

Many criticisms of the effect of the current diversity in accounting methods across firms also fail to recognize the importance of nonaccounting information sources. For instance, Chambers [1974] asserts the following:

> If earnings reports are differentially distorted by the asset valuation and income calculation rules adopted by different companies—and there is considerable evidence of this—the stock market cannot discriminate between the more and the less efficient companies. (p. 49)

Note that the existence of alternative accounting rules does not necessarily imply that the market "cannot discriminate between the more and the less efficient companies." If one assumes no alternative information sources about efficiency, this implication may hold. However, once one recognizes that accounting information is but one of several sources the market may use in assessing efficiency, statements such as the "stock market *cannot* discriminate" have less force. What would such alternative sources be? Some sources could relate to specific *firms*—e.g., dividend announcements, capital-expenditure announcements, product and outlet announcements, personnel changes, and insider trading reports. Alternatively, other sources could relate to the efficiency of one *industry* vis-à-vis others—e.g., information from trade associations (e.g., trends in industry sales of beer); analyses by brokerage houses, Dun & Bradstreet, etc.; publications of consulting firms which specialize in particular industries (e.g., A. M. Best in the insurance industry); and U.S. government statistics such as housing starts, steel production, etc. Some sources of information could also relate to *economy* factors—e.g., statements by Treasury and Federal Reserve Board officials; publications of GNP, economy earnings trends, etc., by government departments; and projections of economic aggregates by economists, econometric models, etc. In short, there are numerous sources of information which can be utilized in assessing the efficiency of individual firms or industries. Given these alternative sources of information, it is far from clear that the effect of firms adopting diverse accounting procedures is that "the stock market cannot discriminate between the more and the less efficient companies."

Statements by Company Officials

Assumptions about capital markets and information are also apparent in statements by company officials about the effects of adopting accounting alternatives. For instance, one company official (quoted in

Sprouse [1964]) presented the following scenario if assets were valued in financial statements at current market prices (e.g., replacement cost):

> This is like a nightmare.... I can see management sitting around the table saying "What do you think we should make our income this year to maximize the price of our stock?" (p. 47)

Even if management reports a higher reported earnings due to an asset revaluation, it does not necessarily follow that the market will accept the revaluation at face value. Other information sources (e.g., real estate trade bulletins) may be used as a check on the market price of the firm's securities.

A similar *mechanistic* perspective is implicit in a statement by a company official (quoted in Backer [1970]) concerning the allocation of costs between interim accounting periods:

> "Yes, if we had abnormally high profits in a quarter we would try to find a way to throw some sales into the next quarter. To do otherwise might mislead stock-holders...."
>
> "*We try to level the quarters to avoid an unfavorable impact on the market price of our stock.* Our objective is to make quarterly figures representative of the economic situation rather than to follow accounting rules. When nonrecurring sales of land occur, or heavy sales in early quarters make earnings unrepresentative of the year's results, we try to make sure that earnings reported for the quarter are not misleading." (p. 216, emphasis added)

Note that the fact that "heavy sales" occur in "early quarters" does not mean that reporting "low" interim earnings in later quarters will have "an unfavorable impact on the market price of the stock." At a minimum, the pattern of past interim sales would reveal this seasonal feature of the business. In a market which uses alternative information sources, this seasonality would be recognized in interpreting the interim earnings figures in the low-activity quarters.

NOTES

[1]Some important early papers in this literature are Fama and Laffer [1971], Hirshleifer [1971], and Marshall [1974].

[2]The economics literature on information and economic behavior is a rapidly growing one. See, for instance, Spence [1973], Stiglitz [1975], and the "Symposium on the Economics of Internal Organization" in the Spring 1975 issue of the *Bell Journal of Economics*.

[3]A variety of alternative definitions of market efficiency have been proposed. For instance, Rubinstein [1975] proposes the following definition:

> Security prices are said to fully reflect information set ϕ_t if the prices are identical to the prices that would be generated in an otherwise identical economy where ϕ_t was the information set of every investor. (p. 820, paraphrased)

Note that the Rubinstein definition relies on equality of prices, whereas the Fama definition relies on equality of distributions of prices. See Beaver [1976] for further discussion of alternative definitions of market efficiency and the different concerns of authors that give rise to these different definitions.

[4]Grossman and Stiglitz [1976] have provided analytical results in which this case is shown to exist.

[5]Further discussion of these issues is in May and Sundem [1973] and Gonedes [1976].

[6]Relaxing the assumption that "all information is available to all market participants" raises interesting issues of economic behavior when individuals have unequal endowments of information. The "signaling literature" in economics (e.g., Spence [1973]) contains an extensive discussion of this topic. Gonedes et al. [1976] provide an interesting analysis of voluntary corporate forecasting of earnings within a framework that admits unequal endowments of information.

[7]For a good introduction to this area, see Chatlos [1975].

[8]In the matter of *Cady Roberts & Company*, 40 Securities and Exchange Commission 907, 912 (1961).

[9]See Shaw [1975] for a good overview of various approaches used in technical analysis.

[10]Fama [1976, Chapter 5] notes that in interpreting the "random-walk" evidence as consistent with capital market efficiency, it is assumed that the equilibrium return on a security is constant through time.

[11]Fama's [1970] review paper contains an excellent survey on studies examining systematic patterns in past security prices or returns. See also Granger [1972].

[12]From *Security Analysis* by Graham et al. Copyright ©1962 by McGraw-Hill, Inc. Used with permission of McGraw-Hill Book Company.

QUESTIONS

QUESTION 7.1: Random Walks and Efficient Markets

Malkiel [1975] commented as follows: "'Random walk' is a real obscenity on Wall Street. It is an epithet that the academic world insultingly hurls at the professional soothsayers. In essence, the random walk theory espouses the belief that future stock prices cannot be predicted" (p. 16).

REQUIRED

(1) Critically discuss this comment.
(2) Suppose that one could reject, at a 5% significance level, the hypothesis that a random-walk model described the daily stock return behavior of a particular stock. Would this result imply an inefficient capital market?

QUESTION 7.2:   Fundamental Analysis Approach to Investment
            Decision Making

Graham et al. [1962] discuss ways in which discrepancies between market price and intrinsic value originate. The following three ways in which market price may exceed intrinsic value were outlined:

a. *General Speculative Enthusiasm—The Typical Bull Market.* The majority of common stocks are overvalued at the height of a typical bull market. The degree of overvaluation varies greatly, however, depending on the degree of speculative emphasis and on accidental factors. Stocks of lowest value are often overvalued proportionately more than others. Their subsequent price decline is that much greater....

b. *Specific Enthusiasm or Overbullishness.* Many securities sell too high in normal markets. The most important group, we believe, is that of the "blue chips"—the prosperous leaders of industry—whose popularity for many years has given their price level a strong upward bias. Certain industries will attract a tenacious bullishness that gives strange results from the analyst's viewpoint....

c. *Overvaluations within a Company.* When a company has senior issues and common stock, and all its securities are of speculative caliber, the common usually sells too high because of the speculator's frequent exclusive interest in common stocks and his preference for low-priced issues....

These overvaluations within a company are not so much in a class by themselves as they are vivid illustrations of the general tendency for speculators to buy regardless of price. When a senior issue is available for comparison, the fact of overvaluation may often be established almost mathematically. (pp. 693–695)

The following four ways in which intrinsic value may exceed market price were outlined:

a. *General Pessimism.* The typical bear market or sometimes a temporary "scare market."

b. *Specific Pessimism or Disfavor.* It is our thesis that the stocks of companies with disappointing showings usually sell lower than they should, for the same basic reason that stocks as a whole sell too low during periods of depression. The significance of the unfavorable conditions is exaggerated. If this view is correct, the "poorer issues" will normally be undervalued in the market in relation to the better issues, with the possible exception of low-priced stocks as a whole, which attract a special sort of speculative interest. Broadly speaking, this generalization is valid.

Our view is based on the principle that in the majority of cases companies showing an unfavorable trend of earnings will reach a bottom at some time and that thereafter their earnings will fluctuate irregularly around some indicated average or normal base. The market price will usually have fallen well below the value indicated by the latter as well as by the asset-value factors. Consequently there is an undervaluation and a practical opportunity for profitable purchase.

c. *The Factor of Unfamiliarity or Neglect.* Undervaluation may often be explained in part by the public's unfamiliarity with the issue. It is assumed that if the stock were better known it would sell higher. We are inclined to believe that neglect of an issue almost always implies some lack of confidence about its future. For a company of any size at all, there are enough people interested in its affairs to create a buying interest in the shares if they have the requisite confidence in its future. It is because this confidence is lacking that the stock remains definitely undervalued.

Our viewpoint is supported by the price behavior of these secondary issues both during bull markets and when some unusually favorable development is taking place in the company's position. At such times sufficient interest develops in this type of concern to create a fair degree of market activity at rising prices. In a typical case the stimulus comes from the groups familiar with the company's operations, and it may be communicated rapidly to the public by brokerage houses and financial services which are attracted to the issue for a transitory period. In this way the undervaluation is ended and in fact may give way to overvaluation.

d. *The Factor of "Complication."* When a security is subject to a serious corporate or legal complication, it is likely to sell for less than its value....

Both the investing public and the speculative public shy away from all types of long-drawn-out litigation or corporate readjustments. This is true to such an extent that a suit intended to get *better* treatment for a security in a readjustment plan will usually put its price *down*, merely because it adds the factor of uncertainty and long delay. (pp. 695–698)

REQUIRED

(1) What does the term *intrinsic value* of a security mean? What role does accounting information play in estimating intrinsic value?

(2) Critically discuss the above extracts. What assumptions about information and capital markets are apparent in these extracts?

(3) What problems might an analyst face when using the above guidelines to identify stocks whose market price is above or below intrinsic value?

QUESTION 7.3: Accounting Diversity and Stock Prices

In a speech criticizing the diversity in generally accepted accounting priniciples, Spacek [1959] commented as follows:

Now, what do these principles of accounting which are called "generally accepted" mean to you as managers? As managers of your own businesses, you can disregard the "generally accepted principles of accounting" and their misleading influence, since you are accountable only to yourselves. But as managers of publicly owned companies, your stockholders will be your employers.

Your stockholders will be interested primarily in profits and high market values for their investments. In most cases the owners (stockholders) will judge the extent of your success on the relative performance of your company's stock in the market. The prices at which the stock market values your stock will depend on the financial position and the earnings of your company.

For instance, it is common practice, in measuring market values, to multiply the earnings per share by a current rule-of-thumb multiplier that may seem reasonable under current conditions. A stock may sell, for example, at 10, 12, 15 or more times earnings, according to the industry, the market conditions, etc. Therefore, as the earnings to which such a multiplier is applied vary, the market price of the stock will also vary.

Spacek examined two hypothetical companies which were alike in every respect except for the following differences in the accounting principles used in their annual reports:

Company A	Company B
Uses LIFO (last in, first out) for pricing inventory	Uses FIFO (first in, first out)
Uses accelerated depreciation for book and tax purposes	Uses straight-line
Charges research and develop ment costs to expense currently	Capitalizes and amortizes over five-year period
Funds the current pension costs—i.e., current service plus amortization of past service	Funds only the present value of pensions vested
Pays incentive bonuses to officers in cash	Grants stock options instead of paying cash bonuses
Credits gains (net of tax thereon) directly to earned surplus (or treats them as special credits below net income)	Includes such gains (net of income tax thereon) in income

Company A reported earnings per share of $.80, while Company B reported $1.79. Spacek then provided the following estimates of the market prices of these companies:

Market Value at	Company A	Company B
10 times earnings	$8.00	$17.93
12 times earnings	9.60	21.52
15 times earnings	12.0	26.90

He concluded his talk as follows:

It is wholly possible to have the stock of these two comparable companies selling at prices as much as 100% apart, merely because of the differences in accounting practices.

You can judge for yourself whether, if you were a stockholder, you would rather have the accounting of Company A or that of Company B followed by your company, if it meant the stock would bring you twice as much cash value upon sale. The answer is too obvious to dwell upon.

Now, I want to emphasize again how important it is to let your management accounting practices find the truth as it actually is, regardless of the vagaries of the accounting practices that may be followed in reporting to the public.

(1) Critically discuss the above extracts. What *assumptions* about information and capital markets are apparent in Spacek's comments?

(2) What forces might operate in the capital market such that companies A and B in the above scenario might not "sell at prices as much as 100% apart, merely because of the differences in accounting practices?"

(3) How would you examine if the assumptions noted in (1) are descriptive of actual markets?

QUESTION 7.4: Reporting Rules for Marketable Equity Securities

The debate in the early 1970's over reporting rules for marketable equity securities represented an interesting interplay between the accounting and finance literature. On May 25 and 26, 1971, the *Accounting Principles Board* (APB) held a public hearing on "Accounting for Investments in Equity Securities Not Qualifying for the Equity Method." The primary issue discussed was whether such investments should be reported at current market value or historical cost in published financial statements. Four basic ways of reporting changes in current market values were discussed at this public hearing:

1. *Realized gains and losses only in net income.* Only realized gains and losses would be reported in the statement of income. Unrealized gains and losses would be reported in a reserve or in ownership equity accounts and would not affect the determination of net income.

2. *No gains and losses reported in net income.* No gains and losses, realized or unrealized, would be reported in the statement of income. Generally, a separate statement, or schedule, of gains and losses on investments would be presented in the financial report.

3. *Gains and losses in net income on a yield basis.* The gains and losses from changes in fair value would be included in the statement of income by means of an amortization of the net unrealized gains over current and designated future periods. Proponents of this view assert that investments in equity securities are motivated by expectations of a long-term yield (dividends plus net capital gains) and that income from such investments should be reported on a basis reflective of long-term yields. As a corollary to this view, the balance of gains not realized at any date is considered to be a valuation reserve related to fair value of the investments or a deferred credit awaiting income recognition on a systematic and rational basis.

4. *Both realized and unrealized gains and losses in net income.* Realized and unrealized gains and losses would be included in the statement of income

with no deferment or amortization. Proponents of this view assert that only this method of reporting gains and losses is consistent with the reporting of investments at fair value in the balance sheet. Just as fair value in the balance sheet presents more useful economic information than does cost, recognition of gains and losses in periods of value changes best reflects the economic consequences of the holding of equity investments. This method of income reporting is considered to overcome the possibility of management of earnings by selection of securities to be sold, to result in all economic effects of the investments being reported in the statement of income in the period in which the effects occurred, and to avoid any artificial normalizing or smoothing of gains and losses. (reported in Arthur Andersen and Company [1971, pp. 2–4])

The majority of the *AICPA Committee on Insurance Accounting and Auditing* argued that the appropriate criteria for choosing reporting rules for marketable equitable securities was which measure best represented realizable value on the balance sheet. They then recommended use of the *yield method*:

The use of a yield method is advocated...not as a means of arbitrarily smoothing the effects of market volatility, but rather because it is the only method which addresses itself to the important consideration of realizable values.... Quoted market values at any given point in time are not conclusive evidence as to what ultimate realizable values will be in a long-term investment portfolio. The only justification for using quoted values as of the close of business at a specific date from an economic point of view is to assume that the portfolio is going to be liquidated immediately. This is a liquidating concept and it is for this reason that quoted values may not be proper when following a going concern concept which requires that consideration be given to long-term experience. (reported in Arthur Andersen and Company [1971, pp. 283–284])

Beaver [1971] took issue with the conclusion that the yield method results in a better measure of realizable value than does the use of current market value. After summarizing evidence from the finance literature that was consistent with daily security price changes behaving as a random walk, he concluded the following:

The present value of the future expected realizable value of a security will always be equal to its currently observed market price. This statement holds regardless of the expected holding period of the security, and no prediction of the expected holding period is required. Moreover, there is no need to predict the expected future rate of return or percentage price change, because it appears both in the numerator and denominator of the calculation and cancels out. The result is an extremely simple rule for measuring the realizable value of the security. Yet the current market value rule, in spite of its simplicity, has extensive theoretical and empirical research to support its validity as the best measure of net realizable value. It is rare when a combination of simplicity and theoretical correctness is possessed by the same measure....

A constant lament in accounting is that we do not have sufficient evidence upon which to base policy decisions regarding appropriate reporting rules for financial statement preparation. The area of the valuation of marketable securities is rare in the sense that extensive evidence exists, supporting the current market value rule with remarkable consistency. Conversely, there is no theory to support a moving average rule, and in fact available research suggests serious deficiencies in such a rule. Therefore, it would be particularly unfortunate if this research were ignored in the formation of accounting policy for marketable equity securities. (pp. 60–61)

Morris and Coda [1973] disagreed with Beaver's conclusions. They argued that a moving average of past security prices is a better predictor of realizable value than is the current market price:

Recent appreciation is less certain, and therefore only a small portion should be recognized in the accounts.... [Under the current market price rule] there would be no distinction between companies that have volatile earnings because of fluctuating sales and those that have volatile earnings because of writeups and subsequent writedowns of the same assets. If such fluctuations were frequent and severe, accountants may face criticism for misstating assets and/or income. In extreme cases it would be possible for companies to appear solvent one year and insolvent the next year while holding the same assets. Undue reliance by accountants upon a single quoted amount from a stock exchange that is known to be volatile, and therefore unreliable, could provide some basis for legal action, however unfair this might appear to be....

The behavior of stock prices is capricious in the short run. Market prices published in the *Wall Street Journal* seem to be endowed with an undeserved reverence; after all, they can be influenced by emotional factors such as a political shock, current general optimism or pessimism, and glamour as well as other short-term factors such as interest rates and supply and demand of money. Therefore, logic would indicate that a single quoted market price at a random date is an unreliable predictor of future cash flows (net realizable values) for long-term investments. (pp. 50, 52)

REQUIRED

(1) Beaver [1971] argued that the evidence from the finance literature strongly supports the random-walk model as a description of the changes in daily security prices. What is the random-walk model? Discuss the evidence from one study that supports the random-walk model. What implications does the random-walk model have for the technical analysis approach to investment decision making?

(2) Design an empirical study that would examine if a moving-average model is a better predictor of net realizable value than is the current market price.

(3) The insurance industry strongly opposed including annual realized and unrealized gains and losses on marketable securities in income. (Marketable securities comprise 25–30% of the assets of many property-liability insurance companies.) One insurance company execu-

tive argued as follows:

> Earnings including unrealized capital gains and losses in income, with the concomitant distortion of net operating results, may confuse and mislead all but the most perceptive person.... The primary purpose of insurance accounting should be to smooth earnings from year to year, thereby increasing public confidence in the insurance industry. (*Best's Review*, Mar. 1975, p. 32)

The executive recommended annual realized gains or losses be included in the income statement and annual unrealized gains or losses be reported in a separate statement. Comment on this argument. You should make reference to the material discussed in Chapter 7 in your comment.

REFERENCES

ARTHUR ANDERSEN AND COMPANY. *APB Public Hearing on Accounting for Investments in Equity Securities Not Qualifying for the Equity Method: Cases in Public Accounting Practice Volume 8.* Arthur Andersen and Company, Chicago, 1971.

AXELSON, K. S. "A Businessman's Views on Disclosure." *The Journal of Accountancy* (July 1975): 42–46.

BACKER, M. *Financial Reporting for Security Investment and Credit Decisions.* National Association of Accountants, New York, 1970.

BEAVER, W. H. "Reporting Rules for Marketable Equity Securities." *The Journal of Accountancy* (Oct. 1971): 57–61.

———. "Market Efficiency." Unpublished Paper, Stanford University, Stanford, Calif., 1976.

BERNSTEIN, L. A. "In Defense of Fundamental Investment Analysis." *Financial Analysts Journal* (Jan.–Feb. 1975): 57–61.

BRILOFF, A. J. *Unaccountable Accounting.* Harper & Row, New York, 1972.

CHAMBERS, R. J. "Stock Market Prices and Accounting Research." *Abacus* (June 1974): 39–54.

CHATLOS, W. E. "Inside Information and the Analyst." In S. N. Levine (ed.), *Financial Analyst's Handbook I—Portfolio Management.* Irwin, Homewood, Ill., 1975: 74–86.

DEMSKI, J. S. "Choice Among Financial Reporting Alternatives." *The Accounting Review* (Apr. 1974): 221–232.

FAMA, E. F. "The Behavior of Stock Market Prices." *Journal of Business* (Jan. 1965): 34–105.

———. "Efficient Capital Markets: A Review of Theory and Empirical Work." *Journal of Finance* (May 1970): 383–417.

———. *Foundations of Finance*. Basic Books, New York, 1976.

FAMA, E. F., and LAFFER, A. B. "Information and Capital Markets." *Journal of Business* (July 1971): 289–298.

GONEDES, N. J. "The Capital Market, the Market for Information, and External Accounting." *The Journal of Finance* (May 1976): 611–630.

GONEDES, N. J., DOPUCH, N., and PENMAN, S. H. "Disclosure Rules, Information-Production, and Capital Market Equilibrium: The Case of Forecast Disclosure Rules." *Journal of Accounting Research* (Spring 1976): 89–137.

GRAHAM, B. DODD, D. L., and COTTLE, S. *Security Analysis: Principles and Techniques*, 4th ed. McGraw-Hill, New York, 1962.

GRANGER, C. W. J. "Empirical Studies of Capital Markets: A Survey." In G. P. Szego and K. Shell (eds.), *Mathematical Methods in Investment and Finance*. North-Holland, Amsterdam, 1972: 469–519.

GROSSMAN, S., and STIGLITZ, J. "On the Impossibility of Informationally Efficient Markets." Unpublished Paper, Stanford University, Stanford, Calif., 1976.

HIRSHLEIFER, J. "The Private and Social Value of Information and the Reward to Inventive Activity." *American Economic Review* (Sept. 1971): 561–573.

LOOMIS, P. "Loomis on Inside Information." *Financial Analysts Journal* (May–June 1972): 20–25, 82–88.

MACNEAL, K. *Truth in Accounting*. 1970 Reprint by Scholars Book Company, Lawrence, Kans., original edition 1939.

MALKIEL, B. G. *A Random Walk Down Wall Street*, Norton, New York, 1975.

MARSHALL, J. M. "Private Incentives and Public Information." *American Economic Review* (June 1974): 373–390.

MAY, R. G., and SUNDEM, G. L. "Cost of Information and Security Prices: Market Association Tests for Accounting Policy Decisions." *The Accounting Review* (Jan. 1973): 80–94.

MORRIS, W. J., and CODA, B. A. "Valuation of Equity Securities." *The Journal of Accountancy* (Jan. 1973): 48–54.

NORR, D. *Accounting Theory Illustrated*, Volume II. First Manhattan Company, New York, 1975.

RUBINSTEIN, M. "Securities Market Efficiency in an Arrow-Debreu Economy." *American Economic Review* (Dec. 1975): 812–824.

SHAW, A. R. "Technical Analysis," In S. N. Levine (ed.), *Financial Analyst's Handbook I— Portfolio Management*. Irwin, Homewood, Ill., 1975: 944–988.

SPACEK, L. "Business Success Requires an Understanding of Unsolved Problems of Accounting and Financial Reporting." Speech Presented at Harvard University, Cambridge, Mass., 1959. Reprinted in J. Lorie and R. Brealey (eds.), *Modern Developments in Investment Management*. Praeger, New York, 1972: 630–644.

SPENCE, A. M. "Job Market Signalling." *Quarterly Journal of Economics* (Aug. 1973): 355–379.

SPROUSE, R. T. (reporter). *The Measurement of Property, Plant and Equipment in Financial Statements*. Harvard University, Cambridge, Mass., 1964.

STIGLER, G. J. "Imperfections in the Capital Markets." *Journal of Political Economy* (June 1967): 287–292.

STIGLITZ, J. E. "Information and Economic Analysis." In J. M. Parkin and A. R. Nobay (eds.), *Current Economic Problems*. Cambridge University Press, New York, 1975: 27–52.

WATERFIELD, R. H. "Our Approach To Serving the Life Insurance Industry." *Arthur Young Journal* (Winter 1974): 2–9.

CHAPTER

PORTFOLIO THEORY AND ASSET PRICING MODELS[1]

Portfolio theory is a structured approach to investment choice under uncertainty. In Section 8.1 we shall outline the central ideas in portfolio theory. The implications for capital asset pricing of assuming that investors adopt a portfolio theory approach are discussed in Section 8.2.

8.1 PORTFOLIO THEORY

Portfolio theory was initially developed by Markowitz [1952; 1959] as a normative approach to investment choice under uncertainty. The theory can be viewed as a simplification of the decision theory framework outlined in Chapter 1. Two important assumptions in this simplification are that security returns are (multivariate) normally distributed[2] and that investors are risk-averse.[3] These assumptions imply two features of investment decisions under uncertainty:

(1) Two statistics are sufficient to describe the distribution of future returns of a portfolio; i.e., the mean and variance of the distribution, and

(2) Investors prefer higher expected returns to lower expected returns for a given level of portfolio variance and prefer lower variance to higher variance of portfolio returns for a given level of expected returns.

The assumption that investors are risk-averse is an important one. It implies the reasonable prediction that investors will attempt to diversify their portfolio rather than hold the single asset with the highest expected return.

In portfolio theory, the concern of the investor is with the distribution of the return on the *portfolio*. The characteristics of *individual securities* are only important in terms of their effect on the distribution of the portfolio return. To model the relationship between the returns on a portfolio and the returns on the securities in that portfolio requires the use of some basic laws of probability theory. The results of these probability laws will be noted in the following discussion.[4]

A Expected Return on a Portfolio

Let $\tilde{R}_i$ be the return on security i and $\tilde{R}_p$ be the return on a portfolio of securities.[5] Then

$$E\left(\tilde{R}_p\right) = \sum_{i=1}^{n} X_{ip} E\left(\tilde{R}_i\right), \tag{8.1}$$

where X_{ip} = the ith stock's proportionate weight in portfolio p. This result follows from the law of probability that the weighted sum of random variables is the sum of the weighted means that make up the sum.

Assume two securities with $E(R_1)=.12$ and $E(R_2)=.14$. If one invests 70% of funds in security 1 and 30% in security 2, then

$$E(\tilde{R}_p)=.7\times.12+.3\times.14=.126.$$

That is, a portfolio's expected return is the weighted average of the expected values of its component securities—the weights are the current market values of these securities.

B Variance of the Return on a Portfolio

The expression for the variance of the portfolio returns is

$$\sigma^2(\tilde{R}_p)=E\left\{\left[\tilde{R}_p-E(\tilde{R}_p)\right]^2\right\}. \qquad (8.2)$$

Given (8.2) and the probability law that

$$\sigma^2(X_{ip}R_i)=X_{ip}^2\sigma^2(\tilde{R}_i), \qquad (8.3)$$

then

$$\sigma^2(\tilde{R}_p)=E\left\{\sum_{i=1}^{n}X_{ip}\left[\tilde{R}_i-E(\tilde{R}_i)\right]\right\}^2. \qquad (8.4)$$

The expression in (8.4) can be better understood by considering a two-security portfolio.

A Two-Security Portfolio

For a two-security portfolio, on expansion (8.4) becomes

$$\sigma^2(\tilde{R}_p)=X_{1p}^2E\left[\tilde{R}_1-E(\tilde{R}_1)\right]^2+X_{2p}^2E\left[\tilde{R}_2-E(\tilde{R}_2)\right]^2$$
$$+2X_{1p}X_{2p}E\left\{\left[\tilde{R}_1-E(\tilde{R}_1)\right]\left[\tilde{R}_2-E(\tilde{R}_2)\right]\right\}. \qquad (8.5)$$

The third component on the right-hand side of (8.5) includes the pairwise covariance between $\tilde{R}_1$ and $\tilde{R}_2$: $E\{[\tilde{R}_1-E(\tilde{R}_1)][\tilde{R}_2-E(\tilde{R}_2)]\}$. This covariance term measures the degree of covariation or comovement between the returns on security 1 and security 2.

The covariance between the returns on securities i and j is usually denoted σ_{ij}. By definition,

$$\sigma_{ij}=r_{ij}\cdot\sigma_i\cdot\sigma_j, \qquad (8.6)$$

where r_{ij} = the correlation coefficient between the returns on security i and security j,[6]

σ_i = standard deviation of the returns on security i.

A more succinct representation of (8.5), using (8.6), is

$$\sigma^2(\tilde{R}_p) = X_{1p}^2\sigma^2(\tilde{R}_1) + X_{2p}^2\sigma^2(\tilde{R}_2) + 2X_{1p}X_{2p}r_{12}\cdot\sigma(\tilde{R}_1)\cdot\sigma(\tilde{R}_2). \quad (8.7)$$

EXAMPLE ONE: Assume equal investment in two securities (X_{1p} = .5, X_{2p} = .5) with equal variances [$\sigma^2(\tilde{R}_1) = \sigma^2(\tilde{R}_2) = .03$].

$$\sigma^2(\tilde{R}_p) = (.5)^2 \times .03 + (.5)^2 \times .03 + 2 \times .5 \times .5 \times r_{12} \times \sqrt{.03} \times \sqrt{.03}$$
$$= .0075 + .0075 + .015r_{12}.$$

The benefits of portfolio diversification can be illustrated by examining the effect on $\sigma^2(\tilde{R}_p)$ of different values of r_{12}.

One extreme case is where $r_{12} = 1$; i.e., the two securities' returns are perfectly positively correlated:

$$\sigma^2(\tilde{R}_p) = .0075 + .0075 + .015 = .03.$$

In this specific example, the variance of the portfolio is the same as the variance of either security. Consider now the case where $r_{12} = .1$; i.e., the two securities' returns are weakly positively correlated:

$$\sigma^2(\tilde{R}_p) = .0075 + .0075 + .0015 = .0165.$$

Note the reduction in $\sigma^2(\tilde{R}_p)$ relative to the case where $r_{12} = 1$. Finally, consider the other extreme case of $r_{12} = -1$; i.e., the two securities' returns are perfectly negatively correlated:

$$\sigma^2(\tilde{R}_p) = .0075 + .0075 - .015 = 0.$$

The portfolio variance is now zero. A perfectly hedged portfolio has been formed. This situation is where there is maximum benefit from diversification.

EXAMPLE TWO: Assume unequal investment in two securities (X_{1p} = .6, X_{2p} = .4) with unequal variances [$\sigma^2(\tilde{R}_1) = .04, \sigma^2(\tilde{R}_2) = .09$].

$$\sigma^2(\tilde{R}_p) = (.6)^2 \times .04 + (.4)^2 \times .09 + 2 \times .6 \times .4 \times r_{12} \times \sqrt{.04} \times \sqrt{.09}$$
$$= .0144 + .0144 + .0288r_{12}.$$

When $r_{12} = 1$, then

$$\sigma^2(\tilde{R}_p) = .0144 + .0144 + .0288 = .0576.$$

When $r_{12} = .1$, then

$$\sigma^2(\tilde{R}_p) = .0144 + .0144 + .00288 = .03168.$$

Note the reduction in portfolio variance relative to where $r_{12} = 1$.

Finally, consider the case where $r_{12} = -1$:

$$\sigma^2(\tilde{R}_p) = .0144 + .0144 - .0288 = 0.$$

As with Example One, it is possible to eliminate uncertainty about the portfolio return by creating a perfectly hedged portfolio.

The weights in both examples were deliberately chosen to illustrate the potential benefits from portfolio diversification. For the two-asset portfolio, maximum benefit from diversification occurs when $r_{12} = -1$ and X_{1p} and X_{2p} are inversely proportional to their standard deviations, i.e., when

$$\frac{X_{1p}}{X_{2p}} = \frac{\sigma(\tilde{R}_2)}{\sigma(\tilde{R}_1)}. \tag{8.8}$$

Thus, in Example Two with $\sigma(\tilde{R}_1) = .2$ and $\sigma(\tilde{R}_2) = .3$, the maximum benefit from diversification occurs when X_{1p}/X_{2p} is in the ratio of $.3/.2$. Given that the security weights in a portfolio must sum to 1, this implies that $X_{1p} = .6$ and $X_{2p} = .4$.

An N-Security Portfolio

In the N-security portfolio,

$$\sigma^2(\tilde{R}_p) = \sum_{i=1}^{n} \sum_{j=1}^{n} X_{ip} X_{jp} \sigma_{ij}. \tag{8.9}$$

By noting that when $i = j$

$$\sigma_{ij} = \sigma_i^2 = \sigma_j^2,$$

(8.9) can be factored into an expression separately containing variance and covariance terms:

$$\sigma^2(\tilde{R}_p) = \sum_{i=1}^{n} X_{ip}^2 \sigma^2(\tilde{R}_i) + \sum_{i=1}^{n} \sum_{\substack{j=1 \\ j \neq i}}^{n} X_{ip} X_{jp} \sigma_{ij}. \tag{8.10}$$

In general, the number of variance terms in (8.10) is N and the number of covariance terms is $[N(N-1)]/2$. Thus, for a 10-security portfolio, $\sigma^2(\tilde{R}_p)$ will contain 10 variance terms and 45 covariance terms. For a 100-security portfolio, $\sigma^2(\tilde{R}_p)$ will contain 100 variance terms and 4,950 covariance terms. Note that it does not necessarily follow that because there are numerically more covariance than variance terms in $\sigma^2(\tilde{R}_p)$ that the contribution of the covariance terms to $\sigma^2(\tilde{R}_p)$ is dominant. It also depends on the relative size of the variance and covariance terms. Empirically, however, covariance terms are the major contributors to $\sigma^2(\tilde{R}_p)$ in large well-diversified portfolios. For instance, Fama [1976, Chapter 7] demonstrates that for a 50-security portfolio the covariance terms constitute approximately 90% of $\sigma^2(\tilde{R}_p)$.

C   Efficient Portfolios and the Dominance Principle

The dominance principle in portfolio theory states that an investor will (1) prefer the portfolio with the highest expected return for a given risk level and (2) prefer the portfolio with the lowest risk level for a given level of expected return. To illustrate this principle, consider the second two-security example in the previous subsection, i.e., where $\sigma^2(\tilde{R}_1)=.04$ and $\sigma^2(\tilde{R}_2)=.09$. Assume that

$$E(\tilde{R}_1)=.008$$
$$E(\tilde{R}_2)=.014$$
$$r_{12}=.1.$$

For the case where $X_{1p}=.6$ and $X_{2p}=.4$,

$$E(\tilde{R}_p)=.0104$$
$$\sigma^2(\tilde{R}_p)=.03168.$$

Contrast this case with investing all funds in security 1:

$$E(\tilde{R}_1)=.008$$
$$\sigma^2(\tilde{R}_p)=.04.$$

From a risk-averse investor's perspective, the above two-stock portfolio *dominates* the single-stock portfolio—it has a higher expected return and a lower variance.

Portfolio theory analysis involves constructing the set of efficient portfolios and then choosing among these efficient portfolios on the basis of the investor's preferences as regards risk and return. An *efficient*

FIGURE 8.1   The Efficient Frontier

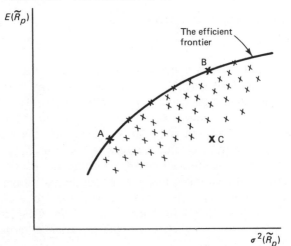

portfolio is a portfolio that has the highest expected return for a given risk level or the lowest risk level for a given level of expected return. The set of efficient portfolios forms the *efficient frontier*. Figure 8.1 illustrates these concepts. It is apparent that portfolio A dominates C and portfolio B also dominates C. No dominance relation exists between A and B as they are on different points of the efficient frontier. The choice between A and B (and other points on the frontier) will depend on the investor's preferences. A retired couple concerned with obtaining a small variance portfolio may prefer A, whereas a recently graduated MBA concerned with high returns may prefer B.

D Benefits of Portfolio Diversification

The variance of a portfolio will, in general, depend on three different factors:

(1) The variance of each security,
(2) The covariance of each security with other securities, and
(3) The number of securities (and their weightings) in the portfolio.

As a preliminary pass to illustrating the benefits of diversification, assume that the returns of each security are independent of the returns of other securities (i.e., $\sigma_{ij}=0$ for all i and j and $i \neq j$) and that there is equal weighting of securities in the portfolio. Given these assumptions, (8.10) becomes

$$\sigma^2(\tilde{R}_p)= \sum_{i=1}^{n} X_{ip}^2\sigma^2(\tilde{R}_i)$$

$$=\frac{1}{N^2} \sum_{i=1}^{N} \sigma^2(\tilde{R}_i), \qquad (8.11)$$

where $X_{ip}=1/N$. If we further assume that the largest security variance is M, then

$$\sigma^2(\tilde{R}_p) \leqslant \frac{NM}{N^2} = \frac{M}{N}. \qquad (8.12)$$

Consider the case where $M=.025$. The behavior of $\sigma^2(\tilde{R}_p)$ for portfolios of different securities is plotted in Figure 8.2. A striking feature of this figure is that a substantial reduction in $\sigma^2(\tilde{R}_p)$ occurs with a relatively small portfolio size. For example, when

$$N=1, \qquad \sigma^2(\tilde{R}_p)=.025$$
$$N=5, \qquad \sigma^2(\tilde{R}_p)=.005$$
$$N=10, \qquad \sigma^2(\tilde{R}_p)=.0025$$
$$N=15, \qquad \sigma^2(\tilde{R}_p)=.0017.$$

FIGURE 8.2 Benefits from Diversification—I

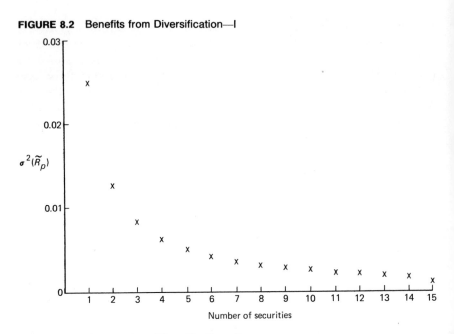

FIGURE 8.3 Benefits from Diversification—II

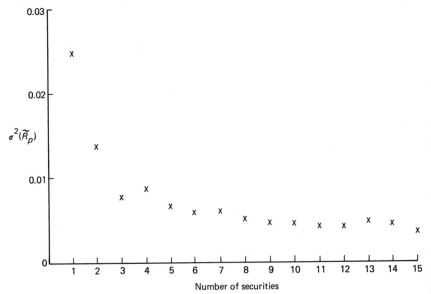

That is, the reduction in portfolio variance is more dramatic when the portfolio size is increased from one to five securities than when it is increased from five to ten securities.

As a more realistic example of the gains from portfolio diversification, we randomly selected equally weighted portfolios of increasing size from all securities listed on the NYSE. Monthly returns over the January 1971 to December 1975 period were used in the example. Figure 8.3 plots the behavior of $\sigma^2(\tilde{R}_p)$ as the number of securities in the portfolio is increased. The pattern in Figure 8.3 is, not surprisingly, less smooth than that for the hypothetical example in Figure 8.2. The general tenor of the pattern in both figures, however, is the same. The portfolio variance decreases markedly when the portfolio size is initially increased. The benefits of diversification then become much less dramatic for increases in the portfolio size beyond (say) ten securities. An important proviso to these results is that the increase in the number of securities is associated with smaller and smaller fractions of the portfolio being invested in each security. Should the fraction invested in some securities be kept constant when the number of securities is increased, the benefits from diversification will be less marked than in Figures 8.2 and 8.3.[7]

E The Market Model

For even a moderately sized portfolio of N securities, (8.1) and (8.9) require estimation of a large number of inputs—N expected returns, N variances, and $[N(N-1)]/2$ covariances. Concern with the computational burden in deriving these estimates led Sharpe [1963] to develop the following *market model*:

$$\tilde{R}_{it} = \hat{\alpha}_i + \hat{\beta}_i \tilde{R}_{mt} + \hat{\epsilon}_{it}, \qquad (8.13)$$

where $\tilde{R}_{it}$ = return on security i in period t,

$\tilde{R}_{mt}$ = return on the market portfolio in period t.

The assumption was made that $E(\hat{\epsilon}_i) = 0$ and $\tilde{\epsilon}_{it}$ and $\tilde{R}_{mt}$ are independent. The $\hat{\beta}_i$ term in (8.13) is termed the *beta* or *relative risk* of a security.

Given (8.13) and the above assumptions, the expected return and variance of an equally weighted portfolio become

$$E(\tilde{R}_p) = \alpha_p + \beta_p \cdot E(\tilde{R}_m) \qquad (8.14)$$

$$\sigma^2(\tilde{R}_p) = \beta_p^2 \sigma^2(\tilde{R}_m) + \frac{1}{N^2} \sum_{i=1}^{N} \sigma^2(\tilde{\epsilon}_i), \qquad (8.15)$$

where $\alpha_p = (1/N)\sum_{i=1}^{N}\alpha_i$, and $\beta_p = (1/N)\sum_{i=1}^{N}\beta_i$. An important result relating to (8.15) is that the second term on the right-hand side becomes relatively less important as N increases. In large well-diversified portfolios, the $\beta_p^2 \sigma^2(\tilde{R}_m)$ component is the major contributor to $\sigma^2(\tilde{R}_p)$.[8] This result is of fundamental importance in portfolio theory. An individual security may have a "large" variance, yet have a "low" covariance with the market portfolio. This security would then be viewed as a "low"-risk security when viewed as a component of a diversified portfolio.

To illustrate the market model, we estimated (8.13) for *International Harvester* using monthly security returns over the January 1971 to December 1975 period (60 observations). A value-weighted index of all NYSE stocks was used for $\tilde{R}_m$. The estimated model, using ordinary least

TABLE 8.1 Market Model Parameter Estimates for Dow-Jones Firms
for January 1971–December 1975

Company	$\hat{\alpha}$	$t(\hat{\alpha})$	$\hat{\beta}$	$t(\hat{\beta})$	R^2	$\bar{R}_i$	$\sigma(\hat{\xi}_i)$
Allied Chemical	.0086	1.010	.997	5.870	.373	.0122	.066
Aluminum Co. of America	.0049	.429	.662	2.927	.129	.0072	.088
American Brands	.0016	.264	.820	6.748	.440	.0045	.047
American Can	.0016	.256	.566	4.447	.254	.0036	.049
AT&T	.0050	1.086	.589	6.442	.417	.0071	.035
Bethlehem Steel	.0114	1.158	1.120	5.734	.362	.0153	.076
Chrysler Corp.	−.0112	−.839	1.217	4.575	.265	−.0069	.103
Du Pont	.0017	.227	.866	5.689	.358	.0048	.059
Eastman Kodak	.0061	.936	.979	7.620	.500	.0095	.050
Esmark, Inc.	.0077	.798	.862	4.477	.257	.0108	.075
Exxon Corp.	.0068	1.187	.724	6.322	.408	.0094	.044
General Electric	.0005	.083	1.271	11.112	.680	.0050	.044
General Foods	−.0036	−.416	1.068	6.153	.395	.0002	.067
General Motors	−.0009	−.126	.805	5.765	.364	.0020	.054
Goodyear Tire	−.0030	−.377	1.045	6.628	.431	.0007	.061
International Harvester	.0020	.201	.931	4.691	.275	.0053	.077
International Nickel	−.0064	−.792	1.006	6.216	.400	−.0029	.063
International Paper	.0113	1.379	.988	6.045	.387	.0148	.063
Johns Manville	−.0048	−.507	.912	4.853	.289	−.0015	.073
Minnesota Mining & Manu.	.0023	.322	1.163	8.283	.542	.0064	.054
Owens Illinois	.0010	.122	1.020	6.418	.415	.0046	.062
Procter & Gamble	.0074	1.407	.871	8.286	.542	.0105	.041
Sears Roebuck	−.0021	−.320	1.023	7.892	.518	.0015	.050
Standard Oil of California	.0059	.688	.919	5.348	.330	.0092	.067
Texaco	−.0023	−.331	.877	6.294	.406	.0008	.054
Union Carbide	.0102	1.362	1.231	8.236	.539	.0146	.058
U.S. Steel	.0160	1.828	.871	4.999	.301	.0191	.068
United Technology	.0115	1.018	.820	3.639	.186	.0144	.087
Westinghouse	−.0104	−.932	.962	4.353	.246	−.0069	.086
Woolworth	−.0034	−.319	1.161	5.496	.342	.0007	.082
Averages	.0025	.360	.945	6.052	.378	.0059	.063

squares,[9] was

$$\tilde{R}_{it} = .0020 + .931\tilde{R}_{mt} + \hat{\epsilon}_{it}$$
$$\underset{t=.201}{} \quad \underset{t=4.691}{}$$
$$R^2 = .275; \quad \sigma(\hat{\epsilon}_i) = .077.$$

These estimates predict that if $\tilde{R}_m$ goes up .01 in a month, the expected return on *International Harvester* will go up by .00931 to be .01131:

$$E(R_{it}|R_{mt}) = .0020 + .931 \times .01 = .01131.$$

The R^2 of .275 means that 27.5% of the variance in the return on *International Harvester* is explained by variations in the returns on the market portfolio.

What do the betas of other securities look like? As an initial pass, we replicated the procedures used for *International Harvester* on all the other stocks in the Dow-Jones Index. Table 8.1 lists the estimates of several *market model* parameters for each of the 30 Dow-Jones stocks. The average $\hat{\beta}_i$ of .945 indicates that these stocks were, on average, marginally less risky than the market portfolio ($\beta_i = 1$) over the 1971–1975 period. Table 8.2 lists average industry betas presented in Rosenberg and Guy [1976]. These

TABLE 8.2   Average Industry Betas

Industry	Average Beta	Industry	Average Beta
Air transport	1.80	Energy raw materials	1.22
Real property	1.70	Tires, rubber goods	1.21
Travel, outdoor recreation	1.66	Railroads, shipping	1.19
Electronics	1.60	Forest products, paper	1.16
Miscellaneous finance	1.60	Drugs, medicine	1.14
Nondurables, entertainment	1.47	Miscellaneous, conglomerate	1.14
Consumer durables	1.44	Domestic oil	1.12
Business machines	1.43	Soaps, cosmetics	1.09
Retail, general	1.43	Steel	1.02
Media	1.39	Containers	1.01
Insurance	1.34	Agriculture, food	.99
Trucking, freight	1.31	Nonferrous metals	.99
Aerospace	1.30	Liquor	.89
Producer goods	1.30	International oil	.85
Business services	1.28	Banks	.81
Apparel	1.27	Tobacco	.80
Construction	1.27	Telephone	.75
Motor vehicles	1.27	Energy, utilities	.60
Photographic, optical	1.24	Gold	.36
Chemicals	1.22		

SOURCE: Rosenberg and Guy [1976, Table 2].

average betas were estimated using the 101 months of security returns from April 1966 to August 1974. The averages in Table 8.2 are consistent with there being considerable differences in the average betas of various industries.

The market model was initially proposed to reduce the number of inputs required in portfolio analysis. It can also be justified in the context of an equilibrium asset pricing model. Indeed, this justification is now the most appealing one. In Section 8.2 we shall discuss both theory and evidence pertaining to equilibrium asset pricing models.

8.2. ASSET PRICING MODELS

A   Theoretical Models

Assume that all investors adopt a portfolio theory approach to investment choice. What does this assumption imply about the setting of aggregate market prices? In answering this question, the following additional assumptions will be made:

(1) All investors have the same expectations about means, variances, and covariances of assets;

(2) All investors have a common time horizon (a single period) for investment decision making; and

(3) All assets are sold in complete and perfect markets (with zero transaction costs).

Given these assumptions, assets will be priced in equilibrium according to the following model (see Black [1972]):

$$E(\tilde{R}_i) = E(\tilde{R}_0) + \beta_i\big[E(\tilde{R}_m) - E(\tilde{R}_0)\big], \qquad (8.16)$$

where $E(\tilde{R}_0)$ = expected return on a minimum variance portfolio whose returns are uncorrelated with those of the market portfolio,

$$\beta_i = \frac{\text{Cov}(\tilde{R}_i, \tilde{R}_m)}{\sigma^2(\tilde{R}_m)}.$$

If one makes the additional assumption that there exists a risk-free asset with a single rate that investors can borrow and lend at, the following special case of (8.16) describes asset pricing in equilibrium (see Sharpe [1964] and Lintner [1965]):

$$E(\tilde{R}_i) = R_f + \beta_i\big[E(\tilde{R}_m) - R_f\big], \qquad (8.17)$$

where R_f = the return on a riskless asset.

A numerical example will illustrate the predictions of these models. Consider (8.17) and assume that $E(R_m) = .01$ per month and $R_f = .002$ per month. Figure 8.4 displays the relationship between expected return and beta. For example, if

$$\beta = 0, \qquad E(\tilde{R}_i) = .002 + 0 \times (.01 - .002) = .002$$
$$\beta = .5, \qquad E(\tilde{R}_i) = .002 + .5 \times (.01 - .002) = .006$$
$$\beta = 1, \qquad E(\tilde{R}_i) = .002 + 1 \times (.01 - .002) = .010$$
$$\beta = 1.5, \qquad E(\tilde{R}_i) = .002 + 1.5 \times (.01 - .002) = .014.$$

The capital market line in Figure 8.4 is the set of efficient portfolios when investors can borrow and lend at a riskless rate. In equilibrium, all investors would hold combinations of the riskless asset and the market portfolio.

In general, the asset pricing model in (8.16) predicts that

(1) There is a positive linear relationship between expected return and beta, and

(2) The only parameter explaining differences in the expected returns of securities is beta.

Given the assumption that there exists a risk-free asset, there is the additional prediction of (8.17) that

(3) $E(\tilde{R}_0) = R_f.$

These predictions have been the subject of detailed testing. In the next subsection we shall discuss the results of these tests.

FIGURE 8.4   Capital Asset Pricing

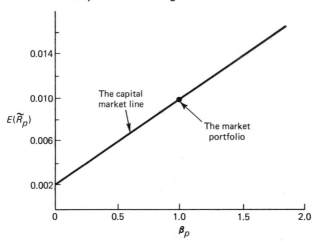

B Evidence on Theoretical Models

The most detailed tests of the asset pricing models described previously have utilized data on NYSE stocks. A feature of these tests is the procedures adopted to reduce nontrivial methodological problems in the analysis. These problems are briefly noted below.

Methodological Problems in Tests of Asset Pricing Models

The first problem is that (8.16) refers to ex ante magnitudes (expected return and risk over a holding period), whereas only ex post data are available for testing. It is possible that expectations can systematically differ from realizations over short periods of time. For this reason, studies have used data covering extended time periods; e.g., Black et al. [1972] used 420 monthly observations (January 1931–December 1965), Fama and MacBeth [1973] used 402 monthly observations (January 1935–June 1968), and Foster [1977] used 528 monthly observations (January 1931–December 1974). The assumption in these studies is that at least over a 30- to 40-year period there should be a reasonable correspondence between expectations and realizations.

A second problem in testing (8.16) arises from measurement errors in estimates of β_i. At the individual security level, there is considerable measurement error. Consider the estimated β_i for *International Harvester* presented in Section 8.1E. The estimated β_i from (8.13) was .931 with a standard error of .199. This means that the 95% confidence interval for β_i is from .533 to 1.329. There is considerably less measurement error in the estimates of the betas of portfolios. To illustrate this point, we formed an equally weighted portfolio of the 30 Dow-Jones stocks and estimated (8.13) over the January 1971–December 1975 period:

$$\tilde{R}_{pt} = .0025 + .945\,\tilde{R}_{mt} + \hat{\epsilon}_{it}$$
$$\quad\;\; t=1.139 \qquad t=21.482$$
$$R^2 = .888; \qquad \sigma(\hat{\epsilon}_i) = .017.$$

The standard error of $\hat{\beta}_p$ was .044. This means that the 95% confidence interval for $\hat{\beta}_p$ is from .857 to 1.033. Note the substantially smaller confidence interval for the $\hat{\beta}_p$ of the Dow-Jones portfolio than for the $\hat{\beta}_i$ of *International Harvester*. In an attempt to reduce the measurement error in estimates of individual security betas, the more extensive tests of asset pricing models have used portfolio returns rather than individual security returns. Stocks have been put into portfolios so as to maximize the dispersion in ex post portfolio betas; hopefully, the procedures used have also resulted in portfolios with the maximum dispersion in ex ante estimates of beta.

A third problem in testing (8.16) is that the R_m in the theoretical model is a value-weighted index of the returns of all available assets, e.g., stocks, bonds, real estate, and human capital. Unfortunately, it is difficult to obtain reliable market price quotations (and thus also the appropriate returns and value weights) on many assets. Most studies have used indexes restricted to NYSE securities because there is reliable and easily available market price data on them. If these indexes do not approximate the returns on a minimum variance portfolio, misleading inferences about the relationship between expected return and risk may be made.[10]

Some Results of Asset Pricing Model Tests

What evidence is there of a positive relationship between expected return and beta? Black et al. [1972] provide evidence on this question for all NYSE stocks for the 1931–1965 period. Ten portfolios were formed in 1931 (and rebalanced each subsequent year) to maximize the dispersion in the ex post portfolio betas (termed systematic risk in Black et al.). Monthly portfolio returns were measured after subtracting an estimate of R_f. Figure 8.5 plots the data for $\hat{\beta}_p$ and $(\overline{R_p - R_f})$ for the ten portfolios in the study. Note that the pattern in Figure 8.5 is consistent with a positive relationship between expected return and beta. The Fama and MacBeth [1973] and Foster [1977] papers also report a similar finding.

Given that the portfolio returns in Figure 8.5 are estimated as $(\overline{R_p - R_f})$, the Sharpe-Lintner asset pricing model (8.17) predicts that the

FIGURE 8.5   Risk-Return Relationships for NYSE Stocks

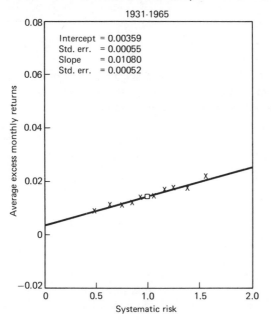

Source: Black et al. [1972, Figure 1]

capital market line should pass through the origin. This is not apparent in the data. Indeed, Black et al. [1972] present detailed evidence inconsistent with the Sharpe-Lintner model's prediction that $E(\tilde{R}_0) - R_f = 0$. Using similar procedures, Fama and MacBeth [1973] report a similar result. One limitation of this evidence against the Sharpe-Lintner model is that an equally weighted index of NYSE stocks was used in computing the portfolio betas. Recall that the theoretical model specifies the use of a value-weighted index of all assets. In Foster [1977], the effect of using a value-weighted index of NYSE stocks as opposed to an equal-weighted index of NYSE stocks was examined. Use of the value-weighted index reduced (but did not eliminate) the violations from the Sharpe-Lintner model observed in Figure 8.5. Note, however, that although the index used in this paper was value-weighted, it was restricted to NYSE stocks. For this reason, the results cannot be viewed as a definitive test of the Sharpe-Lintner model prediction that $E(\tilde{R}_0) - R_f = 0$.

A detailed description and critique of tests of asset pricing models is beyond the scope of this section.[11] Suffice it to note that there is considerable evidence supporting the prediction of a positive relationship between expected return and beta.[12] Tests of other asset pricing model predictions [e.g., linearity, no rewards to nonbeta risk measures, and the Sharpe-Lintner prediction that $E(\tilde{R}_0) - R_f = 0$] are less conclusive. Note, however, that nontrivial problems occur in empirical work in this area. The more definitive tests of asset pricing models are yet to be done.[13]

8.3 SUMMARY

The portfolio theory and asset pricing models described in this chapter play an important part in analysis of the role of financial statement information in capital markets. With the foundations laid in this and prior chapters, we now have a solid base to examine issues such as the role of accounting data in risk assessment and the association between security returns and accounting earnings. These and related topics are examined in subsequent chapters.

NOTES

[1]This chapter is meant to provide a concise summary of several important threads of the finance literature, i.e., portfolio theory and asset pricing models. For further discussions, see Fama [1976] and Sharpe [1970; 1978].

[2]The available evidence suggests that a normal distribution is a good approximation to the distribution of monthly security returns. See, for example, Officer [1971] and Blattberg and Gonedes [1974].

[3]Sharpe [1970] contains a lucid exposition of risk aversion as related to investment decisions.

[4]Fama [1976, Chapter 2] provides a good discussion of probability laws used in portfolio analysis.

[5]The return on a security is computed as

$$\left(\frac{P_t + D_t}{P_{t-1}} - 1 \right)$$

where P_t = closing price in period t,

D_t = dividends paid in period t.

[6]The correlation coefficient (r_{ij}) is the product moment correlation coefficient. See Chapter 6 (footnote 8) for a description of this correlation coefficient.

[7]The above example was restricted to NYSE securities. It also appears possible to increase diversification by investing in (1) other U.S. investment media (e.g., bonds and real estate) and (2) securities listed on foreign exchanges—see, for example, Robichek et al. [1972] and Solnik [1974].

[8]The proviso that the portfolio is well diversified is important. For portfolios that are heavily concentrated in (say) one industry, the $\beta_p^2 \sigma^2(\tilde{R}_m)$ component could considerably underestimate $\sigma^2(\tilde{R}_p)$ for even a large portfolio. For evidence that industry as well as market factors explain variations in realized security returns, see King [1966] and Meyers [1973].

[9]In Chapter 9 we shall discuss adjustments that might be made to ordinary least-squares estimates of β_i in (8.13) to obtain more efficient estimates of the beta of each security.

[10]Further discussion of methodological problems in empirical tests of asset pricing models can be found in Miller and Scholes [1972] and Roll [1977].

[11]See Fama [1976, Chapter 9] and Roll [1977] for detailed discussions of these topics.

[12]Tests of asset pricing models on foreign capital markets have also reported a positive relationship between expected returns and beta. See, for example, Ball et al. [1976] on the Australian capital market.

[13]It is likely that in future work extensions of the equilibrium asset pricing models discussed in this chapter will also be tested. For an example of an extension, see Merton [1977].

QUESTION 8.1:   Portfolio Risk and Return

Some relevant data pertaining to three Dow-Jones stocks over the January 1971–December 1975 period are

		$\sigma(\tilde{R}_i)$	$\hat{\beta}_i$
A:	Aluminum Company of America	.093	.662
B:	Eastman Kodak	.070	.979
C:	Union Carbide Corp.	.085	1.231

The pairwise correlations between the returns of these three securities are

$$r_{AB}=.137$$
$$r_{AC}=.476$$
$$r_{BC}=.422.$$

REQUIRED

(1) Using the Sharpe-Lintner asset pricing model and assuming that $E(\tilde{R}_M)=.010$ per month and $R_f=.002$ per month, calculate the expected return on each stock. Why is $E(\tilde{R}_B)>E(\tilde{R}_A)$ when $\sigma(\tilde{R}_A)> \sigma(\tilde{R}_B)$?

(2) Compute the expected return and variance of equally weighted portfolios of the following stocks:
   (a) A and B.
   (b) A and C.
   (c) B and C.
   Why is $\sigma^2(\tilde{R}_p)$ for (b) $>\sigma^2(\tilde{R}_p)$ for (a)?

(3) Given that $\sigma(\tilde{R}_B)=.070$ and $\sigma(\tilde{R}_C)=.085$, examine the effect on the $\sigma^2(\tilde{R}_p)$ of an equally weighted portfolio of B and C when
   (a) $r_{BC}=1.$
   (b) $r_{BC}=0.$
   (c) $r_{BC}=-1.$
   Comment on the results. What portfolio weights for B and C would create a perfectly hedged portfolio $[\sigma^2(\tilde{R}_p)=0]$ when $r_{BC}=-1$?

(4) A portfolio manager of a pension fund for workers in the oil industry recently commented that he attempted to maintain a well-diversified portfolio. He also commented that he avoided investing in *Exxon*,

Standard Oil of Indiana, Texaco, and other oil stocks. Oil stocks comprise approximately 15% of the market value of all stocks in *Standard & Poor's 500 Stock Index.* How do you reconcile these two comments by the portfolio manager?

QUESTION 8.2: Portfolio Analysis Using the Market Model

Concern with reducing the number of parameters to be estimated in portfolio theory led Sharpe [1963] to develop the market model:

$$\tilde{R}_i = \hat{\alpha}_i + \hat{\beta}_i \tilde{R}_m + \hat{\epsilon}_i.$$

Assuming the validity of the market model, the expected return and variance of an equally weighted portfolio are

$$E(\tilde{R}_p) = \alpha_p + \beta_p \cdot E(\tilde{R}_m)$$

$$\sigma^2(\tilde{R}_p) = \beta_p^2 \sigma^2(\tilde{R}_m) + \frac{1}{N^2} \sum_{i=1}^{N} \sigma^2(\hat{\epsilon}_i),$$

where

$$\alpha_p = \frac{1}{N} \sum_{i=1}^{N} \alpha_i$$

$$\beta_p = \frac{1}{N} \sum_{i=1}^{N} \beta_i.$$

Estimates of $\hat{\alpha}_i$, $\hat{\beta}_i$, and $\sigma^2(\hat{\epsilon}_i)$ for seven Dow-Jones stocks using *monthly returns* over the January 1971–December 1975 period are

		$\hat{\alpha}_i$	$\hat{\beta}_i$	$\sigma^2(\hat{\epsilon}_i)$
1.	Esmark	.0077	.862	.0056
2.	Du Pont	.0017	.866	.0035
3.	Procter & Gamble	.0074	.871	.0017
4.	Johns Manville	−.0048	.912	.0053
5.	General Motors	−.0009	.805	.0029
6.	Standard Oil of Calif.	.0059	.919	.0045
7.	American Brands	.0016	.820	.0022

Over this same period $\sigma^2(\tilde{R}_m) = .0026$.

REQUIRED

(1) Fill in the spaces in the following table for equally weighted portfolios of sizes 3 to 7. The portfolio of size 3 includes *Esmark,*

Du Pont, and *Procter & Gamble*; the portfolio of size 4 includes *Esmark*, *Du Pont*, *Procter & Gamble*, and *Johns Manville*, etc. Assume that $E(\tilde{R}_m) = .010$ per month.

N	$E(\tilde{R}_p)$	β_p	$\beta_p^2\sigma^2(\tilde{R}_m)$	$\dfrac{1}{N^2}\displaystyle\sum_{i=1}^{N}\sigma^2(\epsilon_i)$	$\sigma^2(\tilde{R}_p)$
1	.01632	.862	.001932	.005600	.007532
2	.01334	.864	.001941	.002275	.004216
3					
4					
5					
6					
7					

(2) Plot $\sigma^2(\tilde{R}_p)$ as a function of N. Comment on the results.
(3) Estimate the importance of the

$$\frac{1}{N^2}\sum_{i=1}^{N}\sigma^2(\epsilon_i)$$

term in $\sigma^2(\tilde{R}_p)$ for the portfolios of sizes 1 to 7. Comment on the results.
(4) Assuming the validity of the market model, how many parameters must be estimated when calculating $E(\tilde{R}_p)$ and $\sigma^2(\tilde{R}_p)$ for the seven-stock portfolio? How does this number of parameters compare with the number that must be estimated for the original portfolio theory model developed by Markowitz?

QUESTION 8.3:   The Fundamental Analystics Contest

(Any similarity between this contest and the *Value Line* contest is far from coincidental. See Shelton [1967] and Kaplan and Weil [1973] for discussion of the *Value Line* contest.)

Fundamental Analystics, a firm that sells recommendations on stocks, advertises that a contest is to be held. Investors will be allowed to enter two equally weighted portfolios of 25 NYSE stocks each. *Fundamental* will choose one portfolio of 25 NYSE stocks. This portfolio will comprise those 25 stocks that they think have the greatest price appreciation potential over the next six months. Their choice of stocks will be based on "fundamental analysis" in the best traditions of Graham and Dodd. *Fundamental* will award $100 to each portfolio that beats their portfolio over the next six months. The portfolio that beats *Fundamental's* portfolio by the largest amount will be awarded $100,000.

The rules of the contest are

(1) Each participant is to print the names of the stocks in his two portfolios and deliver them to *Fundamental* by January 10th. An equal amount will be assumed invested in each stock in each portfolio at the close of the market on January 15th.

(2) Six months later, on July 15th, the closing prices for each stock will be adjusted for stock splits, stock dividends, and other capital changes. No adjustment will be made for cash dividends paid in the six months. Then the percentage change in the price of each stock will be calculated. The total change in each portfolio will be determined by averaging the percentage changes of all 25 stocks.

REQUIRED

(1) Assume you are attempting to win a $100 prize. Describe how you would select the 25 stocks in each portfolio. Make explicit any assumptions that underlie your stock selections.

(2) Assume you are attempting to win the $100,000 prize. Repeat the analysis in (1).

QUESTION 8.4:   Rate Regulation for Southern Bell

(This case draws heavily on rate regulation testimonies that were kindly provided by James Bicksler.)

The Sharpe-Lintner capital asset pricing model can be used to derive the expected return on equity securities of a firm, given estimates of R_f, β_i, and $E(\tilde{R}_M) - R_f$. One area in which this model has found applications is in rate regulation. The following details are taken from the *Testimony of James L. Bicksler Before the South Carolina Public Service Commission* (Docket No. 76-352-C). This testimony concerned estimation of a fair rate of return for *Southern Bell Telephone Company*.

In the *Hope* decision [Federal Power Commission v. Hope Natural Gas Co., 320 U.S. 591 (1944)] it was stated that

> From the investor or company point of view it is important that there be enough revenue not only for operating expenses but also for capital costs of the business. These include service on the debt and dividends on the stock. By that standard the rate to the equity owner should be commensurate with the returns on investments *in other enterprises having corresponding risks.* That return, moreover, should be sufficient to assure confidence of the financial integrity of the enterprise, so as to maintain its ability to attract capital. (p. 603)

A variety of approaches have been used to estimate "the required rate of return," e.g., (1) taking the current bond yield and adding an "appropriate" risk premium for the equity shares and (2) taking the dividend yield and adding an "appropriate" adjustment for growth in earnings. These and similar approaches have been criticized due to their having no theoretical support from an equilibrium model of risk and return under uncertainty.

The capital asset pricing model has been proposed as an alternative method of estimating the required equity rate of return. This was the approach adopted by Bicksler. He estimated the "upper limit to the equilibrium rate of return" for *Southern Bell* as 10.45% based on the following estimates:

(1) Return on risk-free asset (R_f). The 30-day Treasury Bill rate at November 12, 1976 of 4.65% was used.

(2) Beta (β). The Vasicek [1973] approach to estimating the beta or relative risk was used. The estimate was derived by regressing monthly returns of *Southern Bell* on a value-weighted index of all NYSE stocks over the January 1971–December 1975 period (60 monthly observations). The beta was estimated to be .617 with a standard error of .081. Thus, the 95% confidence interval of the beta was from .455 to .779.

(3) Risk premium of the market portfolio $[E(\tilde{R}_m) - R_f]$. An instrumental variable procedure similar to that in Black et al. [1972] was used to estimate the risk premium over the January 1931–December 1975 period. This procedure yielded an estimate of 7.44% for the risk premium.

Given these estimates, Bicksler estimated "the upper limit to the equilibrium or fair rate of return for Southern Bell" as 10.45%:

$$E(\tilde{R}_i) = R_f + \beta[E(\tilde{R}_m) - R_f]$$
$$= 4.65\% + .779 \times 7.44\%$$
$$= 10.45\%.$$

REQUIRED

(1) Evaluate the following criticism of Bicksler's approach made in an earlier Georgia rate regulation hearing (see Georgia Public Service Commission Docket No. 2944-U, October 1976):

Dr. Bicksler's cost of capital determination is based solely on the application of a mathematical formula designed for portfolio analysis and classroom discussion of the theoretical behavior of capital markets.

(2) Evaluate the following criticisms of Bicksler's approach also made in the Georgia rate regulation hearing:

No one actually knows the current risk-free rate, today's beta for AT&T, or the current market risk premium. They are nothing more than estimates. The estimates are subject to major errors and are dependent upon the inputs used and time chosen. Although the theory is simple and the equation takes on the appearance of exactness, the answer derived is only as good as the judgments and data used. Speculation does not become exact merely because it takes on the form of a mathematical equation.

(3) In the *Southern Bell* case, one expert witness argued that the available evidence did not support the capital asset pricing model's prediction of a positive relation between expected return and risk. The evidence he cited was that in a recent period the spread between "Bell System equity and both government bonds and commercial paper returns [was] negative.... This is clearly inconsistent with the relative risk of equities vis-à-vis debt instruments." How would you respond to this evidence?

QUESTION 8.5:   Capital Asset Pricing and Rule 10b-5 Cases

Legal decisions in Rule 10b-5 cases contain interesting discussions of several issues raised in Chapters 7 and 8, e.g., about information and capital markets and about the pricing of capital assets—see Leas [1974]. Rule 10b-5 of the Securities and Exchange Act of 1934 states the following:

It shall be unlawful for any person, directly or indirectly, by the use of any means or instrumentality of interstate commerce, or of the mails, or of any facility of any national securities exchange,

(1) To employ any device, scheme, or artifice to defraud,

(2) To make any untrue statement of a material fact or to omit to state a material fact necessary in order to make the statements made, in the light of the circumstances under which they were made, not misleading, or

(3) To engage in any act, practice, or course of business which operates or would operate as a fraud or deceit upon any person, in connection with the purchase or sale of any securities.

This question will examine Chasins v. Smith, Barney & Co. [438 F. 2d 1167 (1970)]. The following details are paraphrased from the U.S. Court of Appeals hearing. Chasins was the muscial director of a New York City radio station and was the commentator on a musical program sponsored by Smith, Barney & Co., Inc., a stock brokerage firm. According to Chasins, it was due to this relationship that he opened his brokerage account with Smith, Barney by orally retaining it to act as his stockbroker.

Between July 19, 1961 and August 22, 1961 Chasins made the following purchases of over-the-counter stocks:

Date	Number of Shares	Company
7/19/61	200	Welch Scientific Co.
7/19/61	200	Tex-Star Oil & Gas Corp.
7/19/61	200	Howard Johnson Co.
8/22/61	200	Welch Scientific Co.

The total cost of the securities to Chasins was $34,950.

Preceding the four sales of July and August 1961, Smith, Barney sent Chasins a written analysis of his then-current security holdings and its recommendations in regard to his objective of aggressive growth of his holdings. The recommendations included strong purchase recommendations for the securities of Welch Scientific, Tex-Star Oil and Gas Corporation, and Howard Johnson Company. Chasins subsequently sold these securities on June 28, 1962, for $16,333.36.

At a district court hearing, it was disclosed that at least at the time of the four transactions in question, Smith, Barney was "making a market" in those securities; i.e., it was maintaining a position in the stocks on its own account by participating in over-the-counter trading in them. There was no testimony that Chasins had any knowledge or notice that Smith, Barney was "making a market" in the securities of the three companies. The decision of the district court ruled that although Smith, Barney had not violated any common law fiduciary duty to Chasins, Smith, Barney had violated Rule 10b-5 in not disclosing its market making (or dealer) status in the securities that it recommended Chasins purchase. Damages were awarded to Chasins in the amount of $18,616.64, with interest. This constituted the difference between the price at which Chasins purchased the securities from Smith, Barney and the price at which he later sold them (prior to discovering Smith, Barney's market making in the securities).

In the U.S. Court of Appeals, Smith, Barney contended that failure to disclose their "market making" role in the securities exchanged over the counter was not failure to disclose a material fact. They also contended that the district court's holding went further than any other decision in this area and that no court had ever found failure to disclose a "market making" role by a stock-brokerage firm to a client-purchaser to be a violation of Rule 10b-5. Smith, Barney's final challenge was to the amount of damages awarded to Chasins. They claimed that only the difference between the price charged him on his purchases and the fair market value on the purchase dates could be granted. They submitted an affidavit on the issue of damages indicating that the price Chasins paid for his purchases was the same as that generally available from other dealers for the same securities.

The Court of Appeals upheld the decision of the district court and reaffirmed the $18,616.64 measure of damages.

REQUIRED

(1) Assume you were the Chief Judge of the Court of Appeals. How would you respond to the arguments Smith, Barney presented to overturn the district court decision?

(2) Evaluate the approach used to obtain the $18,616.64 measure of damages to Chasins.

(3) Propose an alternative method for assessing damages in Chasins v. Smith, Barney & Co.

REFERENCES

BALL, R., BROWN, P., and OFFICER, R. R. "Asset Pricing in the Australian Industrial Equity Market." *Australian Journal of Management*, Vol. 1 (1976): 1–32.

BLACK, F. "Capital Market Equilibrium with Restricted Borrowing." *Journal of Business* (July 1972): 444–454.

BLACK, F., JENSEN, M., and SCHOLES, M. "The Capital Asset Pricing Model: Some Empirical Tests." In M. C. Jensen (ed.), *Studies in the Theory of Capital Markets*. Praeger, New York, 1972: 79–121.

BLATTBERG, R., and GONEDES, N. "A Comparison of the Stable and Student Distributions as Statistical Models for Stock Prices." *Journal of Business* (Apr. 1974): 244–280.

FAMA, E. F. *Foundations of Finance*. Basic Books, New York, 1976.

FAMA, E. F., and MACBETH, J. D. "Risk, Return and Equilibrium: Empirical Tests." *Journal of Political Economy* (May–June 1973): 607–636.

FOSTER, G. "Asset Pricing Models: Further Tests." Report 7703, Center for Mathematical Studies in Business and Economics, Jan. 1, 1977, University of Chicago, Chicago (forthcoming in *Journal of Financial and Quantitative Analysis*).

KAPLAN, R. S., and WEIL, R. L. "Risk and the Value Line Contest." *Financial Analysts Journal* (July–Aug. 1973): 56–61.

KING, B. F. "Market and Industry Factors in Stock Price Behavior." *Journal of Business* (Jan. 1966): 139–190.

LEAS, P. J. "The Measure of Damages in Rule 10b-5 Cases Involving Actively Traded Securities." *Stanford Law Review* (Jan. 1974): 371–397.

LINTNER, J. "The Valuation of Risk Assets and the Selection of Risky Investments in Stock Portfolios and Capital Budgets." *Review of Economics and Statistics* (Feb. 1965): 13–37.

MARKOWITZ, H. "Portfolio Selection." *Journal of Finance* (Mar. 1952): 77–91.

―――. *Portfolio Selection: Efficient Diversification of Investments.* Wiley, New York, 1959.

MERTON, R. C. "A Reexamination of the Capital Asset Pricing Model." In I. Friend and J. L. Bicksler (eds.), *Risk and Return in Finance,* Volume 1. Ballinger Publishing, Cambridge, Mass., 1977: 141–160.

MEYERS, S. L. "A Re-Examination of Market and Industry Factors in Stock Price Behavior." *Journal of Finance* (June 1973): 695–705.

MILLER, M., and SCHOLES, M. "Rates of Return in Relation to Risk: A Re-Examination of Some Recent Findings." In M. C. Jensen (ed.), *Studies in the Theory of Capital Markets.* Praeger, New York, 1972: 47–78.

OFFICER, R. R. "A Time-Series Examination of the Market Factor of the New York Stock Exchange." Unpublished Ph.D. Dissertation, University of Chicago, Chicago, 1971.

ROBICHEK, A. A., COHN, R. A., and PRINGLE, J. J. "Returns on Alternative Investment Media and Implications for Portfolio Construction." *Journal of Business* (July 1972): 427–443.

ROLL, R. "A Critique of the Asset Pricing Theory's Tests, Part 1: On Past and Potential Testability of the Theory." *Journal of Financial Economics* (Mar. 1977): 129–176.

ROSENBERG, B., and GUY, J. "Prediction of Beta from Investment Fundamentals: Part Two, Alternative Prediction Methods." *Financial Analysts Journal* (July–Aug. 1976): 62–70.

SHARPE, W. F. "A Simplified Model for Portfolio Analysis." *Management Science* (Jan. 1963): 277–293.

―――. "Capital Asset Prices: A Theory of Market Equilibrium under Conditions of Risk." *Journal of Finance* (Sept. 1964): 425–442.

―――. *Portfolio Theory and Capital Markets.* McGraw-Hill, New York, 1970.

―――. *Investments.* Prentice-Hall, Englewood Cliffs, N.J., 1978.

SHELTON, J. P. "The Value Line Contest: A Test of the Predictability of Stock-Price Changes." *Journal of Business* (July 1967): 251–269.

SOLNIK, B. H. "Why Not Diversify Internationally?" *Financial Analysts Journal* (July–Aug. 1974): 48–54.

VASICEK, O. A. "A Note on Using Cross-Sectional Information in Bayesian Estimation of Security Betas." *Journal of Finance* (Dec. 1973): 1233–1239.

CHAPTER **9**

RISK ASSESSMENT
AND
FINANCIAL INFORMATION

In this chapter we shall examine the relationship between the riskiness of a firm's securities and aspects of its underlying activities. We shall concentrate on the beta (β), or relative risk measure, of a security. Recall from Chapter 8 that the Sharpe-Lintner capital asset pricing model specifies that beta is the only security-specific parameter affecting differences in their expected returns; i.e.,

$$E(R_i) = R_f + \beta[E(\tilde{R}_m) - R_f], \tag{9.1}$$

where

$$\beta = \frac{\text{Cov}(\tilde{R}_i, \tilde{R}_m)}{\sigma^2(\tilde{R}_m)}.$$

In the more general Black asset pricing model, beta is also the only security-specific parameter leading to differences in their expected returns. In Section 9.1 we shall examine techniques to estimate beta from past security returns. Theoretically derived relationships between beta and the financing, investment, and production decisions of firms are discussed in Section 9.2. The association between beta and accounting variables is examined in Section 9.3. In Section 9.4 we shall examine the important issue of predicting beta from past security market and accounting data.

The major reason for studying these topics relates to the role of beta in portfolio theory and asset pricing models—see Chapter 8. Additional reasons include cost of capital estimation and portfolio performance evaluation. Given estimates of R_f, $E(\tilde{R}_m)$, and β_i, (9.1) can be used to determine the equilibrium expected return on a security. This expected return is an estimate of the cost of equity capital to the firm and thus can be used in a firm's capital budgeting decision.[1] Moreover, for regulated industries, the cost of capital is one factor in the determination of allowable rates to be charged. There are several examples in which (9.1) has been used in testimony concerning the rates to be charged by electric utilities, telephone companies, etc.[2] The other additional reason for studying the issues discussed in this chapter is portfolio performance evaluation. Portfolios with different risk levels have different expected returns, and it is important that these differences be taken into account when assessing their ex post performance. At a minimum, this involves estimating the betas of each portfolio and risk-adjusting the ex post returns of each portfolio. Chapter 12 contains further discussion of some issues involved in this application of asset pricing theory.

9.1 SECURITY RETURN ESTIMATES OF BETA

Past security returns constitute the data base most frequently used to estimate beta. Security return estimates of the betas of the 30 Dow-Jones stocks over the 1971–1975 period were presented in Chapter 8. The estimated betas ranged from .566 for *American Can* to 1.271 for *General Electric*. These estimates were from the *market model*, using the ordinary least-squares technique:

$$\tilde{R}_{it} = \hat{\alpha} + \hat{\beta} \tilde{R}_{mt} + \hat{\epsilon}_{it}, \qquad (9.2)$$

where $\tilde{R}_{it}$ = monthly return on security i in period t,

$\tilde{R}_{mt}$ = monthly return on the market portfolio in period t.

Sixty monthly security returns were used to estimate (9.2). Why 60 months, and why ordinary least squares? These choices were influenced by data availability considerations and the results of published research. The choice of 60 months was based on the results in Bogue [1972] and Gonedes [1973].[3] Sixty months appear to be a reasonable compromise between having sufficient observations to efficiently estimate (9.2) and not going back so far in time that we are dealing with a structurally different firm. Ordinary least squares (OLS) was chosen due to the ready availability of an OLS statistical package. OLS is a relatively simple technique to understand and has been used extensively in the estimation of beta.

It is important to note, however, that there is now considerable evidence that OLS estimates of beta are *not* unbiased estimates of the underlying beta of a firm's securities. The average beta of all securities is 1. This average of 1 is the prior probability of what an individual firm's security beta will be, without any knowledge of the characteristics of the firm, its industry, etc. Given this prior probability of 1, it is reasonable not to place all weight on the estimate of a beta found in any one sample of security returns. Rather, if one observes a beta of (say) 1.5 from a sample of 60 monthly security returns, it is probable that the underlying beta lies closer to 1 than the sample estimate of 1.5.

Evidence consistent with the above argument is presented by Blume [1975]. Using monthly data on the security returns of 800 securities over the 1954–1968 period, Blume estimated (with OLS) two seven-year betas (1954–1961, 1962–1968). Then, the betas covering the 1954–1961 period were ranked from highest to lowest and placed in eight portfolios of 100 securities. The first portfolio included the 100 securities with highest estimated betas...the eighth portfolio included the 100 securities with the lowest estimated betas. The average beta of each portfolio was estimated for both the 1954–1961 period and the 1962–1968 period. Results are presented in Table 9.1. If the 1954–1961 estimates of beta greater (less) than 1 are overestimates (underestimates) of the underlying beta, one would expect the 1962–1968 beta to be closer to 1 than the 1954–1961 beta. This pattern is strongly evident in the data in Table 9.1. After further analysis, Blume concluded that this reversion of estimated betas toward the mean of 1 was due to both

(1) Statistical factors—the estimated 1954–1961 beta being a biased estimate of the underlying 1954–1961 beta, and

(2) Economic factors—firms taking on new projects with betas closer to 1 than their existing portfolio of projects, or the beta of the existing portfolio of projects moving closer to 1 over time.

Evidence similar to that in Table 9.1 has also been presented by other authors—e.g., Bogue [1972].

TABLE 9.1   Betas and Their Regression Tendencies

	Beta of Portfolios	
Portfolio	Grouping Period 7/1954–6/1961	First Subsequent Period 7/1961–6/1968
1	.37	.62
2	.56	.68
3	.72	.85
4	.86	.85
5	.99	.95
6	1.11	.98
7	1.23	1.07
8	1.43	1.25

SOURCE: Blume [1975, Table 1].

Research in both universities and investment firms has produced a variety of techniques to adjust for the mean reversion due to statistical factors. We shall outline the technique developed by *Merrill Lynch*. *Merrill Lynch* first uses ordinary least squares to gain a preliminary estimate of beta ($\hat{\beta}_{OLS}$)—60 monthly security returns are used. Then it adjusts $\hat{\beta}_{OLS}$ as follows:

$$\hat{\beta} = .35 + .65\hat{\beta}_{OLS}. \tag{9.3}$$

This adjustment has the effect of pulling the OLS estimated beta toward the mean of 1. As an illustration, consider the OLS estimated betas of five

Dow-Jones stocks presented in Chapter 8:

General Electric	1.271
F. W. Woolworth	1.161
Eastman Kodak	.979
American Brands	.820
American Can	.566

Using the *Merrill Lynch* technique (9.3), the revised estimates of beta become

General Electric	1.176
F. W. Woolworth	1.105
Eastman Kodak	.986
American Brands	.883
American Can	.718

Note that the revised estimates have been pulled closer to the population mean of 1.[4]

Stability of Beta

An investor is interested in the expected risk of his portfolio over the chosen horizon period. In examining the usefulness of using a beta estimated over a past period, it is important to examine the stability of beta over time. Interesting evidence on this topic has been provided by Sharpe and Cooper [1972]. For each year from 1931 to 1967, the betas of securities with available data on the *CRSP* file were estimated using the past 60 months of security returns. The betas in each year were ranked from highest to lowest and placed in ten *risk-return* classes. The first *risk-return* class comprised those securities with the highest estimated betas over the past 60 months, etc. This procedure was repeated each year. Then, the percentage of stocks remaining in the same risk-return class in adjacent one-year and five-year periods was computed. If the relative rankings of betas were stable over time, each firm would remain in the same risk-return class.

The proportion of stocks whose estimated betas remained in the same risk-return class and within one risk-return class for adjacent one-year and five-year periods is presented in Table 9.2. Not surprisingly, there is more instability in adjacent five-year rankings of beta than in adjacent one-year periods. Note that only 35.17% of stocks in the top risk-return class in one five-year period were in the same class in the next adjacent five-year period.[5] These results suggest that, at the individual security level, there is nontrivial instability in estimated betas over time.[6]

TABLE 9.2   Proportion of Stocks in Specified Risk-Return Classes
in Years $T+1$ and $T+5$, Classified by
Risk-Return Classes in Year T

Risk-Return Class	Proportion in Same Risk-Return Class		Proportion Within One Risk-Return Class	
	In Year $T+1$	In Year $T+5$	In Year $T+1$	In Year $T+5$
10	.7417	.3517	.9129	.6927
9	.4989	.1835	.8800	.5373
8	.4091	.1638	.8307	.4534
7	.3564	.1327	.7836	.4092
6	.3452	.1389	.7758	.3927
5	.3535	.1361	.7799	.4170
4	.3807	.1320	.8018	.4022
3	.4268	.1588	.8418	.4458
2	.5091	.2145	.9023	.6089
1	.7471	.4047	.9340	.6230

SOURCE: Sharpe and Cooper [1972, Table III].

Why might the betas of securities change over time? To answer this question, it is necessary to examine the relationship between the characteristics of a firm (e.g., its financing, investment and production decisions) and its beta. In Sections 9.2 and 9.3 we shall examine theory and evidence on this topic.

9.2   ECONOMIC DETERMINANTS OF BETA

The relationship between the characteristics of a firm and the beta of its securities has been explored at a theoretical level in several important papers.[7] We shall briefly outline the approach adopted in these papers and the evidence presented to support the theoretical analysis.

A   Capital Structure

The relationship between capital structure and beta was first examined by Hamada [1969]. He showed that borrowing by a firm, while maintaining a fixed amount of equity, increased the risk of the stock to the investor. Hamada's results imply that part of the cross-sectional dispersion in the betas of firms is explained by cross-sectional dispersion in their debt to equity ratios. The empirical test of this theoretical result—Hamada

[1972]—used rates of return on 304 NYSE stocks over the 1948–1967 period. The 304 firms were from nine reasonably homogeneous industries, e.g., petroleums, utilities, and department stores. The (1) actual rates of return and (2) the *implied* rates of return on these stocks had no debt and preferred stock been issued were estimated. The approximations used to estimate the implied rates of return used information on the interest payments on debt and the market value of debt. Market model regressions were separately run using the actual and implied rates of return. The hypothesis was that the estimated β_i from actual returns would exceed the estimated β_i from implied returns, i.e., that the addition of leverage increased beta and thus expected return. This hypothesis was supported by the data. Hamada concluded that leverage "explained as much as 21 to 24 per cent of the value of the mean β" (p. 442).

The prediction that financial leverage is a determinant of beta has been supported in other empirical exercises. For instance, in the Beaver et al. [1970] paper, to be discussed in Section 9.3, there is a consistently significant correlation between the beta and the total liabilities to total assets ratio of 307 NYSE stocks over the 1947–1956 and the 1957–1965 periods.

B Operating Leverage

Operating leverage refers to the ratio of fixed to variable operating costs. Several authors have shown analytically that the higher the ratio of a firm's fixed to variable operating costs, the higher the beta or relative risk of a firm's securities.[8] The Lev [1974] paper is of added interest due to its empirical testing of this analytical result.

Lev [1974] demonstrated that, other things being equal, the higher the operating leverage of a firm, the higher the volatility of stock returns. This result was then extended to the covariability of security returns. It was demonstrated that "the [relative] risk of common stocks should be positively associated with the degree of operating leverage" (p. 632). Lev tested this result with firms from the (1) electric utility, (2) steel, and (3) oil industries over the 1949–1968 period. The following regression was central to the test:

$$\beta_i = \hat{a}_0 + \hat{a}_1 V_i + \hat{e}_i, \tag{9.4}$$

where β_i = security return estimate of beta (relative risk),

V_i = estimate of the variable cost component of total costs.

The operating leverage hypothesis predicted that $\hat{a}_1$ should be negative —the higher the variable cost component of total costs, the lower the beta or relative risk. The following results were obtained:

	$\hat{a}_1$	$t(\hat{a}_1)$	R^2
Electric utilities	−6.912	−2.060	.08
Steel manufacturers	−1.340	−2.408	.23
Oil producers	−.274	−1.157	.05

The $\hat{a}_1$ coefficients were all in the direction predicted. The explanatory power (as measured by the R^2) of the model, however, was relatively small for electric utilities and oil producers.

One problem in empirically testing the operating leverage hypothesis is the difficulty of estimating the fixed and variable cost components of a firm. Information on these components is rarely disclosed in annual reports. Even using internal data, there are difficult estimation issues to address, e.g., deciding on the relevant range, deciding the time period over which it is constant, and deciding on the appropriate measure of output for a multiproduct company. Given these estimation problems, the low explanatory power of (9.4) noted above is not surprising.

C Line of Business Activity

The beta of a portfolio is the weighted average of the betas of the securities in that portfolio. By an extension of this result, it can be argued that the risk components of a multiactivity firm's security are the weighted average of the risk components of the activities of the firm. This argument has motivated analytical work on the risk of multiactivity firms.[9] Rubinstein [1973], for instance, demonstrated that a positive relationship existed between the beta of a firm and its operating risk. He then further explored the determinants of operating risk of a multiactivity firm in terms of familiar accounting variables such as fixed cost and variable costs per unit of output. The operating risk of a M activity firm was derived to be

$$\sum_{M=1}^{M} \alpha_M (P_M - V_M)\rho(Q_M, R_M) \cdot \sqrt{\mathrm{Var}\frac{Q_M}{\alpha_M \cdot V_j}} , \qquad (9.5)$$

where α_M = proportion of assets devoted to product line M,

P_M = sales price per unit,

V_M = variable cost per unit,

Q_M = output in units,

R_M = rate of return on the market portfolio of risk assets,

V_j = present total dollar value of the securities of the firm.

In this formulation, α_M measures the importance of each activity to the firm, $P_M - V_M$ reflects the operating leverage of the activity, $\rho(Q_M, R_M)$ the "pure influence of economy-wide events" on the output of the activity, and $\sqrt{\text{Var}(Q_M/\alpha_M V_j)}$ the "uncertainty of output per dollar of assets." One assumption underlying the above expression is that all assets and all fixed costs can be uniquely identified with any one product line. Empirical research on models such as (9.5) would be desirable. It is through such research that the effect on risk estimation of such "seemingly unrealistic" assumptions can be discovered.

Viewing the beta of a multiactivity firm as a weighted average of the betas of the individual activities yields an alternative estimation technique for the risk of a firm's securities:

$$\beta_i = \sum x_a \beta_a \qquad (9.6)$$

where $x_a = $"importance" of activity a in firm i,

$\beta_a = $beta of activity a.

Using the Rubinstein [1973] framework, the x_a weights in (9.6) would be the total assets used in each activity. Figures for these weights, however, are not frequently disclosed in annual reports. An interesting unresolved issue is whether the more frequently disclosed divisional revenue or operating profits enable an analyst to efficiently estimate the x_a weights in (9.6). Another interesting unresolved issue is how the diversity across firms in their line of business disclosure would affect the use of (9.6) in beta estimation. When estimating the β_a component of (9.6) several options are available. One option is to use the average security market estimate of the betas of all listed firms operating in activity a. Another option is to estimate β_a from the accounting data of firm i, e.g., using the regression model of the Bildersee [1975] study discussed in Section 9.3.

This section was motivated by the following question: Why might the beta of securities change over time? We now have some factors that might explain the changes, i.e., a change in financial leverage of a firm, a change in its operating leverage, and a change in its line of business. In Section 9.3 we shall provide some further evidence on this question.

9.3 ASSOCIATION BETWEEN BETA AND ACCOUNTING VARIABLES

The association between security market estimates of risk and accounting variables has been extensively examined. In some cases the accounting variables used in this research have been guided by some

... In many other papers, more heuristic justifications for ...mined have been presented. Some representative examples are examined below.

...riate Analysis

In univariate analysis, the association between beta and a single accounting variable is examined. Given that beta is a covariability measure, a natural accounting variable to use is the expected covariability of a firm's earnings with the earnings of all other firms (termed an *accounting beta*). This covariability can be estimated using the index models discussed in Chapter 5. The first published example of this analysis is Ball and Brown [1969]. The sample examined was 261 NYSE firms over the 1946–1966 period. There were three steps in the analysis:

(1) Estimate the security market beta (β^S) for each firm—monthly returns over the 1946–1966 period were used,

(2) Estimate the accounting beta (β^A) for each firm—annual earnings over the 1946–1966 period were used, and

(3) Estimate the correlation between the market estimated betas from (1) and the accounting estimated betas from (2).

Three different earnings measures were separately examined. The Spearman rank correlations from (3) were[10]

Operating income	.64
Net income	.58
Available for common	.53

These results indicate a significant correlation between security-market- and accounting-based estimates of beta. Note, however, that they do not necessarily imply a causal relationship between the two estimates of beta; one can never infer causal relationships from correlation statistics.

The analysis in Ball and Brown [1969] was conducted at the individual security level. An important extension is the analysis of the association issue at the portfolio level. There are both economic and statistical motivations for using portfolios. The major thrust of portfolio theory is that risk should be examined from a portfolio rather than an individual security perspective. Beaver et al. [1970] state this economic motivation for using portfolios in an association study as follows:

> The primary justification for the analysis of portfolios is that the portfolio, rather than the individual security, is the relevant decision-prediction entity for investors just as the variance of return of the portfolio, not the variance of an individual security's return, is the relevant concept of risk. (p. 669)

The statistical motivation for examining portfolios is due to measurement error at the individual security level. Only 20 observations were used to estimate the accounting beta in the Ball and Brown [1969] study. In similar studies, as few as 10 observations have been used in the analysis. Given these small samples, one suspects a nontrivial amount of measurement error in the sample estimates of β^A at the individual firm level. A common statistical approach to such measurement error is to use a grouping procedure.[11] If an appropriate grouping procedure is chosen, the measurement error will be reduced by the procedure.[12]

The most extensive analysis at the portfolio level is by Beaver and Manegold [1975]. The sample comprised 254 *Compustat* firms over the 1951–1969 period. There were four steps in the analysis:

(1) Estimate the security market beta (β^S) for each firm—monthly returns over the 1951–1969 period were used,

(2) Estimate the accounting beta (β^A) for each firm—annual earnings over the 1951–1969 period were used,

(3) Rank the 254 stocks on the basis of β^S, place each in a portfolio of five (ten) securities, and calculate the average β^S and β^A for each portfolio, and

(4) Estimate the correlation between the portfolio security market betas and accounting betas from (3).

The Spearman rank correlations for two annual accounting earnings variables that were separately examined were

	Single-Security Level	Five-Security Portfolio Level	Ten-Security Portfolio Level
Net income / Total assets	.41	.60	.69
Net income / Net worth	.46	.69	.74

Two features of these results are noteworthy. *First*, forming portfolios appears to have reduced measurement error in the variables as witnessed by the higher correlations at the portfolio level vis-à-vis at the single-security level. *Second*, at the portfolio level there is a strongly significant association between security-market- and accounting-based estimates of beta.

Other Accounting Variables

The accounting beta estimated from an index model is a relatively unfamiliar accounting variable. There is much research into the association between security market estimates of beta and more familiar accounting variables. An early and influential study in this area was by Beaver et al. [1970]. The sample examined was 307 NYSE firms listed on the *Compustat* tape over the 1947–1965 period. The 1947–1956 and 1957–1965 subperiods were examined separately. The following financial variables were correlated with the security market beta (β^S):

(1) *Earnings variability.* The standard deviation of the earnings to price ratio over the subperiod.

(2) *Dividend payout ratio.* Average ratio over the subperiod.

(3) *Accounting beta* (β^A). Estimated from an index model over the subperiod.

(4) *Leverage.* Average debt to total assets ratio over the subperiod.

(5) *Growth.* Average rate of change in assets over the subperiod.

(6) *Size.* The natural logarithm of total assets.

(7) *Liquidity.* Average current ratio over the subperiod.

The above variables were chosen as they "captured most of the important relationships suggested in the literature" (p. 660). This literature was interpreted as implying (1) positive correlations between β^S and earnings variability, accounting beta, leverage, and growth and (2) negative correlations between β^S and dividend payout and asset size.

Spearman rank correlations between the above accounting variables and β^S for the 1947–1956 and 1957–1965 periods are presented in Table 9.3. These correlations are for the individual security level and the five-security portfolio level. Several features of the results are important. *First,* earnings variability, payout, accounting beta, and leverage all show consistently significant correlations with the security market beta in both periods. For these four variables, the correlations at the portfolio level are always higher than at the individual security level. *Second,* the correlations

TABLE 9.3 Correlations Between Security Market Beta
and Accounting Variables: 1947–1965

	1947–1956 Period		*1957–1965 Period*	
	Individual Level	*Portfolio Level*	*Individual Level*	*Portfolio Level*
Earnings variability	.66	.90	.45	.82
Dividend payout	−.49	−.79	−.29	−.50
Accounting beta	.44	.68	.23	.46
Leverage	.23	.41	.22	.48
Asset growth	.27	.56	.01	.02
Asset size	−.06	−.09	−.16	−.30
Liquidity	−.13	−.35	.05	.04

SOURCE: Beaver et al. [1970, Table 5].

TABLE 9.4 Correlations Between Security Market Beta and
Accounting Variables: 1960–1968

		Individual Security Level	*Portfolio Level*
A.	*Covariability Measures*		
	1. $D + E + P$	.36	.88
	2. Dividends	.15	.12
	3. Price-earnings multiple	.29	.69
	4. Earnings	.24	.62
	5. Operating income	.21	.72
B.	*Averages of 1960–1968 Ratios*		
	6. Dividend payout	$-.37$	$-.76$
	7. Asset growth	.21	.56
	8. Total debt/total assets	.24	.53
	9. Pretax interest coverage	$-.23$	$-.41$

SOURCE: Thompson [1976, Table 4].

for the growth, size, and liquidity variables are either insignificant or inconsistent between the two periods examined.

Univariate results similar to those in Beaver et al. [1970] have been presented in many subsequent papers. The Thompson [1976] study is illustrative of these papers. The sample examined was 290 *Compustat* firms over the 1960–1968 period. Correlations at the individual security and the ten-security portfolio level were examined. One set of accounting variables was estimated in what was termed *covariant form*, i.e., the β from an index model using a financial variable of firm i as the dependent variable and the economy average of the financial variable as the independent variable. Five variables were estimated in covariant form: (1) a combination of dividends, earnings, and the price-earnings multiple $(D + E + P)$; (2) dividends; (3) the price-earnings multiple; (4) earnings; and (5) operating income. The 1960–1968 average values of four additional financial variables were also estimated. The correlation between these nine variables and the security-market-estimated beta are presented in Table 9.4.[13] In general, the results indicate a strong association between security market estimates of beta and accounting variables.

B Multivariate Analysis

An important extension of univariate analysis is multivariate analysis, i.e., the association between security market estimates of beta and N (where $N > 1$) accounting (and other) variables. The most common approach is via a multiple regression model with the security market estimate of beta as the dependent variable and accounting variables as the independent variables.

The Bildersee [1975] study will be examined to illustrate this approach. The sample was 71 manufacturing and retail firms which had both common and nonconvertible preferred stocks traded on the NYSE over the 1956–1966 period. Correlations between the security market beta (for the common stock) and 11 accounting variables were first examined on a univariate basis. Then, a multiple regression analysis was run. Bildersee used a stepwise regression program to choose those accounting variables which contributed most to explaining variations in the dependent variable. In Appendix 9.A we shall describe and illustrate the use of stepwise regression in deciding the variables to include in such a model. The final regression reported by Bildersee [1975] contained the following six independent variables:

$$X_1 = \text{Debt to equity ratio}$$
$$X_2 = \text{Preferred stocks/common stocks ratio}$$
$$X_3 = \text{Sales to common equity ratio}$$
$$X_4 = \text{Current assets to current liabilities ratio}$$
$$X_5 = \text{Standard deviation of earnings to price ratio}$$
$$X_6 = \text{Accounting } \beta \text{ estimated from } index\ model.$$

Panel A of Table 9.5 presents the correlation coefficient for each of these six variables. The highest correlation was for X_1—$r_1 = .364$. That is, variations in the debt to equity ratio explained 13.25% ($R^2 = .364 \times .364$) of variations in the security market beta. Panel B of Table 9.5 presents the estimated coefficients for the multiple regression model with all six inde-

TABLE 9.5   Security Market Betas and Accounting Variables: 1956–1966

	Correlation Coefficient
A. *Univariate Analysis*	
X_1 (debt to equity)	.364
X_2 (preferred stocks/common stocks)	.221
X_3 (sales/common equity)	.319
X_4 (current assets/current liabilities)	−.261
X_5 (standard deviation of earnings to price ratio)	.319
X_6 (accounting beta)	.132
B. *Multivariate Analysis*	

$$\hat{\beta}_i^S = .923 + .416X_1 - .630X_2 + .023X_3 - .042X_4 + 4.032X_5 - .081X_6$$
$$\quad\ \ t=2.664 \quad t=-1.543 \quad t=1.758 \quad t=-1.005 \quad t=2.613 \quad t=-2.680$$

SOURCE: Bildersee [1975, Tables 3 and 5].

pendent variables—the adjusted $R^2 = .239$. Thus, the addition of the extra five variables to X_1 explained a further 10% of the variation in the security market betas of the 71 firms.

C Some General Comments

Some general comments are warranted on the association studies discussed in Section 9.3.

1. Most studies on the association between security market estimates of beta and accounting variables have lacked an explicit theoretical underpinning; i.e., the choice of variables has not been guided by a theoretical model linking the firm's financing, investment, and production decisions with the beta of its securities. Rather, a *brute empiricism* approach is apparent in many studies. As a consequence, generalizations based on this empirical research are difficult. Indeed, there are apparent inconsistencies in the variables reported as significant in different studies. At this stage, the studies discussed in Section 9.2 represent the most promising line of research in this area.

The lack of a theoretical model to guide the choice of variables and their form could, in part, explain the low explanatory power of several of the multivariate models. For example, in Bildersee [1975], the stepwise regression procedure was used to determine the variables that maximized the R^2. After intensive searching of 11 variables, the final model was only able to explain 23.9% of the variation in the betas of firms. Hopefully, with more concern with modeling what ratios should be related to beta, the explanatory power of these models can be increased.

2. There have been limited efforts to utilize the more refined techniques of estimating betas from security returns in the studies examined. For instance, both Bildersee [1975] and Thompson [1976] used OLS estimates of beta in their univariate and multivariate analyses. There is now evidence that OLS estimates of beta are biased. At a minimum, the techniques referred to in Section 9.1 could be used to adjust OLS estimates for the statistical mean reversion phenomena. In several studies—Melicher and Rush [1974] and Griffin [1976]—the concern has been with explaining changes in the estimated beta of firms over two periods. In this context, use of OLS estimates for the beta of each period could introduce considerable noise into a model trying to explain beta changes by reference to changes in financial ratios. Such exercises also face the additional problem of specifying the time period when changes in financial ratios would be expected to be reflected in changes in security market betas. Given a forward-looking capital market, it may well be that changes in security market betas lead (anticipate) changes in accounting variables.

3. A major purpose of examining the association between accounting variables and security market estimates of beta is to be able to predict the beta of a future period. Tests using correlation coefficients, multiple regression coefficients, etc., do not directly address the beta prediction issue. More direct tests of this issue are presented in Section 9.4.[14]

9.4 PREDICTING BETA

Choosing a portfolio with a specified level of risk for a future horizon period entails predicting the betas of individual securities. As beta is an ex ante concept—and thus unobservable—nontrivial issues arise in how to evaluate alternative methods for its prediction. Ideally, one would want to assess the alternative methods for forecasting beta on the basis of some *loss function*, e.g., comparing the expected utility of using various estimates of beta vis-à-vis the expected utility of using the "true" ex ante beta. At present, there is limited analysis using this approach.[15] Rather, a variety of surrogate approaches to evaluating alternative prediction methods for beta has been used. While these approaches are more tractable than attempts to incorporate a loss function into the analysis, their relationship to the more general "loss function" evaluation rule is yet to be explored.

One approach has been to use a security return beta estimate in the period being predicted as the proxy for the ex ante beta of the period. Another approach has been to assume the validity of an asset pricing model and to evaluate alternative beta forecast methods by their ability to forecast the actual security returns in the future period. Both approaches are illustrated in this section.

A Predicting Security Return Estimates of Beta

The paper by Beaver et al. [1970] contains one of the first efforts at comparing alternative methods of predicting security return estimates of beta. Two periods were used in the analysis—1947–1956 (period 1) and 1957–1965 (period 2). Security return estimates of beta were derived from a market model regression for each period. Let $\hat{\beta}_{1i}^s$ be the security return estimate of the beta of firm i in period 1. One method of predicting β_{2i}^s examined was

$$E(\beta_{2i}^s) = \hat{\beta}_{1i}^s; \qquad (9.7)$$

i.e., the security return beta in 1957–1965 was predicted to be the same as the comparable estimate in 1947–1956. Another prediction method examined utilized accounting data. The first stage in this method was a regression of $\hat{\beta}_{1i}^s$ against seven accounting variables in period 1. These seven variables were those detailed in Section 9.3A. The final model chosen was

$$E(\hat{\beta}_{2i}) = 1.016 - .584 P_{1i} + .835 G_{1i} + 3.027 V_{1i}, \qquad (9.8)$$

where P_{1i} = average payout ratio of firm i in period 1,

G_{1i} = average growth rate in total assets of firm i in period 1,

V_{1i} = variability in earnings of firm i in period 1 (standard deviation of the earnings to price ratio).

Thus, if $P_{1i} = .482$, $G_{1i} = .085$, and $V_{1i} = .062$ (average period 1 values for the firms in the sample), $\hat{\beta}_{2i}$ would be predicted as

$$E(\beta_{2i}) = 1.016 - .584 \times .482 + .835 \times .085 + 3.027 \times .062$$
$$= .993.$$

The forecasts of (9.7) and (9.8) were evaluated using the forecast error measures described in Chapter 4. These error measures for predicting the betas of portfolios of five securities were

	Security Return Prediction Model (9.7)	Accounting Prediction Model (9.8)
Mean error (%)	−.006	−.003
Mean-square error (%)	.030	.016
Mean absolute error (%)	.139	.104

Thus, at the portfolio level, the accounting-variable-based model (9.8) provided an improvement in forecasting ability over the security return beta prediction model (9.7).

Since the Beaver et al. [1970] paper was published, advances in knowledge about the time-series behavior of *both* security return estimates of beta and accounting variables have been made, e.g., Blume [1975] and the material in Chapter 4. An interesting extension would be to incorporate such advances into the prediction models examined above. Hopefully, such an extension would also draw on the theoretical advances on "the economic determinants of security risk" (see Section 9.2) when deciding both the structure and variables to be included in the prediction models.

B   Predicting Future Security Returns

The variable being forecast in the Beaver et al. [1970] paper was the security return beta estimate. An alternative approach is to forecast future security returns, conditional on a forecast of beta. This approach has been explored by Rosenberg and others in several papers. In Rosenberg and McKibben [1973], the basic approach to be applied in a sequence of studies was outlined. The assumed model for the return on security i in period t was the familiar market model:

$$\tilde{R}_{it} = \alpha + \beta_{it}\tilde{R}_{Mt} + \epsilon_{it}. \tag{9.9}$$

Then, beta was said to be a function of a set of j *descriptors* (W_{jit}) that represent characteristics of the firm i in period t, i.e.,

$$\beta_{it} = \sum_{j=1}^{J} b_j W_{jit} + \epsilon_{it}. \tag{9.10}$$

Substituting (9.10) into (9.9) yielded

$$\tilde{R}_{it} = \alpha + \sum_{j=1}^{J} b_j W_{jit}\tilde{R}_{Mt} + u_{it}. \tag{9.11}$$

The generalized least-squares regression technique was applied to (9.11) to yield estimates of α and the b_j coefficients.

Initially 32 descriptors (W_{jit}'s) were selected as possible characteristics of the firm that could describe beta. These 32 descriptors included 20 "accounting-based descriptors" (e.g., the operating profit margin and the quick ratio), 7 "market-based descriptors" (e.g., security-return estimated beta and share turnover), and 5 "market valuation descriptors" (e.g., dividend yield and the earnings/price ratio). Selection of the 32 variables and of the final regression model was described as follows:

> The 32 descriptors were selected, without any prior fitting to the data, on the basis of studies reported in the literature and the authors' intuition.... The regressions were conducted in a predesigned sequence. First, all 32 descriptors were included in regressions. Those descriptors insignificant at the 90 percent level were deleted. This cutoff was selected on the basis of the results. (p. 325)

The final regression, estimated on annual data for 558 firms over the 1954–1966 period, included 13 independent variables. The regression model was then used to predict annual security returns over the 1967–1970 period. The actual values of the independent variables and $\tilde{R}_{Mt}$ in (9.11) over this period were assumed known, and the forecast of the conditional annual return on each security was made. Then the mean-square error of the forecast was calculated. As a bench mark, several alternative methods of forecasting beta were also examined. The result was that although the regression model had the lowest mean-square forecast error (.0725), its performance over a model assuming the beta of all firms to be the market average of 1 was minimal—the mean-square error of the latter model was .0739.

Several features of the Rosenberg and McKibben [1973] approach should be noted. *First*, the approach combines both accounting and nonaccounting information in a single forecast model. The motivation for combining these information sets is that each may yield some unique information pertinent to forecasting beta. By incorporating both information sets into a single forecasting model, more efficient forecasts may be obtained than from the exclusive use of either information set. *Second*, the approach to model construction and variable choice is relatively heuristic. Ideally, the model and variables should have had a more direct linkage to a theoretical model of security risk determination.

In Rosenberg and Marathe [1975] the above approach was extended in several directions. More companies were included in the analysis, quarterly as well as annual accounting data were used, monthly security returns rather than annual security returns were used in estimating the "market-based descriptors," and the number of descriptors initially examined was increased from 32 to 80 variables. The measure of forecast ability was the percentage of the variability in future security returns that could be explained by various beta forecasting methods. The period of analysis was 1956–1974. The forecast bench mark was a method "essentially identical to the Merrill Lynch prediction rule" (p. 134) for beta.[16] The percentage of variability explained by the "Merrill Lynch...rule" was given a score of 1. Other forecasting methods were expressed as multiples of this bench mark. Thus, a score above 1 indicated that a beta forecasting method explained more variability of the future returns than did the "Merrill Lynch...rule." The relative scores from using various information sets for predicting beta were

Market variability descriptors	1.57
Fundamental descriptors	1.45
Market variability descriptors and fundamental descriptors	1.86

Thus, Rosenberg and Marathe produced important evidence of the potential benefits of combining both accounting and nonaccounting variables when forecasting beta.[17] Using both information sets explained 18% (1.86/1.57) more of the variance in future security returns than using only the "market-based descriptors" and 28% (1.86/1.45) more than using only the "fundamental" descriptors.[18]

9.5 SUMMARY

Analytical and empirical work into the relationship between a firm's financing-investment-production decisions and its security risk shows much promise of increasing our knowledge of how constructs such as variable and fixed costs and financial leverage are related to security risk assessment. Work into the effects of jointly combining both accounting and security market information in risk assessment also holds much promise. Ideally, the analytical work noted above should guide the choice of the model and its variables when jointly combining accounting and security market information in risk assessment.

APPENDIX 9.A   THE STEPWISE MULTIPLE REGRESSION TECHNIQUE

This is a mechanical technique for selecting the independent variables to include in a regression model. Suppose the concern is with the following model:

$$\beta_i^S = \alpha + \beta_1 X_{1i} + \beta_2 X_{2i} + \ldots + \beta_N X_{Ni}, \qquad (9.12)$$

where β_i^S = security market estimate of the beta of firm i's securities,

X_{ji} = jth financial ratio of firm i.

Stepwise regression can be used to decide how many financial ratios to include as independent variables in (9.12).

Stepwise regression will be illustrated with a sample of 12 firms. The betas and the following five financial ratios are presented below:

(1) Current ratio (CR),

(2) Quick ratio (QR),

(3) Debt to equity ratio (DE),

(4) Times-interest-earned ratio (TIE), and

(5) Return on assets ratio (ROA).

The ratios are for 1974 and the betas were estimated over the 1973–1975 period.

		β_i^S	CR	QR	DE	TIE	ROA
1.	American Brands	.854	1.939	.438	1.136	2.901	.071
2.	Armco Steel	.735	2.027	1.084	.854	6.943	.087
3.	Ashland Oil	1.019	1.788	1.137	1.325	4.796	.075
4.	Continental Airlines	2.061	.692	.584	3.368	1.195	.041
5.	Lykes-Youngstown	.359	1.642	1.063	1.260	4.092	.084
6.	Mobil Oil	.903	1.119	.742	1.089	7.973	.080
7.	Quaker State	1.607	2.774	1.367	.616	8.658	.132
8.	Standard Oil (Ind.)	.456	1.512	1.105	.740	9.658	.115
9.	Standard Oil (Ohio)	.595	1.881	1.304	.835	3.034	.060
10.	Sun Oil	.455	1.357	.812	.731	7.636	.100
11.	TWA	2.437	1.001	.736	3.485	.631	004
12.	U.S. Steel	.751	1.663	1.263	.733	7.849	.088

The criterion we shall use in deciding if a variable warrants inclusion in a model is as follows: Does its inclusion increase the adjusted R^2?

The *first step* in the procedure is to separately regress each financial variable against β_i^S. The results were

	Adjusted R^2
$\beta_i^S = 1.61 - .37CR_i$	.000
$\beta_i^S = 1.70 - .70QR_i$	.008
$\beta_i^S = .28 + .55DE_i$	.651
$\beta_i^S = 1.65 - .12TIE_i$	.215
$\beta_i^S = 1.95 - 11.92ROA_i$	.291

The debt to equity ratio explains the most variation in β_i^S and is thus chosen as the first independent variable to enter the regression model.

The *second step* is to separately regress the DE variable and each of the other four variables against β_i^S. The results were

	Adjusted R^2
$\beta_i^S = -1.05 + .79DE_i + .62CR_i$	.778
$\beta_i^S = -.26 + .63DE_i + 45QR_i$	.647
$\beta_i^S = -.24 + .69DE_i + .06TIE_i$	.648
$\beta_i^S = -.57 + .76DE_i + 7.26ROA_i$	.658

The current ratio, when added to the debt to equity ratio, explains the most variation in β_i^S of all the combinations examined in this second step —it increases the adjusted R^2 to .778. Thus, the current ratio warrants inclusion in the regression model.[19]

The *third step* is to regress separately the DE, CR, and each of the remaining three variables against β_i^S. The results were

	Adjusted R^2
$\beta_i^S = -1.09 + .79DE_i + .60CR_i + .07QR_i$	.752
$\beta_i^S = -2.24 + 1.09DE_i + .76CR_i + .11TIE_i$	.864
$\beta_i^S = -1.58 + .92DE_i + .59CR_i + 5.24ROA_i$	.777

Using the adjusted R^2 criteria, the times-interest-earned ratio now enters the regression model—the adjusted R^2 is increased from .778 to .864.

Results of the *fourth step* were

	Adjusted R^2
$\beta_i^S = -2.20 + 1.09DE_i + .81CR_i$ $+ .11TIE_i - .15QR_i$	.848
$\beta_i^S = -2.12 + 1.05DE_i + .87CR_i$ $+ .15TIE_i - 6.62ROA_i$	.865

Note that the adjusted R^2 when the return on assets ratio is added increases only marginally from the model selected from the third step—i.e., it increases from .864 to .865.

If one chose to include the return on assets ratio in the model, one would then proceed to the *fifth step*. The results were

	Adjusted R^2
$\beta_i^S = -2.02 + 1.05DE_i + .96CR_i + .17TIE_i$ $-7.64ROA_i - .24QR_i$	.854

Inclusion of the quick ratio decreases the adjusted R^2 of .865 in the fourth step to .854. Using the above-noted criteria, it would be excluded from the regression model.

Thus, using the above stepwise regression procedure the debt to equity ratio, the current ratio, and the times-interest-earned ratio would be included in the model. Inclusion of the return on assets ratio is very marginal. The quick ratio would be excluded from the model.

The stepwise procedure for selecting variables to include in a model is an extreme example of brute empiricism. It should be used with considerable appreciation of its lack of a theoretical underpinning. It also suffers from being overly influenced by the specific characteristics of the sample being examined.

NOTES

[1] See, for instance, Fama and Miller [1972] or Haley and Schall [1973].

[2] Myers [1972] and Bicksler [1977] provide discussions of this issue and references to expert testimonies at rate regulation hearings.

[3] The use of daily security returns would encounter econometric problems arising from nontrading in securities. See Fisher [1966] for a description of this problem and Scholes and Williams [1976] for estimation techniques to minimize the econometric problems when estimating betas from daily data.

[4] Other adjustment techniques are more involved than that used by *Merrill Lynch*. They include weighted regression techniques (weighting the most recent observations heaviest) and Bayesian regression techniques— see Bogue [1972, Chapter VIII] and Vasicek [1973].

[5] In part, the higher stability in adjacent one-year periods is due to overlapping data bases used to estimate beta; e.g., the 1931–1935 and

1932–1936 betas have 48 out of 60 monthly observations in common when estimating beta.

[6]There is considerably more stability in the estimated betas of portfolios over time. For instance, Beaver et al. [1970] reported that the Spearman rank correlation between adjacent betas of 307 NYSE stocks for the 1947–1956 and 1957–1965 periods was .626 at the individual security level, .876 at the 5-security portfolio level, and .989 at the 20-security portfolio level.

[7]An excellent survey paper on these topics is Rubinstein [1973]. See also Myers [1977]. An interesting early attempt at modeling in this area is Pettit and Westerfield [1972].

[8]See, for example, Rubinstein [1973], Lev [1974], and Percival [1974].

[9]See, for instance, Fama and Miller [1972] and Rubinstein [1973].

[10]The Spearman rank correlations are for the index models estimated with first differences of earnings. Recall from Chapter 5 that first differences is generally a better specification of the index model than are the levels of earnings. The Ball and Brown [1969] results were consistent with this general rule.

[11]Another possible approach to obtaining more efficient estimates of accounting betas is to use quarterly rather than annual accounting data. Use of quarterly data, however, raises some important problems associated with seasonality. The results in Griffin [1976] suggest that considerable specification issues need to be addressed before quarterly accounting data yields more efficient estimates of accounting betas than use of annual accounting data.

[12]Ideally, the variable used to place the observations into groups should be correlated with the "underlying" accounting beta but uncorrelated with the measurement error in the estimates of the accounting beta—see Johnston [1972].

[13]The low correlation between the security market beta and the "covariant" dividend variable is not surprising. A time-series regression of the dividends of firm i against the dividends of all firms has severe estimation problems due to the policy of dividend stabilization followed by many firms.

[14]An interesting issue is whether the capital market adjusts for differences in the accounting techniques of firms when assessing the riskiness of securities. For some preliminary evidence see Eskew [1975].

[15]See Brown [1976] and Klein and Bawa [1976] for some preliminary exploration of this approach.

[16]The "Merrill Lynch prediction rule" used in Rosenberg and Marathe [1975] was

$$\hat{\beta} = .44 + .56\hat{\beta}_{OLS},$$

where $\hat{\beta}_{OLS}$ = the OLS estimate of beta.

[17]It is important to note that Rosenberg and Marathe assumed fore-knowledge of the "fundamental descriptors" in the period being forecast. In practice, the forecasting ability of their techniques would be jointly dependent on the structural model and the ability to forecast the "fundamental descriptors" in the structural model.

[18]Predictions of beta (and other variables) using the above approach are available to subscribers to the *Fundamental Risk Measurement Service* (FRMS) (Barr Rosenberg and Associates, Berkeley, California).

[19]One should be careful about assuming that because a variable is insignificant on a univariate basis that it will also be insignificant on a multivariate basis. See Cochran [1964] for an analysis of how seemingly insignificant variables on a univariate basis may be very important when combined with other variables. For instance, he noted that variables with negative correlations could increase the discriminatory power of a multiple regression model. In the example in Appendix 9.A, the current ratio has the lowest adjusted R^2 in the first step but is the second variable to enter the multiple regression. The product moment correlation between DE and CR is $-.6883$ (between beta and CR it is $-.3010$).

QUESTIONS

QUESTION 9.1:   Security Risk and Accounting Variables

The following data are the betas and selected 1974 financial ratios of nine companies. The betas were estimated using ordinary least squares with monthly returns over the 1973–1975 period.

Companies	Beta	Debt to Equity	Times Interest Earned	Current Ratio	Return on Equity
1. Bethlehem Steel	1.018	.724	8.776	1.631	.081
2. National Airlines	2.216	1.847	2.662	1.127	.074
3. Northwest Airlines	1.617	.900	3.945	.815	.068
4. Phillips Petroleum	1.117	.673	9.135	1.649	.113
5. Republic Steel	.909	.631	9.379	1.856	.088
6. Shell Oil	1.170	.722	11.209	1.628	.106
7. Standard Oil (Calif.)	.915	.669	16.020	1.423	.086
8. Union Oil of Calif.	.596	.692	7.705	1.526	.089
9. U.S. Tobacco	1.056	.659	6.000	2.111	.120

REQUIRED

(1) Which financial ratio(s) would you expect to be correlated with beta? Provide support for your answer.

(2) What is the Spearman rank correlation between beta and the following financial ratios:

(a) Debt to equity,

(b) Times interest earned,

(c) Current ratio, and

(d) Return on equity?

Comment on the results.

(3) The above estimates of beta were derived from an OLS regression. Estimate the betas of these nine companies using the *Merrill Lynch* technique described in Section 9.1. Would the use of the *Merrill Lynch* beta estimates affect the correlations computed in (2)?

(4) [Access to a computer is necessary for this subpart of Question 9.1.] Using the stepwise regression technique, which financial ratios would you include in a multiple regression model explaining differences in the betas of the above nine firms? A variable should be included if its inclusion increases the adjusted R^2 of the model. Critically evaluate the above stepwise regression approach to gaining insight into what aspects of a firm's financing, investment, and production characteristics are important in assessing the beta of its securities.

QUESTION 9.2:   Market vs. Book Value Estimates of Leverage

There has been much argument in the financial accounting literature over whether market or book values should be adopted when using leverage ratios to assess the riskiness of a firm's securities. Consider the long-term debt to equity ratio. The market value alternative would use the current market values of both the long-term debt and the shareholders' equity of each company. The book value alternative would use the figures reported in the financial statements of each company.

REQUIRED

(1) What problems may an analyst encounter in estimating the market values of long-term debt and equity of companies?

(2) Design a study that would examine if a portfolio manager would prefer the use of market or book values when using leverage ratios to assess the riskiness of a firm's securities.

QUESTION 9.3:   Leverage Ratios, Lease Accounting,
                and Betas of Airline Companies

There has been considerable debate over whether leases are debt in the same sense as corporate bonds, debentures, etc. An interesting issue related to this debate is whether the capital market, when assessing the risk of securities, is cognizant of leases not reported on the balance sheet. Prior to the issuance of FASB Statement No. 13 (*Accounting for Leases*) in 1976, airline companies did not report leases on their balance sheets. Question 6.5 provided sufficient information to calculate the debt to equity ratios (with and without leases included on the balance sheet) of the 11 major U.S. airlines. The following are statistics from market model OLS regressions of each airline's security returns against the value-weighted index of all NYSE stocks over the January 1971–December 1975 period:

		$\hat{\alpha}$	$\hat{\beta}$	R^2
1.	American	−.011	1.773	.378
2.	Braniff	.007	2.212	.502
3.	Continental	−.010	2.009	.394
4.	Delta	.003	1.446	.518
5.	Eastern	−.016	1.818	.328
6.	National	−.001	2.251	.489
7.	Northwest	.004	1.685	.469
8.	Pan American	−.007	2.389	.408
9.	Trans World	−.003	2.425	.418
10.	United	.009	1.669	.350
11.	Western	.009	1.909	.433

REQUIRED

(1) Calculate the Spearman rank correlation between the debt to equity ratios and betas of these 11 companies with

    (a) Lease obligations excluded from the balance sheet, and

    (b) Lease obligations included as long-term debt on the balance sheet.

Is there evidence that the capital market was cognizant of the lease obligations of airlines when assessing the riskiness of their securities?

(2) What factors, other than financial leverage examined in (1), could explain the relatively high betas of companies in the airline industry?

(3) The following statement was made against the accounting alternative of reporting leases on the balance sheet:

Capitalizing leases will result in a drying up of bank and capital market financing available to the nation's airline industry. Airline companies will be perceived as too risky by the nation's banking and investment communities.

As a member of the FASB, how would you evaluate this statement when deciding on reporting methods for leases?

QUESTION 9.4: Beta Estimation for Multiactivity Firms

The line of business disclosure reported by three companies is presented below.

1. *Eaton Yale and Towne Inc., 1969 Prospectus*

1968

Sales (000's)	$896,531
Net income	49,199

The following details were also provided in the prospectus:

> EYT's four more important product lines, which contributed an aggregate of approximately 63% of net sales during 1968, are classified pursuant to the Standard Industrial Classification Code published by the U.S. Bureau of the Budget, and are listed below with the approximate percentage of net sales contributed by each such product line.

SIC Code	Classification	
3714	Motor vehicle parts and accessories	29%
3537	Industrial trucks, tractors, trailers and stackers	15%
3599	Miscellaneous machinery	10%
3566	Mechanical power transmission equipment	9%

> EYT's remaining fourteen product lines, similarly classified, contributed an aggregate of approximately 37% of net sales during 1968.

> Profit margins vary among the product lines and may vary within a single product line from year to year.

2. ITT (International Telephone and Telegraph), Annual Report 1975

Sales (000,000's)

Continuing operations:	1975
Telecommunications	$3,620
Natural resources	643
Industrial products	2,332
Food products	1,416
Automotive and consumer products	1,555
Hotels and business services	1,214
Defense and space	558
	11,338
Hartford Casualty and Life	1,955
Other insurance and finance	644
	13,937
Divestible operations:	
Under consent decrees	—
Other	30
Total	$ 13,967

Income (000,000's)

Continuing operations:

Telecommunications	$ 190
Natural resources	57
Industrial products	55
Food products	15
Automotive and consumer products	13
Hotels and business services	(23)
Defense and space	7
	314
Hartford Fire	82
Other insurance and finance	9
	405

Divestible operations:

Under consent decrees	—
Other	(7)
Total	$ 398

3. *Litton Industries, Inc., Annual Report 1976*

Sales (000's)	*1975*
Business systems and equipment	
Business machines	$446,609
Typewriters/copiers	284,903
Specialty paper/printing	142,991
Office furnishings/fixtures	147,408
Defense, commercial, and marine systems	
Navigation systems	$286,278
Communications/data processing	196,663
Shipbuilding	689,748
Industrial systems and equipment	
Machine tools	$223,678
Material handling	81,513
Electronic components	305,389
Professional services and equipment	
Microwave ovens	$129,400
Medical products	220,776
Publishing	57,888
Resource allocation	159,632
Operating Profit (000's)	
Business systems and equipment	($5,021)
Defense, commercial, and marine systems	(50,889)
Industrial systems and equipment	72,928
Professional services and equipment	48,104

REQUIRED

(1) Assume each of the above companies has recently been listed on a stock exchange (i.e., no past security returns are available; assume that financial statements for the prior five years are available). Outline two alternative approaches to estimating the current period's beta of these companies. What problems may exist in implementing these approaches?

(2) Assume that each of the above companies has been publicly listed for at least ten years. A portfolio manager interested in predicting next period's beta of these companies' securities has access to at least three information sets for each company:

(a) Past security returns,

(b) Past accounting data, and

(c) A combination of (a) and (b).

Why might the portfolio manager not want to exclusively rely on (a)? How would you provide evidence on whether the portfolio manager can obtain "better" estimates of beta with (c) rather than (a) or (b)?

(3) Norr [1974] made the following statement on the diversity in approaches used to report line of business information:

Probably segment reporting has been the most meaningful advance in analysis in the post-war period.... Management is in the best position to classify its segments. But, in view of the poor response in recent years, I believe we have no choice; we must go to an SIC code with an increased number of segments...to be disclosed in interim and annual reports." (pp. 8, 9)

How might line of business disclosure along SIC codes facilitate risk assessment by external analysts?

REFERENCES

BALL, R., and BROWN, P. "Portfolio Theory and Accounting." *Journal of Accounting Research* (Autumn 1969): 300–323.

BEAVER, W. H., KETTLER, P., and SCHOLES, M. "The Association Between Market-Determined and Accounting-Determined Risk Measures." *The Accounting Review* (Oct. 1970): 654–682.

BEAVER, W. H., and MANEGOLD, J. "The Association Between Market-Determined and Accounting-Determined Measures of Systematic Risk: Some Further Evidence." *Journal of Financial and Quantitative Analysis* (June 1975): 231–284.

BICKSLER, J. L. "The Usefulness of Beta Risk for Estimating the Cost of Capital." In I. Friend and J. L. Bicksler (eds.), *Risk and Return in Finance*, Volume 1, Ballinger Publishing Company, Cambridge, Mass., 1977: 81–100.

BILDERSEE, J. S. "Market-Determined and Alternative Measures of Risk." *The Accounting Review* (Jan. 1975): 81–98.

BLUME, M. E. "Betas and Their Regression Tendencies." *Journal of Finance* (June 1975): 785–795.

BOGUE, M. C. "The Estimation and Behavior of Systematic Risk." Unpublished Ph.D. Dissertation, Standford University, Stanford, Calif., 1972.

BROWN, S. H. "Optimal Portfolio Choice Under Uncertainty." Unpublished Ph.D. Dissertation, University of Chicago, Chicago, 1976.

COCHRAN, W. G. "On the Performance of the Linear Discriminant Function." *Technometrics* (May 1964): 179–190.

ESKEW, R. K. "Association Between Accounting and Share Price Data." *The Accounting Review* (Apr. 1975): 316–324.

FAMA, E. F., and MILLER, M. H. *The Theory of Finance*. Holt, Rinehart and Winston, Inc., New York, 1972.

FISHER, L. "Some New Stock Market Indices." *Journal of Business* (Jan. 1966): 191–225.

GONEDES, N. J. "Evidence on the Information Content of Accounting Numbers: Accounting-Based and Market-Based Estimates of Systematic Risk." *Journal of Financial and Quantitative Analysis* (June 1973): 407–444.

GRIFFIN, P. A. "Relative Risk and Risk Estimates Derived from Quarterly Earnings and Dividends." *The Accounting Review* (July 1976): 499–515.

HALEY, C., and SCHALL, L. *The Theory of Financial Decisions*. McGraw-Hill, New York, 1973.

HAMADA, R. S. "Portfolio Analysis, Market Equilibrium and Corporate Finance." *Journal of Finance* (Mar. 1969): 13–31.

———. "The Effect of the Firm's Capital Structure on the Systematic Risk of Common Stocks." *Journal of Finance* (May 1972): 435–452.

JOHNSTON, J. *Econometric Methods*, 2nd ed. McGraw-Hill, New York, 1972.

KLEIN, R. W., and BAWA, V. S. "The Effect of Estimation Risk on Optimal Portfolio Choice." *Journal of Financial Economics* (June 1976): 215–231.

LEV, B. "On the Association Between Operating Leverage and Risk." *Journal of Financial and Quantitative Analysis* (Sept. 1974): 627–641.

MELICHER, R. W., and RUSH, D. F. "Systematic Risk, Financial Data, and Bond Rating Relationships in a Regulated Industry Environment," *Journal of Finance* (May 1974): 537–544.

MYERS, S. C. "Finance Theory in Rate Cases." *Bell Journal of Economics and Management Science* (Spring 1972): 58–97.

———. "The Relation Between Real and Financial Measures of Risk and Return." In I. Friend and J. L. Bicksler (eds.), *Risk and Return in Finance*, Volume 1, Ballinger Publishing Company, Cambridge, Mass., 1977: 49–80.

NORR, D. *Accounting Theory Illustrated*, First Manhattan Company, New York, 1974.

PERCIVAL, D. R. "Operating Leverage and Risk." *Journal of Business Research* (Apr. 1974): 223–227.

PETTIT, R. R., and WESTERFIELD, R. "A Model of Capital Asset Risk." *Journal of Financial and Quantitative Ananlysis* (Mar. 1972): 1649–1677.

ROSENBERG, B., and MARATHE, V. "The Prediction of Investment Risk: Systematic and Residual Risk." *Proceedings of the Seminar on the Analysis of Security Prices*. Center for Research in Security Prices, Graduate School of Business, University of Chicago, Chicago, Nov. 1975: 85–159.

ROSENBERG, B., and MCKIBBEN, W. "The Prediction of Systematic and Specific Risk in Common Stocks." *Journal of Financial and Quantitative Analysis* (Mar. 1973): 317–334.

RUBINSTEIN, M. E. "A Mean-Variance Synthesis of Corporate Financial Theory." *Journal of Finance* (Mar. 1973): 167–181.

SCHOLES, M., and WILLIAMS, J. "Estimating Betas From Daily Data." Unpublished Paper, University of Chicago, Chicago, 1976.

SHARPE, W. F., and COOPER, G. M. "Risk-Return Classes of New York Stock Exchange Common Stocks, 1931–67." *Financial Analysts Journal* (Mar.–Apr. 1972): 46–54.

THOMPSON, D. J. "Sources of Systematic Risk in Common Stocks." *Journal of Business* (Apr. 1976): 173–188.

VASICEK, O. A. "A Note on Using Cross-Sectional Information in Bayesian Estimation of Security Betas." *Journal of Finance* (Dec. 1973): 1233–1239.

CHAPTER **10**

CAPITAL ASSET
PRICES AND
FINANCIAL INFORMATION

In this chapter, theory and evidence pertaining to the role of financial statement information in the setting of capital asset prices are discussed. Most work in this area has concentrated on the pricing of common stocks. Note, however, that this work also has implications for capital assets whose price is related to common stock prices, e.g., convertible preferred securities and options. There are several reasons this work is important. One reason relates to the role of information in the setting of equilibrium asset prices—see Chapter 7. The discussion in Section 7.1 indicated that changes in disclosure may affect the ability of the capital market to discriminate between assets which in the absence of information would be treated as identical. In this chapter we shall examine if information about earnings and other variables is important in this discriminating (screening) process.

The material in this chapter also is important to security analysts. The use of a model relating the price of a security to financial statement information occupies an important place in many security selection decisions. The models used range from simple price-earnings multiples to more complex models such as those used by *Value Line* and *Wells Fargo*. An assumption underlying the use of these models is that financial statement information is an important determinant of security prices. Several such models will be examined in this chapter.

Models of security price determination also play an important role in accounting research. Many statements in the accounting literature imply that there is a mechanistic relationship between reported accounting numbers and stock prices—several such statements were quoted in Appendix 7.A. In this chapter we shall illustrate how one can use security price valuation models to examine the descriptive validity of these statements. Note that the validity of these statements is especially pertinent to the investment community. One method proposed for detecting under- or overvalued securities involves adjusting the reported earnings for items such as the earnings of unconsolidated subsidiaries or the unrealized appreciation of fixed assets. If the capital market is already making such adjustments, an analyst needs to look for other methods of analysis in his search for under- or overvalued securities.

In Section 10.1 we shall examine partial equilibrium models of asset pricing. These models have theoretical underpinnings in resource allocation under uncertainty. In Section 10.2 we shall examine asset valuation models used in the investment community. These models generally have a less rigorous theoretical underpinning than those discussed in Section 10.1. Moreover, whereas the main purpose of the models discussed in Section 10.1 is to understand (explain) asset pricing, those in Section 10.2 are often developed to detect mispricing (under- or overvaluations) of capital assets. In Section 10.3 we shall illustrate how the models discussed in prior sections can be used to examine the capital market reaction to alternative accounting measurement rules.

10.1 THEORETICAL MODELS OF ASSET VALUATION

The simplest form of a valuation model is for the certainty case in which all assets yield uniform, sure income streams in perpetuity. Given the market rate of interest (r) and appropriate assumptions about capital markets (e.g., perfect capital markets), the equilibrium market value of the firm (V) is

$$V = \frac{I}{r}, \qquad (10.1)$$

where $I =$ the (uniform) income per period generated by the assets currently held. Extensions of this model have taken various forms. One form is to retain the assumption of certainty but relax the assumption that the assets generate a uniform income per period. For instance, Miller and Modigliani [1961] derived the following valuation model for a firm with a *constant growth* in earnings:

$$V_t = \frac{X_{t+1}}{r} + \frac{X_{t+1}}{r} \left[\frac{k(r^* - r)}{r - kr^*} \right], \qquad (10.2)$$

where $V_t =$ value of the firm at the end of period t,

$X_t =$ earnings generated by the firm in period t,

$r =$ market rate of interest,

$k =$ proportion of the firm's earnings invested each year (assumed constant),

$r^* =$ rate of return on the investment.

In this formulation, V_t is a function of both a no-growth component [first term on the right-hand side (RHS)] and a growth component (second term on the RHS). Note that growth in (10.2) has a precise meaning; it is investments for which $r^* > r$. If $r^* = r$, the second-term on the RHS of (10.2) becomes zero and V_t is exactly determined as per (10.1).

Another extension of the simple certainty case in (10.1) is to recognize uncertainty. Depending on the assumptions made, different valuation models can be derived. We shall concentrate in this section on two valuation models that are derived from partial equilibrium theories of asset valuation under uncertainty, i.e., the Miller-Modigliani risk-class firm valuation model and the Sharpe-Lintner equity valuation model.[1]

A Risk-Class Valuation Model

Using assumptions such as rational investors, perfect markets, and no taxes, Modigliani and Miller [1958] derived the following valuation model for a no-growth firm in risk-class k:

$$V_i = \frac{1}{\rho_k} \cdot \overline{X}_i, \qquad (10.3)$$

where V_i = sum of the market values of all firm i's securities,

$\overline{X}_i$ = expected level of average annual earnings generated by the assets that firm i currently holds,

$1/\rho_k$ = market's capitalization rate for the expected value of uncertain, pure equity earnings streams of firms in risk class k.

Two firms are in the same risk class if investors perceive that whatever values their earnings and investment outlays take, they will always be proportional by a factor λ—i.e., they are perfectly correlated.[2] In empirical applications of the risk-class model, firms operating in a "relatively homogeneous" industry have been said to constitute a risk class. Two such industries that have been examined are electric utilities and railroads.[3]

The first detailed empirical examination of the risk-class model was the Miller and Modigliani [1966] analysis of the valuation of 63 electric utilities in 1954, 1956, and 1957. To recognize "other factors that influence real-world valuations" (p. 343), adjustments to (10.3) for the corporate tax (τ) on $\overline{X}$ and the tax savings for corporate debt interest were added. Additional terms representing (1) "the size of the electric utility" and (2) its "growth potential" were also added. Note that the addition of these latter two terms was based on intuition rather than being implied by a theory of firm valuation under uncertainty. The following structural equation was used to estimate the parameters of the valuation model:

$$(V_i - \tau D_i) = \hat{a}_0 + \hat{a}_1 \overline{X}_i (1-\tau) + \hat{a}_2 \overline{\Delta A}, \qquad (10.4)$$

where V_i = market value of firm i's securities,

τ = corporate tax rate,

D_i = market value of debt of firm i,

$\overline{X}_i(1-\tau)$ = the *tax-adjusted* current earnings,

$\overline{\Delta A}$ = average growth rate in total assets over the past four years.

The reciprocal of the $\hat{a}_1$ coefficient is an estimate of the cost of capital for the firm's risk class.

Empirical results for (10.4) are presented in Table 10.1. The valuation model explained variations in electric utility valuation very well—the R^2 ranged from .56 to .77. Two features of the results are important from a financial statement analysis perspective. *First*, the coefficient on the earn-

TABLE 10.1   Risk-Class Valuation Model of Electric Utility Companies

	Size Coefficient $(\hat{a}_0)$	Earnings Coefficient $(\hat{a}_1)$	Growth Coefficient $(\hat{a}_2)$	Multiple R^2
1954	$-.205$ $t = -2.93$	19.2 $t = 44.65$	.466 $t = 2.74$	.56
1956	$-.111$ $t = -1.59$	16.6 $t = 42.56$	.926 $t = 4.41$	.76
1957	$-.277$ $t = -3.46$	16.0 $t = 36.36$	1.39 $t = 5.65$	.77

SOURCE: Miller and Modigliani [1966, Table 1].

ings term is highly significant. Indeed, Miller and Modigliani [1966] subsequently estimated that the earnings term explained from 68.1% of total valuation in 1957 to 75.9% of total valuation in 1954. *Second*, current earnings is used to approximate the capitalized earnings power of assets currently held. Miller and Modigliani [1966] reported that current earnings provided more efficient estimates of $\overline{X}_i$ than did "equally weighted two- and five-year averages of past reported earnings" (p. 357). This result is consistent with the time-series results for annual earnings discussed in Chapter 4.

A second extensive application of the risk-class model is Brown's [1968] analysis of valuation in the railroad industry. The sample included 45 U.S. railroads. The period examined was 1954–1963. Results for (10.4) for this sample are presented in Table 10.2. The results support the findings of Miller and Modigliani [1966] in a different industry. Note,

TABLE 10.2   Risk-Class Valuation Model of Railroads

	Size Coefficient $(\hat{a}_0)$	Earnings Coefficient $(\hat{a}_1)$	Growth Coefficient $(\hat{a}_2)$	Multiple R^2
1954	1.36 $t = 1.24$	13.02 $t = 30.28$	-1.09 $t = -1.85$	.79
1956	$-.54$ $t = -.34$	10.56 $t = 12.72$	$-.78$ $t = -.94$	.81
1957	1.26 $t = .71$	9.11 $t = 13.01$	-1.23 $t = -1.76$	.73
1960	11.58 $t = 4.83$	13.10 $t = 13.37$	-1.61 $t = -1.64$	.75
1963	$-.38$ $t = -.20$	15.25 $t = 25.85$	-3.92 $t = -6.64$	.92

SOURCE: Brown [1968, Table IV.5].

especially, the significance of the earnings term in every year examined. The lowest t statistic on the earnings term was 12.72 in 1956. As noted in Chapter 2, a t statistic greater than 2 is statistically significant at the .05 level for the sample size examined.

The risk-class valuation model thus appears to have had several successful applications. Note, however, that the model requires firms to all be in the same risk class. The industries examined were chosen due to their being reasonably homogeneous. It is unlikely that many other industries with a sufficient number of firms to efficiently estimate (10.3) are available.

B Sharpe-Lintner Equity Valuation Model

The theoretical underpinning of this valuation model is the Sharpe-Lintner asset pricing model discussed in Chapter 8.[4] The valuation model for an all-equity firm (see Fama and Miller [1972, Chapter 7]) is

$$P_i = \frac{E(\tilde{V}_i) - S_M\left[\mathrm{Cov}(\tilde{V}_i, \tilde{V}_M)/\sigma(\tilde{V}_M)\right]}{1 + R_f}, \tag{10.5}$$

where P_i = equilibrium market value of firm i at period 1,

$\tilde{V}_i$ = market value of firm i at period 2,

$\tilde{V}_M$ = market value of all firms at period 2,

$S_M = [E(\tilde{R}_M) - R_f]/\sigma(\tilde{R}_M)$,

R_f = risk-free rate of interest.

R_M = return on the market portfolio.

Thus, the numerator of (10.5) includes the expected market price at period 2 less an adjustment for the nondiversifiable risk attaching to the period 2 value; this numerator is discounted using the risk-free rate of interest.

In an empirical application of this model, Litzenberger and Rao [1971] examined equity valuation in the electric utility industry over the 1960–1966 period. The estimated model was

$$P_i = \hat{\gamma}_1 E_i + \hat{\gamma}_2 R_i + \hat{\gamma}_3 G_i, \tag{10.6}$$

where P_i = price to book value ratio,

E_i = expected rate of return on book value,

R_i = nondiversifiable risk of earnings to equity,

G_i = expected rate of growth of book value.

Note that as with the growth term in (10.4), G_i in (10.6) was added due to the intuition of the authors rather than being implied by a theoretical model of equity valuation under uncertainty.

The Sharpe-Lintner valuation model, if descriptively valid, implies the following: (1) The reciprocal of γ_1 should approximate an exogenous

TABLE 10.3 Sharpe-Lintner Valuation Model of Electric Utility Companies

	Earnings Coefficient $(\hat{\gamma}_1)$	Risk Coefficient $(\hat{\gamma}_2)$	Growth Coefficient $(\hat{\gamma}_3)$	R^2	Estimated R_f $(1/\hat{\gamma}_1)$	Exogenous R_f
1960	16.7	−22.1	1.7	.55	.060	.052
	$t=22.57$	$t=-2.95$	$t=2.79$			
1961	18.7	−12.0	2.3	.52	.053	.047
	$t=16.55$	$t=-1.07$	$t=2.88$			
1962	17.8	−11.4	1.5	.57	.056	.047
	$t=24.38$	$t=-1.27$	$t=1.90$			
1963	19.8	−16.2	2.4	.56	.051	.044
	$t=25.06$	$t=-1.53$	$t=2.0$			
1964	20.2	−17.8	3.7	.57	.050	.045
	$t=24.63$	$t=-1.50$	$t=2.47$			
1965	19.9	−4.8	5.7	.55	.050	.046
	$t=23.98$	$t=-.30$	$t=2.19$			
1966	17.3	−10.4	3.6	.50	.057	.049
	$t=48.06$	$t=-2.12$	$t=1.33$			

SOURCE: Litzenberger and Rao [1971, Table 1].

estimate of R_f, and (2) γ_2 should be negative—the negative coefficient is a consequence of the risk aversion assumption used in deriving the theoretical model. Table 10.3 details estimates from (10.6) of γ_1, γ_2, and γ_3 and the R^2 over the 1960–1966 period. An exogenous estimate of R_f (interest yield on Standard & Poor's *BBB Composite Utility Bond Index*) is also provided. Note that the estimates of R_f $(1/\hat{\gamma}_1)$ provided by the model were reasonably close to the exogenous estimate of R_f. Moreover, the coefficient on the risk term $(\hat{\gamma}_2)$ was consistently negative. On balance, the theoretical valuation model appeared to adequately describe valuation of electric utility stocks. From a financial statement analysis perspective, it is important to note that the coefficient on the earnings term was statistically significant in every year examined.

The motivation behind the above partial-equilibrium models was whether necessarily simplified models could yield useful insights into asset valuation under uncertainty. Based on the above empirical results, it does appear that the models do yield useful insights; they do help explain differences in the prices of capital assets at a point in time.

10.2 INVESTMENT MODELS OF ASSET VALUATION

The investment community has developed many different valuation models to use in security selection decisions. A common feature of almost all of these models is the use of financial statement data, especially data about earnings, or earnings growth. These models are used to predict an *appropriate price* (or P/E ratio). An associated investment decision is usually based on the sign and extent of the differences between the appropriate price and the actual price.

A survey of "practitioners' evaluation methods" by Bing [1971] gives insight into various approaches used in practice. A questionnaire was sent to "leading financial institutions" to obtain "specific information regarding their techniques and implied theories of equity appraisal." Of the 34 replies, 15 were from commercial banks and 11 from mutual fund organizations. The most popular approaches involved the use of price to earnings multiples, e.g.,

(1) Compare the present actual P/E multiple with a normal multiple for the stock in question, and

(2) Compare P/E multiple and growth of individual stock with industry group multiple and growth.

The use of the term "normal" P/E or "normal" price was mentioned by many respondents to the questionnaire. In this section we shall consider several specific models used to estimate the "normal" P/E multiple or price.[5]

A   The Meader Model

Meader [1935] represents one of the earliest uses of regression models for determining "basic common stock values." He regressed the mean 1933 prices (P_i) of 502 NYSE stocks against the following five variables:

$$S_i = \text{Turnover (shares traded)}$$
$$B_i = \text{Book value per share}$$
$$W_i = \text{Net working capital per share}$$
$$E_i = \text{Earnings per share}$$
$$D_i = \text{Dividends per share.}$$

The estimated relationship was

$$P_i = 1.7 + 1.35 S_i + .12 B_i + .20 W_i + 3.0 E_i + 8.4 D_i. \qquad (10.7)$$

Meader repeated this regression for each year from 1930 to 1939. His conclusion in 1940 was

> If any general conclusion can be drawn from this 10-year series of multiple correlation studies, it is a negative one. The assumption that current dividends and earnings, among other bits of arithmetic, are acceptable criteria of investment value when tested quantitatively by market prices over an extended period did not yield close or consistent results. (Meader [1940, p. 890])

The above model is mainly of interest from a historical perspective. The approach adopted, however, is not unlike that adopted in more recent papers. The Whitbeck-Kisor model—developed at *The Bank of New York* —is another example of the use of regression models in security selection.

B   The Whitbeck-Kisor Model

Whitbeck and Kisor [1963] used a multiple regression equation to predict a "normal" P/E ratio. The independent variables used were

G_i = Expected rate of growth in earnings per share of firm i

PR_i = Expected payout ratio of firm i

R_i = Expected standard deviation of earnings about a trend for firm i.

Analysts provided estimates of each of these three variables. The following cross-sectional multiple regression was then run:

$$\frac{P_i}{E_i} = \hat{\alpha} + \hat{\beta}_1 G_i + \hat{\beta}_2 PR_i + \hat{\beta}_3 R_i. \tag{10.8}$$

A cross-sectional regression on 135 stocks in June 1962 produced the following:

$$\frac{P_i}{E_i} = 8.2 + 1.5 G_i + 6.7 PR_i - .2 R_i. \tag{10.9}$$

Using (10.9) and the following analysts' forecasts of G_i, PR_i, and R_i for *IBM* and *General Motors*,

	IBM	*General Motors*
G_i	17%	3%
PR_i	.25	.75
R_i	5%	20%

the theoretical P/E ratios were calculated as

$$IBM: \quad P/E = 8.2 + 1.5 \times 17 + 6.7 \times .25 - .2 \times 5$$
$$= 34.4$$
$$GM: \quad P/E = 8.2 + 1.5 \times 3 + 6.7 \times .75 - .2 \times 20$$
$$= 13.7.$$

The actual P/E ratios at the time of the forecast were 35.3 for IBM and 15.4 for General Motors. Then Whitbeck-Kisor divided the market P/E ratio by the theoretical ratio; a ratio greater than 1 indicated an overvalued stock, whereas a ratio less than 1 indicated an undervalued stock. They inferred IBM was appropriately priced ($35.3/34.4 \cong 1$), whereas General Motors was $\cong 12\%$ overvalued. Although Whitbeck-Kisor recognized that the theoretical P/E ratios may change over time, they argued "that the market price of the stock will seek this level faster than the theoretical price itself will change" (p. 59).

The most detailed test of the investment performance of the Whitbeck-Kisor model was performed by Malkiel and Cragg [1970]. They first regressed the P/E ratios of 178 firms against an earnings per share growth forecast (G_i), the payout ratio (PR_i), and an earnings variability or risk (R_i) measure—i.e., (10.8). An interesting part of this exercise was the use of earnings per share growth forecasts made by investment analysts. These forecasts were obtained from 17 investment firms. Results of the regressions for 1961–1965 are presented in Table 10.4. Several features of these results are noteworthy. First, the explanatory power of the model appears to be very good—the R^2 ranges from .70 to .85.[6] Second, the most significant variable each year is the forecast of EPS growth. Third, the coefficients of the model appear unstable over time; e.g., the coefficient on the dividend payout term ranges from .78 in 1962 to 7.62 in 1963. The instability in the coefficients could be a symptom of the lack of any theoretical model of asset valuation under uncertainty to guide the choice of variables to include in the regression. It also could be induced by statistical reasons. If the independent variables are multicollinear, different samples can give quite different estimates of the coefficients in a regression model—see Johnston [1972].[7]

Malkiel and Cragg then regressed the one-year return on a stock for $t+1$ against an estimate of the under- or overvaluation from the Whitbeck-Kisor model at t:

$$R_{t+1} = \hat{\alpha} + \hat{\beta}_1 \left[\frac{P/E_t - \widehat{P/E_t}}{\widehat{P/E_t}} \right], \qquad (10.10)$$

TABLE 10.4 Whitbeck-Kisor Price-Earnings Valuation Model

	$\hat{\alpha}$	EPS Growth, $\hat{\beta}_1$	Dividend Payout, $\hat{\beta}_2$	Earnings Variability, $\hat{\beta}_3$	R^2
1961	4.73	3.28 $t=14.47$	2.05 $t=.47$	$-.82$ $t=-1.09$	.70
1962	11.06	1.75 $t=13.99$	.78 $t=.31$	-1.61 $t=-4.11$	.70
1963	2.94	2.55 $t=19.67$	7.62 $t=2.95$	$-.27$ $t=-.69$	.75
1964	6.71	2.05 $t=18.24$	5.33 $t=2.44$	$-.89$ $t=-2.48$	.75
1965	.96	2.74 $t=26.50$	5.01 $t=2.44$	$-.35$ $t=-1.14$	.85

SOURCE: Malkiel and Cragg [1970, Table 2].

where R_{t+1} = one-year return on a stock in period $t+1$,

P/E_t = actual price to earnings ratio at the end of period t,

$\widehat{P/E}_t$ = predicted price to earnings ratio from the Whitbeck-Kisor model.

If the model was successful in security analysis, Malkiel and Cragg hypothesized that the estimated β_1 coefficient would be negative *and* significant. The following results were obtained:

	$\hat{\beta}_1$	$t(\hat{\beta}_1)$	R^2
1961	−.25	−3.08	.09
1962	.21	1.93	.03
1963	−.20	−2.55	.04
1964	.00	.00	.00
1965	−.01	−.11	.00

Only two out of five years was the $\hat{\beta}_1$ coefficient negative *and* significant. Moreover, the explanatory power of the independent variable in (10.10) appears to be weak to nonexistent.[8]

C The Wells Fargo Model[9]

The model used by *Wells Fargo Investment Advisors* combines both traditional valuation theory (see Section 10.1) with *capital market theory* (see Chapter 8). The *first* stage of the analysis is based on the following valuation model:

$$P_i = \frac{D_1}{1+R} + \frac{D_2}{(1+R)^2} + \frac{D_3}{(1+R)^3} + \dots + \frac{D_N}{(1+R)^N},$$

where P_i = price of security i,

D_j = dividends paid in year j,

R = expected return on security i.

For each security in their *Security Market Line* service (345 as of March 1977), *Wells Fargo* analysts provide the following estimates:

(1) Earnings and dividends per share for each of the next five years.

(2) A fifth-year normalized EPS growth rate and normalized dividend payout ratio.

(3) The number of years before a steady-state growth and payout are to be assumed, which is the beginning of the terminal period, or maturity, if you will.

(4) The pattern of growth to be expected between the fifth year and the year of "maturity," the choices being
    (a) a slow decay in the growth rate,
    (b) a linear decay, or
    (c) a rapid decay.
(5) A terminal growth rate [and] payout ratio.... (Fouse [1976, p. 38])

These estimates are combined into estimates of the future dividend stream. The discount rate that equates this future dividend stream with the current price is then determined. This rate is termed the *expected return* and is said to be the "single most important piece of information to have about a common stock" (Fouse [1977, p. 40]).

The second stage of the analysis determines the expected return on each security *conditional* on estimates of its risk and liquidity. A research memorandum of *Wells Fargo Investment Advisors* (dated April 11, 1977) describes this step as follows:

Risk and Return

In general, investors price common stocks to provide additional expected return where additional risk must be taken. Modern capital theory defines the relationship between risk and return by a "Security Market Line," where expected return is plotted against systematic risk (Beta). Beta represents the risk that cannot be diversified away by merely combining stocks in a portfolio.

Although [Beta] is generally measured by regressing past price changes of a stock against price changes of the stock market, Beta can be both analytically as well as empirically related to such fundamental variables as variability in earnings, leverage and the cyclicality of sales. The Security Analysis Group looks at historical Beta calculations based on price changes and accounting data in addition to business prospects in determining risk assignments. The Common Stock Guidance List is then broken into five Risk Sectors for coding and risk management purposes (Risk Sector 1 = lowest risk...Risk Sector 5 = highest risk).

Liquidity Adjustment

In addition to adjusting expected return on the basis of relative riskiness, we have found that investors are willing to give up some expected return in order to own stocks which can be purchased and sold in size without affecting price. This requires another adjustment. By using a measure of market liquidity supplied by Amivest Company, we can empirically determine how much return investors are willing to give up in order to own a liquid stock. (p. 2)

The research memorandum then illustrated how these two stages are combined to form a judgment of the relative attractiveness of a security:

Measure of relative attractiveness
= Expected return − Risk adjustment + Liquidity adjustment.

The following examples of five companies in risk sector 2 were given:

Company	Expected Return	Risk Adjustment	Liquidity Adjustment	Measure of Relative Attractiveness
Citicorp	14.3%	12.9%	.5%	1.9%
St. Joe Minerals	13.9	12.9	−.2	.8
Caterpillar	12.8	12.9	.6	.5
Boeing	11.8	12.9	.3	−.8
Dr. Peper	12.2	12.9	−.2	−.9

The *Wells Fargo* system represents an interesting blend of theory and pragmatism. Note that financial statement information is used in determining both the expected return and the risk of each security. At present, no detailed analysis of the performance of the *Wells Fargo* system has been published. Thus, it is an open issue whether their measures of relative attractiveness enable one to select securities (or portfolios of securities) that subsequently earn abnormal returns.[10]

D   The Value Line Investment Survey Model

The *Value Line model* is of considerable interest due to some evidence of its success in detecting under- or overvalued securities. Stocks are placed in one of five categories based on their estimated price performance in the next 12 months. The current system—see Bernhard [1975]—consists of four components. The first three components have been part of the system for some time:

1.   *The Non-Parametric Value Position.*

The non-parametric value position of a stock is a function of the "order" of its latest relative reported earnings and relative price in relation to the past 10 year's experience. Relative earnings and relative prices are defined as the stock's latest 12 months earnings and price divided by the average earnings and prices of all Value Line stocks for the same period. If a stock's relative earnings are currently the highest in the past 10 years, its earnings rank is 10; if lowest, 1. The same applies to the latest 12 month average price. The higher the earnings rank relative to the price rank, the more undervalued is the stock on the basis of its latest 12 months earnings. The process of assigning an order or rank to relative earnings tends to tame and normalize the earnings data, which in its original form, particularly as far as highly cyclical stocks are concerned, is all too often unmanageable.

In addition to the current earnings and price ranks, a price momentum factor is included in order to predict future relative price action. The price momentum factor for a stock is determined by dividing the stock's latest 10 week average relative price by its 52 week average relative price.

An electronic computer was used to test the discriminating ability of these variables. A multiple regression analysis was performed covering some 13,000 observations and 12 years of market experience. The results clearly indicated that these factors were significantly related to relative price movement in the year ahead. A formula was produced which combined earnings rank, price rank, and price momentum into a composite number which could then be ranked from 1630 to 1,1630 being the best. The number 1630 is used because it represents the number of stocks regularly supervised by The Value Line Investment Survey.

2. *Earnings Momentum.*

This component of the Value Line next 12 month ranking system is a function of the year-to-year change in quarterly earnings per share of each stock relative to that of all stocks under regular supervision. Numerous tests with past data demonstrate conclusively that this "earnings momentum" factor has an important bearing on the subsequent price performance of individual securities and helps refine the selection of favorably situated stocks in terms of the two other value criteria described above. No attempt is made to rank all stocks successively from 1630 to 1, based on the exact earnings changes from a year ago (the implied accuracy would be far greater than could be obtained in practice). Rather, all stocks reporting earnings on a quarterly basis are assigned to one of three equal categories—and ranked 1200, 800 or 400 respectively—depending upon the relative "earnings momentum" of the latest quarter. The most favorable quarterly earnings comparisons (the top one-third) are assigned the number 1200, the middle third, 800 and the lowest third, 400. (The scaling of these numbers is chosen to maintain comparability with the ranking method applied to the "magnitude" and "non-parametric" value criteria.) In assigning ranks, allowance is made, whenever possible, for "special" factors affecting earnings in a specific quarter, such as strikes, accounting adjustments, special tax credits, other non-recurring income and expenses, etc.

3. *Earnings Surprise Factor.*

Tests have indicated that when a company reports quarterly earnings significantly different from those estimated in the Survey, sharp price movements follow. In the Value Line Ranking System, this factor is treated as follows:

Deviation between Actual & Value Line's Estimated Quarterly Earnings	Assigned Numbers
−30% or more	−400
−15 to −29%	−200
−14 to +14%	0
+15% to +29%	+200
+30% & over	+400

As in the case of earnings momentum, the number assigned to the quarterly earnings deviations between actual and estimate is chosen to maintain comparability with the ranking method applied to the "magnitude" and "non-parametric" value criteria. (pp. 37–38)

The fourth component in the *Value Line Investment Survey* model was added in July 1976.[11] *Value Line* [1976] reported that addition of the factor was based on internal studies indicating that "there is a statistical significance in the judgment of *Value Line* analysts as a predictor of future relative price performance":

> 4. *An Analyst Judgment Factor.*
>
> Analysts' judgment can help the ranking system take account of such considerations as backlog trends, incoming order rates, facilities utilization, competitive factors, labor problems, product quality and numerous other nonquantifiable variables. This new factor—the analyst's judgment—will account for only about 20% of a stock's ranking. The other 80% will continue to be determined by completely objective, mathematical disciplines applied to actual price and earnings data. (p. 1)

After each stock has been classified on the basis of the above four components, the individual ranks are summed and the composite numbers arranged into five categories:

Top 100	Group 1
Next 300	Group 2
Middle 830	Group 3
Next 300	Group 4
Bottom 100	Group 5

Figure 10.1 presents the ten-year record of the five *Value Line* groups over the 1965–1974 period. The returns for each group assume an investor bought an equal dollar amount of every stock ranked 1 (highest) for price performance at the beginning of each year. The investor holds that list unchanged for a whole year and then at the end of the year revises his list, dropping out all stocks no longer ranked 1 and replacing them with stocks that had taken their place in the group 1 rankings. The same procedure was repeated for stocks in the other four groups. Note that the price performance of each group does appear consistent with *Value Line's* predictions; e.g., group 1 has the highest price appreciation, and group 5 has the greatest price depreciation.

The results in Figure 10.1 do not necessarily imply that *Value Line* is able to detect under- or overvalued securities. In testing this ability, it is necessary to posit a model of capital asset pricing. If one assumes that the Sharpe-Lintner asset pricing model is descriptively valid, then

$$E(\tilde{R}_i) - R_f = \beta\left[E(\tilde{R}_M) - R_f\right]. \qquad (10.11)$$

If the betas of *Value Line's* five groups systematically differ, then it is possible that the pattern in Figure 10.1 is consistent with (10.11). Evidence on this issue is provided by Black [1973]. Black conducted an extensive

FIGURE 10.1 Ten-Year Record of Price Performance of Value Line Groups

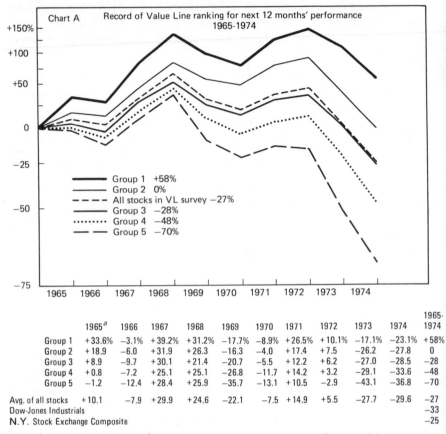

	1965[a]	1966	1967	1968	1969	1970	1971	1972	1973	1974	1965-1974
Group 1	+33.6%	−3.1%	+39.2%	+31.2%	−17.7%	−8.9%	+26.5%	+10.1%	−17.1%	−23.1%	+58%
Group 2	+18.9	−6.0	+31.9	+26.3	−16.3	−4.0	+17.4	+7.5	−26.2	−27.8	0
Group 3	+8.9	−9.7	+30.1	+21.4	−20.7	−5.5	+12.2	+6.2	−27.0	−28.5	−28
Group 4	+0.8	−7.2	+25.1	+25.1	−26.8	−11.7	+14.2	+3.2	−29.1	−33.6	−48
Group 5	−1.2	−12.4	+28.4	+25.9	−35.7	−13.1	+10.5	−2.9	−43.1	−36.8	−70
Avg. of all stocks	+10.1	−7.9	+29.9	+24.6	−22.1	−7.5	+14.9	+5.5	−27.7	−29.6	−27
Dow-Jones Industrials											−33
N.Y. Stock Exchange Composite											−25

[a]April through December–all other years cover a 12-month period

Source: Bernhard [1975, p. 5].

analysis of the performance of the *Value Line* system. He assumed the following strategy over the 1965–1970 period:

> The rankings of Value Line were collected from their published reports, taking every fourth report beginning in April, 1965, when the current ranking system went into effect. We constructed portfolios of all the stocks in each group, and weighted each stock equally each month. This weighting scheme implied that each month we sold some of the stocks that had gone up since the previous month, and bought more of some of the stocks that had gone down. We sold the stocks that left a particular group, and bought the stocks that had come into that group. (p. 12)

Thus, five portfolios were constructed, with each portfolio representing one of the *Value Line* groups. Black estimated the following regression model using the monthly security returns of each portfolio:

$$R_{it} - R_{ft} = \hat{\alpha}_i + \hat{\beta}_i (R_{Mt} - R_{ft}) + \hat{u}_{it}, \qquad (10.12)$$

where R_{it} = return on *Value Line* group i (where $i = 1$ to 5), in time t,

R_{ft} = commercial paper rate at time t,

R_{Mt} = equally weighted average of the returns of the stocks in *Value Line* in time t.

The betas of each portfolio over the 1965–1970 period were

	β
Group 1	1.11
Group 2	1.03
Group 3	.98
Group 4	.96
Group 5	1.03

If there were no difference in the risk-adjusted performance of the five *Value Line* groups, the intercepts of the regression (10.12) for each group would be approximately the same. The results indicated otherwise:

> When the portfolio was revised on a monthly basis, the extra returns earned by the Rank 1 and Rank 5 stocks were respectively 10 per cent per year and −10 per cent per year. Ranks 1 and 2 had t values of around 4.0 in our statistical tests of significance, and Ranks 4 and 5 had t values of around −4.0. If these statistical tests are appropriate, then the possibility that this performance could have occurred by chance is one in 10,000. The tests indicate that the success of the rankings was very consistent over time. (pp. 12–14)

The above results are rather impressive. Assuming the descriptive validity of the Sharpe-Lintner asset pricing model, they suggest *Value Line* is able to detect under- or overvalued securities. It should be noted, however, that criticisms have been made of both the asset pricing model assumed and the statistical significance tests used by Black.[12] It would be interesting to examine the performance of the *Value Line* system in the period since 1970 using more recently developed approaches to estimating and testing the significance of abnormal security returns (see Appendix 11.A).

10.3 VALUATION MODELS AND ACCOUNTING ALTERNATIVES

In this section, we shall illustrate the use of (1) price to earnings ratios and (2) the Sharpe-Lintner equity valuation model to provide evidence on three accounting issues—i.e., (1) accounting for depreciation,

(2) accounting for R & D costs, and (3) accounting for marketable securities. The main issue addressed is whether capital markets take the reported earnings number at face value or whether there is explicit recognition of the valuation methods underlying the computation of reported earnings.

A Accounting for Depreciation

Beaver and Dukes [1973] provide an interesting analysis of whether the capital market recognizes the depreciation method underlying the computation of earnings when setting price/earnings ratios. The sample of firms examined included (1) 54 firms which used accelerated depreciation for tax reporting and straight-line depreciation for external reporting and (2) 69 firms which used accelerated depreciation for both tax and external reporting. The (1) sample is hereafter referred to as A/S firms and the (2) sample as A/A firms. The period of analysis was 1950–1967. The average price to earnings ratios for this period for the two samples were

A/S Firms	A/A Firms
15.08	16.61

Several factors that could explain these different average P/E ratios for the A/S and A/A groups were then examined: (1) differences in risk, (2) differences in growth potential, and (3) differences in accounting measurement methods recognized by the market.

Beaver and Dukes [1973] computed for each firm (1) a risk measure —the beta or relative risk, and (2) an earnings growth measure—the annual rate of growth in earnings assuming continuous compounding over the 1950–1967 period. The averages of (1) and (2) for the two groups were

	A/S Firms	A/A Firms
Beta	1.009	1.003
Growth	.045	.043

Thus, neither of these factors appeared to explain the above differences in average P/E ratios of the two groups. To explore further the differences in accounting methods explanation, the earnings of the A/S group were converted to what they would have reported using accelerated depreciation. The method used in this conversion utilized information in the deferred tax account. Having put the two groups on a comparable depreciation base, the implied average P/E ratios were:

A/S Firms	A/A Firms
16.20	16.61

Note that much of the difference in reported P/E ratios disappeared when differences in depreciation methods were taken into account. This result is consistent with a capital market recognizing the depreciation method used in computing earnings when setting the P/E ratios of firms.

B Accounting for Research and Development

The *FASB Statement Standard No. 2* (1974) has specified that expensing of research and development costs is the only acceptable accounting treatment. Firms are explicitly prohibited from capitalizing such expenses in their audited financial statements. Note, however, that investors are not likewise restricted in their interpretation of the earnings of companies engaged in research and development. An interesting issue is whether the capital market adjusts the reported earnings of firms which differ markedly in R & D expenditure.

Dukes [1976] provided evidence on this issue for 41 firms over the 1960–1968 period. These firms were from three industries—chemicals, drugs, and electronics. The Sharpe-Lintner equity valuation model (see Section 10.1B) was used in the empirical analysis. This study is of added interest in that many of the econometric problems encountered in cross-sectional work were described in detail. The final method of analysis involved the use of a dummy variable representing the research intensity of each industry.[13] Dukes concluded the following:

> The results obtained are consistent with the hypothesis that reported earnings are systematically adjusted before they are impounded into security prices, that the adjustment is largely industry specific, and that, for this sample of firms, the adjustment appears to be directly related to the research intensity of the industry. The evidence is consistent with the hypothesis that investors *do not* naively use the information signals certified by the accountant. (pp. 53–54)

This result, as Dukes [1976] was careful to point out, does not necessarily imply that capitalization of R & D is the "optimum" reporting policy. The problems in making such policy decisions are discussed in Chapter 16.

C Accounting for Marketable Securities

The evidence on this accounting issue comes from the Foster [1977] study of the valuation of 22 property-liability stocks over the 1968–1972 period. The 22 stocks were those with available data over the 1964–1972 period in the A. M. Best *Insurance Securities Research Service*. This *Service* summarizes information from the annual convention statements that insurance companies file with State Insurance Commissioners. A uniform set of accounting procedures is used in these convention statements. The fact that all companies used uniform accounting procedures meant that a potentially important source of *noise* in many cross-sectional studies using accounting data was substantially reduced.

At the time of the study, property-liability companies included realized but excluded unrealized capital gains and losses on marketable securities from the income statement. In 1968, the *Accounting Principles Board* considered alternative rules of accounting for the gains and losses on marketable securities. The APB's initial preference was to let both the annual realized and unrealized capital gains flow through the income statement. This preference met with severe opposition from insurance industry officials and security analysts—see Horngren [1973]. One argument presented to justify this opposition was that investors and the capital market ignored the gains and losses on equity securities. For instance, the Chairman of the Adjusted Earnings Committee of the Association of Insurance and Financial Analysts stated the following at an Accounting Principles Board Public Hearing:

> I would say that there's no evidence in the market place that investors pay any price for realized or unrealized capital gains of an insurance company.... The valuation of fire-casualty companies is heavily, massively weighted toward profitability in underwriting, or lack thereof, and this factor far outweighs in investors' minds whether the company is consistently earning stock market profits or not. (Arthur Andersen [1971, p. 144])

The above and similar statements implied that the returns from a sizable proportion of the assets of property-liability companies were ignored by the capital market. For the 22 companies examined, the average proportion of the common stock portfolio to total assets ranged between 21.2% and 26.7% over the 1964–1972 period. The Foster [1977] study provided evidence on the descriptive validity (at the aggregate market level) of the above argument.

The theoretical equity valuation model used in the study was the Sharpe-Lintner equity valuation model—see Section 10.1B. Results were presented for three earnings measures of property-liability companies:

(1) Underwriting earnings (U),
(2) Underwriting + investment earnings ($U + I$), and
(3) Underwriting + investment + capital gains earnings ($U + I + C$).

In examining the relative association of these three earnings measures, two criteria were used:

(1) *Economic criteria*—e.g., (a) which measure gave estimates of marginal time preference of investors closest to an exogenous estimate and (b) which measure gave a negative coefficient on the risk term (i.e., implied risk aversion).

(2) *Statistical criteria*—e.g., (a) which measure best explained (on a R^2 basis) cross-sectional differences in the dependent variable and (b) which measure gave statistically significant coefficients on the independent variables.

Note that one advantage of using a theoretical equity valuation model is that there are ex ante predictions as to the signs and coefficients of the independent variables.

On both economic and statistical criteria, the U series was the least associated with stock prices. The choice between the $U + I$ and the $U + I + C$ series turned on the significance and stability of the coefficient on the risk term. This coefficient was more significant and more stable with the $U + I + C$ series. For example, the t statistic on the risk term was significant at the .05 level for each of the five years with the $U + I + C$ series, while the risk term was statistically significant with the $U + I$ series in only two of the five years. Given that there were significant differences in the risks of the 22 companies examined (e.g., the betas ranged from .389 to 1.327), this evidence was consistent with the $U + I + C$ series being more highly associated with stock prices than the $U + I$ series. This finding was inconsistent with statements of security analysts and insurance industry officials that "there's no evidence in the market place that investors pay any price for realized or unrealized (capital) gains from the common stock portfolios of an insurance company." The fact that such capital gains were reported in footnotes, surplus statements, etc., rather than included in reported earnings, did not appear to create a substantive interpretation problem to the capital market.

10.4 SUMMARY

In this chapter we have examined theoretical and investment models of security valuation and empirical evidence on their descriptive validity. Two major conclusions of this chapter are

(1) There is theoretical and empirical support for earnings being an important determinant of security prices, and

(2) There is evidence that the capital market reacts not to the earnings numbers per se but rather to the earnings number conditional on the set of measurement rules used to derive that number.

The (2) conclusion is consistent with the capital market using a broad-based information set when setting equilibrium market prices for capital assets.

NOTES

[1]The state preference model is another theoretical model of security valuation. In this model the market value of a security is the sum of the market values of the state-contingent claims the security represents—see Hirshleifer [1970]. This model has not had any empirical applications to security valuation. This lack of empirical application is partially explained by the absence of observable and agreed upon state definitions.

[2]In the initial exposition of the risk-class model—Modigliani and Miller [1958]—a different definition of a risk class was used. See Fama and Miller [1972, p. 161] for discussion of alternative definitions of a risk class.

[3]A second motivation for examining utilities and railroads is the consistency in accounting methods used by these firms in the statements they file with regulatory bodies. Consistency in accounting methods means a reduction in an important source of noise in cross-sectional analysis.

[4]The Sharpe-Lintner capital asset pricing model is a single-period model, and similarly the equity valuation model is strictly a single-period model. Nontrivial theoretical issues arise when extensions to multiperiod valuation models are made—see Long [1972] and Granger [1975]. Note that the definition of expected earnings in a multiperiod model is less clear. For instance, if earnings follow an autoregressive process of order n, the expectations of the one-step-ahead, two-step-ahead,...,n-step-ahead forecasts of earnings will differ. Some procedure for translating this vector of expected future period earnings into a scalar is required.

[5]One problem that is given limited attention in the literature is the calculation of the P/E ratio itself. Suppose one were computing the 1977 P/E ratio for a company with a December 31 fiscal year. One alternative would be to use the December 31 price per share and the 1977 EPS. One "limitation" of this alternative is that the 1977 EPS is not typically announced until January or February 1978—thus the December 31 price would not impound all information about the 1977 EPS. Another alternative is to use the current price per share and the EPS of the four most recently announced quarters. Other alternatives, such as use of the average

of the January 1 and December 31 prices and the average of the last two (five) years' EPS, have also been tried.

[6]Malkiel and Cragg [1970] also estimated (10.8) using historical data for G_i as opposed to expectations of security analysts. The R^2's with the historical data were consistently below those for the expectations data; e.g., in 1963 the R^2 was .49 using historical data as opposed to .75 using expectations data. It is difficult to interpret these differences in R^2's. It could well be that the analysts' estimates of (say) EPS growth are *not* formed independently of the current P/E multiple. When using expectations data there is the danger that the whole exercise is circular.

[7]Granger [1972], in a review of numerous studies relating price to earnings, dividends, etc., noted that one general conclusion was

> There is no stability in the estimates of the coefficients of a model derived from a sequence of cross-sectional data sets through time. This is an extremely damaging observation, throwing considerable doubt both on the reality of the model and also on its usefulness as a predictive tool.... What causes this coefficient instability? A whole variety of technical statistical reasons can be proposed but the most important reason is likely to prove to be model misspecification.... (pp. 503–504)

[8]It should be noted that the performance test used by Malkiel and Cragg had limited theoretical underpinnings. See Chapter 12 for further discussion of performance evaluation.

[9]The following description is based (in part) on Fouse [1976; 1977]. William Fouse of *Wells Fargo Investment Advisors* kindly provided some additional internal research memorandums describing the *Wells Fargo* approach.

[10]Some evidence on the performance of the measures of relative attractiveness is available from *Wells Fargo Investment Advisors* (San Francisco, California).

[11]The analyst's judgment factor replaced the magnitude of over- or undervaluation factor in the pre-July 1976 *Value Line* system. The magnitude factor measured the disparity between the current price/earnings ratio of a stock and its five-year average price/earnings ratio. *Value Line* [1976] reported that this factor had "been found to be of only marginal significance, contributing little to the ability of the system in recent years" (p. 1).

[12]The available evidence is more consistent with the Black asset pricing model having descriptive validity—see Black et al. [1972]. The criticism of Black's statistical significance tests arises due to the returns on the five portfolios being highly correlated with each other. In this situation, Black should have used a T^2 multivariate test (see Morrison [1967]) rather than a sequence of five univariate t tests on the portfolio returns of each ranking group. Whether this would dramatically alter Black's results is not known.

[13]The definition of research intensity was the ratio of R & D expenditures in period t to reported earnings at $t-1$. The sample of firms chosen were those that reported information on "R and D expenditures ... somewhere in the annual report for the period 1955 through 1967" Dukes [1976, p. 18.]

QUESTIONS

QUESTION 10.1:   EPS Growth Estimates and Security Valuation Models

In several studies, security analysts' estimates of EPS growth have been found to be an important variable explaining variations in the price to earnings ratios of companies. For instance, in the Malkiel and Cragg [1970] study the t statistic on the EPS growth term ranged from 13.99 in 1962 to 26.50 in 1965 (see Table 10.4). This result is puzzling, considering the evidence consistent with annual earnings behaving as a random walk—see the results from mean/median studies described in Chapter 4. Malkiel and Cragg commented on this evidence as follows:

> It may be argued that one should not put so much reliance on either past or expected growth rates to explain security prices since there is considerable evidence that earnings growth is "higgledy piggledy".... This may be true and yet security analysts may continue to estimate the worth of shares and their anticipated future returns on the basis of the anticipated growth rate of the security's earnings. As is well known from work on the term structure of interest rates, expectations need not be correct to be an important determinant of the yield curve. (p. 604)

REQUIRED

(1) How would you explain the significance of the EPS growth term in the Malkiel and Cragg study?
(2) Comment on the explanation offered by Malkiel and Cragg.

QUESTION 10.2:   Evaluating Low P/E Investment Strategies

Hobie Leland, Jr. is in charge of an investment division of the *El Camino Bank*. For some detailed empirical work, he develops a data base that contains all NYSE stocks that were continuously listed over the 1949–1975 period. The data base contains the following items for all companies with December 31 fiscal years:

(1) Monthly security returns,

(2) December 31 closing security prices, and

(3) Annual earnings per share (restated to take account of prior mergers, divestitures, etc.).

The monthly security returns on *Standard & Poor's Composite Index* are also included for the 1949–1975 period.

A recently hired employee named Oscar decides to use the data base to test the performance of the following investment approach: Rank the stocks in terms of their P/E ratios, and invest in those in the lowest P/E decile. Oscar computes the P/E ratios of all stocks in 1949 (i.e., December 31, 1949 price/annual earnings per share in 1949), ranks them from highest to lowest, and assumes equal investment in those in the lowest decile. He holds each stock for one year and then assumes sale at the December 31, 1950 price. The average return is calculated as the average of the percentage gain on each stock in the lowest decile portfolio. This procedure is repeated for each year over the 1951–1975 period. Oscar is ecstatic when he reads the computer printout of the results:

Average annual return on the lowest P/E decile portfolio = 21%
Average annual return on the *Standard & Poor's Composite Index* = 13%.

Oscar takes the results to Hobie and recommends the bank adopt the low P/E decile strategy for its discretionary accounts. Hobie is skeptical of Oscar's results and seeks your assistance.

REQUIRED

(1) What problems exist in drawing inferences from the above results about the performance of the low P/E decile strategy of Oscar?

(2) Devise a more refined test of whether the bank can earn abnormal returns using the low P/E decile strategy.

QUESTION 10.3:   The Price-Earnings Gap and Accounting Methods

There is considerable cross-sectional diversity in the P/E ratios of firms. One hypothesized explanation for this P/E diversity is that investors look behind the reported earnings of companies and make off-the-income-statement adjustments. Good and Meyer [1973] examined this issue over the 1966–1972 period. They motivated their analysis as follows:

Investors are becoming familiar with the wide range of options permitted by Generally Accepted Accounting Principles. They see daily evidence that managements use accounting flexibility to manipulate reported results. In addition,

there is a growing recognition of the potential distortions resulting from application of accounting principles that do not require adjustments for the effects of
inflation. In short, investors are becoming increasingly aware that reported
earnings no longer provide a firm base for security valuation.... This article,
while necessarily limited in scope and lacking in precision, attempts to determine if consistently applied accounting adjustments would help to explain a
substantial portion of the price-earnings gap which has developed over the past
several years. (pp. 43, 44)

Two groups of stocks were examined in the article: (1) group A comprising
8 "high-quality, superior-growth" stocks (Kodak, Xerox, Minnesota
Mining, Coca-Cola, Avon, Johnson and Johnson, Merck, and J. C.
Penney) and (2) group B comprising 40 stocks that were representative of
those in the *Standard & Poor's* 500 *Stock Index* population. Adjustments
were made for two factors: (a) depreciation and (b) special items:

Depreciation: This "adjustment" entails the application of an inflation factor to
depreciation accounts. The adjustment attempts to approximate the under-state-
ment of depreciation allowances resulting from persistent inflation over the past
two decades.... The adjustment was made in three steps:

Step 1

Income statements of all companies were adjusted to a straight-line depreciation basis. This provided a consistent base against which an inflation factor
could be applied to depreciation expense. Reported depreciation, of course, is
based on the cost of assets stated in historical dollars rather than current
dollars.

Straight-line depreciation figures for those companies using straight-line depreciation in reports to shareholders are readily available. The problem of estimating straight-line depreciation for those companies using accelerated depreciation in shareholder reports was approached as follows:

A series of hypothetical depreciation situations was set up relating average
asset life and growth rate of capital expenditures to the ratio of accelerated
depreciation to gross plant and equipment. For instance, the ratio of depreciation to gross plant and equipment for a hypothetical company (using sum-of-
years'-digits depreciation) with an average depreciable asset life of 10 years and
a capital expenditure growth rate of 10 per cent was found to be approximately
11.5 per cent. By working out a number of hypothetical situations using a range
of average asset lives and growth rates, a series of curves was developed
showing the relationship among average asset life, capital expenditure growth
and the accelerated depreciation/gross plant and equipment ratio. Since capital
expenditure growth rates and the ratio of accelerated depreciation to gross
plant and equipment can be calculated from available data, the average life of
depreciable assets can be estimated using the series of curves. With the
average life estimate in hand, the calculation of straight-line depreciation is a
matter of simple division.

Step 1 can be illustrated using the figures for Caterpillar Tractor Company in
1972. The ratio of reported accelerated depreciation to average gross plant and

equipment was 7.6 per cent. The capital expenditure growth rate over a 10 year period was about 15 per cent. (Appropriate growth rates for capital expenditures were often difficult to determine, but the data showed little sensitivity to this variable.) The curves constructed from hypothetical depreciation situations suggested an average asset life of about 15 years which in turn indicated that the ratio of straight-line depreciation to average gross plant and equipment would have been about 6.6 per cent. A decrease in depreciation from 7.6 per cent of gross plant and equipment to 6.6 per cent would have resulted in a reduction in depreciation expense of $12–$13 million and an increase in earnings of slightly more than 6.0 per cent.

Step 2

Deferred taxes were added back to earnings for all companies using straight-line depreciation. Since a reserve for deferred taxes was not established when the provision for accelerated depreciation was adjusted to straight-line, this step was necessary to avoid penalizing the straight-line companies (which must set up deferred taxes to cover the difference between depreciation reported to shareholders and accelerated depreciation used for tax purposes.) Also, adding back these deferred taxes is consistent with the "total dividend" concept discussed in the main body of the article. Such taxes may never have to be paid provided capital expenditures continue to grow. The deferred tax account, therefore, may constitute excess cash flow which could be distributed to shareholders or reinvested for expansion.

Step 3

After all companies in the indices had been adjusted to a straight-line basis, depreciation expense was restated to reflect general price-level changes. The adjustment was made as follows:

The year in which assets subject to depreciation were acquired was estimated by applying depreciation/gross plant and equipment ratios to capital expenditures. As an example, consider a company with a depreciation/gross plant and equipment ratio of 10 per cent in 1972. The 1972 reported depreciation was assumed to be composed of 10 per cent of 1972 capital expenditures, 10 per cent of 1971 capital expenditures, and 10 per cent of capital expenditures in each prior year. The 10 per cent depreciation/gross plant and equipment ratio was applied to capital expenditures for a maximum of 15 years prior to the base year until enough depreciation was accumulated to equal the 1972 reported depreciation figure. Any depreciation not accounted for by 1958 was assumed to be on equipment acquired in 1957.

GNP Implicit Price Deflator figures were then used to restate depreciation taken on assets acquired in each year in "current" dollars. For instance, if an estimated $1000 of the total $10,000 of depreciation expensed by Company X in 1972 applied to machinery acquired in 1966, the $1000 was restated to $1300 to reflect inflation from 1966 to the end of 1972. The logic supporting the adjustment, as mentioned previously, is that the expense of depreciating the 1966 machine should be stated in 1972 dollars and not in 1966 dollars, since it would cost at least $1300 to replace the machine in 1972. The difference between $1000 and $1300 was reported as earnings by Company X before this adjustment, but actually would not qualify under the total dividend concept since the

$300 will not be available for distribution or expansion. It will have to be reinvested simply to keep the business operating at its 1972 level. (pp. 81–82)

Special Credits and Charges: The adjustment...involves the charging or crediting of "special" items directly to income over a five year period. This adjustment recognizes the fact that "special" charges often reflect an accumulation of expenses which should have been spread over several years of reported

FIGURE 10.2 Price/Earnings Ratios

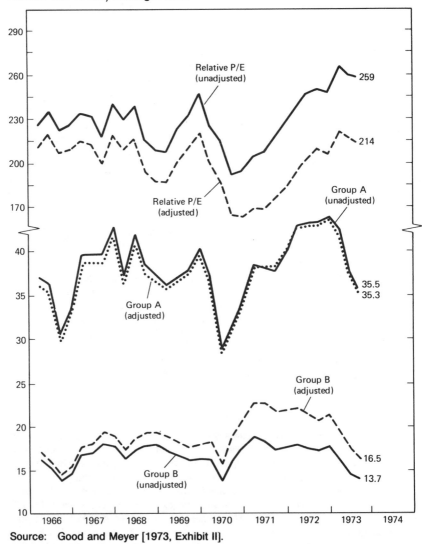

Source: Good and Meyer [1973, Exhibit II].

earnings.... The effects of the special items were spread over five years, centered on the year reported, to recognize three factors: 1) management has flexibility in the timing of special charges and credits, 2) the events leading to a special item are seldom confined to a single fiscal year, and 3) there is an apparent tendency to write off more than necessary in order to facilitate future earnings gains. (pp. 44, 83)

Good and Meyer then calculated the average P/E ratios of the two groups using (1) reported earnings—termed unadjusted P/E ratio, and (2) reported earnings adjusted for depreciation and special credits and charges as noted above—termed adjusted P/E ratio. They also calculated the ratio of group A's P/E to group B's P/E—this ratio was termed the relative P/E. Their hypothesis was that if accounting differences explained part of the difference in the average P/E ratios of groups A and B, the relative P/E should be less when adjusted earnings were used vis-à-vis when reported earnings were used. The results are reported in Figure 10.2. The results were consistent with their hypothesis; e.g., the relative P/E in 1973 decreased from 259 for unadjusted earnings to 214 for adjusted earnings. They concluded that "investors have come to realize that the meaning of reported earnings varies widely among companies" (p. 49).

REQUIRED

(1) Evaluate the above approach to determining if part of the diversity in P/E ratios is explained by market recognition that "the meaning of reported earnings varies widely among companies."

(2) Evaluate the above evidence as regards market recognition of depreciation and special item differences. In answering this question, you should consider the rationale Good and Meyer give for making the adjustments and the specific approximating techniques they use.

(3) What factors other than accounting methods might explain the differences in the average P/E ratios of groups A and B?

QUESTION 10.4:   Rate Regulation for Electric Utilities

[This case draws heavily on material prepared by Herman G. Roseman for rate regulation testimony for *Arkansas Power and Light Company* (Arkansas Public Service Commission Docket No. U-2762, October 1976). Herman Roseman kindly provided a copy of his testimony and his related research in this area.]

Expert witness testimony at rate regulation hearings often contains interesting discussions about the association between security prices and financial statement information. In this question we shall consider testimony by Herman G. Roseman at an *Arkansas Power and Light Company* 1976 rate regulation hearing. Roseman [1976] argued that a key consideration in such rate decisions was the price to book value ratio of the electric utility being regulated:

> *An important—perhaps the most important—goal of rate-of-return regulation today is the achievement and maintenance of an appropriate price-book ratio. If a utility's price-book ratio is too low, this will mean that it may not be able to raise equity capital in the amounts required to serve the public, and such amounts that it does raise will dilute book value per share, unfairly depriving existing investors of part of their ownership share of the company. The price-book ratio of any utility depends principally upon the relationship between the actual return it earns and its cost of equity capital (which itself depends on the cost of money and on the relative riskiness of the utility's stock). If the actually earned return rises, the price-book ratio will rise. If the cost of equity declines, the price-book ratio will rise. (pp. 9–10, emphasis added)*

It was proposed that the cost of common equity capital be determined by finding that accounting "rate of return on equity which, if actually earned, would have brought the price of its stock into equality with its book value per share. This rate of return may be defined as the 'barebones cost of common equity'.... This cost of equity is 'barebones' since it does not provide for the costs of insurance [i.e., underwriting] or market pressure associated with the sale of new stock" (Roseman [1976, p. A4]).

Accounting for Funds During Construction

An important issue in electric utility rate regulation is the method of accounting for funds during construction (AFDC). The issue arises (in part) from the lengthy time required to construct, plants for electric utilities. Assume that $1 million is to be expended each year from 1977 to 1982 for constructing an electric utility plant. The assumption underlying the AFDC accounting rule is that the cost of money tied up in the $1 million is just as much an expense of building the plant as is the costs of materials, labor, etc. Electric utilities can estimate the cost of money tied up in constructing a plant and debit that amount to the construction work in progress (CWIP) account. The corresponding credit ends up on the income statement along with the revenues the electric utility receives. When the plant is finished, the balance in the CWIP account is transferred to the utility plant account. For a description of the technical issues involved in determining both the rate of interest (e.g., the prime rate cost of short-term money vs. the approximate cost of borrowed money) and the base of construction expenditures (e.g., month ending balance of expenditures vs. the average of the month's beginning and ending balances), see

Pomerantz and Suelflow [1975]. The IRS allows utilities to capitalize AFDC for public financial reporting yet expense it for tax purposes.

The percent that the AFDC credit comprises of reported income has increased since the 1960s. The following figures are for "AFDC as Percent of Net Income Available for Common" for the electric utility industry over the 1965–1975 period:

1966	4.9%	1971	24.2%
1967	6.8%	1972	28.2%
1968	10.1%	1973	29.5%
1969	13.8%	1974	34.4%
1970	19.4%	1975	38.9%

There has been much argument that the AFDC component of net income is of "lesser quality." For instance, Roseman [1976a] made the following comment in rate regulation testimony for *Arkansas Power and Light Company*:

> In the eyes of investors, AFDC represents "paper earnings," i.e., lower quality earnings than if derived from current revenues. At a time when investors are concerned that regulators may not be allowing adequate rates of return, and that utilities may not even be able to earn the returns they are allowed, the fact that a large portion of the reported earnings is not actually earned, but is a "mere" accounting entry, creates special concern. This concern of investors about the deteriorating quality of earnings must become a concern of regulators and ratepayers when investors are being called upon to provide unprecedented amounts of money for construction. (p. 7)

As part of his testimony, Roseman presented a "statistical model on determinants of utility price-book ratios." This model included a variable that was hypothesized to capture investor reaction to the AFDC component of net income. The model is described in more detail in Roseman [1976]:

> The statistical model is a study of factors determining the price-book ratios of 94 electric utilities in the first three quarters of 1975. The 94 electric utilities used are those companies listed on the New York Stock Exchange for which data are available in *The Value Line Investment Survey*.... Having derived an equation which tells us the relationship between the price-book ratio and the rate of return on common equity, we can then determine for any given company what its rate of return would have had to have been in order for the price-book ratio to equal 1.0 or 1.1 (or any specified number).
>
> In this model, the dependent variable which I was trying to explain was the recent price-book ratio. The measure I used was the average of the closing prices for January through September 1975, divided by book value per share as of year-end 1974....

I considered and tested a total of 46 variables which might affect price-book ratios.... Using stepwise regression techniques I arrived at [a] list of [7] variables which provides the best fit to the data. (pp. A1–A2)

Table 10.5 details these 7 variables, their regression coefficients, t statistics, and the mean values of each variable for the 94 companies in the regression. The multiple correlation coefficient (R) was .877, "indicating an excellent fit to the data" (p. A4). The regression coefficient for the AFDC variable was −.00268—"this indicates that *investors were discounting the value of that portion of earnings which was comprised of AFDC*...if AFDC as a percent of net income increases by 1 percentage point, the price-book ratio will *decrease* by .00268" (p. A3, emphasis added).

The regression model was then used to determine the cost of equity capital. Roseman [1976] gave the following example to illustrate his approach:

Suppose we have fit the following regression equation to the data:

$$\frac{P}{B} = .05 + .04R_{74} + .06R_{75} - .12X$$

TABLE 10.5 Determinants of Price/Book Value Ratios of Electric Utilities

Variable	Description	Regression Coefficient	t Ratio	Mean
Constant term	—	.22275	3.550	—
X_1	Rate of return on common equity, 1974	.02552	3.769	10.5035
X_2	Square of rate of return on common equity, 1973	.00098	2.700	127.793
X_3	Square of rate of return on common equity, Value Line estimate for 1975	.00132	3.725	130.899
X_4	Accounting method: 1 if flow-through, 0 if not flow-through	−.13413	−6.176	.43617
X_5	Oil as percent of all fuels used in generation, 1974	−.00087	−2.358	20.1383
X_6	AFDC as percent of net income for common, 1974	−.00268	−4.909	34.3554
X_7	Ratio of dividends to cash flow, 1974	.55466	5.096	.408772

where P/B is the price-book ratio, R_{74} and R_{75} are the rates of return on common equity for 1974 and 1975, respectively, and X is a proxy for all other variables. Suppose that for a particular company, the value of X is 2.5. We now ask the following question: at what stable rate of return on equity (such that $R_{74} = R_{75}$) would the price-book ratio equal 1.0? We express this algebraically as follows:

$$1.0 = .05 + .04R_{75} + .06R_{75} - .12(2.5)$$
$$1.0 - .05 + .30 = .10R_{75}$$
$$R_{75} = 12.5\%.$$

Thus, for this particular company, the barebones cost of equity capital would be 12.5 percent.

Calculations of the cost of equity of the [94] electric utilities have been made.... The rate of return required to bring market price into equality with book value per share is 12.95 percent for the average of the 94 electric utilities.... This [estimate of] the barebones cost of equity capital excludes any allowance for issuance costs and market pressure associated with the sale of new stock. In order to be able to sell stock without dilution, the average utility would require a rate of return of about 14 percent. (p. A3)

REQUIRED

In answering this question, it may be useful to also read Question 8.4.

(1) Assume you have been hired to prepare testimony that comments on Roseman's approach to estimating the cost of equity capital. What key points would you make in your testimony?

(2) Describe an alternative approach to estimating the cost of equity capital of electric utilities.

(3) Evaluate the approach used to demonstrate that "investors were discounting the value of that portion of earnings which was comprised of AFDC."

REFERENCES

ARTHUR ANDERSEN and COMPANY. *APB Public Hearing on Accounting for Investments in Equity Securities Not Qualifying for the Equity Method: Cases in Public Accounting Practice*, Volume 8, Chicago, 1971.

BEAVER, W. H., and DUKES, R. E. "Tax Allocation and δ Depreciation Methods." *The Accounting Review* (July 1973): 549–559.

BERNHARD, A. *Investing in Common Stocks*. Arnold Bernhard and Co., New York, 1975.

BING, R. A. "Survey of Practitioners' Stock Evaluation Methods." *Financial Analysts Journal* (May–June 1971): 55–60.

BLACK, F. "Yes, Virginia, There is Hope: Tests of the Value Line Ranking System." *Financial Analysts Journal* (Sept.–Oct. 1973): 10–14.

BLACK, F., JENSEN, M. C., and SCHOLES, M. "The Capital Asset Pricing Model: Some Empirical Tests." In M. C. Jensen (ed.), *Studies in the Theory of Capital Markets*. Praeger, New York, 1972: 79–121.

BROWN, P. "Some Aspects of Valuation in the Railroad Industry." Unpublished Ph.D. Dissertation, University of Chicago, Chicago, 1968.

DUKES, R. E. "An Investigation of the Effects of Expensing Research and Development Costs on Security Prices." In M. Schiff and G. Sorter (eds.), *Proceedings of the Conference on Topical Research in Accounting*. New York University, New York, 1976: 147–193.

FAMA, E. F., and MILLER, M. H. *The Theory of Finance*. Holt, Rinehart and Winston, Inc., New York, 1972.

FOSTER, G. "Valuation Parameters of Property-Liability Companies." *Journal of Finance* (June 1977): 823–836.

FOUSE, W. L. "Risk and Liquidity: The Keys to Stock Price Behavior." *Financial Analysts Journal* (May–June 1976): 35–45.

———. "Risk and Liquidity Revisited," *Financial Analysts Journal* (January/February 1977): 35–45.

GOOD, W. R., and MEYER, J. R. "Adjusting the Price-Earnings Ratio Gap," *Financial Analysts Journal* (November/December 1973): 42–49, 81–84.

GRANGER, C. W. J. "Empirical Studies of Capital Markets: A Survey," in G. P. Szego and K. Shell (eds.), *Mathematical Methods in Investment and Finance* (North-Holland, Amsterdam, 1972): 469–519.

———. "Some Consequences of the Valuation Model When Expectations Are Taken to be Optimum Forecasts," *Journal of Finance* (March 1975): 135–145.

HIRSHLEIFER, J. *Investment, Interest and Capital*. Prentice-Hall, Englewood Cliffs, N.J., 1970.

HORNGREN, C. T. "The Marketing of Accounting Standards," *Journal of Accountancy* (Oct. 1973): 61–66.

JOHNSTON, J. *Econometric Methods* (Second edition). McGraw-Hill, New York, 1972.

LITZENBERGER, R. H., and RAO, C. U. "Estimates of the Marginal Rate of Time Preference and Average Risk Aversion of Investors in Electric Utility Shares: 1960–66," *Bell Journal of Economics and Management Science*: (Spring 1971): 265–277.

LONG, J. B. "Consumption-Investment Decisions and Equilibrium in the Securities Market," in M. C. Jensen (ed.), *Studies in the Theory of Capital Markets*. Praeger, New York, 1972: 146–222.

MALKIEL, B. G., and CRAGG, J. C. "Expectations and the Structure of Share Prices," *American Economic Review* (September, 1970): 601–617.

MEADER, J. W. "A Formula for Dermining Basic Values Underlying Common Stock Prices," *The Annalist* (November 29, 1935): 749.

——. "Stock Price Estimating Formulas, 1930–39," *The Annalist* (June 27, 1940): 890.

MILLER, M. H., and MODIGLIANI, F. "Dividend Policy, Growth and the Valuation of Shares." *Journal of Business* (Oct. 1961): 411–433.

——. "Some Estimates of the Cost of Capital to the Electric Utility Industry." *American Economic Review* (June 1966): 334–391.

MODIGLIANI, F., and MILLER, M. "The Cost of Capital, Corporation Finance and the Theory of Investment." *American Economic Review* (June 1958): 261–297.

MORRISON, D. F. *Multivariate Statistical Methods.* McGraw-Hill, New York, 1967.

POMERANTZ, L. S., and SUELFLOW, J. E. *Allowance for Funds Used During Construction.* Michigan State University, East Lansing, Mich., 1975.

ROSEMAN, H. G. "The Economic Advantages of Putting Construction-Work-in-Progress in the Electric Utility Rate Base," Appendix 1 to *Written Submittal of Regulated Utility Group* (United States of America Before the Federal Power Commission, Docket No. RM75-13, March 1, 1976) Washington, D.C.

——. *Prepared Testimony of Herman G. Roseman* (Arkansas Public Service Commission Docket No. U-2762, Oct. 1976), Little Rock, Ark.

VALUE LINE INVESTMENT SURVEY. *Improvements in the Value Line Performance Ranking System.* Arnold Bernhard and Co., New York, July 9, 1976.

WELLS FARGO INVESTMENT ADVISORS. *Security Market Line Report.* Wells Fargo Bank, San Francisco, 1976.

WHITBECK, V. S., and KISOR, M. "A New Tool in Investment Decision-Making." *Financial Analysts Journal* (May–June 1963): 55–62.

CHAPTER 11

CAPITAL ASSET RETURNS

AND

FINANCIAL INFORMATION

Accounting information is but one of many sources that capital markets may use in the revision of the prices of capital assets such as common stocks, preferred stocks, and corporate bonds. Other sources include dividend information, product and outlet information, management change information, and insider trading information. What evidence is there that accounting information plays an important role in the capital asset price revaluation process? What evidence is there that the capital market reacts to accounting earnings in the mechanistic way suggested by some authors quoted in Chapter 7? What evidence is there about the timeliness of accounting data? These and related issues are discussed in this chapter.

These issues are of major importance to many groups—e.g., investment analysts, corporate management, and accounting policy makers. Consider the *fundamental analysis* approach to investment choice (see Chapter 7). A major part of this analysis examines trends in the financial statements of corporations. If there is no association between such trends and stock market returns, then this analysis is likely to be unrewarding. Moreover, even if there is such an association, the question of the timeliness of accounting data is important. If competitive information sources can provide the capital market with the information in annual reports at an earlier date, then a revaluation of the fundamental analysis approach seems warranted. In Chapter 12 the above points are discussed in more detail. In Chapter 12 we shall discuss the implications of the material examined in Chapters 7–11 for the use of accounting information in investment decisions.

11.1 STOCK RETURNS AND ACCOUNTING EARNINGS

A Annual Earnings

In this section, we shall examine if there is a contemporaneous relationship (association) between accounting earnings changes and stock returns. Important evidence on this issue was provided by Ball and Brown [1968].[1] This paper examined if the capital market reacted differently to a set of firms with positive earnings changes vis-à-vis a set of firms with negative earnings changes. The market reaction was examined in the 12 months up to and including the earnings announcement and the 6 months subsequent to that announcement. The Ball and Brown research design, adopted in many subsequent papers, involved several steps:

Step One: *Select Sample of Firms.* The sample comprised 261 New York Stock Exchange firms over the 1957–1965 period. This set of firms was chosen due to having earnings data available on the *Compustat* tape and security returns data available on the *CRSP* monthly tape.

Step Two: *Select Earnings Announcement Date.* U.S. firms generally release details of annual earnings through three main media:

(1) An estimate by a company official after the end of the fiscal year but before the end-of-year results are fully determined;

(2) A preliminary release of earnings, sales, etc., prior to the issuance of the annual report; and

(3) The annual report.

Not all firms use medium (1), and those officials who do estimate earnings frequently do not give point estimates. Ball and Brown chose the date the preliminary earnings were reported in the *Wall Street Journal* as their announcement date. The median time between the end of the fiscal year and the preliminary earnings announcement ranged from 56 calendar days in 1957 to 39 calendar days in 1965.

Step Three: *Estimate Sign of Earnings Change.* Two models were used to classify firms into those with positive earnings changes and those with negative earnings changes. The first model was the following index model:

$$\Delta Y_{i,t} = \hat{\alpha} + \hat{\beta} \Delta X_{M,t} + \hat{e}_{it}, \tag{11.1}$$

where $Y_{i,t}$ = earnings of the ith firm in period t,

$X_{M,t}$ = average earnings of all other *Compustat* firms in period t,

Δ = first differences operator.

Chapter 5 contains a detailed discussion of index models and an illustration of how one can use (11.1) to estimate the firm-specific change in earnings ($\hat{e}_{it}$). Firms that had a positive (negative) $\hat{e}_{it}$ were classified as having a positive (negative) earnings change.

The second model used to classify firms into positive and negative earnings changes was the random-walk model (see Chapter 4):

$$E(Y_{i,t}) = Y_{i,t-1}. \tag{11.2}$$

A firm had a positive change if $Y_{i,t} > E(Y_{i,t})$ and a negative change if $Y_{i,t} < E(Y_{i,t})$.

Several features of the above models are important. *First*, both models gave earnings changes that were, on average, serially uncorrelated. For instance, the median first-order autocorrelation of the residuals for each firm in (11.1) was $-.05$. This means that the composition of the two earnings change groups changed each year. This changing composition adds strength to the internal validity of the experiment. A *second* feature of the two models was that they were differently affected by the diversity across firms in accounting techniques used to calculate earnings. The index model (11.1) uses the earnings of all other firms to construct the market index of earnings. Thus, any cross-sectional diversity in accounting techniques will affect the estimation of e_{it}. In contrast, the random-walk model (11.2) uses only information about firm i; it avoids problems posed by the diversity in accounting methods used by different firms. Both models (11.1) and (11.2) are affected by changes in accounting methods by the same firm over time.

Step Four: *Estimate Security Returns in Period Surrounding Earnings Announcement.* Ball and Brown adopted what we shall refer to as the cumulative abnormal return (CAR) methodology in estimating security returns in the period surrounding the earnings announcement.[2] A detailed description and illustration of this methodology is provided in Appendix 11.A. The CAR methodology estimates the firm-specific change in the returns on a security. The model estimated by Ball and Brown—termed the market model (see Chapter 8)—was

$$\tilde{R}_{it} = \hat{\alpha} + \hat{\beta}\tilde{R}_{mt} + \hat{U}_{it}, \tag{11.3}$$

where $\tilde{R}_{it}$ = return on security i in period t and $\tilde{R}_{mt}$ = return on an equally weighted index of all NYSE securities in period t. The residual ($\hat{U}_{it}$) in (11.3) estimates the effect on the returns of security i of firm-specific information made available in period t. The estimates of U_{it} for each firm were cumulated for the 12 months up to and including the earnings announcement and the 6 months subsequent to that announcement. The average cumulative abnormal return for the firms with (1) positive earnings changes and (2) negative earnings changes were then calculated. The average cumulative abnormal return of a policy of investing long in type (1) firms and selling short in type (2) firms was also calculated (termed composite CAR).

Results. Figure 11.1 presents the behavior of the CAR of the positive and negative earnings change firms for the earnings per share variable; positive and negative earnings changes were estimated with (11.1). Note that positive earnings change firms had positive cumulative abnormal security returns and that negative earnings change firms had negative cumulative abnormal security returns. Note also that most of the change in the abnormal security return occurred prior to the month that annual earnings were announced in the *Wall Street Journal*. Ball and Brown, after further analysis, concluded the following about the "content and timeliness" of annual income numbers:

FIGURE 11.1 Annual Earnings and Stock Returns: NYSE
Firms

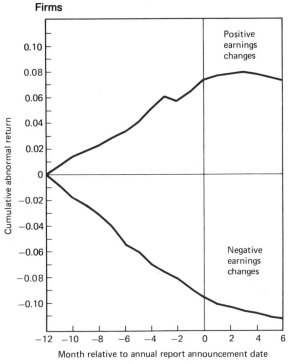

Source: Ball and Brown [1968, Figure 1].

Of all the information about an individual firm which becomes available during a year, one-half or more is captured in that year's income number. Its content is therefore considerable. However, the annual income report does not rate highly as a timely medium, since most of its content (about 85 to 90 percent) is captured by more prompt media which perhaps include interim reports. Since the efficiency of the capital market is largely determined by the adequacy of its data sources, we do not find it disconcerting that the market has turned to other sources which can be acted upon more promptly than annual net income. (pp. 176–177)

The results in Figure 11.1 imply that if an investor knew the sign of the change in earnings per share 12 months in advance of its public release, he could earn an abnormal return of 8.3% by investing long in positive earnings change firms and selling short in negative earnings change firms. Ball and Brown also examined three other earnings variables in addition to EPS: net income, net income after extraordinary items, and a cash flow approximation. The results were similar to those reported in Figure 11.1. Note that Ball and Brown examined the association between a single accounting variable (i.e., earnings) and abnormal security returns. In Section 11.4 we shall examine studies that adopted a multivariate perspective to the association issue.

Annual Earnings: Extensions

A crucial element in the Ball and Brown [1968] study was the estimation of the change in earnings of each firm. Two models—an index model and a random-walk model—were used in discriminating between positive and negative earnings change firms. In Beaver and Dukes [1972] both the set of models for estimating earnings changes and the set of earnings variables were expanded. This expansion was an attempt to examine the sensitivity of the Ball and Brown [1968] results to model specification issues. A set of 123 NYSE firms over the 1963–1967 period was used in the analysis. In general, the results in Beaver and Dukes [1972] strongly supported those in Ball and Brown [1968]. There was a strong association between the sign of the earnings change and the sign of the cumulative abnormal security return in the 12 months up to and including the month of the earnings announcement. Moreover, there was little evidence of abnormal price movement in the 12 months subsequent to the earnings announcement. This result is consistent with a market which reacts quickly to the information contained in the annual earnings announcement.

Annual Earnings: Other Markets and Other Countries

The above results pertain to NYSE firms. A major issue is whether the same results hold for other U.S. securities markets (e.g., the American Stock Exchange and the over-the-counter market) and for the securities markets of other countries. It has been argued that such markets—comprising smaller firms and in most cases having less actively traded stocks—are more likely to exhibit market inefficiencies. The evidence from two studies—one on the over-the-counter (OTC) market and one on the Australian securities market—will be briefly outlined. Further evidence on this issue is presented in Section 11.2. Evidence from non-NYSE markets is important as there is a limited amount of information one can extract from any one data base. If the results found on the NYSE are supported for other data bases, one's confidence in their generality (rather than their being period- or sample-specific) is increased.

The OTC Market. Foster [1975] examined the capital market's reaction to the annual earnings of 73 stock insurance companies, 63 of whom were listed on the OTC market. The period of analysis was 1965–1972. The methodology was similar to that adopted in Ball and

Brown [1968]. One distinctive feature of Foster [1975] was the separate analysis of the three subearnings series of insurance companies, i.e.,

(1) Underwriting earnings,

(2) Investment earnings—comprising mainly interest coupons from bonds or mortgages and dividends from common stocks, and

(3) Capital gains and losses (both realized and unrealized) on marketable equity securities.

These three series represent the three main activities (*lines of business*) of insurance companies. Index models for the annual earnings of each series were estimated. The sign of the residual from the index model for each subearnings series was used to distinguish between positive and negative earnings changes.

Results for the underwriting and investment series are presented in Figure 11.2. The results for the capital gains series closely resemble the

FIGURE 11.2 Annual Earnings and Stock Returns: OTC Firms

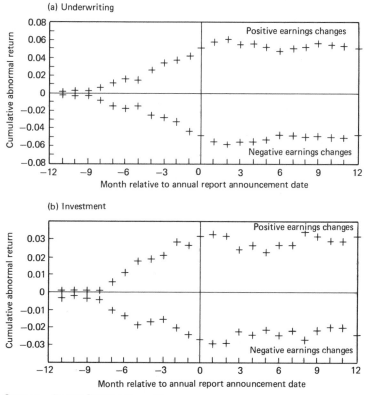

Source: Foster [1975, Figure 1].

reported patterns. Two features of this pattern are important. *First*, the capital market progressively discriminates between the positive and negative earnings change groups for each series in the 12 months up to and including the earnings announcement month. *Second*, most of the capital market's reaction occurs prior to the annual earnings announcement month. Note, however, that there is a slight upward (downward) drift for positive (negative) change firms for the underwriting series in the 2 months subsequent to the earnings announcement month. These slight post-announcement month drifts are also apparent in the Ball and Brown [1968] results reported in Figure 11.1.[3]

The Australian Securities Market.   The Australian stock exchanges are, on any size measure, a small fraction of the size of the NYSE. It is of interest to examine if the typical NYSE reaction detailed in Figure 11.1 also applies to these exchanges. Brown [1970] examined this issue for 118 Australian companies over the 1959–1968 period. The methodology was similar to that in Ball and Brown [1968]. The random-walk earnings

FIGURE 11.3 Annual Earnings and Stock Returns: Australian Firms

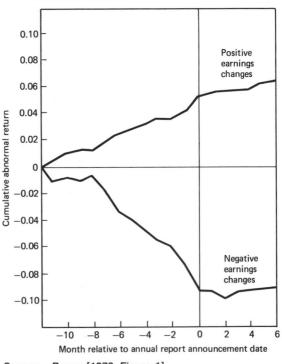

Source: Brown [1970, Figure 1].

expectations model (11.2) was used to classify firms into those with positive and negative earnings changes in each year. Results are presented in Figure 11.3. Note the similar patterns in Figure 11.3 for Australian companies and Figure 11.1 for NYSE companies.[4]

B Interim Earnings

Interim earnings releases represent one medium by which the capital market may anticipate the final annual earnings number of a firm. For industrial U.S. firms, the interim reporting period is usually every quarter. A substantive issue is whether the capital market uses interim reports in revaluing security prices. Evidence on this issue has been provided by several authors, e.g., Brown and Kennelly [1972] and Foster [1977]. The latter study is of particular interest in that daily price data, rather than monthly price data, were used in the analysis. Daily data enable one to more adequately examine the speed with which quarterly earnings are impounded into security prices.

The Foster [1977] study examined the market's reaction to the quarterly earnings of 69 NYSE firms over the 1963–1974 period. The methodology was similar to that of the Ball and Brown [1968] study with two exceptions. One exception was the use of several earnings expectations models that were specifically related to the time-series properties of quarterly data (e.g., the seasonality property). One such model was

$$E(Q_t) = Q_{t-4} + \delta, \qquad (11.4)$$

where Q_t = the quarterly earnings in quarter t and δ = a drift term. The above and other quarterly time-series models are described in more detail in Chapter 4. The second exception was that the CAR was estimated using the *companion portfolio* technique described in Appendix 11.A. Using the sign of the forecast error from (11.4) as the sign of the quarterly earnings change, the CAR was computed for the positive and negative earnings change groups. The composite CAR was also computed. A chi-square (χ^2) statistic was computed to assess the statistical significance of the association between earnings changes and abnormal security returns.

> CHI-SQUARE (χ^2) STATISTIC: This statistic examines whether N groups differ with respect to some characteristic and therefore with respect to the relative frequency with which the group members fall in several categories. Suppose there are two groups: a positive earnings change group ($E+$) and a negative earnings change group ($E-$). Suppose also there are two categories: CAR for a firm is positive (CAR+), and CAR for a firm is negative (CAR−). Then a χ^2 statistic would indicate the association between the $E+/E-$ groups and the CAR+/CAR− groups. Suppose the following

pattern was observed for 40 firms:

	$E+$	$E-$
CAR+	18	2
CAR−	2	18

This pattern indicates a strong positive association between the sign of the earnings change and the sign of the CAR. χ^2 provides a statistical test of the significance of this association:

$$\chi^2 = \sum_{i=1}^{r} \sum_{j=1}^{k} \frac{(O_{ij} - E_{ij})^2}{E_{ij}},$$

where O_{ij} = the observed number of cases categorized in the ith row of jth column and E_{ij} = the number of cases expected to be categorized under the assumption of no association between the sign of the earnings change and the sign of the CAR. The higher the χ^2 value, the more significant is the association examined. For the above example, $E_{ij} = 10$ for each of the above four cases. Thus

$$\chi^2 = \frac{(18-10)^2}{10} + \frac{(2-10)^2}{10} + \frac{(2-10)^2}{10} + \frac{(18-10)^2}{10}$$
$$= 6.4.$$

Using the above 2×2 table, significance levels for the χ^2 are

Level	χ^2
.10	2.71
.05	3.84
.01	6.64

Thus, the 40 observations exhibit a significant association between the sign of the earnings change and the sign of the CAR at the .05 level. See Hollander and Wolfe [1973] for further description of this test.

CAR results from Foster [1977] for the 60 trading days up to and including the announcement of quarterly earnings in the *Wall Street Journal* are presented in Table 11.1. Note that firms with positive interim earnings changes exhibited positive cumulative abnormal security returns and vice versa. Moreover, the relationship between the sign of the earnings change and the sign of the CAR in all four quarters combined, and for each fiscal quarter, is highly statistically significant; e.g., for all four quarters combined $\chi^2 = 130.08$.[5]

TABLE 11.1 Quarterly Earnings Changes and Stock Returns

	CAR Positive Earnings Change Group	CAR Negative Earnings Change Group	Composite CAR	χ^2
All four quarters combined	.0213	−.0326	.0253	130.08
First fiscal quarter	.0267	−.0359	.0300	33.03
Second fiscal quarter	.0156	−.0359	.0229	41.45
Third fiscal quarter	.0312	−.0345	.0323	42.48
Fourth fiscal quarter	.0111	−.0243	.0158	12.80

SOURCE: Foster [1977, Table 5].

To gain insight into the relationship between the results for quarterly earnings and annual earnings, the firms in Foster [1977] were classified each year into one of five categories. These categories were based on the number of quarters each year that had positive earnings changes. The five categories were

A:	+ + + +
B:	+ + + −
C:	+ + − −
D:	+ − − −
E:	− − − −

where + is a positive earnings change quarter and − is a negative earnings change quarter. Thus category A included those observations in which all four quarters had positive changes. Category C included observations in which *any* two of the four quarters had positive earnings changes, etc. The *annual* CAR's for these five categories were

Category	CAR
A	.129
B	.039
C	−.011
D	−.074
E	−.162

That is, in explaining differential annual abnormal security returns of firms, the categorization of their quarterly earnings changes is an important factor. Those firms which had all four quarters of earnings changes of the same sign had, on average, the largest annual abnormal security returns. This evidence is consistent with the security market reacting to the size as well as the sign of the annual earnings change.[6]

The above results suggest that interim reports represent one medium by which the capital market anticipates the annual earnings number. These results, however, do not imply that the purpose of releasing interim reports is to enable prediction of the annual earnings number. We view the interim report as one of many information media that a firm provides to the capital market. Its informativeness will be determined by whether it provides new information pertinent to assessing the return distributions of a security.

Interim Earnings: Seasonality Adjustments

Another issue examined in Foster [1977] was whether the capital market adjusted for the seasonality in quarterly earnings. Many corporate officials, in opposing interim disclosure rules, have argued that investors would be "confused" or "misled" by the interim results of seasonal firms. The following industry statement, taken from Taylor [1963, p. 133], is illustrative of this concern:

> Instead of clarifying the picture, the issuance of a semi-annual report by this company would serve to confuse those dealing in Brown-Forman issues. This is because our business is highly seasonal in nature.

To examine this seasonality issue, two earnings expectations models that suppressed any seasonality in quarterly earnings were also used to classify firms into (1) positive and (2) negative change firms. If the market is cognizant of seasonality, these two nonseasonal models will misclassify a higher proportion of positive and negative change firms. The composite CAR's of these two models were insignificant from zero (χ^2 of .02 and .00). These insignificant χ^2's contrast markedly with the χ^2 of 130.08 reported in Table 11.1. These results are consistent with the capital market adjusting for seasonality when interpreting each quarter's earnings change. This adjustment appears to take the form of an earnings expectations model that incorporates seasonality in the past quarterly series.

Interim Earnings: Speed of Market Adjustment

In an efficient capital market, new information will be rapidly impounded into security prices in an unbiased manner. One study has reported a less than rapid adjustment of security prices to the information in quarterly earnings announcements. Joy et al. [1977] examined the market reaction to the interim earnings announcements of 96 NYSE firms over the 1963–1968 period. For a group of firms with large positive unexpected earnings changes, the postannouncement abnormal return for a 26-week period was over 4.0%; the comparable figure for large negative earnings changes was -2.5%. These results suggest market inefficiency with respect to publicly available interim earnings information. It is important that their generality to other time periods and other companies be examined.[7]

11.2 CAPITAL MARKET REACTION TO CORPORATE ANNOUNCEMENTS

The results examined in Section 11.1 indicate a strong contemporaneous association between earnings changes and security price changes in the 12 (3) months up to and including the month annual (interim) earnings are publicly announced. What evidence is there of a significant reaction by the capital market at the time earnings are announced? In this section we shall concentrate on the short-run reaction of the capital market to earnings and other corporate announcements. Both the trading volume reaction and the security price reaction will be documented.

A Trading Volume Reaction to Earnings Announcements

It is important to note that trading volume can occur for a variety of factors, e.g.,

(1) Investors purchasing/selling capital assets so as to coordinate their income earning and income spending activities.

(2) Investors purchasing and selling to maintain a diversified portfolio.

(3) Investors purchasing/selling due to
    (a) Changes in the risk of their portfolio or
    (b) Changes in their own risk preferences.

(4) Investors purchasing/selling due to taxation reasons—e.g., the differential tax on capital gains vis-à-vis other income.

(5) Investors purchasing/selling due to new information causing a revision of their probability assessments of the distribution of returns.

These factors are not necessarily exhaustive or mutually exclusive. They do imply, however, that in examining the volume reaction to (say) an earnings announcement it is necessary to control for other factors that may induce trading volume.

Annual and Interim Earnings Announcements

Beaver's [1968] study of the trading volume reaction to annual earnings announcements is a good example of controlling for non-earnings-related factors inducing trading volume. A set of 143 firms over the

1961–1965 period was the sample studied. This sample was restricted to non-December 31 fiscal year firms, thus minimizing the effect of December–January tax-induced trading volume. The sample was also restricted to firms which had no dividend announcement in the week of the earnings announcement—thus, the effect of one potentially important nonearnings impetus to trading volume was minimized. Similarly, Beaver examined volume in the earnings announcement period relative to that in the nonannouncement period—thus, trading volume due to factors that induce continuous trading [e.g., (1)] was taken into account in the experiment.

The following measure of weekly trading volume was used by Beaver:

$$V_{it} = \frac{\text{Number of shares traded in week } t}{\text{Number of shares outstanding in week } t} \times \frac{1}{\substack{\text{Number of trading days} \\ \text{in week } t}}.$$

Results for the 17-week period surrounding (and including) the earnings announcement week are presented in Figure 11.4. The dotted line denotes the average V_{it} in the nonreport period. There was a "rather dramatic increase in volume in the announcement week (week 0). The mean volume in week 0 is 33 per cent larger than the mean volume during the nonreport period and it is by far the largest value observed during the 17 weeks. Investors do shift portfolio positions at the time of the earnings announce-

FIGURE 11.4 Volume Reaction to Annual Earnings Announcements

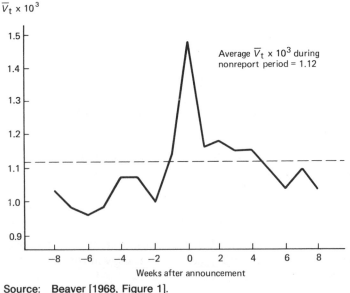

$\overline{V}_t \times 10^3$

Average $\overline{V}_t \times 10^3$ during nonreport period = 1.12

Weeks after announcement

Source: Beaver [1968, Figure 1].

ment and this shift is consistent with the contention that earnings reports have information content" (p. 74).[8]

How does one reconcile this finding with the Ball and Brown [1968] result that most of the information content of the annual earnings report is captured by more prompt media? An important explanation appears to be the relative power of the Ball and Brown and Beaver methodologies to capture any effect at the earnings announcement date. Ball and Brown classified firms into positive and negative earnings change groups based on knowledge of the sign of the annual change 12 months in advance of its public release. As one approaches the announcement date, information about the first three quarters earnings and dividends as well as about other cues such as corporate forecasts and production reports have become publicly available. The effect is that as one approaches the announcement date, models classifying positive and negative earnings change firms based only on the sign of the annual earnings change become increasingly misspecified. The Beaver approach requires no assumption about the sign of the annual earnings change; thus, it avoids the problems associated with specifying the sign of the earnings change for each firm.

EPS Estimate Announcements by Company Officials

The Beaver [1968] results are consistent with at least two hypotheses:

Hypothesis A: Investors react to the announcement per se

Hypothesis B: Investors react to the information contained in the announcement.

Sterling [1970], for instance, would argue that Hypothesis A may be the descriptively valid one:

> Accounting reports have been issued for a long time, and their issuance has been accompanied by a rather impressive ceremony performed by the managers and accountants who issue them. The receivers are likely to have gained the impression that they ought to react, and have noted that others react, and thereby have become conditioned to react. (p. 453)

Using the results in Foster [1973], it is possible to discriminate between these two hypotheses. This paper examined the trading volume and security price reaction to estimates of earnings per share (EPS) announced by company officials *after* the end of the fiscal year but before the preliminary earnings announcement.

The sample in Foster [1973] included 68 estimates made over the 1968–1970 period. The accuracy of the estimates was examined by computing the mean absolute percentage error:

$$\frac{\text{Estimated EPS} - \text{Actual EPS}}{\text{Estimated EPS}}.$$

The average error was only 1.8%. In contrast, if EPS was predicted to be the same as the previous year's EPS, the average absolute error was 26.7%. The sample differed from that in Beaver [1968] in one important respect —it was confined to December 31 fiscal year firms. As there was no available evidence that Beaver's results applied to such firms, the trading volume reaction to a set of 68 December 31 fiscal year firms with no EPS estimate by a company official was also examined.

The trading volume reaction to the following three announcements was examined:

Group I firms (No EPS estimate group)

(1) Preliminary earnings announcement

Group II firms (EPS estimate group)

(2) EPS Estimate by company official
(3) Preliminary earnings announcement

Hypothesis A would predict a significant volume reaction to, at least, announcements (1) and (3). Hypothesis B would predict a significant volume reaction to, at least, announcements (1) and (2). For Group I, there was a 47% increase in V_{it} at the preliminary earnings announcement week, relative to the average of the 16 weeks surrounding that announcement. For Group II there was a 51% increase in V_{it} at the week the estimate was made, relative to the average V_{it} for the 16 weeks surrounding the EPS estimate; for this same group of firms, there was only a 1% increase in V_{it} at the week the preliminary earnings report was released. These results are consistent with Hypothesis B; i.e., the market reacts to the information contained in the announcement rather than to the announcement per se. If that information has already been conveyed to the market by a more timely medium, then there will be little reaction at the preliminary announcement date.

B Security Price Reaction to Earnings Announcements

Two main approaches have been used to examine the security price reaction to earnings announcements. The first approach requires no assumption about the sign of the earnings change. The second approach uses the CAR methodology outlined in Section 11.1. Examples of both approaches will be illustrated.

One approach to examining the price reaction to information has examined the volatility of the residual ($\hat{U}_{it}$) from a market model regression—i.e., (11.3). Beaver [1968] provides an early example of this approach. The price reaction (R) was measured by

$$R = \frac{\hat{U}_{it}^2}{\text{Var}(\hat{U}_{it})}, \qquad (11.5)$$

where $\text{Var}(\hat{U}_{it})$ was the variance of the residual in the period not surrounding the earnings announcement. Beaver argued that "above normal price activity is what would be expected if changes in equilibrium prices are more likely to occur when earnings reports were released" (p. 81). The sample of firms was the same 143 NYSE firms discussed in Section 11.2A. The results closely mirrored those reported in Figure 11.4 for the volume reaction to earnings announcements. The magnitude of the price change in the earnings announcement week was 67% higher than the average during the nonreport period. Above normal activity (approximately 10–15% higher) was also found for the two weeks after the announcement week.

Beaver's [1968] approach to examining the price reaction to earnings announcements has been applied to the earnings announcements of firms listed on a variety of other stock exchanges. For instance, May [1971] applied it to the interim earnings announcements of 105 American Stock Exchange (ASE) firms over the 1964–1968 period. Results are presented in Figure 11.5. The general pattern is similar to that reported by Beaver [1968]; i.e., a significant price reaction in the week earnings is announced. Hagerman [1973] also applied Beaver's methodology to the quarterly and annual earnings announcements of 97 bank stocks listed on the over-the-counter market over the 1961–1967 period. The results indicated a significant price reaction in the week earnings are announced. There was also an above-normal reaction in the week subsequent to the announcement week.

The Beaver [1968] approach requires no assumption about the sign of the earnings change. An alternative approach is to use the CAR approach outlined in Section 11.1. Foster [1977] used this approach to examine the price reaction to the quarterly earnings announcements of 69 NYSE firms over the 1963–1974 period. Table 11.2 details the behavior of the composite CAR in the 20 trading days surrounding each quarterly earnings announcement. The χ^2 corresponding to the association between (1) the sign of the earnings change for the quarter and (2) the sign of the relative risk-adjusted security return on the relevant *day* is also presented in Table 11.2. The quarterly earnings announcement date (0) is the day earnings are announced in the *Wall Street Journal*. For many companies, this information is made available to the NYSE, etc., on the day prior to its publication in the *Journal*. Thus either day -1 or 0 in Table 11.2 could be the effective announcement date.

It is on trading days -1 and 0 that the χ^2 in Table 11.2 is the highest of all those reported. For all four quarters combined, the χ^2's at the days

FIGURE 11.5 Price Reaction to Quarterly Earnings Announcements: ASE Firms

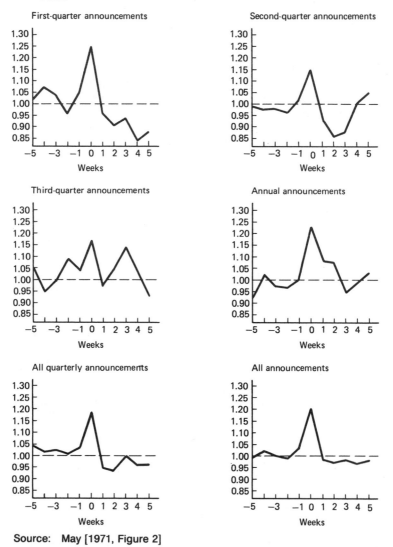

Source: May [1971, Figure 2]

−1 and 0 are 55.08 and 66.87, respectively. The next highest χ^2 is 8.90 on the sixth trading day prior to the earnings announcement. The cumulative abnormal return in the 21 days up to and including the earnings announcement was .0162—approximately 50% of this abnormal return occurred in the day prior to and the day that earnings were announced in the *Wall Street Journal*. Figure 11.6 presents the behavior of the CAR for the

TABLE 11.2 Cumulative Average Residual for Trading Days Surrounding Quarterly Earnings Announcement

Trading Days Surrounding Announcement	All Four Quarters		First Quarter		Second Quarter		Third Quarter		Fourth Quarter	
	Composite CAR	χ^2	Composite CAR	χ^2	Composite CAR	χ^2	Composite CAR	χ^2	Composite CAR	χ^2
−20	.0004	7.07	.0005	5.05	.0009	3.27	.0006	1.82	−.0002	.00
−15	.0017	0.85	.0030	.24	.0025	.00	.0034	.44	−.0022	2.96
−10	.0041	1.65	.0075	.50	.0025	1.27	.0059	1.82	.0003	4.66
−9	.0040	0.96	.0074	1.33	.0020	.88	.0062	1.60	.0005	.83
−8	.0045	1.12	.0081	.01	.0029	.38	.0065	1.20	.0007	.27
−7	.0048	.49	.0081	1.22	.0022	.24	.0076	1.67	.0010	.50
−6	.0059	8.60	.0087	.70	.0036	1.85	.0091	7.09	.0020	.95
−5	.0062	.79	.0088	1.01	.0033	2.82	.0092	.14	.0037	1.56
−4	.0072	4.26	.0102	2.30	.0048	5.92	.0101	.00	.0038	.01
−3	.0075	1.05	.0110	2.31	.0058	1.64	.0099	.86	.0031	.02
−2	.0082	8.90	.0115	3.12	.0074	2.71	.0110	3.42	.0031	.41
−1	.0124	55.08	.0148	8.09	.0120	23.85	.0156	14.63	.0073	10.43
0	.0162	66.87	.0184	23.35	.0166	12.15	.0197	23.69	.0104	9.99
1	.0168	3.81	.0188	1.57	.0170	.72	.0204	.11	.0109	4.52
2	.0170	.91	.0192	1.80	.0171	.51	.0212	2.25	.0103	2.42
3	.0170	.17	.0201	1.97	.0163	1.70	.0216	.11	.0099	.35
4	.0173	1.31	.0210	.35	.0161	.00	.0215	.34	.0107	1.10
5	.0169	4.93	.0210	.25	.0152	.08	.0211	6.10	.0100	1.31
6	.0169	.34	.0210	.08	.0153	.13	.0209	.49	.0101	.02
7	.0169	.35	.0209	.20	.0149	.09	.0217	1.61	.0101	.02
8	.0174	5.67	.0216	.94	.0134	3.12	.0233	12.93	.0113	4.16
9	.0176	.51	.0219	.05	.0135	.17	.0233	.31	.0116	1.05
10	.0178	2.86	.0218	.29	.0148	2.04	.0229	1.12	.0117	.20
15	.0183	.09	.0215	.13	.0169	.13	.0235	2.14	.0111	.58
20	.0189	.29	.0201	.20	.0192	2.78	.0242	.39	.0122	.01

SOURCE: Foster [1977, Table 6].

FIGURE 11.6   Quarterly Earnings and Stock Returns: NYSE Firms

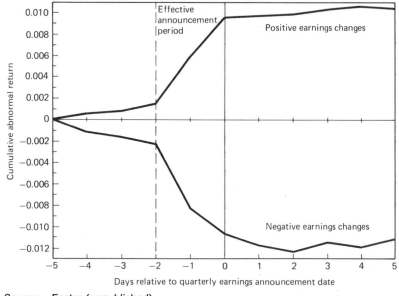

Source: Foster (unpublished).

positive earnings change group and the negative earnings change group for the 10-day period surrounding the quarterly announcement. The marked different announcement effect for these two groups is readily apparent: Positive earnings change firms have a positive abnormal return reaction, while negative earnings change firms have a negative abnormal return reaction.

C   Other Corporate Announcements

The capital market reaction to a variety of other corporate announcements has been examined. Two such announcements—corporate forecasts and corporate dividends—will be briefly examined in this section.

Corporate Forecasts

In Section 11.2 it was illustrated that estimates of annual EPS by corporate officials, made after the end of the fiscal year but before the release of preliminary earnings, induced both trading volume and security price reaction at the time of public release. Corporate officials also release forecasts of EPS, earnings, etc., prior to the end of the fiscal year. At present, these forecasts are voluntarily released by corporate officials. Detailed analysis of the capital market reaction to such forecasts is provided by Patell [1976]. Patell examined the common stock price behavior which accompanied the voluntary disclosure of 336 forecasts of annual earnings per share during the years 1963–1967. It was noted that a variety of factors may influence the market reaction to a forecast, e.g., its imputed accuracy, its newness (prior public nonavailability of the forecast's content), and the imputed motivation for the act of voluntary disclosure. Using a technique similar to that in Beaver [1968]—see the R statistic in (11.5)—Patell found, on average, a significant price reaction in the week of the forecast. This result is consistent with the capital market viewing a corporate forecast (or the act of making the forecast) as a signal pertinent to the valuation of stock prices.

Corporate Dividends

Dividend policy is one means by which management may signal their expectations as to future prospects of a firm. Lintner [1956], based on interviews with corporate management, reported that management is reluctant to reduce dividend payments and generally only increases dividends when it is confident that future earnings will be sufficient to maintain the increased dividend payments. Spangler [1973] examined if the capital market distinguished between firms whose dividend payments were increased and firms whose dividend payments were decreased. The sample examined was all NYSE common stocks over the July 1962–June 1972 period. All changes in dividend amounts of at least 1% magnitude were analyzed—a total of 4,117 observations representing about 1,150 companies. The sample was classified as follows:

(1) All decreases—6.5% of sample,
(2) Small increases (less than 10%)—42% of sample,
(3) Medium increases (10%–25%)—42% of sample, and
(4) Large increases (greater than 25%)—9.5% of sample.

Results for these four groups, for the 21-trading-day period surrounding (and including) the dividend announcement date, are presented in Table 11.3.

The key feature in Table 11.3 is that the sign and size of the security return is positively associated with the sign and size of the dividend change. Results also presented by Spangler indicated that the most significant stock market reaction for each group occurred on the day of and the day subsequent to the dividend announcement. These results are consistent with the capital market viewing dividend changes as providing information pertinent to the valuation of stock prices.[9]

In Sections 11.2A and 11.2B we detailed the capital market's reaction to annual and interim earnings. In this section we illustrated that annual and interim earnings are only one of several information sources that are

TABLE 11.3 Dividend Changes and Stock Returns

Trading Days Surrounding Announcement	All Dividend Decreases	Dividend Increases		
		< 10%	10–25%	> 25%
− 10	− .00217	.00044	.00082	.00053
− 5	− .00755	.00149	.00333	.00666
− 4	− .01054	.00091	.00443	.00895
− 3	− .01334	.00123	.00564	.01345
− 2	− .01806	.00168	.00577	.01598
− 1	− .01980	.00332	.00738	.01823
0	− .04953	.00680	.01409	.02634
+ 1	− .07628	.00994	.01890	.03209
+ 2	− .07743	.01098	.02050	.03213
+ 3	− .07730	.01182	.02130	.03103
+ 4	− .07767	.01159	.02146	.03348
+ 5	− .07915	.01245	.02179	.03399
+ 10	− .08227	.01170	.02062	.03306

SOURCE: Spangler [1973, Tables 1–4].

used by the capital market. At a minimum, corporate forecasts and dividend change announcements also provide information pertinent to security price revaluation.[10] These other sources of information represent one possible means by which the capital market progressively discriminates between positive and negative earnings change firms in the 12 months up to and including the annual earnings announcement. In an efficient market, it is to be expected that the most timely sources of information will be used in the security price revaluation process.

11.3 STOCK RETURNS AND ACCOUNTING ALTERNATIVES

The results in Section 11.1 indicated a significant association between accounting earnings changes and stock price changes. A question arises whether the association is a mechanistic one; i.e., does the aggregate market naively react to a positive (negative) reported earnings change with an upward (downward) revaluation of the stock price, or does it also look at economic aspects underlying the reported earnings number? As noted in Chapter 7, a mechanistic perspective is implicit in many statements in the accounting literature. It is also implicit in many statements by company officials about the effect of proposed accounting changes on stock prices. In this section, we shall examine two different approaches that shed light on the mechanistic argument, i.e., the capital market's reaction to (1) accounting changes and (2) nonreported earnings measures.

A Accounting Changes

A common motivation attributed to management for changing
accounting techniques is an attempt to maintain or boost stock prices. For
instance, a *Business Week* (November 2, 1968) article made the following
comment on the switch by many steel companies to straight-line depreciation:

> For steel executives, the next best thing to import quotas would be a surge in
> their company's stock prices. To attract investors companies are switching
> accounting methods to straight-line depreciation.... Though they may be just
> playing with numbers, steelmen hope all this will make their stocks more
> attractive to investors and boost price-earnings ratios.

Similarly, Kaplan and Roll [1972] made the following statement:

> Company executives must believe such practices affect securities prices or they
> would not take the trouble to change accounting procedures, hinder interperiod
> and intercompany comparisons, and incur a qualification or supplementary
> statement in the auditors' reports. (pp. 226–227)

"Cosmetic reasons," however, are not the only reason that may induce
management to change accounting techniques. Indeed, there are many
reasons (or alleged reasons) for management changing accounting techniques. These reasons can be found in statements in (1) annual reports, (2)
the financial press, and (3) the accounting literature.[11] Examples of reasons
for accounting changes given in annual reports include

(1) *Compliance with FASB Statements*

> *In accordance with Statement No. 2 of the Financial Accounting Standards
> Board* (F.A.S.B.) all research and development costs are expensed as incurred
> and 1974 results have been restated for previously deferred development costs.

> *In accordance with Statement No. 8 of the F.A.S.B.* the company changed its
> method of translating foreign currencies at current instead of historical ex-
> change rates. (*Xerox Corporation*, 1975 Annual Report, p. 17)

(2) *Compliance with AICPA Industry Audit Guides*

> *In accordance with the American Institute of Certified Public Accountants
> (A.I.C.P.A.) published investment company industry audit guide*, the small busi-
> ness investment company has changed its method of accounting for invest-
> ments. In prior years, investments were stated at cost less an allowance for
> possible losses. In connection with the change, investments are stated at fair
> value as determined by the Board of Directors. (*Commerce Group Corporation*,
> 1975 Annual Report, p. 12)

(3) *Compliance with Internal Revenue Service Regulations*

> *In the first quarter of fiscal year 1975, the Company modified its method of
> valuing domestic inventories to the full absorption method, pursuant to recent*

Internal Revenue Service regulations, by changing the composition of elements of overhead costs included in inventory. (*International Harvester*, 1975 Annual Report, p. 9)

(4) *Conformity to Industry Practice*

Effective January 1, 1975, the company adopted the straight line method of computing depreciation for financial statement purposes. *The reason for this change in policy is the desire to conform to prevailing industry practice.* (*Anheuser-Busch*, 1975 Annual Report, p. 30)

(5) *Taxation Savings*

In 1974, the company extended, where it considered appropriate, the last-in, first-out method of accounting to additional domestic inventories. In prior years such inventories were valued generally on the first-in, first-out method. *This accounting change was made to reduce the effect of inflation on income and to obtain the related tax benefit.* (*Rockwell International*, 1975 Annual Report, p. 38)

(6) *"Better Match Costs and Revenues"*

In the fourth quarter of 1975 the company changed its policy of valuing certain domestic inventories from the first-in, first-out (FIFO) to the last-in, first-out (LIFO) basis. *The change was made to reduce the impact of inflation on inventory valuation and effect a more appropriate matching of current costs with current revenues.* (*Woolworth Company*, 1975 Annual Report, p. 22)

Not surprisingly, the financial press has not always accepted, at face value, the reasons given by management for accounting changes. For instance, one paper raised the possibility that changes in revenue recognition rules by *Pan American World Airways* in 1975 were related to avoiding covenants on bank loan agreements.[12] The impact of accounting rules on management incentive schemes has also been suggested as an important factor in accounting change decisions.[13] The accounting literature has noted the importance of many of the motivations noted previously but has not yet developed any detailed analysis of the accounting change decision. Indeed, very little in the form of a developed theory of accounting change decisions exists. The consequence of such limited knowledge is that studies examining the market's reaction to changes have had to adopt an assumption regarding the net effect of factors associated with the change. Two such studies will be examined: Ball [1972] and Sunder [1973; 1975].

Accounting Changes—Ball [1972]. Ball examined the market reaction to 267 changes over the 1947–1960 period. These changes included 85 inventory changes, 75 depreciation changes, and 52 subsidiary accounting changes. Ball assumed that the net effect of these changes, at the change announcement date, was no real increase in the value of the firms. He examined the hypothesis that "the market cannot distinguish real from accounting effects on reported income" (p. 32).

A feature of Ball [1972] was the detailed analysis of techniques for computing the CAR. Inferences in the study were based on the behavior of a CAR computed from a two-factor cross-sectional model (see Appendix 11.A). The relative risks of each firm were recomputed each month to control for risk changes in the sample. The behavior of the average CAR for these 267 changes is presented in Figure 11.7. Ball [1972] interpreted the results as follows:

> The year of the accounting change does not appear to exhibit any unusual behavior for the average firm. The average [residual] in the month of accounting change is 0.12 of 1 percent. Hence, there is little unusual price behavior in that month, indicating that there is little market adjustment of a consistent sign associated with the release of the income report. In the 19 months after the accounting change there is little abnormal price movement. In short, changes in accounting techniques do not appear to be associated with market adjustments in a consistent direction for the average firm. (pp. 22–23)

Ball also computed the χ^2 between the sign of the earnings change and the sign of the abnormal return in the announcement month for the 267 accounting change observations. The resultant χ^2 was insignificantly different from zero ($\chi^2 = .05$). This χ^2 differs strongly from that typically found for samples not chosen on an accounting change criterion. For instance, the comparable χ^2 for the firms in Ball and Brown [1968] was 28.0. This result is strong evidence against a mechanistic relationship between reported accounting earnings and stock prices.

FIFO/LIFO Changes—Sunder [1973; 1975]. Sunder examined a relatively homogeneous accounting change sample—a set of 155 firms

FIGURE 11.7 Accounting Changes and Stock Returns

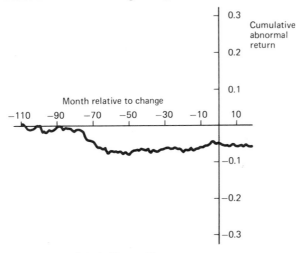

Source: Ball [1972, Figure 5].

changing inventory valuation methods over the 1946–1966 period. This sample was of added interest due to a U.S. Tax law requiring that a firm using LIFO for tax purposes must also use LIFO for financial reporting. Note that if a company has rising input prices, use of LIFO vis-à-vis FIFO will generally reduce reported income. Thus, proponents of the mechanistic hypothesis regarding reported earnings and stock prices would argue that the price of the firms changing to LIFO would decrease. In contrast, Sunder hypothesized that firms changing to LIFO would increase in price.[14] This hypothesis was based on deferment of taxation payments:

> LIFO results in lower taxable and reported earnings. If the marginal tax is positive, the tax liability of the firm is also lower. Even if inventory holding gains are realized in a subsequent period, tax payments on these gains are postponed until such time. This amounts to an interest-free loan to the firm from the tax authority. The value of the firm increases because the present value of net cash flows to the firm is higher. (Sunder [1973, p. 9])

Results from Sunder [1975] for the sample of 129 firms changing to LIFO are presented in Figure 11.8. The CAR was computed using the one-factor market model. The relative risk of each firm was reestimated each month

FIGURE 11.8 LIFO Accounting Changes and Stock Returns

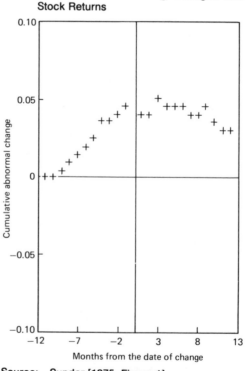

Source: Sunder [1975, Figure 1].

in an attempt to control for possible risk changes of firms. Note that (1) the stock price rises in the 12 months up to and including "the change month" and (2) there is little abnormal return in the months subsequent to the change. The results are inconsistent with the mechanistic hypothesis; lower earnings associated with a LIFO change are not "viewed by the stock market as a sign of averse performance on the part of the firm" (p. 34). Several factors could explain the increase in price in the 12 months up to "the change month"; e.g., (1) accounting change firms are those which ex post had better than average business performance, or (2) the cues which triggered the accounting change by management became apparent to the market in the 12 months prior to the change.[15]

Mechanistic Hypothesis vs. Market Efficiency

Tests of the mechanistic hypothesis, via accounting change studies, have examined if positive earnings changes for change firms were associated with positive price changes and vice versa. To reject the hypothesis it was sufficient to find no such positive association. On this score, both Ball [1972] and Sunder [1973; 1975] reject the mechanistic hypothesis.[16] The question of whether these studies are consistent with capital market efficiency is a much deeper issue. One would need to independently predict the "appropriate" reaction (both its magnitude and its timing) of the capital market to the change and then examine if the observed change was similar to the *appropriate reaction*. As noted earlier, very little in the form of a developed theory of accounting change decisions exists. The notion of an "appropriate" reaction is ill-defined and, as yet, poorly operationalized. For this reason, we choose to interpret the accounting change literature as tests of the mechanistic hypothesis rather than as tests of market efficiency.

The same issue arises in examining the capital market reaction to accounting alternatives. Although the literature on accounting alternatives is voluminous, there is little theory that predicts the degree of association between earnings measures computed via accounting alternatives and stock returns. In the next section, we shall examine the capital market's reaction to nonreported earnings measures. For reasons discussed above, the issue addressed in the next section is the mechanistic hypothesis rather than whether the market "appropriately" reacts to accounting alternatives.

B Nonreported Accounting Alternatives

Does the capital market look beyond the reported income number? In this section, we shall examine the issue from yet another perspective. Specifically, we shall examine whether the capital market makes some systematic adjustments to the reported earnings of companies. Two accounting methods will be examined: (1) depreciation methods and (2) life insurance underwriting earnings methods.

Depreciation Methods

Beaver and Dukes [1973] examined the market's reaction to the depreciation expense reported by 54 firms that used straight-line depreciation for reporting but accelerated depreciation for taxation. The period of analyses was 1963–1967. As noted in Chapter 6, information in the deferred tax account can be used to compute alternative depreciation methods. By the use of this information, earnings measures reported under a variety of depreciation methods were calculated. Then the CAR for the 12 months up to and including the earnings announcements was computed for the earnings measure associated with each depreciation method.

The depreciation expense yielding the highest CAR was larger than that reported for the straight-line method. This result is consistent with the capital market not taking the reported earnings at its face value. Whether this larger imputed depreciation expense represent an attempt by the capital market to use a *current cost* depreciation method was not explored by Beaver and Dukes.

Life Insurance Underwriting Earnings Methods

Prior to 1973, most life insurance companies reported a *statutory* underwriting measure in their financial statements to stockholders. This measure differed in two important respects from earnings computed under generally accepted accounting principles (GAAP):

(1) The costs of writing new policies were charged to operations as incurred, whereas premiums were taken into income over periods covered by the related policies, and

(2) The interest rate assumptions used in computing the reserves of life insurance companies were generally less than the actual return on their investments.

Since 1973, all life insurance companies have been required to report *adjusted* (i.e., GAAP) earnings in their financial statements.

During the pre-1973 period, many financial analysts, *Standard & Poor's*, and *A. M. Best* presented adjusted earnings in their investment advisory services. These adjusted earnings numbers were computed from information contained in the statutory financial statements that insurance companies must file with state insurance commissioners. The main adjustments made were (1) to capitalize costs of new policies and amortize them over the expected life of the policy and (2) to use currently earned rates of return on investments when computing the reserves of life insurance companies. The market's reaction to the statutory measure and an adjusted earnings measure was examined by Foster [1975]. The familiar CAR methodology was adopted. The adjusted earnings measure had a stronger association with security price changes over both the 1965–1968 and 1969–1972 periods. This result was consistent with the market using a broad-based information set when interpreting the reported statutory earnings of life insurance companies.

11.4   MULTIVARIATE ANALYSIS OF ACCOUNTING/NONACCOUNTING DATA

In prior sections of this chapter we have examined the association between security returns and *single* accounting variables or between security returns and *individual* corporate announcements. We shall now briefly examine evidence on the association between security returns and multiple variables (announcements). It should be noted that work in this area is less developed than is the previous work discussed in this chapter. There are two main approaches to incorporating multiple variables into the analysis. The first approach extends the CAR methodology to incorporate multiple variables. The second approach uses a cross-sectional model in which the dependent variable (Y) is (abnormal) security return and the independent variables (X_i's) are financial ratios and market variables.

A   CAR Extensions

An example of extending the CAR methodology to incorporate multiple variables is Foster [1975a]. The multiple variables were the subearnings series of insurance companies, representing results of their three main lines of business, i.e., underwriting results, investment results, and capital gains on marketable securities. Using these three series, it is possible to present evidence on whether the market discriminated among firms which had differing combinations of the eight possible combinations of subearnings changes; e.g., was a firm which had positive changes on all three series distinguished from a firm which had a positive change on underwriting but negative changes on the investment and capital gains series?

Given CAR results for each single series detailed in Foster [1975a], it was predicted that

$$CAR_1 > CAR_2 > CAR_3 > CAR_4 > CAR_5 > CAR_6 > CAR_7 > CAR_8,$$

FIGURE 11.9 Security Market Reaction to Subearnings Changes

	Subearnings Category	CAR	Number of Observ.
1.	$U_p I_p C_p$	.102	47
2.	$U_p I_p C_n$	.065	64
3.	$U_p I_n C_p$	.054	64
4.	$U_p I_n C_n$	.021	47
5.	$U_n I_p C_p$	−.023	40
6.	$U_n I_p C_n$	−.038	63
7.	$U_n I_n C_p$	−.060	75
8.	$U_n I_n C_n$	−.083	64

Tree branches: U_p → $U_p I_p$ (1,2), $U_p I_n$ (3,4); U_n → $U_n I_p$ (5,6), $U_n I_n$ (7,8).

KEY: U = underwriting earnings
I = investment earnings
C = capital gains and losses on marketable securities
p = positive earnings change
n = negative earnings change

Source: Foster [1975a, Table 1].

where CAR_i is the cumulative abnormal return for a particular combination of the subearnings changes. Results are presented in Figure 11.9. The CAR results in Figure 11.9 are in the order predicted. The observed ordering was statistically significant at at least the .01 significance level. These results are consistent with the capital market reacting to the three subearnings series of insurance companies.[17]

B Cross-Sectional Extensions

The basic model used in cross-sectional analyses of the capital market reaction to multiple variables is

$$Y_i = f(X_1, X_2 ..., X_n). \qquad (11.6)$$

The dependent variable is (abnormal) security return. Independent variables examined have ranged from financial ratios to security market variables (e.g., average trading volume of a security). Either ordinary least squares or discriminant analysis has been used in estimating (11.6). Examples of this approach include Nerlove [1968], O'Connor [1973], Benishay [1973], and Gonedes [1974]. The choice of the model, its functional form (linear, multiplicative, etc.), and the specific variables in each of the above and similar studies have been relatively heuristic. For instance, Nerlove [1968] noted the following:

> It would be less than honest if I did not now confess that my initial formulations differed from the formulations reported.... Eleven explanatory variables were used in various combinations in regressions designed to explain differences among rates of return for various time periods. Of these eleven, five were dropped or modified and replaced by a number of other variables. (pp. 317–318)

The most common basis for choice of variables is frequency of their reference in the accounting literature or frequency of their use in prior empirical studies.

The lack of a theoretical underpinning for the model examined is one possible explanation for the seemingly inconsistent conclusions from individual studies. For instance, O'Connor [1973] used a stepwise OLS regression model to examine what ratios best explain variations in abnormal security returns. Out of an initial set of ten financial ratios, five ratios remained as significant explanatory variables of abnormal security returns: total liabilities to net worth, cash flow per share, current liabilities to inventories, income to net worth, and working capital to sales. Ratios representing similar aspects of liquidity, leverage, profitability, and turnover were not found to be statistically significant in each of the Nerlove [1968], Benishay [1973], and Gonedes [1974] studies. It is unlikely that useful generalizations will be gained by further such cross-sectional studies until some theoretical underpinning (however simplified) for the chosen model, its function form, and its specific variables is developed.

11.5 SUMMARY

The evidence on the relationship between capital asset returns and financial information is compelling on the following issues:

(1) There is a positive contemporaneous association between the sign and size of the accounting earnings change and the sign and the size of the security price change.

(2) Much of the market's reaction to accounting earnings is anticipatory; more timely information sources than the earnings announcement are used in the security price revaluation process.

(3) Notwithstanding (2), there is a significant security price and trading volume reaction to the information contained in interim and annual earnings announcements.

(4) There is not a mechanistic relationship between reported accounting numbers and stock returns; the market uses a broad-based information set in interpreting the information content of reported accounting numbers.

In Chapter 12 we shall discuss the implications of the issues and evidence examined in this and prior chapters for investment decisions.

**APPENDIX 11.A   ESTIMATING THE ABNORMAL RETURNS
OF A SECURITY**

A key issue underlying the evidence examined in Chapter 11 is the estimation of the cumulative abnormal return (CAR) measure. This measure is also important in evaluating alternative approaches to investment choice and in evaluating security recommendations made by analysts —see Chapter 12. In this appendix, the theoretical underpinning of the measure and some empirical issues in its estimation are discussed.

The most appealing theoretical framework for the CAR technique is within the context of a capital asset pricing model. Consider the Sharpe-Lintner asset pricing model outlined in Chapter 8:

$$E(\tilde{R}_{it}) = R_{ft} + \beta_i \left[E(\tilde{R}_{mt}) - R_{ft} \right], \qquad (11.7)$$

where R_{it} = return on asset i in period t,

R_{ft} = return on a risk-free asset in period t,

R_{mt} = return on the market portfolio in period t,

β_i = relative risk of asset i.

Using (11.7) in an empirical study means replacing expected returns by realized returns:

$$\tilde{R}_{it} = R_{ft} + \hat{\beta}_i \left(\tilde{R}_{mt} - R_{ft} \right) + \hat{U}_{it}, \qquad (11.8)$$

where $\hat{U}_{it}$ is a residual whose expectation is zero. Equation (11.8) is usually rearranged as follows when estimating β_i:

$$\tilde{R}_{it} - R_{ft} = \hat{\beta}_i \left(\tilde{R}_{mt} - R_{ft} \right) + \hat{U}_{it}. \qquad (11.9)$$

Equation (11.9) can be estimated with ordinary least squares (usually with the intercept suppressed to zero). Given the OLS estimate of β_i, the abnormal return of security i in period t ($\hat{U}_{it}$) is

$$\hat{U}_{it} = \left(\tilde{R}_{it} - R_{ft} \right) - \hat{\beta}_i \left(\tilde{R}_{mt} - R_{ft} \right). \qquad (11.10)$$

It is important to note that when using (11.10) to (say) examine the capital market reaction to an earnings announcment, we are *jointly* testing the hypothesis that the Sharpe-Lintner model is a descriptively valid model of asset pricing and that the earnings have information content.

An Example

Data for *Jos. Schlitz Brewing Company* will be used to illustrate the computation of the cumulative abnormal return measure for the 12 months up to and including the 1973 annual earnings announcement. The preliminary 1973 earnings of \$53,675,000 (1972 earnings = \$37,539,000) was announced in the *Wall Street Journal* on February 12, 1974. Thus the 12 months of interest are March 1973–February 1974. Table 11.4 contains details of $\tilde{R}_i$ [column (1)], $\tilde{R}_m$ [column (2)], and R_f [column (3)] over the March 1973–February 1974 period. The proxy for R_f is the return on government bonds with 1 month to maturity. A value-weighted index of all NYSE stocks is the proxy for R_m. Table 11.4 also contains the excess returns for *Schlitz* [$\tilde{R}_{it} - R_{ft}$: column (4)] and the market [$\tilde{R}_{mt} - R_{ft}$: column (5)].

TABLE 11.4   CAR Estimation for Jos. Schlitz Brewing Company

Month	R_{it} (1)	R_{mt} (2)	R_{ft} (3)	$R_{it} - R_{ft}$ (4)	$R_{mt} - R_{ft}$ (5)
March 73	.095	−.004	.005	.090	−.009
April 73	−.055	−.044	.005	−.060	−.049
May 73	.064	−.019	.006	.058	−.025
June 73	−.044	−.009	.005	−.049	−.014
July 73	.082	.051	.006	.076	.045
August 73	−.025	−.031	.008	−.033	−.039
September 73	−.114	.051	.006	−.120	.045
October 73	.096	−.001	.007	.087	−.008
November 73	−.188	−.117	.005	−.193	−.122
December 73	.107	.014	.006	.101	.008
January 74	−.040	−.001	.006	−.046	−.007
February 74	−.028	.004	.006	−.034	−.002
				$\sum_{t=1}^{12} = -.123$	$\sum_{t=1}^{12} = -.177$

KEY: R_{it} = monthly return on *Jos. Schlitz Brewing Company*,

   R_{mt} = monthly return on market index,

   R_{ft} = monthly return on a risk-free asset.

Excess returns for the 60 months prior to March 1973 were used to estimate (11.9)—$\hat{\beta}_i = 1.087$ for this period. This $\hat{\beta}_i$ implies, for instance, that when the excess return on the market $(\tilde{R}_{mt} - R_{ft})$ is 1%, the "normal" excess return on *Schlitz* $(\tilde{R}_{it} - R_{ft})$ is 1.087%. The abnormal returns for each month in the 12-month period are estimated as follows:

$$\hat{U}_{it} = (\tilde{R}_{it} - R_{ft}) - 1.087 \times (\tilde{R}_{mt} - R_{ft}). \quad (11.11)$$

Thus, for March 1973,

$$\hat{U}_{it} = .090 - 1.087 \times (-.009) = .100.$$

For April 1973,

$$\hat{U}_{it} = -.060 - 1.087 \times (-.049) = -.007.$$

Similarly, for May 1973,

$$\hat{U}_{it} = .058 - 1.087 \times (-.025) = .085.$$

The cumulative abnormal return is estimated as follows:

$$CAR = \sum_{t=1}^{12} \hat{U}_{it}$$
$$= .100 + (-.007) + .085 \ldots = .069. \quad (11.12)$$

The cumulative excess return for the market over this 12-month period was $-.177$. Given a $\hat{\beta}$ of 1.087, *Schlitz's* "normal" cumulative excess return would have been $-.192$. However, *Schlitz's* actual excess return was only $-.123$. Thus, the cumulative abnormal return was .069. Note that this positive cumulative abnormal return was also associated with a positive earnings change for 1973 earnings vis-à-vis 1972 earnings.

Methodological Refinements

Developments in asset pricing theory have implications for the estimation of abnormal returns. Empirical testing of the Sharpe-Lintner asset pricing model has suggested that the following more general asset pricing model has greater descriptive validity (see Chapter 8):

$$E(\tilde{R}_{it}) = E(\tilde{R}_{zt}) + \beta_i [E(\tilde{R}_{mt}) - E(\tilde{R}_{zt})], \quad (11.13)$$

where $\tilde{R}_{zt}$ = the return on an asset whose returns are uncorrelated with $\tilde{R}_{mt}$. Estimation of abnormal returns using (11.13) has been done with the following two-factor model:

$$\tilde{R}_{it} - \tilde{R}_{zt} = \hat{\beta}_i (\tilde{R}_{mt} - \tilde{R}_{zt}) + \hat{U}_{it}. \quad (11.14)$$

The model is referred to as a two-factor model because both the R_{mt} and R_{zt} factors are random variables. Ball [1972] contains a detailed description and an application of using (11.13) to estimate abnormal returns.

A more recent approach to estimating abnormal returns is the *companion portfolio* approach developed by Black and Scholes [1973]. Abnormal returns are estimated by "subtracting from the measured stock return the return on a 'companion' portfolio that has about the same dependence on $\tilde{R}_m$ and $\tilde{R}_z$ as the stock" (p. 11): i.e.,

$$\hat{U}_{it} = \tilde{R}_{it} - \tilde{R}_{pt}, \tag{11.15}$$

where $\tilde{R}_{pt}$ = the return on companion portfolio p in period t. At present, research is being conducted into alternative ways of constructing efficient companion portfolios. For instance, Black and Scholes [1973] proposed the following method:

> The method we use to select a comparison portfolio is very simple. We construct ten portfolios with a wide range of β's. Then we define the "adjusted return" on a stock as the return on the stock minus the return on the comparison portfolio containing that stock. Thus when we put together the adjusted returns for a number of stocks in a given portfolio, we can have some assurance that the composite portfolio will be approximately independent of $\tilde{R}_M$ and $\tilde{R}_z$, since securities in a given comparison portfolio will have approximately the same β as one another, and thus will have approximately the same dependence on $\tilde{R}_M$ and $\tilde{R}_z$. (pp. 11–12)

The Foster [1977] paper examined in Chapter 11 used abnormal returns computed by the above companion portfolio technique. For an alternative approach to forming a companion portfolio, see Gonedes [1975].

Statistical refinements in estimating relative risk also have implications for estimating abnormal returns. Considerable evidence exists that some of the assumptions underlying important properties of OLS estimates of beta (relative risk) do not hold. For instance, there is evidence of nonconstant variance in security returns (Rozeff and Kinney [1976] and Morgan [1976]). There is also evidence that relative risk changes over time (Blume [1975]). In general, these results and others have given rise to less reliance on ordinary least-squares estimation techniques and more reliance on techniques such as Bayesian regression analysis and generalized least-squares analysis.

NOTES

[1]Benston [1967] also examined some related issues. We shall concentrate on the Ball and Brown [1968] paper in part because of its greater influence on subsequent developments in accounting thought.

[2]There are several alternative names in the accounting literature for the CAR methodology, e.g., API (abnormal performance index) and CAE (cumulative average error). For ease of exposition, we shall always use the CAR title even though the study being described may have used a different title for the methodology.

[3]There are several explanations for these slight postannouncement month drifts. One is that they are an artifact of inadequate controls in the

research methodology. The other explanation is that the market does not instantaneously impound all the information in the earnings release. See Ball [1976] for detailed discussion of these explanations.

[4]For evidence relating to other non-U.S. capital markets, see Lev and Yahalomi [1972] on the Tel Aviv Stock Exchange, Deakin et al. [1974] on the Tokyo Stock Exchange, and Forsgardh and Hertzen [1975] on the Stockholm Stock Exchange.

[5]The above results for interim earnings pertain to a sample of 69 NYSE firms over the 1963–1974 period. Brown [1972] and Brown and Hancock [1974] report many similar results for the interim earnings of Australian companies over the 1960–1969 and 1964–1970 periods, respectively.

[6]These results were previously unpublished. Earlier evidence consistent with the market reacting to the size of the quarterly earnings change was presented by Beaver [1974].

[7]Ball [1976] argues that the techniques used by Joy et al. [1977] to determine large unexpected earnings changes accentuate the experimental problems in cumulative abnormal return estimation. He offers alternative explanations to market inefficiency for their results.

[8]Kiger [1972] has reported similar results for interim earnings announcements of 30 NYSE firms in 1968 and 1969.

[9]The results in Table 11.3 are consistent with at least two hypotheses. One hypothesis is that dividend policy per se affects security returns. The alternative hypothesis is that dividend policy per se does not affect security returns; the observed reaction to dividend changes is due to their conveying information about management's expectations of future prospects of a company. The available evidence (e.g., Black and Scholes [1974]) is more consistent with the latter hypothesis.

[10]The evidence in Sections 11.1 and 11.2 is based on studies using monthly, weekly, or daily security returns. There is now evidence of *within* daily market reaction to information. Dann et al. [1977] examined the speed of market reaction to large block sales. They report that "within 15 minutes of the block transaction, prices appear to be essentially unbiased estimates of the closing price for the day of the block transaction" (p. 21).

[11]See Watts and Zimmerman [1976] and Gonedes [1976] for analysis of various motivations for firms making accounting changes.

[12]See the *Wall Street Journal* (May 29, 1975), "Pan American Had April Profit, Tied to Accounting Method."

[13]See Watts and Zimmerman [1976].

[14]The assumptions made by Sunder [1973, pp. 8–9] when hypothesizing that changes to LIFO would increase the value of the firm included

(1) Inventory prices are expected to increase,

(2) Marginal tax rate of the firm is positive,

(3) Discounted net cash flow concept of valuation of firm is used,

(4) Firms using LIFO maintain stable or increasing year-end inventory in order to prevent realization of inventory holding gains, and

(5) Accounting changes are not accompanied by change in the internal decision process of the firm which may systematically alter the reported earnings or value of the firm.

See Sunder [1976] for a closer examination of these assumptions under certainty and uncertainty and their effect on the LIFO/FIFO decision.

[15]See Ball [1972, pp. 25–26] and Demski [1973] for a good discussion of the problems associated with studying the capital market reaction to inventory changes. See also Gonedes and Dopuch [1974].

[16]Other studies on the market reaction to "accounting changes" are also, on balance, inconsistent with the mechanistic hypothesis—e.g., the Kaplan and Roll [1972] study on depreciation and investment credit changes and the Hong et al. [1976] study on purchase vs. pooling choices when accounting for mergers. See also Cassidy [1976] for analysis of some anomalies in the Kaplan and Roll [1972] investment credit results.

[17]In using this design it is important that (1) the earnings changes on each series be uncorrelated with changes on the other series, and (2) the information on each series be released at the same time. If either of these conditions is not met, it can be misleading to draw inferences about the information content (or lack thereof) of various combinations from Figure 11.9. In Foster [1975a] both conditions (1) and (2) were satisfied. Griffin [1976] and Gonedes [1976a] also used a design similar to that in Figure 11.9. Griffin examined earnings, analysts' forecasts of earnings, and dividends. Gonedes examined earnings, dividends, and extraordinary items. Neither condition (1) nor (2) was met in these two papers. Violating (1) means one may be picking up the effect of the magnitude of the change in the first series categorized. Violating (2) means one ignores the important aspect of the timeliness of various signals to the capital market.

QUESTIONS

QUESTION 11.1: Cumulative Abnormal Return Estimation

The 1974 preliminary annual earnings of three companies were announced in the *Wall Street Journal* on the following dates:

American Hospital Supply Corporation	11 February 1975
Bethlehem Steel Corporation	30 January 1975
Coca-Cola Company	6 March 1975

Details of the 19ʺ0–1974 earnings (in $000's) of these three companies are

	American Hospital	Bethlehem Steel	Coca-Cola Company
1970	$25,650	$ 90,071	$146,876
1971	$29,163	$139,239	$167,815
1972	$33,893	$134,584	$190,157
1973	$39,859	$206,609	$214,981
1974	$46,327	$342,034	$195,972

Table 11.5 details the monthly security returns on these securities, a value-weighted market index, and an estimate of the return on a riskless asset over the January 1974–March 1975 period.

TABLE 11.5   CAR Estimation

	American Hospital	Bethlehem Steel	Coca-Cola Company	R_M	R_f
January 1974	−.0575	.0152	−.0711	−.0085	.0063
February 1974	−.0658	.0530	−.0213	.0019	.0058
March 1974	.0691	−.0800	−.380	−.0217	.0056
April 1974	−.0034	.0040	−.0420	−.0373	.0075
May 1974	−.0082	−.0976	.0154	−.0272	.0075
June 1974	.0276	.0619	.0129	.1017	.0060
July 1974	−.1242	−.0042	−.2118	−.1722	.0070
August 1974	−.1739	−.0628	−.1454	−.0828	.0060
September 1974	−.2930	−.0909	−.2882	−.1170	.0081
October 1974	.5461	.1300	.2293	.1657	.0051
November 1974	−.1166	−.0442	−.1344	−.0448	.0054
December 1974	−.0048	−.0613	−.0185	−.0177	.0070
January 1975	.2670	.2714	.2571	.1251	.0058
February 1975	−.1011	−.0237	.0488	.0674	.0043
March 1975	.0684	.1519	.1388	.0237	.0041

(1) Compute the cumulative abnormal return (CAR) of each security in the 12 months up to and including the month the 1974 preliminary annual earnings were announced in the *Wall Street Journal*. Compute the CAR as follows:

$$\hat{U}_{it} = \left(\tilde{R}_{it} - R_{ft}\right) - \hat{\beta} \times \left(\tilde{R}_{Mt} - R_{ft}\right).$$

Over the period examined, the beta of each security was estimated to be

	$\hat{\beta}$
American Hospital	1.71
Bethlehem Steel	1.12
Coca-Cola Company	1.42

(2) What evidence is there of an association between the sign of the earnings change and the sign of the CAR in the 12 months up to and including the earnings announcement?

(3) Assume that in July 1974, *Bethlehem Steel* acquired a 60% interest in American Hospital and that it had to issue long-term debentures to raise the necessary finance. These debentures increased its long-term debt equity ratio from .3 to 1.2. What effect may this merger have on inferences drawn from the behavior of the CAR for *Bethlehem Steel* computed in (1)?

QUESTION 11.2:   Earnings Reports and Stock Returns

Benston [1976] made the following comments in a *Fortune* (April 1976) article entitled "There's No Real News in Earnings Reports":

> The formal presumption about corporate annual reports is that they contain *news*. And the essence of the news is thought to be in the financial statements.
>
> I am one of a number of academic scholars who have been studying the validity of that thought. More precisely, the question we sought to answer was whether the financial statements released by corporations are of any practical use to investors—whether they can be used to make buy and sell decisions that are any better than those that could be made before the release date.
>
> Many investors, I suppose, will find this question very peculiar indeed. It is obvious that published financial statements like those in annual reports do contain data that are recent and unobtainable from other sources. To be sure, preliminary earnings may have already been reported in the financial press or announced in releases mailed to shareholders. But other figures—e.g., on depreciation, interest charges, purchases and sales of assets—are generally available only in the annual report.
>
> And, presumably, all this information is important. The Securities and Exchange Commission has labored mightily to ensure its disclosure and to establish rather detailed regulations about the manner of its presentation.
>
> Yet all the studies—including my own—suggest that the information in annual reports has already been discounted by the market by the time investors receive it. Nor is that all. The studies have also concluded that those preliminary earnings announcements—which reach investors with a much shorter time lag than that affecting annual reports—have also been discounted by the market. The news is old before it is released.
>
> I am aware that this finding collides with the common-sense view of thousands of investors (and with the view of the SEC). Some comment on the findings may be in order.
>
> One possible explanation of this blow to common sense is that the studies are invalid. Perhaps our statistical techniques are not really adequate to measure the impact of financial data on stock prices. We may have estimated the amount of unanticipated earnings incorrectly. Or we may not have adjusted adequately for other events that also affect share prices and that may have obscured the impact of the financial-statement publication. Conceivably, more exact studies will show different results.

Some scholars who accept our basic finding—that earnings reports do not affect stock prices—have a different explanation for the phenomenon than the one I am putting forward (i.e., that the market already "knows" what is in the reports). Their explanation is that financial statements just don't measure a company's position very well.

For example, it is clear that depreciation based on the original cost of plant and equipment does not measure adequately the cost to a company in current dollars of using its assets. Another example: accountants generally write off as a current expense all the amounts invested in advertising and research and development, even though these expenditures will generate future revenues.

Of still greater importance, perhaps, financial statements accord no recognition at all to many events that affect the value of a company to investors—basic changes in a company's competitive position, for example, or new government regulations, or the departure of key company personnel. Therefore, the argument goes, the reason the market ignores financial statements is that they simply don't reflect reality. (pp. 73, 74)

REQUIRED

Critically evaluate the above comments. Cite evidence from specific studies detailed in Chapter 11 in your answer.

QUESTION 11.3:   Accounting Earnings and Stock Returns

The Ball and Brown [1968] paper discussed in Chapter 11 examined whether the capital market distinguished between firms whose earnings increased vis-à-vis firms whose earnings decreased. Chambers [1974] made the following comments on this paper:

The study is in essence a study of the responses of the market to changes in reported net income. The data used are the reported net income figures of 261 firms, the announcement dates, and the movements in security prices before and after announcement dates. The general conclusions were (1) "that the information contained in the annual income number is useful in that if actual [reported] income differs from expected income, the market typically has reacted in the same direction," and (2) "most of the information contained in reported income is anticipated by the market before the annual report is released," some of the developed statistics suggesting "not only that the market begins to anticipate forecast errors in the 12 months preceding the report, but also that it continues to do so with increasing success throughout the year" (pp. 169–171).

At first glance it seems as though conclusion (1) says something quite firm about the information content of income numbers. But on closer inspection it appears that the form of the exercise binds it to a kind of circularity. The market's forecasts of reported incomes are based on previously *reported* incomes of other firms (p. 161); the change in incomes of the subject firms is the change in *reported* incomes; the observed price movements are responses to expected reported incomes and actual *reported* incomes. The exercise is throughout concerned with expected and actual *reported* incomes; it can throw no light whatever on the question of the propriety of different methods of income calculation.

The efficient market hypothesis entails that stock prices adjust rapidly to new information as it becomes available. But it says nothing about the quality of that information. It is conceivable that reported income figures can vary in the same direction (and even by the same percentage) as the substantive increments in net wealth without any close correspondence with those increments; traditional accounting has been shown to tolerate very great differences in the amounts of income reported after applying different permissible rules to the same objects and events. It is also conceivable that reported income figures can vary continuously in one direction while the substantive increments in net wealth vary both upwards and downwards; income-smoothing is a well-documented practice. It is also conceivable that reported income figures may turn out (and some have turned out), after some time has elapsed (months later or years later), to have been greatly in error, leading in the upshot to major 'corrections' of the figures and in some cases to outright failure. The study of short-term price movements can capture none of this; and any study which ignores failures (the source data of Ball and Brown and others relate to companies still listed) disregards a significant part of the population of accounting phenomena. It is conceivable, furthermore, that reported income figures can be made to be consistent with stock prices by book entries after the close of the year, since what is reported is at the discretion of company officers; and there is some evidence of this having been done by at least some companies in some years.... The point of these observations is that even though the market may readily adjust to information which becomes available, it has no ready means of countering (and Ball and Brown's study says nothing about its capacity to counter) false, misleading and erroneous figures.

Consider the securities market now as a capital-rationing or capital-directing device. An efficient market, in the fullest sense, would, by the prices established in it, secure the support of enterprises or projects of companies which have demonstrated earning capacity superior to that of other companies. But if earnings reports are differentially distorted by the asset valuation and income calculation rules adopted by different companies—and there is considerable evidence of this—the stock market cannot discriminate between the more and the less efficient companies.

The Ball and Brown paper (like others in the same stream) alludes to the fact that other sources of information are available to the market besides the earnings report. There may be sources of hints and clues, giving investors grounds for beliefs and expectations. But there is only one potential source of "hard" information on earnings, information which should serve as a corrective of the beliefs based on hints and clues, and that is the annual report. Some have held that those who are prepared to pay for it can get better information of the same general kind. But this contention will not stand up unless one first concedes that there is better information. What information is better information is a proper subject of accounting research. But inquiries of the style of Ball and Brown's do not touch it. Nor can they, since they are firmly based on what accounting is.

One more point seems worth making. There is abundant evidence of the dissimilarity of ways of computing net income; a glance at *Accounting Trends and Techniques* of any year will confirm this. It follows that the reported net incomes of companies are heterogeneous; the only thing they have in common is their label. The common label and the setting in which the figures occur (duly attested financial statements), it is reasonable to suppose, would induce readers to interpret them alike, as being derived from substantially similar processes. But this error should not be made by anyone knowledgeable about accounting processes. We do not attribute the error to Ball and Brown. But they brush it aside. For them the information content of all income numbers (note "numbers," not "measurements") is the same kind of information content, whether any test of a different kind shows some of them to be highly conservative, grossly liberal, vagrant or false. (pp. 47–49)

REQUIRED

(1) What major criticisms is Chambers making in the above comments?

(2) Critically evaluate these criticisms. Cite evidence from specific studies detailed in Chapter 11 in your answer.

QUESTION 11.4: LIFO/FIFO Accounting Changes and Stock Returns

1. The decision of *Chrysler Corporation* to switch from the LIFO to FIFO inventory valuation method (for tax and reporting purposes) was explained in the President's Letter in the *1970 Annual Report* as follows:

Sales of Chrysler Corporation and consolidated subsidiaries throughout the world in 1970 totaled $7.0 billion, compared with $7.1 billion in 1969. Operations for the year resulted in a net loss of $7.6 million or $0.16 a share, compared with net earnings of $99.0 million or $2.09 a share in 1969.

Net earnings for 1969 are restated to reflect a retroactive change in the company's method of valuing inventories, from a LIFO (last-in, first-out) to a FIFO (first-in, first-out) cost basis, as explained in the notes to financial statements. The LIFO method reduces inventory values and earnings in periods of rising costs. The rate of inflation in costs in 1970 and for the projected short term future is so high that significant understatements of inventory values and earnings result. The use of the LIFO method in 1970 would have reduced inventory amounts at December 31, 1970 by approximately $150 million and did reduce inventory amounts reported at December 31, 1969 by approximately $110 million. Also, the use of the LIFO method in 1970 would have increased the loss for the year by approximately $20.0 million, and its use in 1969 reduced the earnings as reported for that year by $10.2 million. The other three U.S. automobile manufacturers have consistently used the FIFO method. Therefore the reported loss for 1970 and the restated profit for 1969 are on a comparable basis as to inventory valuation with the other three companies. Prior years' earnings have been restated to make them comparable.

Results of operations for the first three quarters of 1970 were previously reported on the LIFO method of valuing inventories. The restated results, on the

FIFO method of valuing inventories, for the four quarters of 1970 are as follows:

	Net Earnings (Loss) (Millions)	Earnings (Loss) A Share
1st Quarter	$(27.4)	$(0.57)
2nd Quarter	10.1	0.21
3rd Quarter	2.1	0.05
4th Quarter	7.6	0.15
1970	$(7.6)	$(0.16)

A footnote to the 1970 financial statements gave further details of the inventory change:

Inventories—Accounting Change

Inventories are stated at the lower of cost or market. For the period January 1, 1957 through December 31, 1969 the last-in, first-out (LIFO) method of inventory valuation had been used for approximately 60% of the consolidated inventory. The cost of the remaining 40% of inventories was determined using the first-in, first-out (FIFO) or average cost methods. Effective January 1, 1970 the FIFO method of inventory valuation has been adopted for inventories previously valued using the LIFO method. This results in a more uniform valuation method throughout the Corporation and its consolidated subsidiaries and makes the financial statements with respect to inventory valuation comparable with those of the other United States automobile manufacturers. As a result of adopting FIFO in 1970, the net loss reported is less than it would have been on a LIFO basis by approximately $20.0 million, or $0.40 a share. Inventory amounts at December 31, 1969 and 1970 are stated higher by approximately $110.0 million and $150.0 million, respectively, than they would have been had the LIFO method been continued.

The Corporation has retroactively adjusted financial statements of prior years for this change. Accordingly, the 1969 financial statements have been restated resulting in an increase in Net Earnings of $10.2 million, and Net Earnings Retained for Use in the Business at December 31, 1969 and 1968 have been increased by $53.5 million and $43.3 million, respectively.

For United States income tax purposes the adjustment to inventory amounts will be taken into taxable income ratably over 20 years commencing January 1, 1971.

An article in the *Wall Street Journal* (February 9, 1971) predicted that as a result of the change *Chrysler's* tax bill was increased by $53 million.

REQUIRED

(1) What factors may have motivated Chrysler to make the LIFO to FIFO change?

(2) Why would the "other three U.S. automobile manufacturers have consistently used the FIFO method" over the LIFO method?

2. Sunder [1973] hypothesized the effect of a LIFO to FIFO change on the economic value of the firm as follows:

Realization of inventory holding gains results in higher reported as well as taxable earnings in the current and future accounting periods. Increased tax liability on realized inventory holding gains reduces the economic value of the firm. *Thus the economic value and reported earnings change in opposite directions.* (pp. 9–10)

REQUIRED

(1) What assumptions are implicit in the statement that "economic value and reported earnings change in opposite directions" when a U.S. firm changes from LIFO to FIFO?

(2) Assume that associated with a LIFO to FIFO change the "increased tax liability on realized inventory holding gains reduces the economic value" of firm XYZ. When would you expect this reduction in economic value of XYZ to be impounded into the security price of XYZ?

3. Sunder [1975] examined the cumulative abnormal return (CAR) behavior of 21 firms which changed from LIFO to FIFO during the 1946–1966 period. The last month of the fiscal year during which the change was made was assumed to be the month when the information about the accounting change became available to the market. The behavior of the CAR for the 24 months surrounding the date of the accounting change was

Months Prior to Accounting Change	CAR	Months Subsequent to Accounting Change	CAR
−11	.0239	1	.0189
−10	.0249	2	.0278
−9	.0100	3	.0350
−8	.0224	4	.0336
−7	.0202	5	.0160
−6	.0345	6	.0048
−5	.0408	7	−.0064
−4	.0670	8	.0154
−3	.0322	9	.0178
−2	.0330	10	.0246
−1	.0221	11	.0007
0	.0162	12	.0037

REQUIRED

(1) What evidence is there that the capital market treated the accounting change as implying that the "economic value and reported earnings" of these 21 firms changed in opposite directions?

(2) Compare and contrast the CAR behavior for the above 21 firms with the CAR behavior Sunder [1975] reported for 118 firms who changed to the LIFO inventory method—see Figure 11.8.

QUESTION 11.5: Market Reaction to Replacement Cost Disclosures

In 1977, the top 1,000 large nonfinancial U.S. corporations were required to disclose in the 10-K statements they filed with the SEC details about the replacement cost of inventories and fixed assets. One of the earliest reporters of this information was *Western Union Corp. Western Union* issued a prospectus (dated February 16, 1977) for a new offering of preferred stock. The prospectus noted net income (in $000's) for the 1972–1976 period as

1972	$32,161
1973	$26,897
1974	$35,018
1975	$33,087
1976	$34,000

Details of the replacement cost disclosures presented in the 1977 prospectus are included:

Replacement Cost Information (Unaudited)

In the communication industry, technological advances have been such that equipment is rarely replaced in kind. However, in compliance with rules of the Securities and Exchange Commission, the Corporation has estimated the cost of replacing its plant and equipment and material and supplies as of December 31, 1976, together with estimated depreciation based on replacement cost for the year then ended. The data in the following table should be read in conjunction with the comments below.

	Estimated Replacement Cost	Comparable Historical Cost
	(thousands)	
At December 31, 1976:		
Plant and Equipment:		
Outside communications plant and real estate	$ 308,881	$ 180,903
Equipment furnished customers	691,995	436,262
Inside communications plant	931,369	685,425
Other operating plant	148,132	110,963
Noncapitalized financing leases	77,280	89,783
Gross Plant & Equipment	2,157,657	1,503,336
Allowance for depreciation and amortization	543,650	389,294
Net Plant & Equipment	$1,614,007	$1,114,042
Material and supplies	$ 55,467	$ 55,467
For the Year 1976:		
Depreciation and amortization expense:		
Teletypewriter terminals on customer's premises (see below)	$ 44,067	$ 23,733
All other plant and equipment	101,533	74,075
Total	$ 145,600	$ 97,808

The following table reconciles the historical cost amounts for which replacement cost data are provided above, to the related totals shown in the financial statements:

	Gross Plant and Equipment	Allowance for Depreciation and Amortization
	(thousands)	

At December 31, 1976:

Items for which replacement cost data are provided above	$1,503,336	$ 389,294
Less: Present value of future rentals for noncapitalized financing leases as determined at inception of the leases	(89,783)	(26,727)
Add items for which no replacement cost has been estimated:		
Research and development	27,419	23,128
Plant under construction	169,670	—
Certain fully depreciated and other assets which management does not intend to replace (principally equipment utilized for the Autodin system, equipment located on railroad properties, and the TWX acquisition adjustment)	219,829	138,472
Total as shown on the accompanying balance sheet	$1,830,471	$ 524,167

	Depreciation and Amortization Expense (thousands)

For the Year Ended December 31, 1976:

Items for which replacement cost data are provided above	$ 97,808
Less: Imputed depreciation expense on noncapitalized financing leases	(3,863)
Add: Amortization of research and development	3,777
Depreciation of certain assets which management does not intend to replace	13,350
Total as shown in the accompanying statement of income	$111,072

The data set forth above represent management's estimate of the cost of replacement of productive capacity that would be incurred at December 31, 1976 if such assets were all replaced at that time based on current technology. However this should not be interpreted to indicate that management has present plans to replace such assets, or that future replacement would take place in the form and manner assumed in developing these estimates. In addition these replacement cost data are not necessarily indicative of the amounts for which such assets could be sold, nor are they necessarily representative of costs that might be incurred in a future period.

In fact replacement of plant is a continual process, and thus takes place over many years. In the past decade the Corporation has expended over $1 billion to expand and modernize its physical plant, and significant capital expenditures are expected to continue to be incurred for this purpose every year for selected portions of plant and equipment. An exception to this general rule would be teletypewriter terminals leased to customers, which account for the following amounts included above:

	Estimated Replacement Cost	Comparable Historical Cost
	(thousands)	
Net book value	$365,645	$197,114
Depreciation expense	$ 44,067	$ 23,733

Since 1973 Telex and TWX subscribers have been permitted to provide their own terminals, and since 1974 the Telegraph Company has promoted the sale of its terminals to subscribers, having sold 31,000 of its terminals to date. The Telegraph Company intends to continue this program, and therefore does not anticipate replacing that portion of its plant and equipment represented by teletypewriter terminals leased to customers.

An article in *Fortune* (March 1977) included the following comment on the market reaction to the above information:

The SEC has held that all large corporations must now publish figures showing what their depreciation charges would have been if fixed assets and inventory were valued at replacement cost. The main thought behind this new requirement is that, in an age of inflation, depreciation based on original cost does not adequately measure a company's ability to replace its productive capacity.

The SEC has been cagey about what it expected to happen when the new reports were published. It said that the reports would give investors "a better understanding" and would "improve investment decision-making." The commission said nothing about the effect of this superior thinking on stock prices. But presumably there would be some effect; it just doesn't seem reasonable to impose heavy new accounting expenses (and the SEC admits they're heavy) on business unless some tangible results are anticipated.

If the SEC was expecting the new rules to have some stock-market consequences, it must have been confounded by the Western Union case. The prospectus filed by the company last month shows that, with traditional accounting methods, it earned about $34 million for all of 1976. That figure is roughly what Wall Street was expecting, based on the quarterly reports issued during the year. However, replacement-cost accounting wipes out the entire profit and leaves the company with a $500,000 deficit. You might think that qualifies as a stunner.

The stock market's response suggests that it had known this all along. On the day the prospectus was issued, Western Union was off all of 1/8, closing at 19—close to where it had been for several weeks. Two weeks later, the price was still around 19.

The stock market is really pretty damn smart. (pp. 129–130)

REQUIRED

(1) Assume that prior to 1977 the SEC commissioned you to prepare a report on the likely consequences of replacement cost disclosures on the capital market. Present your conclusions, making explicit any assumptions and evidence that is important in your report.

(2) Comment on the conclusion drawn in the *Fortune* article that, based on the reaction to the *Western Union* case, "the stock market is really pretty damn smart."

(3) Assume that subsequent to 1977 the SEC commissioned you to study the capital market reaction to the replacement cost disclosures of the 1,000 large nonfinancial corporations. The basic issue to be addressed is whether the capital market perceived the disclosures to provide new information pertinent to revaluing security prices. Describe any problems you expect to encounter in your study.

REFERENCES

BALL, R. J. "Changes in Accounting Techniques and Stock Prices." *Empirical Research in Accounting, Selected Studies* (1972): 1–38.

———. "Anomalies in Relationships Between Securities' Yields and Yield-Surrogates." Unpublished Paper, University of Chicago, Chicago, Oct. 1976.

BALL, R., and BROWN, P. "An Empirical Evaluation of Accounting Income Numbers." *Journal of Accounting Research* (Autumn 1968): 159–178.

BEAVER, W. H. "The Information Content of Annual Earnings Announcements." *Empirical Research in Accounting: Selected Studies*, 1968. Supplement to *Journal of Accounting Research* (1968): 67–92.

———. "The Information Content of the Magnitude of Unexpected Earnings." Unpublished Paper, Stanford University, Stanford, Calif., 1974.

BEAVER, W. H., and DUKES, R. E. "Interperiod Tax Allocation, Earnings Expectations and the Behavior of Security Prices." *The Accounting Review* (Apr. 1972): 320–332.

————. "Delta-Depreciation Methods: Some Empirical Results." *The Accounting Review* (July 1973): 549–559.

BENISHAY, H. "Market Preferences for Characteristics of Common Stocks." *The Economic Journal* (Mar. 1973): 173–191.

BENSTON, G. "Published Corporate Accounting Data and Stock Prices." *Empirical Research in Accounting: Selected Studies, 1967.* Supplement to *Journal of Accounting Research* (1967): 1–54.

BENSTON, G. J. "There's No Real News in Earnings Reports." *Fortune* (Apr. 1976): 73–75.

BLACK, F., and SCHOLES, M. "The Behavior of Security Returns Around Ex-Dividend Days." Unpublished Paper, University of Chicago, Chicago, 1973.

————. "The Effects of Dividend Yield and Dividend Policy on Common Stock Prices and Returns." *Journal of Financial Economics* (May 1974): 1–22.

BLUME, M. E. "Betas and Their Regression Tendencies." *Journal of Finance* (June 1975): 785–796.

BROWN, P., "The Impact of the Annual Net Profit on the Stock Market." *The Australian Accountant* (July 1970): 277–282.

————. "Those Half-Year Reports." *Society Bulletin No. 13.* Australian Society of Accountants, Melbourne, 1972.

BROWN, P., and HANCOCK, P. "Profit Reports and the Share Market." Unpublished Paper, University of Western Australia, Perth, W.A., 1974.

BROWN, P., and KENNELLY, J. "The Information Content of Quarterly Earnings: An Extension and Some Further Evidence." *Journal of Business* (July 1972): 403–415.

CASSIDY, D. B. "Investor Evaluation of Accounting Information: Some Additional Empirical Evidence." *Journal of Accounting Research* (Autumn 1976): 212–229.

CHAMBERS, R. J. "Stock Market Prices and Accounting Research." *Abacus* (June 1974): 39–54.

DANN, L. Y., MAYERS, D., and RAAB, R. J. "Trading Rules, Large Blocks and the Speed of Price Adjustment." *Journal of Financial Economics* (Jan. 1977): 3–22.

DEAKIN, E. B., NORWOOD, G. R., and SMITH, C. H. "The Effect of Published Earnings Information on Tokyo Stock Exchange Trading." *International Journal of Accounting* (Fall 1974): 124–136.

DEMSKI, J. S. "Discussion of Relationship Between Accounting Changes and Stock Prices: Problems of Measurement and Some Empirical Evidence." *Empirical Research in Accounting: Selected Studies, 1973.* Supplement to *Journal of Accounting Research* (1973): 46–54.

FORSGARDH, L. E., and HERTZEN, K., "The Adjustment of Stock Prices to New Earnings Information." In E. J. Elton and M. J. Gruber (eds.), *International Capital Markets*. North-Holland, Amsterdam, 1975: 68–86.

FOSTER, G. "Stock Market Reaction to Estimates of Earnings Per Share by Company Officials." *Journal of Accounting Research* (Spring 1973): 25–37.

———. "Accounting Earnings and Stock Prices of Insurance Companies." *The Accounting Review* (Oct. 1975): 686–698.

———. "Security Price Revaluation Implications of Sub-Earnings Disclosure." *Journal of Accounting Research* (Autumn 1975a): 283–292.

———. "Quarterly Accounting Data: Time-Series Properties and Predictive-Ability Results." *The Accounting Review* (Jan. 1977): 1–21.

GONEDES, N. J. "Capital Market Equilibrium and Annual Accounting Numbers: Empirical Evidence." *Journal of Accounting Research* (Spring 1974): 26–62.

———. "Risk, Information, and the Effects of Special Accounting Items on Capital Market Equilibrium." *Journal of Accounting Research* (Autumn 1975): 220–256.

———. "Section 8 of Discussion Notes for Business 430: Analysis of Financial Statements—Accounting Procedures." Unpublished Paper, University of Chicago, Chicago, 1976.

———. "Corporate Signaling, External Accounting and Capital Market Equilibrium: Evidence on Dividends, Income and Extraordinary Items." Center for Mathematical Studies in Business Economics, University of Chicago, Chicago, 1976a.

GONEDES, N. J., and DOPUCH, N., "Capital Market Equilibrium, Information Production, and Selecting Accounting Techniques: Theoretical Framework and Review of Empirical Work." *Studies in Financial Accounting Objectives: 1974*. Supplement to *Journal of Accounting Research* (1974): 48–129.

GRIFFIN, P. A. "Competitive Information in the Stock Market: An Empirical Study of Earnings, Dividends and Analysts Forecasts." *Journal of Finance* (May 1976): 631–650.

HAGERMAN, R. L. "The Efficiency of the Market for Bank Stocks: An Empirical Test." *Journal of Money, Credit and Banking* (Aug. 1973): 846–855.

HOLLANDER, M., and WOLFE, D. A., *Non Parametric Statistical Methods*. Wiley, New York, 1973.

HONG, H., KAPLAN, R. S., and MANDELKER, G., "Pooling vs. Purchase: The Effects of Accounting for Mergers on Stock Prices." Working Paper 26-74-65, GSIA, Carnegie-Mellon University, Pittsburgh, 1976.

Joy, O. M., Litzenberger, R. H., and McEnally, R. W. "The Adjustment of Stock Prices to Announcements of Unanticipated Changes in Quarterly Earnings." Stanford University, Stanford, Calif., 1977 (forthcoming in *Journal of Accounting Research*).

Kaplan, R. S., and Roll, R. "Investor Evaluation of Accounting Information: Some Empirical Evidence." *Journal of Business* (Apr. 1972): 225–257.

Kiger, J. E. "An Empirical Investigation of NYSE Volume and Price Reactions to the Announcement of Quarterly Earnings." *Journal of Accounting Research* (Spring 1972): 113–128.

Lev, B., and Yahalomi, B. "The Effect of Corporate Financial Statements on the Israeli Stock Exchange." *Management International Review* (1972): 145–150.

Lintner, J. "Distribution of Incomes of Corporations among Dividends, Retained Earnings and Taxes," *American Economic Review* (May 1956): 97–113.

May, R. "The Influence of Quarterly Earnings Announcements on Investor Decisions as Reflected in Common Stock Price Changes." *Empirical Research in Accounting: Selected Studies* (1971): Supplement to *Journal of Accounting Research* (1971): 119–163.

Morgan, I. G. "Stock Returns and Heteroscedasticity." *Journal of Business* (Oct. 1976): 496–508.

Nerlove, M. "Factors Affecting Differences Among Rates of Return on Investments in Individual Common Stocks." *Review of Economics and Statistics* (Aug. 1968): 312–331.

O'Connor, M. D. "Usefulness of Financial Ratios to Investors." *The Accounting Review* (Apr. 1973): 339–352.

Patell, J. M. "Corporate Forecasts of Earnings Per Share and Stock Price Behavior: Empirical Tests." *Journal of Accounting Research* (Autumn 1976): 246–276.

Rozeff, M. S., and Kinney, W. R. "Capital Market Seasonality: The Case of Stock Returns." *Journal of Financial Economics* (Oct. 1976): 379–402.

Spangler, C. W. "The Effects of Unanticipated Changes in Dividends on Security Returns." Unpublished Master of Science Thesis, M.I.T., Cambridge, Mass., 1973.

Sterling, R. T. "On Theory Construction and Verification." *The Accounting Review* (July 1970): 444–457.

Sunder, S. "Relationship Between Accounting Changes and Stock Prices: Problems of Measurement and Some Empirical Evidence." *Empirical Research in Accounting: Selected Studies, 1973.* Supplement to *Journal of Accounting Research* (1973): 1–45.

————. "Accounting Changes in Inventory Valuation." *The Accounting Review* (Apr. 1975): 305–315.

————. "Optimal Choice Between FIFO and LIFO." *Journal of Accounting Research* (Autumn 1976): 277–300.

Taylor, R. G. "An Examination of the Evolution, Content, Utility and Problems of Published Interim Reports." Unpublished Ph.D. Dissertation, University of Chicago, Chicago, 1963.

Watts, R. L., and Zimmerman, J. L. "Towards a Positive Theory of the Determination of Accounting Standards." Working Paper 7628, University of Rochester, Rochester, 1976 (forthcoming in *The Accounting Review*).

CHAPTER **12**

INVESTMENT DECISIONS: IMPLICATIONS OF THE EVIDENCE

What implications does the material in prior chapters have for investment decisions? In Section 12.1 we shall address this issue for an investor who assumes that the capital market is efficient with respect to publicly available information. Then in Section 12.2, investment choice in a near-efficient market is considered. The important topic of performance evaluation is discussed in Section 12.3.

12.1   INVESTMENT CHOICE IN AN EFFICIENT MARKET

The implications of efficient markets for investment choice are often misstated or misunderstood. Consider the following comment by Bernstein [1975]:

> Among the investment lessons that the efficient markets hypothesis teaches us are the following...
> —Random selection of securities is as good as any other. Therefore, practice your dart throwing skill.
> —A buy-and-hold policy is as good as any other. Therefore, it is not necessary to follow and keep up with the fundamentals of the companies in which you own securities. (p. 59)

Neither of these "lessons" is implied by an efficient capital market. Constructing a portfolio that suits the risk-return and other preferences of an investor is considerably more involved than implied by the above comment. The key elements of investment choice in an efficient market—high diversification, low turnover, and risk control—will be noted below.

A   Random Selection of Securities?

Investors differ on several dimensions pertinent to security selection. Consider risk preferences. In general, it is not the case that all investors want to hold a portfolio with a beta of 1. For instance, an investor approaching retirement may prefer a portfolio with lower risk than the market portfolio. For this investor, a policy of placing all funds in a randomly selected set of securities would be inappropriate; the best estimate of the beta of a portfolio formed via random selection is 1 and this is deemed too risky by the investor. In deciding what is the appropriate risk-return trade-off for each investor, it is important to know the slope of the efficient frontier. Assuming a Sharpe-Lintner asset pricing model, this slope will depend on R_f and $E(\tilde{R}_M)$. Figure 12.1 and Figure 12.2 present

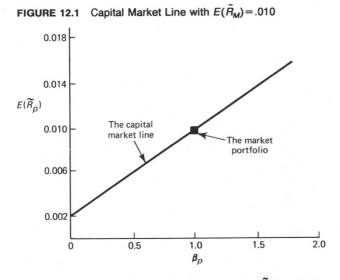

FIGURE 12.1   Capital Market Line with $E(\tilde{R}_M)=.010$

two different efficient frontiers: In Figure 12.1, $E(\tilde{R}_M)=.010$ per month and $R_f=.002$ per month, while in Figure 12.2 $E(\tilde{R}_M)=.018$ and $R_f=.002$. These differences in $E(\tilde{R}_M)$ imply that the market's reward for bearing a unit of risk is lower in Figure 12.1. In Figure 12.1 a portfolio with $\beta=.5$ has an expected return of .006 per month, while in Figure 12.2 a portfolio with $\beta=.5$ has an expected return of .010 per month.

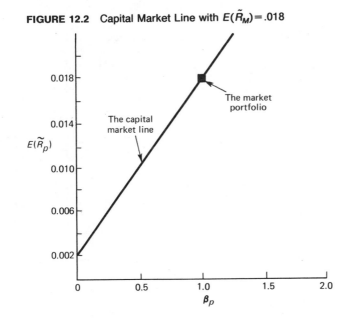

FIGURE 12.2   Capital Market Line with $E(\tilde{R}_M)=.018$

The slopes of the efficient frontiers in Figures 12.1 and 12.2 were for two hypothetical cases. In practice, investors have to use available information to estimate the slope of the efficient frontier facing them at a particular instant. The work of Ibbotson and Sinquefield [1977] illustrates one approach to this estimation issue. They first examined the historical record of several security market series over the 1926–1976 period. The results are reported in Table 12.1. Thus, over this period common stocks had both higher return and higher risk than long-term corporate bonds, government bonds, and U.S. Treasury bills. They then used this information and information about the capital market's year-by-year forecasts of interest rates (as revealed in the government bond yield curve) to predict the expected return on stocks and bonds over the 1977–2000 period. Their prediction of the expected geometric return was 12.5% per year for common stocks, 7.6% for long-term corporate bonds, 7.1% for long-term government bonds, and 5.5% for U.S. Treasury bills. The Ibbotson and Sinquefield [1977] approach illustrates one way of gaining information about the slope of the efficient frontier. For an investor assuming an efficient market, this information is one of the most important he can acquire when making his portfolio selection decisions.

TABLE 12.1 Investment Total Annual Returns: 1926–1976

Series	Geometric Mean (%)	Arithmetic Mean (%)	Standard Deviation (%)	Distribution
Common stocks	9.2	11.6	22.4	
Long-term corporate bonds	4.1	4.2	5.6	
Long-term government bonds	3.4	3.5	5.8	
U.S. Treasury bills	2.4	2.4	2.1	
Inflation	2.3	2.4	4.8	

−50%   0   50%

SOURCE: Ibbotson and Sinquefield [1977, Exhibit 3].

Dividend Preferences of Investors

A random selection of securities will, on average, result in a portfolio with a dividend yield approximating that of the market portfolio. Yet, some investors desire a portfolio with quite different dividend yield characteristics. These desires arise (in part) from the differential tax treatment of dividends and capital gains. Capital gains for individuals are taxed at lower rates and only when realized. As a result, individual investors in high tax brackets will generally prefer returns in the form of capital gains rather than dividends. In contrast, a corporation may prefer dividend returns to capital gains returns due to 85% of corporate dividends not being subject to corporate income tax.

Choosing a portfolio to match these different dividend preferences of investors is considerably more involved than "randomly selecting securities." Sharpe and Sosin [1976] provide a good analysis of some of the trade-offs involved in choosing a portfolio with a dividend yield different from the market average. They first examined the dispersion across securities in dividend yield. Starting in 1927 the dividend yield of each NYSE stock was calculated and that stock placed into one of ten yield deciles. Decile 10 contains the 10% of the stocks with the lowest current yield...decile 1 contains the highest 10%. The realized dividend yield of each decile portfolio was computed for the next year. This procedure was repeated for each year up to 1968. The result was ten portfolios that systematically differed as regards dividend yield—see Table 12.2. The annual excess return (i.e., $\tilde{R}_p - R_f$) and beta of each portfolio are also presented in Table 12.2.[1] Although there is nothing in theory that suggests dividend yield and beta should be negatively correlated, empirically they

TABLE 12.2   Dividend Yields of NYSE Stocks: 1927–1968

Portfolio	Dividend Yield (%)	Excess Return (%)	Beta
10	.90	20.43	1.52
9	2.08	17.47	1.33
8	2.98	16.10	1.19
7	3.72	15.26	1.09
6	4.31	14.56	1.02
5	5.11	13.75	.94
4	5.81	13.11	.86
3	6.40	12.74	.81
2	6.97	12.46	.80
1	8.10	13.12	.82

SOURCE: Sharpe and Sosin [1976, Figures 1–3].

appear to be—the Spearman rank correlation between the dividend yield and the beta of the ten portfolios in Table 12.2 is −.96. This negative correlation creates problems in portfolio design. Sharpe and Sosin note that it is extremely difficult to construct well-diversified portfolios that have both high (low) dividend yield and high (low) betas. They conclude the following:

> It should not prove difficult to construct a portfolio with relatively little non-market risk, average market risk (i.e., a beta value of 1.0) and yield differing from the market average by up to 100 basis points.... On the other hand, attempts to depart substantially from the market average yield may seriously degrade risk-adjusted performance. Holding total risk constant, any attempt to alter yield from the market average by 200 to 300 basis points may result in a decrease of 25 to 75 basis points in total return. This penalty may be necessary in some circumstances, but should not be borne lightly or unwittingly. (p. 41)

In designing a portfolio of securities that has characteristics markedly different from the market portfolio one will, in general, encounter problems in achieving diversification. Attempts to minimize the effects of this limited diversification require the extensive use of computer algorithms. In this context, a simple *random selection* approach is unlikely to result in a diversified portfolio that is consistent with the objectives of the investor.[2]

B Buy and Hold Policy?

It is a common misinterpretation of the efficient markets model that a *buy and hold* policy is the appropriate portfolio strategy. Over time a buy and hold policy can result in a portfolio that is both inadequately diversified and not consistent with an investor's risk preferences.[3] Consider an investor who wishes to maintain a portfolio with a beta or relative risk of 1.4. Over time, the relative weights of the stocks in the portfolio will change as each stock exhibits differential price behavior. It will only be by coincidence that these changing weights will result in the portfolio beta of 1.4 remaining constant.

The above problem arises due to the weights in the portfolio changing over time. Another problem arises because the betas of individual stocks in the portfolio may change over time. Indeed, there is considerable evidence that changes in the risks of stocks occur—see Chapter 9. Firms, for instance, do change their capital structure over time, do change their operating leverage, and do change their lines of business activity. These changes in the economic characteristics of firms can induce changes in the betas of their securities.

The result of these factors is that portfolio rebalancing is necessary to maintain a portfolio that is both diversified and consistent with an investor's objectives. This rebalancing is achieved by buying and selling individual securities. Hence, in any rebalancing exercise it is important to assess the beta of individual securities. It is in this phase of investment analysis that accounting information can play a role. For instance, Rosenberg and Marathe [1975] illustrate the gains from combining both accounting and nonaccounting information in beta assessment—see Chapter 9.

The above discussion indicates that a literal interpretation of the buy and hold statement provides, in general, an inappropriate guideline for investment decisions. The phrase "passive portfolio strategy" appears a more descriptive phrase for investment choice in a market which "fully reflects available information." Black [1971] describes the *passive strategy* as follows:

> It is important for the investor to choose a well-diversified portfolio and it is important for him to choose a portfolio that fits his objectives, including his tax status and his ability to tolerate fluctuations in the value of his portfolio. But once he has a portfolio, he should make changes only to keep it diversified, to fit it to changing objectives, to generate cash, or to realize tax losses. (p. 22)

One tool that an investor can use in a passive portfolio strategy is an index fund. These funds are described below.

C Index Funds as a Diversification Tool

An important element of an investment strategy in an efficient market is the construction of a well-diversified portfolio. Index funds can provide this diversification with a minimum level of transaction costs. An index fund is a portfolio that attempts to match the performance of a chosen index. The index funds of the following institutions will be used to illustrate important features of these funds:

(1) *American National Bank and Trust Company of Chicago* (Chicago, Illinois),

(2) *Batterymarch Financial Management Corp.* (Boston, Massachusetts),

(3) *First Index Investment Trust* (Valley Forge, Pennsylvania), and

(4) *Wells Fargo Bank* (San Francisco, California).

Each of the funds operated by these institutions attempts to match the performance of *Standard & Poor's 500 Stock Index*. A variety of factors will affect the extent to which each fund will match this index, e.g., the number of stocks held, transaction costs, management fees, and the procedures used for reinvesting dividends. Changes in the companies in the index[4] and changes in the number of shares outstanding of those in the index (e.g., through a company repurchasing stock) will also affect the ability of the fund to match the index.

At presént there is debate over the construction of index funds. One policy (followed essentially in the index fund operated by *Wells Fargo*) is to purchase all stocks in *Standard & Poor's Stock Index* in their value-weighted proportions. However, in an effort to reduce transactions costs, several funds have attempted to hold fewer stocks.[5] The *First Index Investment Trust* provided the following details on the construction of its fund:

> The Trust's investment policy will be to attempt to duplicate the investment performance of the Index by owning as many of the 500 stocks contained in the Index as is feasible. These stocks will generally be selected for the Trust's portfolio in order of their weightings in the Index (based on each stock's total market value), beginning with the heaviest-weighted stocks. The Trust will own no fewer than the 200 stocks having the largest weightings, which presently represent more than 85% of the total weighting of the Index and thus are largely responsible for its performance. These stocks would also presently represent more than 85% of the value of the Trust's portfolio.

> The remainder of the portfolio may include both a representative sampling of the other 300 stocks in the Index and slightly larger proportionate holdings of the first 200 stocks, which will be selected according to statistical methods approved by the Trustees. It is believed that this policy will result in a close correlation between the investment performance of the Trust and that of the Index. (*Preliminary Prospectus*—July 30, 1976, p. 2)

First Index stated that based "on the performance of model portfolios and various other studies" they expected the following: "the correlation between the performance of the Trust and that of the Index will be above 0.98" (p. 5).

In contrast, *American National Bank and Trust Company of Chicago* does not always hold all of the large stocks in the *Standard & Poor's Stock Index* in their Employee Benefit Index Fund:

> American National...buys only 250 or so of the S & P stocks, but they are not all the largest. American National uses what is known as a "stratified sampling" method to select its stocks. The companies in the S & P are divided into ten groups on the basis of their weights and risk levels. A computer then selects from among the ten groups to build a portfolio that has the overall risk characteristics and industry diversification of the S & P. (Ehrbar [1976, p. 152])

The quarterly return performance of the *American National's* Employee Benefit Index Fund over the 1974–1976 period suggests that even without holding all 500 stocks in the *Standard & Poors Stock Index*, they have been able to match the index "reasonably well":

Quarters	S & P 500	Employee Benefit Index Fund
1974, 1	−2.80	−2.80
1974, 2	−7.56	−7.43
1974, 3	−25.19	−25.62
1974, 4	+9.43	+9.04
1975, 1	+22.93	+23.40
1975, 2	+15.32	+15.67
1975, 3	−10.95	−11.12
1975, 4	+8.63	+8.64
1976, 1	+14.97	+14.88
1976, 2	+2.48	+2.67
1976, 3	+1.91	+2.06
1976, 4	+3.14	+2.11
	24.92	23.63

Batterymarch [1977] purchases "capitalized-weighted positions in the 250 companies of the *Standard & Poor's 500* that have the largest capitalization and that pass through our prudence screens" (p. 9). They provide the following result on the performance of the fund over the January 1975–December 1976 period:

$$\tilde{R}_{p,t} = -.072 + .989\tilde{R}_{M,t},$$

where $\tilde{R}_{p,t}$ = return on *Batterymarch* fund in month t,

$\tilde{R}_{M,t}$ = return on *Standard & Poor's 500 Stock Index* in month t.

A critical element in a passive portfolio strategy is the reduction of transactions costs. On this score, index funds are very attractive to an investor who decides that the search for under- or overvalued securities is an unrewarding activity. Transaction costs can be reduced in both the initial construction of the portfolio and in its ongoing operation. For instance, *American National Bank* [1976] notes that since the inception of their index fund they have been "incurring trading costs of less than 0.2%. This is well below the $1\frac{1}{2}$–3% that has been estimated as the trading cost for conventional portfolios" (p. 8).

Another (related) advantage of an index fund is a reduction in turnover. For instance, the *Fourth Quarter Report* (December 31, 1976) of the *Wells Fargo Bank* Index Fund noted the following:

The Index Fund is designed to operate with low turnover, thus significantly reducing transaction costs as compared with conventionally-managed portfolios. Sales turnover resulting in transactions costs to participants occurs only when the Standard and Poor's Corporation removes a stock from the Index or when our own screening activities eliminate an issue. The Index Fund's sales turnover calculated by taking sales as a percentage of the average monthly market value, was 3.73% in 1976. Of the total turnover 2.71% was incurred in July 1976 when the Index was redefined to include the Finance Industry. Since Standard & Poor's stated policy for the administration of the Composite Stock Price Index has been to hold composition changes to a minimum (for the 1966–1975 period, an average of 6.7 deletions per year were experienced) it is reasonable to consider July's turnover experience as a non-recurring event. (p.2)

American National Bank [1976] noted that for their Employee Benefit Index Fund they have a "negligible turnover rate (about 2%) as compared to the institutional average turnover rate of 25%" (p. 8).

One problem in wider acceptance of index funds is uncertainty over how the courts will view an investment trustee who places all his equity money in an index fund. Traditionally, courts have been concerned about the investment characteristics of individual securities when deciding on the prudence of investment trustees.[6] In an efficient market, concentration at the individual security level appears misplaced. The concern with individual securities is only with regard to their contribution to portfolio risk and return. Langbein and Posner [1976] have provided a detailed analysis of trust investment law from an efficient market perspective. They concluded that although existing law appears consistent with concentration on individual security characteristics,[7] it would be naive to assume the courts would remain ignorant of efficient capital markets research:

> We began with the question whether trust law would permit the trustee to implement the lessons of capital market research and adopt a buy-the-market investment strategy. We think we should conclude our review of the trust law by warning fiduciaries that they cannot "play safe" by ignoring the new learning and continuing uncritically to put trust money into old-fashioned, managed portfolios. When market [index] funds have become available in sufficient variety and their experience bears out their prospects, courts may one day conclude that it is imprudent for trustees to fail to use such vehicles. Their advantages seem decisive: at any given risk/return level, diversification is maximized and investment costs minimized. A trustee who declines to procure such advantages for the beneficiaries of his trust may in the future find his conduct difficult to justify. (p. 30)

Although the proportion of investment money placed in index funds is currently small, it appears safe to assume that this proportion will be an increasing one in the future.[8]

12.2 INVESTMENT CHOICE IN A NEAR-EFFICIENT MARKET

Although much of the available evidence is consistent with the efficient markets model, there are several notable studies inconsistent with the model. The Jaffe [1974] study of the capital markets' reaction to publicly released insider trading information is an important exception. Corporate officials who qualify as *insiders* are required to file details of their trading in securities of the relevant company with the *Securities and Exchange Commission*. The SEC publishes this information in the *Official Summary of Insider Trading*. The summary is compiled from month-end reports of insiders and is in print approximately five weeks after the last transaction. Jaffe reported that a policy of investing in stocks in which evidence of "intensive" insider trading was publicly available would have yielded an eight-month cumulative abnormal return of 4.93%. This abnormal return was different from zero at at least the .001 significance level.[9] Another study that is inconsistent with the efficient markets models is Black's [1973] analysis of the *Value Line Investment Survey* recommendations over the 1965–1970 period—see Chapter 10. Yet another study suggesting a less than instantaneous reaction to publicly available information is the Joy et al. [1977] analysis of the capital market reaction to interim earnings over the 1964–1968 period—see Chapter 11. The results of these studies and much anecdotal evidence have led some to argue that although the efficient markets model may explain much of capital market behavior, there do exist nontrivial departures from efficiency that can be detected and exploited by investors. The phrase "active portfolio management" is used to describe an investment approach that attempts to detect and exploit perceived departures from efficiency.

A Directions for Security Analysis

Suppose an analyst believes that he can detect situations in which the market does not instantaneously impound all available information. What guidance can we offer him? The *first* guidance is for the analyst to decide where he thinks his comparative ability lies—e.g., is it in forecasting the overall market or in detecting individual securities that are mispriced? Table 12.3 presents a matrix that is taken from Ambachtsheer [1972]. The message of this matrix is that different strategies are appropriate for different kinds of comparative advantages. As an aside, note that the bottom right-hand section of the matrix represents the situation discussed in Section 12.1, i.e., investment choice in an efficient market.

The *second* guidance is for the analyst to *document as well as possible that his judgment is not one that has already been reached by the market.* Assume an analyst, after studying a "mosaic of information," concludes that the expected EPS of a company is $3.20, as opposed to last year's EPS of $4.00. Furthermore, suppose the current EPS forecasts reported by several other analysts are in the $4.80–$5.00 range. The analyst must decide if the impact of the $3.20 forecast is already impounded into the security price of the stock. An analysis of the security returns since the past

TABLE 12.3   Investment Strategies and Investment Abilities

Specific Security Return Forecasting Ability \ *Market Return Forecasting Ability*	*Good*	*Poor*
Good	1. Run concentrated portfolio 2. Manage beta around long-term average˜ desired	1. Run concentrated portfolio 2. Keep beta at desired long-term average
Poor	1. Run well-diversified portfolio 2. Manage beta around desired long-term average	1. Run well-diversified portfolio 2. Keep beta at desired long-term average

SOURCE: Ambachtsheer [1972, Table 1].

earnings announcement can be useful in this decision. In making this analysis, it would be important to control for market factors and any specific corporate announcements (e.g., for dividends) in the period examined. The CAR technique described in Appendix 11.A could be used to control for movements in the market index. The results described in Chapter 11 also provide evidence on the "typical" reaction of stocks to a dividend announcement. Suppose after controlling for market movements and all observable information announcements that the cumulative abnormal return (CAR) since the last annual earnings announcement is −20%. This negative CAR does not necessarily mean that this abnormal return is due to a market consensus of a decrease in EPS. However, given the attempts to control for other factors, there would be an increased probability that the market consensus of the change in EPS to be reported by the company is at least in the direction predicted by the analyst.

What Variables To Predict?

The evidence examined in Chapter 11 highlights the potential gains from predicting financial variables more efficiently than predictions implicit in capital asset prices. For example, by perfectly predicting the *sign* of the annual earnings change 12 months in advance of its public release, a simple trading strategy yielding approximately a 7% abnormal return could be devised—see Ball and Brown [1968]. By perfectly predicting the *sign* of the quarterly earnings change 1 month in advance of its public release, a trading strategy yielding a 1.6% abnormal return could be devised—see Foster [1977].

The CAR techniques used to estimate the above abnormal returns could also be applied to help determine which other financial variables are likely to be worth forecasting. For instance, suppose it is determined that, using the approach in Ball and Brown [1968], there are no abnormal returns from knowing a firm's current ratio 12 months in advance. With this evidence an analyst may revise his assessments about allocating scarce resources to the forecasting of this ratio. As in any empirical exercise, the results of any CAR experiment apply strictly to the sample examined and the techniques used. For instance, it may well be that a multivariate perspective would reveal that advance knowledge of a current ratio is of potential significance. In designing such experiments, it is important to draw on both theoretical and empirical findings. More confidence can be placed in an empirical study when there is a theoretical underpinning to both the techniques used in the analysis and in the rationale for the observed findings.

B Assess the Extent of Comparative Advantage

It is important that an analyst who believes he can detect divergences between current market prices and *intrinsic values* assess the extent of his comparative advantage. The perceived potential gains from detecting over- and undervalued securities should be balanced against the costs of using the fundamental analysis approach to investment choice. Those costs can be substantial. For instance, there are costs of acquiring and analyzing information to obtain an estimate of intrinsic value. There are transaction costs in buying and selling securities perceived as "mispriced." There are also costs of holding an undiversified portfolio in a market which only rewards investors for incurring nondiversifiable risk. An undiversified portfolio is implicit in a fundamental security analysis approach. Those securities perceived to be undervalued (overvalued) will be given a higher (lower) weighting vis-à-vis their weighting in a portfolio which attempts to approximate the market portfolio.[10]

Some results by Sharpe [1975] on one security analysis approach—*market timing*—indicate the importance of an analyst assessing the extent of his comparative advantage. A market timing approach attempts to hold common stocks during *bull* markets and cash equivalents during *bear* markets. The key problem is obviously to predict when bull and bear markets will occur. Sharpe assumed that the investor received perfect foreknowledge of the one-year-ahead returns on both cash equivalents and stocks. Using this knowledge, the investor invested in stocks if their return exceeded cash equivalents and in cash equivalents if their return exceeded stocks. This procedure was repeated for each year of the 1934–1972 period. The annual return on this perfect foreknowledge strategy was 15.25%. In contrast, a policy of *passive investment* in common stocks over this period would have yielded an annual return of 12.76%.

An analyst would, of course, have less than perfect knowledge of next year's returns. A crucial issue is how superior his predictive ability must be to justify a market timing approach to investment. Sharpe concluded that for a realistic set of assumptions one had to correctly predict the timing of the market "three times out of four, merely to match the performance" of a passive portfolio policy of investing in a common stock market portfolio:

> If he is right less often, his relative performance will be inferior. There are two reasons for this. First, [he] will often have his funds in cash equivalents in good market years, sacrificing the higher returns stocks provide in such years. Second, he will incur transaction costs in making switches, many of which will prove to be unprofitable. (p. 67)

The requirement that an analyst be able to predict the timing of the market returns for stocks and cash equivalents in more than three years out of four is obviously quite a stringent one.

12.3 PERFORMANCE EVALUATION

Performance evaluation is a vital activity in assessing the various approaches to investment decision making. Indeed, one of the strongest arguments for a passive approach to portfolio management comes from studies examining the performance of actively managed funds. Performance evaluation is also important for investors who perceive they have a comparative advantage in detecting mispriced securities. Over time these investors should be able to demonstrate that their selections yield abnormal returns.

A Risk-Return Evaluations

A performance bench mark based on the Sharpe-Lintner asset pricing model has been used in many studies of performance evaluation. In this section we shall illustrate this bench mark. Recall that the Sharpe-Lintner asset pricing model (see Chapter 8) is

$$E(\tilde{R}_i) = R_f + \beta_i \left[E(\tilde{R}_M) - R_f \right]. \qquad (12.1)$$

Rearranging (12.1) to the excess returns formulation yields

$$E(\tilde{R}_i) - R_f = \beta_i \big[E(\tilde{R}_M) - R_f \big]. \qquad (12.2)$$

Equation (12.2) is the theoretical underpinning to the *alpha* evaluation measure proposed by Jensen [1968]:

$$\big[\tilde{R}_i - R_f\big] = \hat{\alpha} + \hat{\beta}_i \big[\tilde{R}_M - R_f\big] + u_i. \qquad (12.3)$$

The theoretical model predicts that $\hat{\alpha}$ should be zero. Assume an analyst recommends holding *Diamond Shamrock Corp.* over the January 1, 1973–December 31, 1975 period. Using ordinary least squares to estimate (12.3) yielded

$$\big[\tilde{R}_i - R_f\big] = \underset{t=3.010}{.0386} + \underset{t=5.342}{1.1624} \times \big[\tilde{R}_M - R_f\big]. \qquad (12.4)$$

The $\hat{\alpha}$ of .0386 for *Diamond Shamrock* has a $t=3.010$; one can reject the hypothesis of no abnormal returns at a 5% significant level. This does not necessarily mean that the security analyst who made the recommendation possessed superior investment skills. The problem of sampling variation needs to be considered.

Consider the hypothesis that an analyst had no "superior ability" and his buy recommendations yielded positive abnormal returns 50% of the time and negative abnormal returns the other 50% of the time. If one examined the recommendations of this analyst and found that 75% of the recommendations had positive abnormal returns, what inferences about the initial hypothesis could be made? A significant factor in this decision would be the number of recommendations examined. If the initial hypothesis is correct and 4 recommendations were examined, the probability of finding a *success rate* of $\geq 75\%$ is .3125.[11] In an examination of 8 recommendations, the corresponding probability drops to .145. In a sample of 12 recommendations, this probability further drops to .073. The message is clear. The more recommendations examined, the more confidence one has in drawing conclusions about whether an analyst has "superior" ability.

It is important to note that when using (12.2) and (12.3) in performance evaluation, we are testing the joint hypothesis that the Sharpe-Lintner asset pricing model is descriptively valid and that the analyst had no "superior ability." As noted in Chapter 8, it is an unsettled question whether Sharpe-Lintner is a descriptively valid model of the pricing of traded securities. Thus, questions arise as to the appropriateness of its use as a performance bench mark.[12] Performance evaluation is one area where the results of more definitive tests of asset pricing models (e.g., through the use of indexes better approximating that used in deriving the theoretical model) would be particularly useful.

B Performance of Mutual Funds

There is now substantial evidence that, using (12.2) and (12.3) as a bench mark, the performance of mutual funds is consistent with portfolio managers having no superior ability to either time the market or to detect mispriced securities. We shall briefly examine the Jensen [1968] study and note the results of several subsequent studies.

Jensen [1968] examined the performance of 115 open-end mutual funds over the 1945–1964 period. The average beta of these funds was .840, with a range of .219–1.405. The alpha (α) in (12.3) was estimated for a variety of returns measures—e.g., (1) fund returns *gross* of all management expenses and (2) fund returns net of all expenses such as bookkeeping and research. For returns measured gross of expenses, the average $\hat{\alpha}$ was $-.004$ per year; the average $\hat{\alpha}$ when returns were measured net of expenses was $-.011$. These results indicate that, *on average*, the 115 mutual funds did not earn abnormal returns over this period even before taking into account the management expenses. Jensen also examined whether there was consistency over time in the abnormal performance of individual funds; he reported there was "surprisingly little evidence that indicates any individual funds in the sample might be able to forecast prices" (pp. 414–415).

Conclusions similar to those of Jensen [1968] have been reported in many studies of portfolio performance such as in the McDonald [1974] study of 123 mutual funds over the 1960–1969 period and in the Schlarbaum [1974] study of the portfolio performance of 20 property-liability companies over the 1958–1967 period.

12.4 SUMMARY

If an investor accepts that the efficient markets model is a good description of the capital market, a passive portfolio approach—emphasizing high diversification, low turnover, and risk control—is the appropriate investment strategy. The role of financial statement information in such a strategy is primarily in risk assessment—see Chapter 9. If an investor decides that he can detect situations in which departures from efficiency exist, the role of financial statement information is expanded. The valuation models used by *Wells Fargo* and *Value Line*—see Chapter 10—are illustrative of how financial statement information can be combined with other information in an attempt to detect mispriced securities. Attempts to exploit any perceived inefficiencies involve trading off the higher expected abnormal returns against higher transaction costs and the holding of a less

diversified portfolio. Over time, advocates of an active approach to investment choice should be able to demonstrate that their selections earn
abnormal returns.

NOTES

[1]See Black and Scholes [1974] for earlier analysis of differences across
securities in dividend yield.

[2]The Sharpe-Sosin conclusions as regards dividend yield also apply to
beta. For instance, it is difficult to maintain a well-diversified portfolio
with a beta considerably above that of the market. If one were to rank all
stocks on beta and choose the top decile, the portfolio would be overly
concentrated in specific industries due to an industry effect in the betas of
securities. There is also evidence that higher-beta stocks have higher
residual risk—the implication is that it takes more stocks to achieve a given
level of diversification for a high-beta portfolio than for a low-beta
portfolio. See Klemkosky and Martin [1975]. See also Johnson and Shannon [1974] for discussion of algorithms to obtain diversified portfolios.

[3]Only under very specific conditions will a buy and hold policy result
in a fully diversified portfolio, i.e., if all stocks in the market are bought in
their value-weighted proportions and there are no repurchases or new
issues of stocks by currently listed companies and no stocks are newly
listed on the market.

[4]An example of a change in the *Standard & Poor's 500 Stock Index*
occurred on June 30, 1976. The number of industrials and utilities was
reduced from 425 to 400 and 60 to 40, respectively. A new finance
component (e.g., banks and insurance companies) was added to the index.

[5]Another motivation for not investing in all stocks in an index is
related to trust investment law. This issue is discussed subsequently in this
section. This motivation explains why the index funds operated by *Wells
Fargo* do not always include all 500 stocks in the *Standard & Poor's Stock
Index*. Information provided by *Wells Fargo Investment Advisors* indicated
that on "February 1, 1977, *Wells Fargo's* S & P 500 Index Fund included a
total of 495 issues...in approximately their capitalization weightings. The
five issues not present failed to meet *Wells Fargo's* prudence screen, which
is applied in order to comply with legal counsel's interpretation of the
Employee Retirement Income Security Act of 1974 (ERISA)."

[6]Compare the following statement in the 1974 *Spitzer* case:

> The focus of inquiry...is...on the individual security as such and factors
> relating to the entire portfolio are to be weighted only along with others in

reviewing the prudence of the particular investment decisions. (323 N.E. 2d 700, 703)

[7]This conclusion appears consistent with the use of "prudence screens" by several index funds when building their portfolios. For instance, Batterymarch [1977] noted the following:

We use a version of Professor Edward Altman's "Z-score" program for analyzing each stock in our index-matching universe, the top S & P 350. The results of this bankruptcy forecasting program are used in screening out possible imprudent situations. (p. 18)

Chapter 14 contains analysis of bankruptcy prediction models (including Altman's model). See Bines [1976] for further discussion of legal aspects of portfolio management.

[8]Ehrbar [1976] provides a good presentation of the case for index funds. An interesting discussion of the problems encountered by the *Wells Fargo Bank* in creating and marketing an index fund is described in Black and Scholes [1974a].

[9]The *Value Line Investment Survey* now includes information on insider trading activity in each of the stocks in its service. It may be unwise to assume Jaffe's results will continue given the publicity of his prior successful investment strategy and the now more readily available information about insider trading activity.

[10]More detailed analysis of trade-offs involved in using a fundamental approach in a near-efficient market is provided in Treynor and Black [1973]. See also Fama [1972] and Hodges and Brealey [1973].

[11]These probabilities were calculated using the binomial probability function. See Dyckman and Thomas [1977] for a description of the use of this function.

[12]The alpha evaluation measure itself has also been questioned. See Roll [1977].

QUESTIONS

QUESTION 12.1:   A Defense of Fundamental Analysis

The following extracts are taken from an article by Bernstein [1975] entitled "In Defense of Fundamental Investment Analysis":

The basic purpose of this article is to present a defense of the function and value of fundamental investment analysis and its special branch, financial statement analysis, as an indispensable, rational and useful approach to reaching investment decisions. (p. 57)

Raw Data and its Evaluation

The reasoning behind EMH's (efficient market hypothesis's) alleged implication for the usefulness of security analysis fails to recognize the essential difference between information and its proper interpretation. Even if all the information on a security at a given point in time is impounded in its price, that price may not reflect value. It may be under- or over-valued depending on the degree to which an incorrect interpretation or evaluation of the available information has been made by those whose actions determine the market price at a given time.... Information may be readily available to all those who want to perform the necessary rigorous and demanding work required for its proper analysis. And yet, often after months and even years, the publication of an interpretation or an inevitable action flowing as a consequence of old and known information, results in sudden and dramatic price adjustments to the newly perceived "reality."

Example 1: In recent years the publication of critical articles on accounting practices in industries such as land sales and computer leasing have resulted in sharp declines in the affected companies' securities. And yet, these critical reviews were not new information; it was rather the interpretation of known data that caused the sharp price declines.

Example 2: Even a superficial analysis of the 1972 Annual Report of Consolidated Edison would have revealed that (a) in the three years, 1970 to 1972, the company spent $1,350 million for net construction without any significant increase in profitability to justify such investment, (b) the company borrowed $650 million in 1970 to 1972, covered interest payments less than two times in 1972 and decreased working capital by $76 million in the same year, and (c) in the face of such deterioration of financial strength the company paid common dividends of $134 million out of earnings totaling $148 million that year. And yet, not until the company omitted the common stock dividend a year later, did a complete interpretation of this information come to be reflected in the price of the stock. Although the information was there, a long time elapsed before it was efficiently interpreted by the market. (p. 58)

The Value of Models and Theories

Although models and the theories that describe the workings of such models are designed to increase our understanding of reality so that we can operate in it on an intelligent and informed basis, they are abstract simplifications of reality. EMH is an outgrowth of the never ceasing efforts by students of the stock market to understand it. In order to represent a valid description of reality, a model must describe most of the evidence, not merely selected evidence, and it must square with common sense and with logic. Moreover, *the model, to be of value, must be useful. That is, its implications must yield superior investment predictions.*

EMH meets only part of the foregoing requirements for a valid stock market model. The challenges discussed above represent serious and unresolved inconsistencies and incompatibilities between the efficient market model and market reality. Even more important for our discussion here, *the conclusions derived from EMH regarding the value of fundamental security analysis are impractical and do not lend themselves to rational implementation. How many investors could be persuaded to entrust the fate of their capital to the throw of a dart, to a blind belief that at any given moment a security sells at a fair price*

because it reflects all that is known about it, or to a simple buy-and-hold policy?
(p. 59, emphasis added)

What all this indicates is that the market mechanism is so vast and so complex that no single formula or model can even begin to describe it comprehensively. Broad-brush studies and inferences about market behavior which hope to focus on one variable while keeping all others constant attempt the impossible. This may be a major reason why EMH and its implications fail to describe the market reality completely. (p. 61, emphasis added)

REQUIRED

(1) How would you examine if the instances cited in Examples 1 and 2 were inconsistent with an efficient capital market?

(2) Comment on the statement "the model, to be of value, must be useful. That is, its implications must yield superior investment predictions."

(3) How would you respond to the statement that "the conclusions derived from EMH regarding the value of fundamental analysis are impractical... because it reflects all that is known about it, or to a simple buy-and-hold policy?"

QUESTION 12.2:   The Index Funds Debate

Since the early 1970's, there has been a growing interest in index funds. The reaction of the investment community to these funds has been mixed. The following discussion appeared in the *Weekly Staff Letter* (December 18, 1975) of *David L. Babson and Company, Inc.* (Boston, Mass.).

INDEX FUNDS: WHY THROW IN THE TOWEL?

One of the most prevalent investment myths of the late 1960's was that any professional portfolio manager worth his salt could beat the 8–9% historical return of the market averages by at least 50%. Many firms cited 15% a year as a rock-bottom expectation for the long pull, and a few even talked up their ability to make 25%.

But in the changed investment climate of the 1970's, the averages themselves have not been matching their historical return. Moreover, studies have shown that only a small minority of pension and mutual funds have been keeping up with Standard & Poor's index of 500 stocks.

So lately, a tiny but growing number of companies administering pension accounts have placed part of their investment assets in so-called index funds. These are common stock portfolios which either duplicate the structure of the S & P 500 or consist of 100 or more S & P issues selected to "track" the overall index.

The idea is that since the average investment can't produce "average" results, the way to be sure of getting them is via the index fund approach. This has the added "advantage" of doing away with the need for analytical judgment and attendant investment fees.

The portfolio manager is in essence replaced by a computer which scans the continually changing structure of the S & P and keeps the fund's diversification in line with that of the index. In the process, brokerage fees are held down since these funds have low "portfolio turnover" rates.

As a recent article in the *Wall Street Journal* stated: "Index funds represent an outgrowth of the random walk thesis, which in its most advanced form holds that the stock market is almost perfectly 'efficient'—that is, at any moment, individual stocks are priced about where they should be, based on all known information."

The random walk theory, developed by several university professors, further presumes that any investment manager cannot beat the stock market over the long run except by chance. They claim that picking stocks by throwing darts at a board is as valid an approach as any other. This lends support to the idea of using index funds as a means of assuring "average" equity results.

Several clients have asked us about this new investment technique. So we are devoting this week's Letter to explaining our opinion.

1. *The Basic Purpose of Owning Common Stocks*: This is no different today from what it has been right along—namely to obtain a rising flow of earning power and dividend-paying ability. In an inflationary climate, the increase should be sufficient to offset the erosion in purchasing power.

Back in the mid-1960's, the standard investment view was that (a) inflation would continue indefinitely but at a modest rate and (b) stocks—virtually all stocks—were preferable to bonds as inflation hedges. But, as it has since been proven, inflation doesn't automatically inflate stock prices. This is because it actually hurts the earnings of nearly every company.

When inflation crept along at 1–2% annually—as it did up to the early 1960's—the damage was concealed by the 4–5% rate of basic progress which most good companies were able to make. However, as the inflation rate speeded up in the late 1960's and early 1970's, it became harder and harder for corporate earning power to keep pace. Over this entire period, only a minority of companies have made satisfactory headway against the strong inflationary tide.

2. *A Look at the Record*: The following table compares the 1966–1975 earnings and dividend record of the S & P 500 and our firm's index of 12 seasoned growth stocks. Note that the S & P's progress has not kept pace with inflation while that of the 12 growth companies has done so by a wide margin:

| | In Current Dollars | | | | In Constant Dollars | | | |
| | Earnings | | Dividends | | Earnings | | Dividends | |
Index 1966 = 100	S & P 500	12 Growth	S & P 500	12 Growth	S & P 500	12 Growth	S & P 500	12 Growth
1975	137	249	129	246	83	150	78	149
1974	160	246	125	224	105	162	82	147
1973	147	215	118	192	107	157	86	140
1972	116	182	108	177	90	141	84	137
1971	97	156	107	169	77	125	86	135
1970	91	139	109	153	76	116	91	128
1969	104	132	110	140	92	117	97	124
1968	104	119	107	123	97	111	100	115
1967	96	108	102	111	93	105	99	108
1966	100	100	100	100	100	100	100	100

The shares of leading companies which have maintained superior earnings growth since the speed-up of inflation have, as a group, provided better investment results than the Dow Average or the S & P 500. This can be seen in the table below.

	Total Investment Return* Since End of 1965	
	10 Years	Annual Avg.
Dow 30	+29%	+2.6%
S & P 500	+33	+2.9
DLB 12 Growth	+97	+7.0
Corporate Bonds	+15	+1.4
Treasury Bills	+82	+6.2
Consumer Price Index	+70	+5.5

*Capital appreciation and dividends combined.

Most investors who have concentrated on owning the type of stocks represented by our 12-company index have had superior results since the mid-1960's (as well as in early periods). For example, the next table traces the average year-by-year return of two mutual funds which have consistently followed the investment philosphy and policy our firm has advocated over the years:

	Total Investment Return			
	S & P 500	Dow 30	Average of Two Mutual Funds	
			Total Return	Turnover Ratio
1975*	+33.5%	+41.3%	+19.8%	NA
1974	−26.3	−23.5	−25.8	3.3%
1973	−14.7	−13.3	−12.4	7.7
1972	+18.9	+18.5	+27.0	11.4
1971	+14.2	+9.8	+18.2	11.2
1970	+3.9	+9.2	−3.3	16.6
1969	−8.4	−11.8	+3.6	13.5
1968	+11.0	+7.9	+12.8	9.6
1967	+23.9	+19.2	+25.9	NA
1966	−10.0	−15.8	−4.3	NA
1965	+12.5	+14.4	+22.9	NA
Total				
1964–75	+51.0%	+45.5%	+98.2%	—

*Through December 11   NA = Not Available

Note that the two mutual funds have not done nearly as well as the market indexes in 1975. Yet their return over the entire period shown has been twice as great. No single investment approach can beat the S & P every quarter or every year, but why does it have to?

One of the unfortunate developments in the portfolio management field in recent years has been the excessive preoccupation with short-term results. Rather than sticking with a well-thought-out, long-range plan, many fund managers have been chasing one investment rainbow after another—often switching to a new strategy just as economic events were about to blow it out of the water.

Another reason for below-average results has been the ridiculously high portfolio turnover ratios—another reflection of trying to "beat the market" every quarter. Statistics of the past decade indicate that the higher the turnover, the poorer the long-term results—and, conversely, the lower the turnover, the better the results.

Advocates of index funds say that they keep total management costs to a minimum largely because portfolio turnover is only 2–4% vs. 20% or 30% for conventionally managed funds. But there is no law that says that a non-indexed portfolio has to be churned. The record of the two mutual funds shows that above-average results can be attained with a modest amount of buying and selling.

3. *Favorable Investment Characteristics Are Not Randomly Distributed:* We believe the record clearly shows that the shares of leading companies with a good combination inflation-resistant characteristics have, as a group, provided the best results since the mid-1960's. In the final analysis, selecting investments according to their underlying characteristics is the most important function the portfolio manager can perform.

Over a long span, the difference can be substantial. For example, the two stocks that carry the biggest weight in the S & P 500 are IBM and American Telephone. They equal 11% of the index's current weighting, which is based on the sum total of the share price times the number of shares outstanding for each of the 500 issues.

Why is it that $100,000 invested in IBM 25 years ago is now worth $4.7 million or 22 times more than an equal amount invested in Telephone at the same time? And why is the annual income from that $100,000 in IBM now at a yearly rate of $148,000 or 10 times more than the current income from the equivalent investment in Telephone? It's not that IBM is that much better managed or so much luckier but simply because its characteristics are greatly different from those of the other company.

It makes a lot more sense to us to choose investments based on the characteristics you want rather than on trying to match the performance of an index composed of 500 companies whose characteristics range from uniquely desirable to dreadfully bad.

Actually, 11 of the 12 stocks in our index are included in the S & P. As a group, they account for nearly 20% of the total weighting. There are many more S & P issues which have the inflation-resistant characteristics we think are so important for favorable long-term results.

So if one is going to index his portfolio to a group of companies, why not index it towards the kind one favors and away from those one has less confidence in? Better yet, why index at all—simply diversify!

4. *What's So Great About Matching the S & P?:* Index funds are a negative approach. The S & P itself represents two-thirds of the market value of all stocks

and so by definition cannot provide above-average results. If you settle for simply matching it, you're throwing in the towel—you're conceding defeat.

The basic job of professional managers is to set, carry out and adhere to an investment philosophy aimed at producing effective long-term results. If this approach is consistently followed, the comparison with the averages will take care of itself.

REQUIRED

(1) What major criticisms of index funds are being made in the *Babson Weekly Staff Letter*? How would you respond to these criticisms?

(2) Assume you have been hired to construct and manage an index fund to match the *Standard & Poor's 500 Stock Index*. What major issues would you consider when constructing and managing the fund?

(3) Comment on the following letter to the editors of *Fortune* (August 1976) in response to an article by Ehrbar [1976] that outlined the case for index funds:

Believers in index funds build their faith on the random walk theory, which is premised upon the wealth of information on companies made universally available by armies of security analysts and required public disclosures. However, the analysts exist (and are paid handsomely) because it is generally believed that the information is valuable. If everyone believed the random walk theory, no one would pay analysts, but then the information supply would drop. Thus, the random walk theory can be true only if it is *generally not believed*. And index funds can outperform money managers only if they are generally not bought. (p. 99)

QUESTION 12.3: Investment Choice by the Acorn Fund

The following extract is taken from the *First Quarter Report* (March 31, 1976) of the *Acorn Fund, Inc.*, a no-load fund managed in downtown Chicago (only six miles away from the "Temple of the Efficient Market"!):

Why We Avoid "Efficiency"?

Most security analysts and portfolio managers spend almost all of their time studying perhaps 300 big companies. Recent legislation, such as the Employee Retirement Income Security Act of 1974 (ERISA), has narrowed this focus. The very large effort expended studying these stocks means that that which *can* be known *is* known, and so, to the extent intelligent analysts can predict, the stock prices are determined according to an "efficient" market process. This theory is defined by Lorie and Brealey in *Modern Developments in Investment Management*, as follows:

"One of the most important ideas in the field of investments is that capital markets are 'efficient.' This does not mean that papers get shuffled cheaply and quickly; rather, it means that new information is widely, quickly, and cheaply available to investors, that this information includes what is knowable and relevant for judging securities, and that it is very rapidly reflected in security prices."

If you follow the reasoning of the efficient market hypothesis to its logical conclusion, you should not try to get above-average performance by selecting stocks from a list of the 200 or 300 major "blue-chip" companies on which most institutions concentrate. For this kind of portfolio, a dart-throwing approach (which can be computerized into an Index Fund) will do as well as most portfolio managers, despite their skill and effort.

As a portfolio manager, one cannot hope to know more about Eastman Kodak or Avon Products than other analysts know. The chance to make an above-average return on investments has to be in the less "efficient" part of the market, by studying companies which are not under minute and constant scrutiny by a large group of analysts. In the past five years, as security analysts concentrate more and more on fewer stocks, there are many more possibilities of finding a group of smaller companies with excellent prospects, but selling at prices which still offer a chance to make an above-average return on our total portfolio *without greater risk*.

Will the price of such stocks ever go up, or is it possible these stocks will stay ignored? In our opinion, the sound economic values of these companies get reflected in their stock prices sooner or later. As evidence of this upgrading, the appreciation in Acorn Fund for the first quarter of 1976 speaks for itself. There are four different ways in which a stock price can rise, as illustrated by several current or former Acorn stocks:

(1) Growth: As the company grows, the market price of the stock will go up in line with earnings, dividends, and book value (Midwestern Distribution).

(2) Acquisition: The company can be acquired by a larger company at a price well above the market (Storm Drilling and Rehab, both in 1974).

(3) Repurchase: If a stock sells well below its economic value, the company may repurchase sizeable blocks of its own shares (Northwest Industries, Storer).

(4) Revaluation: As a company grows and prospers, it can cross the threshold of institutional interest, at which time the Ugly Duckling is pronounced a Swan, and its price-earnings ratio substantially increases (Houston Oil).

Good quality smaller companies can produce stock market profits by all four mechanisms, while the established favorite stocks have only the first—one out of four. We therefore spend our time looking at stocks which are not covered by a lot of analysts, so that the price is not set by the "efficient" process. Most Acorn portfolio stocks will be in the "inefficient" market.

Not only are smaller companies the best place to look for profits in a theoretical sense, but often in a practical way as well. A small company can be more easily understood than a large company and can be more responsive to positive developments in a specific area. For instance, a gas discovery by Houston Oil and Minerals causes the stock to jump, while Exxon would not even quiver after a similar discovery. The management of a good small company tends to be aggressive, cost conscious, entrepreneurial, and responsive, compared with large companies which tend toward conservatism and bureaucracy.

REQUIRED

(1) Comment on the distinction *Acorn* draws between the top 200–300 major stocks and those stocks in "the less efficient part of the market."

(2) How would you examine if "smaller companies can produce stock market profits by all four mechanisms [growth, acquisition, repurchase, and revaluation], while the established favorite stocks have only the first [growth]?" What problems would occur in making this examination?

(3) Estimating (12.3) with monthly security returns of *Acorn* over the January 1973—December 1976 period yielded:

$$\left(\tilde{R}_i - R_f\right) = \underset{t=.699}{.00411} + 1.1782 \times \underset{t=12.090}{\left(\tilde{R}_M - R_f\right)}$$

$$\text{Adjusted } R^2 = .755; \qquad \text{Durbin-Watson} = 1.562$$

Is there evidence that *Acorn* possessed superior investment skills over this period?

QUESTION 12.4: Briloff and the Capital Market

The security price behavior of individual stocks at the time of articles alleging "specific accounting abuses" is often cited as evidence inconsistent with market efficiency—see, for example, Bernstein [1975]. Consider the security price behavior of *McDonald's Corporation* at the time of the release of a *Barron's* article by Abraham J. Briloff. See the following attachments:

A. The article by Briloff, "'You Deserve a Break': McDonald's Burgers Are More Palatable Than Its Accounts," from *Barron's* (July 8, 1974).

B. Press releases from *McDonald's Corporation* (July 8, 1974) and *Arthur Young and Company* (July 10, 1974) responding to the article. These press releases appeared in *Barron's* (July 15, 1974).

C. Details of security price and return behavior of *McDonald's* in the period surrounding release of the *Barron's* article.

REQUIRED

(1) Describe and comment on the following criticisms made of *McDonald's* financial reporting and financial management:

(a) Accounting for employee compensation,

(b) Use of pooling accounting for acquisitions, and

(c) The considerations paid for acquisitions.

(2) What sources of information does Briloff use in his analysis? Are these sources all "publicly available?"

(3) How would you explain the drop in the stock price of *McDonald's* over the July 1, 1974–July 11, 1974 period? (Note: From the January 1969–December 1973 monthly security returns, *McDonald's* beta was estimated to be 1.70.)

Attachment A   "You Deserve a Break...."
McDonald's Burgers Are More Palatable
Than Its Accounts
By Abraham J. Briloff*

Some of the sizzle seems to have gone out of McDonald's Corp. In one uptown New York City neighborhood residents are fighting plans to locate one of the company's emporiums on their block. Downtown, on Wall Street, "Big Mac" also has slipped a bit. Thus, citing cost pressures, some security analysts have begun to look for slower growth in future years, the result of which has been to drop the stock, an institutional favorite, seven points in one recent five-day session.

Nonetheless, at a recent price of close to 48, or about 40 times last year's earnings, it's evident that the company which gave the world Ronald McDonald—"the most popular clown character in the country"—scarcely lacks for friends. Nor is the fact hard to understand. After all, in just the past decade, McDonald's has come far and fast. In contrast to '63 revenues of $18 million and net of $1.05 million, last year the fast-food chain—with 2,897 restaurants around the globe—rang up revenues of $592 million and profits of $52 million. And, if anything, 1974 should be still better. The other day, in connection with an announcement regarding plans to postpone a previously proposed 700,000-share secondary, but to go ahead with a $50 million sinking-fund debenture offering, McDonald's disclosed that in the first five months, sales were up 27%, earnings, 30%.

Bitter With the Sweet

Yet it has long been my thesis—it almost can be put down as a law—that wherever ants swarm, the pot not only will contain a bit of honey, but also will be filled with accounting ploys. And McDonald's, I suggest, is very much a case in point. For one thing, the company has used pooling accounting to the hilt, thereby exaggerating earnings (and growth) and proving that the 1970 changes in the accounting rules regarding business combinations still permit major distortions. For another, important questions must be raised as to whether significant compensation in stock paid to employes—measuring in the millions of dollars—has been reflected on the books. In short, there is less to McDonald's bottom line than meets the eye.

One part of my study developed "serendipitously." Thus, on opening the file of documents submitted to the SEC-New York Stock Exchange during 1973–74, I was greeted by a huge batch of so-called SEC forms 144 ("Notice of Proposed

*Dr. Briloff is Professor of Accountancy at the Bernard Baruch School of Business of the City University of New York.

Sale of Securities"). A cursory examination indicated that a significant number was filed by executive and other employes of the corporation stating that the shares being sold were received by gift from Ray A. Kroc (McDonald's founding father and chairman of its board) on September 25, 1972.

Among those reporting sales of shares received in this fashion (and the number of such shares) I found: Steven J. Barnes, Executive Vice President, President International Division, 2,250; G. Brent Cameron, Executive Vice President, 2,000; Gerald Newman, Executive Vice President, Controller, 3,000; Robert A. Papp, Vice President, 2,400; James C. Schindler, Executive Vice President-Design, 2,350; Paul D. Schrage, Executive Vice President, 1,400; and Donald Smith, Executive Vice President, 1,350.

There were many with more modest numbers—some 50, some 100; there was Richard E. Poucher, the Remodelling Manager, who reported 650 shares. Knowing I could not find all the 144s (they're thrown into a file folder most haphazardly, and then researchers like myself mess up the order even more), I proceeded to track down the SEC form 4 ("Statement of Changes in Beneficial Ownership"), which Mr. Kroc had to file for his September 1972 transactions. It showed a September 25, 1972, gift of 198,850 shares, of which 50,000 went to his foundation, leaving 148,850 shares—all of them, presumably, to those selected from among McDonald's employes, executives and others.

The significance of this putative gift transaction is that in September 1972 certain selected corporate employes received more than $8 million in compensation benefits (McDonald's was selling at 55 at that time) which were not reflected as a corporate expense. It is true that actual payment was not made by the corporation, per se. It was, instead, made by someone described in an October 1973 prospectus, as one who "may be deemed to be a 'parent' of the company, as that term is defined in Rules and Regulations under the Securities Act of 1933, as amended. As of the date of this Prospectus, Mr. Kroc owned approximately 18.0% of the Company's common stock of record and benefi-cially....

Considering the persons to whom the shares were given, their position in the company, and especially their apparent lack of any relationship to Mr. Kroc (excepting through the corporation), I maintain that the $8 million was an additional corporate cost. It should have been reflected as such, presumably in 1972, unless the stock was not capable of being freely traded until the following year—in which event the cost might well have been shown in the 1973 state-ments. But the transaction was the equivalent of Mr. Kroc contributing the $8 million in stock to McDonald's capital surplus, followed by the corporation's paying out these shares as bonuses to the selected group of employes.

Interestingly, had Mr. Kroc followed the long road to his objective of recognizing the special contribution by certain employes to his company's accomplish-ments, it could have availed itself of about $4 million in tax savings. As it is, the deduction is lost, though the question regarding the taxability of these payments as income to the employes is, for me, an open one.

That the entire matter had received most thoroughgoing consideration at the highest levels of the McDonald's hierarchy is evidenced by an August 18, 1973, memorandum from the company's corporate counsel saying, in part:

"This memorandum supplements our memorandum of September 26, 1972, with respect to your gift of McDonald's Corp. common stock from Ray A. Kroc. If you should decide to sell all or any part of your gift shares under Rule 144, you may be required, as explained in our previous memorandum, to file a form 144.

"...The form... is a complicated one and in the past several months numerous persons have raised questions regarding its proper completion. Accordingly, to assist you, we enclose a sample Form 144."

I must presume this $8 million in added compensation for the chosen few also came to the auditors' attention. Was this not, then, a matter of sufficient substance to warrant full disclosure in the statements—if not as an actual cost, then surely among the footnotes? Remember, $8 million was more than 20% of the 1972 net income, and 15% of the 1973 amount.

'73 Distribution

During 1973, Mr. Kroc's generosity was more modest. An October, 1973, prospectus recites: "On the date of this Prospectus Mr. Kroc is transferring 16,500 of his shares as gifts to 330 employes, principally restaurant managers and field consultants who have performed for the Company in an outstanding manner. No recipient will receive more than 100 shares." Since the shares were then selling at 71 this payment aggregates $1.2 million—for which there is neither mention nor, from all indications, a deduction in the 1973 financials.

That McDonald's most prestigious auditors failed to reflect or at least disclose this cost is incomprehensible to me. An American Institute of Certified Public Accountants' Interpretation issued June 1973 (but undoubtedly known to the auditors well before they certified the 1972 statements, since Arthur Young had its representation on the Accounting Principles Board) dealt explicitly with the problem.

It states the question, in part, as follows: "Should a corporation account for plans or transactions (plans), if they have characteristics otherwise similar to compensatory plans adopted by corporations, that are established or financed by a principal stockholder (i.e., one who either owns 10% or more of the corporation's common stock or has the ability, directly or indirectly, to control or influence significantly the corporation)?"

And observes: "If a principal stockholder's intention is to enhance or maintain the value of his investment by entering into such an arrangement, the corporation is implicitly benefiting from the plan by retention of, and possibly improved performance by, the employe. In this case, the benefits to a principal stockholder and to the corporation are generally impossible to separate. Similarly, it is virtually impossible to separate a principal stockholder's personal satisfaction from the benefit of the corporation....

"The economic substance of this type of plan is substantially the same for the corporation and the employe whether the plan is adopted by the corporation or a principal stockholder. Consequently, the corporation should account for this type of plan when one is established or financed by a principal stockholder unless (1) the relationship between the stockholder and the corporation's employe is one which would normally result in generosity (i.e., an immediate family relationship), (2) the stockholder has an obligation to the employe which is completely unrelated to the latter's employment (e.g., the stockholder transfers shares to the employe because of personal business relationships in the past, unrelated to the present employment situation), or (3) the corporation clearly does not benefit from the transaction (e.g., the stockholder transfers shares to a minor employe with whom he has had a close relationship over a number of years).

Occam's Razor

"This type of plan should be treated as a contribution to capital by the principal stockholder with the offsetting charge accounted for in the same manner as compensatory plans adopted by corporations.

"Compensation cost should be recognized as an expense of one or more periods...."

Nor can the auditors gain comfort from the June, 1973, dating. These AICPA interpretations are not intended to establish new dogma; they are merely interpretative of that which is already presumed to prevail. All that the publication does is to give wider circulation to the wisdom already expected to be possessed by firms like McDonald's auditors. But, then, to apply Occam's Razor: Even if AY were not aware of this interpretation when they certified the 1972 statements a few months prior to its promulgation, or otherwise deemed it to be inoperative, how could they have overlooked or ignored it in late 1973 when they lent their expertise to a $68 million prospectus, or in early 1974 when they were signing the 1973 accounts?

I contend that traditional wisdom going back a score of years would have dictated that these "gifts" be accorded accounting significance. I maintain that the now traditional Accounting Chapter 13B, would embrace this kind of transaction, especially since Mr. Kroc does benefit importantly from the executives' and other employes' contribution to the corporate bottom line. I realize that reflecting these millions in costs would have had an adverse effect on McDonald's income statements and possibly also an inimical effect on the share prices. That would, of course, be regrettable. But regrettable or not, the accounting profession is supposed to be committed to full and fair disclosure—regardless.

And with that thought in mind, let's begin our examination of McDonald's business acquisition practices. Here we start with a test of your financial acumen. Assume then that you are given the following collage of income statements for 90 restaurants covering the past four years:

	Revs.	Net Inc.	Return
	—000 Omitted—		On Sales
Year 1	$19,590	$1,252	6.4%
Year 2	21,692	525	2.4
Year 3	29,951	1,053	3.5
Year 4	37,314	844	2.3

Query: How much would you be willing to pay for this erratic income pattern averaging less than $1 million annually? Would you expect to pay as much as $50,360,000?

A Matter of Value

Believe it or not, that's precisely the amount which McDonald's paid out in stock during 1973 for restaurants acquired in transactions accounted for as poolings of interest. Moreover, in the Listing Applications filed with the New York Stock Exchange, McDonald's states:

"Prior to the commencement of negotiations in connection with the (acquisitions), the company (McDonald's) through certain of its officers, employees and agents, investigated the financial condition, properties, management and markets of the companies and the value of the stock and assets which were to be acquired.... The purchase price agreed upon was based upon the underlying value of the assets and earning power of the acquired business."

To properly view the "underlying value," let's look at the composite balance sheet of the acquired companies. It won't be found anywhere in the documents, but is derived by a process which I will dub "differential calculus," i.e., comparing McDonald's December 31, 1972, balance sheet as originally included in its 1972 shareholders' report with the revised balance sheet as of the same date, included for comparative purposes in the 1973 report. The differences between the two balance sheets are supposed to represent the amounts which had to be added, *hunc pro tunc*, because of the 1972 pooling accountings.

Based on these calculations, the 90 units had an aggregate working capital deficit of $2.8 million, $10.7 million in depreciated plant and equipment plus $1.4 million in intangibles and miscellaneous assets—for an aggregate $9.3 million. And, after deducting long-term liabilities (of $3.5 million), shareholders' equity amounted to just $5,840,000, for which, remember, McDonald's paid out over $50 million in stock.

10 Cents on the Dollar

It may be that, as McDonald's undoubtedly astute "officers, employees and agents" discerned the underlying values in the land, inventories, buildings and the like, the *real* value really exceeded $50 million. But here's the whole point of this "dirty pooling" syndrome: because of the way in which McDonald's accounted for this $50-odd million, you'd never know it. Thus, McDonald's books picked up no more than the $5,840,000 as the cost. That works out to about 10 cents on the dollar when contrasted with the true cost. And that was only in 1973. During its existence as a public corporation McDonald's paid out some $90 million in stock but booked this cost at only about $10 million.

So what? Well, instead of depreciating the $90 million real cost, McDonald's will be charging off just $10 million against subsequent operations. If this unaccounted-for $80 million cost were spread over 20 years (the rough mean point of the useful lives of the buildings and equipment), it would mean that McDonald's annual income would be reduced by $4 million—and without, it might be added, any tax abatement since the acquisitions appear to have been on a tax-free swap basis. This in itself would have an 8%–10% adverse impact on the "bottom line."

Possibly of even more dramatic impact, a full, true and realistic accounting for the $90 million could have a deleterious impact on the amounts reportable by McDonald's, should it turn around and relicense the acquired franchises or proceed to sell off any land and other real estate picked up in these transactions. I have no way of determining how much of the company's recently reported income from initial license fees and/or gains from restaurant sales stemmed from these pooling acquisitions, but it is interesting that such sales are becoming an increasing practice with this Hamburger Empire. While gains on property dispositions aggregated $1,701,000 during 1970, and slightly more than that in 1971, they doubled (to $3,408,000) for 1972 and mushroomed to $5,553,000 last year. And this may be a mere portent of even greater things to come, since the first quarter 1974 report discloses that during the first three months of this year, $3,667,000 in gains on sales of restaurant businesses were booked, almost tripling the $1,371,000 in such gains for the corresponding period last year.

Subtle Approach

Meanwhile, there is yet another, possibly more subtle way in which McDonald's particular pooling practices will have a salutary effect on the dynamics of its year-to-year growth curve. As noted, the companies pooled during 1973 previously showed about $1 million in aggregate income. These acquisitions were of restaurants run as "mom and pop" establishments—sometimes as corporations, sometimes as partnerships or sole proprietorships. But all could be fairly classified as closely-held small enterprise.

As a certified public accountant with some sophistication in accounting for small enterprises I maintain that such businesses are intuitively committed to minimizing reported income—to produce the irreducibly lowest tax. We achieve this, all according to Hoyle, by using conservative inventory valuations, accelerating depreciation writeoffs and the like. (And since these companies cannot afford two sets of books, their accounting books are identical with those presented to the tax collector—a practice which is not in vogue with major corporations.) And then, assuming the corporate form of organization, we avoid the double taxing process by passing out all or almost all of the income as salaries to the shareholder-executives and their families.

This ultraconservatism could work in McDonald's favor since, even assuming the same level of operations, the diversions and bookkeeping conservatism will cease—producing the appearance of progress.

Nor, from all indications, were the acquired companies' books certified by independent accountants prior to their takeover by McDonald's. It might well be a reasonable presumption that before McDonald's auditors permitted their client to absorb the acquired numbers into the corporate books they would have meticulously scrutinized the accounts, or at least made certain that some other independent accountant's credentials were "on the line"—especially, since each of its Listing Applications in this kind of a transaction carries the legend: "For accounting purposes, the acquisition will be treated as a pooling of interests. Such accounting treatment has been reviewed and approved by Arthur Young & Co., the Company's Independent Certified Public Accountants, as being in accordance with generally accepted accounting principles."

Fruitless Search

Here, again, I'm sorry to disillusion you. Arthur Young's imprimatur notwithstanding, I cannot find certified statements for the companies acquired in the

1973 acquisitions. Illustrative of the statements AY must have relied on are those included in Listing Application No. B-3428, the last of McDonald's for 1973. It covers "A maximum 10,000 additional shares of common stock to be issued in connection with the merger of Kaplan Enterprises Inc. into McDonald's Corporation," and is certified by none other than Saul Kaplan, the president of the acquired company, to wit:

"I, Saul Kaplan, President of Kaplan Enterprises Inc., hereby certify that I have examined the accompanying balance sheet of Kaplan Enterprises Inc. as of April 30, 1973, and the statement of income of Kaplan Enterprises Inc. for the year ended April 30, 1973, and that, in my opinion, said statements present fairly the financial position of said Company on April 30, 1973, and the results of its operations for the year then ended, in accordance with generally accepted accounting principles applied on a consistent basis."

The statements of Kaplan Enterprises Inc. (McDonald's-Kenner, Louisiana) which Mr. Kaplan certified may be summarized as indicated in Tables I and II.

An especially intimate insight into the absurdities of pooling can be gained by focusing on McDonald's acquisitions during the last six months of 1973, when it issued a mere 61,318 shares with a not-so-mere aggregate value of $2,360,000.

Again, using differential calculus, it turns out that the aggregate balance sheets of these pooled companies looked like this:

Total Current Assets		Precisely Zero
Total Current Liabilities		$638,000
Deficit in Working Capital		($638,000)
Fixed Assets:		
Land	$80,000	
Buildings & Equipment		
(net of depre-		
ciation)	646,000	726,000
Other Assets (A		
negative amount)		(239,000)
Deficit in Net Assets		($151,000)

Put simply, McDonald's took over a composite balance sheet with a negative net worth of $151,000 and issued $2,360,000 of its stock.

And what about the income statement of these acquired companies? Again, fussing with numbers in prospectuses and annual reports, subtracting one from the other, and extracting other significant numbers from the mass of data, I come up with the following for these 1973 second half poolings.

	Gross Revs.	Net Inc.
1969	$1,943,000	$118,000
1970	2,455,000	132,000
1971	2,849,000	122,000
1972	2,834,000	79,000

Now, considering this piddling earnings pattern and the even more dismal composite balance sheet, would you be willing to pay out more than $2 million for these fast-food purveyors? The answer is yes, but only if there are some assets which are off the balance sheet—the kind that you could surface at will to report cozy profits if the going got rough.

But if that were the case should not GAAP be constrained to set forth these hidden assets? And aren't the accountings less than candid if you subsequently floated those hidden values through your income statements, making it appear that you're doing great?

Stock Exchange

Nor, by way of an aside, have these antics ended. A NYSE Listing Application (B-4228) filed May 29, 1974, tells about "a maximum of 40,000 shares...to be issued in exchange for all of the assets of Seattle Food Service Corp. and Tacoma Food Service Corp." The shares to be issued were stated to be worth $1,805,000. For what? the *combined* shareholders' equity for both corporations was a MINUS $34,947.50; the *combined* profits for the three months ended March 31, 1974, before taxes, $3,760.37. On whose authority were these statements issued? ".I (Peter G. Tjenos), President of Tacoma Food Service Corp. and Seattle Food Service Corp., hereby CERTIFY...." *Plus ca change, plus c'est la meme.*

Let us now look at the full-year 1973 poolings from another perspective. As we know, McDonald's gave up $50,360,000 of its shares but yet booked this cost at only $5,840,000 net of liabilities—suppressing $44,520,000. In recording these poolings, McDonald's charged its fixed asset accounts with $10,704,000 net of accumulated depreciation, as follows:

Land	$1,861,000
Buildings	
(on owned land)	a3,241,000
Buildings	
(on leased land)	a1,145,000
Equipment, Furniture,	
Fixtures, Signs	a4,457,000
Total Charge to	
Fixed Assets	$10,704,000

a—Net of accumulated depreciation.

From McDonald's 1973 form 10-K we learn that the average cost of a new restaurant built in 1973 aggregated $375,000—$101,000 for land, $177,000 for building and $97,000 for equipment, etc. Using these data, and on the assumption that half the restaurants were on owned land and the other half on leased land, 90 brand new restaurants (i.e., the number acquired on the 1973 poolings) would have cost an aggregate of $29,205,000.

Goodwill or Not?

Mind you I'm computing the cost of brand new buildings and equipment—not the retreads acquired from the prior owners. Since my $29,205,000 exceeded the net book cost (of $10,704,000) by $18,501,000 I will assume that that part of the $44,520,000 in excess cost paid on the poolings might charitably be attributed to the acquired land, brick and mortar. But what shall we do with the remaining $26,019,000? I suppose the accountants' broad brush would call it goodwill. But then where is the goodwill in a situation where the average earnings are less than $1 million on an adjusted capital amount of $24,341,000 ($5,840,000 as booked plus the added $18,501,000 assigned to fixed assets)?

By my unsophisticated, simplistic tastes a goodwill factor of $26 million presumes an excess earnings sum of about $4 million in perpetuity (thereby allowing a 15% pretax return on the investment—which is rather modest by 1973 standards, considering the risks inherent in this business). As I have commented, would that I could see such a return in the aggregate, much less as *excess* earnings, for the 90 restaurants pooled in the 1973 acquisitions.

Differential Accounting

To make matters even more incomprehensible this is not a situation where McDonald's picked up a brand new income stream when it incurred the $50 million cost for the 90 acquired restaurants. To the contrary, the financial statements (again, requiring my differential calculus) demonstrate that during 1972 the companies pooled in 1973 actually contributed $3,603,000 in Rentals, $970,000 in Service Fees and $65,000 in Licenses—a total of $4,638,000. This means that McDonald's 1973 poolings merely leveraged that amount from a Rental-Service Fee position to a Profit from Sales position with but an $844,000 differential. If this differential is worth $50 million, as McDonald's thought, well, so be it. As I said, for me it's incomprehensible.

When reflecting on McDonald's "nickel and dime" pattern of poolings I almost yearn for the far more dramatic and flamboyant exploits of the poolers of old—the Lings, Littons, Leascos, Gulf & Westerns and ITTs. At least they were in hot pursuit of what Leasco's Saul Steinberg called that "Racquel Welch prize"—that which was "big and beautiful." For them a Saul Kaplan Enterprises would be *infra dig.*

TABLE I Kaplan Enterprises Inc.

Balance Sheet as of April 30, 1973:

Current Assets		$51,389.75
Fixed Assets (net of Depreciation)		15,972.96
Other Assets (including $5,686.24 as Unamortized Franchise Fee)		26,150.24
Total Assets		$93,512.95
Current Liabilities	$4,863.63	
Non Current Liabilities	4,761.12	
Shareholders' Loans	39,000.00	$48,624.75
Stockholders' Equity:		
Capital Stock	$5,000.00	
Net Income, year ended 4/30/73	69,888.20	
Distributions to Stockholders	(30,000.00—)	44,888.20
Total Liabilities & Equity		$93,512.95

TABLE II

Income Statement for the Year Ended April 30, 1973:

Net Sales		$557,091.77
Cost of Sales		229,568.31
Gross Profit on Sales		327,523.46
Operating Expenses		
Payroll—Manager	$12,999.81	
Payroll—Others	102,917.17	
Other	61,326.47	
Other Expenses	71,154.45	
Depreciation & Amortization	9,237.36	
Income Taxes	Zero	257,635.26
Net Income		$ 69,888.20

But alas! This is the sad state which was permitted, if not encouraged, by Accounting Principles Board Opinion No. 16, the one hammered out in 1970 and which was going to make business combinations accounting go legitimate. And well the opinion might have (just as its predecessor, Accounting Research Bulletin 48, might have) if the field rules were implemented with responsibility, and a consummate commitment to truth, fairness and full disclosure in our financial reporting practices.

McDonald's accounting, to reiterate, was all determined by Arthur Young & Co. to be fair in accordance with GAAP (generally accepted accounting principles). GAAP-fair nonetheless, they have overstated the company's income and, worse yet, induce the capability for future earnings exaggeration. In short, to adapt the company's anthem, those of us committed to a standard of full and really fair disclosure "deserve a break today from McDonald's."

Attachment B   Press release
from McDonald's Corporation

OAK BROOK, Ill., July 8, 1974—Fred L. Turner, president of McDonald's Corporation, stated: "A current Barron's article concerning the Company's accounting practices is distorted and misleading. The Company has consistently complied with generally accepted accounting principles.

"The article attacks pooling of interests accounting and its use by McDonald's, even though this method is in accordance with generally accepted accounting principles and is widely used. Among many other misleading statements, the article implies that a substantial amount of McDonald's income has been generated from license fees and gains on the sales of restaurants acquired in pooling of interests transactions. In fact, the Company has sold only two restaurants of the more than 200 it has acquired in pooling of interests transactions in the last five years.

"The article criticizes the Company for acquiring restaurants with modest net income and assets. The Company determines the amount it will offer for a restaurant, based not on historical cost or earnings history of the restaurant, but on its evaluation of the prospects of the restaurant under Company management. McDonald's believes that its earnings history speaks for itself as to its judgment on acquisitions.

"The article's analysis of the gifts made by Mr. Ray Kroc, chairman of the board of McDonald's, omitted several material facts. The gifts referred to by the article included gifts to relatives, friends and other non-employees of McDonald's. The gifts were made by Mr. Kroc in celebration of his 70th birthday, at which time he also gave $7.5 million to charity.

"McDonald's is proud of the record it has achieved and the business and accounting practices it has followed."

Press Release
from Arthur Young & Company

CHICAGO, Ill., July 10, 1974—Robert G. Ettelson, Senior Partner of the Chicago office of Arthur Young & Company, has stated that the article in the July 8 issue of Barron's concerning accounting practices of McDonald's Corporation, and referring to its certified public accountants, Arthur Young & Company, contains inaccurate and misleading statements.

The Barron's article asserts that McDonald's reported income has been overstated, apparently due to the use of "pooling of interests" accounting for business combinations rather than "purchase" accounting, and non-recognition of alleged compensation expense in connection with stock given to employees by Mr. Ray Kroc, Chairman of the Board of McDonald's Corporation. To the extent the assertion relates to pooling versus purchase accounting, it is clear that the accounting for business combinations is dictated by existing accounting principles. McDonald's accounting complied with applicable accounting principles and the author does not claim otherwise. The author's dislike of pooling accounting is well known, but his attack should be directed against those having the responsibility for the establishment of accounting principles and not, in an unfair manner, against a company which is properly following the required accounting principles.

With respect to the compensation issue, the article refers to an accounting interpretation issued in June, 1973, which relates to issuance of shares to employees by major stockholders. The author implies that this required McDonald's to treat as compensation expense in its accounts the gifts of McDonald's stock given by Mr. Kroc in 1972 on the occasion of his 70th birthday, as well as gifts of a smaller number of shares announced to certain employees early in 1973. The author states that, "These AICPA (American Institute of Certified Public Accountants) interpretations are not intended to establish new dogma; they are merely interpretative of that which is already presumed to prevail." This statement is contradicted by the statement of the AICPA accompanying these interpretations, which states, "The purpose of the interpretations is to provide guidance on a timely basis... and to clarify points on which past practice may have varied and been considered generally accepted.... Unless otherwise stated, the interpretations are not intended to be retroactive." No retroactivity was required with respect to the Interpretation discussed in the article. Mr. Ettelson added that, in the view of his firm, no accounting would be required even under current accounting rules for the major gifts by Mr. Kroc in 1972. Furthermore, no accounting was required for the lesser number of shares announced to recipients prior to the issuance of the Interpretation in June 1973.

The Barron's article also implies that Arthur Young relied on the opinion of officers of selling companies acquired by McDonald's Corporation in determining the appropriate accounting treatment to be accorded these business acquisitions. This is erroneous.

The author further implies that, in reporting on the combination of the accounts of McDonald's with those of the acquired businesses, Arthur Young relied on the opinion of officers of the selling companies. This is also erroneous.

Attachment C   A.   Daily Security Price Behavior of McDonald's

	McDonald's Price	Trading Volume (000's) in McDonald's	S & P Composite
7/1/74	$48\frac{1}{8}$	957	86.02
7/2/74	47	671	84.30
7/3/74	$47\frac{7}{8}$	569	84.25
7/4/74 (holiday)	—	—	—
7/5/74	$47\frac{5}{8}$	229	83.66
7/8/74	$38\frac{3}{8}$	2,360	81.09
7/9/74	$39\frac{2}{8}$	1,900	81.48
7/10/74	$36\frac{4}{8}$	1,479	79.99
7/11/74	$38\frac{6}{8}$	1,311	79.89

B.   Monthly Security Return Behavior of McDonald's

	Return on McDonald's	Return on S & P Composite	Return on Treasury Bills
Jan. 1974	−.0586	−.0084	.0063
Feb. 1974	−.0484	.0019	.0058
Mar. 1974	.0194	−.0218	.0057
Apr. 1974	.0166	−.0373	.0074
May 1974	.0187	−.0272	.0076
June 1974	−.1216	−.0128	.0060
July 1974	−.2063	−.0760	.0070
Aug. 1974	−.0789	−.0826	.0059
Sept. 1974	−.2964	−.1171	.0080
Oct. 1974	.4315	.1665	.0053
Nov. 1974	−.0391	−.0453	.0051
Dec. 1974	−.1328	−.0179	.0068

REFERENCES

AMBACHTSHEER, K. "Portfolio Theory and the Security Analyst." *Financial Analysts Journal* (Nov.–Dec. 1972): 33–36.

AMERICAN NATIONAL BANK AND TRUST COMPANY OF CHICAGO. *Index Funds and Investment Strategy*. American National Bank, Chicago, 1976.

BALL, R., and BROWN, P. "An Empirical Evaluation of Accounting Income Numbers." *Journal of Accounting Research* (Autumn 1968): 159–178.

BATTERYMARCH FINANCIAL MANAGEMENT CORPORATION. *Batterymarch Index-Matching*. Batterymarch, Boston, Mass., 1977.

BERNSTEIN, L. A. "In Defense of Fundamental Investment Analysis." *Financial Analysts Journal* (Jan.–Feb. 1975): 57–61.

BINES, H. E. "Modern Portfolio Theory and Investment Management: Refinement of Legal Doctrine," *Columbia Law Review* (June 1976): 722–798.

BLACK, F. "Implications of the Random-Walk Hypothesis for Portfolio Management." *Financial Analysts Journal* (Mar.–Apr. 1971): 16–22.

———. "Yes, Virginia, There Is Hope: Tests of the Value Line Ranking System." *Financial Analysts Journal* (Sept.–Oct. 1973): 10–14.

BLACK, F., and SCHOLES, M. "The Effects of Dividend Yield and Dividend Policy on Common Stock Prices and Returns." *Journal of Financial Economics* (May 1974): 1–22.

———. "From Theory to a New Financial Report." *Journal of Finance* (May 1974a): 399–412.

BRILOFF, ABRAHAM J. "'You Deserve a Break': McDonald's Burgers Are More Palatable Than Its Accounts" *Barron's* (July 8, 1974).

DYCKMAN, T. R., and THOMAS, L. J. *Fundamental Statistics for Business and Economics*. Prentice-Hall, Englewood Cliffs, N.J., 1977.

EHRBAR, A. F. "Index Funds—An Idea Whose Time Is Coming." *Fortune* (June 1976): 144–154.

FAMA, E. F. "Components of Investment Performance." *Journal of Finance* (June 1972): 551–567.

FOSTER, G. "Quarterly Accounting Data: Time-Series Properties and Predictive Ability Results." *Accounting Review* (Jan. 1977): 1–21.

HODGES, S. D., and BREALEY, R. A. "Portfolio Selection in a Dynamic and Uncertain World." *Financial Analysts Journal* (Mar.–Apr. 1973): 50–65.

IBBOTSON, R. G., and SINQUEFIELD, R. A. *Stocks, Bonds, Bills and Inflation: The Past (1927–1976) and the Future (1977–2000).* Financial Analysts Research Foundation Monograph, New York, 1977.

JAFFE, J. F. "Special Information and Insider Trading." *Journal of Business* (July 1974): 410–428.

JENSEN, M. C. "The Performance of Mutual Funds in the Period 1945–1964." *Journal of Finance* (May 1968): 389–419.

JOHNSON, K. H., and SHANNON, D. S. "A Note on Diversification and the Reduction of Dispersion." *Journal of Financial Economics* (Dec. 1974): 365–372.

JOY, O. M., LITZENBERGER, R. H. and MCENALLY, R. W. "The Adjustment of Stock Prices to Announcements of Unanticipated Changes in Quarterly Earnings." Stanford University, Stanford, Calif., 1977 (forthcoming in *Journal of Accounting Research*).

KLEMKOSKY, R. C., and MARTIN, J. D. "The Effect of Market Risk on Portfolio Diversification." *Journal of Finance* (Mar. 1975): 147–154.

LANGBEIN, J. H., and POSNER, R. A. "Market Funds and Trust-Investment Law." *American Bar Foundation Research Journal* (Volume 1976, Number 1): 1–34.

MCDONALD, J. G. "Objectives and Performances of Mutual Funds." *Journal of Financial and Quantitative Analysis* (June 1974): 311–333.

ROLL, R. R. "Why the Securities Market Line Cannot Distinguish Superior Assets (or Portfolios) from Inferior Assets (or Portfolios), ex post or ex ante," Study Center in Managerial Economics and Finance, Working Paper 4-77, U.C.L.A., Los Angeles (March, 1977).

ROSENBERG, B., and MARATHE, V. "The Prediction of Investment Risk: Systematic and Residual Risk." *Proceedings of the Seminar on the Analysis of Security Prices.* Center for Research in Security Prices, Graduate School of Business, University of Chicago, Chicago, (Nov. 1975): 85–159.

SCHLARBAUM, G. C. "The Investment Performance of the Common Stock Portfolios of Property-Liability Insurance Companies." *Journal of Financial and Quantitative Analysis* (Jan. 1974): 89–106.

SHARPE, W. F. "Likely Gains From Market Timing." *Financial Analysts Journal* (Mar.–Apr. 1975): 60–69.

SHARPE, W. F., and SOSIN, H. B. "Risk, Return and Yield: New York Stock Exchange Common Stocks, 1928–69." *Financial Analysts Journal* (Mar.–Apr. 1976): 33–42.

TREYNOR, J. L., and BLACK, F. "How To Use Security Analysis To Improve Portfolio Selection." *Journal of Business* (Jan. 1973): 66–86.

IV

OTHER APPLICATIONS

CHAPTER **13**

BOND RATINGS,
BOND YIELDS,
AND
FINANCIAL INFORMATION

Bonds available for investment range from the issues of small municipalities such as Pascagoula, Mississippi to those of large corporations such as *American Telephone and Telegraph*. Investigation of the relationship between bonds and financial information has taken two main directions. One direction is to predict the bond ratings of agencies such as *Fitch*, *Moody's*, and *Standard & Poor's*. The other direction is to predict the yields on publicly traded corporate and municipal bonds. In Section 13.1 we shall discuss bond ratings and bond yields. Models using financial information to predict corporate and municipal bond ratings are examined in Section 13.2. The relationship between bond yields and financial information is analyzed in Section 13.3.

13.1 BOND RATINGS AND BOND YIELDS

A Bond Ratings

There are three main bond rating companies in the United States: *Fitch Investors Service*, *Moody's Investors Service*, and *Standard & Poor's Corporation*. *Fitch* has been rating long-term corporate debt since 1923. *Moody's* began issuing ratings in 1909 with the publication of John Moody's *Analysis of Railroad Investments*. *Standard & Poor's* started issuing ratings in 1941. It was formed from the merger of *Poor's Publishing Company* and *Standard Statistics Company*. Prior to 1968, rating agencies did not charge the corporations or municipalities being rated. On March 1, 1968, *S & P* commenced the policy of rating municipal bonds only upon request and only upon payment of a fee. All three agencies have now instituted a fee system for rating either corporate or municipal bonds.

Each agency rates a wide variety of debt instruments, e.g., the bonds of industrials, public utilities, airlines, bank holding companies, hospitals, and state and local governments and the commercial paper of real estate investment trusts. All three agencies use nine rating categories:

Moody's	Fitch / Standard & Poor's
Aaa	AAA
Aa	AA
A	A
Baa	BBB
Ba	BB
B	B
Caa	CCC
Ca	CC
C	C

Bonds rated Aaa (AAA) are judged to be of the "best quality"—for example, in *Moody's* system they are those that "carry the smallest degree of investment risk." Bonds rated C are those with the lowest rating—for example, in *Moody's* system they are those "regarded as having extremely poor prospects of ever attaining any real investment standing."[1]

What Does a Bond Rating Measure?

The following statement from *Moody's* on municipal bond ratings gives some insight on this question:

> A municipal bond rating is a judgment of the investment quality of a long term obligation issued by a state or one of its subdivisions. It is based on an analysis that must ask, first, what has the debtor pledged to pay and, second, what is the likelihood that he will be able to keep his promises.
>
> The rating...is a statement about the debtor's condition and the probability that he can and will do what he says regarding the debt. It is an evaluative assessment of the protections afforded the bondholder. (*Moody's* [1974, p. 1])

The term *default risk* is generally used in describing what a bond rating purports to measure. It should be noted, however, that this term is not unambiguous. Default could range from temporary payments difficulty with time extension of interest payments to legal bankruptcy with the use of formal (legal) procedures to recover outstanding principal and interest. What weighting is placed on the possibility of such situations when assigning a specific rating is not made explicit by the rating agencies. Moreover, additional factors such as marketability are also said to be considered in bond rating.

Bond Ratings and Default Experience

For corporate bonds, there is some evidence that in the 1900–1943 period there was an inverse relationship between bond rating and default experience. Hickman [1958, p. 10] reports the following default rates over the 1900–1943 period:

Rating Group	Default Rate
I (Aaa)	5.9
II (Aa)	6.0
III (A)	13.4
IV (Baa)	19.1
V–IX (Ba–C)	42.4

Default in these percentages was defined to include (1) failure to pay full interest or principal when due and (2) an exchange where the new security received was worth less than par. Comparable figures for the post-World

War II period are difficult to interpret due to the very few defaults on rated corporate bonds.[2]

The default experience of rated municipal bonds in the pre-World War II period appears to be less impressive than that for corporate bonds. Of the 264 largest municipal bond issues that went into default in the 1930's, 78% were rated Aaa or Aa.[3] Since World War II, however, there have been very few defaults on rated municipal bonds. For instance, only 7 municipal bonds rated by *Moody's* have defaulted since the Depression. All 7 were limited liability revenue bond issues (see Report of Twentieth Century Fund Task Force on Municipal Bond Credit Ratings [1974]).

B Bond Yields

The current yield and the yield to maturity are two terms frequently used in the bond investment literature. The current yield of a bond is the coupon rate of the bond expressed in dollars, divided by the current market price. Assume a 7% coupon bond (interest paid semiannually) with par value of $1,000, 30 years to maturity, and a current market price of $857. The current yield of this bond is

$$\frac{\$70}{\$857} = 8.17\%.$$

This yield calculation is analogous to the dividend yield calculation for common stocks.

The yield to maturity of a bond is calculated to take the following into account: Even though the above bond is selling for $857 now, it will be worth $1,000 at maturity. The yield to maturity is equivalent to the rate of interest, compounded semiannually, at which you would need to invest the $857 market price now to "guarantee" $35 every half-year and have $1,000 at the maturity date of the bond. In terms of present value calculations, it is the rate of interest that makes

$$\text{Present value of } \$1,000, 30 \text{ years hence} + \frac{\text{Present value}}{\text{of a 30-year semiannual annuity of } \$35} = \$857.$$

For this bond, the yield to maturity is 8.3%.[4] In Section 13.3, the issue of what factors determine differences in the yield to maturity of different bonds is examined.

An interesting issue is the relationship between bond ratings and bond yields to maturity. Empirically, they are highly correlated. The lower the bond rating, the higher the average yield to maturity in that rating category. Table 13.1 presents the average yield of industrial, public utility, and municipal bonds in each of *Moody's* top four rating classes over the 1966–1975 period. The lower average yields of municipals vis-à-vis in-

TABLE 13.1   Rating Classes and Bond Yield Averages

	Industrials				Public Utilities				Municipals			
Year	Aaa	Aa	A	Baa	Aaa	Aa	A	Baa	Aaa	Aa	A	Baa
1966	5.12	5.15	5.26	5.68	5.19	5.25	5.39	5.60	3.67	3.76	3.95	4.21
1967	5.59	5.55	5.72	6.21	5.58	5.66	5.87	6.15	3.74	3.86	4.08	4.30
1968	6.12	6.24	6.39	6.90	6.22	6.35	6.51	6.87	4.20	4.31	4.54	4.88
1969	6.93	7.05	7.26	7.76	7.12	7.34	7.54	7.93	5.45	5.58	5.82	6.07
1970	7.77	7.94	8.33	9.00	8.31	8.52	8.69	9.18	6.12	6.28	6.49	6.75
1971	7.05	7.23	7.61	8.37	7.72	8.00	8.16	8.63	5.22	5.36	5.61	5.89
1972	6.97	7.11	7.36	7.99	7.46	7.60	7.72	8.17	5.04	5.19	5.38	5.60
1973	7.28	7.40	7.63	8.07	7.60	7.72	7.84	8.17	4.95	5.09	5.29	5.47
1974	8.42	8.64	8.90	9.14	8.71	9.04	9.50	9.84	5.89	6.04	6.30	6.53
1975	8.61	8.90	9.21	10.26	9.03	9.44	10.09	10.96	6.42	6.77	7.37	7.62

SOURCE: Moody's Investors Service [1976; 1976a].

dustrials and public utilities partly reflects the tax-exempt feature of municipal bonds. It is sometimes argued that the relationship between bond ratings and bond yields is a causal one. That is, the rating given a bond will "determine within limits" the interest rate an issuer must pay on the bond—e.g., see Goodman [1968]. An alternative explanation of the data in Table 13.1 is that bond ratings and bond yields are correlated because they are both influenced by the same underlying economic factors, e.g., interest coverage and profitability of the company issuing the bond.[5]

13.2   BOND RATINGS AND FINANCIAL INFORMATION

Models to predict the rating categories assigned to corporate or municipal bonds have generally taken the following form:

$$Z_i = f(X_{i1}, X_{i2}, \ldots, X_{in}) \tag{13.1}$$

where Z_i = rating of bond of firm (municipality) i,

X_{ij} = value of the jth variable of firm (municipality) i.

Discriminant analysis is the most frequently used technique in estimating these models of bond rating. Prior to describing this technique, it is useful to discuss the potential uses of such models.

Models to explain or predict bond ratings can be useful to the rating agencies themselves. It is important to these agencies that there be consistency at a point in time in the ratings assigned to individual bonds. The incorporation of a model into the rating process is one way of *reducing inconsistencies between individual ratings*. The model could be used in an initial stage of the analysis to form a preliminary rating of the bond. Then individual raters could exercise judgment on factors or interrelationships not captured by the model to decide the final rating of the bond. Moreover, the model could provide important *information to rating agencies on the judgment process of their raters*. It is a frequent finding in the human judgment literature that judges (raters) overestimate the weight actually given to minor cues and underestimate the weight given to major cues in their tasks (see Slovic and Lichtenstein [1971]). Developing a model that examines whether this finding occurs for the judgment of bond raters could provide valuable information when deciding on the scope of, and variables examined in, future rating engagements. Finally, a bond rating model can also be useful to agencies in their ongoing activity of reevaluating currently rated bonds. The model could be used as a *screening device to signal changing economic conditions of companies or municipalities*.

Rating models can also be important to investors in corporate and municipal bonds. Not all bonds are rated by *Fitch, Moody's*, or *Standard & Poor's*. Many corporations and municipalities privately place bonds with insurance companies, banks, etc. The Joint Bank Examination Procedure (issued July 15, 1949—quoted in *Moody's Investors Service* publications) states that banks are restricted to Group 1 securities for their investment portfolios:

> Group 1 securities are marketable obligations in which the investment characteristics are not distinctively or predominantly speculative. This group includes general market obligations in the four highest grades and unrated securities of equivalent value.

A bond rating model could be useful in screening bonds that are "of equivalent value" to those in the four highest rating grades.[6]

A An Example: Discriminant Analysis Model of Municipal Bond Rating

Discriminant analysis is a classificatory technique that has a wide number of uses in financial analysis. We shall illustrate the linear discriminant analysis technique. The following description is intended to convey some intuitive understanding of the technique. Any user of linear discriminant analysis should consult the technical literature on this and other available classificatory techniques.[7]

Several assumptions underlie the following example:

(1) There are two discrete and known groups,

(2) Each observation in each group has a set of two characteristics (variables), and

(3) The two variables arise from multivariate normal populations. The variance/covariance matrix of the two variables is assumed to be the same for each group, but the means of the two variables in each group are different.

Given these assumptions, the following linear discriminant function can be used for classificatory purposes:

$$Z_i = aX_i + bY_i. \tag{13.2}$$

The example used for illustrative purposes is the classification of ten municipal bonds into two groups: (1) those rated A or above by *Moody's* in 1975 ($\geqslant$ A), and (2) those rated Baa or below by *Moody's* in 1975 ($\leqslant$ Baa). The two variables used in the analysis are

$X_i =$ Assessed property valuation per capita of municipality i.

$Y_i =$ General obligation bonded debt per capita of municipality i.

The ten municipalities, their values for the above two variables, and the actual ratings for their general obligation bonds are detailed in Table 13.2. The municipalities used to estimate the discriminant function are termed the *estimation sample*. The steps in using a discriminant model are illustrated below.

Step One: *Estimate Discriminant Function.* In the two-group case with the above assumptions, the discriminant function that "best" distinguishes between the two groups is found by maximizing the ratio of the *between*

TABLE 13.2 Discriminant Analysis Example: Estimation Sample

Municipality	Assessed Property Valuation Per Capita ($'s)	General Obligation Bonded Debt Per Capita ($'s)	Moody's Bond Rating
1. Arlington, Mass.	6,685	116	Aa
2. Highland Park, Ill.	6,360	87	Aa
3. Springdale, Ohio	11,806	272	Aa
4. El Cerrito, Calif.	2,957	53	A
5. La Grange, Ga.	3,183	47	A
6. Pampa, Tex.	2,408	188	A
7. Coon Rapids, Minn.	2,703	613	Baa
8. Hot Springs, Ark.	1,212	43	Baa
9. Mauldin, S.C.	1,054	366	Baa
10. Pascagoula, Miss.	2,684	149	Baa

group sum of squares of the Z_i scores to the *within* group sum of squares of the Z_i scores. The coefficients of this function are calculated as follows:

$$a = \frac{\sigma_y^2 \cdot d_x - \sigma_{xy} \cdot d_y}{\sigma_x^2 \cdot \sigma_y^2 - \sigma_{xy} \cdot \sigma_{xy}} \qquad (13.3)$$

$$b = \frac{\sigma_x^2 \cdot d_y - \sigma_{xy} \cdot d_x}{\sigma_x^2 \cdot \sigma_y^2 - \sigma_{xy} \cdot \sigma_{xy}}, \qquad (13.4)$$

where σ_y^2 = variance of Y_i,

σ_x^2 = variance of X_i,

σ_{xy} = covariance of X_i with Y_i,

d_x = difference between the mean X_i for group 1 and the mean X_i for group 2,

d_y = difference between the mean Y_i for group 1 and the mean Y_i for group 2.

For the data in Table 13.2,

$$\sigma_x^2 = \frac{1}{N-1} \Sigma \left(X_i - \bar{X} \right)^2 = \$10,861,900$$

$$\sigma_y^2 = \frac{1}{N-1} \Sigma \left(Y_i - \bar{Y} \right)^2 = \$32,790$$

$$\sigma_{xy} = \frac{1}{N-1} \Sigma \left(X_i - \bar{X} \right)\left(Y_i - \bar{Y} \right) = -\$16,187$$

$$d_x = \$5,566 - \$1,913 = \$3,653$$

$$d_y = \$127 - \$292 = -\$165.$$

Substituting these values in (13.3) and (13.4) yields

$$a = .000329$$
$$b = -.004887.$$

Thus, the estimated discriminant function is

$$Z_i = .000329 X_i - .004887 Y_i. \qquad (13.5)$$

This function implies that the higher the assessed property valuation per capita, the higher the bond rating, and the higher the general obligation bonded debt per capita, the lower the bond rating. These implications are consistent with prescriptions given in the municipal bond rating literature.

Given the ratios in Table 13.2 and the discriminant function (13.5), the estimated Z_i scores are

Arlington, Mass.: $Z = .000329 \times 6685 - .004887 \times 116 = 1.632$

Highland Park, Ill.: $Z = .000329 \times 6360 - .004887 \times 87 = 1.667$

The Z_i score for all ten municipalities (ranked from highest to lowest Z_i) is

TABLE 13.3 Discriminant Analysis Example: Estimation Sample

Municipality	Predicted Z Score	Moody's Bond Rating	
Springdale, Ohio	2.555	Aa	
Highland Park, Ill.	1.667	Aa	
Arlington, Mass.	1.632	Aa	
La Grange, Ga.	.817	A	
El Cerrito, Calif.	.713	A	
Hot Springs, Ark.	.188	Baa	Misranked
Pascagoula, Miss.	.154	Baa	municipalities
Pampa, Tex.	−.126	A	
Maudlin, S.C.	−1.441	Baa	
Coon Rapids, Minn.	−2.106	Baa	

presented in Table 13.3. The mean Z scores for the two categories of bonds are

Bonds rated A or above	1.210
Bonds rated Baa or below	−.801

Step Two: *Choose Cutoff Point for Discriminant Function.* It is apparent from Table 13.3 that the discriminant function does not correctly rank the municipalities according to their bond ratings. One A-rated bond (Pampa) is given a Z score below that of two Baa-rated bonds (Hot Springs and Pascagoula). The choice of the cutoff point for predicting (1) bonds rated A and above and (2) bonds rated Baa or below will depend on the probability of bonds being misclassified and the cost of the misclassifications associated with each cutoff point considered. In general, the decision theory approach outlined in Chapter 1 should guide the choice of the cutoff.[8]

A frequently used criterion in choosing the cutoff point is minimize the total number of misclassifications in the estimation sample. We shall assume that the only cutoff points considered in this criterion are the midpoints of the Z scores of adjacently ranked bonds. Thus, for instance, the cutoff point between *Arlington* and *La Grange* that is considered is 1.2245 (midpoint between 1.632 and .817). The total number of misclassifications for several alternative cutoff points in Table 13.3 are

Cutoff Point				Total Number of Misclassifications
Predict ⩾ A	if	$Z_i >$	1.2245	3
Predict ⩾ A	if	$Z_i >$	.765	2
Predict ⩾ A	if	$Z_i >$	.4505	1
Predict ⩾ A	if	$Z_i >$	.171	2
Predict ⩾ A	if	$Z_i >$	.014	3
Predict ⩾ A	if	$Z_i >$	−.7835	2
Predict ⩾ A	if	$Z_i >$	−1.7735	3

Thus, the cutoff point which minimizes the total number of misclassifications in the estimation sample is predict a bond rating of A or above if the municipality's Z score exceeds .4505. Only *Pampa* is incorrectly predicted to be a Baa or below with this cutoff point.

Step Three: *Examine Predictive Ability of Discriminant Model on Validation Sample.* The estimates of a and b in (13.5) will reflect not only any underlying population differences between bonds rated $\geqslant A$ and bonds rated $\leqslant$ Baa but also *specific characteristics* of the firms in the estimation sample. Moreover, in many cases the variables used in the final discriminant function are selected from a larger set initially considered. The final set chosen is comprised of those which work best (e.g., result in minimum misclassifications) on the estimation sample. In this context, there is a *search bias* in the estimation sample that leads to an overestimate of the predictive ability of the model on samples independent of that used to select the final variables.[9]

In this situation, it is advisable to examine how well the estimated discriminant function performs on a new sample of rated municipal bonds. This new sample is generally referred to as a *validation* or *hold-out* sample. Table 13.4 presents values of X_i, Y_i, the predicted Z_i score, and the actual bond rating for ten new municipalities. Similar to the sample used to estimate the model, the predicted Z_i scores do not perfectly rank the municipalities by actual bond rating. How would a cutoff point of .4505 perform on the new sample? Two bonds would be misclassified—*Dodge City* and *Cambridge* are misclassified as Baa or below.

TABLE 13.4   Discriminant Analysis Example: Validation Sample

Municipality	Assessed Property Valuation Per Capita ($'s)	General Obligation Bonded Debt Per Capita ($'s)	Predicted Z_i Score	Moody's Bond Rating	
Palo Alto, Calif.	6,114	110	1.474	Aa	Predicted as $\geqslant A$
Homewood, Ill.	4,134	34	1.194	A	
Portland, Maine	11,271	562	.962	Aa	
East Lansing, Mich.	2,835	64	.620	A	
Dodge City, Kan.	2,781	98	.436	A	
Flagstaff, Ariz.	1,616	50	.287	Baa	
Cambridge, Mass.	3,270	278	−.282	Aa	Predicted as $\leqslant$ Baa
Bogalusa, La.	1,796	333	−1.036	Baa	
Aspen, Colo.	11,274	1,159	−1.954	Baa	
Cape Coral, Fla.	25,763	2,304	−2.783	Baa	

A convenient way to summarize the predictions of a discriminant model is via the following classification matrix (also called a *confusion* matrix):

		Actual Rating	
		$\geqslant$ A	$\leqslant$ Baa
Predicted Rating	$\geqslant$ A	a_{11}	a_{12}
	$\leqslant$ Baa	a_{21}	a_{22}

If the discriminant model correctly predicts the group to which each observation belongs, all observations will be on the main diagonal of the matrix, i.e., in the a_{11} and a_{22} elements. The percentage correctly predicted is calculated as

$$\frac{a_{11}+a_{22}}{a_{11}+a_{12}+a_{21}+a_{22}}.$$

Table 13.5 illustrates the classification matrices for the municipal bond rating example. A cutoff point of predict A or above if $Z > .4505$ is assumed.

The above example illustrated *linear* discriminant analysis for classifying observations into one of *two* groups on the basis of *two* variables. Many extensions of this example are possible: e.g., one could classify observations into one of n groups on the basis of m variables. When the

TABLE 13.5 Discriminant Analysis Example: Classification Matrices

A: Estimation Sample

		Actual Rating	
		$\geqslant$ A	$\leqslant$ Baa
Predicted Rating	$\geqslant$ A	5	0
	$\leqslant$ Baa	1	4

% Correct = 90%.

B: Validation Sample

		Actual Rating	
		$\geqslant$ A	$\leqslant$ Baa
Predicted Rating	$\geqslant$ A	4	0
	$\leqslant$ Baa	2	4

% Correct = 80%.

equal variance/covariance matrix assumption of *linear* discriminant analysis appears inappropriate, techniques such as *quadratic* discriminant analysis may be applied.[10] The reader should be aware that the technical literature on classificatory techniques (of which discriminant analysis is but one) is a vast and expanding one.

B Corporate Bond Rating

Corporate bonds rated by agencies include those of industrial, airline, bank, electric and gas utility, insurance, and railroad companies. Statistical studies of the ratings of corporate bonds have generally restricted themselves to specific segments of the corporate bond market. In this section, we shall examine studies on the rating of (1) industrial bonds and (2) electric utility bonds.

Rating of Industrial Bonds

The Pinches and Mingo [1973] study examined all newly issued industrial corporate bonds that were rated between Aa and B by *Moody's* over the January 1967–December 1968 period. The full sample comprised 180 bonds—132 bonds were randomly assigned to an estimation sample and 48 to a validation sample. Note that by restricting the sample to only newly rated bonds, the problem posed by any lag by rating agencies in revising the existing rating of a bond to changed financial fortunes of a company was avoided.

The first stage in the empirical analysis was the choice of independent variables. Pinches and Mingo chose 35 financial variables that could potentially be used in rating industrial bonds. They then used factor analysis in an attempt to identify "basically independent dimensions of the data" (p. 4). Seven factor patterns were identified for these 35 financial variables. The factor patterns were said to represent (1) size, (2) financial leverage, (3) long-term capital intensiveness, (4) return on investment, (5) short-term capital intensiveness, (6) earnings stability, and (7) debt and debt coverage stability. The financial variable most highly correlated with each factor was then chosen to be included in the discriminant function.[11]

The next stage in the analysis was estimation of the discriminant model. The final model chosen included five of the seven financial variables selected in the first stage:

(1) Years of consecutive dividends,

(2) Issue size,

(3) Net income and interest to interest,

(4) Long-term debt to total assets, and

(5) Net income to total assets.

A dummy variable representing the subordination status (1 = subordinated; 0=not subordinated) of the bond was also included as a separate variable.

With these variables in the estimated discriminant function predictions of bond ratings were made. The matrix of actual and predicted bond ratings for the original sample of 132 bonds is presented in Table 13.6. The total number of bond ratings correctly predicted is obtained by summing the main diagonal entries of the matrix—92 of the 132 bonds ($\cong 70\%$) are on the main diagonal. Note, however, that the discriminant model predicts different rating classes with differing success—Aa (71%), A (85%), Baa (16%), Ba (89%), and B (74%). The discriminant model predicted within one classification (either one higher or lower) of the actual rating for 130 of the 132 bonds. For the validation sample of 48 bonds, 65% of the ratings were correctly predicted; see Table 13.6—47 bonds were predicted within one classification of the actual rating. In this sample, there were also

TABLE 13.6 Predicting Industrial Bond Ratings

A: Estimation Sample

		Actual Rating				
		Aa	A	Baa	Ba	B
Predicted Rating	Aa	10	2	0	0	0
	A	4	22	8	0	0
	Baa	0	0	4	0	0
	Ba	0	2	13	39	6
	B	0	0	0	5	17

% Correct = 70%.

B: Validation Sample

		Actual Rating				
		Aa	A	Baa	Ba	B
Predicted Rating	Aa	1	0	0	0	0
	A	3	9	2	1	0
	Baa	0	0	0	0	0
	Ba	0	0	7	15	3
	B	0	0	0	1	6

% Correct = 65%.

SOURCE: Pinches and Mingo [1973, Tables 6 and 7].

considerable differences in the percentages correctly predicted—Aa (25%), A (100%), Baa (0%), Ba (88%), and B (67%). Note that for both the estimation and validation samples the discriminant model had considerable difficulty in predicting Baa bonds—4 out of 25 correct in the original sample and 0 out of 9 correct in the validation sample. Pinches and Mingo attributed this problem to the specific independent variables included in the model not discriminating very effectively between bonds rated Baa and bonds rated in adjacent categories.

Pinches and Mingo [1975] extended their 1973 study in an attempt to improve the prediction of Baa bonds. This extension was important as Baa is the lowest acceptable "investment quality" rating for the bond investments of many institutions. Separate discriminant functions were estimated for subordinated and nonsubordinated bonds. A quadratic rather than a linear discriminant function was also used in this extension. The total percentage of bond ratings correctly predicted increased from 70% to 75% —the percentages correct for each class were Aa (71%), A (83%), Baa (48%), Ba (91%), and B (100%).

Extensions of prior studies are all too rare in the financial analysis literature. Most (if not all) empirical studies involve some methodological choices that subsequent developments call into question. Although these developments may cast doubts on the findings of prior studies, it is generally only by replicating the empirical analysis that the precise effect of these developments can be determined. In the Pinches and Mingo case, the effect was an increase in the correct prediction rate for Baa bonds from 16% in their 1973 paper to 48% in their 1975 paper.

Ratings of Electric Utility Bonds

Altman and Katz [1976] examined the ability of a discriminant model to predict the ratings of electric utility bonds over the 1969–1971 period. The sample examined was all first mortgage bonds which received an identical rating by both *Moody's* and *Standard & Poor's* in a particular year—88 bonds in 1969, 84 bonds in 1970, and 87 bonds in 1971. Based on "prior related studies, discussions with public utility company officers, rating agency statements and the experience of the researchers" (p. 213), 30 financial ratios were originally selected. The final discriminant function included 14 of these 30 variables. Of particular interest were some financial ratios specifically related to the electric utility industry, e.g., (maintenance + depreciation)/operating revenue and the three years' growth rate of kilowatt-hour sales. For the validation sample, the discriminant function predicted the actual bond rating 77% of the time. The percentages correct for the individual rating categories were Aaa (52%), Aa (88%), A (75%), and Baa (50%).

C Municipal Bond Rating

The term *municipal bond* is generally understood to encompass all bonds issued by state and local governments. The principal classification of municipal bonds is into *general obligation* and *revenue* bonds:

(1) *General obligation bonds* are secured by the issuer's pledge of its full faith, credit, and taxing power for the payment of principal and interest, and

(2) *Revenue bonds* are payable only from the revenues derived from a particular faculty that is acquired or constructed with the bond funds, e.g., a tollway.

Statistical attempts to explain or predict the ratings on municipal bonds have concentrated on the general obligation bonds of local governmental units.

The factors reported to be considered in rating general obligation bonds include both quantitative and qualitative factors. For instance, Sherwood [1976] reported that *Standard & Poor's* considers at least the following ten factors while rating municipal bonds: (1) details of the issuer's overall debt, (2) the total assessed valuations of property over the last four years, (3) tax collection details for each of the last four years, (4) population of the municipality, (5) the two most recent annual reports and its most recent budget,[12] (6) the assessed property valuation of each of the ten largest taxpayers, (7) details of the municipality's economy, (8) the school enrollment in each of the last ten years, (9) the borrowing plans for the next five years, and (10) the capital improvement program for the next five years. While some of these factors are easily quantifiable, others are not; e.g., it is easier to quantify the population of the municipality than to quantify the diversification of the municipality's economy.

Rating of General Obligation Municipal Bonds

Two related attempts to explain or predict the ratings on general obligation bonds will initially be examined—Carleton and Lerner [1969] and Horton [1970]. Both studies were supported by the *Federal Deposit Insurance Corporation*. Carleton and Lerner used discriminant analysis in analyzing the ratings of 691 general obligation bonds. These bonds were selected from the 1967 edition of *Moody's Municipal Bonds* (details of the selection criteria were not given). A sample of 491 bonds was used as the estimation sample; 200 bonds were used as a validation sample. Based on a literature review and conversations with bond rating analysts, the following independent variables were used in the discriminant analysis:

$X_1 = 1$ if a school district, zero otherwise,

$X_2 =$ Debt to assessed property valuation,

$X_3 =$ Debt per capita,

$X_4 =$ Logarithm of population—used as a proxy for the economic
diversity of a community,

$X_5 =$ Logarithm of debt—also used as a proxy for economic diversity, and

$X_6 =$ Average current tax collection rate

Carleton and Lerner hypothesized that higher values of variables X_1 to X_3 would be associated with lower bond ratings, while higher values of variables X_4 to X_6 would be associated with higher bond ratings.

Table 13.7 gives the classification matrices for both the estimation sample of 491 bonds and the validation sample of 200 bonds. If the statistical model correctly predicted the actual rating of each bond, then all observations would be on the main diagonal of the matrices in Table 13.7. For the estimation sample, only 39% of the observations are correctly classified, while the comparable figure in the validation sample is 35%. Note that the discriminant function predicted within one rating class from the actual rating 84% of the time in the estimation sample and 85% of the time in the validation sample. On balance, the above results appear far

TABLE 13.7 Predicting Municipal Bond Ratings

A: Estimation Sample

		Actual Rating				
		Aaa	Aa	A	Baa	Ba
	Aaa	3	21	27	5	0
Predicted Rating	Aa	1	29	47	21	0
	A	1	18	95	34	1
	Baa	0	5	72	57	2
	Ba	0	1	9	33	9

% Correct = 39%.

B: Validation Sample

		Actual Rating				
		Aaa	Aa	A	Baa	Ba
	Aaa	1	6	10	2	0
Predicted Rating	Aa	0	11	17	10	1
	A	0	7	41	27	2
	Baa	1	1	32	14	1
	Ba	1	0	3	10	2

% Correct = 35%.

SOURCE: Carleton and Lerner [1969, Tables 5 and 6, reprinted with permission].

from impressive. Any detailed evaluation of these results, however, would require consideration of the costs of misclassifying the actual bond ratings. These costs would depend on the specific context in which the discriminant model was used.

Horton [1970] further examined some issues raised in the Carleton-Lerner (C-L) paper. One specific issue examined was the classification of bonds into those rated Baa and above and those rated Ba. This classification is important due to only bonds rated Baa and above being considered of "investment grade" by many banks, insurance companies, etc. In the C-L sample, there were only 12 Ba bonds out of the 491 in the estimation sample and 6 out of the 200 in the validation sample. Horton used a sample of 75 randomly chosen "investment-quality" bonds (Baa and above) and 75 randomly chosen "non-investment-quality" bonds. Nine more independent variables (e.g., per capita income of the district) were added to the six used by C-L. Using a cutoff criterion of maximize the percentage classified as correct in the estimation sample, Horton correctly classified 84% of the 150 bonds. On a validation sample of 25 investment-quality bonds and 25 non-investment-quality bonds, he correctly classified 80%. It is important to note that there was a different misclassification rate for investment-quality bonds (72% correctly classified) than for non-investment-quality bonds (88% correctly classified). Horton commented that by using a different original cutoff point, he could increase the percentage of non-investment-quality bonds correctly classified. This increase, however, was associated with a decrease in the investment-grade bonds correctly classified.

The choice of 1 Ba bond to every 1 Baa or above bond in the samples examined by Horton creates problems in generalizing the results to other samples. Typically, the percentage of Ba bonds in a random sample of general obligation bonds is quite small. In this case, use of the discriminant functions developed for Horton's sample could give very different misclassification rates on random samples of general obligation bonds.[13]

Rating General Obligation Bonds of U.S. Cities

Another examination of municipal bond rating is Michel's [1976] analysis of the ratings of the 50 largest U.S. cities (except New York, Washington, and Honolulu) over the 1962–1971 period. A discriminant model was built using 1962–1966 annual data for *Moody's* bond ratings and 12 financial variables for each city. The 12 financial variables included

(1) Total bonded debt per capita,

(2) Total revenue per capita,

(3) Federal and state aid as a percentage of debt services, and

(4) Pension fund obligations as a percentage of total revenues.

The variables were "selected because of the importance attributed to them by municipal fiscal authorities and because they are frequently cited as indicative of the risk of municipal obligations" (p. 5). Having used the 1962–1966 data as the estimation sample, Michel then used the 1967–1971 data for the cities examined as the validation sample. The classification matrices for both the estimation and validation samples are presented in Table 13.8. The percentage classification rates (60% on estimation sample, 58% on validation sample) were interpreted as indicating that "the variables typically used to assess risk do not accurately reflect the underlying risk associated with municipal issues or that the bond ratings do not effectively incorporate the risk of an issue, or both" (p. 17).

The percentage classification rates for municipal bond rating studies are generally below those for corporate bond rating studies. The reason for this difference is unclear. One possible explanation is the alleged greater problems existing in municipal financial reporting. There have been complaints over nondisclosure of both pension liabilities and long-lived assets and over the lengthy delays that occur in municipalities presenting their financial statements—see the Report of the Twentieth Century Fund Task Force on Municipal Bond Credit Ratings [1974]. The Coopers and Lybrand/University of Michigan [1976] study reported that 80% of the 46 cities studied did not disclose the actuarially computed value of unfunded

TABLE 13.8   Predicting Bond Ratings of U.S. Cities

A: Estimation Sample

		Actual Rating			
		Aaa	Aa	A	Baa
Predicted Rating	Aaa	12	4	4	0
	Aa	10	57	25	9
	A	3	29	60	0
	Baa	0	6	1	5

% Correct = 60%.

B: Validation Sample

		Actual Rating			
		Aaa	Aa	A	Baa
Predicted Rating	Aaa	12	2	6	1
	Aa	8	69	31	11
	A	0	24	44	0
	Baa	0	7	4	6

% Correct = 58%.

SOURCE: Michel [1976, Tables 7 and 8].

vested pension liabilities in their annual reports. Details of accrued cost of vacation and sick leave benefits were not disclosed by 84% of the sample. Investments in long-lived assets (e.g., city halls and police cars) were not revealed by over 25% of the cities examined. It is an open issue whether such disclosure problems explain (even in part) the generally lower classification rates for municipal bond rating studies.

D Some General Comments

The above studies examined are representative of what is an expanding literature on models for predicting bond ratings.[14] Some general comments on this literature are in order.

1. The models are attempting to capture the human judgments of bond raters. It is surprising that most prior studies have ignored the vast literature on human judgment modeling in the psychology literature; e.g., the Slovic and Lichtenstein [1971] review paper referred to over 100 studies on human information processing. This literature emphasizes that the failure of a linear (quadratic) model to predict a bond rater's judgment may say as much about the consistency of the rater's judgment as about any misspecification in the linear (quadratic) model. In several bond rating studies, the erroneous conclusion was drawn that the failure to predict ratings necessarily meant that the chosen model omitted an important variable(s) considered by the rating agencies. Another reason for the failure of the models to predict ratings could arise from "rating lag"; i.e., even though the underlying economic circumstances of a firm may have changed, the rating agency has not recently reexamined its prior rating.

2. One of the problems in generalizing from this research is the diversity in approaches used to both (1) chose the initial set of variables and (2) reduce this set of variables to those included in the discriminant function. In some studies, only the vaguest details on these issues are given. In part, this diversity in approach is attributable to the lack of an explicit and testable statement of what a bond rating represents. Nonetheless, more specific details on variable choice and the criteria used to include and exclude variables from the discriminant function are warranted in future studies. Ideally, there should be some underlying "economic rationale" for the variables included in the model. One has more confidence that variables will possess some predictive value when there is such a rationale for their inclusion.

3. The problem of operationalizing specific variables in bond rating models is often a difficult one. Consider modeling the terms of a bond indenture agreement. These agreements are reported to be important in bond rating (Sherwood [1976]). Given the numerous terms and covenants

in these agreements and the diverse remedies provided for lack of compliance, devising a single variable (or set of variables) to capture *differences* in them across firms seems monumental. Not surprisingly only the crudest modeling has been employed, e.g., use of a dummy variable to capture the subordination status of the bond. Consider also modeling the economic diversification of a municipality. This variable is frequently cited as important in municipal bond rating. The measure used to represent this variable in several studies—logarithm of the size of population—appears to be relatively "crude." One can think of large municipalities heavily dependent on one industry and smaller municipalities having at least four or five separate industries providing employment opportunities, taxation revenues, etc. Yet, one important test when evaluating these measures/proxies for variables is whether models incorporating them lead to better decisions than models which exclude them. On this test, even "crude" measures of variables may be warranted in a specific decision context.

4. An interesting issue is whether bond rating agencies adjust for cross-sectional differences in the accounting methods used by companies or municipalities. For instance, do they treat the reported debt to equity ratio of a company capitalizing lease financing differently from a company which does not capitalize leases? As another example, do they recognize differences across municipalities in the divergence between the assessed valuation of property and the market valuation of property? Although there are isolated comments on these questions, there is not extensive empirical evidence on whether the choice of accounting method influences the assigned ratings of bonds.[15]

13.3 BOND YIELDS AND FINANCIAL INFORMATION

There is at present little developed theory of bond pricing under uncertainty.[16] Much of the literature on bond pricing first assumes a certainty case and illustrates how present value discounting methods can be used to determine the bond price. When uncertainty is introduced, four factors that are said to affect the yields to maturity of bonds are generally outlined:

(1) Interest rate risk—i.e., the effect of unexpected changes in interest rates on bond market prices,

(2) Purchasing power risk—i.e., the effect on bondholders when the coupons on bonds are paid in nominal and not real dollars,

(3) Default risk—i.e., the inability of a company to meet its financial obligations when they fall due, and

(4) Marketability risk—i.e., the possibility that bonds may have to be sold at a discount due to the lack of an active market in the bonds.

It should be noted that these four factors are not derived from a developed theory of bond pricing under uncertainty. Rather, they appear to have been heuristically developed to explain empirically observed differences in yields across bonds at a point in time or differences in yields of the same bond over time. This lack of a theoretical model of bond pricing under uncertainty makes interpretation of empirical work explaining differences in bond yields somewhat difficult. Nonetheless, the existing empirical work is of interest as it suggests variables that potentially could be integrated into a theoretical analysis.

A   Corporate Bond Yields

The first detailed empirical analysis of factors explaining differences in corporate bond yields is Fisher [1959]. To control for nonfirm specific factors that may influence bond yields, Fisher examined risk premiums rather than yields to maturity—"the risk premium on a bond...[is] the difference between its market yield to maturity and the corresponding pure rate of interest" (p. 221). The pure rate of interest was defined as "the market yield on a riskless bond maturing on the same day as the bond under consideration" (p. 221). Both *default risk* and *marketability risk* were hypothesized to be the determinants of risk premiums. The three variables used as proxies for default risk were

$X_1 =$ Earnings variability, measured as the coefficient of variation on earnings after tax of the most recent nine years

$X_2 =$ Solvency, measured as the length of time since one of the following events occurred—"firm was founded, the firm emerged from bankruptcy, or a compromise was made in which creditors settled for less than 100 percent of their claims" (p. 224)

$X_3 =$ Equity/debt ratio, measured as "ratio of market value of the firm's equity to the par value of its debt" (p. 224).

The variable used as a proxy for marketability risk was

$X_4 =$ Total market value of the publicly traded bonds the firm has outstanding.

Cross-sectional regressions were run for 71 firms in 1927, 45 firms in 1932, 89 firms in 1937, 73 firms in 1949, and 88 firms in 1953. Results when all 366 bonds were pooled were

$$Y_i = .987 + .307X_{1i} - .253X_{2i} - .537X_{3i} - .275X_{4i} \qquad (13.6)$$
$$t = 9.59 \qquad t = -7.03 \qquad t = -17.32 \qquad t = -13.10$$

where Y_i = the risk premium of corporate bond i. All four variables were statistically significant from zero and in the direction Fisher hypothesized. Moreover, the R^2 of (13.6) was .75, implying the above variables explained considerable variation in risk premiums on bonds. The lack of a theoretical model underlying the Fisher results means that omitted variables could be a potential problem in interpreting the above results. Fisher [1959, p. 235], for instance, noted the possibility of provisions in bond indenture agreements being important variables in addition to X_1 to X_4. As noted in the prior section, however, operationalizing differences in indenture provisions across firms is no easy task.

B Municipal Bond Yields

The methodology developed by Fisher [1959] has also been applied to municipal bond yields. Hastie [1972] hypothesized that default risk and marketability were determinants of municipal bond yields. Default risk was estimated by four factors:

(1) Overall debt to "true value" of taxable property,

(2) Default history,

(3) Economic diversification, and

(4) Percentage of college students to issuer's population.

Marketability risk was estimated by three factors:

(1) Size of the offering,

(2) Net debt of the issuer, and

(3) Past population growth.

Although Hastie [1972] was able to explain as much as 86% of the variability on the yields of a sample of municipal bonds, there was considerable instability in the estimated coefficients over time and on subsamples of the bonds at a point in time.

At the present stage in research, it is unlikely that much insight will be generated by further similar cross-sectional regressions of yields on corporate or municipal ratios. Prior analytical modeling of bond pricing offers more promise of yielding testable propositions that can increase our understanding of the bond market.

13.4 SUMMARY

The analysis of corporate and municipal bonds is attracting increasing attention. Attention has focused on predicting both bond ratings and bond yields. Although there is evidence that financial statement information can make an important contribution in these predictions, much analysis remains to be done. Relative to research on common stocks, we have little evidence on the speed of the reaction of the bond market to corporate announcements such as annual and interim earnings. Similarly, we also have little evidence on whether bond raters or the bond market reacts to accounting data in the mechanistic way posited in some statements detailed in Chapter 7.

NOTES

[1] *Standard & Poor's* and *Fitch* do have three additional categories (DDD, DD, and D) for bonds in default.

[2] Ross [1976] noted that in the post-World War II period no industrial or utility had gone into default while still rated in one of the first four bond rating categories. See also Johnson [1967] for analysis of bond ratings and default experience.

[3] These figures would have been more informative if details about the number of issues in each rating class had also been provided.

[4] In practice, most calculations of yield to maturity are made by reference to a *yield book*. This book is organized into tables representing different coupon rates. For each coupon rate, there is a table which contains (a) the yield to maturity, (b) the current market price, and (c) the years to maturity. Given two of these three variables, the third can be determined by reference to the table. See Homer and Leibowitz [1972] for further discussion of yield to maturity and related concepts.

[5] The evidence on whether bond ratings, per se, influence bond returns or bond yields is conflicting. Studies concluding that there is an influence include Rubinfeld [1973], Katz [1974], and Grier and Katz [1976]. Studies concluding that there is no observable influence include Hettenhouse and Sartoris [1976], and Weinstein [1977]. See also, West [1973].

[6] One problem in using a model estimated with rated bonds to predict the ratings of privately placed bonds could arise if there are substantive economic differences between the two groups of bonds, i.e., if there is a self-selection bias in having as an estimation sample only those companies which applied for a rating.

[7]See, for example, Cooley and Lohnes [1971] and Press [1972]. Joy and Tollefson [1975] and Eisenbeis [1977] provide a good discussion of issues that arise when using discriminant analysis in financial contexts.

[8]See Press [1972] for application of the decision theory approach to deciding cutoff points in a discriminant model.

[9]See Frank et al. [1965] for discussion of this issue.

[10]Eisenbeis [1977] provides a good discussion of the issues to be considered when choosing between various discriminant techniques. He also discusses the implications for discriminant analysis when the assumption of normality of the variables is violated. Note that for several accounting ratios there is considerable evidence that normality is not a descriptively valid assumption—see Chapter 6.

[11]The use of factor analysis as a screening device to choose financial ratios for a discriminant function is not without problems. Eisenbeis [1977] notes the following: "If classification accuracy is a primary goal, then the criterion for keeping or deleting variables and dimensions should be related to the overall efficiency of the classification results.... It would seem inappropriate to discard variables...without first examining the overall classification results to determine what the effects or costs of dimension reduction really are" (p. 21).

[12]There is considerable debate over both the form and content of the financial reports of municipalities—see the Report of the Twentieth Century Task Force on Municipal Bond Credit Rating [1974], the Coopers and Lybrand/University of Michigan [1976] report, and Davidson et al. [1977].

[13]Morrison [1969] and Eisenbeis [1977] provide further discussion of this problem.

[14]Other studies in this literature include Horrigan [1966], Pogue and Soldofsky [1969], West [1970], and Ang and Patel [1975].

[15]Harmelink [1973] reported some evidence pertaining to the "general policyholders' ratings" assigned by A. M. Best to property-liability insurance companies. The sample comprised 55 companies with B+ or lower ratings and 55 companies with A or A+ ratings. The period of analysis was 1960–1970. He reported that either excluding or including the capital gains or losses on the marketable securities of P-L insurance companies produced similar predictive results with a linear discriminant model.

[16]By a "developed theory of bond pricing under uncertainty" we mean something akin to the capital asset pricing model that was outlined in Chapter 8. The finance literature on this topic, however, is in a state of flux. There is much current work on adapting the Black and Scholes [1973] option pricing model to other corporate liabilities. See, for example, Merton [1974] and Black and Cox [1976].

QUESTIONS

QUESTION 13.1: Bond Ratings and Bond Yields

It is commonly argued that there is a causal link between bond ratings and bond yields. For instance, Goodman [1968] commented as follows:

> Ratings normally are assigned to large, widely-known issues of municipal bonds prior to public sale by the issuer. Investors are so accustomed to the system that almost automatically, a rating will determine within certain limits the interest rate the issuer must pay on its bonds. (p. 60)

Design an empirical study that would provide evidence on whether the relation between bond ratings and bond yields (see Table 13.1) is a causal one.

QUESTION 13.2: Statistical Models of Bond Rating

There has been some criticism of the use of statistical models to predict bond ratings. For example, Albert C. Esokait, a senior vice-president of *Moody's*, was quoted in *Forbes* (September 1970) as follows:

> [Bond rating] is not a number game. You couldn't rate bonds on a computer. It would blow a gasket. Bond-rating is a comprehensive analysis of the position of a company in whatever industry it is in. (p. 19)

Another executive of *Moody's*, J. Phillips, stated the following:

> [Bond rating] is a question of examining each area of information, and their interrelationships and making a judgment modified as necessary by evidence and experience. *There is no way to cram them all into a single formula, which invariably produces the right answer.* The stumbling block is weighting and most disagreements on ratings spring from different weights attached to the factors in analysis by different analysts. (Phillips [1975, p. 377], emphasis added)

H. R. Fraser, an executive of *Standard & Poor's*, made the following comment on a paper (Altman and Katz [1976]) using discriminant analysis to predict the bond ratings of electric utilities:

> Can a reasonably accurate classification of utilities into their observed bond rating categories be made using only published financial data plus a multivariate model?...I came to the conclusion that ignoring basic fundamentals and using only the financial data published by a rating agency could result in some very dangerous assumptions, no matter what set of ratios or type of model was used.

Furthermore, unless the fundamentals, their trends, and management's approach to these developments were analyzed, the probability of accurately predicting future rating changes would be something less than the flip of a coin. (Fraser [1976, p. 240])

REQUIRED

(1) Comment on the above statements by executives of rating agencies.

(2) What purposes could the statistical bond rating models examined in Chapter 13 serve?

(3) It has been argued that "there is no way of demonstrating whether the rating agencies are right or wrong" in their rating decisions. Do you agree?

QUESTION 13.3:   Rating General Obligation Municipal Bonds

1. Hobie Leland, Jr. has just been appointed to the municipal investment division of the *Down-Under Bank*. His first task is to build a linear discriminant model for predicting whether bonds will be rated (1) A or above *or* (2) Baa or below. His superior provides him with details (from *Moody's Municipal and Government Manual*) of the population, general obligation debt, assessed property valuation and the current *Moody's* rating for 12 general obligation bonds. Hobie calculated the following financial ratios for each municipality:

$X_{1,i}$ = General obligation debt per capita of municipality i

$X_{2,i}$ = Assessed property valuation per capita of municipality i

$X_{3,i}$ = General obligation debt to assessed property valuation of
municipality i.

The values of X_1, X_2, X_3 and the current rating for each municipal bond are presented in Table 13.9. After trying all combinations of X_1, X_2, and X_3 in linear discriminant models, Hobie chooses the following discriminant model:

$$Z_i = -.00435 X_{1,i} + .00064 X_{2,i}.$$

He chooses the cutoff point which minimizes the total number of misclassifications. The exact cutoff point is the midpoint between the Z scores of the adjacently ranked bonds.

REQUIRED

(1) Given the minimize the total number of misclassifications criterion, what cutoff point should Hobie choose? Present the classification matrix for the above model with this cutoff point.

(2) Under what circumstances would a criterion different from minimize the total number of misclassifications be appropriate for *Down-Under*?

TABLE 13.9 Municipal Bond Rating: Estimation Sample

City	General Oblig. Debt Per Capita (X_1)	Assessed Value Per Capita (X_2)	General Oblig. Debt to Assessed Value $\times 10^2$ (X_3)	Rating
Austin, Tex.	192	5,905	3.25	Aa
Corpus Christi, Tex.	266	4,188	6.35	Aa
Fresno, Calif.	52	3,011	1.73	Aa
East Cleveland, Ohio	32	2,286	1.40	A
Franklin, Tenn.	41	2,428	1.69	A
Rome, Ga.	160	4,515	3.54	A
Crowley, La.	100	870	11.49	Baa
Franklin, Pa.	157	2,478	6.34	Baa
Great Bend, Kan.	144	2,597	5.54	Baa
Hamtramck, Mich.	62	4,725	1.31	Baa
Midfield, Ala.	360	1,652	21.79	Baa
Vicksburg, Miss.	128	2,137	5.99	Baa

(3) What problems may occur in measuring the municipal variables chosen by Hobie's superior?

2. Hobie remembers that it is advisable to use a validation or hold-out sample to test the predictive ability of the discriminant function chosen in 1. He collects information for another 12 general municipal bonds—see Table 13.10.

TABLE 13.10 Municipal Bond Rating: Validation Sample

City	General Oblig. Debt Per Capita (X_1)	Assessed Value Per Capita (X_2)	General Oblig. Debt to Assessed Value $\times 10^2$ (X_3)	Rating
Bristol, Conn.	269	4,687	5.74	Aa
Monterey, Calif.	44	4,977	.88	Aa
Anaheim, Calif.	49	4,378	1.12	A
Jonesboro, Ark.	91	956	9.52	A
Peekskill, N.Y.	113	2,945	3.84	A
Scottsdale, Ariz.	98	3,141	3.12	A
Tempe, Ariz.	165	2,924	5.64	A
Barstow, Calif.	148	2,423	6.11	Baa
Dayton, Kent.	120	2,445	4.91	Baa
Escondido, Calif.	136	4,230	3.22	Baa
Port Needles, Tex.	262	4,117	6.36	Baa
Ruston, Lou.	187	1,035	18.07	Baa

REQUIRED

(1) Examine the predictive ability of the cutoff point chosen in 1(1) on the validation sample of 12 general obligation municipal bonds. Present the classification matrix for this validation sample.

(2) Hobie is disappointed by the results for the validation sample. What factors may explain these results?

(3) Hobie's superior is disillusioned by the performance of Hobie's model on the validation sample. He examines discriminant functions using all combinations of the variables in Table 13.10 and reports that the following model has fewer misclassifications on Table 13.10 data than does Hobie's model:

$$Z_i = -.00023X_{2,i} - .2166X_{3,i}.$$

Can you defend Hobie's model choice vis-à-vis the above model chosen by his superior?

QUESTION 13.4:   Rating Water Revenue Bonds

The bonds of *water works* comprise a large segment of the municipal revenue bond market. The areas looked at in rating these bonds include the debt of the water works, its financial operations, technical details of the plant, and the economy of the area served by the water works. Since the interest and principal repayments are to be derived from the future revenues, particular attention is paid to the ability of the water works to generate revenues sufficient to cover operating expenses and interest and principal repayments. Some financial ratios used in the analysis of water bonds include the following:

Financial Ratio	Average of 95 Water Systems Rated by Moody's (1975)
$X_1 =$ *Operating ratio*—operating and maintenance expenses (excluding depreciation) divided by total operating revenues	59.3%
$X_2 =$ *Net take-down*—net revenues (gross revenues less operating and maintenance expenses) divided by system gross revenues	44.2%
$X_3 =$ *Debt service safety margin*—system gross revenues less operating and maintenance expenses and less current debt service divided by system gross revenues	22.8%

TABLE 13.11   Water Revenue Bonds

		X_1	X_2	X_3	*Bond Rating*
		A.	*Estimation Sample*		
1.	Evanston, Ill.	38.86	61.14	45.20	Aa
2.	Moline, Ill.	42.97	57.03	44.00	A
3.	Napa, Calif.	56.79	43.21	17.30	A
4.	Pinellas, Fla.	20.88	79.12	54.10	A
5.	St. Petersburg, Fla.	38.02	61.98	68.30	A
6.	Bedford, Ind.	69.04	30.97	12.80	Baa
7.	Hazelton, Pa.	66.84	33.16	16.10	Baa
8.	Petaluma, Calif.	55.27	44.73	29.60	Baa
9.	Sarasota, Fla.	55.35	44.65	26.10	Baa
10.	Vacaville, Calif.	61.59	38.41	23.60	Baa
		B.	*Validation Sample*		
1.	Decatur, Ill.	54.48	45.52	27.30	A
2.	Elgin, Ill.	54.91	45.09	23.30	Aa
3.	Hollywood, Fla.	21.45	78.55	49.20	A
4.	Merced, Calif.	10.79	89.21	48.50	A
5.	Riverside, Calif.	54.44	45.56	18.20	A
6.	Chesterfield, Va.	50.44	49.56	29.40	Baa
7.	Cocoa, Fla.	53.75	46.25	17.00	Baa
8.	Monroeville, Ill.	64.72	35.28	6.80	Baa
9.	Mount Vernon, Ill.	64.30	35.70	2.70	Baa
10.	Niles, Ill.	83.95	16.05	7.20	Baa

KEY: X_1 = operating ratio (%),
X_2 = net take-down (%),
X_3 = debt service safety margin (%).

Table 13.11 (panel A) lists 1975 values of these ratios for ten water works and the corresponding rating of the revenue bonds—these bonds comprise the estimation sample.

An analyst decides to examine the ability of a parsimonious linear discriminant function to predict whether the ratings are (1) A or above *or* (2) Baa or below. After some experimentation with the above three ratios, he decides on the following function:

$$Z_i = -.09157X_{1,i} + .00537X_{3,i}.$$

REQUIRED

(1) What relationship between bond ratings and the values of X_1, X_2, and X_3 would you predict to exist? Is there evidence in Table 13.11 (panel A) that the relationships you predict do occur for these ten water bonds? (It is sufficient to compare the mean values of each ratio for bonds rated A or above and bonds rated Baa or below.)

(2) Using as your criterion minimize the total number of misclassifications, what cutoff point would you choose for the above linear discriminant function? Only consider cutoff points that are midpoints between the Z scores of adjacently ranked bonds. Present the classification matrix for the above model with this cutoff point.

(3) Table 13.11 (panel B) presents information on another ten revenue bonds of water works. These bonds will serve as a validation sample. Why is it advisable to examine the predictive ability of the above discriminant function on a validation sample? Present the classification matrix from using the cutoff point chosen in (2) on the validation sample.

(4) Analysts rating water revenue bonds report that an important variable they consider is the rating of the general obligation bond of the municipality in which the water works operates. Why would an analyst be concerned with the general obligation bond when the municipality does not pledge its full faith, credit, and taxing power for the payment of principal and interest on the revenue bond?

REFERENCES

ALTMAN, E. I., and KATZ, S. "Statistical Bond Rating Classification Using Financial and Accounting Data." In M. Schiff and G. Sorter (eds.), *Proceedings of the Conference on Topical Research in Accounting.* New York University, New York, 1976. 205–239.

ANG, J. S., and PATEL, K. A. "Bond Rating Methods: Comparison and Validation." *Journal of Finance* (May 1975): 631–640.

BLACK, F., and COX, J. "Valuing Corporate Securities: Some Effects of Bond Indenture Provisions." *Journal of Finance* (May 1976): 351–367.

BLACK, F., and SCHOLES, M. "The Pricing of Options and Corporate Liabilities." *Journal of Political Economy* (May–June 1973): 637–659.

CARLETON, W. T., and LERNER, E. M. "Statistical Credit Scoring of Municipal Bonds." *Journal of Money, Credit and Banking* Vol. 1 (Nov. 1969): 750–764.

COOLEY, W. C., and LOHNES, P. R. *Multivariate Data Analysis*. Wiley, New York, 1971.

COPPERS & LYBRAND. *Financial Disclosure Practices of the American Cities: A Public Report*. Coopers & Lybrand, New York, 1976.

DAVIDSON, S., GREEN, D. O., HELLERSTEIN, W., MADANSKY, A., and WEIL, R. L. *Financial Reporting by State and Local Government Units*. Center for Management of Public and Nonprofit Enterprise, University of Chicago, Chicago, 1977.

EISENBEIS, R. A. "Pitfalls in the Application of Discriminant Analysis in Business, Finance and Economics." *Journal of Finance*: 875–900.

FISHER, L. "Determinants of Risk Premiums on Corporate Bonds." *Journal of Political Economy* (June 1959): 217–237.

FRANK, R. E., MASSY, W. F., and MORRISON, D. G. "Bias in Multiple Discriminant Analysis." *Journal of Marketing Research* (Aug. 1965): 250–258.

FRASER, H. R. "Comment on 'Statistical Bond Rating Classification Using Financial and Accounting Data.'" In M. Schiff and G. Sorter (eds.), *Proceedings of the Conference on Topical Research in Accounting*. New York University, New York, 1976: 240–244.

GOODMAN, R. M. "Municipal Bond Rating Testimony." *Financial Analysts Journal* (May–June 1968): 59–65.

GRIER, P., and KATZ, S. "The Differential Effects of Bond Rating Changes Among Industrial and Public Utility Bonds by Maturity." *Journal of Business* (Apr. 1976): 226–239.

HARMELINK, P. J. "An Empirical Examination of the Predictive Ability of Alternate Sets of Insurance Company Accounting Data." *Journal of Accounting Research* (Spring 1973): 146–158.

HASTIE, K. L. "Determinants of Municipal Bond Yields." *Journal of Financial and Quantitative Analysis* (June 1972): 1729–1748.

HETTENHOUSE, G. W., and SARTORIS, W. L. "An Analysis of the Informational Value of Bond-Rating Changes." *Quarterly Review of Economics and Business* (Summer 1976): 65–78.

HICKMAN, W. B. *Corporate Bond Quality and Investor Experience*. National Bureau of Economic Research, New York, 1953.

HOMER, S., and LEIBOWITZ, M. L. *Inside the Yield Book*. Prentice-Hall, Englewood Cliffs, N.J., 1972.

HORRIGAN, J. O. "The Determination of Long Term Credit Standing with Financial Ratios." *Empirical Research in Accounting: Selected Studies, 1966*. Supplement to *Journal of Accounting Research* (1966): 44–62.

HORTON, J. J. "Statistical Classification of Municipal Bonds." *Journal of Bank Research* (Autumn 1970): 29–40.

JOHNSON, R. E. "Term Structures of Corporate Bond Yields as a Function of Risk of Default." *Journal of Finance* (May 1967): 313–345.

JOY, O. M., and TOLLEFSON, J. O. "On the Financial Applications of Discriminant Analysis." *Journal of Financial and Quantitative Analysis* (Dec. 1975): 723–739.

KATZ, S. "The Price Adjustment Process of Bonds to Rating Reclassifications: A Test of Bond Market Efficiency." *Journal of Finance* (May 1974): 551–561.

MERTON, R. C. "On the Pricing of Corporate Debt: The Risk Structure of Interest Rates." *Journal of Finance* (May 1974): 449–470.

MICHEL, A. J. "Municipal Bond Ratings: Discriminant Analysis Approach." Paper Presented at Financial Management Association Meetings (Montreal), 1976.

MOODY'S INVESTORS SERVICE, INC. *Pitfalls in Issuing Municipal Bonds.* Moody's, New York, 1974

MOODY'S INVESTOR SERVICES, INC. *Moody's Corporate Bond Yield Averages by Rating.* Moody's, New York, 1976.

———. *Moody's Municipal Bond Yield Averages by Rating.* Moody's, New York, 1976a.

MORRISON, D. G. "On the Interpretation of Discriminant Analysis." *Journal of Marketing Research* (May 1969): 156–163.

PHILLIPS, J. "Analysis and Rating of Municipal Bonds." In S. N. Levine (ed.), *Financial Analysts Handbook 1—Portfolio Management.* Irwin, Homewood, Ill., 1975: 371–380.

PINCHES, G. E., and MINGO, K. A. "A Multivariate Analysis of Industrial Bond Ratings." *Journal of Finance* (Mar. 1973): 1–18.

———. "The Role of Subordination and Industrial Bond Ratings." *Journal of Finance* (Mar. 1975): 201–206.

POGUE, T. F., and SOLDOFSKY, R. M. "What's in a Bond Rating?" *Journal of Financial and Quantitative Analysis* (June 1969): 201–228.

PRESS, S. J. *Applied Multivariate Analysis.* Holt, Rinehart and Winston, Inc., New York, 1972.

REPORT OF THE TWENTIETH CENTURY FUND TASK FORCE ON MUNICIPAL BOND CREDIT RATINGS. *The Rating Game.* Twentieth Century Fund, New York, 1974.

ROSS, I. "Higher Stakes in the Bond-Rating Game." *Fortune* (Apr. 1976): 133–142.

RUBINFELD, D. "Credit Ratings and the Market for General Obligation Municipal Bonds." *National Tax Journal* (Volume XXVI, 1973): 17–27.

SHERWOOD, H. C. *How Corporate and Municipal Debt Is Rated.* Wiley, New York, 1976.

SLOVIC, P., and LICHTENSTEIN, S. "Comparison of Bayesian and Regression Approaches to the Study of Information Processing in Judgment." *Organizational Behavior and Human Performance* (Nov. 1971): 649–744.

WEINSTEIN, M. I. "An Examination of the Behavior of Corporate Bond Prices." Draft of Ph.D. Dissertation, University of Chicago, Chicago, 1977.

WEST, R. R. "An Alternative Approach to Predicting Corporate Bond Ratings." *Journal of Accounting Research* (Spring 1970): 118–127.

———. "Bond Ratings, Bond Yields and Financial Regulation: Some Findings." *Journal of Law and Economics* (Apr. 1973): 159–168.

FINANCIAL DISTRESS PREDICTION

Prediction of the financial distress of corporations, municipalities, universities, and other institutions is a subject of much interest and research. In Section 14.1 we shall examine a variety of reasons for this subject attracting attention. Some problems in defining *financial distress* are discussed in Section 14.2. Univariate and multivariate models for predicting distress are examined in Sections 14.3 and 14.4. Some general comments on research in this area are made in Section 14.5.

14.1 IMPORTANCE OF PREDICTING FINANCIAL DISTRESS

One of the main reasons for developing models to predict financial distress revolves around public policy issues. In certain industries, regulatory bodies have been set up to monitor the financial solvency and stability of companies. For instance, state insurance commissioners are concerned with protecting the policyholders of insurance companies registered in that state. Part of their activities involves detecting companies that appear to be showing signs of *financial distress*.[1] Similarly, the Interstate Commerce Commission (ICC) is concerned that the nation's railroads remain viable economic units. The bankruptcy of the *Penn-Central Transportation Company* prompted the following comment by the chairman of the ICC:

> Beyond the Penn-Central investigation, the ICC probably will develop a number of rulemaking procedures aimed at fashioning guidelines for providing "early warnings" of impending bankruptcies of other roads. (quoted in Altman [1973, p. 184])

The models examined in Sections 14.3 and 14.4 are illustrative of several approaches the ICC could use to predict impending bankruptcies.[2] The *Federal Deposit Insurance Corporation* (FDIC) is likewise concerned with minimizing the number of *financially distressed* firms (banks) under its jurisdiction. Indeed, it has devoted considerable resources to developing distress prediction models for U.S. banks.[3]

Models for predicting financial distress could also be important in legal decisions. Consider antitrust cases. Blum [1974] has noted that one defense against violating an antitrust law is the so-called *failing company doctrine*. This doctrine can apply where one of two merging companies is likely to fail and where the "failing" company has received "no offer to merge from a company with which a merger would have been legal." The "rationale of the Doctrine is that the likely harm to communities, employees, creditors, and owners associated with a failing business that might be forced into a liquidation proceeding outweighs harm to competition caused by allowing a failing and presumably weak but still intact firm to merge with a competitor" (pp. 1–2). Use of a model for predicting "failure" provides the court with some evidence as to which firms may fall within the failing company doctrine defense against antitrust laws.

Distress prediction models can also provide useful information to the management and investors of corporations. Bankruptcy can mean that a firm incurs both direct and indirect costs—see Warner [1976]. Direct costs include fees to professionals such as accountants and lawyers. Indirect costs include the lost sales or profits due to the constraints imposed by the court or the court-appointed trustee. Although there is limited empirical evidence on the numerical magnitude of these two types of costs,[4] both represent an external drain on the value of the assets underlying an investor's claim. It may well be that if early warning signals of bankruptcy were observed, these costs could be reduced by arranging a merger with another firm or adopting a corporate reorganization plan.

Research on financial distress prediction has relevance to lending institutions, both in deciding the conditions under which new loans are given and in devising policies to monitor existing loans. Consider the design of restrictive covenants in bond indenture or loan agreements. Many such covenants contain provisions related to the value of the current ratio or the dollar magnitude of working capital. Such specific provisions assume that these variables are important in discriminating between "good" and "bad" loans. By empirically testing financial variables in a distress prediction model, it is possible to examine the descriptive validity of this assumption. It may well be that variables other than conventional liquidity measures are more effective indicators of subsequent financial distress.

Altman and McGough [1974] have noted that models predicting financial distress may also be of assistance to an auditor. When issuing an opinion on the financial statements of a corporation, an auditor is generally required to make an assumption as to whether the business will remain as a going concern. Although the final decision must rest on the auditor's judgment, his decision can be aided by a model that predicts distress.

14.2 PROBLEMS IN DEFINING FINANCIAL DISTRESS

The literature on financial distress is largely composed of two streams: (1) a descriptive-oriented branch outlining bankruptcy acts and legal cases on these acts and (2) an empirical branch in which models to predict the financial status (e.g., bankrupt/nonbankrupt) of corporations are examined.[5] Underlying both streams of this literature is some ambiguity over what the term *financial distress* means. This ambiguity is not surprising when it is realized that if one views liquidation of a corporation as definitive evidence of it losing its existence, there is a continuum of events that can lead up to liquidations, e.g., declining share of major product markets, deferment of payments to short-term creditors, omission of a preferred dividend, and filing of a Chapter X or XI bankruptcy. Both the legal system and the empirically based classificatory models seek to determine points on this continuum that can serve as criteria for distinguishing *distressed* from *nondistressed* firms.[6]

Chapter XI of the Bankruptcy Act is a voluntary proceeding in which a firm continues to operate while it tries to work out a plan for the payment of its debts or a reconstruction of the debtors' claims. There can be important reasons why a firm will file for Chapter XI bankruptcy, even though it is not legally forced to do so. The court can provide a firm protection from lawsuits against the firm, from mortgage foreclosure, etc. Under a Chapter X Bankruptcy Act filing, a trustee appointed by the court is responsible for running the firm. Note, however, that the trustee can delegate his authority to run the firm to the old management. The use of a Chapter X or Chapter XI filing for bankruptcy does not necessarily mean that the corporation is to be liquidated. Corporations can reemerge from bankruptcy proceedings as viable entities and subsequently become competitive and profitable firms in their industry.

The problem of defining financial distress in the not-for-profit sector of the economy is an especially difficult task. Suppose a private university is having extreme difficulty meeting running expenses out of tuition fees, grants, and endowment income. Several options may be open to the university trustees. One is to formally close the university and sell its physical facilities. A second option is to seek a merger with another university. Yet another option is to reduce research grants drastically and library acquisitions and to increase existing faculty teaching loads when resignations occur. The last option may result in important changes in the "goals" of the university. In an empirical study, it would be relatively easy to use the first option as a sign of financial distress. It would be considerably more difficult to set up criteria for classifying universities who chose the last option as being in a financially distressed or nondistressed category.[7]

Given the ambiguity in the term *financial distress*, it is not surprising that different authors have used different criteria of distress. For instance, in Beaver [1966] a firm was "said to have failed when *any* one of the following events have occurred: bankruptcy, bond default, an overdrawn bank account, or nonpayment of a preferred stock dividend" (p. 71). In contrast, Deakin [1972] defined failure "to include only those firms which experienced bankruptcy, insolvency, or were otherwise liquidated for the benefit of creditors" (p. 168). Although these different criteria of distress make generalizations from this research difficult, it is far from clear that any agreed upon set of criteria will be quickly forthcoming. The reader is well advised to always determine the specific criteria used when an author determines that a firm is "financially distressed."

14.3 UNIVARIATE MODELS OF DISTRESS PREDICTION

A univariate approach to predicting financial distress involves the use of a single variable in a prediction model. There are two key assumptions in this approach:

(1) The distribution of the variable for distressed firms differs systematically from the distribution of the variable for the nondistressed firms, and

(2) These systematic differences can be capitalized on for prediction purposes.

The univariate approach will be illustrated by a case study of U.S. railroad bankruptcies in the 1970–1971 period.

A An Example: Predicting Railroad Bankruptcies[8]

In 1970, several large Class I U.S. railroads filed for bankruptcy under provisions of the National Bankruptcy Act, e.g., *Boston and Maine Corporation* and the *Penn-Central* railroad complex. How well did the financial statements issued in the year prior to 1970 predict this bankruptcy? To examine this question, a sample of ten railroads was chosen to build a univariate prediction model. The following two ratios were calculated for each company from the 1969 statements filed by these railroads with the *Interstate Commerce Commission*:

(1) *Transportation expenses to operating revenue* (TE/OR).   Transportation expenses are primarily the actual cost of train operations and include the wages of train crews and fuel costs. Operating revenues comprise mostly freight revenues. They also include passenger revenues and revenues from miscellaneous sources such as mail express.

(2) *Times interest earned* (TIE).   Interest charges are for fixed interest obligations. Earnings are before interest and tax. A negative value of this ratio implies that the company had negative earnings (a loss) before interest and tax payments.

For simplicity, it is assumed that these two ratios are normally distributed. Table 14.1 details the ten railroads and the 1969 values of the two ratios for each railroad. This sample is used to build several univariate bankruptcy prediction models and is referred to as the *estimation sample*.

Distribution Differences Between Ratios of Bankrupt and Nonbankrupt Railroads

The first assumption in the univariate approach is that the distribution of the ratio differs between the bankrupt and nonbankrupt railroads. The assumption of normality for each ratio implies that either the mean or the variance of the distribution differs between the two groups of railroads. In this section we shall concentrate on differences in means. For the TE/OR ratio, the means of the two groups are

Nonbankrupt railroads	.356
Bankrupt railroads	.473

That is, the bankrupt group spends more (on average) of each dollar of operating revenue on transportation expenses such as train crew wages and fuel costs. The means for the TIE ratio of the two groups are

Nonbankrupt railroads	2.49
Bankrupt railroads	−.26

Thus, the nonbankrupt group evidences a greater ability (on average) to generate revenues sufficient to cover fixed interest obligations. On balance, these differences suggest that at least one year prior to bankruptcy the financial ratios of the bankrupt and nonbankrupt railroads appear to be

TABLE 14.1   Railroad Bankruptcy Prediction Example: Estimation Sample

	TE/OR	*TIE*
Nonbankrupt in 1970		
1. Ann Arbor Railroad (Mich.)	.524	−1.37
2. Central of Georgia Railway (Ga.)	.348	2.16
3. Cincinnati, New Orleans and Texas Pacific Railway (Ohio)	.274	2.91
4. Florida East Coast Railway (Fla.)	.237	2.82
5. Illinois Central Railroad (Ill.)	.388	3.10
6. Norfolk and Western Railway (Va.)	.359	2.81
7. Southern Pacific Transportation Co. (Del.)	.400	3.56
8. Southern Railway Company (Va.)	.314	3.93
Bankruptcy Filings in 1970		
9. Boston and Maine Corporation (Del.)	.461	−.68
10. Penn-Central Transportation Co. (Pa.)	.485	.16

markedly different. A statistical significance test for the difference between the means of the two groups was used and supported the above conclusion at the .05 level for each ratio.[9]

Predictive Ability Tests

An important issue is whether one can use the above-noted differences in mean values of the ratios for predictive purposes. The univariate approach to prediction that will be outlined is the *dichotomous classification test* developed by Beaver [1966]. This approach involves ranking the railroads by the value of a ratio and then visually inspecting the data to determine an "optimal" cutoff point for predicting a railroad as bankrupt or nonbankrupt. The rankings of companies for each ratio are presented in Table 14.2. For simplicity, it will be assumed that the only cutoff points considered are the midpoints between the adjacently ranked ratios; e.g., for the TE/OR ratio, the first cutoff point considered is .5045, which is midway between the .524 of *Ann Arbor Railroad* and the .485 of *Penn-Central*. A type I prediction error occurs when a bankrupt (B) railroad is predicted to be nonbankrupt (NB). A type II error occurs when a nonbankrupt (NB) railroad is predicted to be bankrupt (B).

The type I, type II, and total number of errors (misclassifications) from using several alternative cutoff points of the TE/OR ratio are

Cutoff Point	Number of Type I Errors	Number of Type II Errors	Total Number of Errors
Predict B if TE/OR > .5045	2	1	3
Predict B if TE/OR > .473	1	1	2
Predict B if TE/OR > .4305	0	1	1
Predict B if TE/OR > .394	0	2	2
Predict B if TE/OR > .3735	0	3	3

The cutoff point which minimizes the total number of misclassifications (errors) is predict B if a railroad's TE/OR ratio > .4305. Only one railroad is misclassified using this model, i.e., *Ann Arbor Railroad*. For the TIE ratio, the cutoff point which minimizes the total number of misclassifications is predict B if a railroad's TIE ratio < 1.16. This cutoff point also misclassifies only one railroad.

The technique of choosing the cutoff point based on the ten railroads in the estimation sample runs the danger that specific characteristics of the firms in the two categories will overly influence the value of the cutoff point. Ideally, one wants any differences between the bankrupt and nonbankrupt firms that are incorporated into the univariate prediction model to reflect only the underlying population differences between these two

TABLE 14.2 Railroad Bankruptcy Prediction Example:
Dichotomous Classification Test: Estimation Sample

Railroad	Ratio	Actual Status in 1970
1. Ranking on TE/OR Ratio		
Ann Arbor Railroad	.524	NB
Penn-Central Transportation	.485	B
Boston and Maine	.461	B
Southern Pacific Transportation	.400	NB
Illinois Central Railroad	.388	NB
Norfolk and Western Railway	.359	NB
Central of Georgia Railway	.348	NB
Southern Railway	.314	NB
Cincinnati, New Orleans and Texas Pacific	.274	NB
Florida East Coast Railway	.237	NB
2. Ranking on TIE Ratio		
Southern Railway	3.93	NB
Southern Pacific Transportation	3.56	NB
Illinois Central Railroad	3.10	NB
Cincinnati, New Orleans and Texas Pacific	2.91	NB
Florida East Coast Railway	2.82	NB
Norfolk and Western Railway	2.81	NB
Central of Georgia Railway	2.16	NB
Penn-Central Transportation	.16	B
Boston and Maine	−.68	B
Ann Arbor Railroad	−1.37	NB

groups. In this situation, it is important to examine the predictive ability of the univariate model on an independent sample of railroads. This independent sample is termed the *validation* (or hold-out) sample. During 1971, only one Class I U.S. railroad filed for bankruptcy—*Reading Company*. This railroad and nine other nonbankrupt railroads in 1971 were used as the validation sample. Details of these companies and the 1970 values of the TE/OR and TIE ratios are in Table 14.3.

Table 14.4 summarizes the prediction results for the validation sample. Use of the .4305 cutoff point for the TE/OR ratio results in no type I errors and two type II errors—*Erie-Lackawanna* and *Chicago, Milwaukee, St. Paul and Pacific*. For the TIE ratio, the 1.16 cutoff point results in no type I errors and three type II errors—*Erie-Lackawanna, Chicago, Milwaukee, St. Paul and Pacific*, and *Bangor and Aroostock*. The *Erie-Lackawanna* railroad filed for bankruptcy in 1972.

TABLE 14.3 Railroad Bankruptcy Prediction Example: Validation Sample

	TE/OR	TIE
Nonbankrupt in 1971		
1. Akron, Canton and Youngstown Railroad (Ohio)	.382	1.85
2. Alabama Great Southern Railroad (Ala.)	.305	4.05
3. Atchison, Topeka and Santa Fe Railway (Kan.)	.373	4.72
4. Bangor and Aroostock Railroad (Me.)	.341	.88
5. Burlington Northern Incorporated (Del.)	.425	2.73
6. Chesapeake and Ohio Railway (Va.)	.395	3.12
7. Chicago, Milwaukee, St. Paul and Pacific Railroad (Wis.)	.437	.27
8. Erie-Lackawanna Railway Co. (Del.)	.469	.22
9. St. Louis Southwestern Railway Co. (Mo.)	.352	46.70
Bankruptcy Filing in 1971		
10. Reading Company (Pa.)	.451	.40

TABLE 14.4 Railroad Bankruptcy Prediction Example: Dichotomous Classification Test: Validation Sample

Railroad	Ratio	Actual Status in 1971	
1. *Ranking on TE/OR Ratio*			
Erie-Lackawanna	.469	NB	
Reading Company	.451	B	Predicted bankrupt
Chicago, Milwaukee, St. Paul and Pacific	.437	NB	
Burlington Northern	.425	NB	
Chesapeake and Ohio	.395	NB	
Akron, Canton and Youngstown	.382	NB	
Atchison, Topeka and Santa Fe	.373	NB	Predicted nonbankrupt
St. Louis Southwestern	.352	NB	
Bangor and Aroostock	.341	NB	
Alabama Great Southern	.305	NB	
2. *Ranking on TIE Ratio*			
St. Louis Southwestern	46.70	NB	
Atchison, Topeka and Santa Fe	4.72	NB	
Alabama Great Southern	4.05	NB	Predicted nonbankrupt
Chesapeake and Ohio	3.12	NB	
Burlington Northern	2.73	NB	
Akron, Canton and Youngstown	1.85	NB	
Bangor and Aroostock	.88	NB	
Reading Company	.40	B	Predicted bankrupt
Chicago, Milwaukee, St. Paul and Pacific	.27	NB	
Erie-Lackawanna	.22	NB	

General Comments on the Railroad Example

1. The criterion used for choosing the cutoff points for each ratio was minimize the total number of misclassifications. This criterion will not always lead to a unique cutoff point. Consider the following ranking of five companies:

Railroad	TE/OR	Actual Status
A	50	B
B	49	NB
C	48	B
D	47	NB
E	46	NB

A cutoff point of predict B if TE/OR > 49.5 and predict B if TE/OR $>$ 47.5 will both lead to one company being misclassified. In general, the choice of the cutoff point will depend on the probability of firms being misclassified and the cost of the misclassifications associated with each cutoff point considered.

2. The dichotomous classification test of Beaver [1966] is but one of several univariate approaches to predicting bankrupt firms. An alternative approach is to use the mean or median values of the ratio in the estimation sample. The mean TE/OR ratio for the ten railroads in the estimation sample is .356. Using a mean ratio univariate model implies predicting bankruptcy if the ratio $> .356$ and predicting nonbankruptcy if the ratio $\leqslant .356$. (How does this model perform on the estimation and validation samples?)

3. If several univariate models are used, it is possible that they may yield conflicting predictions for a firm. Consider the *Bangor and Aroostock Railroad* in the validation sample (Tables 14.3 and 14.4). Based on its TIE ratio of .88, it would be incorrectly predicted to be bankrupt in 1971. Yet, its TE/OR ratio of .341 gives the opposite prediction. The multivariate prediction models examined in Section 14.4 are motivated in part by attempts to resolve such conflicting predictions.

B   Mean Ratios of Distressed/Nondistressed Firms: Evidence

Comparisons of the mean ratios of distressed and nondistressed firms have a long history in the published literature.[10] An important study is Beaver [1966]. One part of Beaver's study was a comparison of the mean financial ratios of 79 *failed* firms and 79 *nonfailed* firms. A firm was designated as failed when any one of the following events occurred in the 1954–1964 period: bankruptcy, bond default, an overdrawn bank account, or nonpayment of a preferred stock dividend. The 79 nonfailed firms were selected using a *paired-sample* design—for each failed firm, a nonfailed firm of the same industry and asset size was selected. The means of 30 financial ratios were computed for each of the failed and nonfailed groups in each of the five years before failure.[11] Beaver called this comparison of mean ratios a *profile analysis*. It examines if there are observable differences in the mean ratios of the two sets of firms. Results for six financial ratios are presented in Figure 14.1.[12] In general, there is a marked difference in the behavior of the mean financial ratios of the two groups. The cash flow to total debt and the net income to total assets ratios appear to exhibit the most marked differences as early as five years before failure.

One limitation of the comparison of the mean financial ratios test is that it examines only one point on the distribution. Differences between the means could be induced by several extreme observations in either one of the groups examined. Apart from these extreme observations, there could be almost complete overlap in the distribution of the ratio of both groups. There are several options one can use to increase confidence that there are distribution differences in the ratios of distressed and nondistressed firms. One option is to use a median rather than a mean ratio comparison test. Another option is to use a statistical significance test, e.g., a test for equality of means. Yet another option is to conduct a univariate predictive test of the kind outlined in the railroad bankruptcy prediction example presented earlier in this chapter.[13]

C Univariate Prediction Tests: Evidence

The dichotomous classification test outlined earlier was first used extensively by Beaver [1966]. The sample was the 79 *failed* and 79 *nonfailed* firms described in the prior section. The cutoff point was chosen by arraying the values of each ratio and choosing the value which minimized the total misclassification percentage. The sample was randomly divided into two subgroups. The cutoff point chosen on the first subgroup (the *estimation sample*) was used to classify firms in the second subgroup (the *validation sample*) as *failed* or *nonfailed*. The percentage misclassification rates for six ratios for each of the five years before failure are presented in Table 14.5. These percentages are for the validation sample of firms. The cash flow to total debt and net income to total assets ratios predict with similar success in each of the three years prior to "failure"; e.g., both misclassify only 13% of the firms one year prior to "failure."

One interesting result in Beaver [1966] was that the cutoff point criterion of minimize the total number of misclassifications resulted in different percentages of type I and type II errors. In particular, nonfailed firms were correctly predicted to a greater extent than the failed firms. For

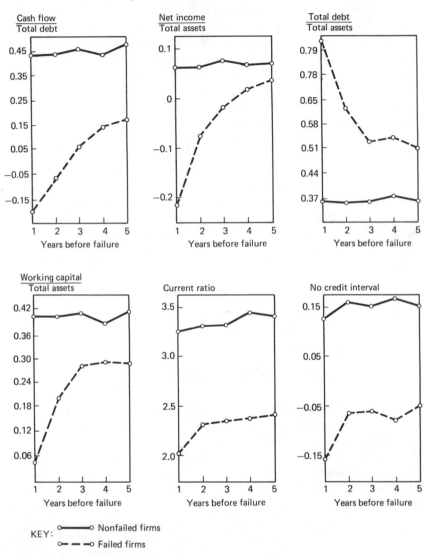

FIGURE 14.1   Profile Analysis: Mean Ratios of Failed and Nonfailed Firms

KEY: o——o Nonfailed firms
       o— —o Failed firms

Source: Beaver [1966, Figure 1].

TABLE 14.5 Univariate Failure Prediction: Dichotomous Classification Test: Percentage Misclassification Rates

Ratio	Year Before Failure				
	1	2	3	4	5
Cash flow / Total debt	.13	.21	.23	.24	.22
Net income / Total assets	.13	.20	.23	.29	.28
Total debt / Total assets	.19	.25	.34	.27	.28
Working capital / Total assets	.24	.34	.33	.45	.41
Current ratio	.20	.32	.36	.38	.45
No credit interval	.23	.38	.43	.38	.37

SOURCE: Beaver [1966, Table 3].

instance, the type I and type II error percentages for the cash flow to total debt ratio were

Year Before Failure	Type I Error Percentage	Type II Error Percentage	Total Misclassification Percentage
1	.22	.05	.13
2	.34	.08	.21
3	.37	.08	.23
4	.47	.03	.24
5	.43	.05	.22

In a decision context, any differential penalties between type I and type II errors would need to be explicitly taken into account when choosing the cutoff point in a univariate prediction model.[14]

In a subsequent paper, Beaver [1968] attempted to gain further insight into the reasons for the results in Table 14.5. In particular, he examined reasons for the relatively poor predictive performance of the liquidity ratios. Based on an analysis of the components of each ratio, he concluded the following:

My interpretation of the finding is that the cash flow, net income, and debt positions cannot be easily altered and represent permanent aspects of the firm. Because failure is so costly to all involved, the permanent, rather than the short-term, factors largely determine whether or not a firm will declare bankruptcy or default on a bond payment. For example, if a firm is in a poor liquid asset position but has good profit prospects, more than likely it will be able to obtain the necessary funds to meet maturing obligations. Conversely, even if a firm has the liquid assets to meet the obligations due, it may be unwilling to forestall the inevitable and will not wait until its liquid asset reservoir is exhausted before declaring bankruptcy. (p. 117)

In a related exercise, Deakin [1972] replicated Beaver's analysis on a different sample of firms over a different time period. The sample comprised 32 firms which "experienced bankruptcy, insolvency or were otherwise liquidated" in the 1964–1970 period. Each of the 32 failed firms was "matched with a nonfailed firm on the basis of industry classification, year of the financial information provided and asset size" (p. 168). The results of the univariate prediction tests were quite similar (although with somewhat higher percentage misclassification rates) to those reported in Beaver [1966].

14.4 MULTIVARIATE MODELS OF DISTRESS PREDICTION

One limitation of the univariate approach is that different ratios can imply different predictions for the same firm. It is not surprising that attempts have long been made to combine the information in several financial ratios into a single index. For instance, Wall [1936] outlined the following system of weighting ratios to arrive at a single index:

		Weights
1.	Current ratio	25%
2.	Worth to debt	25%
3.	Worth to fixed assets	15%
4.	Sales to receivables	10%
5.	Sales to inventories	10%
6.	Sales to fixed assets	10%
7.	Sales to worth	5%

The ratios of a specific firm were given the above weights and then added to give an overall rating for the firm. Although Wall's model has its limitations (e.g., the arbitrary choice of the weights), it is an interesting early effort in the now increasingly popular area of multivariate financial model building.

There are several issues in multivariate model building:

(1) What form should the model take (e.g., linear or multiplicative)?
(2) What variables should be included?
(3) What weights should be applied to the variables?

Ideally, some economic theory of financial distress should help guide the decisions on these issues. Unfortunately, there is very little available theory a model builder can draw upon. In this situation, it is not surprising that published analysis has mostly been of a *brute empirical* kind. The most common statistical tool used in multivariate distress prediction modeling is linear discriminant analysis. Chapter 13 contains a description and illustration of this technique for predicting municipal bond ratings. We shall further illustrate use of the technique by reference to the railroad bankruptcy example used previously.

A An Example: Predicting Railroad Bankruptcies

In this example, there are two discrete and known groups: railroad nonbankrupt in year t or railroad bankrupt in year t. Each railroad has two financial variables that will be used in the multivariate model: the transportation expense to operating revenue ratio (TE/OR)—X_i—and the times-interest-earned ratio (TIE)—Y_i. It is assumed that these two ratios come from a multivariate normal population and that the variances of each ratio for each group are equal.

The linear discriminant analysis model to be used for classificatory purposes is

$$Z_i = aX_i + bY_i. \tag{14.1}$$

Using the data for the estimation sample (Table 14.1), we obtained the following estimate of (14.1):

$$Z_i = -3.366X_i + .657Y_i. \tag{14.2}$$

To illustrate estimation of Z_i for each railroad, consider the *Penn-Central* with TE/OR = .485 and TIE = .16:

$$Z_i = -3.366 \times .485 + .657 \times .16$$
$$= -1.527.$$

Table 14.6 details the ten railroads in the estimation sample ranked on their Z_i scores. The cutoff point which minimizes the total number of misclassifications is $Z = -.640$ (midpoint between .247 and -1.527). This

TABLE 14.6 Railroad Bankruptcy Prediction Example: Z Scores for Estimation Sample

Railroad	Z Score	Actual Status in 1970
Southern Railway	1.524	NB
Florida East Coast Railway	1.054	NB
Southern Pacific Transportation	.991	NB
Cincinnati, New Orleans and Pacific	.989	NB
Illinois Central	.730	NB
Norfolk and Western	.637	NB
Central of Georgia	.247	NB
Penn-Central Transportation	-1.527	B
Boston and Maine	-1.998	B
Ann Arbor Railroad	-2.663	NB

TABLE 14.7 Railroad Bankruptcy Prediction Example:
Z Scores for Validation Sample

Railroad	Z Score	Actual Status in 1971	
St. Louis Southwestern	29.482	NB	
Atchison, Topeka and Santa Fe	1.844	NB	
Alabama Great Southern	1.633	NB	
Chesapeake and Ohio	.719	NB	Predicted
Burlington Northern	.362	NB	nonbankrupt
Akron, Canton and Youngstown	−.071	NB	
Bangor and Aroostock	−.570	NB	
Reading Company	−1.255	B	
Chicago, Milwaukee, St. Paul and Pacific	−1.294	NB	Predicted
Erie-Lackawanna	−1.434	NB	bankrupt

cutoff point misclassifies only one firm—*Ann Arbor Railroad.*

The discriminant function estimated on the 1970 sample can now be used to predict the bankrupt/nonbankrupt status of railroads in 1971. The estimated Z scores for the 1971 sample from Table 14.3 are presented in Table 14.7. Use of the $Z = -.640$ cutoff point correctly classifies the status of eight out of ten railroads. Two nonbankrupt railroads are incorrectly predicted to be bankrupt in 1971: *Chicago, Milwaukee, St. Paul and Pacific* and *Erie-Lackawanna.*

B Multivariate Models: Evidence

A representative example of multivariate model building for predicting corporate bankruptcy is Altman [1968]. The sample of firms included 33 manufacturers that filed a bankruptcy petition under Chapter X of the Bankruptcy Act during the 1946–1965 period. These 33 firms were paired with 33 nonbankrupt firms on the bases of similar industry and asset size. The asset size ranged between $1 million and $25 million. For each firm, 22 variables were initially chosen for analysis. The choice criteria were "popularity in the literature" and "potential relevancy to the study." These 22 ratios were classified into five ratio categories: liquidity, profitability, leverage, solvency, and activity. One ratio from each category was chosen for inclusion in the discriminant model. These five variables were

$X_1 =$ Working capital to total assets
$X_2 =$ Retained earnings to total assets
$X_3 =$ Earnings before interest and taxes to total assets
$X_4 =$ Market value of equity to book value of total debt
$X_5 =$ Sales to total assets.

TABLE 14.8 Mean Ratios of Bankrupt/Nonbankrupt Firms
in the Altman [1968] Study

	Bankrupt Group Mean	Nonbankrupt Group Mean
Working capital to total assets (X_1)	−.610	.414
Retained earnings to total assets (X_2)	−.626	.355
Earnings before interest and taxes to total assets (X_3)	−.318	.153
Market value of equity to book value of debt (X_4)	.401	2.477
Sales to total assets (X_5)	1.50	1.90

SOURCE: Altman [1968, Table 1].

Table 14.8 presents the mean ratios of the two groups of firms one year prior to the bankruptcy. The discriminant function chosen after "numerous computer runs" was[15]

$$Z_i = .012X_1 + .014X_2 + .033X_3 + .006X_4 + .010X_5.$$

For the sample of 66 firms used to estimate the above function, the total misclassification rate was 5%—the type I error was 6%, while the type II error was 3%. Altman also examined the predictive ability of financial ratios from the financial statements issued two years prior to bankruptcy. Not surprisingly, the predictive ability was less than that for one year prior to bankruptcy—the total misclassification rate was 17%, with a type I error of 28% and a type II error of 6%.

The predictive ability results for one year prior to bankruptcy are quite impressive. However, these results could reflect

(1) Population differences in the financial ratios of bankrupt and non-bankrupt firms,

(2) Sample characteristics of the specific 66 firms examined, and

(3) Search bias from using 22 variables and then choosing the 5 that "worked best" on the estimation sample.

It is primarily the type (1) factor that is of concern to the model builder. One check on the influence of factors (2) and (3) is to examine the predictive ability of the discriminant model on a sample not used for estimation purposes. Altman used two validation samples in his analysis. The first was a sample of 25 bankrupt firms whose asset size range was the same as that of the initial bankrupt group. Twenty-four of these 25 firms were correctly predicted to be bankrupt. The second validation sample comprised 66 nonbankrupt firms which had "suffered temporary profitability difficulties" but did not become bankrupt. The discriminant model correctly predicted 52 out of the 66 as nonbankrupt.

Small Business Distress Prediction

The incidence of distress in small firms is much greater than in the larger firms included in the Altman [1968] sample. Dun & Bradstreet [1976] provide the following details on the percentage of all 1975 business firm failures, classified by size (based on the dollar value of liabilities):

Less than $100,000	$100,000 to $1 Million	Over $1 Million
65.6%	30.3%	4.1%

A study on distress prediction for small businesses is Edmister [1972]. Forty-two firms which defaulted on a small business loan were matched with a sample of nondefaulting firms. The mean total asset size of the firms was $164,940. Nineteen ratios were initially selected on the basis of having "been advocated by theorists or been found to be significant predictors of business failure in previous empirical research" (p. 1479). Using a stepwise discriminant procedure, these 19 ratios were reduced to 7 in the final discriminant function. On the estimation sample, the total misclassification rate was 7%; there was a type I error of 15% and a type II error of 5%. Although no hold-out sample was used, Edmister did present simulation tests supporting the statistical significance of the above classification results.

14.5 SOME GENERAL COMMENTS

The literature on financial distress prediction is both diverse and rapidly growing.[16] Some general comments on the existing state of this literature appear warranted.

1. One limitation of much of the published research arises from the retrospective or *ex post* nature of the analysis, i.e., the estimation and validation samples both include firms that are known to have failed on a set date. Thus, it is possible in the research to compare the financial ratios of failed and nonfailed firms one year, two years, etc., prior to failure. Yet, in decision-making contexts, one knows neither which firms will fail nor the date on which they fail. To demonstrate that the results of this research have direct applicability to decision contexts, *it would be necessary to make ex ante predictions about the failure (and its timing) of firms currently nonfailed.* Some analysis in the Altman [1973] study on railroad bankruptcy

illustrates the use of discriminant models for ex ante predictions. Altman estimated a linear discriminant function using an estimation sample that included 21 railroads that went bankrupt between 1939 and 1970. He then computed Z scores for all Class I U.S. railroads with available data as of December 31, 1970. Fourteen out of 55 railroads were predicted to be in a "financially distressed state." Of these 14, 6 had already petitioned for bankruptcy. Of the remaining 8 railroads, only 1 went bankrupt in the year subsequent to that used to estimate the Z score (1971). This predictive performance contrasts sharply with the 2% misclassification percentage rate Altman reported for the estimation sample. Note, however, that the predictions made using the December 31, 1970 financial information were of an ex ante or prospective kind, whereas those for the estimation sample were of an ex post or retrospective kind.

2. A major criticism of many studies is the limited attempts made to develop any theory of financial distress that would specify the variables to be included in the discriminant function. A brute empiricism approach of choosing (say) 20 to 40 variables and then using a stepwise discriminant model to select the variables in the final discriminant function has been used in several studies. This approach is limited in its ability to provide generalizable results as to what financial variables are likely to be consistent predictors of financial distress.

3. The question of what is the appropriate bench mark for judging the predictive ability of a univariate or multivariate model is a difficult one. Studies that have used equal samples of bankrupt and nonbankrupt firms have generally used a random prediction model as a bench mark. That is, if 100 firms were examined, the following prediction results are used as the bench mark:

		Actual	
		B	NB
Predicted	B	25	25
	NB	25	25

Some comments by Neter [1966] on the use of equal samples of bankrupt/nonbankrupt firms and the use of the random prediction bench mark are worth repeating:

> In a comparison of the predictive power of predictions from ratios with those from a naive model, the question always arises as to how "naive" the naive model should be.... I suspect very much that a banker is not going to be faced with 50 percent failed firms and 50 percent nonfailed firms. Let us take a proportion that may be more realistic.... Suppose that the banker is faced with 99 nonfailed firms for every failed firm. The random prediction model would

have a predictive power as follows:

$$(.99)(.99)+(.01)(.01)=.9802.$$

This follows since the banker predicts with probability .99 that the firm will not fail; 99 percent of the time he will be faced with nonfailed firms, 1 percent of the time he predicts failure and 1 percent of the time he will actually be faced with a failed firm. So, about 98 percent of the time the banker would make a correct prediction with this randomized model scheme. But there is no law that says the naive model must be a randomized model. What if we consider a very simple pure strategy: always predict nonfailure. How often will the banker then be right? He will be right 99 percent of the time.

This suggests that a pure strategy might be a more reasonable naive model than a randomized strategy in this case....

Where the failed and nonfailed firms are equally frequent, the two naive models perform equally well. As soon as one gets away from the 50:50 situation, however, I would submit that the randomized strategy is a little too naive. (p. 115)

Note that it does not necessarily follow that a decision maker should always predict nonfailure in the above example—the costs of incorrectly predicting failed and nonfailed firms would also need to be considered.

A problem related to Neter's comments is the use of samples of 50% distressed/50% nondistressed firms when the population that inferences are made about is not 50%/50%. In the Dun & Bradstreet [1976] survey of business failures in the 1920–1975 period, the failure percentages ranged from 1.54% in 1932 to .04% in 1945—the 1975 rate was .43%. Misleading inferences about the ability of a model to predict business failure may occur when there is such a divergence between the sample priors of distressed/nondistressed firms used to estimate a model and the population priors that describe the underlying population.[17]

4. The methodologies chosen in some papers have important limitations that should be considered in interpreting their results. The requirement of some studies that a firm have at least five years of financial data available omits from the analysis a segment of firms (newly formed firms) in which the incidence of corporate failure is relatively high. The Dun & Bradstreet [1976] survey notes that 46.4% of the failures that occurred in 1975 were businesses that had been in existence four years or less. This statistic suggests that age may well be an important variable when building a discriminant model to predict failure. (Note that the X_2 variable in Altman [1968]—retained earnings to total assets—may be capturing this effect.)

The use of a paired-sample design where firms are matched on size and industry criteria effectively precludes these variables as indicators of financial distress in the study. Yet there is considerable evidence that both size and industry groups contain important information on distress likelihood. Evidence on size was quoted earlier in this chapter. Dun & Bradstreet [1976] gives the following industry information on the 1975 failure rate per 10,000 operating concerns:

	Failure Rate Per 10,000 Operating Concerns
Manufacturing	
Furniture	103
Apparel	99
Textiles	90
Lumber	44
Chemicals and drugs	38
Stone, clay and glass	25
Retail	
Infants' and children's wear	90
Men's wear	73
Shoes	43
Bakeries	26
Jewelry	21
Groceries, meats and produce	16

Thus, there do appear differences across industries in their observed failure rates. Incorporating these differences into a discriminant model could well improve its predictive ability.

5. The importance of using validation samples is by now generally well recognized in this literature. The specific hold-out sample techniques used, however, have varied—e.g., Beaver [1966] randomly divided his sample into two and estimated the model on one subsample and validated it on the other subsample; Altman [1968] used all his initial sample for estimation but used two new samples (neither similar to the estimation sample) for validation purposes; and Edmister [1972] used simulation evidence. These different hold-out techniques are another reason it is difficult to make generalizations from this research.

In some areas of financial distress analysis, the percentage of the total population in the distressed category will be relatively small. For example, in the model predicting Class I railroads that filed for bankruptcy in the 1970–1972 period, there would only be 5 observations in the bankrupt class and over 50 in the nonbankrupt class. In this context, splitting the sample in half to obtain a hold-out sample would accentuate the problem of efficiently estimating the parameters of the discriminant model. Moreover, it would also accentuate the problem of the specific characteristics of the individual bankrupt railroads overly affecting the estimated discriminant function. Users of classificatory techniques are well advised to examine some of the hold-out sample designs developed for use in such contexts—e.g., the Lachenbruch design.[18]

6. The use of accounting data in distress prediction models also warrants more caution than has been apparent in some studies. The computed financial ratios jointly reflect the underlying economic events affecting a firm and the specific accounting techniques used by the firm. It is quite possible that the predictive ability of prediction models will be affected by the diversity across firms and over time in accounting techniques. For instance, it is possible that the predictions of a model estimated prior to 1974 will be affected by the large number of firms making switches to the LIFO inventory valuation method in that year. There are several options open to an analyst in this context. One option is to restrict the model to firms who use the same accounting methods. Another option is to attempt to explicitly adjust the reported financial statements to obtain more consistency in accounting methods. The techniques outlined in Section 6.3 are illustrative of this approach.

A related issue is whether the consistent use of one accounting method vis-à-vis another will affect the predictive ability of a financial distress prediction model. An initial study on this issue is Elam [1975]. This study examined whether the "addition of capitalized lease data to a firm's financial statements will increase the power of financial ratios for predicting firm bankruptcy" (p. 28). A sample of 48 bankrupt firms was matched (on industry and year of bankruptcy criteria) with 48 nonbankrupt firms. The period of analysis was 1966–1972. Both sets of firms reported uncapitalized long-term leases in footnotes to their financial statements. Univariate and multivariate prediction models were examined in the analysis. Elam concluded that there was little difference in predictive ability when ratios were computed with or without the long-term leases capitalized on the balance sheet.[19, 20]

14.6 SUMMARY

There is an underlying thread to much of the vast literature on financial distress prediction, i.e., the attempt to capture systematic differences between distressed and nondistressed firms or institutions and then utilize these differences for predictive purposes. Although much interesting work in this area has been published, more attention is needed to develop some theory of financial distress that could help guide researchers on what variables to incorporate into predictive models.

NOTES

[1]See Trieschmann and Pinches [1973] and Pinches and Trieschmann [1974; 1977] for distress prediction models in the insurance industry.

[2]See Altman [1973] for a distress prediction model for Class I U.S. railroads.

[3]Sinkey [1975] is a good illustration of FDIC research in this area. Chapter 15 contains a discussion of distress prediction in the banking industry.

[4]The Baxter [1967] article is widely cited as evidence of significant direct bankruptcy costs. Baxter reported that legal fees in large *personal* bankruptcy cases totaled about 20% of the individual's assets. Warner [1976] examined legal costs of 11 railroads which filed for bankruptcy between 1930 and 1955. These costs represented, on average, 2.5% of the market value of the debt and equity claims as of three years prior to bankruptcy filing.

[5]There is also a small but growing literature on theoretical issues related to financial distress—e.g., Gordon [1971], Stiglitz [1972], Higgins and Schall [1975], and Lintner [1977]. The only detailed theoretical model on distress prediction is Wilcox's [1971] adaptation of the *gambler's ruin model*. For an empirical test of this model, see Wilcox [1973].

[6]Gordon [1971] proposed that a "corporation is in a state of distress when there is a nontrivial probability that it will not be able to pay the interest and principal on its debt" (p. 348). The issue of what is a "nontrivial probability" was not addressed by Gordon.

[7]Schipper [1977] contains further discussion of the problems of deciding on operational criteria for determining if a private college is distressed or nondistressed. She defined distress as "the imminent cessation of existence as an independent entity or a decision to do so. Any private college which closes its doors (or whose trustees vote to do so), declares bankruptcy, or is taken over by another entity for financial reasons ceases to exist for the purpose of this study" (p. 3).

[8]The case study is used only for exposition purposes. A more extensive analysis would require a larger sample. For a detailed study on predicting U.S. railroad bankruptcies, see Altman [1973]. See also the papers in the "Lessons of the Penn-Central Debacle" section of the May 1971 issue of the *Journal of Finance*.

[9]The statistical test used (a t test for equality of means) assumed the variances of each variable for the two groups were the same but unknown; i.e., we had to use the sample information to estimate it. See Peters and Summers [1968, p. 151] for a description of this test.

[10]Makeever [1971] contains a good description of studies on this topic. A representative early study is Winakor and Smith [1935].

[11]The phrase "years before failure" refers to the number of annual financial statements issued prior to failure. Thus, one year before failure refers to the year of the most recent financial statement issued prior to failure.

[12]The no credit interval ratio in Figure 14.1 is a relatively unfamiliar measure—it is calculated as (cash + marketable securities + receivables − current liabilities)/fund expenditures from operations.

[13]In examining distributional differences as in Figure 14.1, it would be instructive to also present the 95% confidence limits for the means of the failed and nonfailed firms. If a comparison of median financial ratios of the two groups were made, presentation of the interquartile ranges of each group would be instructive.

[14]Lev [1971] used Beaver's sample to examine the predictive power of *decomposition measures*. These measures attempt to capture the relative stability of the composition of financial statements. He concluded that in each of the five years prior to failure, failed firms experienced more substantial changes in assets and liabilities than nonfailed firms. Using the dichotomous prediction test, the misclassification rate of the decomposition measure was comparable to the ratios that performed best in Beaver [1966].

[15]When computing the Z score for each company, the ratios are expressed in absolute percentage terms, e.g., a working capital to assets ratio of 10% is expressed as 10.0 and a sales to total assets ratio of 2.0 or 200% is expressed as 200.0. A Z score of 2.675 was established as a cutoff point; a firm with a Z score less than 2.675 was classified as "failed."

[16]The two multivariate studies examined in Section 14.4 are illustrative of an extensive literature. Some other studies include Hempel [1973] on municipal distress prediction, Bloch [1969] on distress prediction in the savings and loan industry, Altman and Loris [1976a] on distress prediction for over-the-counter broker-dealers, and Schipper [1977] on distress prediction for private colleges.

[17]Eisenbeis [1977] provides extended discussion of this point.

[18]The Lachenbruch technique withholds the observation to be predicted and computes the discriminant function using the $N-1$ observations in the sample. The withheld observation is then predicted. This procedure is repeated until all observations have been predicted—see Eisenbeis and Avery [1972].

[19]Altman [1976] provides further discussion of the Elam results. He notes sufficient problems in the Elam design to make the issue of the effect of lease capitalization on predictive ability unresolved.

[20]The above set of comments is not an exhaustive list of issues that warrant attention in future work. See Joy and Tollefson [1975] and Eisenbeis [1977] for further discussion. Eisenbeis stresses the importance of

examining the appropriateness of the linear discriminant assumption that the variables of each group have equal variances. If the assumption of equal variances is inappropriate, quadratic rather than linear discriminant procedures may be appropriate—see Eisenbeis and Avery [1972].

QUESTIONS

QUESTION 14.1: Profile Analysis of Failed and Nonfailed Firms

There has been much work comparing the financial ratios of failed and nonfailed firms. An illustrative study is Deakin [1972]. Details of the sample selection criteria are as follows:

> Thirty-two failed firms were selected from a population which experienced failure between 1964 and 1970.... The term failure was defined...to include only those firms which experienced bankruptcy, insolvency, or were otherwise liquidated for the benefit of creditors.... Each of my failed firms was matched with a nonfailed firm on the basis of industry classification, year of the financial information provided and asset size [as of five years prior to failure]. (p. 168)

Deakin computed the means of several financial statement items for both the failed and nonfailed firms for each of the five years prior to the bankruptcy, insolvency, or liquidation. These mean financial statement items are presented in Tables 14.9 and 14.10.

REQUIRED

(1) Which financial ratios exhibited the most marked differential behavior for the failed and nonfailed firms in the five years prior to failure? Use the graphical approach illustrated in Figure 14.1.

(2) Compare the results for the Deakin sample in (1) with those of the Beaver [1966] sample discussed in Chapter 14. What problems in comparing the results of these two studies exist?

(3) What problems in drawing inferences about the differential behavior of the ratios of failed and nonfailed firms arise from the sample selection criteria used by Deakin?

(4) "[Profile analysis can demonstrate] that failed and non-failed firms have dissimilar ratios, not that ratios have predictive power. But the crucial problem is to make an inference in the reverse direction, i.e., from ratios to failures" (Johnson [1970, p. 1168]). Do you agree with this statement?

TABLE 14.9 Mean Financial Items of Failed Firms

		Years Before Failure				
		5	4	3	2	1
A.	**Balance Sheet Data**					
1.	Cash & marketable securities	753	1,020	730	511	329
2.	Accounts receivable	1,845	3,164	3,563	2,359	2,090
3.	Inventories	2,827	6,064	7,390	2,525	2,378
4.	Other assets	3,937	7,018	8,332	5,107	5,229
5.	Total assets	9,362	17,266	20,015	10,502	10,026
6.	Current liabilities	3,780	4,820	8,092	6,102	6,860
7.	Other liabilities	2,149	8,617	9,784	3,537	3,408
8.	Net worth	3,433	3,829	2,139	863	−242
9.	Liabilities & net worth	9,362	17,266	20,015	10,502	10,026
B.	**Income & Funds Statement Data**					
10.	Sales	16,508	15,425	18,359	16,656	16,938
11.	Net income	65	−29	−664	−858	−1,309
12.	Cash flow	145	308	−244	−518	−909

TABLE 14.10 Mean Financial Items of Nonfailed Firms

		Years Before Failure				
		5	4	3	2	1
A.	**Balance Sheet Data**					
1.	Cash & marketable securities	981	1,086	1,107	1,304	1,365
2.	Accounts receivable	1,716	1,730	1,837	2,146	2,358
3.	Inventories	3,022	3,000	3,006	3,479	3,974
4.	Other assets	3,678	3,995	4,225	5,243	5,565
5.	Total assets	9,397	9,811	10,175	12,172	13,262
6.	Current liabilities	2,023	2,251	2,370	2,920	3,305
7.	Other liabilities	2,169	2,432	2,479	2,826	3,800
8.	Net worth	5,205	5,128	5,326	6,426	6,157
9.	Liabilities & net worth	9,397	9,811	10,175	12,172	13,262
B.	**Income & Funds Statement Data**					
10.	Sales	16,989	16,395	17,610	20,445	22,426
11.	Net income	206	46	211	426	480
12.	Cash flow	523	381	577	865	941

(This case draws heavily on research reported in Trieschmann and Pinches [1973] and Pinches and Trieschmann [1974]. George Pinches kindly provided a copy of the data base used in the research.)

Statutes in all U.S. states provide for an insurance department which has the responsibility of "supervising insurance companies and enforcing compliance with the law." The concerns of these insurance departments include

(1) Solvency of insurers,

(2) Propriety of premium rates,

(3) Fair dealings with the policyholders, and

(4) Uniform financial reporting.

A number of techniques have been used in the solvency monitoring process: audits of annual statements, screening financial ratios and company data, consumer complaints, and actions by other state insurance departments or industry groups. This case is concerned with the potential use of quantitative prediction models in the solvency monitoring process.

In two related studies, Trieschmann and Pinches [1973] and Pinches and Trieschmann [1974] examined univariate and multivariate financial distress prediction models that could be used in monitoring the solvency of property-liability insurers. A sample comprising both insolvent and solvent firms was used in the research. The selection criteria for the insolvent firms were

(1) Involuntary receivership, rehabilitation, conservatorship, or liquidation between January 1, 1966 and December 31, 1971;

(2) Asset size of at least $100,000;

(3) Availability of two years of financial data;

(4) No overlapping management between distress firms;

(5) No exchanges, bonding, fraternals, or guaranty firms; and

(6) Did not entirely reinsure themselves before distress.

These insolvent firms were matched with solvent firms from a set of firms which met the following criteria:

(1) Property-liability firms licensed in the State of Missouri,

(2) Total asset size of less than $30 million, and

(3) Not affiliated with or owned by another firm with more than $30 million in assets.

This case uses 24 of the 52 firms in the original Trieschmann and Pinches [1973] research. Twelve firms are used for an estimation sample and an additional 12 firms for a validation sample. Each sample includes 6 insolvent firms and 6 *matched* solvent firms. Three variables from the original set of 70 variables are examined. These three variables and the authors' hypotheses about their values for solvent and insolvent firms are

$$X_1 = \text{Cost of stocks/Market price of stocks.}$$

This variable measures *investment management*. Since distressed firms have a higher ratio, one could assume that their stock investments have not increased in value to the same extent that solvent firms' stock investments have. Because market price is in the denominator, a lower ratio reflects better performance. (p. 332)

$$X_2 = \text{Combined ratio.}$$

This ratio is the traditional measure of *underwriting profitability*. One would expect the distress firms ratio to be higher than the solvent firms' ratio. This relationship would reflect on the greater profitability of solvent firms. (p. 332)

$$X_3 = \text{Direct premiums written/Policyholders' surplus.}$$

This ratio is the traditional measure of *underwriting risk* where a high ratio indicates greater underwriting exposure and more risk. (Pinches and Trieshmann [1974, p. 567])

Table 14.11 details names of the firms in the estimation sample and the values of the above ratios. The ratios for the insolvent firms are taken from the last financial statement issued prior to "liquidation," "receivership," etc. The ratios for each solvent firm are taken from the same financial year

TABLE 14.11 Property-Liability Insurers: Estimation Sample

	X_1	X_2	X_3
Solvent firms			
1. LaSalle National Insurance Company	.398	.928	1.050
2. Maine Insurance Company	.757	.960	1.924
3. Wabash Fire & Casualty Insurance Company	.701	.983	2.963
4. Workmen's & Suffolk Mutual Insurance Company	.802	.730	1.768
5. Great Northern Casualty Mutual Company	.705	.965	1.386
6. Highway Insurance Company	.979	.964	4.161
Insolvent firms			
7. Pennsylvania Millers Mutual Insurance	1.545	1.318	7.815
8. Continental Western Insurance Company	.846	1.024	2.737
9. Mid-Continent Casualty Company	.773	1.296	2.869
10. Church Mutual Insurance Company	1.314	1.042	2.187
11. Protective Insurance Company	1.011	.990	9.221
12. Great Central Insurance Company	1.120	.975	8.989

TABLE 14.12   Property-Liability Insurers: Validation Sample

	X_1	X_2	X_3
Solvent firms			
1. Knickerbocker Insurance Company	.600	1.120	.892
2. Mid-Central Mutual Casualty Company	.558	.816	.896
3. Mid-America Mutual Insurance Company	.382	.950	.240
4. State Fire & Casualty Company	.530	.956	2.684
5. St. Lawrence Insurance Company	.851	.890	1.946
6. Reliable Mutual Insurance Company	.602	1.008	4.905
Insolvent firms			
7. Square Deal Insurance Company	1.168	1.077	4.056
8. Druggists Mutual Insurance Company	1.072	1.014	11.720
9. Germantown Insurance Company	1.148	.765	12.643
10. Millers Mutual Fire Insurance Co. of Texas	.984	1.023	2.298
11. National Automobile & Casualty Insurance Co.	.780	1.048	5.475
12. Traders & General Insurance Company	1.000	.996	7.287

that the ratios of the matched insolvent firm are taken from. Table 14.12 provides similar details for the firms in the validation sample.

The X_1 variable was developed by the authors as a measure of *investment management*. The combined ratio (X_2) is the sum of the loss ratio and the expense ratio. These two ratios are calculated as follows:

$$\text{Loss ratio} = \frac{\text{Loss and loss adjustment expenses incurred}}{\text{Net earned premiums}}$$

$$\text{Expense ratio} = \frac{\text{Underwriting expenses incurred}}{\text{Net written premiums}}.$$

The relationship of net premiums written to policyholders' surplus (X_3) is often referred to in the insurance literature. For instance, Evans [1968] reported that a sample of six failed automobile insurance companies had a higher average net premiums written to policyholders' surplus ratio than did a sample of ten surviving automobile insurance companies.

REQUIRED

1. Univariate Prediction Models

   (1) What evidence is there of differences in the mean ratio of the insolvent firms and solvent firms for X_1, X_2, and X_3? Are these differences in the direction predicted by Trieschmann and Pinches?

   (2) For each ratio, choose the cutoff point which minimizes the total number of misclassifications. The exact cutoff point is to be the midpoint between the adjacently ranked ratios. If several

cutoff points give the same total number of misclassifications, choose that cutoff (from these) which minimizes the number of type I errors.

(3) For each ratio, evaluate the predictive ability of the cutoff point developed in (2) on the validation sample. Why is it important to examine the predictive ability of a univariate model on a validation sample?

(4) Evaluate X_1 as a measure of the investment management performance of a property liability insurer.

2. *Multivariate Prediction Models*

(1) Consider the following linear discriminant function, which is based on the estimation sample data:

$$Z_i = -5.822X_{2,i} - .287X_{3,i}.$$

Choose the cutoff point which minimizes the total number of misclassifications in the estimation sample. The exact cutoff point is to be the midpoint between the adjacently ranked Z_i scores. Present the classification matrix for this discriminant function.

(2) Evaluate the predictive ability of the model chosen in (1) on the validation sample. Present the classification matrix for the discriminant function. Why is it important to examine the predictive ability of a multivariate model on a validation sample?

(3) Suppose an insurance regulator decided to adopt the model in (1) for monitoring the solvency of property-liability insurers. Why might the regulator be reluctant to make public details of this model?

QUESTION 14.3: Bankruptcy Prediction and Audit
"Going Concern" Evaluations

An important part of an auditor's examination of a firm's financial statements is expressing an opinion on whether the firm is a going concern. Carmichael [1972] made the following comments on this phase of an audit:

The assumption that an entity is a going concern is made in the absence of evidence to the contrary.... A financially healthy company is characterized by adequate return on investment and sound financial position. When the converse of these two interrelated characteristics exists the company may have a going-concern problem.

The elements of contrary evidence may be classified as follows:

A. Financing problems—difficulty in meeting obligations.
  1. Liquidity deficiency....
  2. Equity deficiency....
  3. Debt default....
  4. Funds shortage....

B. Operating problems—apparent lack of operating success.
    1. Continued operating losses....
    2. Prospective revenues doubtful....
    3. Ability to operate is jeopardized....
    4. Poor control over operations. (pp. 93–94)

This question examines the qualifications (or lack thereof) made by auditors to the statements of three companies that went bankrupt in 1974 and 1975. Details of these qualifications are provided below.

American Beef Packers—main activity was beef packing and processing. It filed under Chapter XI bankruptcy on January 7, 1975. Details of its audit reports were

6/1970–5/1971	Unqualified
6/1971–5/1972	Unqualified
6/1972–5/1973	Unqualified
6/1973–5/1974	Unqualified
6/1974–5/1975	Qualified

Arthur Andersen and Company, the auditor for the 6/1974–5/1975 period (but *not* in the prior years), included the following statement in their audit report:

The Company has filed a petition for an arrangement under Chapter XI of the Bankruptcy Act and has submitted a plan of arrangement to continue operations and defer payment to credits. As of October 3, 1975, the Plan has not been confirmed by the Courts.... The Company's ability to continue operations is dependent upon confirmation of the plan of arrangement and upon the future success of its remaining operations and the possible effect of the matters discussed in the following paragraphs, none of which are not determinable.... In view of the significance of the matters discussed in the preceding paragraphs and the uncertainties which they create, we are unable to express an opinion on the accompanying financial statements or the supporting schedules. (Arthur Andersen and Company, October 3, 1975)

W. T. Grant and Company—main activity was retail trading. It filed for bankruptcy on October 3, 1975. Details of its audit reports were

2/1970–1/1971	Unqualified
2/1971–1/1972	Unqualified
2/1972–1/1973	Unqualified
2/1973–1/1974	Unqualified
2/1974–1/1975	Qualified

The qualified opinion related to (1) a dispute between the IRS and *W. T. Grant* and (2) the "continuing value of an investment" in a subsidiary. The audit report included the following statement:

The continuing value of the Company's total investment in the common stock and convertible notes of Granjewel Jewelers and Distributors, Inc., a 51% owned subsidiary, may be impaired as a result of the potential inability of such subsidiary to continue as a going concern....

Subject to effects, if any, on the financial statements of the ultimate resolution of the matters discussed in the preceding paragraph, the financial statements referred to above present fairly the consolidated financial position of W. T. Grant Company and consolidated subsidiaries at January 30, 1975.... (Ernst & Ernst, April 18, 1975)

Omega Alpha Inc.—main activities were wire and cables, floor coverings, marine repairs and engineering, and finance and bond development. It filed under Chapter XI bankruptcy on September 27, 1974. Details of its audit reports were

7/1970–6/1971	Unqualified
7/1971–6/1972	Qualified
7/1972–6/1973	Qualified
7/1973–6/1974	Qualified

The audit report for the 7/1972–6/1973 period included the following statement:

The financial statements of [several] subsidiaries were examined by other independent accountants whose reports thereon are qualified with respect to (i) the allocation of the goodwill between TMC (Transcontinental Music Corporation) and NAAC et al. (North American Acceptance Corporation), (ii) realization of the goodwill on TMC and (iii) ultimate profitable operations of TMC....

In our opinion, based upon our examination and the aforementioned reports of other independent accountants, and subject to the resolution of the matters described [above], the accompanying financial statements present fairly the respective consolidated and separate financial position of Omega-Alpha, Inc. at June 30, 1973 and 1972.... (Coopers and Lybrand, November 21, 1973)

The audit report for the 7/1973–6/1974 period included the following statement:

Omega-Alpha, Inc. filed for protection under Chapter XI of National Bankruptcy Act on September 27, 1974.... As the effect of this action is not presently determinable, the accompanying statements have been prepared on a going concern basis, reflecting historical costs. The bankruptcy proceedings may, however, require substantial adjustments to assets, which may be subject to forced sale, and liabilities, which may be settled for less than face amounts presented....

As a result of the bankruptcy, litigation, and our inability to satisfy ourselves as to the operations of NAAC, we express no opinion on the aforementioned financial statements and supporting schedules. (Coopers and Lybrand, September 27, 1974)

Table 14.13 presents values for each firm of the five financial ratios used in the Altman [1968] discriminant function detailed in Section 14.4B (the year given refers to the year in which the fiscal year ends).

TABLE 14.13   Financial Ratios of Bankrupt Firms

	X_1	X_2	X_3	X_4	X_5
American Beef Packers					
1971	.134	.096	.074	.478	11.309
1972	.083	.070	.068	.324	8.529
1973	.067	.070	.101	.142	6.752
1974	.050	.103	.133	.106	7.442
1975	(.593)	(.385)	(.587)	.031	10.705
W. T. Grant and Company					
1971	.323	.285	.113	1.439	1.559
1972	.376	.259	.083	1.013	1.459
1973	.312	.235	.076	.687	1.484
1974	.329	.198	.048	.172	1.479
1975	.162	.035	(.193)	.035	1.632
Omega Alpha Inc.					
1971	.162	.003	.010	.080	.180
1972	.073	(.153)	.015	.043	.833
1973	(.046)	(.720)	(.251)	.027	.756
1974	(.558)	(.942)	.017	N/A[a]	1.117

[a]N/A: Omega was delisted during 1974; assume $X_4 = 0$ in 1974.

KEY: X_1 = working capital to total assets,

X_2 = retained earnings to total assets,

X_3 = earnings before interest and taxes to total assets,

X_4 = market value of equity to book value of total debt,

X_5 = sales to total assets.

REQUIRED

(1) Examine whether the Altman [1968] discriminant function,

$$Z = .012X_1 + .014X_2 + .033X_3 + .006X_4 + .010X_5,$$

predicted bankruptcy earlier than did the auditor for each of the above three companies. Comment on the results. Comment also on the relative contributions of the five ratios to the Z scores. (Predict bankruptcy if Z is less than 2.675; ratios should be expressed in absolute percentage terms—see footnote 15.)

(2) What factors would an auditor want to consider when building a discriminant function to aid in his evaluations about whether a firm is a going concern?

(3) The Cohen Commission—Commission on Auditors' Responsibilities [1977]—recommended that the auditor evaluate the adequacy of

disclosure about future uncertainties rather than attempt to predict whether the firm will remain as a going concern:

The most significant uncertainty that can cause a "subject to" qualification under present reporting requirements is doubt about a company's ability to continue to operate as a going concern, but there is no reason to believe that independent auditors are better able to predict continued business success or failure than they are able to predict the outcome of other uncertainties. The auditor's responsibility for "going concern" and other uncertainties should be to evaluate whether the disclosure presented by management includes all the available material information on the potential effect of the uncertainties on the entity's earnings and financial position. (p. xviii)

One reason cited for this recommendation was the following:

Research has shown (i.e., Altman and McGough [1974]) that an analysis of financial statements, using certain simple financial ratios, is a better indicator of a company's future prospects than noting whether the auditor has expressed a qualified opinion or an unqualified opinion. (p. 30)

Critically evaluate this recommendation of the Cohen Commission.

QUESTION 14.4:   Capital Market Reaction to Failed Firms

Two studies have examined the capital market reaction to failed firms: Beaver [1968a] and Westerfield [1970]. These studies are briefly described below.

Beaver [1968a] examined (among other things) the security market returns of (1) 79 failed firms and (2) 79 nonfailed firms vis-à-vis the returns on an equally weighted index of all NYSE stocks:

$$\hat{U}_{it} = \tilde{R}_{it} - \tilde{R}_{Mt},$$

where $\hat{U}_{it}$ = return on security i in period t, adjusted for market-wide events,

$\tilde{R}_{it}$ = return on security i in period t,

$\tilde{R}_{Mt}$ = return on NYSE market index in period t.

The mean annual adjusted returns ($\hat{U}_{it}$) for the (1) and (2) samples of firms were

Years Before Failure	Failed Firms (1)	Nonfailed Firms (2)	Difference (1)−(2)
5	−.08	−.07	−.01
4	−.13	−.04	−.09
3	−.20	−.04	−.16
2	−.21	−.01	−.20
1	−.38	−.06	−.32

Beaver concluded the following:

> Investors appear to adjust to the new solvency positions of the failed firms continuously over the five-year period, but the largest unexpected deterioration still occurs in the final year before failure. (p. 182)

Westerfield [1970] used the cumulative abnormal return (CAR) measure—see Appendix 11.A—in examining the capital market reaction to 20 bankrupt firms in the 10 years (120 months) prior to the bankruptcy declaration. The market model—see Chapter 8—was estimated for each firm using monthly security returns in the initial 4-year period examined (months 120 to 73 prior to bankruptcy). Using estimates of α and β from this initial 4-year period, the monthly abnormal return was

$$\hat{U}_{it} = \tilde{R}_{it} - \left(\hat{\alpha} + \hat{\beta} \times \tilde{R}_{Mt}\right).$$

The abnormal returns ($\hat{U}_{it}$) were cumulated in the 72 months prior to bankruptcy. The average CAR for the 20 bankrupt firms was negative in each of the 60 months prior to bankruptcy. The decline was most marked in the 12 months prior to bankruptcy. The values of the CAR at selected time periods prior to bankruptcy declaration were

	CAR
60 months prior	$-.051$
48 months prior	$-.232$
36 months prior	$-.289$
24 months prior	$-.322$
12 months prior	$-.486$
Month of declaration	$-.760$

REQUIRED

(1) Critically evaluate the above approaches to examining the capital market reaction to bankrupt firms in the period prior to bankruptcy.

(2) Assume you were building a multivariate model to predict bankruptcy. Explain how you could incorporate the Beaver and Westerfield results into the analysis.

(3) Altman [1971] hypothesized that "investors, in general, tend to underestimate the financial plight of those firms that eventually go bankrupt" (p. 79). Based on the Beaver and Westerfield results, he concluded the following:

> It appears that the market began bidding down the prices of the future bankrupt stocks as much as five years prior to bankruptcy. The fact that the market performance continued downward, especially in the year immediately prior to bankruptcy, means that although investors were aware of the firm's deteriorating condition for a long time prior to failure, the situation's seriousness was

consistently underestimated. We conclude..., therefore, that *a model or tech-nique which is capable of predicting impending failure might be a considerable assistance in a short selling context.* (p. 81, emphasis added)

Comment on Altman's conclusion. Design a study to test the statement that "a model or technique...might be of considerable assistance in a short selling context."

REFERENCES

ALTMAN, E. I. "Financial Ratios, Discriminant Analysis and the Prediction of Corporate Bankruptcy." *Journal of Finance* (Sept. 1968): 589–609.

———. *Corporate Bankruptcy in America.* Heath Lexington Books, Lexington, Mass., 1971.

———. "Predicting Railroad Bankruptcies in America." *Bell Journal of Economics and Management Science* (Spring 1973): 184–211.

———. "Capitalization of Leases and the Predictability of Financial Results: A Comment." *The Accounting Review* (Apr. 1976): 408–412.

ALTMAN, E. I., and LORIS, B. "A Financial Early Warning System for Over-the-Counter Broker-Dealers." *Journal of Finance* (Sept. 1976a): 1201–1217.

ALTMAN, E. I., and McGOUGH, T. P. "Evaluation of a Company as a Going Concern." *Journal of Accountancy* (Dec. 1974): 50–57.

BAXTER, N. D. "Leverage, Risk of Ruin and the Cost of Capital." *Journal of Finance* (Sept. 1967): 395–404.

BEAVER, W. H. "Financial Ratios as Predictors of Failure." *Empirical Research in Accounting: Selected Studies, 1966.* Supplement to *Journal of Accounting Research* (1966): 71–111.

———. "Alternative Accounting Measures as Predictors of Failure." *The Accounting Review* (Jan. 1968): 113–122.

———. "Market Prices, Financial Ratios, and the Prediction of Failure." *Journal of Accounting Research* (Autumn 1968a): 179–192.

BLOCH, E. "The Setting of Standards of Supervision of Savings and Loan Associations." In I. Friend (ed.), *A Study of the Savings and Loan Industry.* U.S. Government Printing Office, Washington, D.C., 1969.

BLUM, M. "Failing Company Discriminant Analysis." *Journal of Accounting Research* (Spring 1974): 1–25.

CARMICHAEL, D. R. *The Auditor's Reporting Obligation.* AICPA, New York, 1972.

COMMISSION ON AUDITORS' RESPONSIBILITIES. *Report of Tentative Conclusions*. AICPA, New York, 1977.

DEAKIN, E. B. "A Discriminant Analysis of Predictors of Business Failure." *Journal of Accounting Research* (Spring 1972): 167–179.

DUN & BRADSTREET. *The Business Failure Record 1975*. Dun & Bradstreet, New York, 1976.

EDMISTER, R. O. "An Empirical Test of Financial Ratio Analysis for Small Business Failure Prediction." *Journal of Financial and Quantitative Analysis* (Mar. 1972): 1477–1493.

EISENBEIS, R. A. "Pitfalls in the Application of Discriminant Analysis in Business, Finance, and Economics." *Journal of Finance* (June 1977): 875–900.

EISENBEIS, R., and AVERY, R. *Discriminant Analysis and Classification Procedures*. Heath, Lexington, Mass., 1972.

ELAM, R. "The Effect of Lease Data on the Predictive Ability of Financial Ratios." *The Accounting Review* (Jan. 1975): 25–43.

EVANS, K. C. "Basic Financial Differences of Substandard Automobile Insurers." *Journal of Risk and Insurance* (Dec. 1968): 489–513.

GORDON, M. J. "Towards a Theory of Financial Distress." *Journal of Finance* (May 1971): 347–356.

HEMPEL, G. H. "Quantitative Borrower Characteristics Associated with Defaults on Municipal General Obligations." *Journal of Finance* (May 1973): 523–530.

HIGGINS, R. C., and SCHALL, L. D. "Corporate Bankruptcy and Conglomerate Merger." *Journal of Finance* (Mar. 1975): 93–113.

JOHNSON, C. G. "Ratio Analysis and the Prediction of Firm Failure." *Journal of Finance* (Dec. 1970): 1166–1168.

JOY, O. M., and TOLLEFSON, J. O. "On the Financial Applications of Discriminant Analysis." *Journal of Financial and Quantitative Analysis* (Dec. 1975): 723–739.

LEV, B. "Financial Failure and Information Decomposition Measures." In R. R. Sterling and W. F. Bentz (eds.), *Accounting in Perspective: Contribution to Accounting Thoughts by Other Disciplines*. South-Western, Cincinnati, 1971: 102–111.

LINTNER, J. "Bankruptcy Risk, Market Segmentation and Optimal Capital Structure." In I. Friend and J. L. Bicksler (eds.), *Risk and Return in Finance*, Volume 11. Ballinger Publishing Company, Cambridge, Mass., 1977.

MAKEEVER, D. A. *The Feasibility of a Numberical Scoring System for Commercial Loans*. Harris Trust and Savings Bank, Chicago, 1971.

NETER, J. "Discussion of 'Financial Ratios as Predictors of Failure.'" *Empirical Research in Accounting: Selected Studies, 1966*. Supplement to *Journal of Accounting Research* (1966): 112–118.

PETERS, W. S., and SUMMERS, G. W. *Statistical Analysis for Business Decisions*. Prentice-Hall, Englewood Cliffs, N.J. 1968.

PINCHES, G. E., and TRIESCHMANN, J. S. "The Efficiency of Alternative Models for Solvency Surveillance in the Insurance Industry." *Journal of Risk and Insurance* (Dec. 1974): 563–577.

———. "Discriminant Analysis, Classification Results, and Financially Distressed P-L Insurers." *Journal of Risk and Insurance* (June 1977): 289–298.

SCHIPPER, K. "Financial Distress in Private Colleges." Paper Presented to Conference on Measurement and Evaluation of the Economic Efficiency of Public and Private Nonprofit Institutions. University of Chicago, Chicago, 1977. Published as Supplement to *Journal of Accounting Research*.

SINKEY, J. F. "A Multivariate Statistical Analysis of the Characteristics of Problem Banks." *Journal of Finance* (Mar. 1975): 21–36.

STIGLITZ, J. E. "Some Aspects of the Pure Theory of Corporate Finance: Bankruptcies and Takeovers." *Bell Journal of Economics and Management Science* (Autumn 1972): 458–482.

TRIESCHMANN, J. S., and PINCHES, G. E. "A Multivariate Model for Predicting Financially Distressed P-L Insurers." *Journal of Risk and Insurance* (Sept. 1973): 327–338.

WALL, A. *How To Evaluate Financial Statements*. Harper & Row, New York, 1936.

WARNER, J. B. "Bankruptcy Costs, Absolute Priority, and the Pricing of Risky Debt Claims." Unpublished Ph.D. Dissertation, University of Chicago, Chicago, 1976.

WESTERFIELD, R. "Pre-bankruptcy Stock Price Performance." Working Paper, University of Pennsylvania, Philadelphia, 1970.

WILCOX, J. W. "A Simple Theory of Financial Ratios as Predictors of Failure." *Journal of Accounting Research* (Autumn 1971): 389–395.

———. "A Prediction of Business Failure Using Accounting Data." *Empirical Research in Accounting: Selected Studies, 1973*. Supplement to *Journal of Accounting Research* (1973): 163–179.

WINAKOR, C. H., and SMITH, R. F. *Changes in Financial Structure of Unsuccessful Industrial Companies*. Bulletin No. 51. University of Illinois Press, Bureau of Economic Research, Urbana, Ill., 1935.

CREDIT DECISIONS

AND

FINANCIAL INFORMATION

An important use of financial statement information is in credit decisions by banks and other financial intermediaries. In this chapter we shall examine the potential use of financial information in quantitative approaches to credit decisions. In Section 15.1 we shall outline some important aspects of these decisions. The use of numerical scoring models in consumer and commercial loan decisions is discussed in Section 15.2. Quantitative tools are also useful to the various federal and state agencies regulating the banking industry, e.g., the *Federal Deposit Insurance Corporation*. In Appendix 15.A, models that use financial information in examining the quality of bank loan portfolios and in predicting the financial distress of banks are examined.

15.1 ASPECTS OF CREDIT DECISIONS

Credit decisions by banks and other financial intermediaries embrace many dimensions. Consider when a bank is approached by a new loan applicant. The decision is not simply to grant credit or not grant credit. In the grant credit alternative, decisions about the rate of interest to charge, the amount of the loan, the payment schedule, the security required for the loan, and the restrictions to be placed on the borrower must be made. Having decided to grant an applicant a loan, a bank faces further decisions. The bank may attempt to design an early warning system to anticipate loan defaults. The design of such an early warning system entails decisions about the model to use for predicting default and about the variables to include in the model. If a loan actually defaults, decisions relating to the collection of future payments and repayment of the principal must then be made. In short, there are many aspects of credit decisions. In this section we shall examine attempts to model various aspects of credit decisions.

A Modeling the Loan Officer Function

Hester [1962] provides an interesting analysis of the *loan officer function*. This function was defined as follows:

A loan officer function is a relation which specifies the terms at which a bank with particular characteristics is willing to lend to a borrower with a known profit, balance sheet, and credit history and with particular prospects for the future. It is a generalized supply function for loans in the sense that instead of merely having the amount of loans determined by a set of exogenous variables, it has a set of loan terms including the amount of loans determined by the set of exogenous variables. (p. 3)

The descriptive model developed by Hester was

$$F(R, M, A, S) = G(W_1, W_2, \ldots, W_i; Z_1, Z_2, \ldots, Z_j), \qquad (15.1)$$

where R = loan rate of interest (in percent),

M = maturity of the loan (in months),

A = amount of the loan (in dollars),

S = 1 if the loan is secured and 0 otherwise,

W_i = ith relevant characteristic of loan applicants, $i = 1, 2, \ldots, I$,

Z_j = jth relevant characteristic of lending banks, $j = 1, 2, \ldots, J$.

Using data from individual term loans (i.e., loans with maturities exceeding one year) granted by three large banks, the above model was estimated with regression analysis. Separate regression models were estimated for each R, M, A, and S variable and for each bank. The results of the empirical analysis were consistent with

(1) Banks trading off R, M, A, and S in their term loan decisions;

(2) Four characteristics of applicants being significant determinants of R, M, A, and S: profitability, the current ratio, the size of the applicant's deposit balances at the bank, and the number of years the applicant had been a depositor at the bank; and

(3) Several characteristics of lending banks being significant determinants of R, M, A, and S: a size variable and the ratio of its commercial and industrial loans to its deposits.

The Hester study is important in increasing our understanding of how existing loan decisions are made, e.g., the variables they are placing the greatest weight on in their term loan decisions. One limitation of the analysis arises because the above model (15.1) should have been estimated with a set of simultaneous equations. This approach would have allowed more explicit recognition of the interrelationships between loan applicant characteristics and characteristics of the lending banks.

B Modeling Commercial Loan Decisions

There has been considerable attention paid to modeling human judgment tasks.[1] Cohen et al. [1966] provide an example of human judgment modeling in the banking industry. Their analysis was "intended to provide a rigorous understanding of the types of analyses which bankers undertake and the key factors which influence their decisions to grant business loan requests on either the original or modified terms or to reject them entirely" (p. 219). The first stage of the analysis was development of an overall view of bank procedures for analyzing business loan applications. Bank procedures at two large banks were used as the basis for the model development. Figure 15.1 presents a flowchart of these procedures. Eight main sections to these procedures are distinguished in this flowchart:

FIGURE 15.1   Bank Procedures for Analyzing Business Loan Applications

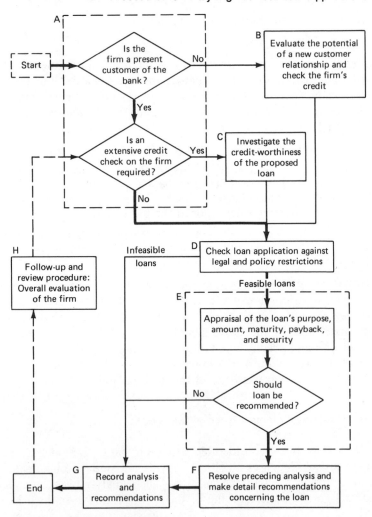

Source: Cohen et al. [1966, Figure 1, Reproduced with permission of the publisher].

A. Status of the firm's customer relationship.

B. Evaluation of a new customer relationship.

C. Credit evaluation.

D. Check on legal and policy restrictions.

E. Appraisal of the loan's purpose, amount, maturity, payback, and security.

F. Detailed recommendations.

G. Record analyses and recommendations.

H. Follow-up and review.

Cohen et al. then developed a computer simulation model that attempted to automate these functions—the simulation model was "intended to make the same decisions on particular business loan applicants that commercial banks actually make" (p. 219).

Of particular interest from a financial statement analysis perspective is the credit evaluation phase of the model. There were five main segments to the credit evaluation model:

(1) Is the bank's share of risk clearly unreasonable?

(2) Does the firm have enough current assets?

(3) Are the firm's current assets sufficiently liquid?

(4) Is the firm financially profitable?

(5) What is the final credit rating of the applicant?

The simulation model used information from both the applicants' financial statements and from *Robert Morris Associate's* industry financial statements for the pertinent industry. Minimum acceptable levels of several ratios were set based on industry averages; e.g., if the ratio of tangible net worth to total debt for a loan applicant was less than the minimum acceptable standard for the industry, the proposed amount of the bank loan was reduced so that the ratio was within the minimum acceptable limits.

Two objectives of the Cohen et al. [1966] analysis were (1) to establish a descriptive theory of how bank credit is allocated to business firms and (2) to determine the potential normative value of applying the credit decision model in practice. The former objective was related to a purpose of descriptive analysis, i.e., to understand the phenomena of interest. At present, there is limited knowledge of bank decision processes. While the Cohen et al. analysis shows how the bank loan application process might be structured, it remains an open issue whether their model adequately captures the key elements of that process. No attempt was made to show that for a new set of loan applicants their simulation model would make the same decisions that would be made using the procedures at the two banks that were used as the basis for the model development.

The second objective of Cohen et al. was based on the assumption that "if a computer program which can generate the same decisions on business loan applications that bankers now make is obtained, it is probable that variations in the program would result in loan decisions which are even better" (p. 221). To explicitly test if variations can result in "better" decisions, it is necessary to provide criteria for judging the quality of decisions. Unfortunately, there is very little in the credit literature that examines what characterizes a "better" decision.[2] This is in contrast to, say, the investment literature where there has been much research on normative approaches to investment choice. Although proposals for using portfolio theory (see Chapter 8) to model the optimal structure of a loan portfolio have been made,[3] little research directly related to bank credit decisions has been published.

15.2 NUMERICAL CREDIT SCORING MODELS

In Chapter 14 we discussed several motivations for extending ratio analysis from a univariate to a multivariate perspective. Numerical credit scoring systems represent one example of multivariate ratio analysis. A numerical credit scoring system weighs factors which distinguish "good" loans from "bad" loans in order to arrive at an overall credit rating. There are several key decisions in designing a credit scoring system:

(1) Deciding the population to which the scoring model is to apply,
(2) Deciding on the form of the scoring model (e.g., additive or multiplicative),
(3) Deciding on the variables to include in the model, and
(4) Deciding on the weights to be applied to these variables.

Ideally, some underlying theory relating loan experience with the characteristics of borrowers and lenders (and possibly other variables representing, say, industry and economic factors) should guide decisions on the above items. At present, no such underlying theory exists. Most model building has either (1) arbitrarily chosen the variables and the weights on these variables or (2) used statistical tools such as stepwise regression analysis or stepwise discriminant analysis to choose the variables and their respective weights.

The above decisions are not made on a once and for all basis. Rather, as more information about the population to which the model relates is gained, revisions in the model form, its variables, and their weights can be made. Indeed, one benefit of a credit scoring system is that it facilitates constant monitoring and control over the risk of incoming accounts. By comparing the characteristics of applicants on which the model was built with the characteristics of applicants currently applying for loans, it is possible to ascertain if there is some stability in the credit population. Moreover, by comparing the predictions of the credit scoring model (e.g., as regards the percent of defaults) with its subsequent experience, it is possible to determine areas where some revision of the model may be appropriate.

A   An Example: A Scoring System for Paper Companies

Details of actual credit scoring systems used by banks and other financial intermediaries are confidential. If loan applicants knew the variables and the weights in a scoring model, they might attempt to "tailor" their financial statements to fit the specific characteristics of the scoring system. Thus, it is not surprising that there is little published information on scoring systems actually used in the field. The example of a scoring system to be presented (from the *Annual Compilation of Financial Ratios of Selected Paper Companies*, Consolidated Papers, Inc. [1977]) is not directly linked to loan evaluation decisions. It was devised to give some insight into the "financial condition" of U.S. paper companies. The format of this scoring system, however, is not unlike those in operation in some banks and credit departments.[4]

Table 15.1 details the 11 ratios and their respective weights in the scoring system. The maximum number of total points a company can receive is 160. Consolidated Papers [1977] notes that "the weighting of these various ratios is arbitrary and the resulting ranking is also arbitrary. Different rankings can easily be obtained by using other weighting factors." Table 15.2 gives the financial ratios of selected paper companies for fiscal years ending in 1976. The aggregate score of each company is also provided.

B   Consumer Credit Scoring Models

An early example of a consumer credit scoring model is the system developed by *Spiegels, Incorporated* for its mail-order business—see Wells [1963]. In 1934 they began handling new customers' applications by a *vital question* system. Four principal questions were scored, and if the customer's total score exceeded a stated total, he was given credit without further analysis. If the score did not exceed the stated total, the mail order was held for further credit analysis.

A more recent application of credit scoring to personal loan evaluation is that of Apilado et al. [1974]. Data were obtained "from the records of 307 commercial banking offices and eighteen finance companies located in a relatively high industrialized southwestern state" (p. 276). The accounts were taken from the *closed loan files* of the banks and finance

TABLE 15.1 Scoring System for Paper Companies

Column 1: Current Assets to Current Liabilities		Column 2: Net Profit to Net Sales		Column 3: Capital Turnover		Column 4: Return on Capital Employed	
Ratio of	*Points*	*Ratio of*	*Points*	*Ratio of*	*Points*	*Ratio of*	*Points*
4.00 and over	10	10.0 and over	20	1.5 and over	20	10.0 and over	30
3.75–4.00	9	9.0–10.0	18	1.4–1.5	18	9.0–10.0	25
3.50–3.75	8	8.0–9.0	16	1.3–1.4	16	8.0–9.0	20
3.25–3.50	7	7.0–8.0	14	1.2–1.3	14	7.0–8.0	15
3.00–3.25	6	6.0–7.0	12	1.1–1.2	12	6.0–7.0	10
2.75–3.00	5	5.0–6.0	10	1.0–1.1	10	5.0–6.0	8
2.50–2.75	4	4.0–5.0	8	.9–1.0	8	4.0–5.0	6
2.25–2.50	3	3.0–4.0	6	.8– .9	6	3.0–4.0	4
2.00–2.25	2	2.0–3.0	4	.7– .8	4	2.0–3.0	2
1.75–2.00	1	1.0–2.0	2	.6– .7	2	1.0–2.0	0
1.50–1.75	0	.0–1.0	0	.5– .6	0	.0–1.0	2^a
1.25–1.50	1^a	1.0^a– .0	2^a	.4– .5	2^a	1.0^a– .0	4^a
1.00–1.25	2^a	2.0^a–1.0^a	4^a	.3– .4	4^a	2.0^a–1.0^a	6^a
.75–1.00	3^a	3.0^a–2.0^a	6^a	.2– .3	6^a	3.0^a–2.0^a	8^a

Column 5: Net Profit to Shareholders' Equity		Column 6: Noncurrent Liabilities to Shareholders' Equity		Column 7: Net Sales to Working Capital		Column 8: Cost of Sales to Inventory	
Ratio of	*Points*	*Ratio of*	*Points*	*Ratio of*	*Points*	*Ratio of*	*Points*
30–32	15	.00– .10	10	0– 2	10	15–16	15
28–30	14	.10– .20	9	2– 4	9	14–15	14
26–28	13	.20– .30	8	4– 6	8	13–14	13
24–26	12	.30– .40	7	6– 8	7	12–13	12
22–24	11	.40– .50	6	8–10	6	11–12	11
20–22	10	.50– .60	5	10–12	5	10–11	10
18–20	9	.60– .70	4	12–14	4	9–10	9
16–18	8	.70– .80	3	14–16	3	8– 9	8
14–16	7	.80– .90	2	16–18	2	7– 8	7
12–14	6	.90–1.00	1	18–20	1	6– 7	6
10–12	5	1.00–1.10	0			5– 6	5
8–10	4	1.10–1.20	1^a			4– 5	4
6– 8	3	1.20 and over	2^a			3– 4	3
4– 6	2					2– 3	2
2– 4	1					1– 2	1
0– 2	0						
Less than 0	1^a						

TABLE 15.1

Column 9: Fixed Assets to Shareholders' Equity		Column 10: Total Liabilities to Shareholders' Equity		Column 11: Noncurrent Liabilities to Working Capital	
Ratio of	Points	Ratio of	Points	Ratio of	Points
50– 60	10	25– 40	10	0– 30	10
60– 70	9	40– 55	9	30– 60	9
70– 80	8	55– 70	8	60– 90	8
80– 90	7	70–*85	7	90–120	7
90–100	6	85–100	6	120–150	6
100–110	5	100–115	5	150–180	5
110–120	4	115–130	4	180–210	4
120–130	3	130–145	3	210–240	3
130–140	2	145–160	2	240–270	2
140–150	1	160–175	1	270–300	1
150 and over	0	175–190	0	300–330	0

[a] Indicates negative ratios or points.

SOURCE: Consolidated Papers, Inc. [1977].

companies. A sample of 950 accounts was used in the analysis—one half were "good" loans (paid as agreed) and one half were "bad" loans (charged off). Thirteen variables relating to each account were initially examined—e.g., amount of loan, age of borrower, marital status, home status, and gross monthly income. On a univariate analysis, the following variables were found to be the best predictors of credit risk:

(1) Home status (own free and clear, buying, renting, other),
(2) Checking account (yes or no),
(3) Purpose of loan, and
(4) Terms of loan (number of monthly payments).

Among the variables least effective on a univariate basis were the sex of the borrower and the number of dependents of the borrower.

Multiple discriminant analysis was then applied to the initial sample of 950 accounts. The final discriminant function included 8 of the 13 variables. A stepwise discriminant procedure was used in choosing these variables. The final discriminant function included variables for home status, checking account, purpose of the loan, number of dependents, number of monthly payments, age of borrower, amount of loan, and marital status. On a hold-out or validation sample of 835 accounts (404 "bad" and 431 "good"), 299 of the "bad" accounts were correctly classified (type I error of 26%) and 313 of the "good" accounts were correctly classified (type II error of 27.38%). These percentage errors are, to say the least, quite "high." One reason for these high error rates appears to be that

TABLE 15.2 Financial Ratios of Selected Paper Companies, Fiscal Year Ending in 1976

Relative Position 1976	1975	Company	Fiscal Year Ending 1976	Score (maximum possible 160)	Total Net Sales $(000)	Price Earnings Ratio 3/31/77	Cash Dividend Payout (2-Yr. Avg.) (%)	Col. 1 Current Assets to Current Liabilities Times	Pos.	Col. 2 Net Profit to Net Sales %	Pos.
1	2	Union Camp	12/31	122	$ 1,002,983	12	33.0	3.77	2	11.83	2
2	1	Badger Paper Mills	12/31	120	28,497	7	53.0	4.12	1	5.25	17
3	3	Consolidated Papers	12/31	120	293,234	7	41.1	2.95	6	7.39	8
4	4	P.H. Glatfelter	12/31	119	97,898	6	29.1	3.42	3	12.01	1
5	20	Pentair Industries	12/31	105	90,651	5	8.1	1.82	23	4.80	19
6	—	Williamette Industries[a]	12/31	102	546,143	10	25.5	1.86	20	7.63	7
7	6	Potlatch	12/31	93	624,056	12	26.1	2.34	12	7.65	6
8	11	Great Northern-Nekoosa	12/31	89	844,600	8	28.2	2.45	11	6.90	11
9	8	Mosinee Paper	12/31	89	60,899	4	16.3	2.62	10	8.78	4
10	10	Westvaco	10/31	89	922,355	9	34.7	3.06	5	6.15	12
11	5	Kimberly-Clark	12/31	87	1,585,302	8	35.4	1.82	22	7.65	5
12	15	Mead	12/31	85	1,599,342	8	38.0	1.90	19	5.55	15
13	18	Weyerhaeuser	12/26	84	2,868,379	17	43.1	2.09	16	10.67	3
14	14	Federal Paperboard	1/1/77	82	393,580	6	34.5	2.80	9	5.74	13
15	7	St. Regis	12/31	82	1,642,132	9	36.4	2.87	7	5.56	14
16	19	Georgia-Pacific	12/31	79	3,038,000	15	31.8	1.41	26	7.09	10
17	16	Crown-Zellerbach	12/31	77	2,125,977	10	52.4	2.28	13	4.59	20
18	22	Boise-Cascade	12/31	76	1,931,530	10	24.9	2.09	15	5.22	18
19	13	American Can	12/31	75	3,142,500	8	49.9	2.15	14	3.21	24
20	12	International Paper	12/31	74	3,540,600	10	38.2	1.98	18	7.16	9
21	17	Hammermill	1/2/77	71	689,939	9	46.5	3.25	4	3.30	23
22	24	Champion-International	12/31	61	2,910,523	9	48.5	1.98	17	3.54	22
23	21	Scott Paper	12/31	58	1,373,770	9	36.6	1.53	25	5.32	16
24	23	Wausau Paper	8/31	55	76,262	5	29.3	2.81	8	1.84	25
25	25	Sorg Paper Co.	12/31	47	53,721	—	—	1.79	24	(1.07)	27
26	27	Bergstrom	12/31	31	63,799	31	—	1.82	21	.25	26
27	26	Great Lakes Paper	12/31	8	136,314	22	—	.53	27	3.57	21
—	9	Brown Company[b]	7/31					2.39		2.95	
		Weighted average 1976		79			37.6	2.05		6.22	
		Weighted average 1975		61			34.9	2.10		5.47	
		Total net sales 1976			$ 31,682,986						
		Total net sales 1975			$ 26,453,536						

[a]Included in 1976 for the first time.

[b]Changed fiscal year-end—only eight months' data reported; therefore, not included in totals.

the variables used by Apilado et al. were restricted to those on the initial loan applicant form. Information gained from credit references, etc., was excluded from the study.[5]

Col. 3 Capital Turnover		Col. 4 Return on Capital Employed		Col. 5 Net Profit to Shareholders' Equity		Col. 6 Noncurrent Liabilities to Shareholders' Equity		Col. 7 Net Sales to Working Capital		Col. 8 Cost of Sales to Inventory		Col. 9 Fixed Assets to Shareholders' Equity		Col. 10 Total Liabilities to Shareholders' Equity		Col. 11 Noncurrent Liabilities to Working Capital	
Times	Pos.	%	Pos.	%	Pos.	Times	Pos.	Times	Pos.	Times	Pos.	%	Pos.	%	Pos.	%	Pos.
1.08	21	12.78	1	20.98	3	.43	5	3.56	2	6.24	17	87.88	4	59.00	4	100.34	5
1.70	3	8.93	8	11.30	19	.09	1	3.86	3	6.77	12	51.31	1	26.15	1	16.03	1
1.42	8	10.49	4	13.85	15	.16	2	6.08	14	5.94	22	83.32	3	31.17	2	54.49	2
.93	25	11.17	3	17.80	6	.38	4	3.05	1	8.43	6	91.67	5	57.19	3	84.17	3
2.55	1	12.24	2	32.48	1	.81	22	10.41	22	11.56	1	109.91	11	150.18	24	142.76	9
1.31	12	10.00	5	18.06	5	.54	12	10.98	23	10.03	3	126.55	21	77.69	8	268.36	23
1.19	16	9.10	7	15.17	11	.52	9	7.11	17	6.32	14	121.60	17	71.48	5	196.76	18
1.16	18	8.00	12	14.39	12	.53	11	6.21	15	7.32	8	114.34	13	74.94	7	168.33	15
1.06	22	9.31	6	21.01	2	1.07	24	4.26	4	7.07	10	137.85	25	138.86	23	207.80	20
1.24	14	7.63	14	14.14	13	.61	14	4.90	6	6.62	13	114.86	14	82.77	10	137.15	8
1.15	19	8.80	10	15.75	9	.47	6	7.56	20	4.34	27	100.47	10	79.03	9	183.72	17
1.38	10	7.66	13	15.78	8	.65	17	7.24	19	9.36	4	93.77	6	106.51	20	174.96	16
.83	26	8.86	9	16.25	7	.62	16	5.60	8	5.94	23	125.82	19	85.77	14	240.32	21
1.29	13	7.40	15	14.11	14	.68	18	5.65	10	5.46	25	126.31	20	91.43	16	164.14	14
1.14	20	6.34	17	11.16	20	.52	10	4.84	5	7.13	9	80.36	2	72.58	6	131.12	7
1.22	15	8.65	11	18.09	4	.52	8	13.83	26	6.21	19	133.86	24	91.11	15	318.08	24
1.34	11	6.15	18	12.08	16	.62	15	5.96	13	6.30	15	111.51	12	95.14	17	144.59	10
1.17	17	6.11	19	11.13	21	.52	7	5.94	12	5.49	24	95.38	7	83.13	12	149.98	11
1.63	4	5.23	21	11.97	18	.70	19	5.73	11	6.01	21	97.70	8	124.80	21	111.16	6
1.01	23	7.23	16	15.24	10	.71	20	7.00	16	7.74	7	130.43	23	99.27	18	256.95	22
1.48	6	4.88	23	9.96	23	.81	21	5.37	7	6.92	11	117.19	15	105.21	19	151.31	12
1.40	9	4.96	22	11.98	17	.88	23	7.18	18	6.09	20	123.69	18	132.35	22	204.02	19
1.01	24	5.37	20	10.03	22	.59	13	13.36	25	6.25	16	121.57	16	83.26	13	451.30	26
1.54	5	2.83	24	7.55	25	1.12	25	5.64	9	6.23	18	127.62	22	150.32	25	162.48	13
2.40	2	(2.57)	27	(4.87)	27	.36	3	12.67	24	8.45	5	99.20	9	83.08	11	98.80	4
1.44	7	.36	26	1.15	26	1.76	26	9.01	21	10.05	2	218.67	26	238.73	26	340.09	25
.55	27	1.96	25	7.83	24	1.93	27	—	27	4.51	26	367.65	27	352.83	27	—	27
						.79						111.47		119.11		144.43	
1.18		7.34		14.36		.61		6.64		6.37		114.85		92.24		188.61	
1.08		5.91		11.99		.71		6.25		5.56		120.38		101.35		211.47	

SOURCE: Consolidated Papers, Inc. [1977].

C Commercial Credit Scoring Models

In contrast to the extensive literature on the use of credit scoring models in consumer loan analysis, the literature on applications in the commercial loan area is quite small. Several possible reasons for this situation are outlined by Orgler [1970]:

> First, commercial borrowers do not belong to large homogeneous populations as do customers for consumer credit. This lack of standardization presents a problem in obtaining data for a statistically significant study. Second, there are substantial variations among commercial loans with respect to their size, terms, collateral types, and payment procedure, all of which are relatively uniform in the case of consumer loans. Finally, there is a lack of reliable up-to-date financial data on small commercial borrowers and particularly on those who defaulted in their loans. (p. 436)

The most frequent application of credit scoring in the commercial sector is with respect to trade credit. A study by Ewert [1977] is illustrative of research in this area.[6] The data analyzed were taken from the credit records of a manufacturing company. The sample comprised 507 firms which obtained credit with this company over the 1960–1964 period—298 of the accounts were "good" and 209 were "bad." A "bad" account was defined as one placed for collection with an outside agency or written off in the books of the manufacturing company. The 209 "bad" accounts were all the "bad" accounts of the manufacturer that Ewert could obtain data on. Data could not be obtained on 128 "bad" accounts in the 1960–1964 period. The 298 "good" accounts were randomly drawn from approximately 15,000 accounts defined as "good" over the 1960–1964 period.

The following details on variable choice were given by Ewert:

> There was no shortage of variables to test. Since there is a proliferation of plausible hypotheses and an absence of a general theory about credit worthiness, virtually every piece of information available could be rationalized as a possible discriminator between the goods and bads. Over 100 variables were tested.... Many variables which have been suggested as good indicators of credit worthiness could not be tested because the requisite information was not in the credit files. It was surprising to find the limited amount of information consistently available for most of the customers sampled. For instance, income statements were rarely found in the sample. Slightly less scarce were balance sheets from a year other than the current year. The paucity of data precluded testing income statement ratios and changes in balance sheet ratios. (pp. 89–90)

Three hundred and seven of the 507 firm accounts were used in estimating a model to discriminate between "good" and "bad" accounts. A stepwise regression procedure was used in choosing the independent variables. The final regression function included 17 variables, including 9 based on information provided by trade creditors to *Dun & Bradstreet*, e.g., the percentage of suppliers to the firm who report it to be a slow payer of trade accounts. Financial-statement-based variables included net worth, the current ratio, and the sales to working capital ratio. The validation sample included 100 "good" accounts and 100 "bad" accounts—165 of these accounts were correctly classified (a type I error of 18% and a type II error of 17%).

D Benefits of Credit Scoring Models

The decision of whether to implement a credit scoring model in a firm should be made on a cost-benefit basis (see Chapter 1). In this section, several ways in which the benefits of such systems may be realized are outlined. The discussion is necessarily at an abstract level. Estimation of the numerical extent of these benefits would require much greater specification of a loan decision context than is possible in this chapter.

1. One potentially important benefit of a credit scoring system is quantification of risks in credit decisions. For instance, Ewert [1977, p. 148] presented the following cumulative frequency distribution of "good" and "bad" accounts for the 200 firms in his hold-out sample (the Ewert study is described in Section 15.2C):

Credit Score from Scoring Model	Cumulative Frequencies "Goods"	"Bads"
− .200	0%	0%
.208	0	35
.226	2	36
.245	3	40
.356	6	58
.543	16	76
.577	17	82
.596	20	85
.699	34	97
.763	49	99
.898	75	100
1.200	100	100

Thus, a firm making trade credit decisions with Ewert's model can observe that (say) a decision rule of extend trade credit if the score for an applicant is equal to or greater than .577 will result in approximately 17% of "goods" being misclassified and 18% of "bads" being misclassified. By observing these percentages and the costs of each misclassification, management can make a considered decision on the desired risk level.

2. A credit scoring system can be used to test which variables (financial or otherwise) are important in discriminating between "good" and "bad" credit risks. Collecting and processing financial information is a costly activity, and it is important not to devote resources to collecting information on variables that lack discriminatory power. Note that the importance of a variable should be considered from a multivariate rather than a univariate perspective. The published literature contains several examples of variables which lack significant discriminatory power on a univariate basis, but which appear in a final discriminant function—e.g.,

the number of dependent variables in the Apilado et al. [1974] consumer credit study.

3. Having decided on the attributes of the scoring system, a bank can use the model to process loan applicants in a consistent manner. One limitation of the heuristic system used in some banks is that inconsistent decisions can be made by different loan evaluation officers. Given the increase in government regulations in the bank lending area (e.g., the Equal Credit Opportunity Act of 1975), it is important that a bank be able to document that its loan decisions are being made in a consistent and "objective" manner.

4. Credit scoring systems can assist in the allocation of a loan officer's time and resources. For instance, applicants above a set score could be accepted without further analysis; those below the score could be subject to further credit analysis. Similarly, a credit scoring system could be used as a screening device for the existing set of loans. The financial statements of companies with loans with a bank could be regularly scored and only those failing to reach a certain level subjected to internal review procedures.[7]

E   Some General Comments

Designing a credit scoring system entails some important factors that generally warrant explicit consideration.

1. The sample used in developing the model should correspond to the population to which the scoring model is to apply. In this regard, it is important to distinguish between two populations of interest to a lender:

(1) The population of new applicants, and
(2) The population of accepted applicants.

In many studies, a scoring model is based on a sample of accounts in a firm's files. This sample is appropriate if the concern is with developing internal review procedures to monitor existing accounts. If, however, the concern is with building a model to process new credit applicants, a sample based only on accounts in a firm's files may not be a representative one. These accounts have already been screened as "good" credit risks by the existing system. Thus, it is possible that a variable that is currently used in rejecting new applicants may not show up as a significant discriminatory variable on a model built on only accepted applicants.

It is difficult to overcome this problem when estimating scoring models to process new applicants. One alternative is to accept every applicant for a time period and track the subsequent loan experience.

Another proposed alternative is to include the applicants rejected by the existing system with those accounts initially accepted and subsequently classified as "bad." The latter alternative makes the assumption that the existing system has no type II errors. Yet another alternative is to subjectively estimate what would have been the credit experience if applicants who were rejected by the existing system were accepted.[8]

2. In most bank credit contexts, the number of "bad" loans relative to the number of "good" loans will be quite small. Yet, in many studies the samples used in developing the credit scoring model include 50% "good" and 50% "bad" accounts; i.e., the sample probabilities are dramatically different from the population probabilities of "good" and "bad" accounts. This difference creates severe problems in generalizing the results of research in this area—see Chapter 14 for discussion of this problem.[9]

3. When choosing the appropriate cutoff point for predicting "good" and "bad" credit risks, it is necessary to consider both the probabilities of misclassifying "good" and "bad" credit risks in the loan applicant population of interest and the costs of misclassifying loan applicants. Estimating the latter can be a difficult task. Consider new loan applicants. Predicting a loan will be "bad" when in fact it would not could entail the loss of the contribution margin on the loan plus the possible loss of future business of the applicant. The cost of incorrectly predicting an applicant will be a "good" credit risk will depend (in part) on the stage at which the "bad" status of the loan is detected and the collection costs incurred by the firm on the loan.

4. In building numerical scoring systems and in processing applicants with these models the problem of missing observations can arise; e.g., an applicant only fills out answers to 39 of the 40 questions on an application form. In this case, a firm may deem it not cost-effective to return the application form to the applicant seeking the missing information. Ewert [1977] encountered this problem in estimating a scoring model for processing trade credit applicants. None of the 100 variables examined was available for all firms in the sample. One solution adopted was that "if a few firms (approximately 10 percent or less of all the firms) were missing information for a given variable, the median value for the [combined good and bad] sample was substituted for the missing information" (p. 92).

5. The diversity in accounting techniques used by companies can create difficulties when using a credit scoring system for commercial loan evaluation. In this connection it is useful to distinguish between

(1) Cross-sectional diversity—i.e., differences in accounting techniques used by different firms at a point in time, and

(2) Time-series diversity—i.e., differences in accounting techniques used by the same firm over time.

Consider cross-sectional diversity. If, say, the model is estimated on a primarily FIFO inventory/straight-line depreciation set of firms, then it is possible that a LIFO inventory-accelerated depreciation firm could be rejected credit when it would have been extended credit had it used different accounting techniques. Moreover, in deciding the set of variables to include in the model, any cross-sectional diversity in accounting techniques in the estimation sample could be an important source of noise that causes some ratios to be excluded from the model. There are several alternatives one can adopt in this situation. One alternative is to build separate credit scoring models for each combination of major accounting alternatives. A second alternative is to use adjustment techniques (see Chapter 6) to place all applicants scored by the model on a similar basis as regards accounting techniques. Time-series diversity in accounting techniques can arise from voluntary or required (e.g., by *FASB*) accounting changes. If a model builder decides that the impact of such changes is significant, it may be appropriate to reestimate the model using data derived from the currently adopted accounting techniques.[10]

When faced with accounting diversity, a model builder may decide to include variables in the scoring model that are less affected by either cross-sectional or time-series diversity in accounting techniques, e.g., physical measures or capital market measures such as market value of debt to market value of equity. If one assumes capital market efficiency, capital market measures can be especially useful due to their impounding a very broad information set. Note, however, that capital market measures will only be available for publicly listed firms. From any small loan applicants to banks, such measures would not be available.

15.3 SUMMARY

A major limitation of work in the credit evaluation area is the limited analytical modeling of credit decisions. Another major limitation is that the empirical work has been largely of a brute empiricism kind. More attention needs to be paid to modeling why certain characteristics are associated with loan defaults while others are not.

APPENDIX 15.A BANK REGULATION AND FINANCIAL INFORMATION

Commercial banks are required to meet certain standards in order to maintain deposit insurance (up to $40,000 per account) provided by the *Federal Deposit Insurance Corporation* (FDIC). Adherence to these standards is determined through *bank examinations* by federal and state regulatory agencies. The purposes of a bank examination are stated by the FDIC to be[11]

(1) To determine asset quality;

(2) To determine the nature of liabilities;

(3) To ascertain compliance with laws and regulations;

(4) To evaluate controls, procedures, accounting practices, and insurance;

(5) To evaluate management and its policies; and

(6) To determine capital adequacy.

Two interesting aspects of bank regulation work that involve the use of financial statement information are (1) examining the quality of a bank's loan portfolio and (2) examining the solvency of banks to gain early warning signals of those in the financially distressed category. In this appendix, studies that examine these two aspects are discussed.

1. Examining Loan Quality

The FDIC examines the loan portfolios of banks, and those loans that are considered "doubtful" are placed in a "criticized" category. Orgler [1970; 1975, Chapter 4] used regression analysis to determine what characteristics helped to distinguish FDIC "criticized" loans from "noncriticized" loans. Data were obtained from the files of FDIC examiners in a number of East Coast states. Each "criticized" loan (termed "Bad") was matched with several "noncriticized" loans (termed "Good") from the same industry. The estimation sample contained 75 criticized loans and 225 noncriticized loans. The validation sample consisted of 40 criticized and 80 noncriticized loans. The dependent variable in the regression model was either 1 (loan criticized) or 0 (loan noncriticized). The initial set of independent variables included both financial (over 20 ratios) and nonfinancial ratios. The final regression model selected was

$$Y_i = 1.1018 + .1017X_1 - .3966X_2 - .0916X_3$$
$$- .1573X_4 - .0199X_5 - .4533X_6, \tag{15.2}$$

where $X_1 = 0$ if loan unsecured and 1 if loan secured,

$X_2 = 0$ if past interest payment due and 1 if loan current,

$X_3 = 0$ if firm not audited and 1 if firm audited,

$X_4 = 0$ for a net loss and 1 for a net profit,

$X_5 =$ working capital to current assets,

$X_6 = 0$ for loan criticized by bank examiner during the last examination and 1 if not criticized.

Orgler used two cutoff points when classifying loans: C_1 and C_2, where $C_1 < C_2$. These two cutoff points gave three predicted categories for commercial loans:

$$\hat{Y}_i > C_2 = \text{“Bad” loan}$$
$$C_1 \leqslant \hat{Y}_i \leqslant C_2 = \text{“Marginal” loan}$$
$$\hat{Y}_i \leqslant C_1 = \text{“Good” loan.}$$

The values of C_1 and C_2 were based on an arbitrary decision rule:

> ...the proportion of bad loans classified wrongly as good should be less than 5 percent of all bad loans and that the proportion of bad loans classified correctly as bad should be at least 75 percent of total bad loans (the remainder falls into the "marginal" category). The emphasis on bad loans is explained by the relatively high penalty cost associated with overlooking a potentially bad loan. (p. 61)

The classification matrices for both the estimation and validation samples are in Table 15.3—the cutoff points chosen on the estimation sample were $C_1 = .08$ and $C_2 = .25$.

Orgler proposed that (15.2) be used in the loan review process as follows. First, classify the loans as good, marginal, or bad. Then a bank examiner would review the marginal loans to determine whether they belong to the good or bad category. Finally, he would only examine in detail the loans in the bad category. Thus, it was argued that examiners could be relieved of reviewing the good category of loans (24.1% of the validation sample) and devote their scarce resources to the marginal and bad categories. Similar proposals for this use of credit scoring models in consumer and commercial loan evaluation have also been made. It is interesting to note that the Orgler study is analogous to the bond rating studies examined in Chapter 13. The model in (15.2) is attempting to explain (predict) the judgments of bank examiners, while the models in Chapter 13 were attempting to explain the judgments of bond rating agencies.[12]

Credit Decisions and Financial Information

TABLE 15.3   Predicting Bank Loan Examiner Criticisms

A. Estimation Sample

		Actual	
		Bad	Good
Predicted	Bad	80%	20.4%
	Marginal	16%	54.7%
	Good	4%	24.9%

B. Validation Sample

		Actual	
		Bad	Good
Predicted	Bad	75%	17.5%
	Marginal	22.5%	47.5%
	Good	2.5%	35%

SOURCE: Orgler [1970, Tables 2 and 3, reprinted with permission]

2. Examining Bank Solvency

As a result of information gained in a bank examination, a bank may be placed on a "problem" list. A "problem bank" is a greater risk to the FDIC insurance fund than is a nonproblem bank. The three classes of problem banks, categorized according to their likelihood of needing financial assistance, are[13]

(1) Serious problem—potential payoff (PPO). An advanced, serious bank presenting at least a 50% chance of requiring FDIC financial assistance in the near future.

(2) Serious problem (SP). A banking situation that threatens ultimately to involve the FDIC in a financial outlay unless drastic changes occur.

(3) Other problem (OP). A banking situation involving a significant weakness with a lesser degree of vulnerability than (1) or (2) and calling for aggressive supervision and more than ordinary concern by the FDIC.

The FDIC monitors the financial solvency of banks in an attempt to minimize the number of problem banks and to avoid problem banks requiring FDIC financial assistance.

An illustrative study of FDIC-sponsored research on the characteristics of problem banks is Sinkey [1975]. The sample of firms comprised 90 banks identified as "problems" in 1972 and 20 banks identified as "problems" in 1973. Each problem bank was matched with a nonproblem bank, using the following matching criteria: (1) geographic market area, (2) total deposits, (3) number of banking offices, and (4) Federal Reserve membership status. The composition of the "problem banks" was

(1) Potential payoff (PPO): 2.

(2) Serious problem (SP): 14.

(3) Other problem (OP): 94.

Over 100 variables were initially examined to see if there was a significant difference between the ratios of problem and nonproblem banks on a univariate basis. Table 15.4 presents a profile analysis (mean ratios of problem and nonproblem banks) for five selected ratios over the 1969–1972 period. These five ratios represent the following dimensions of bank finances:

(1) Loan volume—loans/assets,

(2) Capital adequacy—loans/capital plus reserve,

(3) Efficiency—operating expense/operating income,

(4) Sources of revenue—loan revenue/total revenue, and

(5) Uses of revenue—other expenses/total revenue.

For each year for each of these five ratios the mean ratios of the problem and nonproblem banks were statistically different at a 5% significance level.

TABLE 15.4 Profile Analysis of Problem Banks

Financial Ratio	1969	1970	1971	1972
Loans/assets				
1. Problem bank	53.9	55.4	56.9	56.0
2. Nonproblem bank	49.3	48.9	47.8	47.8
Loans/capital plus reserve				
1. Problem bank	648.3	692.2	768.9	838.6
2. Nonproblem bank	564.5	562.5	562.4	577.5
Operating exp./operating inc.				
1. Problem bank	83.9	85.5	89.3	94.1
2. Nonproblem bank	78.5	78.6	81.8	82.4
Loan revenue/total revenue				
1. Problem bank	64.7	65.8	68.8	69.8
2. Nonproblem bank	59.3	59.2	59.9	59.6
Other expenses/total revenue				
1. Problem bank	15.8	16.0	16.3	16.4
2. Nonproblem bank	12.3	13.0	13.2	13.7

SOURCE: Sinkey [1975, Table 3].

Sinkey then used a multiple discriminant analysis model to classify the problem and nonproblem banks on the basis of their financial ratios. Separate functions were estimated in 1969, 1970, 1971, and 1972. In general, six or seven variables were included in each discriminant function. The prediction results for each year were[14]

	Type I Error (predict problem bank as nonproblem)	Type II Error (predict nonproblem bank as problem)	Total Misclassification Rate
1969	46.36%	25.45%	35.91%
1970	42.73%	27.27%	35.00%
1971	38.18%	24.55%	31.36%
1972	28.15%	21.36%	24.76%

Thus, in the years prior to being classified as a problem bank, the discriminant model is progressively better able to classify the banks that were termed problems in 1971 and 1972.

Sinkey noted that the research was part of a project for developing an early warning system to predict problem banks. Several potential advantages of an effective early warning system as a supervisory tool were said to be (1) to enable the banking agencies to more efficiently allocate their resources, (2) to make more efficient use of preexamination data, and (3) to provide bank regulatory agencies with an evaluation of their examination and supervisory performances.[15]

NOTES

[1]An early classic study is Clarkson's [1962] simulation model of the investment decisions of a trust investment officer.

[2]For some initial research, see Edmister and Schlarbaum [1974], Mehta [1974], and Long [1976].

[3]See, for example, Lev [1974, Chapter 11].

[4]Main [1977] illustrates a hypothetical scoring system for consumer credit rating.

[5]Other examples of consumer credit scoring models include Durand [1941], Myers and Forgy [1963], and Main [1977]. See also Orgler [1975, Chapter 5] for a credit scoring model for outstanding consumer loans.

[6]Altman et al. [1974] illustrate use of a credit scoring model for French commercial loan evaluation. Their results are difficult to interpret due to their failure to use a validation sample.

[7]The above list of areas where introduction of a numerical scoring system could be beneficial is not an exhaustive one. For instance, Weingartner [1966] notes the following areas where a scoring system may be beneficial:

> First, by including credit scores in reports, management obtains a running barometer of the quality of credit granted and of the quality of applications turned down. Such information permits monitoring and changing, when necessary, overall policy with respect to consumer loans. In addition, it enables management to make better forecasts of future write-offs. In multibranch operations it helps to oversee decentralized operations and identify weak spots early. Second, a credit scoring system helps in training new credit personnel by systematically displaying the factors considered in judging credit, and associated credit performance with these factors. (pp. 52–53)

[8]See Cohen and Hammer [1966, pp. 127–134] for further discussion of this problem.

[9]See also Eisenbeis [1977] for a more detailed analysis of this problem.

[10]See Abdel-Khalik [1973], Oliver [1972], Kennedy [1975], Libby [1975], and Schwan [1976] for analysis of the effect of different accounting alternatives (disclosure levels, etc.) on bank loan decisions.

[11]See Benston [1973] and Sinkey and Walker [1975].

[12]An important issue is whether bank examiner "criticisms" of loans are good measures of ex ante default risk on loans. On this score, the available evidence (e.g., Wu [1969]) suggests a positive but not highly significant relationship between a loan being "criticized" and its subsequently being "written off." Note, however, that ex post experience may underestimate the predictive ability of examiner "criticisms." A "criticism" of a loan may lead a bank to institute renegotiations with a borrower that avoids the loan's subsequently being "written off."

[13]See Sinkey and Walker [1975].

[14]A Lachenbruch hold-out discriminant analysis technique was used to obtain these prediction results—see Sinkey [1975, pp. 31–33].

[15]Whether federal banking agency classifications of problem banks are effective predictors of likely financial distress is an interesting issue. Benston [1973] noted that of the 56 banks that failed between January 1959 and April 1971, only 41% (22 banks) were classified as "problems" at the time of the bank examination approximately one year before failure (see also Gilbert [1975]). However, in 28 of the other 34 banks that failed, fraud or embezzlement was found to be a major factor. Whether any early warning system relying on discriminant function scores could detect frauds is a doubtful issue. Indeed, it is far from clear that bank examination procedures are (or should be) designed to detect fraud or embezzlement.

QUESTIONS

QUESTION 15.1:   Numerical Scoring for Commercial Loan Decisions

Details of a numerical scoring system for U.S. paper companies are presented in Tables 15.1 and 15.2.

REQUIRED

(1) Consider the companies ranked (in 1976) 1, 10, 14, 17, and 22. Which ratios appear to contribute most to differences in the aggregate scores of these companies?

(2) No adjustment has been made for possible accounting technique differences across the above paper companies. Why might differences in accounting techniques across companies pose a problem for the use of a credit scoring system in commercial loan evaluation? What alternatives may a bank consider to minimize these problems?

(3) In addition to the cross-sectional diversity in accounting techniques referred to in (2), there is also the problem of time-series diversity in accounting techniques. Give several examples of this diversity and what factors may give rise to it. Why might differences in accounting techniques by a firm over time pose a problem for the use of a credit scoring system in commercial loan evaluation? What alternatives may a bank consider to minimize these problems?

QUESTION 15.2:   Restrictive Covenants in Loan Agreements

Many commercial loans contain restrictions on the magnitude of certain financial items or ratios. The following restrictions are illustrative:

> The bank [loan] prohibits the payment of cash dividends; other loan provisions require the maintenance of a ratio of current assets to current liabilities of not less than one to one, a tangible net worth of not less than $600,000, and a ratio of consolidated indebtedness to tangible net worth not to exceed two to one. (*Eanco*, 1975 Annual Report)

> At July 31, 1975 the Company was required to maintain consolidated tangible net worth (as defined) of at least $26,828,000, consolidated working capital (as defined) of not less than $20,000,000, and a consolidated working capital ratio of not less than 1.5 to 1. (*Republic Corporation*, 1975 Annual Report)

REQUIRED

(1) What factors would a bank consider in deciding what restrictive covenants to include in a loan agreement?

(2) A footnote in the 1975 Annual Report of *Republic Corporation* noted that "pursuant to the amended credit agreement, the banks consented to certain transactions which otherwise would have been prohibited." Why would a bank agree to a borrower violating the restrictions in a loan agreement?

(3) Restrictions on the minimum level of the current ratio are often included in restrictive covenants. Critics of this ratio contend that it ignores information about the timing and magnitude of future cash flows (see Chapter 2). Cash-based liquidity ratios, such as the defensive interval measure, have been proposed as alternatives to the current ratio. Design an empirical study to determine the conditions under which a bank would prefer to include restrictive covenants relating to the defensive interval measure rather than to the current ratio.

QUESTION 15.3: Commercial Loan Decisions and Financial Distress Prediction

In Chapter 14 we discussed several studies that examined financial distress prediction, e.g., Beaver [1966] and Altman [1968]. The reception to these papers has been mixed. Bernstein [1974] made the following comment on Beaver [1966]:

> The study focused on experience with failed firms after the fact. While it presented evidence that firms which did not fail enjoyed stronger ratios than those which ultimately failed, the ability of ratios to predict failure has not been conclusively proved. Another important question yet to be resolved is whether the observation of certain types of behavior by certain ratios can be accepted as a better means of the analysis of long-term solvency than is the current use of the various [traditional] tools of analysis. (p. 464)

Soldofsky and Olive [1974] were also less than enthused by the Beaver [1966] and Altman [1968] studies:

> These new studies were admittedly based upon very small samples; the industry designations were broad; and the sample of bankrupt firms spanned periods of more than 10 years in two of the cases. Each of these factors limits the practical usefulness of these studies. The cash flow to debt rule-of-thumb ratio for successful performance is not well known. Some index-of-risk approach might be utilized for future interbusiness credit management, but such innovations require at least a generation before their use becomes widespread. Discriminant scores are difficult to understand.

> Most bankruptcies take place among small and closely held firms, but Altman used a variable that requires the use of market values for equities. However, the technique employed by Altman could be utilized to select another variable of high discriminant ability.

Both Altman and Beaver were pleased with the ability of their results to predict data in the next year after the publication of financial statements. However, time to bankruptcy might be as short as one month, and only in a few cases would it be as long as 12 months. Virtually every credit analyst could look at the trend and level of a few ratios and pick firms for which bankruptcy was likely within the coming year without elaborate statistical analysis. Altman and Beaver's approaches will tend to be expensive since separate studies would be needed for each fairly narrow industry classification such as lumber yards or men and boy's clothing stores.

Trade creditors will find such information useful, but the prediction that a customer is very likely to fail within the next one, two, or three years is not necessarily a reason to withdraw all trade credit. The seller must consider his profit margin on each sale, his investment in the amount of trade credit outstanding, the probable period prior to failure, the probability of failure, and other factors. A detailed analysis may show that sales to firms with a strong probability of failure may still earn a rate of return greater than the cost of capital up to some period, such as 18 months, before the expected failure. (p. 349)

In contrast, Van Horne [1974] is quite optimistic about the potential of such studies:

Several empirical studies [Beaver, Altman] have been undertaken that show great promise for statistically testing the predictive power of financial ratios.... However, the studies described only scratch the surface. The potential for testing empirically the underlying predictive power of financial statement data is enormous. As additional tests are undertaken, we shall have a much better understanding of which ratios are important in predicting certain types of events. As a result, financial ratio analysis will become more scientific than it is now. No longer will we be dependent upon the subjective experience of the analyst in evaluating which ratios are important. With sufficient testing, meaningful bench marks can be established which will make financial analysis truly objective in scope. (p. 670)

REQUIRED

(1) From a commercial loan evaluation officer's perspective, what do you think are the two major limitations of the results of this research? Describe how you would overcome (or minimize) these two limitations if you were designing a study on financial distress prediction for a large commercial bank.

(2) Discuss two *specific* areas in which studies such as Beaver [1966] and Altman [1968] would provide valuable information to loan evaluation officers of a large commercial bank.

(3) It has been proposed that discriminant models, akin to that used by Altman [1968], be used in commercial loan evaluation in place of loan evaluation officers. This proposal is consistent with the following recommendation made in the human judgment modeling literature: "get the human decision maker out of the decision process at

the earliest possible moment" (Rorer [1972, p. 19]). What factors may underlie Rorer's recommendation? Comment on its applicability to commercial loan evaluation.

(4) It has also been proposed that banks who adopt a discriminant model in processing commercial loans publicly disclose complete details of the model and the cutoff points. What arguments for and against this proposal would a bank want to consider?

QUESTION 15.4: Bank Failures and Bank Regulation

In 1973 and 1974 two large U.S. bank failures increased public concern over the procedures for detecting potential failures that were being used by bank regulatory authorities. The two banks were the *United States National Bank of San Diego* (USNB) and the *Franklin National Bank of New York* (Franklin). Sinkey [1975a] provides the following details on the failure of the USNB:

> On November 9, 1972, USNB was placed on the FDIC's troubled-bank list in the "serious problem" classification. The Comptroller's examination...indicated that "classified" assets were 371% of capital and reserves, up from 25% of capital and reserves as of the September 13, 1971 examination report. Furthermore, 86% of the classified assets and $113 million in standby letters of credit were obligations of business enterprises controlled by C. Arnholt Smith, his family or business associates. The [examiner's report] indicated that Mr. Smith had knowingly withheld credit information relating to the classified loans in order to conceal their true quality. (p. 9)

Classified assets are those for which the examiner predicts a potential for probable default. On May 23, 1973, the Comptroller of the Currency forced C. Arnholt Smith to resign the presidency and board chairmanship of USNB. On October 18, 1973, USNB was declared insolvent by the Comptroller of the Currency—it reopened the next day under the banner of *Crocker National Bank of San Francisco*.

Sinkey [1975b] provides the following details on the failure of *Franklin*:

> On May 10, 1974 Franklin National Bank of New York announced that it planned to omit dividend payments on its common and preferred stocks, an unprecedented move for a major money-market bank. Franklin, the twentieth largest bank in the nation at the time, said that it had lost $14 million, mainly because of unauthorized foreign exchange transactions made by one of its traders without the knowledge of the bank's top management. Needless to say, the Franklin story made front-page headlines and television evening newscasts.... Over the six-month period December 31, 1973 to June 30, 1974, Franklin's total deposits declined by $1,022 million, a decrease of 39.3%.... On October 8, 1974, Franklin was declared insolvent by the Comptroller of the Currency but reopened the next day, with the financial assistance of the FDIC, under the banner of European-American Bank and Trust Co. (pp. 10–11)

Table 15.5 presents selected financial items for all California banks and for USNB covering the four years prior to the failure of the USNB. Table 15.6 presents similar data for all New York State banks and *Franklin*. The percentage of other deposits (item 7) for *Franklin* that was comprised of foreign deposits was 14.3% in 1970, 16.3% in 1971, 39.5% in 1972, and 48.9% in 1973. Comparable figures for all New York State banks were not available.

REQUIRED

(1) Compare the profiles of the financial ratios of all California banks vs. USNB and all New York State banks vs. *Franklin* in the four years prior to the failure of each bank. At a minimum you should examine profiles of the following ratios:

Capital Structure

  1. Capital account (item 11)/total assets
  2. Total deposits (items 6 and 7)/capital account (item 11)

Asset and Deposit Structure

  3. Loans (item 4)/total assets
  4. Demand deposits (item 6)/total deposits (items 6 and 7)

Profitability

  5. Net income (item 19)/total assets
  6. Net income (item 19)/capital account (item 11)

Comment on the results from a bank regulator's perspective.

(2) Benston [1973] reported that of the 56 banks that failed between January 1959 and April 1971, only 41% were classified as "problems" at the time of the bank examination, approximately one year before failure. Why might this percentage give a misleading impression of the effectiveness of the FDIC's ability to minimize bank failures?

(3) The risks that banks can assume are constrained by government regulations; e.g., a limit is imposed on the maximum loan each bank can make to one customer, and restrictions are placed on the real estate loans banks can make. Regulators regularly examine banks to determine the quality of their assets and to enforce compliance with banking regulations. It has been proposed that there be a substantial reduction in bank regulations and that banks be allowed to choose the risks they deem appropriate. To protect those holding deposits at banks, related proposals for variable deposit insurance have been made, e.g., Mayer [1965] and Peltzman [1972]. Regulatory authorities under these proposals would charge each bank for FDIC insurance of $40,000 per account based on the assessed risks the bank assumed. The President's Commission on Financial Structure and Regulations

TABLE 15.5 Selected Financial Items of California Banks and USNB ($000,000's)

	All California Banks				United States National Bank (San Diego)			
	1969	1970	1971	1972	1969	1970	1971	1972
Assets								
1. Cash	8,224	8,585	9,932	11,939	72	80	81	137
2. Government securities	9,761	12,145	15,978	15,199	120	134	213	303
3. Other securities	699	1,095	1,061	874	16	15	16	15
4. Loans	32,439	33,886	38,245	45,411	312	347	402	540
5. Other assets	2,675	2,917	3,293	3,607	57	21	25	52
	53,798	58,628	68,509	77,030	577	597	737	1,047
Liabilities and Equity								
6. Demand deposits	19,989	20,713	22,463	26,607	202	212	227	316
7. Other deposits	23,513	28,636	33,699	37,461	223	292	406	574
8. Federal funds	0	0	0	0	24	18	24	49
9. Reserves for loan losses	652	651	667	718	6	6	7	8
10. Other liabilities	6,164	5,008	7,732	7,645	86	32	32	39
11. Capital account	3,480	3,620	3,948	4,599	36	37	41	61
	53,798	58,628	68,509	77,030	577	597	737	1,047

TABLE 15.5

	All California Banks				United States National Bank (San Diego)			
	1969	1970	1971	1972	1969	1970	1971	1972
Operating Revenue								
12. Interest & fees on loans	2,549	2,718	2,687	2,995	24	28	32	37
13. Interest & div. on securities	433	526	663	697	6	7	8	12
14. Other operating income	444	533	599	675	4	5	6	6
	3,426	3,777	3,949	4,367	34	40	46	55
15. Security gains (losses)	(9)	(2)	9	8	0	0	1	1
Expenses								
16. Interest on deposits	1,468	1,549	1,649	1,825	15	16	20	26
17. Provision for loan losses	66	76	103	114	0.25	0.4	1.1	1.6
18. Other expenses	1,495	1,760	1,800	1,990	16	21	22	24
	3,029	3,385	3,552	3,929	31.25	37.4	43.1	51.6
19. Net income (loss)	388	390	406	446	2.25	2.6	3.9	4.4

TABLE 15.6 Selected Financial Items of New York State Banks and Franklin ($000,000's)

	All New York State Banks				Franklin National Bank			
	1970	1971	1972	1973	1970	1971	1972	1973
Assets								
1. Cash	24,328	25,461	29,690	28,589	457	583	1,201	1,201
2. Government securities	18,916	20,318	21,757	20,255	777	639	412	520
3. Other securities	2,810	2,519	3,103	4,616	162	218	237	209
4. Loans	60,546	63,006	74,203	87,861	1,603	1,719	2,079	2,767
5. Other assets	6,027	6,316	7,033	8,167	459	346	431	301
	112,627	117,620	135,786	149,488	3,458	3,505	4,360	4,998
Liabilities and Equity								
6. Demand deposits	54,739	55,830	62,281	63,016	1,164	1,268	1,507	1,410
7. Other deposits	31,976	37,947	43,794	51,821	1,468	1,572	1,954	2,323
8. Federal funds	0	0	0	0	475	278	493	797
9. Reserves for loan losses	1,530	1,522	1,581	1,695	31	31	30	27
10. Other liabilities	16,096	13,053	18,062	22,111	132	134	150	215
11. Capital account	8,286	9,268	10,068	10,845	188	222	226	226
	112,627	117,620	135,786	149,488	3,458	3,505	4,360	4,998

TABLE 15.6

	All New York State Banks				Franklin National Bank			
	1970	1971	1972	1973	1970	1971	1972	1973
Operating Revenue								
12. Interest and fees on loans	4,602	4,119	4,272	6,801	148	133	135	242
13. Interest and div. on securities	926	1,005	1,047	1,094	55	49	47	83
14. Other operating income	1,001	1,122	1,269	1,542	13	14	16	19
	6,529	6,246	6,588	9,437	216	196	198	344
15. Security gains (losses)	(60)	14	3	(16)	(1)	0	1	0
Expenses								
16. Interest on deposits	2,225	2,114	2,343	4,531	120	99	99	236
17. Provision for loan losses	112	164	200	287	3	7	8	12
18. Other expenses	3,290	3,055	3,058	3,478	69	72	77	83
	5,627	5,333	5,601	8,296	192	178	184	331
19. Net income (loss)	842	927	990	1,125	23	18	15	13

[1971] presented the following arguments against variable deposit insurance premiums:

The Commission rejected the variable rate proposal. It recognizes that differences in risk of failure exist and that its recommendation for liberalizing the regulations relating to the asset, liability and capital structures of financial institutions would probably increase these differences. The problem is a practical one. The Commission does not see how differences in risks can be evaluated with sufficient precision to be adequately reflected in insurance assessments. Further, the Commission believes that assessments might be used, albeit unintentionally, to penalize innovative institutions. New and different functions might be regarded as high risk functions. Finally, knowledge that some institutions were paying higher assessments than others could weaken public confidence in those institutions, which would defeat the purpose insurance was designed to achieve. (p. 74)

How could financial statement information be used in a variable deposit insurance premium system? Comment on the reasons offered by the President's Commission against variable deposit insurance premiums.

REFERENCES

ABDEL-KHALIK, A. R. "The Effect of Aggregating Accounting Reports on the Quality of the Lending Decision: An Empirical Investigation." *Empirical Research in Accounting Selected Studies, 1973*. Supplement to *Journal of Accounting Research* (1973): 104–138.

ALTMAN, E. I. "Financial Ratios, Discriminant Analysis and the Prediction of Corporate Bankruptcy." *Journal of Finance* (Sept. 1968): 589–609.

ALTMAN, E. I., MARGAINE, M., SCHLOSSER, M., and VERNIMMEN, P. "Financial and Statistical Analysis for Commercial Loan Evaluation: A French Experience." *Journal of Financial and Quantitative Analysis* (Mar. 1974): 195–211.

APILADO, V. P., WARNER, D. C., and DAUTEN, J. J. "Evaluative Techniques in Consumer Finance Experimental Results and Policy Implications for Financial Institutions." *Journal of Financial and Quantitative Analysis* (Mar. 1974): 275–283.

BEAVER, W. H. "Financial Ratios as Predictors of Failure." *Empirical Research in Accounting: Selected Studies, 1966*. Supplement to *Journal of Accounting Research* (1966): 71–111.

BENSTON, G. J. "Bank Examination." *The Bulletin* of the Institute of Finance, Graduate School of Business Administration, New York University, New York, Nos. 89–90, May 1973: 1–73.

BERNSTEIN, L. P. *Financial Statement Analysis.* Irwin, Homewood, Ill., 1974.

CLARKSON, G. P. E. *Portfolio Selection: A Simulation of Trust Investment.* Prentice-Hall, Englewood Cliffs, N.J., 1962.

COHEN, K. J., and HAMMER, F. S. (eds.). *Analytical Methods in Banking.* Irwin, Homewood, Ill., 1966.

COHEN, K. J., GILMORE, T. C., and SINGER, F. A. "Bank Procedures for Analyzing Business Loan Applications." In K. J. Cohen and F. S. Hammer (eds.), *Analytical Methods in Banking.* Irwin, Homewood, Ill., 1966.

CONSOLIDATED PAPERS, INC. *18th Annual Compilation of Financial Ratios of Selected Paper Companies.* Consolidated Paper, Wisconsin Rapids, Wisc., 1977.

DURAND, D. *Risk Elements in Consumer Installment Financing.* National Bureau of Economic Research, New York, 1941.

EDMISTER, R. O., and SCHLARBAUM, G. G. "Credit Policy in Lending Institutions." *Journal of Financial and Quantitative Analysis* (June 1974): 335–356.

EISENBEIS, R. A. "Pitfalls in the Application of Discriminant Analysis in Business, Finance and Economics." *Journal of Finance* (June 1977): 875–900.

EWERT, D. C. *Trade Credit Management: Selection of Accounts Receivable Using a Statistical Model.*. PSD, College of Business Administration, Georgia State University, Atlanta, Ga., 1977.

GILBERT, R. A. "Bank Failures and Public Policy." *Federal Reserve Bank of St. Louis* (Nov. 1975): 7–15.

HESTER, D. D. "An Empirical Examination of a Commercial Bank Loan Offer Function." *Yale Economic Essays* (1962): 3–57.

KENNEDY, H. A. "A Behavioral Study of the Usefulness of Four Financial Ratios." *Journal of Accounting Research* (Spring 1975): 97–116.

LEV, B. *Financial Statement Analysis: A New Approach.* Prentice-Hall, Englewood Cliffs, N.J., 1974.

LIBBY, R. "Accounting Ratios and the Prediction of Failure: Some Behavioral Evidence." *Journal of Accounting Research* (Spring 1975): 150–161.

LONG, M. S. "Credit Screening System Selection." *Journal of Financial and Quantitative Analysis* (June 1976): 313–328.

MAIN, J. "A New Way to Score with Lenders." *Money* (Feb. 1977): 73–74.

MAYER, T. "A Graduated Deposit Insurance Plan." *Review of Economics and Statistics* (Feb. 1965): 114–116.

MEHTA, D. R. *Working Capital Management.* Prentice-Hall, Englewood Cliffs, N.J., 1974.

MYERS, J. H., and FORGY, E. W. "The Development of Numerical Credit Evaluation Systems." *Journal of the American Statistical Association* (Sept. 1963): 799–806.

OLIVER, B. L. "A Study of Confidence Interval Financial Statements." *Journal of Accounting Research* (Spring 1972): 154–166.

ORGLER, Y. E. "A Credit-Scoring Model for Commercial Loans." *Journal of Money, Credit and Banking*, Vol. 2 (Nov. 1970):435–445. Reprinted by permission.

———. *Analytical Methods in Loan Evaluation*. Lexington Books, Lexington, Mass., 1975.

PELTZMAN, S. "The Costs of Competition: An Appraisal of the Hunt Commission Report." *Journal of Money, Credit and Banking* (Nov. 1972): 1001–1004.

PRESIDENT'S COMMISSION ON FINANCIAL STRUCTURE AND REGULATION. *The Report of the President's Commission on Financial Structure and Regulation*. U.S. Government Printing Office, Washington, D.C., 1971.

RORER, L. G. "A Circuitous Route to Bootstrapping Selection Procedures." *Oregon Research Institute Research Bulletin* (1972):

SCHWAN, E. S. "The Effects of Human Resource Accounting Data on Financial Decisions: An Empirical Test." *Accounting, Organizations and Society* (1976): 219–237.

SINKEY, J. F. "A Multivariate Statistical Analysis of the Characteristics of Problem Banks." *Journal of Finance* (Mar. 1975): 21–36.

———. "The Failure of United States National Bank of San Diego: A Portfolio and Performance Analysis." *Journal of Bank Research* (Spring 1975a): 8–24.

———. "Adverse Publicity and Bank Deposit Flows: The Cases of Franklin National Bank of New York and United States National Bank of San Diego." *Journal of Bank Research* (Summer 1975b): 109–112.

SINKEY, J. F., and WALKER, D. A. "Problem Banks: Identification and Characteristics." *Journal of Bank Research* (Winter 1975): 208–217.

SOLDOFSKY, R. M., and OLIVE, G. D. *Financial Management*. South-Western, Cincinnati, 1974.

VAN HORNE, J. C. *Financial Management and Policy*, 3rd ed. Prentice-Hall, Englewood Cliffs, N.J., 1974.

WEINGARTNER, H. M. "Concepts and Utilization of Credit-Scoring Techniques." *Banking* (Feb. 1966): 51–53.

WELLS, H. L. "New Customer Credit Pointing System." In *Numerical Pointing Plans for Evaluating Consumer Credit Risks*. Philadelphia Credit Bureau, Philadelphia, 1963.

WU, H. K. "Bank Examiner Criticisms, Bank Loan Defaults, and Bank Loan Quality." *Journal of Finance* (Sept. 1969): 697–705.

POLICY
CHOICE

CHAPTER **16**

ACCOUNTING POLICY
DECISIONS

In prior chapters we have concentrated on the use of financial information in credit and investment decisions. In this chapter, we shall examine forces that influence the information set made available to creditors and investors. In particular, the influence of decisions by regulatory bodies such as the Financial Accounting Standards Board (FASB) and the Securities and Exchange Commission (SEC) will be discussed.

Forces other than decisions by regulatory bodies also influence the information set available to creditors and investors. An overview of the existing institutional framework is presented in Figure 16.1. This figure illustrates that market forces as well as decisions by regulatory bodies can be important determinants of the information set available to external parties. For example, even prior to the Securities Exchange Act of 1934, there were strong disclosure forces operating in the capital market. These forces led corporations to disclose much of the information pertinent to security price valuation that was subsequently required by the act. Firms compete with each other in the capital market to attract capital from investors. One way of competing is through the disclosure of additional financial information. Benston [1969] reports that prior to the 1934 act, many corporations were already disclosing sales, cost of goods sold, depreciation, net income, as well as balance sheet information such as current assets and current liabilities. Moreover, there were already in existence *information intermediaries* (e.g., *Moody's*) which gathered and summarized financial information and sold it to creditors and investors.

Another example of how market forces can affect the available information set is in the municipal bond market. Under existing law, municipalities are not required to present annual financial statements to bondholders. Yet, we observe some municipalities publicly reporting such information. One newspaper article (the *Wall Street Journal*, January 6, 1975) noted that since the New York City financial crisis there has been increased market pressure for more disclosure of municipal finances. The article noted that "whatever the law says...bond analysts say the market itself will encourage improved disclosure. A municipality standing on its legal rights to keep mum will pay a penalty—higher borrowing costs."

Figure 16.1 also illustrates that bodies other than the firm itself can provide information pertinent to assessing the distribution of future returns on the firm's securities. Organizations such as brokerage houses, *Moody's*, *Standard & Poor's*, industry associations, etc., all provide information to the capital market. These organizations, like firms, can also be affected by market forces and the decisions of regulatory bodies. Some effects of changes in life insurance financial reporting standards illustrate this point. Starting in 1973, life insurance companies were required to report their

FIGURE 16.1   Forces Affecting Information Set Available to External Parties

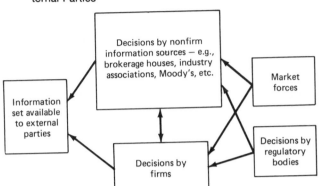

underwriting results using generally accepted accounting principles (GAAP). Prior to this date, most firms reported underwriting results using the accounting principles prescribed by state insurance commissioners. These principles—termed *statutory principles*—differed from GAAP in two main respects:

(1) Costs of writing new policies were expensed in the first year of the policy rather than being amortized over the life of the policy, and

(2) The interest rate assumptions used in computing policy reserves were below the returns insurance companies earned on their investments.

Prior to 1973, various bodies (e.g., *Standard & Poor's* and *A.M. Best*) adjusted the statutory earnings of life insurance companies for differences (1) and (2) noted above. These resultant earnings numbers—termed *adjusted earnings*—were provided to subscribers of the investment services of these firms. Since 1973, however, these bodies have stopped reporting their own adjusted earnings estimates. They now report the GAAP numbers provided in the annual reports of insurance companies. Thus, the effect of the 1973 life insurance reporting requirements has been to transfer the source of (and presumably the costs of preparing) GAAP earnings numbers from several information intermediaries to life insurance companies.

16.1   IMPACT OF ACCOUNTING POLICY DECISIONS

In Chapter 4 it was noted that the accounting numbers reported by firms are a function of both (1) the financing, investment, and production decisions of firms and (2) the accounting methods/disclosure policies used by these firms. In this section we shall present some evidence that both (1) and (2) may be affected by accounting policy decisions. This evidence will be based on the effect (or alleged effect) of *specific* accounting policy decisions on *specific* groups.

A Financing, Investment, and Production Decisions

The accounting for marketable equity securities issue illustrates the potential impact that existing and proposed reporting rules may have for corporate decisions. Under existing reporting rules, only the realized gains and losses on equity securities are included in income. There are statements that these rules influence the investment decisions of corporations. For instance, the second quarter 1974 interim report of *ITT* stated the following:

> *Hartford Fire Insurance Company* invests in common and preferred stocks to produce earnings from a combination of dividends and appreciation. *ITT* believes that stockholders are entitled to participate currently in the earnings generated by appreciation, and since present accounting rules require the sale of securities in order to record such gains, *Hartford* sells securities to realize investment gains.

The Accounting Principles Board (APB) in the 1969–1972 period considered the alternative reporting rule of including both annual realized and unrealized capital gains and losses in income.[1] *The Monumental Corporation* made the following comment on this reporting rule:

> Some have advocated that the realized and unrealized gains should flow into the income statement on an annual basis. Frankly, if this happened, this would make common stocks unattractive for our company.... The reward vis-à-vis bonds and mortgages today is not great enough to face these risks. If the stock of the company declines when it shouldn't, how do you explain why you bought commons when you could have bought bonds at 9 percent? (reported in Arthur Andersen & Co. [1971, p. 71])

That is, *The Monumental Corporation* argued that a particular accounting policy decision would cause them to invest more in bonds and less in common stocks.

As a second example of the potential impact of accounting policy decisions on corporate executives, consider *FASB No. 8* (*Accounting for the Translation of Foreign Currency Transactions and Foreign Currency Financial Statements*). This standard requires monetary assets and liabilities of foreign subsidiaries to be translated using the current exchange rate between the U.S. dollar and the respective foreign currency. Nonmonetary items are to be translated at the exchange rate in effect at the time of the initial transaction. Prior to *FASB No. 8*, many corporations translated current assets and current liabilities using the year-end exchange rate and translated fixed assets and long-term liabilities at the exchange rate in effect at the time of the initial transaction. Some companies have argued that the effect of *FASB No. 8* is a change in the financing, investment, or production decisions of multinational corporations. The following report discusses *Ramada Inn*:

> [One] especially troublesome issue is raised by *FASB No. 8* for those U.S. firms that either themselves or through their subsidiaries have heavy long-term debt in foreign currencies. Since that indebtedness is now exposed, exchange-rate fluctuations can produce significant quarterly translation gains or losses for affected companies. For firms with large long-term foreign-currency indebtedness, the choice of volatile earnings or costly hedge operations in foreign-currency markets clearly is not very attractive.
>
> Some companies probably are going to seek ways to avoid such problems in the future even though difficult adjustments in operations may be involved. A case in point is *Ramada Inn*. In the past that firm largely financed its foreign operations by borrowing long-term in the country of operation and using the proceeds to build hotels.
>
> It repaid the local-currency borrowing out of local-currency earnings.... *Ramada* told FASB—in a response to the Board's initial draft—that the proposed ruling would "essentially force us to finance all future foreign hotels with U.S. Dollars." The company subsequently announced that it is taking this course, though it believes that it runs "counter to what we should do from an economic standpoint." (*Morgan Guaranty Survey*, July 1976, p. 10)

Similar statements on the alleged effect of *FASB No. 8* can be found in the addresses of chairmen or presidents of several other multinational corporations.

B Information Production Decisions

Accounting policy decisions have the potential to impose substantial information production costs on firms. Consider the 1975 SEC proposals for increased disclosure and a limited review by accountants of interim reports.[2] Arthur Andersen & Co. [1975] made the following estimates of increased audit costs:

> These estimates...cover 31 engagements with annual audit fees ranging from $25,000 to $1,100,000.... The cost for limited reviews made on a retrospective year-end basis of quarterly data to be included in notes to annual financial statements would vary from 3 percent to 24 percent of the annual audit fees. Approximately 80 percent of the estimates fell between 5 percent and 18 percent.... These costs do not include additional costs that would be incurred internally by companies to comply with the Commission's proposals. (p. 8)

The American Bar Association (in a March 14, 1975 letter to the SEC) commented on the interim reporting proposals as follows:

> In 1975 dollars, the [audit fees of U.S. manufacturing companies could] easily be
> $763,000,000. Estimates by several public accounting firms of the percentage
> increase in audit fees attributable to the quarterly audit which would be required
> by the Audited Note Proposal range from 20% to 40%.... The low end estimate
> produces a total increase in audit fees of over $150,000,000 a year; an average
> of the low and high end estimates produces a total increase of $229,000,000 a
> year. These figures, of course, do not reflect the substantial in-house costs of
> registrants which would be required to devote employee time to working with
> the independent accountants as they perform their audit functions. (p. 6)

Obtaining estimates of the "in-house costs" referred to by the American
Bar Association is difficult. Some evidence on their nontrivial size is
obtained from another specific accounting policy decision, i.e., the Federal
Trade Commission's (FTC) request for annual line-of-business information.

In 1974 the FTC requested information on the sales and contribution
margins for each line of business of 345 of the largest U.S. manufacturing
companies.[3] The FTC estimated that the average *in-house* cost per company of complying with their regulations was $10,000–$20,000. Several
companies estimated their costs of compliance as follows (see Scheibla
[1975]):

	Initial Start-Up Cost	Annual Maintenance Cost
Beatrice Foods	$1,171,800	$108,680
Procter & Gamble	$1,263,000	$100,000–$150,000
Singer	$ 500,000	$125,000
Westinghouse Electric	$ 438,000	$200,000

In short, policy decisions can impose substantial information production
costs on corporations, although there is some disagreement as to their
exact magnitude.

Corporate Disclosure Decisions

Corporate disclosure decisions can also be affected by accounting
policy decisions. A good illustration of this point is the corporate reaction
in 1975 to the SEC's proposed rules for "Disclosure of Projections for
Future Economic Performance."[4] The proposed rules would have required
a corporation to report a forecast to the SEC within ten days of making the
projection. In addition, the company would have to file a second report if
it concluded that a previous projection was no longer "valid." The response of industry to this proposal was negative.

Burson-Marsteller [1975] provides some survey evidence on this industry response. The chief financial officers of the *Fortune* 1,000 Industrial

Corporations were polled to determine whether they would provide projections if the SEC proposals were enacted. Of the 375 responses, 39% said they made or confirmed projections in 1974. However, if they were required to file the projection as required under the 1975 SEC proposals, (1) 93% said they would not be willing to forecast performance to a member(s) of the investment community, (2) 93% would not grant a press interview if it prompted a management projection, and (3) 92% of the respondents would not confirm or negate a projection made by another individual. Burson-Marsteller also polled 400 security analysts regarding the forecasting proposals. Of the 83 who responded, 93% contended that the SEC proposal "would restrict the flow of information from corporations [to investors] concerning future performance potential" (p. 4).

16.2 ACCOUNTING POLICY CHOICE

Although accounting disclosure decisions of U.S. firms are presently guided (in part) by several regulatory bodies, this has not always been the situation.[5] Indeed, in the nineteenth and early twentieth centuries a market or laissez-faire approach predominated. The AICPA (then the American Institute of Accountants) expressed the following philosophy in a 1932 correspondence with the New York Stock Exchange:

> The more practical alternative is to leave every corporation free to choose its own methods of accounting...but require disclosure of the methods employed and consistency in their application from year to year. (American Institute of Accountants [1934, p. 7])

It was not until 1933 that the SEC was set up to regulate the information released by corporations. It is also primarily since the late 1930's that the AICPA (and its policy bodies such as the APB and FASB) has issued committee reports (opinions, standards, etc.) to influence the reporting practices of corporations. The question arises of why bodies such as the FASB and SEC have seen fit to regulate information flows rather than allow market supply and demand forces to operate.

A Arguments for a Regulatory Approach

Two main reasons appear to underlie arguments for a regulatory approach[6]:

(1) Market forces will lead to an "inefficient" resource allocation, given some economic standard of efficiency, and

(2) Market forces will lead to an "undesirable" resource allocation, given some ethical standard of desirability.

Consider the argument about "inefficient" resource allocation. To provide some structure to this argument, it is useful to briefly note some results from the economics literature. Given certain restrictive assumptions, it can be shown that the equilibrium set of market prices from a perfectly competitive economy achieves an efficient (in the sense of a Pareto-optimal) allocation of resources.[7] In this context, the market approach can be relied upon to achieve an efficient resource allocation. Once the restrictive assumptions are relaxed, however, there is no assurance that a competitive market solution will be an efficient one.

The economics literature has for some time focused on conditions where the market solution results in non-Pareto resource allocations (termed *market failures*). For instance, there has been considerable argument that because of the inability to effectively exclude the nonpurchasers of patents, warrants, etc., there will be underinvestment in research and development—see Arrow [1962]. There has also been a related concern in the accounting literature that because of the inability to exclude nonpurchasers, there will be a non-Pareto optimal production of information by firms—see Gonedes and Dopuch [1974]. Although it has been documented that market failures may occur with respect to information production, it is far from obvious that a policy board such as the SEC or FASB can regulate information production so as to achieve a Pareto-optimal distribution of resources.

Consider now the argument for regulation based on market forces leading to an "undesirable" allocation of resources. This argument is commonly made with respect to regulating the trading activities of corporate officials (i.e., *insider trading*). It is alleged that insiders have access to nonpublic information about a firm's future prospects and that the use of this information for security trading gives them an "undesirable" or "unfair" advantage over external investors. Issues regarding fairness also appear important in proposals for regulating forecasts made by corporate officials. For instance, Gray [1973]—Chairman of the Financial Analysts Federation Special Committee on Corporate Forecasts—stated the following:

> To the extent that forecasts provide genuinely new information (e.g., reflecting a new corporate development), a broad and even distribution would tend to induce a more *equitable* distribution of gains or losses of investors. The immediate price change might be greater because the new forecast would be discounted more uniformly but the net result might be a *fairer* market. (p. 66, emphasis added)

The SEC's 1975 proposals for regulating such forecasts were motivated (in part) by similar concerns. Burton [1974] gave the following as one rationale for the forecasting regulations:

> At the same time as many companies announced their projections publicly, a number of others communicated their expectations to a select few. Favored analysts might be advised of current budget data either directly or by letting them know that their estimates were "in the ballpark." Through a variety of such devices, many corporations sought to be sure that "market" estimates of their earnings were not far off the mark while still not taking any public position on the projected results. While the overwhelming majority of such efforts were done in good faith, the end result was lack of knowledge as to what forecasts were those of management as opposed to those of analysts working independently. In a few cases there was evidence of *selective disclosure* to institutional investors interested in the stock and *unfair* use of such insider information. (p. 86, emphasis added)

Clearly, value judgments are involved in deciding what is an "undesirable" or "unfair" use of insider information. What an external investor might think is an "undesirable" use of inside information, a corporate official might think is very "desirable."

The question of whether the above arguments are sufficient to justify the degree of regulation now in existence is an extremely difficult one to structure, let alone answer.[8] Much work in the industrial organization literature is currently examining the arguments used to justify intervention in market forces by regulatory bodies such as the SEC, the Interstate Commerce Commission, the Federal Communications Commission, the Federal Drug Administration, and the Civil Aeronautics Board. At present, the evidence suggests that these arguments are often based on isolated cases of alleged "inefficiency" or "inequity" or on overestimates of the ability of government agencies to achieve "set goals."[9]

B Implementation Issues

Regulatory bodies such as the FASB and its predecessor the APB face a major difficulty in obtaining acceptance for their chosen alternative. The importance of this aspect has been stressed by several individuals who have been associated with accounting policy decisions, e.g., Horngren [1972; 1973; 1976] and Moonitz [1974]. The investment tax credit scenario is a good illustration. Congress instituted the investment tax credit to stimulate investment in capital assets. The two main accounting alternatives are the deferral method (the tax benefits affect reported income over the life of the purchased asset) and the flow-through method (the tax benefits affect reported income in the year the asset is purchased). In October 1971, the APB issued an exposure draft supporting the deferral method. Horngren [1972] provides the following details on the problems associated with implementing this policy choice:

> Without public support, which usually means without the widespread support of industry, significant changes are seldom possible. Perhaps the situation would be better expressed negatively. If there is widespread hostility to a suggested accounting principle, there is small chance of implementing it—regardless of how impeccable its logic or how heavy the support within the Board.
>
> The investment tax credit is a clear example of the impotence of both the SEC and the APB when hostility is rampant. Let me describe the events without getting tangled in the pros and cons of the conceptual issues:
>
> 1. The APB did not issue its exposure draft of October 22, 1971, until receiving two written commitments. The SEC said it would support the APB position, and the Department of the Treasury indicated that it "will remain neutral in the matter."
> 2. The Senate Finance Committee issued its version of the 1971 Revenue Act on November 9. In response to lobbying, the Committee clearly indicated that companies should have a free choice in selecting the accounting treatment of the new credit.
> 3. On November 12, Treasury sent a letter to the chairman of the Senate Finance Committee that stated: "Since any change in the preexisting well-established financial accounting practice might operate to diminish the job-creating effect of the credit, the Treasury Department strongly supports a continuation of the optional treatment."
> 4. Congress then cut the ground out from under the APB and the SEC by passing legislation that stated that "no taxpayer shall be required, without his consent, to use…any particular method of accounting for the credit."
> 5. The APB's unanimous denunciation of congressional involvement was issued on December 9, 1971. (p. 10)

Horngren used this scenario to illustrate his hypothesis that (1) the SEC has been an active rather than a passive participant in the accounting standard setting process and (2) the existing framework is best characterized as a cooperative effort between the public and private sectors. In a later paper—Horngren [1973]—he noted the following:

> Although most accountants have claimed that the responsibility for the setting of standards has been kept within the private sector, this view is oversimplified and misleading.
>
> The (informal) organizational relationship is similar to that of decentralized management in industry. Exhibit 1 shows a single organization whose products are accounting standards. The key idea is a *decentralized* structure. A crude parallel can be drawn as you descend the chart. Congress has ultimate power, but with rare exceptions has delegated this power to the SEC (and other federal agencies). In turn, the SEC has delegated much of this power to the APB.
>
> Decentralization is frequently defined as the relative freedom to make decisions. Top management adopts decentralization when it believes that lower manage-

EXHIBIT I

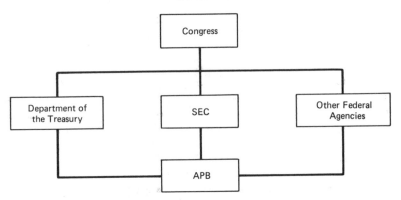

ment has more information and ability to make decisions that obtain the overall goals of the organization. In industry, the extent of decentralization varies from company to company. The heavier the decentralization, the greater the latitude of the lower-level managers to make a host of decisions, including acquisition of materials and equipment and sales of products and services. Decentralization lies along a continuum and is subject to recentralization, either selectively or totally, whenever high-level management so decides.

The implications of this informal decentralized organizational structure are far-reaching. Both the SEC and the APB are subjected to constraints exerted by superior management, Congress, and the entire organizational unit is subjected to the influence exerted by the customers, the parties affected by the standards (reporting companies, practitioners, and users of the reports).

The key to a successful enterprise is to generate a product that is *acceptable* to customers. The decentralized manager may develop what he perceives as a superior product, but his perceptions must overlap with those of his customers. If new standards are proposed that seem unacceptable, the customers must be persuaded otherwise. If the standards are sufficiently unappealing, the customer may complain to higher management (the SEC or Congress). (pp. 61–62)

In addition to illustrating implementation problems facing a policy body,[10] the investment tax scenario also illustrates the heterogeneity in individuals' preferences for information systems. For instance, although the APB preferred the deferral method of accounting for the investment credit, some corporate officials preferred the flow-through method. This heterogeneity in preferences is also apparent in decisions of the FASB. The Chairman of the FASB made the following comments on an accounting for general purchasing power changes project:

It's interesting to see how the powers line up on this issue. Of the large accounting firms, none of whom have a vested interest in the outcome, opinion is diverse: Four favor the proposal, three are against it and two suggest that action be deferred.

Banks and insurance companies, on the other hand, have no such diversity in view. They are absolutely and unequivocally opposed because of the impact that this proposal would have on their earnings: It would tend to reduce them. While they may discuss the issue on conceptual grounds, they arrive at one conclusion: the pragmatic one.

On the other hand, public utilities and transportation companies, which will experience an increase in their earnings should the proposal be adopted in its present form, are also virtually solidly opposed to it. But, note the effect is different; here, earnings are increased. This group either favored the concept of price level adjustments for only depreciation and similar costs and raged against the recognition of gain on long term liabilities or insisted that fixed assets, in their case, should be treated as monetary items. They presented a new set of arguments, but their motivation was equally pragmatic.

We are encountering another power bloc in connection with this project. Small public accounting firms argue that the proposal might increase the amount of work which they do for their clients or, if not done, would require that they qualify their opinions on these reports. These accounting firms have undertaken a vigorous write-in campaign to apprise us of the disastrous consequences of this proposal. What is their real concern? Although their arguments are couched in language questioning the usefulness of price level data and concern over the cost of providing it, the true motivation for the spectacular responses we have received may be the concern, expressed by only a few, that with increased costs their clients may drift to other practitioners not required to insist on compliance with this standard. Is this how accounting principles should be forged? (Armstrong [1977, p. 78])

It is interesting to note that the FASB subsequently withdrew a preliminary exposure draft of a standard that would have required firms to present general price-level-adjusted financial statements in their annual reports.

Obviously the accounting policy maker is operating in an environment where some parties will perceive they benefit from a particular policy decision while other parties perceive they are harmed by the same decision. In this context, societal value judgments inescapably underlie (at least implicitly) accounting policy decisions. Given this social choice perspective, what role can the research that underlies much of the material in prior chapters play in policy decisions? In Section 16.3 we shall discuss this issue in some detail.

16.3 ACCOUNTING POLICY DECISIONS AND RESEARCH

Research of the kind discussed in this book can provide important information to policy makers in at least three ways: (1) provide evidence on the descriptive validity of industry arguments, (2) provide evidence on assumptions implicit in policy decisions, and (3) provide evidence on the consequences of past policy decisions.

A Evidence on Descriptive Validity of Industry Arguments

In Section 16.1 we noted that corporate decisions can be affected by accounting policy decisions. It is not surprising in this situation that one input into policy decisions is arguments by corporate officials about the likely impact of any proposed accounting rule on their industry. The question arises of how a body such as the FASB evaluates these arguments. Consider the testimony by *The Monumental Corporation* quoted in Section 16.1, i.e., that the increased variability in reported income from including unrealized capital gains and losses on equity securities in income would cause "the stock of the company to decline when it shouldn't." The accounting issue here for the insurance industry is not whether such capital gains or losses will be disclosed but rather where they will be disclosed. Such gains are already disclosed in the annual reports of insurance companies. Thus, the FASB must evaluate if the price of insurance stocks will be affected by changing the location of disclosure of an item, i.e., does the *geography* of disclosure matter?

The evidence from the many studies on capital market efficiency (see Chapters 7–11) suggests that a change in the location of disclosure, per se, will not affect aggregate security prices.[11] Indeed, there is evidence in Foster [1977] that the capital market is already including the expected capital gains on equity securities in income when valuing property-liability insurance companies. Given this available evidence, the onus would appear to be on the insurance industry to provide more evidence to support their arguments about the likely impact of the above reporting rule on insurance stocks. This accounting issue underscores the importance of disclosure decisions. In an efficient capital market, the substantive issue as regards affecting security prices is the decision whether to disclose rather than the decision where to disclose.

B Evidence on Assumptions Underlying Policy Decisions

The published standards (opinions, releases, etc.) of accounting policy bodies often state the reasons for, or the assumptions underlying, particular policy decisions. In some cases, very little evidence is given to support these statements or assumptions. Consider the accounting for extraordinary items issue. The assumption underlying the label *extraordinary* is that these items are different from those included in "ordinary" income. For instance, the Committee on Accounting Procedure in *Accounting Research Bulletin No. 43* stated the following:

Only extraordinary items such as the following may be excluded from the determination of net income for the year, and *they should be excluded when their inclusion would impair the significance of net income so that misleading inferences might be drawn therefrom*: (a) material charges or credits specifically related to operations of prior years... ; (b) material charges or credits resulting from unusual sales of assets not acquired for resale and not of the type in which the company deals.... (p. 63, emphasis added)

From a security market perspective, one operational test of the above assumption is that the security price revaluation implications of $1 of extraordinary income is different from the revaluation implications of $1 of income before extraordinary items. This test could be conducted using the cumulative abnormal return (CAR) technique discussed in Chapter 11. If the evidence from an extensive empirical analysis turned out to be inconsistent with this assumption, the strength of the argument supporting the specific reporting rules for extraordinary items would appear to be considerably reduced.[12]

As a second example, we shall consider an assumption made in *APB No. 15* (earnings per share). The APB concluded that convertible debt should be treated as common stock equivalent if, at the date of issuance, the cash yield on the bond is less than $66\frac{2}{3}\%$ of the then-current bank prime interest rate. Frank and Weygandt [1970] examined how well this criterion predicted the actual conversion of 28 convertible bonds that were issued in 1965. All 28 bonds were *not* classified as common stock equivalents (i.e., not likely to convert).[13] Yet by 1968 they reported that significant amounts of conversion (at least 25%) had occurred in 13 cases. In a subsequent article—Frank and Weygandt [1971]—they used discriminant analysis to build a model to predict conversion. Using a validation sample of 97 convertible bonds issued in 1966, they were able to better predict actual conversion than did the APB's model of predict conversion if the cash yield at issuance date is less than $66\frac{2}{3}\%$ of the then-current bank prime interest rate.

C Evidence on the Consequences of Past Policy Decisions

Research on the consequences of past policy decisions can provide useful information on the likely consequences of new policy decisions. There is an underlying similarity to many policy decisions; e.g., they extend the required items to be disclosed, or they change the timing at which required items are to be disclosed. It seems fruitful to learn from the experience of prior policy decisions.

The work of Benston [1973] represents an ambitious attempt to examine the effect of the disclosure rules associated with the Securities Exchange Act of 1934. Among the issues examined were the effect of the disclosure rules on the security returns or betas of publicly listed securities. The research design compared the behavior of security returns and betas in the period prior to the 1934 Act with that in the period subsequent to the

1934 Act. Benston found little observable difference and concluded the following: "All of the many measurements and analyses showed that the 1934 Act's financial disclosure requirements had no measurable effect on the securities of the corporations presumably affected" (p. 153). This finding of no effect could be consistent with at least two hypotheses: (1) The 1934 Securities Act provided no *additional* information that was pertinent to valuing capital market securities, or (2) the 1934 Act did provide additional information which had an effect on security returns or betas, but Benston's research design was not able to detect that effect.[14]

The fact that several hypotheses are consistent with Benston's results is no criticism of the Benston paper. This situation is characteristic of most (if not all) empirical projects. What is required is further research to discriminate among these various hypotheses. This research could examine (1) subsequent disclosure acts or (2) the same disclosure act but with a different methodology. An example of the former is Hagerman's [1975] study of the effect of the 1964 amendments to the Securities Exchange Act on the behavior of bank stocks. Stigler's [1964] study of the related 1933 Securities Exchange Act illustrates the latter.[15] Each of these two studies also reported that the disclosure rules examined had limited (if any) effect on the securities registered under those acts.[16]

Assuming that Benston's research design was adequate to the task, the important question is *why* the finding of no effect. One possible explanation is that, even prior to the Securities Exchange Act of 1934, there were strong market forces motivating firms to provide the information required by the Act. As noted earlier, Benston [1969] reported that prior to the 1934 Act, many corporations were already disclosing sales, cost of goods sold, depreciation and net income, as well as balance sheet information such as current assets and current liabilities. Moreover, note that even for those firms not reporting such items, other information sources may provide similar signals as regards the distribution of future returns on the security, e.g., dividends, and physical production reports. Indeed, one result that is apparent in the efficient market studies examined in prior chapters is that annual and interim reports compete with other sources in providing capital markets with information pertinent to security price revaluation. An important task of a policy body appears to be to determine those items in which accounting has a comparative advantage in reporting—this comparative advantage could arise from information production cost considerations, from timeliness considerations, or from reliability considerations.[17]

The importance of the line of research pursued by Benston [1973] and others lies in its enriching our knowledge about aspects of the environment in which policy decisions are made and implemented. The general presumption is that an understanding of the forces operating in the environment will facilitate the making of predictions about the consequences of specific accounting policy alternatives. At present our knowledge in this area is limited. For instance, we know little about why some firms issue corporate forecasts while others refrain from doing so. We know little about why some firms issue detailed financial information in annual reports while others release only that information required by regulatory bodies. We know little about why some firms change accounting techniques and others do not.[18] The opportunities for research in this area are obviously very extensive.

16.4 SUMMARY

In this chapter we have considered several forces that influence the information set available to creditors, investors, and other external parties, i.e., (1) market forces and (2) policy decisions by regulatory bodies such as the FASB and the SEC. At present, our understanding of how these (and potentially other) forces interact is quite limited. An important area of research is to examine the mechanism by which such forces impact on the information production decisions of (1) internal parties within the firm and (2) nonfirm information intermediaries such as brokerage houses. An examination of this mechanism would enable us to better understand the forces that influence the information set available to external parties.

NOTES

[1]See Horngren [1973] for discussion of APB deliberations on the marketable equity securities issue.

[2]See Green [1977] for discussion of the 1975 SEC interim reporting proposals.

[3]Solomons [1977] provides background details to the FTC line-of-business reporting requirements.

[4]See Chenok [1977] for discussion of the 1975 SEC forecasting proposals.

[5]Hendricksen [1977, Chapters 2 and 3] provides background information on the growth of U.S. regulatory reporting requirements.

[6]Posner [1974] and Stigler [1971] contain excellent discussions on the various theories used to explain the pattern of regulation in the U.S.

economy, e.g., the "public interest" theory, the "capture" theory, and the "economic" theory. Demski and Feltham [1976, Chapter 8] discuss possible reasons for regulation in an accounting context.

[7]Quirk and Saposnik [1968] and Intriligator [1971] contain good summary discussions of the technical literature in which proofs of these results are presented. A Pareto-optimal allocation of resources is one where no individual can be made better off without making any other individual worse off.

[8]In particular, social choice problems arise in deciding what is a preferred level of government regulation. If we make the value judgment that the preferences of the individuals affected by regulation should count, then issues associated with Arrow's [1963] impossibility theorem arise. This theorem states that no social preference function will exist which exhibits "seemingly reasonable" requirements, e.g., that the preference function is not dictatorial, is independent of irrelevant alternatives, and provides a complete, transitive and reflexive ranking of the social alternatives. See Mueller [1976] for a survey of the social choice literature and Demski [1974] for analysis in an accounting context.

[9]Examples of this research include Benston [1969], Comanor and Mitchell [1972], and Peltzman [1973].

[10]Horngren [1976] made the following further comment on the investment tax credit issue:

> When Congress intervened in the 1971 investment credit fiasco, every member of the APB was shocked and disgusted, including me. The Board issued a unanimous denunciation of this meddling by politicians. If we had better understood the political process, we should not have been surprised. Instead, we should have been far better prepared to cope with the interference.
>
> Letters from congressmen and cabinet officers may upset us, but they are the facts of life. To survive, the private policy makers must face these facts skillfully. (p. 94)

[11]If corporate officials do change their investment policy at the time the change in place of disclosure is made, it is possible that aggregate security prices may be affected.

[12]For evidence on the capital market reaction to extraordinary items, see Horwitz and Young [1974], Gonedes [1975], and Eskew and Wright [1976].

[13]See Hofstedt and West [1971] for some corrections to the Frank and Weygandt [1970] paper.

[14]See Gonedes and Dopuch [1974, pp. 93–96] for a critical analysis of the research design used by Benston.

[15]Subsequent discussion of the Stigler [1964] paper in the October 1964 and April 1965 issues of the *Journal of Business* should be read in conjunction with the original articles.

[16]The conclusions of no effect of accounting disclosure regulations have not gone unchallenged—see Somer [1974]. Note also that Collins [1975] and Deakin [1976] have reported finding an effect of SEC or AICPA disclosure requirements. Collins examined the SEC's line of business requirements, while Deakin examined the AICPA's change in reporting requirements for retail land sales companies.

[17]Considerations of this kind appear to underlie several of the recommendations of the Cohen Commission, e.g., the committee recommended the elimination of "subject to" qualified audit opinions—"there is no reason to believe that independent auditors are better able to predict continued business success or failure than they are able to predict the outcome of other uncertainties" (Commission on Auditors' Responsibilities [1977, p. xviii]).

[18]Some evidence on these issues is provided in Gagnon [1971], Warren [1977], Watts and Zimmerman [1976], and Zimmerman [1977]. The last two studies argue that "agency costs" help explain the choice of accounting techniques used by reporting entities. Tests of the validity of this argument need to quantify these agency costs and demonstrate that entities with different agency costs choose different accounting techniques. No such tests have yet been published.

QUESTIONS

QUESTION 16.1:   Accounting Policy Decisions and Efficient Capital Markets

The following questions were raised by Beaver [1973] in an article titled "What Should Be the FASB's Objectives?":

> Was the acrimony arising out of the investment tax much ado about nothing? Does it matter whether special gains and losses are reported in the ordinary income or in the extraordinary item section? When firms switch from accelerated to the straight-line depreciation what is the effect upon investors? Did the Accounting Principles Board allocate its resources in an appropriate manner? If its priorities needed reordering, where should the emphasis have to be shifted? What objectives should be adopted for financial accounting standards? (p. 49)?

After summarizing the results of research on the relationship between financial statement data and security prices, Beaver noted the following:

> The evidence across a variety of contexts, supports the contention that the market is efficient with respect to published information....

> [These] findings have a direct bearing on the questions raised at the outset and suggest that our traditional views of the role of policy-making bodies, such as the APB, SEC and FASB, may have to be substantially altered. (pp. 52, 49)

What are the implications of efficient capital markets for accounting policy decisions by regulatory bodies such as the FASB or SEC?

QUESTION 16.2:   Accounting Principles: Public vs. Private Determination?

Robert Chatov [1977] made the following case in a debate on "Should the Public Sector Take Over the Function of Determining Generally Accepted Accounting Principles?":

Introduction

As our debate topic implicitly and too accurately recognizes, the private sector presently determines generally accepted accounting principles, which is not what was intended by the Congress that passed the 1933 Securities Act and the 1934 Securities Exchange Act. Those acts explicitly authorized development of corporate financial reporting rules in the public sector, and that is where they ought to be formulated today. Whether one favors development of corporate financial reporting rules by the private or the public sector depends upon how one feels about the relative importance of three distinct, frequently contradictory objectives of corporate financial reporting. The three objectives are corporate reporting, investor evaluation and government planning.

Corporate Reporting. To permit the corporation to present the financial information it considers most conducive to its corporate purposes.

Investor Evaluation. To provide investors (broadly defined) with information on a particular corporation, or with data sufficient to permit comparison of two or more corporations, even in different industries.

Government Planning. To provide the basis for a wide range of macroeconomic public policy decisions, such as forecasting the effect of inventory changes, capital investment, R & D expenditures, corporate profitability, etc., on economic activity, and in addition, to allow measurement of competition in different markets; and for the SEC to implement the directive of the securities acts to eliminate speculation in the financial markets that negatively affects the nation's economic health.

These three objectives are mutually exclusive in today's atmosphere of private sector control of the development of corporate financial reporting rules. I am aware that this is a strong statement but I have deliberately left out any qualifiers like "probably" or "potentially" before "mutually exclusive". Today only the first objective is being approximated, as the conglomerate merger movement of the 1960's bore witness. Investor information is inadequate because of the undecipherability of corporate statements, attributable in part to the Security and Exchange Commission's advocated footnote disclosure policy, which was originated in 1935. Secondly, because of the multitude of accounting alternatives available to corporations in reporting their financial position, we have a lack of standardization of accounting conventions within industries no less than between industries. The result is that average investors are clearly incapable of deciphering corporate financial reports, sophisticated investors and financial institutions are similarly disadvantaged, and the government is presented with a mass of data which when aggregated is substantially meaningless. For example, can anyone assert that aggregated corporate profits really mean anything, except to indicate the state of mind of the corporate sector?

I do not believe the development of corporate financial standards should any longer be permitted to be located within the private sector. But before asking why the public sector ought to develop corporate financial reporting rules, and which area of the public sector ought to be doing it, we must first ask why it is that private sector is presently performing this particular function.

Transfer of Authority to the Business Sector

It is an amazing incident in the history of independent regulatory agencies that the SEC transferred its authority under Sections 19 and 13 of the '33 and '34 Acts back to the private sector within three years of beginning its operation. Thereafter the mode of operation between the SEC and the private sector became rigid and institutionalized. I have delineated this complicated event in my book, *Corporate Financial Reporting: Public or Private Control?*, but I will provide in some of my remaining time, a sketch of the unfortunate transfer of authority from the SEC to the private sector.

Corporate registration forms were needed to implement the Securities Acts, and their development became a combined private sector/public sector event. The FTC and the SEC after it, received considerable help from members of both the American Institute of Accountants and the American Society of Certified Public Accountants, the two national professional groups which were to merge in 1936. This assistance established a basis for the interaction between the public and private sectors in the area of corporate financial reporting.

Now the early Commissioners had two alternatives about the way they were going to interpret the Securities Acts. Were they to regard the Acts as a mandate to actually regulate the financial sector, or were the Acts merely intended to enforce adequate disclosure of financial information for the benefit of investors? The early Commissioners chose the less imaginative and less controversial route. They interpreted the Securities Acts as disclosure statutes. This mentality surfaced in the Northern Powers Securities case of 1935. By a 3–2 vote, the Commission permitted an accounting treatment of which all of the Commissioners disapproved, on the grounds that the accounting convention had been disclosed in footnote. The specific matter dealt with the manner of writing off unamortized debt discount. That is not important. What is important is that it indicated the Commission's legalistic approach toward the Securities Act, showing a concern for what the law seemed to demand on a minimal basis rather than what was required for a fair statement of the facts. Voting for the majority were Kennedy, Landis and Mathews. Contra were Healy and Pecora. It was a crucial decision because thereafter it prevented the SEC from developing affirmative requirements for corporate financial reporting. The SEC failure to exercise its accounting rulemaking authority at this point placed it in a permanently disadvantaged position. It also set the basis for the "disclosure mentality" of the SEC, which offers corporations an enormous amount of leeway.

Following the Northern Power securities case the private sector continued a barrage of abuse, faint praise, and opposition, toward the SEC, which contributed to preventing the SEC from operating authoritatively and effectively in the corporate financial control area. In December 1936, in exasperation with the practicing accountants, Landis made a statement in a speech that:

The impact of almost daily tilts with accountants, some of them called leaders in their profession, often leaves little doubt that their loyalties to management are stronger than their responsibilities to the investors.

There was immediate objection from the accounting sector, represented by the American Institute of Accountants, which pleaded for an opportunity to handle the problems mentioned by Landis. For whatever reason, Landis then suggested that an AIA representative contact Carman Blough, then the Commission's Chief Accountant. Blough, with Landis' approval, agreed that the SEC would refer to the AIA all accounting questions coming before the SEC with which the Commission took issue, where accountants had signed the statement. Furthermore, violation cases would also be turned over to the AIA Ethics Committee for action. In January of 1937 Blough sent Starkey of the AIA the first set of accounting questions from the SEC. This, of course, was a critical turning point and it led to institutionalizing the responsibility for accounting principles in the hands of the private sector. By mid-1937 the AIA indicated satisfaction with these arrangements. There was also a slackening of the anxiety expressed by the practicing accountants by this point. All that remained was to announce as official policy that the SEC would avoid creating comprehensive accounting standards in favor of the accounting practitioners, a decision that was made by the Commission in 1937 and communicated to the AIA by Blough at the Institute's fall meeting. The message was that the AIA could make the accounting rules although if they did not do it, the SEC would. Early next year the AIA's Committee on Accounting Procedure was reconstituted in order to undertake the task. The SEC's ASR No. 4 in 1938 made the policy official. In 1937, at the fiftieth anniversary of the AIA, R.H. Montgomery made the Presidental address entitled "What Have We Done and How?" Montgomery indicated the AIA's satisfaction with the SEC authority abdication: He said, "We have survived the Securities and Exchange Commission, which has done a good job."

Private Sector's Administration of Accounting Principles

For the next 20 or so years the administration of corporate financial reporting regulations was in the hands of the American Institute of Accountants' Committee on Accounting Procedure, which very early decided that no comprehensive approach would be taken to the development of accounting principles. Rather, accounting problems would be taken as they came up. The Committee on Accounting Procedure was cleverly designed to prevent accomplishment of any major results. With 22 members widely dispersed geographically, the permanent research staff consisted of a part-time director and one full-time research assistant. The Committee's pronouncements had only a moral authority, although the SEC later required all submitted reports to be compatible with CAP pronouncements. CAP opinions required at least two-thirds approval for release. The CAP's approach was, as described by Carmen Blough, to "put out brush fires." The brush fire approach continued until some 20 years later when the Committee on Accounting Procedure came under such heavy fire from within the profession, that a new organization was felt to be in order. This resulted in creation of the late lamented Accounting Principles Board, which lasted for about 13 years, and was replaced by the Financial Accounting Standards Board, et al.

The operations of the Accounting Principles Board essentially continued what the CAP had done, albeit with a larger research staff, and again demonstrated the private sector's interest in achieving only the first of the three objectives already mentioned, viz, to permit corporations leeway in showing the financial picture best serving its particular purposes. No comprehensive approach to developing internally consistent accounting principles was ever developed: the footdragging of the APB was notorious, coming to the inescapable attention of all interested parties during the conglomerate merger movement. For reasons best known to the accounting profession and the financial sector, even though the abuses of pooling of interest of accounting method was well known to the financial community by 1961, no substantive action was taken by the APB until 1969–70. At this point it was too late to save the APB, and the only question was what was going to replace the APB.

The choice was public sector vs. private sector control. Quite predictably, private sector control won out, since the private sector made the decision. Of course the private sector would take this position since it was to the financial interest of those who were making the decision that prime direction for corporate financial reporting rules remain outside the public authority. This also served the antigovernment ideology that has always characterized both the accounting and the financial sector groups. And it was striking that the SEC was unwilling to make an attempt to do anything about retrieving the authority for developing corporate financial reporting rules from the private sector. It is apparent that the SEC has become so used to an agreeable relationship with the private sector that it has absolutely no interest at all in trying to reacquire financial rulemaking powers since it would involve an enormous battle with the private sector, which the SEC probably would have lost anyhow due to the political pressure that could have been exerted upon them.

What then are the prospects for the FASB? Which is another way of asking, why should we expect a performance by the FASB which will deviate significantly from the performance of the CAP and APB before it? I think there are no substantive differences between the three groups, between the CAP, the APB and the FASB, aside from the blatant joining together of the accounting profession with their corporate clients in the new Financial Accounting Foundation organizations. This can have only one result, as predictable as what happens when the justice of the peace is given a financial interest in the outcome of the traffic violator's trial. The financial accounting rules developed by the FASB will not work to the disadvantage of the corporate sector, particularly since the corporations are so heavily represented on the Financial Accounting Standards Advisory Committee. The passive role of the SEC can be expected to continue, although I must admit that I have been impressed by occasional signs of life from Chief Accountant John C. Burton.

To get back to my initial point, which was, which of the three objectives cited at the outset are going to be satisfied by the Financial Accounting Standards Board? The objective most likely to be satisfied is the first, that of permitting corporations to show those things which they would most like to show, and to devote itself to a continuing avoidance of really controversial issues. This is to be expected, and one ought not to be upset about it. But there ought to be better ways of doing things. My contention is that the public sector has the major interest in and the responsibility for, developing rules for corporate financial reporting. Because of the tradition in the SEC towards having the private sector develop rules of corporate financial reporting, and because developing an intelligible set of corporate financial rules is a scholarly undertaking, not suited to a government agency, I do not recommend that the SEC take over this function.

I suggest that what is needed is a national commission to develop a comprehensive accounting code for industrial corporations within the United States. You may shudder with horror at my assertion that this accounting code ought to provide several things: (1) it ought to provide for uniformity in accounting treatment; (2) it ought to provide the elimination of alternative treatments of accounting; (3) it ought to provide for comparability among the financial reports of different corporations, which should result if the first two objectives are met. Only in this way will investors be able to rely upon corporate financial reports and upon making comparisons between them. Only in this way will the government have reliable financial information which it will be able to appraise on the basis of knowing specifically what is in the reports and their aggregations. And only in this way can we look forward to intelligent and meaningful public policy decisions to be made by government, based on consistent, aggregatable corporate financial data.

REQUIRED

(1) Do you agree with Chatov that "the private sector presently determines generally accepted accounting principles" (p. 117)?

(2) What are the main arguments Chatov presents for having accounting principles set within the public sector? How would you respond to these arguments?

(3) The President of the *Financial Executives Institute* made the following comment at a Senate subcommittee hearing on the accounting profession:

The establishment of accounting standards should remain in the private sector with the oversight of the Securities and Exchange Commission.... The most constructive remark I can offer to this subcommittee is that we keep things as is. I do not mean to keep the status quo—but we should retain and improve on the existing system—because it is workable. (quoted in *This Week in Review*, Haskins and Sells, May 13, 1977)

What specific arguments can you present for the existing system vis-à-vis determination of accounting principles in the public sector?

QUESTION 16.3:   Corporate Forecasting: Fuqua Industries, Inc.

Issues relating to voluntary corporate forecasting raise interesting questions at both the public policy level and the individual firm level. Details of voluntary forecasts released by *Fuqua Industries, Inc.* in the 1972–1975 period are presented in Part 1. The reaction of SEC officials and corporate executives to *Fuqua's* decision to voluntarily release forecasts is outlined in Part 2.

1. *Voluntary Forecasting by Fuqua Industries, Inc.* On December 28, 1972 *Fuqua Industries, Inc.* issued its *Preliminary Annual Report in 1972 and a Look Ahead to 1973*. This report contained unaudited financial statements for 1972 and forecasts of financial items for 1973. The letter to shareholders in this *Preliminary Annual Report* included the following comment:

> This is the first time you have ever received an Annual Report on the last day of a corporate fiscal year. It is even more unique to see included detailed forecasts for the following year's operations.
>
> It should be clearly understood that 1972 figures are unaudited and subject to possible adjustment. However, in a well managed company, the independent auditors do not create financial data but should only have to verify that company figures are accurate and presented in a manner consistent with prior years....
>
> It is clear that the Securities and Exchange Commission will shortly require public companies to make forecasts of future operations. While we are not fully convinced of the merits of making public projections of future earnings, if this is the kind of music we will have to march to, we are willing to lead the band.
>
> We urge you to understand that forecasts of future operations are based on business factors as evaluated by management at the time such forecasts are made. In order not to mislead investors, we believe our 1973 forecasts to be conservative representing our minimum anticipated financial performance as we see economic and competitive factors in December 1972. (p. 1)

Table 16.1 contains an extract from the *Preliminary Annual Report—1972*.
The 1972 Annual Report provided further details of the 1973 forecasts:

> Under the Fuqua planning system, each subsidiary prepares a detailed operating budget for each succeeding 12 months. These budgets are analyzed in great detail by all members of the management team of each operating unit of the company. Subsequently another detailed and objective analysis is made in cooperation with Fuqua officers and financial specialists on the corporate staff....
>
> In the budget review process, the assumptions and the plans for achievement of goals of financial performance of each subsidiary are placed into the context of its particular industry, its competitive situation, as well as overall economic factors. Judgment as to practical performance goals is made. The concluding step is the final operational forecast of each subsidiary, which may be substantially different from the initial efforts.
>
> The reliability of budgeting procedures is naturally greater in some subsidiaries than in others. This may be due to relative uncertainty about forecasting material or labor costs. For example, it is particularly difficult to make accurate forecasts for businesses which are directly affected by weather conditions, while forecasting results of our radio and television stations is relatively easy. (p.3)

TABLE 16.1 Fuqua Industries: Summary of Operations
Years Ended December 31 ($ millions)

			Sales and Revenues			Estimated	Forecast
	1967	1968	1969	1970	1971	1972	1973
Leisure Time							
Snowmobiles & lawnmowers	$ 13.9	$ 21.4	$ 30.9	$ 36.9	$ 45.8	$ 56.0	$ 68.0
Sporting goods	15.9	19.8	24.1	28.3	31.4	37.0	39.0
Marine products	38.4	49.7	49.5	29.7	34.0	41.0	48.0
Entertainment	24.6	24.5	25.0	26.9	27.1	38.0	45.0
Photographic finishing	14.1	17.0	19.6	18.1	17.9	21.0	23.0
Total Leisure	106.9	132.5	149.1	139.9	156.2	193.0	223.0
Transportation	66.5	72.0	97.5	113.2	131.0	140.0	147.0
Shelter[a]	26.0	29.7	37.3	39.4	41.6	61.0	74.0
Agribusiness	18.1	20.9	21.0	28.9	33.0	36.0	40.0
Total continuing operations[b]	217.5	255.1	304.9	321.4	361.8	430.0	484.0
Add: Discontinued Operations	42.4	40.8	43.7	28.5	6.1	—	—
Less: Restatements of businesses purchased	36.7	40.8	11.0	5.5	1.3	—	—
Total sales and revenues	$223.2	$255.1	$337.6	$344.4	$366.6	$430.0	$484.0

TABLE 16.1

	Earnings						% of Total	Compound Annual Growth Rate %	Earnings Forecast 1973
	1967	1968	1969	1970	1971	Estimated 1972			
Leisure Time									
Snowmobiles & lawnmowers	$ 2.4	$ 4.7	$ 5.8	$ 6.2	$ 7.3	$ 9.7	22%	32%	$ 11.4
Sporting goods	1.1	2.0	2.9	3.2	3.1	4.1	9	30	4.1
Boats & boat trailers	1.0	3.6	3.3	.3	.6	3.3	7	27	4.5
Entertainment	2.5	3.2	4.5	4.2	4.5	6.4	14	16	6.8
Photographic finishing	1.6	1.8	1.4	1.0	1.7	2.5	6	9	2.9
Total Leisure	8.6	15.3	17.9	14.9	17.2	26.0	58	24	29.7
Transportation	3.6	4.3	6.0	4.5	9.2	10.0	22	23	10.0
Shelter[a]	.3	2.0	5.9	6.2	4.7	2.8	5	56	5.5
Agribusiness	3.1	3.0	1.5	3.1	5.3	6.7	15	17	6.9
Total continuing operations[b]	15.6	24.6	31.3	28.7	36.4	45.5	100%	23%	52.1
Add: Discontinued operations	1.7	1.6	.5	1.6	(.8)	(.1)			—
Less: Unallocated corporate expenses and corporate interest	.9	1.7	3.9	6.2	7.9	9.7			9.7
Less: Restatements of businesses purchased	1.2	2.7	.3	1.0	.2	—			—
Income before income taxes	15.2	21.8	27.6	23.1	27.5	35.7		19	42.4
Income taxes	7.0	11.0	13.6	11.5	13.5	17.7			21.0
Net operating income	$ 8.2	$ 10.8	$ 14.0	$ 11.6	$ 14.0	$ 18.0		17%	$ 21.4

[a] Does not include Brigadier Industries since acquisition had not been completed.

[b] Includes all continuing companies for all periods regardless of date of acquisition except that Gulf States Theatres is included only for the periods since June 1, 1972. Gulf States Theatres was only a part of a business complex, and accurate data for prior periods on the theatres is not available.

SOURCE: Fuqua Industries, *Preliminary Annual Report 1972 and a Look Ahead to 1973* (p. 6).

The six-month interim report for the period ended June 30, 1973 included the following comment:

At the end of 1972, we made an innovative move by forecasting 1973 sales and earnings, for the entire company by categories of business. The 1973 forecast is updated in this midyear report.

While we have revised our outlook for some classifications of business, the 1973 forecast in total is little changed. Forecasts reflect prospects for future performance as seen at the time they are made. Some events, unforeseen earlier in the year, have made revisions of forecasts for some operations necessary. While business forecasting is not an exact science, we at Fuqua make a continuing effort to improve our ability to anticipate the future. (p. 3)

Table 16.2 contains an extract from this interim report.

Fuqua continued its policy of forecasting in 1974, and in January released aggregate 1973 preliminary results and aggregate 1974 forecasts. On February 8, it released its *Preliminary Results for 1973 and a Look Ahead to 1974.* Comments made in this release included the following:

The detailed operational forecasts are intended to share our internal budget with investors. Forecasts are based on Fuqua's operations as viewed in relation to estimates of general economic conditions as of early February 1974, and are subject to the qualifications that sales and earnings may vary from forecast as economic conditions change during the year. While 1973 preliminary results and 1974 forecasts were announced in early January 1974, this more detailed summary has been delayed to reflect an overview of the general economy which has been subject to unprecedented uncertainties during the past 60 days due to the changing government energy policy.

A major deviation from 1973 forecasts was caused by the inability to foresee the gasoline shortage which had a disastrous effect on the snowmobile industry.... Fortunately, snowmobile business is not a significant part of overall Fuqua operations, representing only 2% of sales. Because of the uncertain future of this business, a decision was made to terminate operations, and results are reported in "discontinued businesses." (p. 1)

An extract from the February 1974 release is presented in Table 16.3.

The 1974 six-month interim report included a 1974 forecast update as well as some explanations for the revisions:

Interest and inflation rates were underestimated when the original 1974 forecasts were made. Increased inventories and receivables require more working capital, thus increasing corporate interest expense. (p. 2)

Table 16.4 presents the updated forecasts from the 1974 six-month interim report. No subsequent forecast updates for 1974 results were provided. The third-quarter 1974 interim report, however, included the following note:

We have begun switching to LIFO inventory from the commonly used FIFO method. LIFO provides a much more accurate method of measuring earnings in a period of inflation. While the change to LIFO will reduce 1974 earnings by an

TABLE 16.2 Fuqua Industries: Financial Data and Forecasts (in thousands)

		Earnings		Forecast—1973		Sales Forecast 1973
	1970	*1971*	*1972*	*Original*	*Latest*	
Leisure Time						
Snowmobiles & lawnmowers	$ 6,206	$ 7,278	$ 9,852	$11,400	$10,200	$66,000
Sporting goods	3,153	3,149	3,993	4,100	4,100	51,000
Marine products	255	557	3,333	4,500	4,500	53,000
Entertainment	4,206	4,504	6,181	6,800	6,400	45,000
Photofinishing	1,038	1,705	2,423	2,900	3,200	24,000
Total	14,858	17,193	25,782	29,700	28,400	239,000
Transportation	4,478	9,233	10,008	10,000	10,000	152,000
Shelter	5,278	3,680	2,812	5,500	8,100	80,000
Agribusiness	1,766	4,595	5,223	6,900	5,300	34,000
Continuing operations	$26,380	$34,701	$43,825	$52,100	$51,800	$505,000
Discontinued businesses	1,920	(388)	1,472	—	700	
Unallocated corporate expenses	(6,161)	(7,861)	(9,822)	(9,700)	(10,000)	
Income before income taxes	22,139	26,452	35,475	42,400	42,500	
Income taxes	11,030	12,959	17,406	21,000	21,200	
Net operating income	$11,109	$13,493	$18,069	$21,400	$21,300	

SOURCE: Fuqua Industries, *Six Month Report For Period Ended June 30, 1973 and Revised 1973 Forecast* (p. 2).

560

TABLE 16.3 Fuqua Industries

				Sales (in millions)		
				1973		
	1970	1971	1972	Dec. 1972 Forecast	Estimated (unaudited)	1974 Forecast
Leisure Time						
Lawn & garden equipment	$ 22.2	$ 26.3	$ 36.0	$ 42.0[b]	$ 54.9	$ 65.0
Sporting goods	22.7	30.1	39.1	39.0	54.7	84.0
Marine products	29.6	34.0	42.4	48.0	49.8	43.0
Entertainment	26.4	25.9	37.2	45.0	46.5	47.0
Photofinishing	17.9	17.8	21.8	23.0	26.2	29.0
Total Leisure	118.8	134.1	176.5	197.0	232.1	268.0
Transportation	112.6	130.5	140.7	147.0	156.6	182.0
Shelter[c]	42.7	45.1	69.2	85.0[b]	90.5	91.0
Total Sales[a]	$274.1	$309.7	$386.4	$429.0[b]	$479.2	$541.0

TABLE 16.3

				1973		
Earnings (in millions)						
	1970	*1971*	*1972*	*Dec. 1972 Forecast*	*Estimated (unaudited)*	*1974 Forecast*
Leisure Time						
Lawn & garden equipment	$ 5.3	$ 5.9	$ 8.9	$ 9.4[b]	$13.2	$14.2
Sporting goods	2.2	3.0	4.0	4.1	4.1	7.6
Marine products	.3	.6	3.3	4.5	4.2	2.7
Entertainment	4.2	4.5	6.2	6.8	6.4	7.0
Photofinishing	1.0	1.7	2.4	2.9	3.3	3.9
Total Leisure	13.0	15.7	24.8	27.7	31.2	35.4
Transportation	4.5	9.2	10.0	10.0	9.8	9.8
Shelter[c]	6.4	5.1	5.6	7.9[b]	10.9	13.1
Total operations[a]	$23.9	$30.0	$40.4	$45.6	$51.9	$58.3
Unallocated corporate expenses and interest	(6.2)	(8.3)	(9.9)	(9.7)	(12.1)	(11.0)
Income before taxes —continuing operations	17.7	21.7	30.5	35.9	39.8	47.3
Income taxes	8.8	10.6	14.6	17.8	19.5	23.3
Net income—continuing operations	$ 8.9	$11.1	$15.9	$18.1[b]	$20.3	$24.0

[a] Includes purchased businesses from date of acquisition and restatement for discontinued operations.

[b] Restated for discontinued businesses: original forecasts, which included discontinued businesses, were $484.0 for total sales and $21.4 for net income.

[c] Stormor division moved from discontinued "Agribusiness" classification to Shelter.

SOURCE: Fuqua Industries, *Preliminary Results for 1973 and a Look Ahead to 1974* (p. 3).

additional 35 to 50 cents per share, the change will also provide us with a tax savings of $3 to $5 million in 1974 and should add substantially to our cash flow in 1975 by reducing our estimated payments....

The change in inventory accounting will make forecasting meaningless this year. (p. 1)

The change to LIFO was made effective January 1, 1974.

On February 21, 1975 *Fuqua* issued a press release that included the following comments:

Net income in 1974 was $9.6 million or $1.07 per share reported on the new LIFO accounting method compared with the $16.5 million or $1.69 per share reported in 1973 when Fuqua was using the traditional FIFO accounting procedure. The company said the switch to LIFO reduced its pretax earnings by $8 million or 47 cents per share after income taxes.

Mr. Fuqua said the company would "reluctantly" discontinue its former practice of making a forecast of future earnings. "Of course, we have the same internal budgets we shared with our stockholders in past years—but this year there is so much uncertainty in the economic outlook that we would have to qualify any forecast as little more than an educated guess," Fuqua said.

Table 16.5 presents an extract from the 1974 *Annual Report*.

2. *Reaction to Fuqua's Forecasting Releases.* Details of the reaction of various parties to *Fuqua's* public release of its 1973 forecasts are provided by John K. Shank and John B. Calfee, Jr., "Case of the Fuqua Forecast," *Harvard Business Review* (November–December, 1973) Copyright ©1973 by the President and Fellows of Harvard College; all rights reserved. The following extracts are taken from that source:

Reaction of Dennis C. Stanfill, Chairman of the Board of *Twentieth Century-Fox Film Corporation*

"I would have recommended against the publication of any earnings forecasts for the upcoming year. The practice is not soundly based and would be counterproductive.

"The concrete, specific number-forecast is misleadingly precise, since it is impossible to explain, with equal precision, the assumptions on which it is based. Many investors may be needlessly made to think that the art of management is an easy one, and that businessmen operate in a world of certainty. This is hardly the case; the very opposite is true.

"Also, while management should be expending its energies on looking ahead to new conditions, a missed forecast would make it necessary to look defensively backward to explain the deviation.

"An executive must also consider the internal effect of forecasts. As it is, most subsidiary executives play it safe and make it difficult to secure reasonably realistic forecasts. They might be inclined to play it even safer if they knew the boss was going to announce publicly a forecast."

Reaction of James Stewart, Chairman of the Board, *Frank B. Hall & Co., Inc.*

TABLE 16.4 Fuqua Industries Annual Earnings and Sales Data—Forecast Update (in millions)

	Earnings				Forecast—1974		Sales Forecast—1974	
	1970	1971	1972	1973	Original	Update	Original	Update
Recreation								
Lawn and garden equipment	$ 5.3	$ 5.9	$ 8.9	$13.2	$14.2	$14.9	$ 65.0	$ 70.0
Sporting goods	2.2	3.0	4.0	4.1	7.6	8.0	84.0	100.0
Marine products	.3	.6	3.3	4.2	2.7	1.7	43.0	40.0
Entertainment	4.2	4.5	6.2	6.4	7.0	8.1	47.0	53.0
Photofinishing	1.0	1.7	2.4	3.3	3.9	4.8	29.0	35.0
Total recreation	13.0	15.7	24.8	31.2	35.4	37.5	268.0	298.0
Transportation	4.5	9.2	10.0	9.8	9.8	9.4	182.0	193.0
Shelter	6.4	5.1	5.6	10.9	13.1	10.2	91.0	90.0
Total operations	$23.9	$30.0	$40.4	$51.9	$58.3	$57.1	$541.0	$581.0
Unallocated corporate expenses and interest	(6.2)	(8.3)	(9.9)	(12.1)	(11.0)	(14.5)		
Income before taxes—continuing operations	17.7	21.7	30.5	39.8	47.3	42.6		
Income taxes	8.8	10.6	14.6	19.5	23.3	21.1		
Income from continuing operations	$ 8.9	$11.1	$15.9	$20.3	$24.0	$21.5		

SOURCE: Fuqua Industries, *Six Month Report and 1974 Forecast Update* (p. 3).

TABLE 16.5 Fuqua Industries

	Sales and Revenues (in millions)				
	1970	*1971*	*1972*	*1973*	*1974*
Recreation					
Lawn & garden equipment	$ 22.2	$ 26.3	$ 36.0	$ 54.9	$ 69.5
Sporting goods	22.7	30.1	39.1	54.7	97.6
Marine products	29.6	34.0	42.4	49.8	39.7
Entertainment	26.4	25.9	37.2	46.5	52.3
Photofinishing	17.9	17.8	21.8	26.2	35.5
Total recreation	118.8	134.1	176.5	232.1	294.6
Transportation	112.6	130.5	140.7	156.6	181.6
Shelter	40.3	42.3	64.3	85.1	74.5
Total[a]	$271.7	$306.9	$381.5	$473.8	$550.7

	Earnings (in millions)				
	1970	*1971*	*1972*	*1973*	*(LIFO) 1974*
Recreation					
Lawn & garden equipment	$ 5.3	$ 5.9	$ 8.9	$13.2	$11.1[b]
Sporting goods	2.2	3.0	4.0	4.1	1.4[b]
Marine products	.3	.6	3.3	4.2	.8[b]
Entertainment	4.2	4.5	6.2	6.4	8.4
Photofinishing	1.0	1.7	2.4	3.3	4.0
Total recreation	13.0	15.7	24.8	31.2	25.7
Transportation	4.5	9.2	10.0	9.8	5.9
Shelter	6.3	4.7	4.0	9.1	3.7[b]
Total operations[a]	23.8	29.6	38.8	50.1	35.3
Unallocated corporate interest and expenses	(6.2)	(8.3)	(9.9)	(12.1)	(15.9)
Consolidated continuing operations before taxes	17.6	21.3	28.9	38.0	19.4
Taxes on income	8.7	10.4	13.8	18.6	9.2
Consolidated continuing operations	8.9	10.9	15.1	19.4	10.2
Unconsolidated subsidiary	—	.2	.8	.9	(.6)
Continuing operations	$ 8.9	$11.1	$15.9	$20.3	$ 9.6

[a] Restated for pooling of interests, discontinued operations, and unconsolidated subsidiary.

[b] Companies in these products lines were switched to LIFO.

SOURCE: Fuqua Industries, *Annual Report 1974* (p. 21).

"There did not appear to be a pressing need that such a forecast be made. In the first place, since the precedent would require bearish years to be forecasted as well, the fact that the preliminary budgets were bullish would not have been a persuasive reason to forecast.

"Secondly, substantial uncertainties existed, not only with respect to the balance of 1972, but also, and more importantly, with respect to 1973. To be specific, the snowmobile and lawn mower lines are obviously dependent on weather conditions as well as on the normal uncertainties inherent in any business. Since these lines represent 22% of 1972 estimated earnings and 18% of 1973 forecasts, the effect of a reasonable error could be significant.

"Thirdly, regardless of the fact that a company is protected against legal liability, a significant later adjustment to forecasts, particularly downward, can create unfavorable stockholder reaction, even though the forecasts were prefaced with multiple 'ifs.' Furthermore, a small stockholder has far less understanding of business than an active partner. Fuqua recognized this and designed a 'simple' format for the 'average' shareholder as opposed to a comprehensive summary of statistics for the security analyst. However, an unsophisticated shareholder's reliance on company forecasts tends to be substantially greater than an analyst's, and his reaction to forecast changes is therefore more drastic."

Reaction of John C. Burton, Chief Accountant, *Securities and Exchange Commission*

"I view Fuqua's 1972 preliminary annual report, which included forecasts by product line for 1973, as a significant step forward in corporate financial reporting.

"I eagerly await the analysis of the actual 1973 results; they should be much more meaningful when compared with the forecast data. They should show how Fuqua combines year-to-date figures with updated statements of expectations as the year progresses. These steps will complete the reporting system that the 1972 report began. In describing a business continuum, it makes no sense to stop reporting as of a particular date. Only a system of reporting that encompasses the past, present, and future on a continually updated basis can provide investors with a meaningful picture of economic activities on which they can base rational investment decisions.

"I believe that such a system will naturally develop because the financial community will demand it and because corporations will decide that the risks associated with not publishing forecasts are greater than those that accompany a carefully thought out plan of forecast publication. It is management's ethical and legal responsibility to treat investors fairly. One way to make sure significant data are not leaked to selected individuals is to forecast them publicly, first!

"I have little doubt that, in another five to ten years, forecasts, analyses of actual results compared to them, and systematic explanations of changes in expectations will be routinely accepted parts of public financial reporting, just as today they are routinely used as part of a modern business's internal information and control system.

"As more people follow Mr. Fuqua into this water, I am confident his judgment that it is temperate and alligator-free will be confirmed. And, he will have had some useful swimming experience."

REQUIRED

(1) Comment on *Fuqua's* 1972 decision to publicly release its forecasts of earnings and sales. You should consider in your answer the comments of Stanfill, Stewart, and Burton quoted in Part 2. Do you agree with Stanfill when he said, "I would have recommended against the publication of any earnings forecasts...?"

(2) Evaluate the accuracy of *Fuqua's* forecasts of the 1973 and 1974 results. What problems arise in making this evaluation? Do you agree with the statement in the 1974 third-quarter interim report that "the change in inventory accounting will make forecasting meaningless this year?"

(3) Discuss *Fuqua's* 1975 decision to discontinue publicly releasing its internal forecasts.

(4) Burton argued (see Part 2) that a system of corporations making public their updated forecasts of sales, earnings, etc., would "naturally develop because the financial community will demand it...." Why might the FASB or SEC not want to rely exclusively on market demand and supply forces in accounting policy decisions in the corporate forecasting area?

REFERENCES

AMERICAN INSTITUTE OF ACCOUNTANTS. *Audits of Corporate Reports.* American Institute of Accountants, New York, 1934.

ARROW, K. J. "Economic Welfare and the Allocation of Resources for Invention." In *The Rate and Direction of Economic Activity: Economic and Social Factors.* National Bureau of Economic Research, Princeton, 1962: 609–625.

———. *Social Choice and Individual Values.* Cowles Foundation Monograph 12. Wiley, New York, 1963.

ARMSTRONG, M. S. "The Politics of Establishing Accounting Standards." *Journal of Accountancy* (Feb. 1977): 76–79.

ARTHUR ANDERSEN & CO. *APB Public Hearing on Accounting for Investments in Equity Securities Not Qualifying for the Equity Method.* Arthur Andersen & Co., Chicago, 1971.

———. *To the Securities and Exchange Commission in Response to Requests for Comments on Proposals Relating to Quarterly Financial Information.* Arthur Andersen & Co., Chicago, 1975.

BEAVER, W. H. "What Should Be the FASB's Objectives?" *Journal of Accountancy* (Aug. 1973): 49–56.

BENSTON, G. J. "The Effectiveness and Effects of the SEC's Accounting Disclosure Requirements." In H. G. Manne (ed.), *Economic Policy and the Regulation of Corporate Securities*. American Enterprise Institute for Public Policy Research, Washington, D.C., 1969: 23–79.

———. "Required Disclosure and the Stock Market: An Evaluation of the Securities Exchange Act of 1934." *American Economic Review* (Mar. 1973): 132–155.

BURSON-MARSTELLER. *Corporate Financial Officers and Security Analysts on the Disclosure of Projections of Future Economic Performance*. Burson-Marsteller, 1975.

BURTON, J. C. "Forecasts: A Changing View from the Securities and Exchange Commission." In P. Prakash and A. Rappaport (eds.), *Public Reporting of Corporate Financial Forecasts*. Commerce Clearing House, New York, 1974.

CHATOV, R. "Should the Public Sector Take Over the Function of Determining Generally Accepted Accounting Principles." *The Accounting Journal* (Spring 1977): 117–123.

CHENOK, P. B. "Earnings Forecasts." In S. Davidson and R. L. Weil (eds.), *Handbook of Modern Accounting*. McGraw-Hill, New York, 1977: 6.1–6.23.

COLLINS, D. W. "SEC Product-Line Reporting and Market Efficiency." *Journal of Financial Economics* (June 1975): 125–164.

COMANOR, W. S., and MITCHELL, B. "The Costs of Planning: The FCC and Cable Television." *Journal of Law and Economics* (Apr. 1972): 177–231.

COMMISSION ON AUDITORS' RESPONSIBILITIES. *Report of Tentative Conclusions*. AICPA, New York 1977.

DEAKIN, E. B. "Accounting Reports, Policy Interventions and the Behavior of Security Returns." *The Accounting Review* (July 1976): 590–603.

DEMSKI, J. S. "Choice Among Financial Reporting Alternatives." *Accounting Review* (Apr. 1974): 221–232.

DEMSKI, J. S. and FELTHAM, G. A. *Cost Determination: A Conceptual Approach*. Iowa State University Press, Ames, 1976.

ESKEW, R. K., and WRIGHT, W. F. "An Empirical Analysis of Differential Capital Market Reactions to Extraordinary Accounting Items." *Journal of Finance* (May 1976): 651–674.

FOSTER, G. "Valuation Parameters of Property-Liability Companies." *Journal of Finance* (June 1977): 823–836.

FRANK, W. G., and WEYGANDT, J. J. "Convertible Debt and Earnings Per Share: Pragmatism vs. Good Theory." *The Accounting Review* (Apr. 1970): 280–289.

———. "A Prediction Model for Convertible Debentures." *Journal of Accounting Research* (Spring 1971): 116–126.

GAGNON, J. M. "The Purchase-Pooling Choice: Some Empirical Evidence." *Journal of Accounting Research* (Spring 1971): 52–72.

GONEDES, N. J. "Risk, Information, and the Effects of Special Accounting Items on Capital Market Equilibrium." *Journal of Accounting Research* (Autumn 1975): 220–256.

GONEDES, N. J. and DOPUCH, N. "Capital Market Equilibrium, Information Production, and Selecting Accounting Techniques: Theoretical Framework and Review of Empirical Work." *Studies on Financial Accounting Objectives*. Supplement to *Journal of Accounting Research* (1974): 48–129.

GRAY, W. S. "Proposal for Systematic Disclosure of Corporate Forecasts." *Financial Analysts Journal* (Jan.–Feb. 1973): 64–71.

GREEN, D. O. "Interim Reports." In S. Davidson and R. L. Weil (eds.), *Handbook of Modern Accounting*. McGraw-Hill, NewYork, 1977: 5.1–5.21.

HAGERMAN, R. L. "Regulation of Accounting Principles." *The Accounting Review* (Oct. 1975): 699–709.

HENDRIKSEN, E. S. *Accounting Theory*, 3rd ed. Irwin, Homewood, Ill., 1977.

HOFSTEDT, T. R., and WEST, R. R. "The APB, Yield Indices, and Predictive Ability." *The Accounting Review* (Apr. 1971): 329–337.

HORNGREN, C. T. "Accounting Principles: Private or Public Sector?" *Journal of Accountancy* (May 1972): 37–41.

———. "The Marketing of Accounting Standards." *Journal of Accountancy* (Oct. 1973): 61–66.

———. "Will the FASB Be Here in the 1980's?" *Journal of Accountancy* (Nov. 1976): 90–96.

HORWITZ, B., and YOUNG, A. "Extraordinary Gains and Losses and Security Prices." *Quarterly Review of Economics and Business* (Winter 1974): 101–110.

INTRILIGATOR, M. D. *Mathematical Optimization and Economic Theory*. Prentice-Hall, Englewood Cliffs, N.J., 1971.

MOONITZ, M. *Obtaining Agreement on Standards in the Accounting Profession*. Studies in Accounting Research No. 8. American Accounting Association, Sarasota, Florida, 1974.

MUELLER, D. C. "Public Choice: A Survey." *Journal of Economic Literature* (June 1976): 395–433.

PELTZMAN, S. "An Evaluation of Consumer Protection Legislation: The 1962 Drug Amendments." *Journal of Political Economy* (Sept.–Oct. 1973): 1049–1091.

POSNER, R. A. "Theories of Economic Regulation." *Bell Journal of Economics and Management Science* (Autumn 1974): 335–358.

QUIRK, J., and SAPOSNIK, R. *Introduction to General Equilibrium Theory and Welfare Economics.* McGraw-Hill, New York, 1968.

SCHEIBLA, S. "Illegal Search and Seizure." *Barron's* (Feb. 17, 1975).

SHANK, J. K., and CALFEE, J. B. "Case of the Fuqua Forecast." *Harvard Business Review* (Nov.–Dec. 1973): 34–43.

SOLOMON, D. "Divisional Reports." In S. Davidson and R. L. Weil (eds.), *Handbook of Modern Accounting.* McGraw-Hill, New York, 1977: 44.1–44.27.

SOMER, A. A. "Financial Reporting and the Stock Market: The Other Side." *Financial Executive* (May 1974): 36–40.

STIGLER, G. J. "Public Regulation of the Securities Markets." *Journal of Business* (Apr. 1964): 117–142.

———. "The Theory of Economic Regulation." *Bell Journal of Economics and Management Science* (Spring 1971): 3–21.

WARREN, C. S. "Characteristics of Firms Reporting Consistency Exceptions—A Cross-Sectional Analysis." *Accounting Review* (Jan. 1977): 150–161.

WATTS, R. L., and ZIMMERMAN, J. L. "Towards a Positive Theory of the Determinantion of Accounting Standards," Working Paper No. 7628. University of Rochester, Rochester, N.Y., 1976 (forthcoming in *Accounting Review*).

WRISTON, W. B. "Accounting to Whom for What?" *Financial Executive* (Sept. 1976): 12–17.

ZIMMERMAN, J. L. "The Municipal Accounting Maze: An Analysis of Political Incentives." *Conference on Measurement and Evaluation of the Economic Efficiency of Public and Private Non-Profit Institutions.* Supplement to *Journal of Accounting Research* (1977).

AUTHOR INDEX

SUBJECT INDEX